KU-258-219

DICTIONARY OF
ISLAMIC ARCHITECTURE

purchased by the

Arab World Education Programme

supported by the Karim Rida Said Foundation

DICTIONARY OF
ISLAMIC ARCHITECTURE

Andrew Petersen

BRITISH MUSEUM

7 OCT 1999

WITHDRAWN

EDUCATION SERVICE
LIBRARY

London and New York

First published 1996
by Routledge
11 New Fetter Lane, London EC4P 4EE

Simultaneously published in the USA and Canada
by Routledge
29 West 35th Street, New York, NY 10001

First published in paperback 1999

© 1996 Andrew Petersen

Typeset in Optima and Palatino by RefineCatch Limited, Bungay, Suffolk
Printed and bound in Great Britain by Clays Ltd, St Ives plc

All rights reserved. No part of this book may be reprinted or
reproduced or utilized in any form or by any electronic,
mechanical, or other means, now known or hereafter
invented, including photocopying and recording, or in any
information storage or retrieval system, without permission in
writing from the publishers.

British Library Cataloguing in Publication Data
A catalogue record for this book is available from the British Library

Library of Congress Cataloging in Publication Data
A catalogue record for this book is available from the Library of Congress

ISBN 0–415–06084–2 (hbk)
ISBN 0–415–21332–0 (pbk)

Contents

10461

BM8 (PET)

Dedication

This book is dedicated to my friend Jamie Cameron (1962-95) historian of James V of Scotland.

Preface

In one of the quarters of the city is the Muhammadan town, where the Muslims
have their cathedral, mosque, hospice and bazar. They have also a qadi and a
shaykh, for in every one of the cities of China there must always be a shaykh
al-Islam, to whom all matters concerning Muslims are referred.

Ibn Battuta, *Travels in Asia and Africa 1325–1354*, Routledge & Kegan Paul, 1929

Abu Abdallah Mahammad of Tangier, also known
as Ibn Battuta, is the most famous of the Arab
travellers. His journeys started with a pilgrimage
(hajj) to Mecca and afterwards he always tried to
travel within a Muslim context whether he was in
Timbuktu or China. What is notable about these
accounts is that they deal with Muslim communities which are remote from the western stereotype
of Muslim society. For example most general
works on Islamic architecture tend to confine themselves to the Middle East and North Africa, neglect-
ing the centuries old Islamic heritage of South-East
Asia, India, East and West Africa. It is an aim of
this book to include as many as possible of these
less well known Muslim cultures whose populations
now outnumber those of the central Islamic lands.

As a corollary to this approach there has been an
attempt to include vernacular architecture rather
than dealing exclusively with well known monumental architecture. As well as being important in
its own right vernacular architecture provides an
architectural context for the more famous monu-

ments. In order to aid the reader's appreciation of
this relationship, vernacular architecture has been
included in regional summaries, which also discuss
the geographical and cultural character of an area.
As a balance to the regional approach there are
also historical accounts dealing with particular dynasties or historic styles.

The encyclopedic nature of this work has meant
that there is little room for theoretical discussions
of aesthetics or meaning. This is not because these
are unimportant considerations but because these
are issues best discussed in a different, more selec-
tive format. The main purpose of this book is to
provide basic information which includes defini-
tions of architectural terms, descriptions of specific
monuments and summaries of regional and historic
groups. Attached to each entry there is a short list
of books for further reading which refers the user
to the principal works on the subject. It is hoped
that the information provided will enable the
reader to gain some appreciation of the diversity
and genius of Muslim culture.

Acknowledgements

First, I must thank my parents who have enabled me to pursue my interest in this subject. Gwendolyn Leick gave me the idea for the book in the first place and subsequently encouraged me in the long process of writing.

The research that I undertook for the book was of two kinds – library based and field work. The library research was carried out in a number of institutions in Europe and the Middle East and I would like to thank everyone who helped me with references or information, in particular: Michael Given, Tony Grey, StJohn Simpson, Benjamin Pickles, Mark Horton, Alistair Northedge, Matt Thompson and Jeremy Johns. The field research was usually carried out as an incidental part of other projects. Several individuals and institutions have been particularly helpful; these are: the British School of Archaeology in Jerusalem, the British School of Archaeology in Iraq, the British Institute at Amman for Archaeology and History, the British Institute in Eastern Africa, the International Merv Project, Dr Julian Reade and the Turkish Government.

Preparation of the manuscript and drawings was helped by a number of people including Heather Nixon, Charles Craske, Crispian Pickles, David Myres and Kate Cheyne. Photographs were provided by a number of people and institutions, in particular I would like to thank Kerry Abbott, Pat and Charles Aithie, Susan Bailey, Rebecca Foote, Cherry Pickles and James Allan. Here I would also like to express my thanks to Mark Barragry and Seth Denbo both of Routledge for their enthusiasm and patience.

Finally, I would like to express my gratitude to my wife Heather Nixon who tolerated and helped with this book for so long.

A

Abbasids

Dynasty which ruled most of the Islamic world between 750 and 945.

In 750 CE there was a revolution against Umayyad rule which began in eastern Iran and rapidly spread over the whole empire. The Umayyads were totally destroyed except for one prince who fled to Spain and established the Umayyad dynasty there. The newly established Abbasids decided to move the capital from Damascus to a city further east, first Raqqa was chosen and then in 762 Baghdad was founded by the Abbasid caliph al-Mansur. Baghdad grew to be one of the biggest and most populous cities in the world based around Mansur's famous round city. In 836 the caliph al-Mu'tassim was unhappy about clashes between the local population and his troops so he established a new capital further north on the Tigris at Samarra. During this period the power of the caliphate began to decline and control over distant provinces was loosened. Several local dynasties grew up including the Tulunids in Egypt, the Aghlabids in Ifriqiyya and the Samanids in Khurassan (eastern Iran). Internal troubles in Samarra caused the caliph al Mu'tamid to move back to Baghdad in 889; at this time Abbasid power outside Iraq was purely nominal. In 945 the Abbasids were replaced by the Shi'a Buwaihid amirs as rulers of Iraq and Iran. For the next two hundred years the Abbasids remained nominal caliphs with no real authority. In the mid-twelfth century the Abbasids were able to reassert some authority when the Seljuk ruler Sultan Muhamad abandoned his siege of Baghdad. During the reign of Caliph al-Nasir (1179–1225) the Abbasids were able to gain control over much of present-day Iraq. The Mongol invasions and sack of Baghdad in 1258 dealt a final blow to the political aspirations of the Abbasids.

Although Abbasid architecture covers a vast area from North Africa to western India, the majority of extant buildings are in the Abbasid homeland of Iraq. Abbasid architecture was influenced by three architectural traditions – Sassanian, Central Asian (Soghdian) and later, during the twelfth and thirteenth centuries, Seljuk. Many early Abbasid structures such as the palace of Ukhaidhir bear a striking resemblance to Sassanian architecture, as they used the same techniques (vaults made without centring) and materials (mud brick, baked brick and roughly hewn stone laid in mortar), and built to similar designs (solid buttress towers). Central Asian influence was already present in Sassanian architecture but it was reinforced by the Islamic conquest of Central Asia and the incorporation of a large number of Turkic troops into the army. Central Asian influence is seen most clearly at Samarra where the wall paintings and some of the stucco work resemble that of the Soghdian palaces at Panjikent. The Abbasid architecture of the twelfth and thirteenth centuries is essentially Seljuk architecture built with Iraqi materials.

In addition to the various influences upon it, early Abbasid architecture can be seen to have developed its own characteristics. One of the most notable features of the Abbasid cities of Baghdad and Samarra is their vast scale. This is most clearly demonstrated at Samarra with its extensive palaces and mosques stretched out for more than 40 km along the banks of the Tigris. The scale of the site led to the development of new forms: thus the great spiral minarets of the Great Mosque and the Abu Dulaf Mosque were never repeated elsewhere (with the possible exception of the Ibn Tulun Mosque). Other developments had far-reaching consequences; for example, the three stucco types developed at Samarra rapidly spread throughout the Islamic world (e.g. the Abbasid mosque at Balkh in Afghanistan) and continued to be used centuries later.

See also: Aghlabids, Baghdad, Balkh, Iraq, Samarra, Tulunids, Ukhaidhir

ablaq

Term used to describe alternating light and dark courses of masonry.

1

Azzam Palace, Damascus. Eighteenth-century example of ablaq masonry, ©Rebecca Foote

It is thought that the origin of this decorative technique may derive from the Byzantine use of alternating courses of white ashlar stone and orange baked brick. The technique of ablaq seems to have originated in southern Syria where volcanic black basalt and white limestone naturally occur in equal quantities. The first recorded use is in repairs to the north wall of the Great Mosque of Damascus which are dated to 1109. In 1266 Sultan Baybars built a palace known as Qasr Ablaq which was built out of bands of light and dark masonry. Although the building has not survived, it demonstrates that the term ablaq was used to describe masonry of this type. In the fourteenth and fifteenth centuries this became a characteristic feature of Mamluk architecture in Egypt, Syria and Palestine. At this stage red stone is also used so that some buildings are striped in three colours, red, black and white. Ablaq continued to be used in the Ottoman period and can be seen in buildings such as the Azzam palace in Damascus. A difference between its use in the Mamluk and the Ottoman periods is that earlier on it was restricted to façades, doorways and windows whereas in the Ottoman period it is used for overall decoration, sometimes including the floors. The technique was also used in Spain and can be seen in the voussoirs of the arcades of the Great Mosque in Córdoba which are red and white.

The technique also seems to have been invented in Europe in the mid-twelfth century although it is not certain whether it was invented independently or copied from Syria. Important European examples are the thirteenth-century churches of Monza, Siena and Orvieto and a four-storey palace in Genoa.

Afghanistan

Mountainous country located between Iran, India and Central Asia.

Most of Afghanistan is either mountain or desert with only 13 per cent of the land under cultivation. The country is dominated by two mountain ranges, the Hindu Kush and the Himalayas. Communication between different areas is difficult and many villages are cut off by snow for half the year. The climate is extreme with temperatures varying from −26 to 50 degrees centigrade. The population is a mixture of ethnic groups including Pushtun, Tajiks, Uzbeks and Turkoman.

Since earliest times Afghanistan's importance has been based on its position between the great civilizations of Iran to the west and India to the south-east. In addition the country formed a route between nomadic Central Asia and the more settled regions to the south. These diverse cultures have all left their mark on the history and archaeology of the country. Before the second century BCE Afghanistan was ruled by the Achaemenids who traced their origins to the conquests of Alexander the Great. From the first century BCE the country was taken over by nomadic groups from Chinese Central Asia, the most significant of which were the Kushans who established a major empire with Buddhism as the official religion. The great Kushan Empire had broken up by the eighth century CE leaving the Sassanians controlling the west and the eastern part in the hands of independent Kushan rulers.

With the fall of the Sassanian Empire the western provinces of Khurassan and Sistan were incorporated into the Islamic Empire although the eastern province of Kabul did not accept Islam until the ninth or tenth century. The first Muslim rulers to control the entire area were the Ghaznavids who seized power from the Samanid rulers of Khurassan in the late tenth century. Under the second ruler, Mahmud, the Ghaznavid Empire was extended to include the Punjab and parts of western Iran. In the late eleventh century the Ghaznavids were threatened by the Seljuks who took over most of Iran and eventually reduced them to the status of vassals. Both the Seljuks and the Ghaznavids were defeated by a local dynasty known as the Ghurids in the late twelfth century. The thirteenth century saw the arrival of the Mongols who incorporated the region into their vast empire. During the fourteenth century the Mongol Empire fragmented and in 1339 Timur established his own empire. Herat was established under the Timurids as capital of the dynasty and became the principal city of the region. A further nomadic invasion at the beginning of the sixteenth century led to the collapse of the Timurid Empire. In 1528 Herat was occupied by the Saffavids whilst the Mughals (descendants of the Timurids) retained control of Kandahar in the south. The decline of these two empires in the eighteenth century led to the establishment of the kingdom of Afghanistan which was able to maintain its independence between the expanding Russian and British empires.

The principal building materials used in Afghanistan are mud brick and pisé, baked brick and stone; wood is fairly rare. The majority of pre-modern buildings in Afghanistan are built of mud brick or pisé and have not survived well the ravages of time. More important buildings are made of baked brick which is often decorated with stucco, painted frescos, tiles or relief brick patterns. There is no tradition of ashlar masonry and stonework usually consists of rubble masonry foundations for mud-brick structures. Exceptions to this usually represent outside influence such as the mosque of Larwand which is Indian in its design and execution.

The oldest identifiable Islamic building in Afghanistan is the ninth-century Abbasid mosque at Balkh. This is a square nine-domed structure with arches resting on four central piers. The north, west and south sides are solid walls whilst the east side opposite the mihrab is an open arcade resting on two round piers. The distinctive feature of the mosque is its stucco decoration which resembles that of Samarra and demonstrates the long distance transmission of ideas and motifs during this period. A more unusual form is the eleventh-century mosque/madrassa at Lashkari Bazar near the modern town of Bust. This is a square mud-brick and pisé structure with external buttress towers and a central courtyard. On the west side of the courtyard there is a small iwan containing a mihrab. The orientation of the building is aligned with the qibla (unlike other buildings on the site) suggesting that it served a religious function, possibly a madrassa. Further east at Ghazni is the palace mosque of Masud III; this is a rectangular structure with a roof supported on six pillars and three doors on the west side. The mihrab is made from marble panels carved with Quranic calligraphy and stylized vegetation. Contemporary descriptions of the city mention a hypostyle mosque supported with wooden columns made of trees imported from India. Unfortunately no mosques of this type have survived although the carved wooden mihrab in the village of Charkh-i Loghar gives an idea of the quality of woodwork of the period.

Mosques of the Ghurid period show a marked Iranian influence which can be seen in buildings such as the mosque and madrassa of Ghiyath al-Din in the village of Ghist. The remains of the building comprise two large domed units made of brick with semi-circular squinches. A better preserved example is the Shahr-i Mashad Madrassa which forms a square courtyard building with domed room. The most notable feature of the building is the decorative brickwork façade which comprises five blind niches and a projecting entrance iwan or pishtaq. The façade is decorated with cut brickwork and stucco which form elaborate patterns and include fifteen bands of inscription. More unusual is the mosque of Larwand which is built entirely of monolithic stone panels and resembles contemporary Indian architecture. The entrance is set within a façade of three arches supported by faceted engaged columns. The doorway itself is decorated with elaborate carving which resembles woodwork. Inside the mosque is covered with a dome which rests on flat corbels.

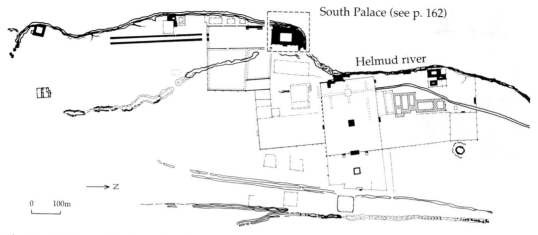

South Palace (see p. 162)

Helmud river

0   100m

Plan of Lashkari Bazar, Afghanistan (after Allen)

Mosques of the Ilkhanid and Timurid periods continued to use the same Iranian forms although a greater variety of vaults was employed. One of the most important innovations was the double dome which was used for tombs and memorials, this comprised a shallow domed ceiling inside and a tall elongated dome outside. The greatest mosque of the Timurid period is the Great Mosque of Herat which was rebuilt during the reign of the Timurid Sultan Husain Baiqara. The mosque is built around a huge brick-paved courtyard with the principal iwan or prayer hall flanked by twin minarets at the west end. Either side of the main iwan are shallower iwans with doors leading to prayer and teaching rooms. Unfortunately the original glazed tilework of the Great Mosque has mostly been replaced although the smaller mosque of Hauz-i Karboz contains a superb example of a tiled Timurid mihrab.

The minarets or memorial towers first erected by the Ghaznavids in the eleventh century are probably the most distinctive feature of Afghan Islamic architecture. The earliest examples are the minaret of Masud III and the minaret of Bahram Shah both at the capital, Ghazni. Each of these structures consists of a baked brick tower standing on an octagonal or cylindrical stone base or socle. The baked brick shafts have a stellate (eight-pointed, star-shaped) plan and are divided into decorative brick panels. The tower of Masud originally stood more than 44 m high but has now been reduced to 20 m. The upper part of both minarets was a cylindrical shaft but these have

now disappeared. Other examples of a related type are the minaret of Zaranj and the minaret of Khwaja Siah Posh, both in Sistan. The Zaranj minaret had an octagonal shaft with a semi-circular flange in the centre of each side whilst the Khwaju Siah Posh minaret comprised sixteen alternating angular and rounded flanges. The culmination of this form is the 65-metre-high minaret of Jam built by the Ghurids in the twelfth century. The height of the structure is further emphasized by its position in a deep valley at the intersection of two rivers. The tower consists of three main sections each in the form of a tapering cylinder. The lowest and largest section is decorated with panels alternating with giant strap-work loops and terminating in a muqarnas corbel balcony. The second and third storeys are each decorated with giant bands of calligraphy.

The first examples of Islamic domestic architecture occur at the site of Lashkari Bazar near the modern town of Bust. The site contains three palaces, the most famous of which is the southern palace which overlooks the Helmud river. This was built around a rectangular courtyard with four iwans (one on each side) leading into separate quarters. The palace was luxuriously decorated with stucco, wall paintings and carved marble panels in a style reminiscent of Abbasid Samarra. In addition to the main palaces there were a number of smaller mansions with a similar design based around a courtyard and iwans. This design was to remain a feature of later Afghan architecture and can be seen in the medieval (thirteenth- to

Twelfth-century minaret, Jam, Afghanistan, ©Ashmolean Museum

fourteenth-century) houses of Dewal-i Khodayda and Gol-i Safed. The village of Dewal-i Khodayda comprises a number of courtyard-iwan houses aligned to protect them from the north-west wind. Gol-i Safed is a walled town with houses of a similar design to Khodayda but more elaborate decoration in the form of blind niches and decorative brickwork.

See also: Herat, Iran, Lashkari Bazar, Mughals, Timurids

Further reading:

F. R. Allcin and N. Hammond (eds), *The Archaeology of Afghanistan from Earliest Times to the Timurid Period*, London, New York, San Francisco 1978.

Agades (also Agadez)

Islamic trading city located in the Aïr region of Niger, West Africa.

The origins of the city are obscure although it is likely that it began as a Tuareg encampment like its western counterpart Timbuktu. The first arrival of Tuareg into the region is not known although Ibn Battuta describes the area as under Tuareg domination in the fourteenth century. In 1405 the Tuareg sultanate of Aïr was inaugurated and it is likely that Agades was founded at this time. Nevertheless, the first Tuareg sultans remained nomads and were not based in the city until the mid-fifteenth century by which time the town was an important entrepôt for the trade between Timbuktu and Cairo. In the early sixteenth century Sonni Ali the emperor of Gao deposed Adil the ruling sultan of Agades and replaced him with a governor. At the same time a Songhay colony was established and Songhay was established as the official language of the city. Although the city was not captured during the Moroccan invasion of 1591, the disruption of the trade routes meant that the city declined and by 1790 it was almost completely deserted. Many of the inhabitants migrated to the Hausa cities of the south. By the mid-nineteenth century the city had recovered and was once more a prosperous trading centre with a mixed population of Berbers from the Algerian Sahara and immigrants from the Hausa cities of Kano and Sokoto.

The main building material in Agades is mud-brick although immediately outside the city in the Tuareg encampments stone is the main material of construction. Most houses are single storey with roofs built from split palm trunks laid diagonally across the corners supporting more beams on top of which are palm frond mats with earth piled on top.

Little remains of the pre-nineteenth-century town although descriptions by early European and Arab travellers give some idea of what the earlier Tuareg city looked like. A sixteenth-century description by Leo Africanus describes the city as built in the 'Barbary mode' (i.e. Berber) which implies that it may have consisted of stone houses like those inhabited by the present-day Tuareg of the region. These houses are simple two-roomed rectangular buildings made of stone and mortar often with mud-brick courtyards and outhouses.

5

The Tuareg nature of the city is further emphasized by the open prayer place (musalla) and shrine known as Sidi Hamada just outside the south walls of the city. The site consists of an open area of ground with a low bank at the east side against which is built a dry stone wall which rises up to the mihrab in the centre. A nineteenth-century description of the southern part of the city mentions a large mud-brick complex surrounded by a walled enclosure crowned with pinnacles. It seems likely that this may have been the citadel of the Tuareg city although it has also been interpreted as a khan. Also in this area were some well-built (stone?) houses amongst which was a building interpreted as a bath house (hammam).

When the city was resettled in the nineteenth century a large northern extension was added which was enclosed within a city wall (katanga). The houses of this period were built of mud and their interiors resembled those of the Hausa cities of northern Nigeria with moulded mud decoration.

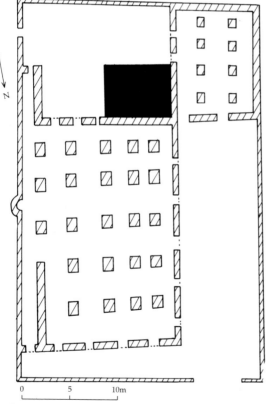

Plan of the Great Mosque, Agades, Niger. Minaret shaded (after Prussin)

The major work of this period was the rebuilding of the minaret of the Great Mosque between 1844 and 1847. The mosque consists of a large rectangular sanctuary with a mihrab in the centre of the east wall and the huge minaret attached to the north-west corner. A nineteenth-century description mentions another ruined minaret to the south of the mosque; this has now entirely disappeared. The present minaret is over 30 m high and tapers from a square base (10 m per side) at the bottom to a square platform (3 m square) at the top. The exterior faces of the minaret are characterized by thirteen layers of projecting palm timbers which act as tie beams for this complex structure. Inside the minaret there is a timber-framed staircase lit by twenty-eight openings (seven on each side). This structure is distinguished from other monumental minarets in the region by its base which consists of four massive earth piers instead of a solid block. The architectural origins of the building are not known although it has been suggested that it bears some similarity to the tapering stone-built minarets of southern Algeria.

See also: Oualata, Timbuktu, West Africa

Aghlabids

Dynasty which ruled the north African province of Ifriqiyya during the ninth century.

Although nominally under Abbasid control, the Aghlabids were able to exercise a great deal of independence. Militarily their great achievement was the conquest of Byzantine Sicily.

The Aghlabids were great patrons of architecture and much of their work has survived. Their work demonstrates a mixture of Byzantine and Abbasid building styles. One of the most important projects was the rebuilding of the Great Mosque of Qairawan and the addition of the huge three-tiered minaret/tower. The Aghlabids were also responsible for major irrigation and water supply systems the most famous example of which are the huge circular cisterns of Qairawan. Much of their effort was also directed towards the development of the coastal towns as bases from which to launch the conquest of Sicily. The military nature of Aghlabid rule is further reflected in the large number of ribats or fortified monasteries which they constructed.

See also: Tunisia

Further reading:

A. Lezine, *Architecture de l'Ifriqiyya: recherche sur les monuments aghlabides*, Paris 1966.

Agra

City in central northern India famous for its Mughal monuments.

Agra is located on the banks of the river Jumna 160 km south of Delhi. Although Agra was an ancient Hindu city the present city was refounded as a capital by Sikander Lodi at the beginning of the sixteenth century. In 1505 Iskander built a mud-brick fortress by the banks of the river at the centre of his new city. However, in 1526 the Lodis were defeated by Babur at the battle of Panipat and Agra was incorporated into the expanding Mughal Empire. Although Agra became one of the principal Mughal cities, little construction took place until 1565 when the third emperor Akbar demolished the old fort of Sikander Lodi and built a new fort faced in red sandstone. For the next eighty years Agra was the imperial capital apart from a brief period between 1571 and 1585 when Akbar moved to nearby Fatehpur Sikri.

The main monuments of Agra are the fort and the Taj Mahal which are located 1.5 km apart on the west bank of the river. The fort consists of a roughly triangular area enclosed by a huge red sandstone wall capped with pointed crenellations. The walls have two main gates (the Delhi Gate and the Amar Singh Gate) and are surrounded by a deep paved moat. The fort is the product of several construction phases the earliest of which belongs to the reign of Akbar. Little of Akbar's original palace survives, except for the enclosure walls and the Jahangari Mahal which is a Hindu-style pavilion in the south part of the building. Most of the interior of the fort may be attributed to the reign of Shah Jahan who also built the Taj Mahal which can be viewed across the water from the private apartments of the palace. Although less rigidly planned, the interior of the Agra Fort bears a striking similarity to the Red Fort in Delhi also built by Shah Jahan. The layout is based around a series of formal gardens and pavilions the most beautiful of which is the Mussaman Burj or octagonal tower which overlooks the river and is capped by an octagonal copper dome. Other important monuments in Agra include the Rambagh, the Chini Ka Rauza and the tomb of Itmad al-Daula. The Rambagh is a formal four-part garden laid out

by the first Mughal emperor Babur. In the centre of the garden is an open octagonal domed pavilion standing on thirty-six columns. The Chini Ka Rauza is a Persian-style tiled tomb crowned with a bulbous dome built for the seventeenth-century poet Afzal Khan. The tomb of Iltimad al-Daula is a square structure with octagonal domed minarets at each corner, the outer surface of the tomb is decorated with carved white marble and geometric marble screen. In the centre of the structure is the tomb of Iltimad al-Daula which is lined with yellow marble and has fine pietra dura stone inlay.

See also: Delhi, India, Mughals, Red Fort, Taj Mahal

Further reading:

M. Ashraf Husain, *An Historical Guide to the Agra Fort based on Contemporary Records*, Delhi 1937.

W. G. Klingelhofer, 'The Jahangiri Mahal of the Agra Fort: expression and experience in early Mughal architecture', *Muqarnas* 5: 153–69, 1988.

E. Koch, 'The lost colonnade of Shah Jahan's bath in the Red Fort at Agra', *Burlington Magazine* 124: 331–9, 1982.

—— 'The Zahara Bagh (Bagh-i Jahanara) at Agra', *Environmental Design* 1986: 30–7.

Ahmadabad

Main city of Gujarat in western India with a mixed Hindu, Muslim and Jain population.

The old city is located on the east bank of the Sabarmati river. Ahmadabad was founded by Ahmad Shah I in 1411 near to the old Hindu town of Asaval which it replaced. The Bhadra towers erected by Ahmad Shah to protect the citadel are the oldest surviving part of the city; however, most of the original fortifications have been destroyed. The city contains some of the best examples of medieval Gujarati architecture which is characterized by its integration of Hindu, Jain and Islamic forms.

At the centre of the city is the Jami Masjid built by Ahmad Shah I and completed in 1424. The plan of the building comprises a huge rectangular courtyard with entrances on three sides and a covered sanctuary to the west. The sanctuary is divided into fifteen domed bays (five wide and three deep) supported on 260 columns. In the centre of the sanctuary façade is the huge main entrance flanked by two tall minarets (now partially demolished). At the end of each of the aisles there is a mihrab made of coloured marble. The central

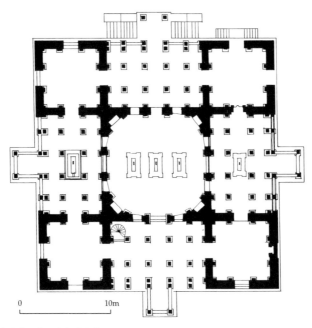

Plan of the tomb of Ahmad Shah, Ahmadabad, India

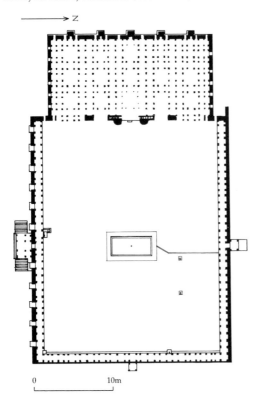

Jami Masjid, Ahmadabad, India

aisle is three times the height of the rest of the building and contains projecting balconies looking in to the central area. To the east of the mosque is the tomb of Ahmad Shah which consists of a square domed mausoleum in the centre with four smaller square domed chambers at the corners and pillared verandas in between.

One of the finest buildings of the city is the Rani Sipri Mosque built in 1514. The building is quite small and has a pronounced Hindu character with elaborate carved decoration and fine perforated jalis or screens.

See also: Gujarat, India

Further reading:

G. Mitchell and S. Shah, *Ahmadabad*, Bombay 1988.

Ajdabiya (Roman Corniclanum)

Prominent Fatimid city in Libiya.

Ajdabiya's owed its importance to its position on the junction of two important routes, the coastal route from Tunisia to Egypt and the desert caravan route from the oases of Jaly and al-Ujlah. Although the site was known in Roman times, it was during the Fatimid period that the city achieved its greatest development.

Several remains of the Fatimid complex have been recovered including a rectangular mud-brick enclosure wall, the qasr or palace and the mosque. The palace is a rectangular stone built structure approximately 22 by 33 m with solid circular corner towers and semi-circular buttress towers. The palace has one entrance in the north wall leading into a courtyard enclosed by apartments. At the opposite end to the corner from the entrance there is a large T-shaped suite of rooms which probably functioned as the royal apartment. The royal apartments were once luxuriously decorated with stucco work.

The most important building at the site is the mosque located in the south-west corner of the complex. Extensive archaeological work on the mosque has defined a Fatimid and pre-Fatimid phase above an earlier Roman site, but only the Fatimid phase has been investigated in any detail. In 912 the Fatimids sacked the town of Ajdabiya and destroyed the mosque building a new one on the site. The Fatimid mosque consists of a rectangular structure (47 by 31 m) built out of mud brick with corners, piers, jambs and other structurally important points built out of stone. There was one entrance in the north-west side opposite the mihrab and several other side entrances, all of which appear to have been plain in contrast to the monumental porches at Mahdiya and Cairo. Inside there is a large courtyard paved with flagstones and a water tank in the middle at the northern end of the mosque. The courtyard is surrounded by arcades and on the south-eastern side is the sanctuary. The latter has a wide central aisle running at right angles to the qibla wall where it meets a transept running parallel to the qibla wall; all the other aisles are aligned at right angles to the qibla.

To the left of the main entrance is a large square block 4 m high which was the base of a minaret with an octagonal shaft. This is the earliest example of this type of minaret which was later developed into the characteristic Cairene minaret form. There are also traces of a staircase built into the wall which have been interpreted as the remains of a staircase minaret used before the erection of the later octagonal one.

Little remains of the mihrab apart from the foundations and some stucco fragments; however, nineteenth-century drawings depict it as a curved recessed niche with a horseshoe arch.

See also: Fatimids, Libiya

Further reading:

A. Abdussaid, 'Early Islamic monuments at Ajdabiyah', *Libiya Antiqua* 1: 115–19, 1964.
—— 'The old Islamic city of Ajdabiyah', in *Some Islamic Sites in Libiya*, Art and Archaeology Research Papers, London 1976, 19–24.
H. Blake, A. Hutt and D. Whitehouse, 'Ajdabiyah and the earliest Fatimid architecture', *Libiya Antiqua* 8: 105–20, 1970.
P. Donaldson, 'Excavations at Ajdabiya, 1976', *Libyan Studies* 7: 9–10, 1976.
D. Whitehouse, 'The excavations at Ajdabiyah: an interim report', *Libyan Studies* 3: 12–21, 1972.
—— 'Excavations at Ajdabiyah: second interim report', *Libyan Studies* 4: 20–7, 1973.

ajimez

Spanish term for pair of windows sharing a central column. This is one of the distinctive features of Islamic buildings in Spain and is especially noticeable on minarets.

Albania

Mountainous country in south-eastern Europe which was incorporated into the Ottoman Empire in the fifteenth century.

The first Ottoman incursions into Albania in the late fourteenth and early part of the fifteenth century were fiercely resisted by the Albanians under their leader Skanderberg who managed to unite the various feudal factions who had previously ruled the country. The resistance of the people together with its mountainous terrain meant that the country was not fully conquered until the late fifteenth century. Few Turks settled in the country which nevertheless converted to Islam. This remained the state religion until the revolution of 1967 when the country became officially atheist. Mosques were converted into museums and minarets were demolished in order to destroy the distinctive Islamic appearance of the cities. In 1991 with the collapse of the authoritarian communist regime Islam has again become the main religion with 72 per cent of the population Muslim and 27 per cent Christian (Greek Orthodox and Catholic). As a result mosques have been reopened with rebuilt minarets. There are substantial numbers of Albanians living abroad particularly in the USA where there are four Albanian mosques (in Detroit, Chicago and Waterbury, Connecticut).

A recent survey has indicated that there may be as many as 800 mosques surviving in Albania along with 300 historical Muslim sites. The mosques in Albania are of two types, the classical Ottoman type derived from Byzantine architecture based on a square domed area with a triple-domed portico and the more common rectangular buildings with wooden painted ceilings which are typical of the Balkans. The oldest Muslim building in the country is the Berat Congregational Mosque built in 1380. Another early mosque is the Ilias Mirahori Mosque in the town of Korçë built in 1494 after the Ottomans had gained control of the whole country. One of the most celebrated mosques in Albania is at Krujë 20 km north of the capital Tiranë. The mosque, located in the grounds of Skanderberg's castle, was built in 1779 and has wooden ceilings painted to look like a dome set on squinches. Another famous building is the Peqin Mosque built in 1822 which incorporates a clock tower into the design of the minaret.

Much of the secular Ottoman architecture in Albania was destroyed in the fierce modernizing programmes of the 1960s and 1970s with the exception of the towns of Gjirokastër and Berat which have been preserved as museum towns. The town of Gjirokastër is built on slopes around the citadel which is located on a high plateau. The town is first mentioned in the twelfth century although the majority of surviving buildings belong to the seventeenth and eighteenth centuries. The typical house in the city consists of a tall stone block structure up to five storeys high with external and internal staircases, a design thought to originate from fortified country houses in southern Albania. The basic form of the house consists of a lower storey containing a cistern and stable with an upper storey reached by a flight of exterior stairs. The upper storey was divided into two units: a guest room, and a winter or family room containing a fireplace. Later on more storeys were added to accommodate extended families; these upper floors were reached by internal staircases. In the seventeenth century houses were built with two wings protecting the lower external staircase.

Berat is a much older city dating back to the Ilyrian period. Initially conquered by the Ottomans in the fourteenth century, it was then recaptured, and not finally occupied by the Turks until 1417. The town is located on the banks of the Osun river and like Gjirokastër is built around a citadel.

The citadel was remodelled by the Turks soon after its capture in 1417 and again in the eighteenth and nineteenth centuries to take account of the use of artillery. Like the fortified houses of Gjirokastër the houses of Berat have external staircases and the main living area of the building is on the upper floor. However, at Berat this feature was designed to overcome the hilly nature of the ground rather than for defensive reasons. Thus to avoid dampness and having to excavate hillsides the houses are built on stone substructures which are sometimes used for storage. The upper parts of Berat houses are built out of timber filled in with lath and plaster and then whitewashed. The verandas sometimes extend along the whole front of the house although in many cases part of the veranda is occupied by a separate room. In the nineteenth century many of these verandas were filled in with large glazed windows. Inside the houses are elaborately decorated with carved and painted woodwork.

Further reading:

R. I. Lawless, 'Berat and Gjirokastër: two museum towns in Albania', in *Islam in the Balkans: Persian Art and Culture of the Eighteenth and Nineteenth Centuries*, Edinburgh 1979, 9–18.
P. Ward, *Albania*, Cambridge and New York 1983.
'Albania', *Aramco World* July/August 1992: 38–47.

albarrani

Spanish term for a tower projecting from the walls of a castle or city fortifications and connected by means of a bridge. The earliest example in Spain is at Mérida and is connected to the ninth-century fortress, but most other examples are later.

Further reading:

J. Zozaya, 'Islamic fortifications in Spain: some aspects', in *Papers in Iberian Archaeology*, BAR, Oxford 1984.

Aleppo (Arabic Halab)

Syria's second city located on the river Qoueiq in north-west Syria.

Aleppo is often regarded as the oldest inhabited city in the world because of its continous history from at least the twentieth century BCE. Although the city was of great significance in Roman and Byzantine times its importance declined during the first three centuries of Islam in favour of the nearby city of Qinnarisin. Under the Hamdanids Aleppo once more became powerful as capital of a dynasty ruling northern Syria; this was short-

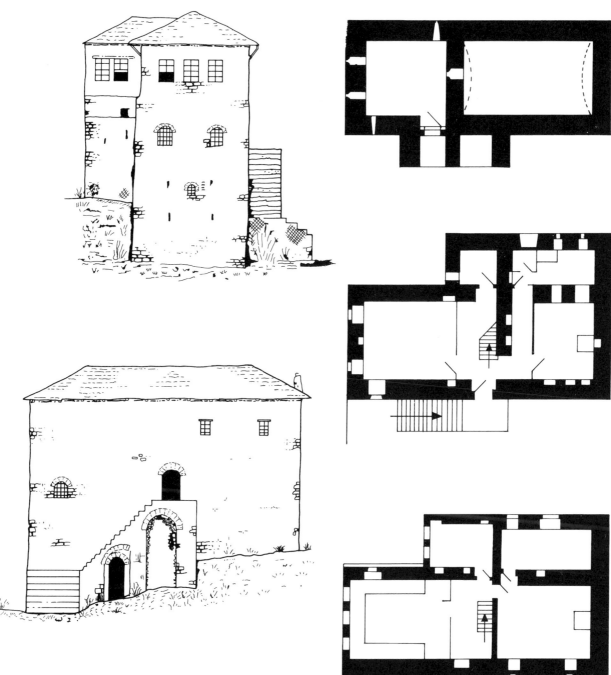

Aleppo (Arabic Halab)

Tower houses in Girokastër, Albania (after Lawless)

0   5

11

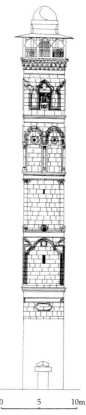

0   5   10m

Eleventh-century minaret of the Great Mosque, Aleppo

lived, however, and the city was not able to recover its status until 1129 when Imad al Din Zengi was made governor. Imad al Din was able to consolidate his position through a series of victories against the Crusaders which established him as premier ruler in Syria. Under Imad and his successors the Zangids and later the Ayyubids the city grew to be one of the great cities of Islam. Despite the Mongol invasions of 1260 and 1400 Aleppo remained a major city throughout the Middle Ages and the Ottoman period.

Although there are the remains of an Umayyad mosque enclosed within the Great Mosque, most of the monuments in Aleppo belong to the period after the eleventh century. During the twelfth and early thirteenth centuries a number of important madrassas were built including al-Zahiriyyah (1217), al-Sultaniyyah (1223) and the Madrassa al-Firdaws which includes a mosque, a school and a turbah. Important public buildings from the fourteenth and fifteenth centuries include the Maristan

(hospital) Arghuni and the Hammam al-Nasiri (public baths).

In spite of the great beauty of Aleppo's madrassas and mosques the best-known feature of the city is its fortifications, particularly the citadel which dominates the old city. Although fortification on the citadel began as early as the tenth century, the most spectacular work dates from the thirteenth century under Ghazi al Malik al-Zahir. During this period the glacis, triple entrance and most of the towers were built. Characteristic features of this work are the monumental inscriptions, carved animal sculpture and massive masonry. In addition to the citadel the old city is enclosed within a medieval wall and gates.

Whilst the medieval period saw the development of Aleppo's fortifications and religious buildings the Ottoman era produced a large number of commercial and industrial buildings. Prominent amongst these are Khan al-Sabun (early sixteenth century), Khan al-Jumruk, Khan al-Wazir and Bayt Dallal (all seventeenth century). These buildings belong to a complex network of suks which extend for a distance of 15 km.

Further reading:

A. Bahnassi, 'Aleppo', in *The Islamic City*, ed. R. B. Serjeant, Paris 1980. This gives a general overview of the city's monuments.
J. Sauvaget, 'Halab', E. I. IV, gives a general history of the city.
Bulletin des Études orientales, esp. 36, 'Études sur la ville d'Alep', 1984, contains recent research.

Algeria

North African country located between Morocco and Tunisia.

Algeria can be divided into three main regions, the Mediterranean coast known as the Tell, the High Plateaux immediately south of the coast and further south the Sahara desert. The Tell is dominated by coastal mountains, although there are three small sections of coastal plain, one at Algiers, one at Oran and one at Annaba. The High Plateaux are more arid with marginal areas for agriculture. The Sahara desert covers four-fifths of the country and links it to West Africa.

Algeria did not exist as a political unit until the Ottoman occupation of the sixteenth century (the country did not include the Sahara regions until the early twentieth century). Before that period it is difficult to separate the history of this area from the rest of North Africa. The first Arab invasion of Algeria occurred in 681 and by the beginning of the eighth century the Byzantine towns of the coast had all surrendered. The predominantly Berber population was converted to Islam relatively quickly and in the early eighth century took part in the conquest of Spain. A notable feature of Algeria at this point was the rapid development of religious sects the most important of which were the Kharijites who established independent rule in the area. The expansion of the Fatimids in the ninth century attracted Berber support particularly along the coast, although those of the south remained opposed to the Fatimid regime. During the eleventh century Berber groups in the south of the country emerged as a coherent political and military force known as the Almoravids. The Almoravids were able to conquer most of Morocco and Algeria and Spain before the end of the eleventh century. Internal disputes meant that the dynasty lasted only fifty years more before being overthrown by the Almohads, another Berber group with similar origins. Like their predecessors the Almohads too had early successes, but did not last much beyond the twelfth century. The political history of the region from the thirteenth to the sixteenth century is quite confused, with various local dynasties trying to establish control over the whole area. The Spanish took advantage of this situation and invaded in 1510. There was strong local resistance to the Spanish invasion and the Ottoman Turks were called in as allies against the Christians. The Turks formally established their rule in 1587 by appointing a governor and defining the present borders of the country. In the early nineteenth century the French occupied the coastal cities to prevent attacks on their ships. This temporary occupation gradually developed into a virtual annexation with French settlers arriving in the country. The occupation lasted until 1962 when Algeria was established as an independent state.

The principal building materials of Algeria are stone, baked brick and mud brick (toub) with wood used as a roofing material. In the coastal cities the quality of the buildings is of a very high standard with ashlar masonry and ornamental stonework in a style similar to North Africa and Spain. South of the coast dressed stonework is very rare and even palatial buildings such as Qal'at Banu Hammad are built out of roughly squared stone. Baked brick is

found mostly in coastal cities such as Tlemcen and Nedroma, although is also used for houses in oasis cities in the east such as Tamelhat where houses have decorative brickwork panels. Roofing tiles made of baked clay are a feature of coastal cities, in particular Tlemcen which is heavily influenced by neighbouring Morocco. Mud brick is used in the High Plateaux regions and in the oasis towns of the desert.

The earliest Islamic architecture which has survived belongs to the Sanhaja Berber dynasties. Excavations at Ashir 170 km due south of Algiers have revealed the remains of a tenth-century palace built by the Zirid dynasty. The palace is a rectangular enclosure (72 by 40 m) with a large central courtyard around which were four separate residences. Across the courtyard from the entrance there was an arcade resting on columns behind which was a domed audience hall. One hundred and fifty kilometres east is the site of Qal'at Banu Hammad capital of the Hammadid dynasty. The city is located high up in the mountains at an altitude of 1,400 m. The city was founded in 1007 by Hammad the father of the dynasty and a relation of the Zirids. Excavations at the site have revealed the Great Mosque and three palaces. In 1015 Hammad broke his allegiance to the Fatimids and pledged his support for the Abbasids. The results of this change of policy can be seen in the architecture of the city; thus a minaret was added to the Great Mosque and the palaces are decorated with carved stone screens reminiscent of contemporary Abbasid stucco work. To the north of Qal'at on the coast is the city of Bougie which became the Hammadid capital from 1060 to 1085, but there are few standing remains of the Hammadid city with the exception of a monumental sea gate.

The south of Algeria was a refuge for Ibadis who rebelled against both the Shi'a orthodoxy of the Fatimids and the Sunni orthodoxy of the Abbasids and their local supporters. In the eleventh century the Ibadis established a capital at the oasis town of Sadrat. Excavations have revealed a number of houses decorated with ornate stucco in the Abbasid style.

The rise of the Almoravids in the eleventh century led to the development of a new mosque form which can be seen in the Great Mosques of Tlemcen, Nedroma, Algiers and Tozeur. This new form preserved the North African tradition of aisles running perpendicular to the qibla with a

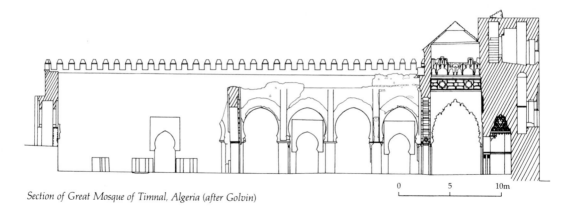

Section of Great Mosque of Timnal, Algeria (after Golvin)

dome in front of the mihrab. The new development was to integrate the lateral arcades into the prayer hall of the mosque and incidentally reduce the size of the courtyard. Another notable feature is that none of the mosques was built with minarets although these were added in later periods.

The breakdown of central political authority after the twelfth century meant that with occasional notable exceptions there were few major architectural projects. In religious architecture this meant the construction of madrassas instead of congregational mosques and in secular architecture it meant the construction of khans/funduqs instead of palaces. A notable exception to this general pattern is the city of Tlemcen which formed the centrepiece of a contest between the Zayyanid and Marinid dynasties. The most ambitious project of the period was the city of al-Mansura outside Tlemcen which was built by the Marinids in 1303 as a base for besieging Tlemcen. After the failure of the first attempt a new siege city was built in 1336. At the centre of this city was the Great Mosque which still survives in its unfinished state. The mosque forms a large rectangle 85 by 60 m and, like the Almoravid mosques, the lateral arcades form an integral part of the prayer hall. The most striking feature of the building is the minaret, at the base of which is the main entrance to the mosque. The minaret is built in a reddish stone decorated with geometric patterns carved into it.

Ottoman architecture was confined principally to the coastal cities with the best examples in Algiers which became the capital at this time. Under French rule Islamic architecture was relegated to a secondary position, although at the beginning of the twentieth century they introduced the West African 'Sudanese Style' to cities such as Ardar in the southern Sahara.

See also: Algiers, Qal'at Banu Hammad

Further reading:

D. Hill and L. Golvin, *The Islamic Architecture of North Africa*, London 1976.

Algiers

Capital city of Algeria.

Algiers is located in the middle of the north coast of Algeria and is built on the site of the Roman town of Icosium. The Muslim city was founded in 944 and rose to prominence under the Almoravids who built the Great Mosque. The city did not become the capital until the Ottoman conquest of the sixteenth century. The city has two seventeenth-century Turkish mosques built in the classical Ottoman style with a large central dome and multiple-domed portico. There are also a number of Turkish mansions in the city built on the wealth derived from attacking Christian ships.

See also: Algeria, Qal'at Banu Hammad

Further reading:

G. Marçais, 'La vie et l'art d'Alger à l'époque Turque', *Communications of the First International Congress of Turkish Art*, Ankara 1986, 251–9.

C. Vincent, 'L'habitation de Grande Kablylie (Algérie)', *Cahiers des Arts et Techniques d'Afrique du Nord* no. 5, 1955, 17–29.

Alhambra

Palace complex in Granada in south-west Spain known for being one of the most beautiful examples of Islamic architecture.

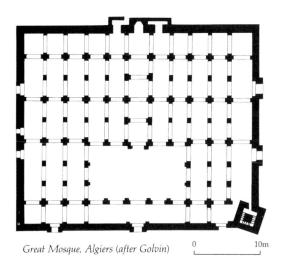

Great Mosque, Algiers (after Golvin)

0   10m.

The name Alhambra, 'The Red Fort', accurately reflects the building's fortified position on a rocky spur in the middle of Granada between the river Darro and the river Genil. The city of Granada first rose to importance in 1012 as capital of the Zirid dynasty who established their base on the site of the Alhambra. Later in 1231 the city was capital of the Nasirid dynasty under Banu al-Ahmar who ruled the province of Andalucía until the final conquest of Ferdinand and Isabella in 1492. As rulers of the last Muslim state in Spain the Nasirids were able to collect some of the most able craftsmen in the peninsula.

The oldest part of the present structure is the Alcazaba which was built in the twelfth century by the Almohads and which protects the western end of the spur on which the Alhambra is built. It is entered through the Puerta de las Armas and enclosed by strong walls which are fortified by rectangular towers. The earliest of these is the Torre Quebrada whilst other early towers are the Torre del Adarguero and the Torre del Homenaje. The Torre del Homenaje was the keep of the Alcazaba and in it the first Nasirid emirs had their apartments. Excavations within the Alcazaba have revealed traces of barracks and a large cistern which date from this early period.

Most of the Alhambra, however, dates from the fourteenth and fifteenth centuries and consists of several palaces built for successive emirs. The earliest of these is known as the Palacio del Partal;

built in the early fourteenth century, it now consists of a tower with an arcaded patio on brick piers. There is also a small mosque built for Yusuf I in 1354 with a small mihrab. The largest and most famous of the palaces is the Palacio de Comares which takes much of its present form from Muhammad V's rebuilding in 1365. The palace is entered through a series of patios or arcaded courtyards with central pools or fountains. The main courtyard for the Comares palace is the Patio de los Arrayanes, on either side of which were the private rooms of the emir's wives. On the northeast side is the entrance to the emir's private quarters known as the Sala de la Barca. This room consisted of a long rectangular chamber with alcoves at either end covered in semi-domes decorated with stars; the area between the alcoves is covered by an inverted boat-shaped vault. These quarters lead via a small mosque to the Salón del Trono or throne room. This room is a large square structure with three deep vaulted recesses on each side formed by the artificially thick walls. The recesses open into paired or single arched windows which overlook the city of Granada whilst the interior of the room is decorated in a profusion of coloured tiles, carved stucco and intricate carpentry.

Later, to distinguish between the personal quarters and formal public reception rooms, Muhammad V created the Patio de los Leones leading on to the Sala des Reyes as a centre for ceremonial. These buildings are regarded by many as the culmination of Islamic palace architecture. The centrepiece of the Patio de los Leones is the fountain, consisting of a polygonal basin supported by marble lions. The Sala des Reyes is a long room or series of rooms opening on to a larger vaulted area, which in turn opens on to the Patio de los Leones. Architecturally this room is a complex structure which questions the distinction between internal and external space. Each of the smaller rooms is decorated with painted ceilings depicting scenes of chivalry and the walls are decorated with intricate stucco work.

See also: Granada, Spain

Further reading:

O. Grabar, *The Alhambra*, London 1978.
W. Irving, *The Alhambra*, London 1906.
F. Prieto-Moreno, *Los Jardines de Granada*, Madrid 1952.
E. Sordo and W. Swaan, *Moorish Spain: Córdoba, Seville and Granada*, London 1963.

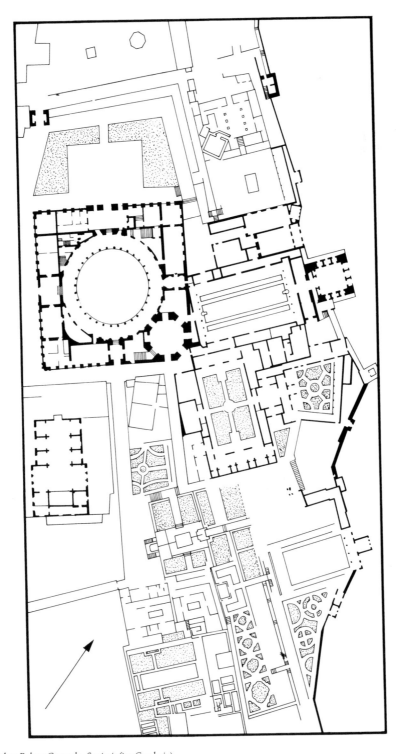

Plan of Alhambra Palace Granada, Spain (after Goodwin)

The Partal Palace Alhambra, © *J.W. Allan, Ashmolean Museum*

Almohads

North African Berber dynasty which ruled over much of North Africa, Spain and parts of sub-Saharan West Africa.

The Almohads originated from the Atlas mountains of Morocco and were led by a religious leader who preached moral reform. They defeated the ruling dynasty of the Almoravids and established the greatest empire of the western Islamic world. In 1170 the capital was moved to Seville from where resistance to the Christian reconquest could be organized.

Almohad architecture is characterized by its mosques and fortifications. The most notable feature of Almohad mosques are the large minaret towers which dominate the great mosques of Seville, Marakesh and Rabat. Under their predecessors, the Almoravids, minarets were thought to be inappropriate and were left out of mosque designs. The Almohads were responsible for reintroducing the minaret, first in a tentative form, as in the minaret of Timnal where it is a low tower behind the mihrab, and later in a monumental form. The design varied from one tower to another but the basic form was a square shaft containing a central core with a vaulted room on each storey. The exterior was usually decorated with windows set within frames made of cusped arches which formed networks of lozenge shapes. The form of these minarets established a tradition which was followed in mosques of the fourteenth century and later.

City walls are equally demonstrative symbols of Almohad ideology with stepped crenellations and decorated gateway façades. The best examples of Almohad fortifications are the city gates at Rabat with their complex bent entrances and monumental façades decorated with cusped arches.

See also: Marakesh, Morocco, Rabat, Seville

Further reading:

H. Basset and H. Terrasse, *Sanctuaires et fortresses almohades,* Paris 1938.

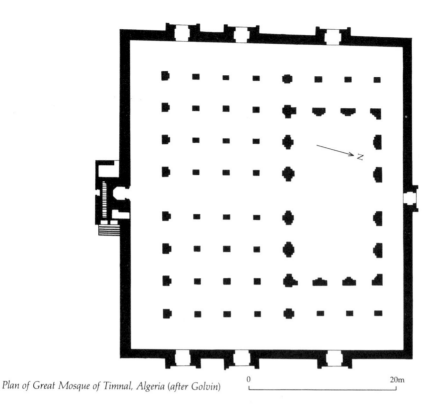

Plan of Great Mosque of Timnal, Algeria (after Golvin)

0   20m

Amman (Roman Philadelphia)

Capital of Jordan containing palace of Umayyad princes.

The Ummayad palatial complex which probably dates from the early eighth century occupies the ancient citadel area in the centre of modern Amman. The most famous part of the complex is the cruciform reception hall which stood at the entrance to the palace. This building consists of four arched iwans set around a central square space which was probably an open courtyard rather than a roofed space. The interior of the courtyard and iwans are decorated with blind niches which are reminiscent of Sassanian buildings in Iraq and further east. Each iwan comprises a tall slightly pointed arch facing the courtyard with a semi-dome behind. In general the form of the building seems to represent an eastern tradition whilst the materials and method of construction suggest a more local (Roman) ancestry.

The rest of the palatial complex forms a rough parallelogram bisected by a central street or processional way. On either side of the central street there are separate buildings or apartments each built around its own courtyard. At the end of the main street a gateway leads into a large courtyard dominated by a large iwan. A door at the back of the iwan gives access to a cruciform domed chamber which may have served as the throne room.

The other important Umayyad building in Amman was the Friday mosque which was demolished and completely rebuilt in 1923. This was a large rectangular building measuring 60 m by 40 m with three entrances on the north side opposite the mihrab. At some later period, probably during the thirteenth century, a square minaret was built at the north-east corner.

See also: Jordan, Umayyads

Further reading:

A. E. Northedge et. al., *Studies on Roman and Islamic Amman*, Oxford 1993.

'Amr, Mosque of

Mosque in Fustat, said to be the oldest mosque in Egypt.

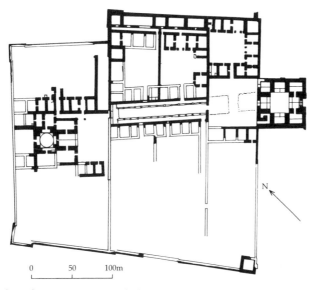

Plan of Umayyad palatial complex, Amman (after Northedge)

The present structure consists of a large roughly square enclosure measuring approximately 120 m on each side. The great variation in the thickness and design of the walls testifies to the building's long history of development and restoration. The first mosque on the site is said to have been built by 'Amr ibn al–'As in 641–42. 'Amr was the chief commander of the Arab troops who won Egypt for Islam and so the building has an historical significance beyond the surviving architecture. Although the remains of this earliest mosque have not survived, there are several historical accounts from which the design of the building can be reconstructed. It consisted of a rectangular structure 29 by 17 m without a concave mihrab and was probably built of mud brick and palm trunks.

Thirty-two years later in 673 the first mosque was pulled down and a larger structure built to accommodate the growing number of Muslims. As well as being larger the new mosque was equipped with four towers which could be used for the call to prayer. These have been interpreted as the first minarets although it is likely that they were not much higher than the roof of the mosque.

The earliest mosque from which any remains survive belongs to the reconstruction of 827 carried out by 'Abd Allah Ibn Tahir. The remains comprise the southern wall of the present mosque which contains blocked-up windows alternating with round-arched niches with shell-like hoods. Both niches and windows are framed by engaged colonettes. Internally there are remains of wooden cornices carved in late Hellenistic style which joined the end columns of the arcades to the wall. Descriptions of the mosque in the tenth century describe it as having glass mosaics on the wall and a bayt al-mal, or treasury, in the centre of the courtyard which together with the four towers suggest a resemblance to the Great Mosque of Damascus.

In later periods several reconstructions and restorations were carried out. The most important changes include those made by Khalif Hakim who added two arcades in the sahn and had the mosaics removed, Sultan Baybars who rebuilt the north wall, the merchants whose restorations were carried out in 1401–2, Murad Bey who strengthened the building and added two minarets in 1797–8. In the restorations of Muhammad Ali in the 1840s the mosque achieved its present form.

Further reading:

D. Berhens-Abouseif, *Islamic Architecture in Cairo: An Introduction*, Supplements to Muqarnas vol. 3, Leiden 1989, 47–50. Contains a general summary and bibliography.

K. A. C. Creswell, *A Short Account of Early Muslim Architecture*, revised and enlarged ed. J. Allan, Aldershot 1989, 8, 15, 17, 46, and chapter 14, 303–14. This gives a detailed account of the building.

Anjar ('Ayn Jar)

Umayyad city in Lebanon.

Anjar was built by the Umayyad caliph al–Walid in 714–15 CE. The city is contained within a rectangular enclosure (370 m north–south and 310 m east–west) supported by a series of solid semi-circular buttress towers and four hollow corner towers. There are four principal gateways and the walls were originally crowned with stepped merlons (crenellation). Internally the city is built to a regular plan recalling earlier Byzantine and Roman cities. There are four principal colonnaded streets which meet at the centre in a tetrapylon. Many of the buildings are built of alternating courses of ashlar blocks and layers of baked brick. There is a series of shop units (3.5 m wide and 5 m deep) lining the main streets behind the colonnades. In the south-east quadrant of the city is a palace within a rectangular enclosure (about 70 by 60 m). The interior of the palace is divided into four units arranged symmetrically; at the south end there is a building with with a triple aisles and an apse resembling a basilical hall, this is duplicated at the north end. To the north of the palace is the mosque which is entered from the west street. The mosque is a rectangular structure (47 by 30 m) with a small central courtyard surrounded by two aisles on the west, east and qibla (south) sides whilst there is one aisle on the north side. On either side of the mihrab are two entrances which lead into a narrow lane that connects with the palace. There is a small bath house next to the north gate which comprises a square vaulted hall, leading via two intermediate rooms into a hot room.

Ankara (Ancyra)

Capital of Republic of Turkey set in the centre of the Anatolian plain.

During the ninth century Anatolia was subject to a number of Arab raids, the most serious of which occupied Ankara for a short period. However, the city was not finally captured until 1071 when it fell to the Seljuk Turks. The oldest surviving mosque in the city is the Aslan Cami built out of wooden columns and reused classical and Byzantine stones. In 1402 the Ottomans suffered a major setback at Ankara when they were defeated by Timur. During the seventeenth century the city was considered to be one of the more important business centres with its own purpose-built bedestan (now the Museum of Anatolian Civilizations). Ankara has some interesting examples of Ottoman domestic architecture with houses built out of wooden frames filled in with brickwork. However, for most of the Ottoman period the city was of minor importance and only rose to prominence when Mustafa Kemal Attatürk chose the city as the site for Turkey's new capital. As a planned city Ankara has some of the best examples of Turkish Republican architecture which is a heavy monolithic architecture reminiscent of Eastern Europe under Communism. The architecture of this period is tempered by conscious references to a Turkish past which include large overhanging eaves and simplified Seljuk-type stonework. Prominent examples of this architecture are the railway station and the offices of the Turkish historical society.

See also: Ottomans, Seljuks, Turkey

Further reading:

H. M. Akok, *Ankari'nin Eski Evleri*, Ankara 1951.
R. Holod and A. Evin, *Modern Turkish Architecture*, Philadelphia 1984.
G. Öney, *Ankara'da Türk Devri Yapilari (Turkish Period Buildings in Ankara)*, Ankara 1971.

appadana

A method of construction whereby a flat roof rests directly on columns (i.e. without intervening arches).

al-Aqmar Mosque

Small Fatimid mosque in Cairo noted for its design and the decoration of the façade.

The mosque is known as al-Aqmar, 'the moonlit', and was founded by Ma'mun al-Bata'ihi, vizier of the Fatimid caliph al-Amir in 1125. The building consists of a small 10-metre square courtyard surrounded by an arcade one bay deep on three sides and three bays deep on the qibla side. Most of the building is made from brick except for the front which faces the main street which is faced in dressed stone.

Architecturally the most important feature of the building is the way the façade is set at a different angle from the rest of the mosque to reconcile the need of having the mosque correctly oriented towards Mecca and the façade facing

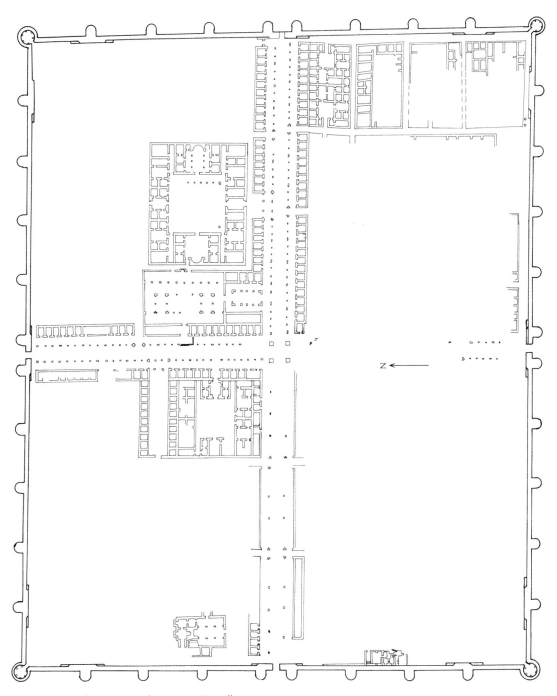

Plan of Umayyad city, Anjar, Lebanon (after Creswell)

Principal street, Anjar, Lebanon

onto the main street. This is the first mosque in Cairo to adopt this arrangement which became common in later mosques. The façade is further emphasized by its decoration and design. It consists of a projecting entrance in the centre flanked by two large niches (only one of these is now visible). The hood of each niche is composed of radiating flutes with a central medallion. The projecting portal consists of a central doorway also with a fluted hood. Either side of the doorway are two smaller niches each with a cusped arch surmounted by a muqarnas moulding. The shape of the arches, the fluted hoods with central medallions and the arrangement of the façade are all features which later become common in Cairene architecture.

Al-Aqmar is also important as it is the first instance of a mosque which incorporates shops into its design. The mosque was originally raised up above street level and the shops were incorporated into the outside walls of the building on a lower level.

See also: Cairo, Fatimids

Further Reading:

D. Berhens-Abouseif, *Islamic Architecture in Cairo: An Introduction*, Supplements to Muqarnas, vol. 3, Leiden 1989, 71–4.

K. A. C. Creswell, *The Muslim Architecture of Egypt*, Oxford 1932–40, 1:241 ff.

C. Williams, 'The Cult of 'Alid Saints in the Fatimid Monuments of Cairo. Part I: The Mosque of Aqmar', *Muqarnas* 1:37 ff., 1983.

al-Aqsa Mosque

The principal mosque of Jerusalem which forms part of the sacred enclosure (haram) with the Dome of the Rock at the centre.

The Aqsa Mosque is located on the southern part of the Haram al-Sharif on an axis with the south door of the Dome of the Rock. In the time of Umar a mosque is known to have been built on the site although it appears to have been a semi-permanent structure made out of re-used material, hastily put together to form a covered prayer area with a shed roof. During the reign of al-Walid the mosque was rebuilt with its present alignment.

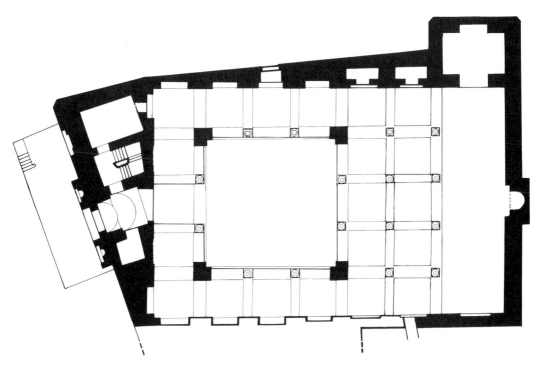

Plan of mosque of al-Aqmar, Cairo (after Williams)

Mosque of al-Aqmar, Cairo, © Creswell Archive, Ashmolean Museum

Only a small part of al-Walid's mosque survives but this indicates that the aisles all ran perpendicular to the qibla wall (as they do today). This arrangement is unusual and recalls the arrangement of Byzantine churches such as the Church of the Nativity in Bethlehem.

The earthquake of 748 severely damaged the mosque which was subsequently rebuilt by the Abbasid caliphs al-Mansur (759) and al-Mahdi (775). The mosque of al-Mahdi had a raised central aisle leading to the mihrab in front of which he built a wooden dome; either side of the central aisle were seven side-aisles. An earthquake of 1033 destroyed the mosque and it was once again rebuilt by the Fatimid caliph al-Zahir in 1035. This mosque had a total of seven aisles, a central aisle with three aisles on either side.

See also: Damascus Great Mosque, Dome of the Rock, Jerusalem, Medina, Palestine, Umayyads

Further reading:

R. W. Hamilton, *The Structural History of the Aqsa Mosque. A Record of Archaeological Gleanings from the Repairs of 1938–42*, Government of Palestine, Jerusalem 1949.

arasta

Turkish term for a street or row of shops whose income is devoted to a charitable endowment or waqf (equivalent to a European shopping arcade).

Arastas are found in most of the regions of the former Ottoman Empire and usually form part of a commercial or religious complex which may include a han (or khan), a mosque and bath house. Many arastas were probably made of wood but these have largely disappeared leaving only those made of more permanent materials. Arastas are often covered over with a barrel vault and have a row of shops either side of a central street, but they can also be open to the sky. Important examples of arastas include the Misir Çarşi in Istanbul, the arasta associated with the Selimiye mosque in Edirne and the arastas at the Sokollu complex at Lüleburgaz and the Selim I complex at Payas both designed by Sinan.

See also: Ottomans

Further reading:

M. Cezar, *Typical Commercial Buildings of the Ottoman Classical Period and the Ottoman Construction System*, Istanbul 1983.

arch

Method of vaulting area between two walls, columns or piers.

Islamic architecture is characterized by arches which are employed in all types of buildings from houses to mosques. One of the most common uses is in arcades where arches span a series of columns or piers to form a gallery open on one side. Arcades are used to line mosque courtyards although they are also used in courtyard houses.

The earliest form of arches employed in Islamic architecture were the semi-circular round arches which were characteristic of Roman and Byzantine architecture. However, fairly soon after the Islamic conquests a new type of pointed arch began to develop. Round arches are formed from a continuous curve which has its centre at a point directly below the apex and level with the springing of the arch on either side. Pointed arches are made by forming each side of the arch from a different centre point, the greater the distance between the two points the sharper the point. In the Dome of the Rock built in 691 the arches supporting the dome are slightly pointed whilst in the cisterns at Ramla built in 759 there is a pronounced point. The arches at Ramla are formed by a separation of the points by a distance of one-fifth the span of the arch; this ratio became standard in many early Islamic buildings.

Another arch form developed during the early Islamic period is the horseshoe arch. Horseshoe arches are those where the arch starts to curve inwards above the level of the capital or impost. Horseshoe arches were developed in Syria in pre-Islamic times and have been recorded as early as the fourth century CE in the Baptistery of Mar Ya'qub at Nisibin. The earliest Islamic monument with horseshoe arches is the Great Mosque of Damascus where the arches of the sanctuary were of slightly horseshoe form. However, the area where horseshoe arches developed their characteristic form was in Spain and North Africa where they can be seen in the Great Mosque of Córdoba. In Tunisia the horseshoe arches of the Great Mosque of Qairawan and the mosque of Muhammad ibn Khairun have a slightly pointed form. Probably the most advanced arch form developed in the early Islamic period is the four-centre arch. This is a pointed arch form composed of four curved sections each with its own centre producing

'Atshan, Khan, Iraq

an arch with steep curves lower down and flattened point at the apex. The earliest occurrence of the four-centred arch is at Samarra at the Qubbat al-Sulaiybiyya. Another arch form which makes its first appearance at Samarra is the cusped arch which is used in the external decoration of the Qasr al-Ashiq. This arch form later became one of the favourite decorative arch forms used throughout the Islamic world from Spain to India.

Arches were not used in India before Islamic times where trabeate construction was the main method of roofing an area. However, arches were regarded as essential by the first Muslim rulers who built arched screens in front of trabeate structures such as the Quwwat al-Islam Mosque in Delhi. Even the screens of the earliest Indian mosques were not composed of true arches but were corbelled structures made to look like arches.

artesonado

Spanish term for wooden panelled ceiling found in Islamic and Mudéjar buildings. Some of the best examples can be found in palaces especially the Alhambra in Granada.

'Atshan, Khan

Small palatial building in the Iraqi western desert between Ukhaidhir and Kufa.

Built of baked brick the design is similar to Ukhaidhir although on a much smaller scale (17 m per side). Externally the building has a simple regular plan consisting of four circular solid corner towers with semi-round towers on three sides and an entrance set between two quarter-round towers on the north side. Internally the building appears to have an irregular plan with long vaulted halls along two sides and a small courtyard decorated with a façade of blind niches. The structure was probably built in the Umayyad period although it has previously been considered an Abbasid (post-750) construction.

See also: Ukhaidhir

Further reading:

B. Finster and J. Schmidt, *Sasaidische und fruhislamische Ruinen im Iraq, Baghdader Mitteilungen* 8, Berlin 1976.

avulu

Turkish term for the courtyard of a mosque which in the summer could be used as an extension of the prayer area.

ayina kari

Mosaic of mirrored glass used in Mughal architecture.

Ayyubids

Medieval dynasty which ruled Syria, Palestine, Iraq, Egypt and Yemen during the twelfth and thirteenth centuries.

The founder of the dynasty was Shirukh, a Kurdish retainer of the Zengid prince Nur al-Din. First Shirukh secured the governorship of Aleppo and later was appointed vizier to the Fatimid ruler of Egypt. Shirukh was succeeded by his nephew Salah al-Din who rapidly extended his position and became ruler of Egypt, Syria and northern Iraq whilst he appointed his brother ruler of Yemen. Salah al-Din's greatest accomplishment was the defeat of the Crusaders and the reconquest of Jerusalem. Salah al-Din died in 1189 and his empire fragmented under his successors who ruled various parts of the empire until the mid-thirteenth century.

Ayyubid architecture was dominated by the need to combat two enemies: the Crusaders in Palestine and the rising threat of Shi'ism and religious dissension. To combat the Crusaders a network of fortresses was built which rivalled those of the Crusaders both in size and technical sophistication. Amongst the best examples of Ayyubid military architecture are Qal'at Rabad at Ajlun in Jordan and Qal'at Nimrud at Banyas in Syria. In addition the fortification of citadels was improved and the famous gateway of the Aleppo Citadel dates from this period. Some of the techniques of fortification were learned from the Crusaders (curtain walls following the natural topography), although many were inherited from the Fatimids (machicolations and round towers) and some were developed simultaneously (concentric planning).

Shi'ism was an equally dangerous threat to the Ayyubids who built a large number of madrassas in both Syria and Egypt. In Egypt the Ayyubids had to reintroduce religious orthodoxy after two centuries of government-imposed Shi'ism. In Syria there was a so a growing threat of Shi'ism in the form of the Assassins who had benefited from the confusion of the Crusader conflict. The Ayyubids tried to promote Sufism as an orthodox alternative and began to build khanqas and Sufi shrines to provide a focus for these activities.

See also: Cairo, Damascus, fortification, Syria, Yemen

Azerbayjan

Country lying south of the Caucasus and east of the Republic of Armenia.

The present Independent Republic of Azerbayjan is the northern part of the Azeri-speaking region which also includes north-western Iran. The capital of the southern part of Azerbayjan is Tabriz whilst the capital of the Independent Republic is Baku. The Independent Republic of Azerbayjan received its name from the Turkish invasion of 1918 although historically it may be identified with the Albania of classical writers. The country lies to the south of the Caucasus and to the east of the Republic of Armenia. More than half of the country is mountainous, though the eastern coastal strip bordering the Caspian Sea is relatively flat. From the twelfth century at least Baku has been known for its natural oil wells which are also the basis of its modern economy. Turkish became the main language of the country after the Seljuk invasions of the eleventh century. Most of the population is Muslim although there are a small number of Zoroastrians with their own fire-temple.

Unlike much of Central Asia and Iran Azerbayjan has its own well-developed, dressed-stone masonry tradition. This can be seen in the tombs, madrassas and mosques of Azerbayjan which have façades carved in relief in a style reminiscent of Seljuk Anatolia. One of the best examples of this stone-working tradition is the palace of the Shirvan Shas in Baku which has monolithic stone columns with austere geometric capitals. Baked brick was also used throughout Azerbayjan, though predominantly in south (now western Iran). One of the most elegant examples of Seljuk brickwork is found in the Gunbad-i-Surkh at Maragha which was built in 1146.

See also: Baku

al-Azhar

One of the main mosques in Cairo and also important as one of the oldest universities.

The name of the mosque, al-Azhar, means 'the flourishing'. The mosque was built in 970 by the Fatimid caliph al-Muciz as the main mosque of the new city of al-Qahira. In 989 the mosque was given the status of theological college to teach the Isma'ili theology. Because of its age and importance the mosque has undergone many alterations and developments although the core of the tenth-century mosque is preserved. The original mosque consisted of a central courtyard with three arcades, two either side of the qibla and the qibla arcade itself. A raised transept runs from the mihrab to the courtyard and there were originally three domes in front of the qibla wall, one above the mihrab and one at either corner.

The plan shares many features with the Fatimid architecture of North Africa, in particular the arrangement of the aisles and the projecting entrance similar to that of Ajdabiya in Libiya.

Later in the Fatimid period the size of the courtyard was reduced by adding four extra arcades around the courtyard. Also a dome was added to the courtyard end of the transept and was hidden by a pishtaq or raised wall above the arcade. Some of the original Fatimid stucco decoration is also preserved, in particular the hood of the prayer niche and on the interior of the arcades. The style is similar to stucco found at Samarra but includes scrolls and palmettes typical of Byzantine decoration.

Further reading:

D. Berhens-Abouseif, *Islamic Architecture in Cairo: An Introduction,* Supplements to Muqarnas, Leiden 1989, 3: 58–63

K. A. C. Creswell, *The Muslim Architecture of Egypt,* Oxford 1952–60, 1: 36 ff.

azulejo

Spanish term for small glazed tiles often used as dadoes in courtyards and palaces.

B

bab

gate.

badgir

Iranian term for wind tower. Tall chimney-like structure which projects above the roof of a building to expel warm air in the day and trap cooler breezes at night.

See also: mulqaf

Badr al-Jamali, Tomb of (also referred to as the Mashhad of al-Juyushi)

Important eleventh-century Fatimid tomb complex in Cairo.

This complex was built by the Armenian general Badr al-Jamali, chief vizier of the Fatimid caliph al-Mustansir, in 1085. Although it is known as a mashhad or tomb complex, the name of the person buried or commemorated is not known (Badr al-Jamali is buried elsewhere).

The complex consists of a prayer room, a small domed room (possibly a tomb) and a tall square minaret built around a small courtyard. The courtyard façade of the prayer room consists of a triple-arched arcade with a large central arch and two smaller side arches. The prayer room is cross vaulted except for the area in front of the mihrab which is covered with a large dome resting on an octagonal drum resting on plain squinches. Both the mihrab and the dome are decorated in stucco work in an Iranian style.

The minaret or tower consists of a tall rectangular shaft with a two-storey structure on the top. This is a square room with a domed octagonal pavilion above it. A significant feature of the design is that at the top of the shaft is a muqarnas cornice which may be one of the first occurrences of this decoration in Egypt. On the roof of the complex are two domed kiosks containing prayer niches. The exact function of these is not known although it has been suggested that they were shelters for the muezzin who would make the call to prayer from the roof similar to the goldasteh found in mosques in Iran.

The exact purpose of this unique building is not known although there have been suggestions that it is a watchtower disguised as a mosque or that it is a victory monument commemorating the victories of Badr al-Jamali.

Further reading:

D. Berhens-Abouseif, *Islamic Architecture in Cairo: An Introduction*, Supplements to Muqarnas, vol. 3, Leiden 1989, 66 ff.
K. A. C. Creswell, *The Muslim Architecture of Egypt*, Oxford 1952–60, 1:155 ff.
F. Shafici, 'The Mashhad of al-Juyushi: Archaeological notes and studies', *Studies in Islamic Art and Architecture in Honour of Professor K. A. C. Creswell*, Cairo 1965, 237 ff.

bagh

Iranian and Mughal term for garden or garden pavilion.

See also: chahar bagh

Baghdad (Madinat al-Salam)

Capital city of Iraq.

Baghdad was founded by the Abbasid caliph al-Mansur in 762. According to historical accounts al-Mansur built a round city with four gates and a palace and mosque at the centre. Leading from the four gates to the centre there were streets lined with shops and markets whilst the area between these streets were quarters reserved for different groups of people. The round shape of the city may be derived from Central Asian ideas of planning or may have some symbolic significance. In any case a round city wall would be both cheaper to build for a given area and would be easier to defend (no weak corner points). The defensive nature of the city is further emphasized by the bent entrances

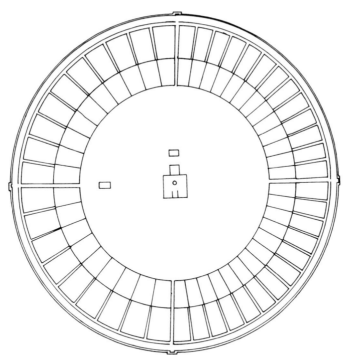

Reconstruction of plan of eighth-century Round City of al-Mansur (Baghdad) (after Creswell)

and the double wall. Unfortunately nothing remains of al-Mansur's city with the possible exception of a mihrab in the Iraq museum. The round city was built on the west bank of the Tigris and shortly afterwards a complementary settlement was founded on the east bank known as Mu'asker al-Mahdi. In 773 al-Mansur moved the markets outside to a place called al-Karkh. From 836 to 892 the capital was transferred to Samarra because of troubles with the caliph's Turkish troops in Baghdad. When Caliph al-Mu'tamid moved back to Baghdad he settled on the east bank of the Tigris which has remained the centre of the city to the present day.

The Buwaihids built a number of important buildings, such as the Bimaristan al-Aduli (hospital) and the Dar al-Alim (house of science) but the Seljuk conquest found the city in a ruinous condition because of the conflict between the Buwaihid amirs and their soldiers. In 1056 Tughril Beg separated his residence from the rest of the city by a broad wall. Although few buildings of the Seljuk period survive, an idea of the appearance of the city in the thirteenth century (before the Mongol invasion) can be gained by looking at the illustrations of al-Wasiti

to the Maqamat of al-Harriri (MS Arabe 5874).

During the period of the later Abbasid caliphate (twelfth to thirteenth century) a massive defensive wall was built around east Baghdad which for centuries marked the boundary of the city. The walls had four gates of which only one survives, the Bab al-Wastani. The gate stood in the centre of a moat and was connected to the city wall and the outside by two brick bridges. The arch of the main entrance is decorated with geometric interlace and is flanked by two lions in relief. Other buildings which survive from this period are the Zummurud Khatun Tomb, the Mustansiriya Madrassa, the building known as the Abbasid palace and two minarets. The Zummurud Khatun Tomb built in 1209 consists of a conical muqarnas dome built on an octagonal base. The sides of the base are decorated with decorative brickwork set over a series of blind niches. Until the eighteenth century a ribat and madrassa built at the request of Zummurud Khatun (mother of the Abbasid caliph al-Nasir) were located near the tomb. The Mustansiriya Madrassa was built between 1227 and 1233 and is the most famous surviving building in Baghdad. It was built by the caliph al-Mustansir and contained four Sunni law schools (i.e. Sha'fi, Hanafi, Maliki and Hanbali). The madrassa is a rectangular courtyard building with four large iwans, one for each law school. The courtyards and iwans are faced with ornate hazarbaf brickwork and carved interlace. The building now known as the Abbasid palace was probably originally the madrassa of al-Sharabiyya built by Sharif al-Din Iqbal in 1230. The building is situated within a rectangular enclosure of 430 square metres and is dominated by a vaulted hall over 9 m high. The brickwork decoration of the building is identical to that of the Zummurud Khatun Tomb. The surviving pre-Mongol minarets belong to the Jami' al-Khaffin and the 'Ami Qumuriyya Mosque; both structures comprise a cylindrical shaft resting on a square base with muqarnas corbelling supporting the balcony.

The most important remains of the Ilkhanid period are Khan Mirjan and the Mirjaniya Madrassa. The khan was built in 1359 to support the madrassa which was completed in 1357. The madrassa is mostly destroyed apart from the gateway which is a monumental portal with carved brickwork similar to that of the Abbasid palace. Khan Mirjan is a remarkable building built around a central covered courtyard. The roof of the courtyard is made of giant transverse vaults which in turn are spanned by barrel vaults. This system made it possible to cover a huge interior space as well as providing light to the interior (through windows set between the transverse vaults).

Many buildings survive from the Ottoman period, the most significant being the shrine of al-Kadhimiyya which houses the tombs of the imams Musa al-Kadhim and Muhammad Jawad. The shrine has been successively rebuilt and much of the structure belongs to the eighteenth or nineteenth century. The shrines stand in the middle of a large courtyard lined with two storeys of arcades. The tombs are covered by tall golden domes and flanked by four minarets, a porch runs around three sides of the tomb structure and there is a mosque on the south side.

The traditional houses of Baghdad are built of brick around small central courtyards. Many houses had projecting wooden balconies often with carved wooden screens. Most of the houses had windcatchers (mulqaf) which would keep the houses cool during the oppressive summer heat.

See also: Iraq

Further reading:
J. Lassner, *The Topography of Baghdad in the Middle Ages*, Wayne State University Press, Detroit 1970.
V. Strika and J. Khalil, *The Islamic Architecture of Baghdad*, Naples 1987.
J. Warren and I. Fethi, *Traditional Houses in Baghdad*, Horsham, UK 1982.

Bahrain

The State of Bahrain comprises a small island on the west side of the Persian/Arabian Gulf located between Qatar and Saudi Arabia.

During Antiquity the island may have been known as Dilmun and during the early Islamic period was known as Awal. The Islamic history of the country is closely tied to its Persian and Arabian neighbours, a fact which is reflected in its architecture and culture. The island seems to have been an important trading centre in the Sassanian period but seems to have missed out from the general economic boom of the early Islamic period. In the tenth century the island escaped from the control of the Abbasid dynasty and became one of the main bases of the Ismaili Carmathian state which controlled much of the northern Gulf during this period. With the collapse of the Carmathians in the tenth century the island came under the control of the Uyunids who were another local dynasty. From the twelfth century onwards Bahrain was under the influence of Persian dynasties who used the island as a trading base with pearls as the basic commodity. In 1504 Bahrain was captured by the Portuguese who controlled the island until 1602 when the country again fell under the influence of Iran. In the 1780s the Khalifa family came from Arabia and established themselves as rulers of the island with British protection. In 1860 Bahrain became a British dependency until its independence in 1971.

The building materials on Bahrain are similar to those used elsewhere in the Gulf and include limestone and coral blocks for masonry and palm trees for wood and thatch. The country contains several early Islamic sites the most famous of which is Qal'at Bahrain on the north coast. The Qal'at as revealed by excavation is a small rectangular building with round corner towers, semi-circular buttress towers and a projecting entrance made out of two quarter circles with a gateway between. Next to this fort is a large fortress built in the thirteenth century which is known as the Portuguese fort because of its restoration in the sixteenth century.

Bahrain contains several historical mosques, the most famous of which is the Suq al-Khamis Mosque founded in the eleventh century. The present building has two main phases, an earlier prayer hall with a flat roof supported by wooden columns dated to the fourteenth century and a later section with a flat roof supported on arches resting on thick masonry piers (this has been dated to 1339). Another distinctive building is the Abu Zaidan Mosque built in the eighteenth century which has a long transverse prayer hall with open sides and a triple arched portico.

The typical Bahrain merchant's house is built around several courtyards each of which forms a separate unit opening on to a series of shallow rooms. Upstairs the arrangement of rooms is repeated but instead of the thick stone walls of the ground floor the walls are built of a series of piers alternating with panels made out of thin coral slabs. Sometimes two layers of coral slabs were used with a cavity in between to provide increased thermal insulation. The temperature of the lower rooms is kept low by various ventilation ducts connected to wind catchers. In addition to coral panels plaster screens are used as a means of ensuring privacy in the upper part of the house. These screens are often decorated with geometric patterns, the most common of which is a series of intersecting rectangles producing a stepped pattern. Most of the traditional houses of Bahrain are located in the Muharraq district of the capital Manama. The most famous house is the palace of Sheikh Isa built in 1830 and recently restored as a national monument. The house is built around four courtyards and includes some beautiful incised stucco panels in the upper rooms.

See also: Kuwait, Oman, Qatar, Saudi Arabia, UAE

Further reading:
S. Kay, *Bahrain: Island Heritage*, Dubai 1985.
C. Larsen, *Life and Land Use on the Bahrain Islands*, Chicago 1983.
R. Lewcock, 'The Traditional Architecture of Bahrain', in *Bahrain through the Ages: The Archaeology*, ed. S. H. Ali al-Khalifa and M. Rice, London 1986.

Baku
Capital of the Independent Republic of Azerbayjan.

Baku is located on a peninsula on the west coast of the Caspian Sea. The city has always been famous for its naturally occurring oil wells although it did not achieve political importance until the fifteenth century, when it was established as the capital of a local dynasty known as the Sherwan Shahs. The Sherwan Shahs had established themselves along the west coast of the Caspian Sea as early as the fourteenth century although they did not move to Baku until their previous capital of Shir'wan was captured by the Qara Qoyonulu in 1426. The Sherwan Shahs were effectively destroyed in 1500 when the Saffavid ruler Isma'il killed the reigning shah. Baku remained part of the Iranian Empire from the sixteenth until the early twentieth century when it was annexed by Russia.

One of the earliest Islamic monuments in Baku is the Kiz Kallesi which is a huge round bastion tower built of brick. The tower was probably built in the eleventh century although the precise date has not been agreed. The tower may have formed part of the city walls of Baku although alternatively it may have been an independent castle or watchtower. The majority of monuments in Baku date from the period of the Sherwan Shahs or later. The most important monuments form part of the royal complex which stands on a hill overlooking the Caspian Sea. All of these buildings are made out of large bluish-grey limestone blocks which are carefully squared and dressed. At the centre of the complex is the palace which was built in the mid-fifteenth century. The layout of the palace is based on two interconnected octagons with two storeys. A tall entrance portal opens into an octagonal hall which in turn leads via a passageway into a smaller hall. The palace complex includes a private mosque which has a cruciform plan entered from monumental portal set to one side. One of the other arms contained a separate women's mosque and there was another prayer hall upstairs. The complex also includes a number of mausoleums the most important of which is the tomb of the shahs. This comprises a square central chamber leading on to four barrel-vaulted side rooms. The dome is slightly pointed and decorated with faceting.

See also: Azerbayjan

Balkh, Hajji Piyadi Mosque (also known as Masjid-i Tarikh, Nuh Gunbad or Masjid-i Ka'b al-Akhbar)
Site of a badly damaged mosque, believed to date from the early Islamic period.

The mosque is situated north-east of the city walls

of Balkh in Afghanistan. Most scholars agree that the monument should be dated to the ninth century CE. Although the roof itself has collapsed the building is regarded as one of the earliest examples of a nine-domed mosque.

The mosque is built out of a combination of baked and unbaked brick and pisé. The extant remains include massive round piers and smaller engaged columns typical of Abbasid architecture.

Further reading:

L. Golombeck, 'Abbasid mosque at Balkh', *Oriental Art* NS 15(3): 173–89, Autumn 1969.

J. D. Hoag, *Islamic Architecture*, New York 1977, 48–9.

Banbhore

Major early Islamic site in Pakistan.

Banbhore is located on the north bank of the Gharro Creek near the Indian Ocean coast in the Pakistani state of Sind. Archaeological work at the site has revealed a long-term occupation from the first century to the thirteenth century CE which includes three distinct periods, Scytho–Parthian, Hindu–Buddhist and early Islamic. It seems probable that the site is the ancient city of Debal referred to in early Muslim accounts of the area and conquered by the Arab general Mohammed ibn al-Qasim in 711.

The city comprises a large area enclosed by a stone and mud wall strengthened by solid semi-circular bastions with three main gateways. The walled area is divided into two parts, an eastern and a western section separated by a fortified stone wall. In the middle of the eastern sector is the congregational mosque. The mosque has a roughly square plan, built around a central courtyard, two arcades on each of the sides except the qibla side which is three bays deep. The mosque has been dated by an inscription to 727 CE, two years after the capture of Debal. Significantly there is no trace of a concave or projecting mihrab which confirms the mosque's early date as the first concave mihrab was introduced at Medina between 707 and 709 (see also Wasit and mihrab).

Remains of houses and streets have been found both within the walls and outside to the north and east. Large houses were built of semi-dressed stone or brick, the smaller houses of mud brick.

See also: Pakistan

Further reading:

S. M. Ashfaque, 'The Grand Mosque of Banbhore', *Pakistan Archaeology* 6: 182–209, 1969.

M. A. Ghafur, 'Fourteen Kufic inscriptions of Banbhore, the site of Daybul', *Pakistan Archaeology* 3: 65–90, 1966.

S. Qudratullah, 'The twin ports of Daybul', *in Sind through the Centuries*, Karachi 1981.

bangala

Mughal and Indian term for roof with curved eaves resembling the traditional Bengali hut.

See also: char-chala, do-chala

Bangladesh

See Bengal

Basra

Early Islamic garrison town and Iraq's principal port.

Basra was founded in 635 as a twin garrison town of Kufa. The purpose was to relieve the pressure of the constant immigration into Iraq as well as to provide a base for the opening of a new front against the Arabs of Bahrain. The majority of Arabs in Basra, unlike those of Kufa, had not taken part in the wars of conquest in Iraq. The first mosque was marked out with reeds and people prayed within the enclosed space without any fixed building. In 665 CE a new mosque was built on the site by Ziyad, governor of Iraq. The mosque was built out of baked bricks with a flat roof supported by teak columns. Unfortunately the expansion of modern Basra has meant that no remains of the early period stand above ground.

See also: Iraq, khatta

bayt

Arabic term for house. In Umayyad and Abbasid architecture it is used to describe the living units within palaces and desert residences.

bayt al-mal

Arabic term for treasury (literally 'house of the money'). In Friday mosques usually an octagonal or square room raised up on columns in the centre of the courtyard.

bazar

Market area in Turkish city.

The Turkish word bazar is derived from the Persian 'pazar'. A Turkish bazar will normally contain a number of specialized buildings such as bedestans, bath houses (hammams), hans (khans) and caravanserais as well as private shops, market stalls and a mosque. One of the earliest examples of a Turkish bazar is that of Bursa which was first developed in the fourteenth century. This complex includes six mosques, three baths, seventeen khans, six madrassas and a bedestan.

See also: arasta, bedestan, Ottomans

bedestan

Special closed form of Turkish market where goods of high value were traded. The usual form of bedestan is a long domed or vaulted hall two storeys high with external shop units.

Originally bedestan referred to the area of a market where cloth was sold or traded from the 'bezzaz han' (cloth market). The earliest bedestans were probably specific areas of a general bazar or market. The earliest known bedestan is the Beyşehir Bedestan built in 1297 according to an inscription above the gateway. The building consists of a closed rectangular courtyard covered by six domes supported on two central piers. There are doorways on three sides and on the outside there are small open shop units, six on the east and west sides and nine on the north and south sides.

During the Ottoman period bedestans developed as a specific building type and became the centre of economic life in a city. Because they could be locked they were often used for jewellery or money transactions and came to be regarded as signs of prosperity in a city. Ottoman bedestans were built in a variety of forms and may include features such as external shops, internal cell units and arastas (arcades). The simplest plan consists of a square domed hall with one or two entrances like those at Amasya or Trabzon. More complicated structures like the Rüstem Pasha Bedestan in Erzerum consist of a central enclosed courtyard surrounded by a closed vaulted corridor containing shop units.

Bengal

Low-lying delta area in the north-west corner of the Indian subcontinent.

The character of Bengal is largely determined by the Ganges and Bramaputra rivers which divide into innumerable branches before entering the sea. Although the area is currently divided between the two modern states of India and Bangladesh it retains a certain homogeneity based on its language (Bangli) and culture.

In the thirteenth century the region was conquered by Muslim Turks who occupied the city of Gaur (Lakhnaw) in north-west Bengal. From this base the areas of Satgaon (south-west Bengal) and Sonargaon (east Bengal) were conquered and incorporated into an independent sultanate in 1352 CE by Iliyas Shah. Despite dynastic changes the area remained independent until the sixteenth century when it was incorporated into the Mughal sultanate, and even then it still retained its identity as a separate province.

Lack of suitable building stone in the area meant that the predominant materials of construction were red clay bricks from the alluvial silts and bamboo and thatch. The majority of buildings were made of bamboo and thatch and consist of a rectangular area which is roofed by a curved thatch roof ('charchala' and 'do-chala'). Most of the more important buildings, however, were made out of brick. In the pre-Mughal period such buildings were faced either with red terracotta plaques or less frequently in stone. From the sixteenth century onwards brick buildings were coated in white plaster.

One of the achievements of Bengali building was its translation of traditional bamboo and thatch architecture into more permanent stone and brick forms. One of the best examples of this is the use of curved roofs from the sixteenth century onwards. There are two main forms of this roof – do-chala and char-chala. A do-chala roof consists of a central curved ridge rising in the middle with curved side eaves and gabled ends. A char-chala roof is made of crossed curved ridges with curved eaves. The earliest surviving example of this roof type in a brick building is the tomb of Fath Khan at Gaur dated to the seventeenth century. This form was so successful that it was used elsewhere in the Mughal Empire, at Agra, Fatehpur Sikri, Delhi and Lahore. In addition to its aesthetic appeal curved roofs also have a practical purpose in an area of high rainfall.

Other characteristic features of Bengali architecture adopted by the Mughals and used elsewhere are the two-centre pointed arch and the use of cusped arches for openings.

The predominant form of Islamic architecture in Bengal is the mosque. In pre-Mughal Bengal the mosque was virtually the only form of Islamic building, although after the sixteenth century a

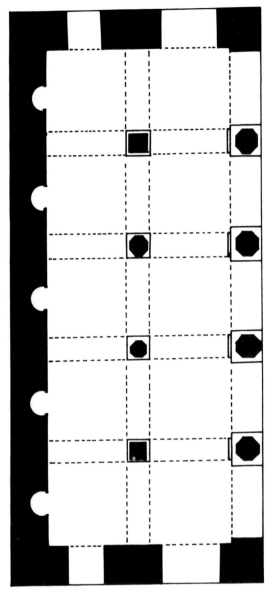

Mosque of Zafar Khan, Ghazi, Bengal. Note multiple mihrabs (after Michell)

mosques. The number of mihrabs is determined by the number of entrances in the east wall. Engaged corner towers are a constant feature of Bengali architecture and may derive from pre-Islamic temples. Curved cornices are probably derived from the curved roofs of bamboo huts; it is possible that they may have a practical function for draining water away from the base of the domes.

During the pre-Mughal sultanate three types of mosque were built, rectangular, square nine-domed and square single-domed.

Mosques built on a rectangular plan are divided into aisles and bays according to the number of domes on the roof. At the east end of each aisle is a doorway and at the west end a mihrab. There are also openings on the south and north sides of the mosque corresponding to the number of bays. The nine-domed mosques are similar to those found elsewhere in the Islamic world, but they differ in having three mihrabs at the west end. The most popular form of mosque in pre-Mughal Bengal was the single-domed chamber. It is likely that this design is developed from the pre-Islamic temple of Bengal.

None of these early mosques was equipped with minarets and sahns as was common in the Middle East but these features were introduced with the Mughal conquest in the sixteenth century. However, the Mughals were also influenced by the local architecture of Bengal and it is from this period that we have the first example of a do-chala roof translated into brick (the Fath Khan Tomb at Gaur, dated to the seventeenth century).

Muslim buildings can be found all over the region of Bengal, although the largest concentrations can be found at Dhaka and Gaur (Lucknow). Calcutta, the capital of Indian Bengal, was founded during the period of British rule in the nineteenth century. As might be expected the early mosques of the city show strong British influence. The descendants of Tipu Sultan built three mosques in the city all with the same double-aisled, multi-domed rectangular plan. The most famous of these buildings, the Tipu Sultan Mosque built by his son Muhammad, is built in the style of a European building with Tuscan colonettes and Ionic columns used for the windows and central piers.

Further reading:

P. Hassan, 'Sultanate mosques and continuity in Bengal architecture', *Muqarnas* 6, 1989. This deals with pre-Mughal architecture.

wide variety of Islamic building types such as the caravanserai and madrassa were introduced. Characteristic features of Bengali mosques of all periods are multiple mihrabs, engaged corner towers and curved cornices. Although multiple mihrabs sometimes occur in North India, Bengal is the only place where they are a constant feature in

G. Michell (ed.), *The Islamic Heritage of Bengal*, Paris 1984. This is the best reference book on Islamic architecture in Bengal.

beteng

Indonesian term for enclosure wall, used to refer to the outer walls of palaces in Java.

Bijapur

City in southern India famous for its sixteenth- and seventeenth-century architecture.

Bijapur is located on an arid plateau between the Krishna and Bhima rivers. The city rose to prominence under the Adil Shahi dynasty who ruled the city from the fifteenth century until its conquest by the Mughals in 1686. Traditionally the dynasty was founded in 1490 when the Turkish governor Yusuf Khan declared the independence of Bijapur. By the sixteenth century the Adil Shahi dynasty ruled a huge area which extended as far as Goa on the western coast.

Since the seventeenth century the city has shrunk so that the present town occupies less than half the original area. The original city walls with a circumference of over 10 km survive to give some idea of the city's original importance. These massive walls are surrounded by a moat and protected by ninety-six bastions. There are five main gateways, each of which consists of a bent entrance protected by two large bastions. Within this huge enclosure there is a smaller walled area known as the Arquila or citadel which forms the centre of the modern town. The city is supplied with water by a series of underground water channels interspersed with water towers to regulate the pressure.

Water is perhaps the most distinctive element in the architecture of Bijapur and is used for ornamental tanks, water pavilions, bath houses and ornamental channels. The Mubarak Khan is one of the best surviving examples of a water pavilion; it consists of a three-storey structure with a shower bath on the roof. Other notable examples include the Jal Mandir Palace once located in the centre of a reservoir (now disappeared) and the Sat Manzili which was originally a seven-storey structure enlivened with water tanks and spouting water.

The city contains several mosques, the largest of which is the Jami Masjid founded in the sixteenth century. The mosque has a rectangular central courtyard containing several fountains in the centre. The mosque sanctuary is nine bays wide and is crowned by a large central dome. One of the more unusual features of the mosque is the stone floor which is divided up into 2,250 individual prayer spaces. Other important mosques in the city are the Jhangari Mosque and the Mecca Masjid which is enclosed within huge walls.

The city contains many tomb complexes the best known of which is the mausoleum of Muhamad Adil Shah II, known as the Gol Gumbaz. Other important mausoleums include the Ibrahim Rauza built between 1626 and 1633. The complex consists of a large square area enclosed within a tall wall and entered via a monumental gateway flanked by twin minarets. In the centre of the complex is a raised platform containing two large buildings either side of a sunken rectangular tank. To the east surrounded by a colonnade is the domed tomb chamber which has an extraordinary suspended stone ceiling. To the west of the pool is the the mosque with four thin minarets, one at each corner. The whole complex is decorated with painted, inlaid and carved ornament in the form of flowers and arabic calligraphy.

See also: Deccan, Gol Gumbaz, India

birka

Arabic term for tank, reservoir or cistern.

blazon

Decorative device or symbol used in Mamluk architecture to denote particular amirs or military dignitaries.

The earliest blazons were circular shields containing a simple symbol. Later these became complex designs divided into three fields with a variety of symbols used to denote different offices (i.e. a napkin represents the master of the robes and a pen box represents the secretary). The earliest example of a blazon was found in the tomb of Sheikh Iliyas in Gaza dated to 1272. Blazons are not used after the Ottoman conquest of 1517.

Further reading:

W. Leaf, 'Not trousers but trumpets: a further look at Saracenic heraldry', *Palestine Exploration Quarterly*, 1982.
L. A. Mayer, *Saracenic Heraldry*, Oxford 1933.

Bosnia

Independent state in south-eastern Europe, previously constituting part of the former Republic of Yugoslavia.

Fourteenth-century composite Mamluk blazon used by warrior class (after Mayer)

Islam was introduced to Bosnia by the Ottoman Turks although it later became the religion of a large proportion of the native Bosnian population. The first Turkish invasion of Bosnia was in 1386 and by 1389 after the battle of Kosovo the Bosnian rulers had accepted Turkish suzerainty. In 1463 the Bosnian king Stjepan Tomasevic failed to pay tribute to the Ottomans resulting in a further invasion of Bosnia. By 1512, with the conquest of the district of Sebrenik, all Bosnia had been incorporated into the Ottoman Empire. After the conquest there was large-scale Islamization which appears to have spread from the towns outwards. During the seventeenth century Bosnia served as a base for the conquest of Hungary whilst during the eighteenth century it became a border area between the Austro-Hungarian and Ottoman empires. In 1878 Bosnia was invaded by the Austro-Hungarian army after the Turks had been forced to leave under the terms of the Congress of Berlin. After the First World War Bosnia was incorporated into the Federal Republic of Yugoslavia until 1992 when it became an independent state.

In general Ottoman buildings in Bosnia reflect the imperial architecture of Istanbul, Bursa and Edirne although there are also elements of a local style. This style seems to have been partly developed by Dalmatian builders from Dubrovnik who were hired to construct some of the monumental buildings. One characteristic of Dalmatian building is the use of small cut stones instead of the bricks more commonly used in Ottoman architecture. Another notable feature of Bosnian architecture is the use of squinches instead of the triangular pendentives more common in Turkish architecture.

Four main periods of Islamic architecture have been identified. The first period which begins with the Turkish conquest is characterized by the founding of cities such as the capital Sarajevo, Banja Luka and Mostar. Also during this period many public buildings and mosques were founded by the Turkish governors and aristocracy. Important buildings from the sixteenth century in Sarajevo include Ghazi Khusraw Bey Cami, the 'Ali Pasha Cami and the Brusa Bedestan. During the second period, in the seventeenth century, the patronage of buildings was mostly by local merchants and includes khans, bath houses and mescits although some imperial buildings were erected such as the Tekke of Hajji Sinan in Sarajevo (1640). During the eighteenth and nineteenth centuries (the third period) there was increased European influence in the architecture as well as fashions imported from Istanbul. An interesting phenomenon is the development of the town of Trevnik as the official residence of the Ottoman vizier. Under the Austro-Hungarian Empire a fourth period can be distinguished which was characterized by an attempt to build non-Turkish Islamic architecture. Many of the buildings of this period were built in 'Moorish Style', the most famous example of which is Sarajevo Town Hall.

See also: Albania, Bulgaria, Ottomans

Further reading:

M. Kiel, 'Some reflections on the origins of provincial tendencies in the Ottoman architecture of the Balkans', in *Islam in the Balkans: Persian Art and Culture of the 18th & 19th Centuries*, Edinburgh 1979.

brickwork

In many areas of the Islamic world brick is the primary building material.

There is an important distinction to be made between fired or baked brick and mud brick. Fired brick requires fuel to heat the kilns, making it relatively expensive, although the firing makes it more durable and therefore more suitable for monumental building. Architecture of the early Islamic period drew on two distinct building traditions each of which used fired brick as a major component. In the Mediterranean area brickwork derived from Byzantine and ultimately Roman traditions whereas in former Sassanian territories it dated back to the ancient civilizations of Mesopotamia and Iran.

In the Byzantine tradition brick was usually used for specific parts of a building such as the dome or as string courses to level off layers of rubble wall. In the area of Syria and Jordan the availability of good quality stone meant that bricks were little used in the Byzantine architecture of the area and consequently were little used in the early Islamic architecture of the area. In the few examples – Mshatta and Qasr al-Tuba – where brickwork is employed it seems to be an import from the Sassanian east rather than a continuation of a local tradition. It is only with the Ottoman conquest of Anatolia that the Byzantine brickwork tradition becomes fully incorporated into Islamic architecture.

In the east (Iran and Iraq), however, brick was employed in the earliest Islamic buildings (i.e. Khan Atshan) as a direct continuation of Sassanian practice. It was in this area that the techniques of decorative brickwork developed using either standard bricks arranged in patterns or specially shaped bricks. Bricks could be laid vertically, sideways, flat on or in a herringbone pattern and were used to form geometric patterns or even inscriptions. Particularly elaborate brickwork was referred to by the Persian term hazarbaf (qv). Brickwork of the Seljuk period, from the eleventh to thirteenth century, in Iran and Central Asia is particularly elaborate using specially manufactured bricks. A particularly good example is Aisha Bibi Khanum Mausoleum at Djambul, Uzbekistan.

See also: hazarbaf, mud brick

Bukhara

Oasis city in the Republic of Uzbekistan, Central Asia.

Bukhara is located in the valley of the Zeravshan river 200 km west of Samarkand. The city was first mentioned by its present name in a seventh-century Chinese text; however the city itself is probably older. The first Arab raid on Bukhara occurred in 674 although it was not finally conquered until 739. During the ninth and tenth centuries the city was under the rule of the Samanids and from 900 was capital of the province of Khurassan. During this period the city flourished and became established as one of the greatest centres of learning in the Islamic world.

Descriptions of Bukhara in the Samanid period indicate that it consisted of two main parts, the citadel and the town itself. The citadel and the town were separate walled enclosures on a high plateau, with a space between them which was later occupied by a congregational mosque. The citadel had a circumference of 1.5 km and contained, besides the palace, the city's first Friday mosque which was built on a pagan temple. The town itself was approximately twice the size of the citadel and was enclosed by a wall with seven gates. Later the whole area of the city and the citadel was enclosed within a wall with eleven gates (visible until 1938). In addition to the city walls there were outer walls which enclosed the villages around the city to protect them from nomad attacks; traces of these walls still survive.

Little is left of the Samanid city except the tenth-century mausoleum of the Samanid rulers known as the mausoleum of Isma'il the Samanid. This is one of the earliest examples of Islamic funerary architecture and consists of a square chamber with a hemispherical dome and decorative brickwork on both the exterior and the interior. The corners of the building are formed by engaged cylindrical brick piers whilst the corners of the dome are marked by small domed finials. In the centre of each side there is a recessed niche containing a door which acts as a focus for the surface decoration. The main form of decoration is small, flat, tile-like bricks laid alternately in vertical or horizontal groups of three. Another decorative technique is bricks laid horizontally in groups of three with one corner projecting outwards producing a dog-tooth pattern. This dog-tooth pattern is used mainly in the spandrels of the door arch which are also decorated with square terracotta plaques. At the top of the exterior façade there is an arcade of small niches which mask the zone of transition and also provide light to the interior. The decoration of the interior is similar to the exterior façade although here tiles are set vertically on end producing a diaper pattern. The dome rests on arched squinches which alternate with arched grilles which admit light to the interior.

The collapse of the Samanids at the end of the tenth century led to the gradual decline of Bukhara under their successors the Kharakhanids. This decline was reinforced by the Mongol invasions of the thirteenth century which twice destroyed the city. There seems to have been no recovery in the

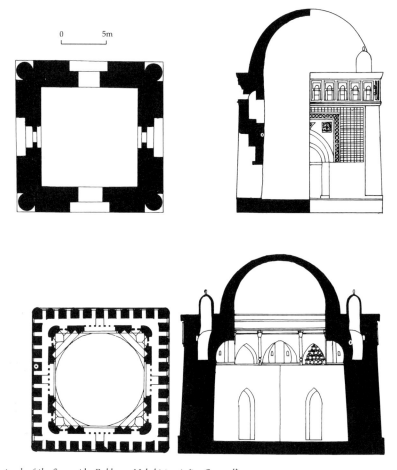

0   5m

Tenth-century tomb of the Samanids, Bukhara, Uzbekistan (after Creswell)

fifteenth century and it was not until the arrival of the Uzbeks in the sixteenth that the city recovered some of its former splendour. There are few structures which survive from the period between the Samanids and the Uzbeks although there are a few important buildings which date from the twelfth century. The most famous of these is the Kaylan Minaret which is a huge tower over 45 m high and is decorated with bands of decorative brickwork. The tower is a tapering cylinder with an arcaded gallery surmounted by an overhanging muqarnas corbel; its form is similar to that of Seljuk towers in Iran with its band of polychrome tile decoration at the top. Another twelfth-century structure demonstrating Seljuk influence is the shrine of Chasma Ayyub with its conical dome. A few buildings

survive from the fifteenth century including the Ulugh Beg Madrassa built in 1417.

Most of the major monuments of Bukhara date from the Uzbek period and include the massive Kukeldash Madrassa, the Divan Begi Mosque and Madrassa and the Kaylan Mosque. The buildings of this period resemble the Timurid buildings of Samarkand which they were clearly intended to imitate in both size and design. Another feature of this period is the grouping of buildings around a focal point or square such as the Lyabi Hauz or the Poi Kaylan in order to increase the visual effect. The Kukeldash Madrassa measures 80 by 60 m and is the largest madrassa in Central Asia although its decoration is surprisingly austere. The Divan Begi Mosque and Madrassa are equally impressive

Tenth-century mausoleum of the Samanids, Bukhara © StJohn Simpson

Minaret of the Kaylan Mosque, Bukhara © StJohn Simpson

with tall pishtaq entrances framed by twin minarets. The largest mosque in the city is the Kaylan Mosque built in the sixteenth century with the twelfth-century minaret nearby. The entrance to the mosque is through a huge entrance iwan or pishtaq decorated with blue glazed tiles covered with yellow flowers and turquoise stars. Within the mosque is a huge courtyard surrounded on three sides by a deep arcaded gallery. At the south-west end is another large iwan which leads to a domed room covered with a mihrab.

During the eighteenth century there was a move away from the monumental architecture of the first Uzbek rulers towards a lighter form of architecture inspired by Saffavid Iran. One of the finest examples of this style is the Masjid-i Jami opposite the Bola Hauz which has a magnificent hypostyle wooden porch supported on twenty wooden columns with painted muqarnas capitals.

See also: Samarkand, Timurids, Uzbekistan

Further reading:

J. Lawton and F. Venturi, *Samarkand and Bukhara*, London 1991.

G. Pugacenkova and L. Rempel, *Bukhara*, Moscow 1949.

L. Rempel, 'The Mausoleum of Isma'il the Samanid', *Bulletin of the American Institute of Persian Art and Archaeology* 4: 199–209, 1936.

Bulgaria

A small country located on the Danube in south-eastern Europe.

Bulgaria borders Turkey, Greece, Serbia, Russia and Romania. The name of the country derives from the Bulgars, a Turkic people who conquered this area in 679 CE and adopted Christianity from the Byzantines in 865. The presence of Islam in Bulgaria is almost exclusively connected with the Ottoman conquest of the region.

The first Ottoman conquest in Bulgaria took place in the mid-fourteenth century when they occupied part of the area now known as Bulgarian

Thrace. In 1396, after Sultan Bayezid's victory at the battle of Nikeboli (Nicopolis), the Danube area of Bulgaria was incorporated into the Ottoman Empire. From the end of the fourteenth century Bulgaria was strongly Ottomanized and new Muslim cities were established especially in the south-east of the country. By the sixteenth century this part of the country was predominantly Muslim and remained so until the nineteenth.

The main building materials used in Bulgaria were similar to those used by the Byzantines and later the Ottomans in Anatolia. These included baked brick on its own, baked brick in combination with ashlar masonry, ashlar masonry, coursed rubble masonry with wood and mud brick and wood. The choice of material depended partly on the area and partly on the status of a particular building.

Bulgaria can be divided into two main regions on the basis of Ottoman architecture: Bulgarian Thrace and the area of the Danube (Danubia). Bulgarian Thrace was the first area conquered by the Ottomans and so has a higher proportion of Ottoman buildings than the rest of the country.

Bulgarian Thrace

One of the oldest Islamic structures in Bulgaria is the turba of Lal Sahin Pasa in Kazanlik, thought to date from the mid-fourteenth century. The turba is an open, domed canopy supported on piers; the entire structure is made out of baked brick.

Most of the surviving Ottoman buildings, however, are in the major cities. Some of the best examples can be found in Plovdiv (Turkish Filibe and Byzantine Philippopolis) in the south-east of Bulgaria near Turkish Thrace. Here the Ottomans founded a new Muslim settlement outside the walls of the Christian one. The focal points of the city were the two mosques located at either end of the city centre. The older of these is the Cumaya Cami or Great Mosque built by Murad II in the 1420s which is reputedly one of the largest and most important mosques in the Balkans. It has nine bays roofed by three central domes and six wooden vaults, and beneath the central dome is a pool or fountain. In general the building resembles that of the Sehadet Cami in Bursa built in 1365. To the south of the Great Mosque is the Zaviye Cami or Imaret Mosque built in 1440 which formed the core of a commercial district with a bedestan

and hammam. The Ottoman town of Filibe was developed between these two mosques and a main street was built to link the two.

To the east of Filibe is the city of Yambol which was established after the Ottoman conquests in 1365. Probably the most important monument at Yambol is the Eski Cami built between 1375 and 1385. This consists of a single-domed unit built of brick and ashlar masonry in the Byzantine and early Ottoman style. In the mid-fifteenth century rooms were added on to the sides and a square minaret was also added. At Yambol too is one of the best preserved examples of an early Ottoman bedestan. This consists of a long hall roofed by four domes and entered through the middle of the long sides. On the outside of the building are thirty vaulted rooms or shop units.

North and West Bulgaria (Danubia)

Outside Thrace Ottoman buildings tended to have more local characteristics. In the area of Danubia a particular form of mosque developed consisting of a spacious wooden rectangular hall with a flat roof or wooden ceiling (sometimes with an inset wooden dome), covered by a gently sloping roof. This roofing system was lighter than a brick or stone dome so that walls could be made thinner and could be built out of coursed rubble rather than ashlar masonry. Two examples of such mosques survive at Vidin on the Danube; the mosque of Mustafa Pasa built in the early eighteenth century and the Ak Cami built in 1800. Both are built out of coursed rubble masonry with flat wooden ceilings under tiled roofs. Another such mosque at Belgradcik (Haci Husseyin Aga) has a carved wooden ceiling in the local Bulgarian style.

A characteristic type of building found in north-east Bulgaria is the tekke or dervish lodge. The Kizane Tekkesi near Nikopol on the Danube is characteristic of the Besiktasi order in the sixteenth century. The complex is built of wood and mud brick and was last rebuilt in 1855. The tekke comprises several elements including a kitchen, guesthouse, assembly hall and the mausoleum of the saint.

Further reading:

M. Kiel, 'Early Ottoman monuments in Bulgarian Thrace', *Belleten* 37 no.152, 1974.
—— 'Urban development in Bulgaria in the Turkish

period: the place of architecture in the process',
International Journal of Turkish Studies 4 no.2: 79–158,
Fall/Winter 1989.

burj

Arabic term for a fortified tower.

Bursa

*Located on the slopes of the Uludag (Great Mountain)
in north-west Anatolia, Bursa became the first capital
of the Ottoman state after its capture from the Byzantines in the fourteenth century.*

The city first came under Turkish control in 1071
after the battle of Manzikert when it was captured
by the Seljuk leader Alp Arslan. In 1107 the city
was recaptured by the Byzantines who retained
their control until 1326, when it was finally taken
by the Ottomans after a ten-year siege. During the
remainder of the fourteenth century Bursa was
established as the Ottoman capital with imperial
mosques, palaces and a flourishing commercial
centre. In 1402, after the battle of Ankara, Timur
marched westwards where he plundered and
burned the city. It quickly recovered and during
the subsequent period one of the city's most important monuments, the Yeşil Cami, was built. However, the city never recovered its former importance
especially as it had been replaced as capital by
Edirne in 1366. In 1429 the city suffered a severe
plague, and the fall of Constantinople in 1453
meant that it was no longer the Asian capital of
the Ottomans. During the sixteenth century Bursa
was merely a provincial city and there are no
major monuments of this period in contrast to
Edirne and Istanbul. In the early nineteenth century
the city was established as the centre of the silk
trade with the first silk factory opened in 1837.

Bursa is dominated by the ancient citadel which
had proved such an obstacle to early Turkish
attacks. The early Ottoman palaces were built of
wood on the spurs of the mountain and none has
survived. However, the commercial centre of the
city, established by Orhan in the fourteenth century, still contains a number of early buildings.
The oldest Ottoman building in Bursa is the Alaettin Cami built in 1335 which consists of a square
domed prayer hall and vaulted portico. Two years
later Orhan built the first of the Bursa T-plan
mosques. It consists of a domed central courtyard

flanked by two student rooms and with a prayer
hall to the south. Orhan's mosque was part of a
complex which included two bath houses and a
soup kitchen. One of the bath houses, known as the
Bey Hammam, has survived in its original form and
is the oldest known Ottoman bath house. The building has the same basic form as later hammams and
consists of a large domed dressing room leading
via an intermediary room to the cruciform domed
hot room. Next door on the same street is the Bey
Han also built by Orhan in the early fourteenth
century. This is a two-storey structure built around
a central rectangular courtyard with an entrance
on the north side and a stable block at the back.
The lower windowless rooms were used for storage
whilst the upper floor contained the rooms for
travellers each with its own chimney.

To the west of Bursa is an area known as
Çekirge which was developed as a royal centre by
Orhan's successor Murat between 1366 and 1385.
At the centre of the complex was the Hüdavendigâr Cami, or royal mosque, which is a unique
example of a madrassa and zawiya in one building.
The lower floor is occupied by the zawiya and
mosque whilst the upper floor is the madrassa. The
zawiya and mosque is built to the same T-plan as
was used earlier in Orhan's mosque whilst the
upper floor is built as a traditional madrassa modified to the shape of the building below. The
arrangement is unusual because the zawiya was
used by mystical dervishes hostile to religious
orthodoxy and the madrassa by students and teachers of orthodox Islamic law. The combination reflects the political situation of the time when the
Ottomans were moving away from their role as
leaders of frontier warriors with traditional dervish
supporters to a more centralized state system relying on religious orthodoxy for support. Like the
Hüdavendigâr Mosque, the Beyazit complex begun
in 1490 includes a zawiya mosque and an orthodox
madrassa although here the two buildings are
separate with the mosque zawiya on a hill and the
rectangular madrassa below. The mosque has the
same T-plan as Orhan's original mosque although
the tall five-domed portico represents an advance
in mosque design.

The main mosque of Bursa is the Ulu Cami
(Great Mosque) built by Beyazit between 1399
and 1400. The mosque covers a large area (63 by
50 m) and is roofed by twenty domes resting on
large square piers. The main entrance and the

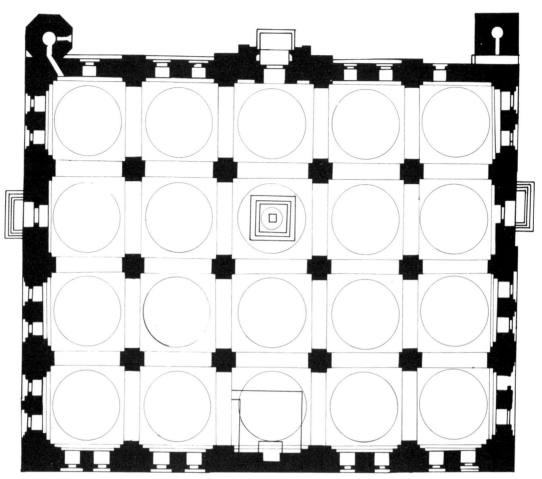

Ulu Cami, Bursa, Turkey (after Goodwin)

mihrab are on the same central axis and there is a sunken pool underneath the second dome in front of the mihrab. The interior is decorated with giant black calligraphy which dates to the nineteenth century but which may be copied from earlier originals.

The culmination of the Bursa T-plan mosques is the Yeşil Cami built by Mehmet I between 1403 and 1421. The building forms the centre of a complex which includes a madrassa, bath house, soup kitchen and the tomb of Mehmet I. The last imperial mosque to be built in Bursa is that of Murat II built in 1447. The building is a simplified version of the T-plan mosque and dispenses with the vestigial entrance vestibules found on the earlier mosques so that the portico leads directly on to the domed courtyard. Although the Mu-

radiye was the last of the Bursa imperial mosques, the Bursa T-plan continued to influence the form of later Ottoman mosques.

Bursa is well known for its bath houses (kapilica) which relied upon naturally occurring warm spring water. The sulphurous spring water occurs naturally at a temperature of 80° which is too hot for human use so that it must be mixed with cold water to achieve a bearable temperature. One of the oldest thermal bath houses is the Eski Kapilica (Old Bath House) rebuilt by Murat I on the site of an earlier Roman bath. Also famous is the Yeni Kapilica built by the grand vizier Rüstem Pasha in the sixteenth century which has a similar plan to the Haseki Hammam in Istanbul built by Sinan.

See also: Ottomans, Yeşil Cami

Further reading:

A. Gabriel, *Une Capitale Turque, Brousse,* Paris 1958.

A. Tuna, *Bursa Yeni Kapilica* (The Yeni Bath House at Bursa), Istanbul 1987.

Byzantine architecture

Architecture characterized by brick and masonry construction, round arches and domes, developed within the Byzantine Empire.

Byzantine architecture was of crucial importance to the development of early Islamic architecture and later the architecture of the Ottoman Empire. At the time of the Islamic conquest of Syria in the seventh century Byzantine was essentially a continuation of Roman architecture. There were, however, a few major differences, the most significant of which was the massive church-building campaign of Justinian (sixth century) which made Christianity the central focus of architecture. Also noticeable in the architecture of this period was the influence of the capital Constantinople on the rest of the empire.

During the ninth to eleventh centuries the Byzantines recovered from the disastrous effects of the Islamic conquests, and in this period there is evidence of Islamic influence on Byzantine architecture, particularly in descriptions of the palaces of Constantinople.

During the fourteenth to fifteenth centuries Byzantine architecture was a major influence on that of the Turkish principalities in Anatolia. In particular the domed basilical church had a formative influence on early Ottoman mosques.

See also: Hagia Sophia, Ottomans, Umayyads

Further reading:

C. Mango, *Byzantine Architecture,* London 1986.

C

Cairo (Arabic: al-Qahira)

Capital of Egypt and one of the most prominent cities of the Islamic world. The English name for the city derives from the French, Le Caire, which in turn is derived from the Arabic al-Qahira. The modern town is composed of the remains of four cities established in this area during the early Islamic period.

At the time of the Islamic conquest the capital of Egypt was Alexandria, although by 641 a new city called Fustat was founded further south on the east bank of the Nile, next to the old Roman fortress town of Babylon. In 750 the newly established Abbasid caliphs established another city or camp known as al-'Askar to the east of Fustat. During the ninth century the semi-autonomous Tulunids expanded further north-east with the establishment of the city of al-Qataic which was based around the grand palace of Ibn Tulun. Under the Fatimids Egypt became the seat of the caliphate and to this end in 971 a new city was founded to the north-east. Originally the city was called al-Mansuriyya, but four years later was renamed al-Qahira 'the victorious', after al-Qahir (the planet Mars), which was in the ascendant at the time of its foundation. Although today the whole city is referred to officially as Cairo or al-Qahira, before the eighteenth century only the original Fatimid capital was referred to by this name whilst the whole city was known as Misr or Masr (literally Egypt).

The original al-Qahira of the Fatimids was a luxurious palace city described by contemporary writers as having marble floors grouted with gold and vast treasure houses filled with beautiful golden objects. From the tenth to the twelfth century Cairo was symbolically divided between al-Fustat, the commercial and popular capital, and al-Qahira, the royal city of the caliphs. The devastation and dislocation brought about in Egypt by the Crusaders changed the old order, so that al-Qahira was no longer exclusively a royal enclosure and instead became the true capital whilst al-Fustat became a dying suburb.

Salah al-Din planned to unite the city by enclosing both Fustat and al-Qahira in massive walls. Although unable to complete this project Salah al-Din was able to build the massive citadel on Muqattam hill. During the Mamluk and Ottoman periods the city continued to grow with suburbs growing up around the citadel and al-Qahira and huge cemeteries extending east and west into the desert.

The Fatimid Cairo

The two most important pre-Fatimid buildings to survive in some form are the mosque of Camr at Fustat and the mosque of Ibn Tulun. Little survives of either, nor of the original mosque of Camr ibn al-'As built in 641 and said to be the earliest mosque in Egypt. The most important feature of the present mosque is that it indicates the position of the original settlement of al-Fustat. The mosque of Ibn Tulun on the other hand represents the remains of the city or settlement known as al-Qataic founded by Ahmad ibn Tulun. In many ways the Tulunid capital resembled the contemporary Abbasid capital at Samarra – from the triple-arched gate, the polo ground and the racecourses, to the extensive use of stucco.

The Fatimid Period (969–1171)

This is earliest time from which a significant number of monuments survive. It was during this period that Egypt became centre of the caliphate which ruled from North Africa to Palestine. Although the Fatimids ruled a vast empire, they were to a certain extent strangers in Egypt as the majority of the population remained Sunni. This alienation is reflected in the way al-Qahira was kept as an official city closed to the general population. The caliphs lived in palaces lavishly decorated with gold and jewels and when they died they were also buried within them. Unfortunately nothing survives of these palaces as they were systematically destroyed by later rulers, although detailed descriptions can be found in the writings of Nasiri Khusraw or al-Maqrizi.

The best surviving examples of Fatimid architecture in Cairo are the mosques of al-Azhar (970) and al-Aqmar (1125) which demonstrate a transition from early Islamic to medieval forms. Despite later accretions, the mosque of al-Azhar represents an early Islamic hypostyle form with three arcades around a central courtyard. The sanctuary is composed of five aisles parallel to the qibla and a central transverse aisle which is emphasized by being both higher and wider than the surrounding roof. Originally there were three domes at the qibla end, one in front of the mihrab and one on either side. Three aisles around a central courtyard and the arrangement of three domes are all features common in early North African mosques. Inside the mosque was lavishly decorated with stucco work, only part of which survives (around the mihrab and on parts of the arcades). The stucco has some Abbasid influence although there are also Byzantine and Coptic elements in the designs.

Built some 150 years later, the mosque of al-Aqmar has a much more sophisticated design, reminiscent of the later medieval buildings of Cairo. It was founded by the vizier Ma'mun al Bata'ihi during the reign of Caliph al-Amir. The interior plan consists of a small central courtyard surrounded on four sides by triple arcades. The sanctuary consists of a small area divided into three aisles parallel to the qibla wall. Initially the mosque would have been covered with a flat hypostyle roof but it is now covered with shallow brick domes. Stylistically the most important feature of the plan is the way the entrance is positioned at an angle to the main building. This feature allows the mosque to be incorporated into a pre-existing street plan whilst having the prayer hall correctly aligned for the qibla. This is one of the earliest examples of this type of plan which was to become more pronounced in Mamluk religious buildings. The other important feature of the al-Aqmar Mosque is the decoration of the façade which was developed in later mosques to be a main feature of the design. The façade is made of stone overlying a brick structure. Today the right hand side is hidden by a later building but it is assumed that it was originally symmetrical with a projecting portal in the middle. The decoration of the façade is dominated by decorated niches with fluted conch-like niches, an arrangement used in more complex forms in later mosques. The al-Aqmar Mosque is also significant as the earliest mosque to incorporate shops in its design (these were below the present street level and have been revealed by excavations). Another important mosque of Fatimid Cairo is that of the caliph al-Hakim built between 990 and 1003. The mosque, which has recently been restored, has a large rectangular courtyard surrounded by four arcades. A transept aisle opposite the mihrab indicates the direction of the qibla which is further emphasized by three domes. The entrance to the mosque is via a large projecting portal similar to that of the mosque of Mahdiyya, the Fatimid capital in North Africa. Probably the most famous feature of this mosque are the minarets at either end of the north façade. They were built in 990 and consist of one octagonal and one cylindrical decorated brick tower; at some later date (probably 1110) the lower parts of these minarets were encased in large brick cubes for some unknown reason.

Apart from mosques, various other types of religious building are known to have been built in Fatimid Cairo including many tombs or mashads devoted to religious personalities. However, most of these have not survived or have been altered beyond recognition as they have been in continuous religious use. An exception to this is the mashad of al-Juyushi also known as Mashad Badr al-Jamali.

This structure consists of two main parts, a domed prayer hall opening on to a courtyard and a large minaret. Although there is a side chamber which may have been a tomb, there is no positive identification of the person commemorated. The prayer hall is covered with cross vaults except for the area in front of the mihrab which is covered with a tall dome resting on plain squinches. The minaret is a tall square tower capped by an octagonal lantern covered with a dome. A notable feature of the minaret is the use of a muqarnas cornice which is the first example of this decoration on the exterior of a building. The roof of the complex also houses two small kiosks whose function has not been resolved. Other notable Fatimid mashads are the tombs of Sayyida Ruqayya and Yayha al-Shabih both in the cemetery of Fustat. The first of these was built to commemorate Sayyida Ruqayya, a descendant of Cali even though she never visited Egypt. The layout of this building is similar to that of al-Juyushi except that the dome is larger and is fluted inside and out. Visually the most impressive feature of this building is the mihrab, the hood of which is composed of radiating flutes of stucco set within a large decorated frame.

The best surviving examples of Fatimid secular architecture are the walls and gates built by Badr al-Jamali between 1087 and 1092. The first walls and gates of Cairo were built of brick during the reign of al-Mucizz but were replaced with stone walls by Badr al-Jamali in the eleventh century. The stone for the walls was mostly quarried from ancient Egyptian structures and many of the stones display hieroglyphic inscriptions and ancient motifs. The walls were built on three levels: a lower level raised slightly above the street level containing shops and the entrances to gates, a middle level containing vaulted galleries and pierced with arrow slits, and an upper level consisting of a parapet protected by large rounded crenellations. The gates are set between large semi-circular or rectangular buttress towers, the lower parts of which are made of solid masonry. The surviving gates of Fatimid Cairo are Bab al-Nasr (Gate of Victory), Bab al-Futuh (Gate of Conquest) and Bab Zuwayla (after a North African tribe prominent in the Fatimid armies). The general appearance of the towers and gates seems to be developed from Byzantine military architecture.

The Ayyubid Period (1171–1250)

The Ayyubid period in Cairo represents a return to orthodox Sunni Islam. One of the consequences of this was that there was not allowed to be more than one Friday mosque in any urban area. Instead the Ayyubid period saw the foundation of many madrassas and khanqas as a means of propagating orthodox law and religion. The earliest such madrassa was that of Imam Shafci founded by Salah al-Din. Although the madrassa has not survived, the connected tomb of Imam Shafci still stands. This is much larger than any of the earlier Fatimid tombs measuring approximately 15 m square underneath the central dome. The wooden cenotaph of the imam survives intact and is decorated with carved geometric designs around bands of Kufic and Naskhi script which are dated to 1178.

The best surviving example of an Ayyubid madrassa is that of Sultan al-Salih Najm al-Din

Ayyub built in 1243. It is built on the site of one of the great Fatimid palaces. Like the Mustansariyya this madrassa was built for all four of the orthodox Sunni rites of Islamic law with a separate area for each rite; today only the minaret, the entrance complex and part of the east courtyard survive. The original plan consisted of two courtyards either side of a passageway. Each courtyard was flanked on two sides by small barrel-vaulted cells and on the other two sides by large iwans. The minaret of this complex is the only surviving Ayyubid minaret of Cairo and consists of a square brick shaft with an octagonal upper part covered with a ribbed dome. The entrance-way includes a decorated keel-arched niche, in the centre of which is a Naskhi foundation inscription; the whole is encased by a muqarnas frame.

One of the finest buildings attributed to the Ayyubid period is known as the 'Mausoleum of the Abbasid Caliphs' because it was used for this purpose after the Mongol sack of Baghdad. Although there is some dispute about its date of construction, it is generally agreed to have been built between 1240 and 1270. The central dome is supported on two tiers of squinches which alternate with similarly shaped windows and muqarnas stucco niches so that the zone of transition becomes two continuous bands of niches. This pattern was later adopted for most domes resting on squinches.

Other important buildings of the late Ayyubid period are the tomb of Sultan Salah al-Din, the mausoleum of Shajarat al Durr and the minaret of Zawiyat al Hunud all dated to around 1250.

Few remains of secular buildings survive with the exception of the citadel and the fortification walls. The citadel was probably the most substantial building of Ayyubid Cairo, its main function being to strengthen and connect the city's walls. It was built on Muqattam hill in the style of Syrian castles of the Crusader period using material taken from several small pyramids at Giza which were demolished for the purpose. Both square and round towers were used to fortify the walls which may reflect two periods of construction, one under Salah al-Din and one under his son and successor al-Malik al-'Adil. Innovations to the fortifications included bent entrances in the gateways and arrowslits which reached the floor.

Bahri Mamluk Period (1250–1382)

The early Mamluk period is architecturally the most prolific period in Cairo with a wide range of major building projects carried out. Many of these buildings have survived demonstrating a diverse range of styles, techniques and designs. During this period some of the major forms of later Cairene architecture were established such as the erection of sabils on street corners often linked to primary schools. During this period there was also considerable foreign influence from Sicily, Iran, North Africa and Spain which was absorbed into the architecture of Cairo.

Congregational mosques were founded during this period after the strict Shafi'ite orthodoxy of the Ayyubid sultans who only permitted one congregational mosque in the city, that of al-Hakim. Under the Mamluks each area had its own Friday mosque and during the fourteenth century madrassas and khanqas were also used as Friday mosques. The earliest and grandest mosque built

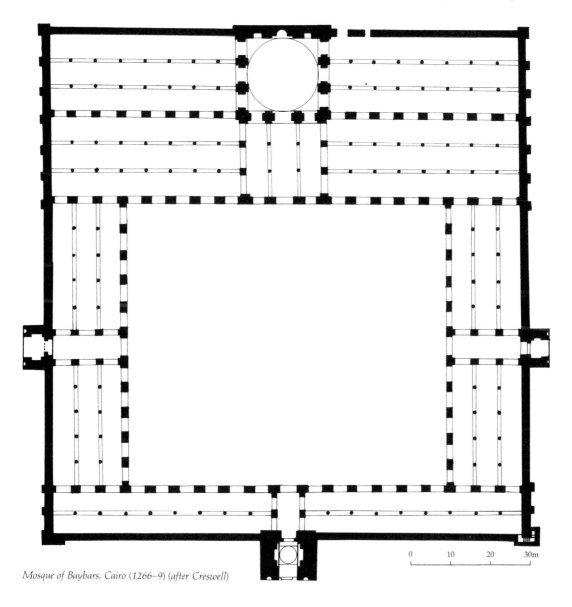

Mosque of Baybars, Cairo (1266–9) (after Creswell)

0   10   20   30m

under the Mamluks was that of Sultan al-Zahir Baybars built between 1266 and 1269. Although partially ruined the general plan of this mosque can be reconstructed – it consists of a large rectangular courtyard with arcades on four sides and projecting entrances on three sides. Most of the arcades rested on columns except for those around the sanctuary which rest on rectangular piers. The outer walls are protected by rectangular buttresses in between which are pointed arched windows with stucco grilles. The walls are built out of stone, and alternate courses are painted to achieve the effect of ablaq masonry; the upper part of the wall is crenellated. There was once a minaret next to the main entrance which has now disappeared. The area in front of the mihrab known as the maqsura was once covered with a large wooden dome decorated in marble; between this and the courtyard was a nine-domed transept.

Another royal mosque of this period is that of Sultan al-Nasir Muhammad at the citadel, built between 1318 and 1385. Like that of Baybars this is a hypostyle mosque built around a rectangular courtyard with a large dome covering the area in front of the mihrab. The most remarkable feature of this mosque are the two cylindrical stone minarets, one opposite the army headquarters and the other opposite the royal palace. The more elaborate of the two faces the palace and is decorated with vertical and horizontal zig-zag patterns with a small solid bulbous dome on the top. The other minaret is similar except that it is less decorated and has a hexagonal pavilion covered by a bulbous dome. The upper portion of each minaret is covered in blue, white and green faience tiles. It seems likely that both the faience decoration and the bulbous domes are copied from similar minarets in Iran, probably Tabriz, where such forms were common at the time.

Other important mosques built during this period were those of Amir Altinbugha al-Maridani built in 1340 and of Amir Aqsunqur built in 1347. Important features of the al-Maridani Mosque include the minaret which is the earliest example of the octagonal minaret with pavilion which was to become typical of later Cairene architecture. The building is also notable for its wooden mashrabiyya screen that separates the maqsura from the rest of the mosque. The mosque of Aqsunqur is a good example of an attempt to use a Syrian building tradition in Egypt. The building was originally roofed with cross-vaults in the Syrian style but later these were replaced with a flat wooden roof.

Probably the most famous building of Mamluk Cairo is the Sultan Hasan Mosque. This was built on a four-iwan plan madrassa and was the first madrassa in Cairo to be accorded the status of a congregational mosque. The building consists of a square central courtyard with four great iwans. The largest of the iwans is a prayer hall behind which is the domed mausoleum. Between the four iwans are four separate courtyards one for each of the orthodox Sunni rites of Islamic law. The building includes several notable architectural features amongst which are the doorway thought to be modelled on that of the Gök Madrassa at Sivas and the floriated stucco inscriptions in the prayer hall.

Mausoleums were a common feature of religious and semi-religious institutions from the early Mamluk period onwards. One of the best examples of this is the mausoleum, madrassa and hospital of Sultan al-Mansur Qalawun built between 1284 and 1285. Today the hospital has disappeared leaving only the madrassa and mausoleum. The madrassa is built on the typical Cairene four-iwan plan with iwans of differing sizes. The largest iwan is that of the prayer hall which is arranged in three aisles like a Byzantine basilica. The most outstanding feature of the complex is the mausoleum itself which consists of a huge rectangular hall with a central dome supported on piers and massive columns arranged in a manner similar to the Dome of the Rock in Jerusalem. The walls are decorated in a wide variety of materials including marble inlay, mother of pearl and coloured stones. The mihrab is one of the largest in Cairo and is decorated with several tiers of blind niches within the niche itself. The importance of the mausoleum is evident from the fact that it had its own madrassa in addition to the madrassa attached.

Although mausoleums did not usually achieve the grandeur of Qalawun's tomb, often the mausoleum was the most impressive part of a complex. Thus the tomb of Sultan Baybars al-Jashankir was an elaborate and richly decorated building in relation to the rather plain khanqa associated with it. Tombs often acted as a focal point for a building and sometimes incorporated foreign features or unusual techniques in order to draw attention to the building and its founder. This can be seen in the madrassa–mausoleum of Amir Sarghitmish built in 1356 where the mausoleum is not placed next to the prayer hall as was usual but instead was built in a position so that its façade and profile were directly on the main street. The mausoleum is covered by a double-shell dome set on an unusually high drum with an exterior moulding of muqarnas marking the transition from drum to dome. This form of dome is not usual in Cairo and may have been copied from similar domes in Samarkand.

Circassian Mamluk Period (1382–1517)

Several developments took place in the fifteenth-century architecture of Cairo which distinguish it from the earlier Mamluk period. These developments were of two basic types: those concerned with the layout and plan of buildings and those concerned with the decoration and construction of buildings.

The biggest factor affecting design and layout was the lack of space in an increasingly crowded area. The most obvious result of this was that mosques tended to be smaller and were designed to fill awkwardly shaped plots. The size of mosques was reduced in a number of ways, the most notable of which was the reduction in size of the central courtyard until it became a small square area in the centre covered by a wooden lantern to admit light. A result of this design change was that the side walls of mosques were now pierced with many windows to make up for the lack of light from the courtyards. Also there was a move away from the hypostyle mosque towards the four-iwan plan used for madrassas. However, the form of the iwans changed from brick or stone vaults to flat wooden roofed units. Another change was that now madrassas did not include accommodation blocks for students who were located outside.

The trend which had begun in the fourteenth century of using madrassas as Friday mosques was extended so that now buildings would fulfil several roles such as khanqa, madrassa and jami. The earliest example of such a combination was the complex of Sultan Barquq built between 1384 and 1386.

One of the exceptions to the decreasing size of mosques is the Khanqah of Sultan Faraj ibn Barquq built between 1400 and 1411. This large complex was deliberately built outside the main urban area in the cemetery on the eastern outskirts of Cairo.

The plan adopted for this building was that of a hypostyle mosque, with a spacious central court-yard containing an octagonal central fountain. Despite its traditional Friday mosque layout this structure contained living units for Sufis as well as two domed mausoleums flanking the sanctuary or prayer hall.

Many of the changes in the architecture of the late Mamluk period are concerned with the building and decoration of domes. Among the most famous features of Cairo are the carved stone domes built during this period. These are fairly unique to Cairo although occasional examples can be found elsewhere, such as the Sabil Qaytbay in Jerusalem which is known to be a copy of similar Egyptian domes. Up to the late fourteenth century most domes in Egypt were either built of wood or brick, and stone domes were only used for the tops of minarets. It is thought likely that this was the origin of the larger stone domes used on tombs. The earliest stone domes had ribbed decoration similar to that seen on the tops of minarets; later this was developed into a swirled turban style as can be seen on the mausoleum of Amir Aytimish al-Bajasi built in 1383. The next stage was zig-zag patterns followed by the intricate star patterns which can be seen on the mausoleums built for Sultan Barbays. Under Sultan Qaytbay an important innovation was made where the star pattern would start at the top, whereas previously decoration had started at the bottom. With the increasing sophistication of dome decoration it was natural that domes were set on higher drums so that they could be seen from far away. The increased confidence in stone carving exhibited in domes is also reflected in the decoration of minarets which are now also carved in stone. One of the earliest examples of this is the minaret belonging to the complex of Sultan Barquq built between 1384 and 1386. The minaret is octagonal throughout and has a central section composed of giant intersecting circles.

Another innovation in the architecture of this period was the triangular pendentive. The earliest examples in Cairo were used in the citadel mosque of al-Nasir Muhammad and were made of wood. Later pendentives were used for stone domes although muqarnas squinches continued to be used. A related feature introduced at this time was the groin vault used in complex arrangements for portals. Often doorways would be covered by a complex groin vault with a small dome in the centre forming a half-star shape.

The Ottoman Period (1517–1914)

The Ottoman conquest of Egypt marks a fundamental change in the architecture of Cairo. Most noticeably, new architectural forms were introduced from Istanbul and Anatolia, whilst several types of Mamluk buildings, such as domed mausoleums or khanqahs ceased to be built.

One of the earliest Ottoman buildings of Cairo is the mosque of Sulayman Pasha built in 1528. This building is almost entirely Ottoman in its construction and shows little relationship to the pre-existing Mamluk architecture. The mosque consists of a central prayer hall flanked by three semi-domes and opening on to a central courtyard enclosed by domed arcades.

In addition to new layouts and forms the Ottomans also introduced new types of buildings such as the takiyya which performed a similar function to the khanqa and madrassa.

Unlike the khanqa or madrassa the takiyya was built separate from the mosque. This was characteristic of Ottoman institutions which were built separately from mosques rather than as buildings with several functions like the madrassa, khanqa, jami combination of the late Mamluk period.

Despite the new styles and forms introduced by the Ottomans many buildings continued to be built in Mamluk architectural style. A good example of this is the mosque and mausoleum of Mahmud Pasha built in 1567 which in many ways resembles the mosque of Sultan Hasan, with a large domed mausoleum behind the prayer hall. The minaret, however, is built in the classic Ottoman style with a tall thin fluted shaft.

Probably the most famous building of Ottoman Cairo is the mosque of Muhammad Cali Pasha built between 1830 and 1848. This building has a classical Ottoman design consisting of a large central domed area flanked by semi-domes and a large open courtyard surrounded by arcades covered with shallow domes. On the west wall of the courtyard is a clock tower including a clock presented by Louis Philippe, King of France. The mosque was designed by an Armenian and is said to be based on the Sultan Ahmet Mosque in Istanbul.

Domestic and Secular Architecture

The continuous development of Cairo has meant that apart from the major monuments very few secular buildings have survived from before the Ottoman period. The earliest evidence for Cairo's houses comes from excavations at Fustat where Iraqi-style four-iwan plan houses were discovered. This style consists of four iwans, one on each side of a central courtyard with a fountain. In each house the main iwan was divided into three, a central area and two side rooms. There are also descriptions of early Islamic Cairo which describe multi-storey apartments.

During the Fatimid period we have the first evidence for the living unit known as the qaca which became the typical living unit of Cairo. This consists of a small courtyard area with two iwans opposite each other. The iwans could be closed off with folding doors whilst the courtyard could be covered over with an awning. On the upper floor overlooking the courtyard were wooden galleries. In Mamluk times the qaca was developed so that the central courtyard became smaller and was covered by a wooden dome or lantern. The central hall or courtyard would often be decorated with coloured marble and finely carved mashrabiyya doorways and screens. The central fountain was usually octagonal and was sometimes fed by a stream of water running from the back wall of the main iwan.

In the late Mamluk and early Ottoman period a particular type of sitting room known as the maqad became popular. This consisted of an arcade on the upper floor level which overlooked the main public courtyard of an important residence. From the sixteenth century onwards important residences would also incorporate an extra kitchen for the preparation of coffee.

In addition to private houses there were from a very early period blocks of houses or apartments which would have been rented by the occupiers. These buildings were known as 'rabc' and consisted of rows of two-storey apartments usually built above shops or khans. One of the earliest examples is the rabc of Sultan al-Ghuri at Khan al-Khalili.

It is known that many of the larger houses had private bathrooms although these would not have included all the facilities available in a public bath house or hammam. Cairo is known to have had a large number of hammams although many of these have recently disappeared. In general the rooms of a bath house were fairly plain with the exception of the maslakh (reception hall) which was often domed and sometimes was supported with columns.

Further reading:

D. Berhens-Abouseif, *Islamic Architecture in Cairo: An Introduction*, Supplements to Muquarnas vol. 3, Leiden 1989. This is the best modern summary of Islamic architecture in Cairo.

K. A. C. Creswell, *The Muslim Architecture of Egypt*, Oxford 1952–60. Contains the most comprehensive discussion and treatment of buildings from the beginning of the Fatimid (969) to the end of the Mamluk (1517) periods.
For domestic architecture see:

J. C. Garcin, B. Maury, J. Revault and M. Zakariya, *Palais et Maisons du Caire: I. D'Époque Mamelouke (XIIIe–XVIe siècles)*, Paris 1982.

B. Maury, A. Raymond, J. Revault and M. Zakariya, *Palais et Maisons du Caire: II. Époque Ottomane (XVIe– XVIIIe siècles)* vol. 2, Paris 1983.
For modern architecture see:

M. al-Gawhury, *Ex-Royal Palaces of Egypt*, Cairo 1954.

A. D. C. Hyland, A. G. Tipple and N. Wilkinson, *Housing in Egypt*, Newcastle-upon-Tyne 1984.

cami

Turkish term for a congregational or Friday mosque as opposed to the smaller mescit.

caravanserai

Roadside building which provides accomodation and shelter for travellers.

The term caravanserai is a composite Turkish term derived from caravan (i.e. a group of travellers) and serai (palace). Generally it refers to a large structure which would be capable of coping with a large number of travellers, their animals and goods. The term first seems to have been used in the twelfth century under the Seljuks and may indicate a particularly grand form of khan with a monumental entrance. During the Saffavid period in Iran (seventeenth to eighteenth century) caravanserais are often huge structures with four iwans.

See also: khan

çarşi

Turkish term for a market.

Central Asia

Central Asia comprises the modern independent republics of Khazakstan, Turkmenistan, Khirgiziya and Uzbekistan.

In pre-Islamic times Central Asia was the home of several important Turkic dynasties the most important of which were the Kushans who ruled over most of the area in the fifth century CE. By the seventh century the western part of the Kushan Empire had been conquered by the Sassanians whilst the eastern part fractured into a number of independent principalities. One of the most important principalities was that of the Sogdians whose art and architecture seem to have been an important influence on Islamic architecture of the ninth century and after.

During the Islamic period the cities of central Asia continued to control the Silk Route and cities

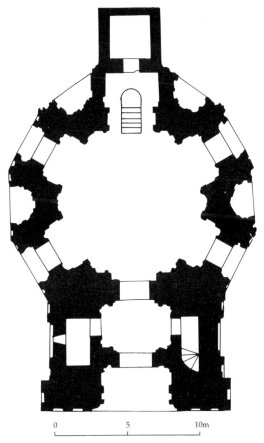

0   5   10m

Plan of Tutabeg Khatun Tomb, fourteenth century, Urgench, Uzbekistan

such as Samarkand, Bukhara and Merv rose to great prosperity.

See also: Turkmenistan, Uzbekistan

çeşme

A Turkish term for a fountain or tap used to provide drinking water. These were often attached to Ottoman monuments to fulfil a charitable purpose.

chahar bagh or char bagh

Iranian and Mughal term for a formal garden laid out in four plots of equal size and divided by axial paths.

See also: gardens, Mughals

chajja

Mughal and Hindu term for projecting eaves or cover usually supported on large carved brackets.

char-chala

Indian roof form with curved eaves and curved surfaces. Derived from Bengali architecture.

See also: bangala, Bengal, do-chala

Char Minar

Ceremonial gateway in Hyderabad which is one of the best examples of south Indian Islamic architecture.

When it was built in 1589 the Char Minar (literally four towers) formed the centre of the city and with the charkaman (four gates) was part of the ceremonial approach to the royal palaces (now destroyed). The building is a square structure with arched gateways in the centre of each side which intersect at the centre. At each of the four corners is a tower or minaret nearly 60 m high and crowned with an onion-shaped bulbous dome. The first storey above the arches contains a circular cistern whilst on the second storey there is a small domed mosque.

See also: Deccan, Hyderabad, India

char su or char taq

Iranian and Mughal term for the intersection of two market streets where there is usually an open square with four arched entrances. (Roughly equivalent to the classical tetra pylon.)

chatri

Mughal and Hindu term for a domed kiosk on the roof of a temple, tomb or mosque. The domes are usually supported on four columns.

chauk

Indian term for an open square or courtyard.

China

There are three main Muslim groups within the Republic of China, these are the maritime communities of the great ports, the urban communities of northern China and the predominantly Turkic people of Central Asia.

Maritime Communities

The development of maritime Muslim communities in China is less well documented than the conquests of Central Asia or the inland settlements of northern China. The first coastal settlements seem to have been mostly in southern and eastern ports and include the cities of Canton, Chuan Chou, Hang Chou in Chekiang Province and Yang Chou on the lower Yangtze. The descendants of these early Muslims are known as Hui (a term also applied to the Muslims of the northern inland cities) and through intermarriage have become culturally Sinicized. This was partly as the result of increased intermarriage and also missionary activity. The prominence of the Muslim communities grew under the Yuan and Ming dynasties so that in the fifteenth century the Chinese navy was commanded by Muslims, the most famous of whom was Cheng Ho, who cleared the China sea of pirates and led an expedition to East Africa.

According to Islamic tradition the first mosques in China belong to the maritime community and were located in the coastal ports. Historical sources suggest that they may have been established in the seventh century by Sa'd bin Abi Waqqas and several other companions of the prophet. There is little archaeological evidence for mosques of this period although there are several mosques which may have been founded at an early date. Probably the oldest of these is the Huai-Shang Mosque in Canton which is referred to as early as 1206, although a mosque probably existed on the site in T'ang times (618–906). The oldest part of the building is the 36-m-high minaret with a thick tapering shaft. As minarets are rare in China it has

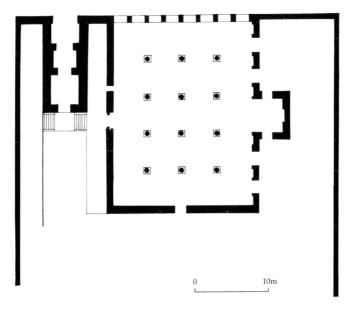

Plan and doorway of the mosque of Chuan Chou, China

been suggested that the minaret functioned as a lighthouse. The rest of the mosque was built in the fourteenth century and is built in Chinese style with green tiled wooden roofs. The Sheng Yu Mosque at Chuan Chou is surrounded by massive granite walls and is the last of seven mosques which once stood in the city. The building was founded in 1009 although most of the building seems to date from the fourteenth century or later. Another early mosque is the Feng-Huan Mosque at Hang Chou which is locally attributed to the T'ang period (according to a seventeenth-century inscription) although it seems more likely that it was established during the Yuan period.

Inland Communities

Away from the coast the Muslims of China may be divided into two main groups, the Turkic- and Persian-speaking peoples of Xinjiang (formerly Chinese Turkestan) and the Chinese-speaking Hui people of Yunnan, Ningxia and Gansu. Initially both these groups were less integrated into Chinese society than their maritime counterparts and their early history is one of conflict rather than acculturation. The first direct confrontation between Arabs and Chinese occurred in 751 at the battle of Talas and resulted in a victory for the Arabs. During the Yuan period (1279–1368) there was increased Muslim presence in central China due to the large numbers of Muslim soldiers introduced by the Mongols. The growth of Muslim communities continued during the Ming period (1368–1644) when there was also a certain amount of Sinicization of the Muslims which is reflected in the architecture. These communities established many of the usual Islamic institutions, including mosques, madrassas and caravanserais although the methods and techniques of construction appear to have been predominantly Chinese.

Traditionally the oldest inland mosque in China is the mosque of Ch'ang-an which is supposed to have been founded in the T'ang period although a Sung or Yuan foundation is now thought more likely. The Great Mosque of Xian at the eastern end of the Silk Route was founded by the Muslim Admiral Cheng Ho in the fourteenth century. Contained within a huge enclosure wall measuring 48 by 246 m this is the largest mosque in China. The layout of this building with its succession of courtyards, green tiled pavilions and tiered pagoda-like minarets resembles a Buddhist temple rather than any traditional mosque form. However, there are many subtle deviations from typical Chinese forms including the east–west orientation (temples were normally oriented east–west) and the wooden dome which is built into the flared pitched roof of the ablutions pavilion. The flat wooden mihrab is contained within a small room which projects from the centre of the west side of the prayer hall. Other historical mosques in central China include the recently renovated Nui Jei Mosque in Beijing which is reputed to have been founded in the tenth century although there is no archaeological evidence for this.

In Central Asia the Muslims retained their ethnic identity so that the Xinjian region has the largest number of Muslims composed of several groups including Uighurs, Khazaks, Khirgiz and Tajiks. The architecture of this region is similar to that of the former Soviet Republics to the west and has little in common with the rest of China. One of the most famous mosques of this region is the Imin Mosque of Turfan built in 1779. The main features of the mosque are the prayer hall and next to it the huge minaret. The minaret is a cylindrical brick-built structure over 44 m tall and decorated with fifteen bands of geometric brickwork. The large prayer hall is built of mud brick and entered through a large iwan flanked by shallow arched niches. Other mosques in Turfan are more modest in scale and usually consist

of a rectangular brick prayer hall with arcades supported on wooden columns. In the city of Urumqui there is a mixture of architectural styles reflecting the cosmopolitan nature of a city on the Silk Route. One of the largest mosques in the city is the Beytallah Mosque which has traces of Persian and Mughal influence. The building consists of a rectangular prayer hall with engaged minarets at each corner and a tall bulbous dome in the centre. Perhaps more unusual is the Tartar Mosque which is a small wooden building with a short square minaret capped with a pointed wooden spire.

See also: Central Asia, Indonesia, Java, Malaysia, Philippines, Uzbekistan

Further reading:

China Islamic Association, *The Religious Life of Chinese Muslims*, Peking 1981.

A. D. W. Forbes, 'Masjid V. In China', *Encyclopedia of Islam* 6: 702–3, 1991.

J. Lawton, N. Wheeler *et al.*, 'Muslims in China', *Aramco World Magazine* 36 no. 4: July/August 1985.

D. Leslie, *Islam in Traditional China*, Canberra 1986.

H. Saladin, 'Monuments musulmanes de Chine et d'Extrème Orient', *Manuel d'art musulmans*, Paris 1907.

—— 'Les mosquées de Pékin', *Revue du Monde Musulmans*, 2: 1907.

coral

Coral is used as a building material for coastal settlements throughout the Indian Ocean, Arabian/Persian Gulf and the Red Sea.

Two main types of coral stone are used for construction: fossil coral quarried from the coastal foreshore, and reef coral which is cut live from the sea bed. Fossil corals are more suitable for load-bearing walls whilst reef corals such as porites are more suitable for architectural features such as door-jambs or mihrab niches. Fossil corals are mostly from an order of coral known as Rugosa which is now extinct. When quarried this coral forms rough uneven blocks known as coral rag. Although this can be cut into rough blocks it cannot be dressed to a smooth finish and therefore has to be used in conjunction with another material to produce an even surface.

Living coral from the reef is easier to cut and dress to a smooth finish although it does require hardening by exposure to the air. The preferred type of reef coral for building is porites because of its compact vascular structure which means it is both strong and easy to carve. However, this is

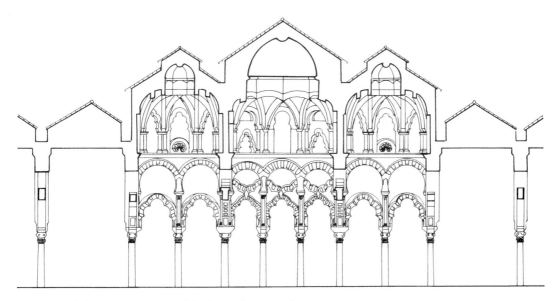

Section through the Great Mosque of Córdoba, Spain (after Barucand)

not the only type used and, at the eleventh-century site of Ras al-Hadd in Oman, at least seven different types were noted. In the Maldives and Bahrain platy corals such as oxypora and montipora are used for partitions.

The origins of coral-building are not well understood although it is generally believed that the technique originated on the coasts of the Red Sea. The earliest example was discovered at the site of al-Rih in the Sudan where a Hellenistic cornice made of coral was found re-used in an Islamic tomb. From the Red Sea the technique spread to the East African coast of the Indian Ocean where its was established as the primary building material for monumental buildings. In the Arabian/Persian Gulf there is another tradition of coral stone construction although the antiquity of this tradition is in doubt as suitable coral has only grown in the area within the last 1,000 years. At the present time the use of coral stone extends over large areas of the Indian Ocean and includes the coastline of India (Gujarat), the Maldives and Sri Lanka. The origins of coral-building in these areas has not been investigated although it generally seems to be associated with Islamic traders.

See also: Bahrain, East Africa, Maldives, Qatar, Saudi Arabia, Sudan, United Arab Emirates

Córdoba

Capital of Islamic Spain (al-Andalus) from 717 until the eleventh century although it continued to be in Muslim hands until its capture by Ferdinand III of Castile.

In Arabic the city was known as Qurtabat al-Wadi al-Kabir and together with Madinat al Zahra' represented the centre of Islamic Spain under the Umayyad dynasty of Spain. It is located on a plateau next to the Guadalquivir river (from Arabic Wadi al-Kabir) which was navigable from the sea in Islamic times. Abd al-Rahman I made it the capital of al-Andalus and laid out the famous Great Mosque of Córdoba (known in Spanish as 'La Mezquita') next to the river. The Great Mosque became the centre of the city which was said to have had fifty mosques in the tenth century. Few of these mosques have survived although the convent of Santa Clara and the church of San Juan are both converted mosques. Santa Clara has fine marble columns and the remains of a minaret whilst San Juan has a minaret which retains its original paired window. In the tenth century Córdoba was famous as the wealthiest city in Europe with paved streets illuminated by street lighting. Some of the atmosphere of the medieval Islamic city can still be recalled in the Jewish quarter to the north of the Great Mosque next to the

Umayyad city walls. Outside the walls Umayyad remains can be seen along the river bank. The bridge known as the Puente Romano was rebuilt in 720 and is 250 m long and rests on sixteen arches. Also alongside the river are remains of water mills which date from Muslim times.

See also: Córdoba Great Mosque, Madinat al-Zahra', Spain.

Further reading:

G. Goodwin, *Islamic Spain: Architectural Guides for Travellers*, London 1990, 39–63.

E. Sordo and W. Swaan, *Moorish Spain: Córdoba, Seville and Granada*, Eng. trans. I. Michael, London 1963.

Córdoba Great Mosque

Principal mosque of Spain under the Umayyads.

The Great Mosque was laid out in 786 by Abd al-Rahman I who built it on the site of a Christian church which the Muslims had previously shared with the Christians. The mosque was supposedly built by a Syrian architect to recall the Great Mosque at Damascus although it has more in common with the Aqsa Mosque in Jerusalem. Less than fifty years later Abd al-Rahman II extended the mosque to the south adding eighty new columns. In 964 al-Hakim II also extended the mosque further south. Towards the end on the tenth century the mosque was once more enlarged by adding fourteen aisles to the east thus balancing the length with the width. Each of these extensions meant building a mihrab further south, each of which was successively more grand. Two of these mihrabs have survived. The earlier, ninth-century mihrab is the size of a large room and has now been converted into the Capilla Villavicosa; it is roofed by a large dome supported on ribs resting on cusped arches. Next to this mihrab is the maqsura or royal enclosure which is equally grand with carved stucco decoration and interlaced cusped horseshoe arches. The tenth-century mihrab consists of an octagonal chamber set into the wall with a massive ribbed dome supported on flying arches. The interior of the dome is decorated with polychrome gold and glass mosaics which may be a gift of the Byzantine emperor. This mihrab suggests the change in status of the Umayyad rulers from amirs to caliphs.

The most remarkable feature of the Great

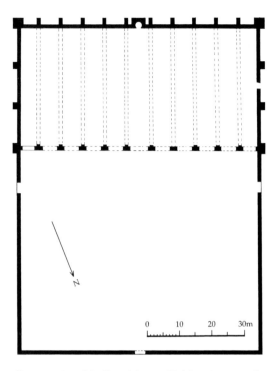

Reconstruction of the Great Mosque, Córdoba (after Creswell)

Mosque are the two-tier free-standing horseshoe arches resting on columns. It is thought that this arrangement is a structural solution to the problem of achieving a high roof with only short columns. The roof of the mosque consists of aisles arranged perpendicular to the quibla wall, a feature elsewhere encountered only in the Aqsa Mosque in Jerusalem.

The appearance of the mosque was ruined in the sixteenth century when a cathedral was built in the middle of the sanctuary, the minaret of the Great Mosque is now encased within the belfry of the cathedral. Diagonally opposite the Great Mosque is the caliph's palace which has now been converted into the archbishop's palace.

See also: Córdoba, Spain

Further reading:

K. A. C. Creswell, *A Short Account of Early Muslim Architecture*, revised and enlarged ed. J. W. Allan, Aldershot 1989, 291–303.

G. Goodwin, *Islamic Spain: Architectural Guides for Travellers*, London 1990, 44–55.

Crusader architecture

European architecture of the Christian states established in Syria and Palestine during the Middle Ages; also architecture associated with those states in other parts of the Middle East or Europe.

The largest concentration of Crusader architecture is to be found in Palestine although Crusader strongholds were also built further afield from the Gulf of Aqaba to Anatolia. The main territories comprising the Crusader dominions were: the kingdom of Jerusalem (roughly equivalent to modern Palestine), the county of Tripoli (centred on the Lebanese port of Tripoli), the principality of Antioch (on the north coast of Syria) and the county of Edessa (with its capital at Urfa).

Although the Crusades continued up until the sixteenth century, the main period of Crusader architecture was from the beginning of the twelfth century to the end of the thirteenth, the period during which the Crusaders occupied Palestine.

Crusader architecture is characterized by high quality ashlar masonry, massive construction and the frequent use of masonry marks. Sculptural decoration and the extensive use of vaulting are other characteristic features. Although the Crusaders built a variety of buildings, including hospices, mills and harbours, their most distinctive work is found in castles and churches.

Generally Crusader castles were a developed form of European fortification with additional features learnt from Byzantine and Islamic military technology. The most common form of fortification was the tower (*tour*) which is equivalent with the Arabic burj. Typically these had two or three vaulted storeys which would provide protection and a good view of the surrounding countryside. The larger castles were all designed for a specific location so that each building has a different plan. Nevertheless each castle would be composed of a number of common features which could include a rock-cut fosse or ditch, a glacis or stone revetment and one or more sets of curtain wall linked by towers, with possibly a keep in the middle. Loopholes tended to be very large with wide reveals.

The churches were often as strongly built as the castles as they were an integral part of Crusader rule. The importance of Jerusalem is notable in the fact that out of 300 churches in Palestine 66 were in Jerusalem. Most Crusader churches were small barrel-vaulted single-cell buildings with an apse at the west end. The larger churches were mainly built on a cross-in-square plan, although it is noticeable that domes were rarely used.

As in other areas it is difficult to assess the relative effects which Crusader, Byzantine and Islamic architecture had on each other. It is, however, possible to see specific areas where there was influence, thus the Muslim castle at Ajlun is obviously similar to Crusader castles. However, the most significant way in which the Crusades influenced Islamic architecture was indirect, through the Venetians who provided the Crusaders with ships.

Further reading:

J. Folda (ed.), *Crusader Art in the Twelfth Century*, Oxford.

T. E. Lawrence, *Crusader Castles*, new edn. with introduction and notes by Denys Pringle, Oxford 1988.

R. C. Smail, *The Crusaders in Syria and the Holy Land*, London 1973.

Cyprus (Turkish: Kibris; Arabic: Qubrus)

Large island off the southern coast of Turkey and east coast of Syria with a mixed Greek- and Turkish-speaking population.

The first Islamic conquest of Cyprus was led by the Arab general Mu'awiya as part of the naval war against the Byzantines who had previously controlled the island. In 653 Abu al-Awar established a garrison on the island which remained until it was withdrawn by the caliph Yazid in 680–83. Cyprus remained nominally under the control of Islam until it was retaken by the Byzantine emperor Nicephorus Phocas in 965. For the next 600 years Cyprus was under a succession of different, mostly Christian rulers, thus in 1189 Isaac Comnenus, governor of the island, seceded from direct Byzantine control. In 1191 the island was captured by Richard I of England and came under western (Frankish) control under the house of Lusignan. Between 1424 and 1426 the island briefly came under the control of the Mamluks of Egypt but was restored to Lusignan control through Venetian intervention. From 1489 to 1570 Cyprus was under direct Venetian rule which was terminated by the Ottoman conquest of 1571. The Ottoman invasion, under Lala Mustapha Pasha, marks the real beginning of Cyprus's long engagement with Islam. However, in many ways the Ottoman conquest had simply replaced one group of rulers with another, leaving the Greek Orthodox population largely intact. This situation was understood by the Ottoman emperor, Selim I, who after the conquest tried to improve the prosperity of the island by populating it with Greek families from the Kayseri region. Ottoman rule ended with the First World War and from 1918 the island was under British rule until it became independent in the 1950s.

The main building material on Cyprus is dressed limestone although baked brick is also used. Also Cyprus differs from its other near-eastern neighbours in having a rich source of high quality timber, enabling buildings to be built with pitched wooden roofs covered with tiles. Although it is known that the early Arab conquerors of Cyprus built several mosques in Nicosia most of these were dismantled or destroyed when Yazid withdrew the garrison in 683. The only Islamic building in Cyprus connected with this period is the tomb of Umm Haram who died near Larnaca during the early Arab invasion. However, the earliest reference to the tomb is 1683 and the main structure on the site today is a tekke (Hala Sultan Tekke) built in 1797. Thus the Islamic architecture of Cyprus is all from the Ottoman period and is closely linked to the Ottoman architecture of Anatolia. There are, however, distinctive features in Cypriot Islamic architecture which may be traced to the fact that the Ottomans converted many of the existing Gothic buildings into mosques or palaces leaving the Greek Orthodox churches untouched. The most spectacular examples of this are the Selimiye Cami in Nicosia and the Lala Mustapha Pasha Cami in Famagusta which are both converted Gothic cathedrals. The Selimiye in Nicosia was a thirteenth-century cathedral (Ayia Sofia) which was converted to a mosque in 1570 by removing the choir and altars and changing the arrangement of windows and doors so that the main entrance was

from the north. At some later date a cylindrical Ottoman minaret was built on to the projecting corner buttresses. The Lala Mustapha Mosque on Famagusta was built in the fourteenth century as the cathedral of St Nicholas, it was badly damaged during the conquest of 1570 and converted into a mosque in 1571 after being stripped of all its internal decoration. Like the Selimiye, the Lala Mustapha Mosque had a minaret added to its west end at a later date. The same procedure was adopted with the Lusignan Palace which was converted into the governor's palace by the addition of a new Ottoman reception room (diwan). Some buildings were converted for different uses, thus the fourteenth-century church of St George of the Latins was converted into the Büyük Hammam of Nicosia by adding an Ottoman-style porch with niches and thickening the walls.

In addition to converting Gothic churches the Ottomans constructed new buildings with Gothic details – thus the minaret of the Cami Kebir (Great Mosque) at Larnaca is built with trefoil panels. Elsewhere Gothic influence on Ottoman buildings can be seen in the use of round windows and the dog-tooth pattern on balcony supports.

See also: Ottomans

Further reading:

Association of Cypriot Archaeologists, *Muslim Places of Worship in Cyprus*, Nicosia 1990.

E. C. Aristidou, *The Tekke of Hal Sultan*, Nicosia 1982.

C. Enlart, *The Gothic Art and the Renaissance in Cyprus*, trans. and ed. D. Hunt, London 1987.

A. C. Gazioglu, *The Turks in Cyprus: A Province of the Ottoman Empire (1571–1878)*, London 1990.

G. Jeffrey, *A Description of the Historic Monuments of Cyprus: Studies in the Archaeology and Architecture of the Island*, Nicosia 1918 and London 1983.

—— *The Mosques of Nicosia*, Nicosia 1935.

D

Damascus

Capital city of Syria and one of the chief cities of the Middle East.

Damascus is located in southern Syria on the banks of the Barada river. The area of Damascus forms an oasis on the edge of the Great Syrian desert. The name Damascus is pre-Semitic and is mentioned in Egyptian texts of the second millennium BCE. The oldest standing remains date from the Roman period and include parts of the city wall, columns marking the lines of street, and the enclosure on which the Umayyad mosque is built. During the Umayyad period Damascus was established as capital of the Islamic world which stretched from Spain to Central Asia. With the establishment of the Abbasid caliphate based in Iraq and later the Fatimid caliphate in Egypt the status of the city declined. In 1154 Nur al-Din established it as his capital, and under his successors the Ayyubids it was once again one of the principal cities of the Islamic world. The Mongol raids of the second half of the thirteenth century reduced the city to a secondary role with Cairo established as the Mamluk capital. The Ottoman conquest in 1516 restored the prosperity which was reinforced by its position as starting point of the Ottoman Hajj caravans. During the eighteenth century the city was eclipsed by the commercial prosperity of Aleppo, though Damascus remained the political capital. With the collapse of the Ottoman Empire in 1918 Damascus was re-established as an Arab capital.

Mud brick and wood are the principal materials of construction for traditional houses. The lower parts of houses have thick walls made out of mud brick which are strengthened at the corners with wooden stakes laid horizontally. The upper parts of the houses are often cantilevered over the street on wooden beams. The walls of the upper part are made out of a wooden framework with bricks laid in between often in a herringbone pattern. The more important monuments are made of stone with baked brick or stone rubble used for domes and vaulting. A characteristic of the monumental masonry of Damascus is the use of ablaq (alternating courses of dark and light masonry) made out of white limestone and black basalt.

There are few standing remains from the Umayyad period with the exception of the Great Mosque which is the oldest major mosque still preserved in its original form. Little was done to alter the pre-Islamic plan of the city and many of the Byzantine buildings were simply converted; thus the caliph's palace, behind the Great Mosque, was formerly the residence of the Byzantine governors. The plan of the city at this time formed a roughly rectangular shape along the banks of the Barada river, a shape which was retained until the expansion during the sixteenth century.

In the three centuries following the fall of the Umayyads Damascus suffered a state of near anarchy. In 1076 strong rule was restored by the Turkoman chief Atsiz ibn Uvak and for the next eighty years the city was ruled by Turkish chiefs or Taabegs. During this period a hospital was built and seven madrassas were established.

With Nur al-Din's capture of Damascus in 1154 the city became the centre of activity directed against the Crusaders who had seized Palestine. During this period there was a great deal of military and religious building. The walls of the city were strengthened with new gateways such as the Bab al-Seghir whilst the older gateways were reinforced. The citadel was also remodelled with a new gate and a large mosque. The number of mosques and madrassas were increased in order to promote orthodox Sunni Islam against both Shi'is and the Christianity of the Crusaders. Other important buildings included the maristan, or hospital, of Nur al-Din and the madrassa and tomb of Nur al-Din. The hospital, which also functioned as a medical school, has a magnificent portal which is a mixture of Roman, Iranian and Mesopotamian styles. Directly above the door is a classic Roman pediment above which there is an arch with a

Entrance to the Hospital of Nur al-Din (built 1154), Damascus, ©Rebecca Foote

muqarnas archway. The top of the structure is crowned with an Iraqi-style conical dome. Inside the hospital is built like a madrassa with four iwans opening on to a central courtyard with a fountain in the centre. One of the iwans is a prayer hall whilst the other is a consultation room. The tomb of Nur al-Din is located on the corner of his madrassa and comprises a square chamber covered with a muqarnas dome resembling that of the hospital and ultimately the conical domes of Iraq.

Under the Ayyubids the madrassa became the main form of religious building with more than twenty examples recorded by Ibn Jubayr in 1184. Most of these tombs were commemorative structures which usually had the tomb of the founder attached. The standard form of Ayyubid tomb was a square room covered with an octagonal zone of transition made up of squinches and blind arches; above this there was usually a sixteen-sided drum which was pierced with windows and arches. The domes are usually tall, slightly pointed structures with broad fluting. The interior of the tombs was usually decorated with painted stucco designs. Important examples include the tomb of Badr al-Din Hassan and the mausoleum of Saladin in the Madrassa Aziziya. The cenotaph of Saladin is made of carved wooden panels whilst the walls were covered with polychrome tiles by the Ottomans in the sixteenth century. Another feature of Ayyubid architecture was the introduction of ablaq masonry.

The Mongol invasion of 1260 put an end to the most brilliant period of Damascus's post-Umayyad history. Although the Mamluks continued to develop the city it was no longer the foremost capital in the region. Baybars, the first Mamluk sultan, was particularly fond of the city and refurbished the citadel as a royal residence for himself. To the west of the city he built another palace known as the Qasr Ablaq which was built out of alternating courses of black and ochre-coloured masonry. Madrassas continued to be built although not on the same scale as before. There was a proliferation of mausoleums and to this period may be ascribed the invention of the double mausoleum where two mausoleums were included within a single complex. Examples of this type of building include the tomb of the Mamluk sultan Kit Bugha and the tomb of the Muhajirin commemorating a Mamluk who had fought the Mongols. The form of these double mausoleums was of two symmetrical domed tombs, with a monumental portal between them which would lead to the madrassa or memorial mosque.

In the later Mamluk period there was a development in the outward appearance of buildings characterized by the growth in the number of decorative octagonal minarets. These towers were decorated with blind niches, muqarnas corbelling elaborate finials and stone inlays. There was also a development of the markets outside the city centre and to this period may be ascribed the development of the suqs known as Taht Qal'a (below the citadel).

The Ottoman conquest of the early sixteenth century re-established Damascus as a regional capital, a position which was reinforced by its position at the start of the Hajj (pilgrimage) route to Damascus. New facilities both religious and practical were built to accommodate the vast numbers of pilgrims coming from Anatolia, Syria and even from Iran. The most important monument was the Tekiyya of Sulayman the Magnificent designed by his architect Sinan and completed in 1555. The

Tekiyya is built on the river bank on the site of the old Mamluk palace, Qasr Ablaq. The Tekiyya comprises a mosque, kitchens and a camping ground for pilgrims. The mosque is built in the classical Ottoman style with a prayer hall covered by a large dome and a double arcade running round it on three sides. The twin minarets are tall pencil-like structures with sharp pointed roofs. The pure Ottoman appearance of the building is modified by the use of alternating black and white (ablaq) masonry. Other Ottoman mosques of the period also display a mixture of local and Ottoman features, thus the Sinaniya (after Sinan Pasha the governor of Damascus, not the architect) mosque has a large central dome in the Ottoman style but the use of ablaq masonry and the monumental muqarnas portal resemble earlier Mamluk buildings.

The Ottoman conquest also brought a fresh impetus to the trade of the city with the establishment of numerous khans. One of the earliest Ottoman examples is Khan al-Haria built in 1572 around a square courtyard with stables and store rooms on the ground floor and accomodation above. In eighteenth-century khans the central courtyard was often smaller and covered with domes. The most famous example of this later type is the As'ad Pasha Khan which is a square building covered with eight small domes and a large central dome supported on marble columns. The eighteenth century also saw the development of domestic architecture influenced by buildings such as the Azzam palace which was built around a courtyard in the traditional Syrian manner but with decoration that recalls the mansions of Istanbul.

See also: Aleppo, Ayyubids, Mamluks, Syria

Further reading:

R. S. Humphreys, 'Politics and architectural patronage in Ayyubid Damascus', *Essays in Honour of Bernard Lewis: The Islamic World from Classical to Modern Times*, ed. C. E. Bosworth, C. Issawi, R. Savory and A. L. Udovitch, Princeton, NJ 1989.

J. G. De Maussion, *Damas, Bagdad, capitales et terres des califes*, Beirut 1971.

J. Sauvaget and M. Ecochard, *Les Monuments Ayyubides de Damas*, Damascus 1938–50.

Damascus Great Mosque

Principal mosque of Damascus founded by the Umayyad caliph al-Walid in 706 CE.

The Great Mosque stands in the centre of the old city of Damascus on the site of the Roman temple platform, or *temenos*. The outer walls of the *temenos* still survive and are distinguished as large blocks of dressed masonry with pilasters set at intervals into the side. At the four corners of the *temenos* there are large square towers and around the edge there were arcades which opened into a large rectangular courtyard. There were four axial doorways to the *temenos*, that on the east being the principal entrance. At the time of the Islamic conquest the Byzantine church of St John stood in the middle of this platform. Immediately after the conquest the Muslims shared this space with the Christians with the Christians retaining possession of their church and the Muslims using the southern arcades of the *temenos* as a prayer area.

In 706 al-Walid destroyed the church and built a mosque along the southern wall of the *temenos*. The layout of the mosque comprised three aisles running parallel to the south (qibla) wall cut in the centre by a raised perpendicular aisle or transept. At the south end of this transept there was a mihrab set into one of the blocked doors of the south façade. Walls were inserted on the west and east sides between the corner towers, and new two-storey arcades were built around the east, north and west sides of the courtyard. The arcades and prayer hall were covered with pitched wooden roofs covered with tiles except for the centre of the transept which had a wooden dome. In the north-west of the courtyard there is an octagonal chamber raised up on eight columns with a pool beneath. This structure functioned as the bayt al-mal or treasury and is found in other early mosques such as Harran and Hamma.

Since the Umayyad period the mosque has been rebuilt several times because of fires (1069, 1401 and 1893) although its basic plan has remained the same. Originally the arcade of the sanctuary façade comprised one pier alternating with two columns but this was subsequently changed to piers only. A range of different arch forms is used in the arcades including round, semi-circular horseshoe and slightly pointed arches. The walls of the mosque are decorated with glass mosaics similar to those in the Dome of the Rock, with depictions of palaces and houses next to a river (possibly the Barada river in Damascus). The long rooms in the east and west sides were lit by marble grilles with geometric interlace patterns based on octagons and circles.

The form of the mosque, particularly the sanctuary façade, was probably derived from Byzantine palatial architecture, possibly the Chalci palace in Constantinople. Later mosques in Syria such as the Great Mosques of Aleppo, Hamma, Harran and Córdoba. The Great Mosque of Diyarbakir built in the Seljuk period is also of this form.

See also: Damascus, Diyarbakir, Harran, Syria, Umayyads

Further reading:

K. A. C. Creswell (mosaics by Marguerite Van Berchem), *Early Muslim Architecture*, Oxford 1969, 1 (1): 156–210, 323–72.

dam

Dams have always been an important factor in Islamic civilization as a means of harnessing scarce or fugitive water supplies. Famous examples of pre-Islamic dams in the Middle East include the Macrib dam in Yemen and the Shallalat dam in northern Iraq. The advantages of dams over cisterns or reservoirs is that a large volume of water can be stored with a relatively small amount of construction work. The simplest forms of dam are made of earth with a clay core whilst more imposing masonry dams are built to contain larger volumes of water. Most dams are associated with irrigation works and are sometimes linked to water mills. However, some of the largest dams are built to provide drinking water for cities; one of the best examples is the Birket al-Sultan in Jerusalem which consists of a large masonry dam built across the wadi Hinon in the sixteenth century. On top of the dam in the centre is a drinking fountain or sebil which supplied water to travellers. One of the greatest examples of Ottoman engineering is the Valide Bend, a large masonry dam constructed in the Belgrade forest in 1769 to supply water to Istanbul.

dar

House or residence. Often implies a house of high status and may be roughly equivalent to mansion.

dar al-imara

Governor's palace. In early Islamic architecture this was usually located at the qibla end of the mosque (i.e. behind the mihrab). This was a safety measure to enable the govenor (or caliph) to enter the mosque without having to pass through other worshippers.

See also: Kufa

dargah or dukka

Covered courtyard in traditional Cairene houses.

Deccan

Region of southern India famous for its distinctive pre-Mughal Islamic architecture.

The Deccan includes the modern Indian states of Maharashtra, northern Andhra Pradesh, northern Karnataka and Goa. Physically the Deccan comprises a plateau bordered by the Arabian Sea to the west and the Bay of Bengal to the east. Each of these coasts is bordered by a range of hills known as the western and eastern Ghats. The central plateau is watered by the Krishna and Godavari rivers which flow eastwards into the Bay of Bengal. The region has a long history of monumental religious architecture with Buddhist cave art at Ajanta and numerous medieval Hindu shrines. Although the coastal regions were exposed to Islam from an early period it was not until the thirteenth century that there were any significant Islamic conquests in the area. In the early fourteenth century the Tughluq ruler of Delhi destroyed the power of the Hindu Hoysala kingdom and for the first time a major Muslim presence was established in the area. In 1338 after his victories in the region Muhammad Tughluq Shah II decided to move his capital from Delhi to Daulatabad, and although the transfer was unsuccessful and most of the population returned to Delhi the conquest established permanent Muslim rule in the region.

Muslim rule in the Deccan was complex and fragmentary, with dynasties established at various capitals gaining the upper hand at different times, until the late seventeenth century when the area was brought into the Mughal Empire. From 1347 to 1422 the central Deccan was ruled by the Muslim Bahmani kings from the newly established fortress city of Gulbarga. In 1424 Sultan Ahmad Shah Bahmani moved the capital to another fortress city Bidar. In 1487 the Bahmani kings were overthrown by the Barid Shahi dynasty who ruled the city until the seventeenth century. However, in 1512 real power passed to the Qutb Shahi sultans who ruled from their capital of Golconda. Although the Mughal conquests effectively ended the independence of the Deccani sultans, the city of Hyderabad managed to survive into the twentieth century as an autonomous state.

The earliest Muslim architecture of the region

was derivative of local architecture, thus the mosque of Daulatabad incorporates many of the features of a Hindu temple. However, the architecture of the newly established fortress cities of Bidar, Golconda, Gulbaraga and Bijapur was a distinctive mixture of Indian and Middle Eastern styles. The defensive architecture of the cities was highly sophisticated using concentric planning and bent entrances. Decoration was in the form of coloured tiles imported from Kashan (Iran), and Persian calligraphers were used to decorate the façades of tombs and mosques. The area developed a distinctive bulbous dome form with petals around the base (or drum) and heavy tiered finials rising from a moulded lotus-shaped apex. Other distinctive architectural features are the use of huge decorative battlements and complex stucco forms. The standard tomb form was a domed square with engaged towers or minar at each corner the finest example of which is the Gol Gumbaz at Bijapur.

See also: Bijapur, Char Minar, Firuzabad (India), Gol Gumbaz (India), Hyderabad.

Further reading:

E. S. Merklinger, *Indian Islamic Architecture: The Deccan,* Warminster 1981.

P. Davis, *The Penguin Guide to the Monuments of India, 2: Islamic, Rajput and European,* London 1989.

Delhi

Capital city of India containing some of the finest examples of Indian-Islamic architecture.

Delhi is located approximately in the centre of northern India between the mountains of the Himalayas and the Rajasthan desert. More immediately the city is located on the banks of the Jumna river and near the Aravalli hills.

The modern city of New Delhi is only the latest in a series of eight cities which have occupied the area of Delhi. Although there were earlier settlements on the site the oldest architectural remains can be attributed to the eleventh-century city built by the Rajput Tomar king Anangpal. In 1193 the city (known as Lal Kot) was captured by the Afghan conqueror Muhammad of Ghur who left the city in charge of his deputy, Qutb al-Din Aybak. By the time of Muhammad of Ghur's death in 1206 Qutb al-Din Aybak had declared himself independent and established himself as the first Muslim ruler of Delhi. In 1304 Ala al-Din Khalji founded a second city known as Siri which was

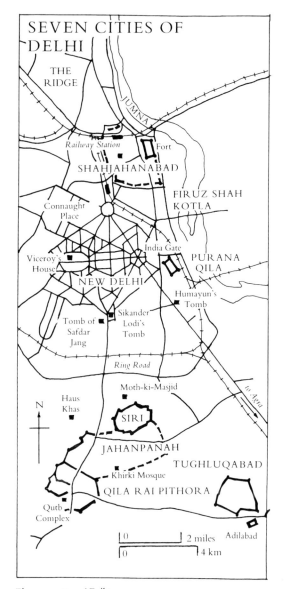

The seven cities of Delhi

located to the north of the first city. Later on, in 1321, a third city known as Tughluqabad after its founder Ghiyath al-Din Tughluq was founded to the east of the first city. However, this city was only used for four years until Muhamd Tughluq founded a fourth city known as Jahanpanah which also only lasted a short time as it was abandoned in 1328 when the ruler moved the capital to Daulatabad in the Deccan. The move to Daulatabad was disastrous and the sultan soon returned to Delhi. In 1354 Firuz Shah Tughluq established Firuzabad as the fifth city located by the river several kilometres to the north. For the next 150 years the area around Firuzabad was developed by successive dynasties although the central area fell into ruin. In 1534 the Bengali ruler Sher Shah founded the sixth city on the ruins of Firuzabad. This remained the centre of the city until 1638 when the Mughal ruler Shah Jahan established the city of Shahjahanabad. This was a huge new development to the north with the Red Fort at its centre. In 1911 Shahjahanabad became Old Delhi when the British laid out the present city of New Delhi.

Remains of all these cities have survived to present a cross-section of the development of Islamic architecture in India. The first city is known as Qila Rai Pithora after the Rajput ruler who built the fortifications. The most significant remains from the first city are the Qutb Minar and Mosque begun by Qutb al-Din Aybak in 1193. The Qutb Mosque complex stands inside the remains of fortification walls which were built by the Rajputs in the twelfth century. Originally the enclosure walls had thirteen gates although only three have survived. Fragments of Hindu temples incorporated into the mosque complex demonstrate the abrupt transition from Hindu to Muslim rule.

Apart from fortifications there are few remains of Siri (the second city of Delhi) because much of the stone was taken in the sixteenth century for use in Sher Shah's city. However, the remains of the third city, Tughluqabad, are remarkably well preserved. The remains consist of a huge irregular four-sided enclosure 1.5 by 2 km which includes a palace area, seven large cisterns, remains of a Friday mosque, the citadel and a tomb complex. The enclosure walls are tapering structures up to 30 m high, pierced with arrow slits and crowned by massive crenellations. Outside the enclosure walls to the south is the tomb of Ghiyath al-Din Tughluq which was originally an island set in an artificial lake and approached via a causeway from the palace complex. The tomb is a square domed building set within its own enclosure

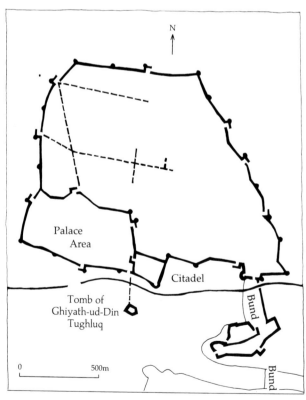

Plan of Tughluqabad, Delhi

and fortified with round bastions. To the east is a similar island structure known as Adilabad. Like the tomb complex this was a fortified area connected to the rest of the city by a causeway; within it was a huge audience hall on pillars built by Muhamad Tughluq.

The remains of the fourth city, Jahanpanah are located to the west of Tughluqabad between Siri and Qila Rai Pithora. Although much of this city has been destroyed the mosque is still standing and has an unusual plan consisting of four open courtyards. There are even fewer remains of the fifth city, Firuzabad, which was later built over by Sher Shah in the construction of the sixth city. The centre of the sixth city is the Purana Qila or 'Old Fort' initially built by the Mughal emperor Humayun and later developed by Sher Shah. The Purana Qila is a rectangular enclosure with huge corner bastions built on the supposed site of the city of Indraprastha mentioned in the Mahabharata. The interior of the fort is largely empty except for the Qala-i-Kuhna Mosque and the octagonal three-storey pavilion known as the Sher Mandal.

The seventh city, Shahjahanabad was founded by Shah Jahan in 1638 and was completed ten years later. Located on the banks of the Jumna river, the new city was dominated by the imperial palace known as the Red Fort. The street plan was based on two main avenues, the Chandni Chowk running east–west and the Faiz Bazar which runs south from the Red Fort. Near the intersection of these streets is the principal mosque of the city. This is one of the largest mosques in India and consists of a huge courtyard over 90 m square with three monumental gateways, a central rectangular cistern and a triple-domed sanctuary flanked by two minarets.

New Delhi is an Anglo–Indian city with few traditional Islamic buildings although the area occupied by the city includes some fine Islamic tombs the most famous of which is that of the second Mughal emperor Humayun.

See also: India, Mughals, Qutb Minar and Mosque, Red Fort

Further reading:

R. E. Frykenberg, *Delhi through the Ages: Essays in Urban History, Culture and Society*, Delhi 1986.

S. A. A. Naqvi, *Delhi: Humayun's Tomb and Adjacent Buildings*, Delhi 1946.

R. Nath, *Monuments of Delhi*, New Delhi 1979.

A. Petruccioli, 'Modelli culturali nell'impianto e nelle transformazioni di Old Delhi', *Storia della città* 31–2: 123–44, 1985.

Y. D. Sharma, *Delhi and its Neighbourhood*, 2nd edn., New Delhi 1974.

desert

The definition of desert varies with different authors, but it is generally agreed that any area with less than 50 mm annual rainfall may be counted as desert. For practical purposes, however, areas with less than 200 mm (the limit of dry farming) may reasonably be regarded as desert. Although deserts are a common feature of the Islamic world, most cities and areas of settlement are either outside this area or located next to large river systems such as the Nile, Tigris, Euphrates and Indus.

Until recently the majority of desert inhabitants have been nomadic pastoralists keeping either sheep and goats or camels and living in some form of tent. Important exceptions to this have been oasis trading settlements, Hajj routes and mining centres which are generally dependent on outside support for their survival. In certain periods, such as the early Islamic, political conditions, or more recently the exploitation of oil in Arabia, have made desert settlements more viable.

The architecture of the desert may be divided into three categories: permanent, semi-permanent and temporary. Temporary structures are either portable tents or made of expendable materials such as palm fronds, requiring minimum input of labour. Semi-permanent structures may be made out of a combination of portable and non-portable materials (e.g. a tent with stone walls) or may be made of perishable materials which need frequent renewal such as the palm-frond huts of the Tihama in Yemen. Permanent structures may be built of pisé, mud brick, baked brick, stone or, more recently, cement blocks and reinforced concrete.

Any desert settlement must make some provision for obtaining and storing water, usually from wells or seasonal rainfall, although occasionally sites are dependent on water brought from elsewhere (this was often the case with Hajj routes). The unpredictability of rain and the high evaporation rates in the desert (in many areas of the Middle East the rate of evaporation can exceed 2,000 mm annually) mean that elaborate water catchment and storage facilities are developed. Sites dependent on seasonal and sometimes erratic rain usually employ a system of dams, cisterns and run-off channels to maximize the catchment area. If water needs to be transported some distance, underground channels (qanats) are built to minimize evaporation.

Further reading:

E. Beazley and M. Howerson, *Living with the Desert: Working Buildings of the Iranian Plateau*, Warminster 1982.

S. Helms (with contributions by A. V. G. Betts, W. and F. Lancaster and C. J. Lenzen), *Early Islamic Architecture of the Desert: A Bedouin Station in Eastern Jordan*, Edinburgh 1990.

dershane

Turkish term for lecture hall or studying room, literally 'room for lessons'. Usually these are larger domed rooms or vaulted iwans on one side of an Ottoman madrassa.

diwan

Term of Iranian origin describing a reception hall, either in a house or a palace. Later on the word is also used to describe a government ministry.

diwan-i amm

Public reception hall.

diwan-i khass

Private reception hall.

Diyarbakir (Amida)

Prominent city on the banks of the Tigris in south-east Turkey famous for its massive black basalt walls which are still largely intact.

Diyarbakir was captured from the Byzantines by Arab armies in 693 and became one of the great Islamic frontier fortresses. On capturing the city the Byzantine cathedral was shared between Muslims and Christians, although by 770 it was again used as a church. Later a Great Mosque was built on the site of the present Ulu Cami which according to a contemporary description (Nasiri Khusraw, 1045) had arcades two tiers high. The Ulu Cami in its present form dates to between 1090 and 1155 according to two inscriptions in the name of the Seljuk leader Malik Shah. The prayer room or sanctuary of the mosque is three aisles wide and covered with a transept in the middle on the axis of the mihrab. This arrangement and the similarity with the Great Mosque in Damascus (once thought to have been a church) has given rise to the

Ulu Cami, Diyarbakir, Turkey

assertion that the building was once a church in spite of contradictory evidence. The similarity with the Great Mosque in Damascus is explained by the fact that Malik Shah also carried out work there and may have used this as a model for that of Diyarbakir.

During the fifteenth century Diyarbakir became capital of the Aq-qoyunulu Turkman dynasty which was given control of the city in return for its support of Timur at the battle of Ankara in 1492. Buildings of the Aq-qoyunulu period provided a model for those of the Ottoman period. Several mosques of this period survive, the most famous of which is that of Kasim Padişah with its large central dome. The minaret is detached and consists of a tall square structure raised on four columns.

After its capture from the Aq-qoyunulu the Ottomans developed Diyarbakir as a regional administrative centre with its own mint. There are several notable sixteenth-century Ottoman mosques in Diyarbakir all built in the ablaq style (striped black and white masonry) with tall minarets with square shafts. Several of the mosques have fine tile decoration similar but inferior to that of Iznik which was probably produced within the city. The first of these is the Fatih Cami built between 1518 and 1520 which consists of a large dome supported by four semi-domes in a quatrefoil pattern. This plan, which is also used in the Peygamber Cami built in 1524, was probably the inspiration for Sinan's use of the plan in the Şehzade Cami in Istanbul. One of the more interesting mosques is the Melek Ahmet Pasha Cami which is built on first-floor level and is entered by a passage under the mosque which leads into a courtyard from which a set of stairs leads up into the prayer room.

Several nineteenth-century konaks (palatial houses) survive in Diyarbakir. One of the best examples is the Gevraniler Konak completed in 1819. The house is built around a courtyard on a vaulted sub-structure which contains cisterns, stables and a bath house. The apartments face north and are arranged as separate pavilions with their own terraces.

See also: Ottomans

Further reading:

D. Erginbaş, *Diyarbakir eveleri*, Istanbul 1954.
J. Raby, 'Diyarbakir: A rival to Iznik', *Istanbuler Mitteilungen* 26: 429–59, 1976.

Djenné (Dienné)

City in central Mali known for its unique mud-brick architecture which is a blend of African and Islamic styles.

The city was founded sometime between 767 and 1250 CE and was converted to Islam by Koy Kunboro, the twenty-sixth chief of the city, between 1106 and 1300. The prosperity of the city was based on the long-distance trans-Saharan trade routes, the most important commodities being gold and salt. The city was conquered by the Moroccans in 1591 who ruled the town until 1780. In the nineteenth century it was incorporated into the theocratic state of Macina, and came under French control in 1898, after which it declined in importance.

The main building material used in Djenné is mud brick, locally known as ferey. The mud bricks are plastered with mud plaster giving buildings a smooth rounded organic look which is offset by the use of bundles of palm sticks projecting from the walls (turon). These palm sticks have a dual function providing both decoration and a form of scaffolding for maintenance. Small cylindrical bricks were used until the 1930s when rectangular bricks were introduced. It is thought that the cylindrical bricks provided greater stability than modern ones, which is why so many older buildings have survived.

The city is built on a small hill between creeks and until recently was surrounded by a wall with eleven gates. The city was divided into quarters according to tribal divisions. More wealthy merchants lived in large monumental courtyard-houses, surrounded by open spaces. The houses were divided into male and female areas, with the men's area on the first floor at the front overlooking the street. The women's area by contrast was usually on the ground floor at the back of the courtyard. Traditionally these houses are decorated with a façade known as the 'Sudan Façade' which includes pillars and decorated entrances as its characteristic features.

The most famous building of the city is the Great Mosque which is said to have been originally built by Koy Kunboro who destroyed his palace to build it. The early mosque is known to have survived to the 1830s when it was destroyed. The present Great Mosque was built in 1909 on the foundations of the earlier structure. It stands on a raised platform approximately 75 m square reached six monumental staircases. The mosque consists of a large internal courtyard surrounded by a corridor, and a huge prayer hall, with a wooden roof supported by ninety rectangular piers. All four faces of the mosque are decorated with round pinnacles or cones, engaged pillars and bundles of palm sticks set into the side. The main entrances to the mosque are on the south and north sides (the east side is the qibla wall). The north side is more decorated than that of the south reflecting its proximity to the richer areas of the city. The east side or qibla wall is supported by three large rectangular towers. On the inside of the mosque a deep recessed mihrab is built into each one of these towers, and the central tower contains in addition a staircase to a platform on the roof, whence the speech of the imam could be relayed to the rest of the town.

P. Maas, *Aramco World*, November/December 1990: 18–29, gives the best recent account of Djenné.

L. Prussin, *The Architecture of Djenné: African Synthesis and Transformation*, Yale 1973.

do-chala

Type of roof with curved eaves, derived from Bengali huts (bangala). Used first in Bengali and later in Mughal architecture.

dome

Circular vaulted construction used as a means of roofing. First used in much of the Middle East and North Africa whence it spread to other parts of the Islamic world, because of its distinctive form the dome has, like the minaret, become a symbol of Islamic architecture.

It seems likely that the dome originated as a roofing method where the absence of suitable timber meant that it was impossible to make a flat timber roof. The earliest domes in the Middle East were associated with round buildings and were produced out of mud brick placed in layers which tilt slightly inwards. Another early method of dome construction which can still be seen in northern Syria and Harran in Turkey is the corbelled dome where mud bricks are placed horizontally in circular layers of diminishing circumference producing a corbelled dome. When the Romans conquered the Middle East the dome was incorporated into Roman architecture and under the Byzantines it became the main method of roofing monumental buildings. The chief advantage of domes is that large areas can be roofed without the interference of columns. At this time the wooden dome was developed which combined the space of dome building with the flexibility and lightness of wood. By the seventh century wooden domes were a normal method of roofing churches so that when the Arabs came to build the Dome of the Rock a wooden dome was used as the most appropriate form for this major religious building. Wooden domes were usually covered with sheets of metal, either copper or lead, as protection against the weather. The exact construction of the domes of the Caliph's Mosque in Baghdad is not known although the fact that it was described as green suggests that it was covered in copper.

Most domes, however, continued to be built of less flexible materials such as stone, mud brick and baked brick. One of the main problems of dome construction was the transition from a square space or area into a circular domed area. Usually there was an intermediary octagonal area from which it is easier to convert to a circular area although there is still the problem of converting from square to octagon. Two main methods were adopted, which are the *squinch* and the *pendentive*. The squinch is a mini-arch which is used to bridge a diagonal corner area whilst a pendentive is an inverted cone with its point set low down into the corner and its base at the top providing a platform for the dome. Squinches are the main method of transition in pre-Ottoman architecture whilst pendentives are more common after the sixteenth century. In India, where there was no tradition of arches before the advent of Islam, domes rest on flat corbels which bridge the corners.

During the medieval period Islam developed a wide variety of dome types which reflect dynastic, religious and social distinctions as much as different construction techniques. One of the most extravagant dome forms is the muqarnas or conical dome which appears as early as the eleventh century in Iraq at Imam Dur. A conical dome consists of multiple tiers of muqarnas which blur the distinction between structure and decoration and between circular and square forms. Later on the idea of the double dome was introduced as it was recognized that there was a conflict between the external appearance of the dome and the aesthetics of the interior of the domed space. The result was tall external domes with shallower interior domes. Increasing emphasis on the exterior can be seen in Cairo and Egypt where masonry domes with intricately carved exteriors were developed. In Iran and Central Asia tall domes were covered in coloured (usually blue) glazed tiles, culminating in the huge bulbous fluted domes on a high circular drum which were characteristic of the Timurid period (fifteenth century). In pre-Mughal India the standard dome form was derived from Hindu architecture and consisted of a squat circular form with a lotus design around the apex and a characteristic bulbous finial. Ottoman architecture adopted the Byzantine dome form and developed it to produce vast domed areas such as that of the Selimiye in Edirne.

Dome of the Rock (Qubbat al-Sakhra)

The third most important shrine of Islam. It is located on the Temple Mount in Jerusalem.

The Dome of the Rock was built by the early caliph Abd al-Malik in 691 and is generally agreed to be one of the oldest Islamic monuments. The building consists of a domed octagonal structure set in the middle of a raised plaza or enclosure known as the Haram al-Sharif or holy place. In the immediate vicinity of the Dome of the Rock are two other buildings of similar antiquity, the Qubbat al-Silsila and the Aqsa Mosque. The Qubbat al-Silsila is a smaller structure immediately to the east of the Dome of the Rock; it shares the same basic plan of an octagonal structure covered with a dome, although unlike the larger monument the sides of the structure are open. The purpose of the Qubbat al-Silsila is unknown although it probably had some ritual function. The Aqsa Mosque has been rebuilt several times so that its original form is difficult to determine although its basic form was probably similar to that of today. The Aqsa Mosque serves as the main place of prayer for the Haram and is located to the south of the Dome of the Rock.

The plan of the Dome of the Rock is based around a central dome resting on a circular drum supported by an arcade. This inner arcade is enclosed by an outer octagonal arcade and a solid octagonal wall which supports the shallow pitched roof around the dome. Both sets of arcades are carried on a mixture of piers and columns; the inner arcade is composed of four piers and twelve columns whilst the outer arcade consists of eight piers and sixteen columns. There are four entrances to the building, one on each of the sides facing the four cardinal points. Each of the eight sides of the outer octagon is divided into seven tall arches or bays, five of the arches on each side are open as doors or windows whilst the two nearest the corners are blind arches. There are twelve more windows in the circular drum below the dome. Directly below the dome is an exposed area of natural rock enclosed by a screen or fence, under-neath this is a small cave with a mihrab reached by a set of steps.

Several forms of decoration are used including mosaics, marble, repoussé metalwork and coloured glass. The mosaics are particularly important examples of the combination of Sassanian and Byzantine motifs which is a characteristic of early Islamic art. Another important feature of the mosaics is that they carry an inscription dating the building to 691. At present only the interior mosaics survive although originally they also covered the outside.

The building has been restored many times in its 1,300-year history. One of the most important restorations was carried out during the sixteenth-century reign of the Ottoman sultan Suleyman the Magnificent. It was during this restoration that the exterior was covered with glazed ceramic tiles which covered the earlier mosaic coating. The tiles were the forerunners of Iznik tiles (q.v.) which became such a significant feature of Ottoman architecture. The present tiles covering the building were added in 1968. At the same time the Dome was covered with gold for the first time, although the present covering dates from 1993.

The Dome of the Rock is generally regarded as an attempt to provide a Muslim alternative to the Church of the Holy Sepulchre which had previously dominated the city of Jerusalem. The plan and design of the Dome of the Rock reflect this rivalry. In religious terms the building is significant because it commemorates the place where Abraham offered his son Isaac as a sacrifice and the place from which Muhammad made his night journey to heaven.

See also: Jerusalem

Further reading:

K. A. C. Creswell, *A Short Account of Early Islamic Architecture*, ed. J. W. Allan, Aldershot 1989.
O. Grabar, *The Formation of Islamic Art*, Yale 1973.

domical vault

A dome which rises from a square or rectangular base without the intervention of a drum, squinches or pendentives.

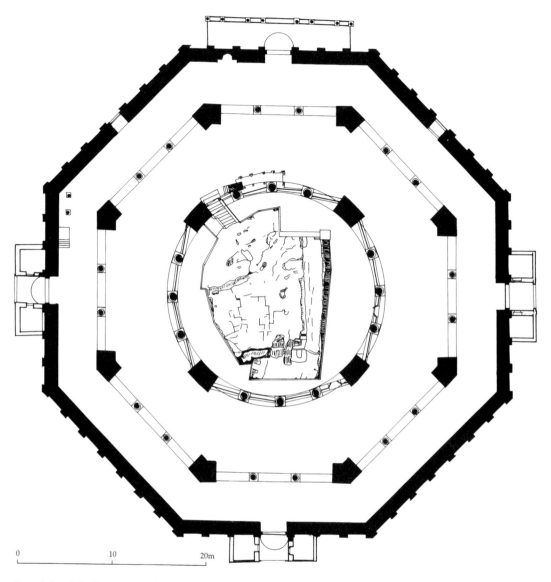

Ground plan of the Dome of the Rock, Jerusalem. Note exposed rock surface in centre (after Creswell)

E

East Africa

Muslim areas of East Africa have traditionally been the coastal strip which extends for over a thousand miles and includes the coasts of Somalia, Kenya, Tanzania (including Zanzibar) and northern Mozambique. This area has a homogeneous culture, known as Swahili, which is distinct from but related to both the Arabic Islamic world and the Bantu-speaking peoples of the interior.

Historical Background

The first documentary evidence concerning the East African coast comes from the first-century CE Periplus of the Erythraen Sea and the fourth-century geography of Ptolemy. The origins and history of Islam on the East African coast are obscure, although historical sources have been supplemented recently by information from archaeological excavations to produce at least an outline picture. Historically the earliest Islamic settlements on the coast took place during the eighth century and this has been confirmed recently by excavations at Shanga in Kenya.

The Swahili culture has traditionally been based on Indian Ocean trade with Arabia, India and the Far East and it is probable that this is how Islam arrived in East Africa rather than by conquest or a policy of colonization. Although it is likely that some Arabs and Persians may have settled on the coast, the overwhelming majority of the population had African origins as is demonstrated by the Swahili language itself which is essentially a Bantu language with many Arabic loan words. There is little documentary evidence of the early period before the arrival of the Portuguese although there are several early buildings which are dated by inscriptions. The earliest of these is a Kufic inscription in the Kizimkazi Mosque in Zanzibar dated to 1107 CE, although the mosque was rebuilt in the eighteenth century according to another inscription in the building. Other early dated monuments are in Somalia, including the Great Mosque of Mogad-ishu built in 1238 and the mosque of Fakhr al-Din in 1269.

In addition to inscriptions there are also various early accounts by travellers. In 1331 the coast was visited by Ibn Battuta who travelled as far south as Kilwa in southern Tanzania and described the people and buildings of the coast, and also in the early fourteenth century a Chinese embassy visited and described the coast.

Through analysis of trade goods, architectural features and local artefacts, archaeology has provided a more detailed model of how Swahili culture developed in the centuries prior to the Portuguese. In the earliest phase of settlement (eighth–ninth century) the main trading partner seemed to be the Persian Gulf; later on with the collapse of the Abbasid caliphate trade seems to be more connected with the Red Sea and ultimately Egypt. During these two early periods the towns of the Lamu archipelago such Manda and Shanga seem to have risen in wealth and importance. Later in the thirteenth century the area around Kilwa in southern Tanzania seems to have risen rapidly in wealth and importance along with the city of Mogadishu in Somalia. This change can partly be explained through the history of local dynasties and partly through the growth of the gold trade which originated in Zimbabwe and made its way via Sofala, Kilwa, Mogadishu and Yemen to the Middle East.

In the sixteenth century the coast was opened to Europeans when the Portuguese established a base in Mombasa as part of the sea route India. For the next two hundred years until the mid-eighteenth century the Portuguese tried to control the trade of the coast against the rival claims of the Dutch and the Omanis. Whilst the rivalry of the maritime powers disrupted trade, the stability of the coastal towns was threatened by the Galla, a nomadic tribe from Somalia, who sacked and pillaged towns as far south as Mombasa. In the mid-eighteenth century the Omanis at last won the struggle for supremacy on the coast when

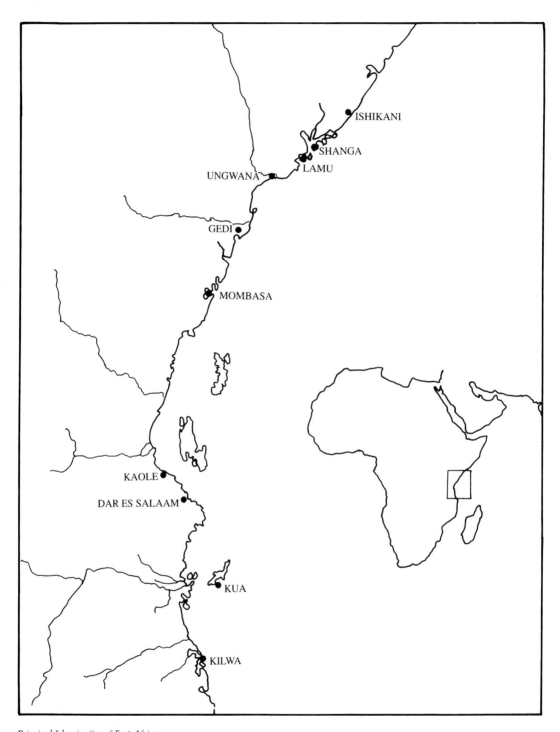

Principal Islamic sites of East Africa

they captured the Portuguese base of Fort Jesus in Mombasa. During the next century Omani power was extended inland and by 1832 their position was so secure that Sultan Sayyid Said moved his capital from Muscat to Zanzibar which remained the capital until the beginning of the twentieth century.

The coast of East Africa is fairly low-lying and is fringed with extensive tracts of mangrove forests intermittently punctuated by inlets and creeks. Occasionally there are groups of islands such as at Kilwa or Lamu forming small archipelagoes and a few larger offshore islands like Zanzibar, Pemba and Mafia. The coast is protected along most of its length by substantial coral reefs which also form the base of most of the coastal foreshore. It is important to note that all the Islamic settlements so far discovered in East Africa are within four miles of the coast and most are considerably nearer. Most sites are located slightly apart from the mainland either on peninsulas which are cut off at high tide or on islands, although many are also located on the shores of creeks or inlets. The main form of communication was by boats with a fairly shallow draught, which could be brought in close to the shore at high tide.

The main building materials were coral, mangrove poles (barriti), coconut thatch (barissti) and mud which were all easily available on the coast. In the absence of any other suitable form of stone on the coast coral was employed as the main building material for stone houses. Two main types were used, reef coral quarried live from the sea and fossil coral which formed the main rock underlying the coast. Usually reef coral was used for the finer decorative elements of a building whilst fossil coral was used for the walls, although there are certain variations on this. Coral was also burnt and used to make lime for plaster and mortar. Mangrove poles were the main type of timber used and were available in considerable quantities as any coastal settlement would involve the clearance of large areas of mangrove. The standard dimensions of mangrove poles are between 1.80 and 2.80 m long which imposes a maximum span on roofs without supports. Barissti or coconut palm was used as a thatch to roof mud-walled houses and to build temporary fishing shelters (bandas). Red mud earth was used either as a building material for walls in wattle-and-daub constructions or as floor make up within stone houses. In most places and at most periods throughout the coast mud wattle-and-daub constructions would have been the predominant form of construction whilst stone was only used for special purposes.

Architecture

Although East Africa has been Islamic for more than 1,000 years the towns or settlements do not contain all the elements usually found in a Muslim town. There are, for example, no public baths or hammams, presumably because of the hot moist climate (although the Omanis built baths on Zanzibar in the nineteenth century). Similarly there are no suqs or open-air markets and no caravanserais or khans. Before the Portuguese period (sixteenth century) there do not seem to have been significant attempts to fortify towns with walls and there are few examples of fortified buildings before this period with the enigmatic exception of Husuni Ndogo (see Kilwa). The reasons for this are presumably connected with the maritime nature of Swahili civilization and its relative remoteness from other Muslim areas. Nevertheless the East African coast does have some outstanding examples of other Islamic building types including mosques, palaces, houses and tombs.

The earliest mosques so far discovered have all been in excavations at Shanga in Kenya where a sequence of five superimposed mosques have been discovered dating from the ninth to the fourteenth centuries. The first three of these mosques (Shanga I–III) are dated to before 900 CE and the earliest appears to have been a small open-air structure surrounded by an enclosure made out of wattle and daub. The structure was rectangular, measuring approximately 5 m north–south by 3.5 m east–west, with rounded corners, an entrance on the south side and a floor made of stamped green earth. No mihrab could be detected in the structure and may not have been thought necessary at this early date in such a small structure, where the orientation of the building and the position of the door opposite the qibla were enough to indicate the direction of Mecca (in East Africa the qibla is due north). The second mosque (Shanga II) was of a similar size and design although it had a more substantial structure with a plaster floor and roof supported on a single central timber post and ten external posts. In the centre of the north wall was a large semicircular post hole which may have been for a wooden mihrab. The next (Shanga III) to be built on the site was largely destroyed by subsequent rebuilding but was of similar dimensions to the two earlier mosques and had a roof supported by at least eight large posts. The first stone mosque (Shanga IV), dated to between 850 and 890, was built directly on top of the previous wooden building (Shanga III) and consisted of a rectangular structure built out of reef coral (also called porites) with a rectangular antechamber at the south end. The latest mosque on the site (Shanga V) is still standing to roof height and is dated to around 1000 CE. It is also a rectangular structure built out of fossil coral (coral rag) with an antechamber at the south end and four large posts to support the roof in the centre. There are entrances to this building on the east and west sides and no traces of a mihrab in the first phase, although this may have been a portable wooden structure.

Unfortunately there are few examples of early mosques to compare with those at Shanga so it is not possible to say how typical they are. However, comparison shows that many of the features at Shanga were developed in later mosques, in particular the absence of an external courtyard with arcades, the rectangular longitudinal alignment of the plan, the use of side rooms, the arrangement of doors either at the south end or from the sides and the gradual introduction of more permanent materials.

Other early mosques include the Kizimkazi Mosque on Zanzibar, the mosque at Manda, the three thirteenth-century mosques in Mogadishu, and the Great Mosque at Kilwa. The Kizimkazi Mosque on Zanzibar was rebuilt in the eighteenth century but has a twelfth-century foundation inscription confirmed by excavations. The plan consists of a narrow rectangular structure with a row of central columns supporting a roof two aisles wide and four bays deep. Excavations at Manda in Kenya have revealed a mosque with a similar plan which may date to the tenth century. Although more complex, the Great Mosque in Mogadishu (1238) is built around the same basic plan and consists of a simple rectangular structure two aisles wide and five bays deep. This building is also unusual for having a minaret, a feature which does not occur elsewhere in

the architecture of East Africa until the nineteenth century.

Of all the mosques on the East African coast the Great Mosque at Kilwa is the most impressive because of its size and antiquity. The mosque basically consists of two parts, an earlier northern part and a much larger southern extension. Beneath the floors of the northern part of the building remains of an earlier mosque have been found which was initially dated to the twelfth century but may well be earlier. Although this mosque was not fully excavated it seems to have had the same design as the twelfth-century mosque which was later built over it. This mosque has a rectangular plan measuring approximately 6 m east–west by 12 m north–south with nine columns arranged in three rows. There is a large deeply recessed mihrab in the centre of the north wall and doorways on the west and east sides. In general this plan conforms to the general type of mosque on the coast although it is much larger than its contemporaries. Sometime in the sixteenth century a massive southern extension (20 m north–south by 15 m east–west) was added with alternating domed and barrel-vaulted chambers supported first on timber columns and later on composite octagonal masonry columns. The whole area was five aisles wide and six bays deep and had entrances on the west and east sides. Attached to the south-east corner of this area was a large masonry dome used as a prayer room by the sultan of Kilwa. The island of Kilwa also contains a nine-domed mosque known as the Small Domed Mosque which is one of the few examples of a Middle Eastern type of mosque in East Africa.

Before the sixteenth century most mosques were rectangular with a single row of columns aligned with the mihrab and a separate room for ablutions to the south. After this time, however, new forms were introduced, including the square-plan mosque as seen in the small mosques at Kua and the main mosque at Songo Mnara. From the fifteenth century onwards it is also possible to see a development of mihrabs from simple recessed niches into much more complex forms with multi-lobed arches recessed several times. From the late eighteenth century onwards carved plaster is used in place of reef coral to decorate the mihrab. Another feature which becomes popular at this period (except in the Lamu area) is the recessed minbar which is set into the north wall of the mosque and is entered either through the mihrab itself or through a separate opening in the wall. Later on, in the nineteenth century, minarets become a feature of mosques for the first time. Previously some mosques had a form of staircase minaret which provided access to the roof from which the call to prayer could be made. The reason for the absence of minarets until this relatively late date is not known, although it is likely that it may have had a religious basis connected with Ibadiism. Certainly the technology for building towers was present as can be seen in the numerous pillar tombs of the coast and structures such as the Mbraaki pillar in Mombasa built in the fourteenth century. Some of the earliest minarets in East Africa were built on the Kenya coast such as at Shella near Lamu and several mosques in Mombasa town.

After the mosques palaces represent some of the best examples of Islamic architecture on the coast. Although not many have survived from the earliest period it is likely that most settlements had some form of palace or great house located next to the main mosque. Excavations at Shanga and Manda (both in Kenya) have revealed early monumental buildings which date to before 1000 CE near the congregational mosque of the settlement. The island of Kilwa contains several palaces, the most famous of which is Husuni Kubwa which may date from the thirteenth century. This is a massive complex over 100 m long which occupies a projecting headland away from the main settlement. The palace has a monumental entrance at the south end which leads into the south court, roughly 40 m square with arcades and rooms arranged on each side. A doorway in the north wall leads on to the central palace area which is in turn divided into four courtyards which have been interpreted as an audience court, a domestic court, a palace court and a courtyard around an octagonal pool. Other palaces on Kilwa include the Makutani Palace (eighteenth century), the Great House next to the Great Mosque (fifteenth century) and Songo Mnara on a nearby island (also fifteenth century).

Husuni Kubwa is certainly the largest pre-nineteenth-century palace on the coast and most subsequent palaces were more like large houses. The fifteenth-century palace at Gedi appears as the largest house amongst several large houses each with similar arrangements of courtyards, storage areas and public and private rooms. The palace was built by the Sheikh of Malindi and was distinguished from other buildings in the town by a royal tomb adjacent to the entrance. The palace consists of a high-walled rectangular enclosure (approximately 35 by 25 m) with a monumental entrance on the east side. The main area of the building is the north courtyard which has been interpreted as an audience hall for the ruler who would have conducted his official business from there. This courtyard leads on to the private quarters of the sultan to the south. The harem courtyard is on the west side of the audience courtyard but separated from it by a wall, and is only accessible by going through the private apartments or by a separate entrance to the palace on the west side which opens directly into the harem area.

At the beginning of the nineteenth century the Omanis introduced a new concept of palace architecture with large multi-storey buildings enclosed within gardens. The earliest of these is the Mtoni Palace built in 1830 around a large square courtyard and with a Persian bath house attached. The largest of the Omani palaces is the Maruhubi Palace which also had a bath house and fort within the gardens which covered 50 hectares.

Houses of the East African coast represent a continuous development of domestic architecture that can be traced back over 1,000 years. Unfortunately most houses were built of impermanent materials such as wattle and daub, so that the surviving stone houses only represent a small proportion of the dwellings in even the wealthiest towns. However, from the available evidence it seems likely that the basic wattle-and-daub house retained a fairly conservative plan through history; thus remains of wattle-and-daub houses at Shanga, Manda and Kilwa seem to be fairly consistent with present-day houses. These consist of a rectangular structure with a pitched roof supported on rafters and posts sunk into the ground. The roofs would be covered in coconut palm thatch (barissti) and the walls made of wattle and daub (thin stakes dug into the ground, interwoven with palm leaves and covered with a protective layer of mud). Wattle-and-daub constructions appear to be the earliest form of housing in Swahili settlements and predate the first stone houses by 200 years.

The earliest coral stone buildings on the coast seem to have been public buildings such as mosques and administrative centres, and the first domestic stone buildings appear to have been palaces. Only in the fifteenth and sixteenth centuries did stone houses become common in the settlements of the coast at places like Songo Mnara and Gedi. At Takwa, a settlement inhabited between the sixteenth and seventeenth centuries, there were over 150 stone houses and one mosque, indicating that stone houses were the norm. However, it was not until the eighteenth and nineteenth centuries that stone houses became common in most of the major settlements. The town of Lamu probably contains the best examples of eighteenth-century domestic architecture on the coast: the typical Swahili house of the period consists of a stone enclosure wall with no outward-facing windows. The entrance to the building is usually a porch with benches either side which forms the only generally accessible part of the house. The porch opens on to a small anteroom which in turn leads out into a courtyard which contains a small bathroom and a well. There is a guest room on one side of the courtyard (usually the north) which is separate from the rest of the house, whilst the private quarters are on the other (south) side of the courtyard. These usually consist of a series of long narrow rooms arranged side by side and opening successively one on to the other. The outer two rooms are the outer and inner living rooms which are both open to receive light from the courtyard. There are usually raised areas at either end of each room which can be curtained off and used for sleeping areas. Behind the inner living room is the harem which is another narrow longitudinal room with wooden doors separating it from the living rooms. Behind this room there is an inner bathroom on one side and a larger room usually with a small blocked doorway to the outside which is used for laying out the dead. The houses are usually decorated with stucco work in the form of niches and large decorative friezes which are mostly concentrated around the harem. Either side of the doorway to the harem are niches, and within the harem itself, set into the wall facing the door, are a large array of niches. The niches were used for displaying valuable imported pottery

although their precise significance is a matter for discussion.

Most houses were single storey and if another level was built this was usually for another house or family unit for the children of the family on the ground floor. When an upper storey was added there was usually an extra single room with a thatched roof added at a higher level which functioned as a kitchen (kitchens were usually in the courtyard so that the smoke could escape). Stone houses were only built by people of high status within the community and could not be bought or sold to outsiders.

Monumental stone tombs are one of the characteristic features of Swahili architecture. Like stone houses tombs made of stone were not available to everyone and were probably reserved for people of wealth or rank; the precise status required is not known, although it has been pointed out that the tomb of the Lamu saint Habib Salih bin Alwi was built of wood as he may have been considered an outsider and therefore not eligible for a stone tomb.

Most tombs consist of a rectangular enclosure of varying dimensions with the east side of the tomb decorated in various ways. Monumental tombs are usually built either next to a mosque (usually the north end) or isolated in the open country. Often they are used as shrines where offerings are left and prayers said on specific days. In Somalia and northern Kenya there is a group of tombs consisting of large enclosures with an average size of 30 m square and a maximum of over 75 m square.

Decoration takes several forms, the best known of which is the pillar; other forms include panelled decoration, stepped ends, and a domed or pitched roof. Pillar tombs consist of a cylindrical or square shafted pillar rising out of the wall of the tomb which is usually decorated with panels. The pillars are sometimes decorated with fluting and Chinese bowls set into the top of the pillar. Pillar tombs are widely distributed and the earliest examples are dated to the fourteenth century. Although most tombs have some form of panelled decoration, in some structures this becomes quite complex and is the main form of decoration as in the Ishakani tomb of north Kenya which is decorated with more than thirty panels with various forms of geometric designs consisting of triangles, diamonds, squares, rectangles and

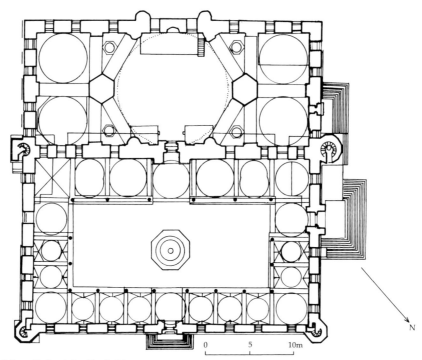

Üç Şerefeli Cami, Edirne, Turkey (after Goodwin)

chevrons. Other panelled tombs are decorated with plain panels alternating with niches. Many tombs are decorated with stepped corners as a main feature of their decoration; this was the predominant form of tomb until the nineteenth century. Although most tombs are open enclosures, occasionally they are covered over either with a dome or a pitched roof. The earliest examples of covered tombs are from Ungwana, where three tombs covered with gabled roofs are dated to the mid-thirteenth century. Domed tombs seem to be much later and only occur after the sixteenth century.

See also: coral, Gedi, Kenya, Kilwa, Lamu, minaret, Somalia, Sudan, Tanzania, Zanzibar

Further reading:

J. de V. Allen and T. H. Wilson, *Swahili Houses and Tombs of the Coast of Kenya*, Art and Archaeology Research Papers, London 1979.

P. Garlake, *The Early Islamic Architecture of the East African Coast*, Memoir no.1 of the British Institute of History and Archaeology in Eastern Africa, Oxford 1966.

M. C. Horton, 'Early Muslim trading settlements on the East African coast: new evidence from Shanga', *Antiquaries Journal* 67: 290–323, 1987.

H. C. Sanservino, 'Archaeological remains on the southern Somali coast', *Azania* 18: 151–64, 1983.

P. Sinclair, 'Chibuene: an early trading site in southern Mozambique', *Paideuma* 28: 148–64.

Edirne (Byzantine: Adrianople)

Major Ottoman city in European Turkey on the main route between the Middle East and Europe.

Edirne was captured in 1362 and rapidly rose to replace Bursa as the Ottoman capital in 1366. During the fifteenth century the city was developed as a major Turkish city with caravanserais, khans and mosques and a royal palace. The capture of Constantinople (later Istanbul) in 1453 meant that Edirne was no longer the capital, although it continued to be one of the first cities of the empire and a country residence for the Ottoman sultans until the nineteenth century. Unfortunately the royal palace which was located on the banks of the Tunca river has disappeared, but photographs and plans show an ancient building considerably altered

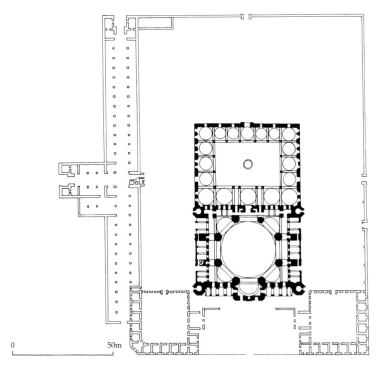

Selimiye Complex, Edirne, Turkey (after Goodwin)

by nineteenth-century additions when it again was used as a residence of the sultans. The best-preserved part of the palace seems to have been the kitchens which provided a model for those of the Topkapisarai.

The oldest surviving mosque in Edirne is known as the Yildirim Cami which is built on the ruins of a church. The date of construction is debated but is believed to be between 1360 and 1390. Other early mosques include the Muradiye Tekke and Mosque built in 1421 which includes both green tiles of the Yeşil Cami (Bursa) type and blue and white Chinese style tiles. Unfortunately the building was heavily damaged in an earthquake of 1751 and much of the original appearance of the mosque has been lost in the eighteenth-century restoration. The largest early mosque at Edirne is the Eski Cami completed during the reign of Mehmet I in 1413. This is a nine-domed building with a portico of five bays on the north side and a minaret at the north-west corner (the second minaret was added twenty years later). The six side domes are hemispherical whilst the central domes on the line of

the mihrab are a variety of shapes (polygonal, octagonal and star-shaped vaults).

Of a similar period but very different style is the Üç Şerefeli Cami begun in 1437. Where the Eski Cami was the last great Ottoman mosque to be built in the multi-domed fashion the Üç Şerefeli was the first of the new type of imperial mosque. It consists of a rectangular courtyard and smaller rectangular prayer area covered by one large dome and four subsidiary domes (two either side). The main dome rests on a hexagonal drum supported by two large octagonal piers. This was a revolutionary design when mosques were either a collection of single-domed units or a large area covered by multiple domes of equal size like the Eski Cami. The Üç Şerefeli was also unique for its time because of its four minarets decorated in a variety of patterns; they were placed at the corners of the courtyard and arranged so that the two smallest were at the front and the tallest minarets were at the back. The tallest minaret is in the north-west corner and is distinguished by its three balconies which give the building its name.

In 1484 Beyazit ordered the construction of a major new mosque and hospital by the side of the Tunca river. The complex covers a large area (approx. 300 by 200 m) and includes the mosque, a hospital, sanatorium and medical school. There is a stone bridge next to the complex which was probably built at the same time. The mosque at the centre of the complex consists of a single-domed unit, flanked by two tabhanes (dervish hostels) and approached via a rectangular arcaded courtyard. The most significant architectural feature of the complex is the hexagonal hospital hall which encloses a central domed hexagonal court leading off to vaulted iwans.

Edirne's continued importance during the sixteenth century is proved by Selim II's choice of the city for his imperial mosque the Selimiye, whose central dome was the largest Ottoman dome and was equal to that of Hagia Sophia with a diameter of 32 m. The mosque forms part of a complex which includes a covered market, a madrassa and primary school. Like the Üç Şerefeli Mosque the Selimiye has four minarets although here one is placed at each corner of the domed prayer hall rather than the courtyard.

See also: Ottomans, Selimiye, tekke

Further reading:

A. Kuran, 'Edirne'de Yildirim Camii' (The Mosque of Yildirim in Edirne), *Belletin*, 28(3): 429–38, 1964.

R. M. Meriç, 'Edirne'nin tarihi ve mimari eserleri hakkinda', in *Türk San'ati Tarihi Araştima ve Incelemeleri*, Istanbul 1963.

R. Meyer-Riefstahl, 'Early Turkish tile revetments in Turkey', *Ars Islamica*, 4: 1937.

R. Osman, *Edirne sarayi*, Ankara 1956.

A. S. Ünver, *Edirne Muradiye cami*'i, Istanbul 1953.

Egypt (excluding Cairo)

Located at the north-eastern tip of Africa forming a bridge between Africa and Asia. The population of the Arab Republic of Egypt is 90 per cent Muslim and 10 per cent Coptic Christian. Despite its vast size (1 million square kilometres) most of the population lives in the region of the Nile Delta between Cairo and Alexandria. The other inhabited area is the Nile valley which runs the whole length of the country from Sudan in the south to the Mediterranean in the north. The rest of Egypt is inhospitable desert with a sparse population.

Egypt is fortunate in having a wealth of building materials at its disposal. The main materials are stone, baked brick, mud brick and wood. In the Delta region (which includes Cairo and Alexandria) suitable building stone is not naturally available, although Ancient Egyptian monuments containing stone imported from Upper Egypt provided a plentiful quarry for many Islamic buildings. Even in Upper Egypt ancient structures were often the most accessible source of building stone. Nevertheless, baked brick was often the preferred material because of its relative cheapness (i.e. transport costs), its versatility and standard size. Mud brick is obviously cheaper than baked brick, can be quickly produced and provides excellent thermal insulation. In pre-modern times mud brick formed the basic building material for most of the country but more recently it is confined to southern Egypt. Date palms form the main natural source of wood and palm wood is used for most traditional architecture. More exotic wood could be imported from Europe or Africa for use in the wealthier houses of Cairo.

Several factors have combined to make the Islamic architecture of Egypt outside Cairo virtually unknown: first, the overwhelming wealth of Cairo's architectural heritage; second, the monuments outside Cairo are often made of mud brick and have survived less well; third, monuments of Egypt's pharaonic past have tended to overshadow those of later periods. In this discussion I have concentrated on the architecture of Upper Egypt which generally receives less attention.

The most important monuments of Upper Egypt are the necropolis of Aswan, the al-'Amri Mosque at Qus and a group of five Fatimid minarets. The necropolis of Aswan is located outside the town of Aswan in Upper Egypt. The necropolis consists of a long strip 500 m wide stretching along the side of the road for nearly 2 km. Within the necropolis there are more than 1000 tombs built which originally had inscriptions dating them to the eleventh or early twelfth century. The tombs represent one of the best examples of medieval funerary architecture in the Middle East. There are several forms of tomb, from simple rectangular enclosures open to the sky to elaborate domed structures with mihrabs and a variety of vaults. Mud brick is the main material of construction although baked brick was used for the domes and some of the arches. The outer surfaces of the tombs were originally covered in lime plaster although in most cases this has now worn off. A character-istic feature of the domed tombs were projecting horns at the angles of the drum which supported the dome. The tombs are also significant as some of the earliest examples of muqarnas squinches.

The city of Qus is located on the east bank of the Nile more than 950 km south of Cairo. Qus replaced Qift as the dominant city of Upper Egypt during the ninth to tenth centuries. The city's main role was as a Nile port for goods coming overland from the Red Sea port of Qusayr. The main monument in the city is the al-'Amri Mosque which is a Fatimid building founded in 1083 although it has later Mamluk and Ottoman additions. The only Fatimid remains are part of the qibla wall which includes the original round-arched mihrab. The most famous part of the complex is the tomb from the Ayyubid period built for Mu-barak ibn Maqlid in 1172. The mausoleum stands on a square base and is similar to some of the later tombs at Aswan with projecting horns on the drum. However, the design is more advanced and includes developed muqarnas niches and a slightly fluted dome pierced with star- and tear-shaped openings.

The five minarets of Upper Egypt which are usually included in any discussion of Fatimid mina-rets are also dated to the eleventh century. The mosque of Abu al-Hajjaj in Luxor is the most famous because of its position on the roof of the Temple of Luxor. The mosque is mostly a nineteenth-century construction but one of the two minarets dates to the eleventh century. The minaret is built of mud brick and has a square base 5 m high surmounted by a tapering cylindrical shaft which reaches a height of nearly 15 m. The top of the minaret is a tall domed pavilion with two tiers of windows. The square base is reinforced with three layers of wooden beams and the stair-case inside is also made of wood. Eighty kilometres south of Luxor is the small market town of Esna. In the centre of the town is the Ottoman mosque of al-'Amri with a Fatimid minaret similar to those of Aswan and Luxor. The square base of the minaret is built out of baked brick with layers of wood inserted every nine courses. The tapering cylindrical shaft is white-washed and may be built of mud brick. The minaret at Aswan is similar with a square base and a tapering shaft, but lacks

Minaret, Aswan, Egypt, © Hutt Archive, Ashmolean Museum

the domed chamber on the top, although the remains of brackets indicate that there was once a superstructure. Externally this building is built of baked brick although the interior is made of unbaked mud brick. Its notable feature is the two bands of brickwork inscription at the top. This is one of the earliest examples of this type of in-scription (hazarbaf) which was later to become a common feature in Islamic architecture. To the south of Aswan near the village of Shellal are two minarets of similar style to the minaret of Aswan and the mosque of Abu al-Hajjaj in Luxor. One of the minarets known as Mashad al-Bahri has a brick inscription similar to that of the mina-ret in Aswan. The other minaret known as al-Mashad al-Qibli is of interest as it stands next to a mosque of approximately the same date. The mosque is built on to a slope so that at one end it rests on a vaulted substructure which over-looks the valley below. The sanctuary of the mosque is covered by six domes and has three minarets in the qibla wall.

See also: Cairo, Fathy, Fustat, Hassan, mud
   brick

Further reading:

J. Bloom, 'Five Fatimid minarets in Upper Egypt', *Journal of the Society of Architectural Historians* 43: 162–7, 1984.

—— 'The introduction of the muqarnas in Egypt', *Muqarnas* 5: 1988.

K. A. C. Creswell, *The Muslim Architecture of Egypt*, 2 vols, Oxford 1952; repr. New York 1978.

F

Fatehpur Sikri

Abandoned city in northern India founded by the Mughal emperor Akbar in 1571.

Fatehpur Sikri derives its name from the village of Sikri which occupied the spot before, the prefix Fatehpur, City of Victory, was added in 1573 after Akbar's conquest of Gujerat in that year. Akbar chose this site for a city out of reverence for Sheikh Salim, a religious mystic of the Chisti order who prophesied that he would have three sons. In order to ensure the efficacy of the prophecy Akbar moved his pregnant wife to Sikri where she had two sons. In response Akbar decided to build an imperial mosque and palace at the village of Sikri. The location of the palace and mosque at the site encouraged further settlement by courtiers, noblemen and their attendants so that within a few years a city had grown up which was enclosed by a defensive wall. The city is built on the ridge of a hill next to a lake which has now dried up, giving rise to the theory that the city was abandoned because its water supply had failed. The centre of the city was the palace and mosque, which are located on the top of the ridge overlooking the lake, while the rest of the city was located on the sides of the ridge away from the lake. The city occupies an area of 5 km square with a wall on three sides and a fourth side open to the lake. There are three main gateways in the city wall between which there are semi-circular buttress towers.

The rise of the city from 1571 was very rapid so that after 1573 it was regarded as the capital of the Mughal Empire. However, after the city was abandoned by Akbar in 1585 to fight a campaign in the Punjab, the city seems to have declined just as rapidly so that by 1610 it was completely abandoned. The reason for the sudden decline of the city is usually given as the failure of the water supply, however the real reason may have been the emperor's loss of interest in the place. As the sole reason for the city's existence seems to have been a whim of the emperor, the fact that he was no longer in residence meant that there was no longer any incentive for anybody else to stay. The effect of the emperor's presence on the place may be gauged from an early description of the town which described the road from Agra to Fatehpur Sikri as completely filled with merchants' shops and stalls as if the two cities were one. A useful analogy may be with the Abbasid capital of Samarra which flourished for fifty years until the caliphs moved back to Baghdad when it declined to the level of a market town.

The first major structure built at the site was Jami Masjid (congregational mosque) which was completed in 1571 the year of Sheikh Salim's death. At the time of its construction it was the biggest mosque in India measuring 160 m east–west by 130 m north–south. The central courtyard is surrounded by arcades of pointed arches which lead into small cell-like rooms. The centre of the west of the courtyard is dominated by the sanctuary which has a huge central iwan leading on to a domed area in front of the main mihrab. Either side of the central dome are two smaller domes each covering the area in front of a smaller mihrab. As elsewhere at Fatehpur Sikri the building is covered with Hindu architectural features, thus the arcade of the sanctuary and the central iwan are capped by lines of chatris and internally the roofs are supported on Hindu-style carved columns, whilst the domes are supported on corbels in the tradition of Indian temple architecture. Approximately in the centre of the north side of the courtyard are two tombs, one belonging to Sheikh Salim and another to his grandson Islam Khan. The tomb of Sheikh Salim consists of a square domed chamber with an outer veranda filled in with a pierced marble screen (jali). The outside of the tomb is protected by a sloping canopy (chajja) supported on snake-like brackets. There are two main entrances to the mosque, a small private entrance from the palace on the east side and a monumental public entrance on the south side. The public entrance is known as the Buland Darwaza and was built in 1576 to commemorate Akbar's victory over Gujarat. The gate's name Buland Darwaza, 'Tall Gate', refers to the gate's outstanding height of 40 m. Like most Mughal mosques this building is raised up on a terrace so that the entrances are approached by flights of steps; in the case of the Buland Darwaza the stairs rise up another 12 m from ground level. The gate has an iwan plan with a large, deep central iwan flanked by two pairs of side iwans. In the middle of the back wall is a smaller gateway leading in to the mosque also flanked by two blind arches of equal size. The frame of the central iwan is surrounded by a monumental inscription and is capped by domed chatris.

The largest building complex at Fatehpur Sikri is the palace, covering an area approximately 250 m square. The layout is similar to that of other imperial Mughal palaces with three main areas, the public area, the mardana or men's area, and the zenana or women's area. Visitors approaching the palace first enter through a gateway to a large arcaded courtyard with the Diwan-i Amm (public audience hall) in the centre of the west side. In other Mughal palaces this is usually a grand, highly decorated building, but in this case it is a small rectangular pavilion with a central bay at the front to accommodate the emperor. There is no direct access from the courtyard to the pavilion which is raised at least 2 m above the level of the courtyard. This arrangement suggests a greater degree of security than at other palaces, a theme which is repeated throughout the palace particularly in the women's quarters.

The overwhelming impression within is of a Hindu palace, with few indications of Islamic design. Immediately behind the Diwan-i Amm is a large courtyard in the centre of which a cross is marked out; this is a giant version of a Pachisi board which is an ancient Indian game. To the north of this courtyard is the most intriguing section of the palace, called the Diwan-i Khass. This is a square two-storey building with a balcony supported on heavy corbels above which is a chajja also supported on heavy corbels. On the roof there are domed chatris at each corner. Inside the building consists of a two-storey hall with a gallery at first-floor level. Bridges which run diagonally from the corners of the gallery connect to a balcony supported by a central pillar. The pillar is richly carved in the Hindu tradition with a mass of heavy corbels supporting the circular balcony above. This arrangement does not correspond to any other private audience room in a Mughal palace, nor is it encountered elsewhere in Mughal architecture. However, the arrangement of a square building with a central pillar may reflect some Hindu mandala whereby the central column represents the axis of the world; in this, if this was also the place where the emperor sat, he would be identifying himself as the axis of the world. In the context of his conquest of Gujarat Akbar may have been wishing to describe himself in Hindu terms of power.

The arrangement of a central column approached by four bridges is repeated in a less formal setting in the courtyard known as the Anup Talao where there is a square pool with a central island approached by bridges from each of the four sides. The Anup Talao forms the central area of the private residence of the emperor and the main part of the mardana, or men's area. To the south of the pool is a pavilion known as the khwabagh or bedroom although its exact use is not known.

The area to the east of the Anup Talao is the zenana, or women's area, separated from the rest of the complex by a long wall. This is the most magnificent part of the palace and was decorated with painting and rich carvings. One of the most highly decorated buildings of the palace is the Sunahra Makan which is decorated with both geometric and figurative wall paintings. The most visible building in this area is the Panch Mahal, a five-storey pavilion crowned with a domed chatri which overlooks the men's area. The heart of the women's area, however, is known as Jodh Bai's Palace, a rectangular courtyard enclosure separate from the rest of the palace. The enclosure is entered through a single fortified gateway on the east side which leads into the rectangular courtyard. The courtyard is surrounded by arcades on all four sides and in the middle of each is a two-storey house with staircases to the upper floors and apartments. To the north of Jodh Bai's Palace is the Hawa Mahal or wind palace, which is a raised pavilion designed to catch the breeze. Another of the residential areas for women is a structure known as Birbal's House which is located to the west of Jodh Bai's Palace and is thought to be one of the earliest parts of the palace (it is dated by an inscription to 1571).

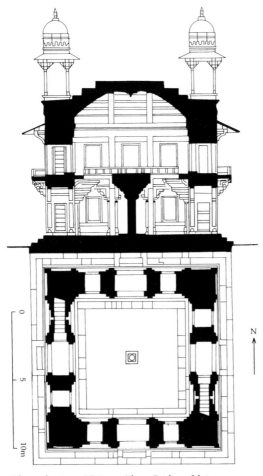

Plan and section of Diwan-i Khass, Fatehpur Sikri

N
↑

the major religions in India at the time and included several Muslim sects, Hindus, Jains, Zoroastrians and Catholic Christians from Goa (Jesuits). The debates took place in a part of the palace known as the Ibadat Khana which is now thought to have disappeared. The end result of the conference was the formulation of a controversial new religion called Din Ilahi of which Akbar was the head. Akbar's interest in other religions may explain why he was prepared to have so much Hindu-style architecture in his palace, in particular the enigmatic form of the Diwan-i-Khass. The design of Fatehpur Sikri is unusual in Mughal architecture as a whole but may be regarded as characteristic of Akbar's reign. Other examples of Akbar's Hindu-style architecture are the Jahangari Mahal in Agra fort, the Ajmer fort in Rajasthan and Akbar's tomb at Sikandara near Agra.

See also: Mughals

Further reading:

M. Brand and G. D. Lowry, *Akbar's India: Art from the Mughal City of Victory*, New York 1985.
—— *Fatehpur Sikri*, Bombay 1987.
S. A. A. Rizvi, *Fatehpur Sikri*, New Delhi 1972.
S. A. A. Rizvi and V. J. Flynn, *Fatehpur Sikri*, Bombay 1975.
G. H. R. Tillotson, *Mughal India*, Architectural Guides for Travellers, London 1990.

Fathy, Hassan

Egyptian architect noted for his use of traditional materials to build modern Islamic structures.

Born in 1900 the son of a wealthy landowner Hassan Fathy was brought up in Cairo, Alexandria and Europe. He studied architecture at the University of Cairo whence he graduated in 1926. In 1927, on his first visit to one of the family estates, he was shocked by the terrible living conditions of the poor and resolved to find a way to house the poor reasonably. He also conceived a love for the Egyptian countryside which was to motivate him for the rest of his life. He realized that imported western material and technology was too expensive and inappropriate for rural housing in Egypt. Instead Fathy thought that mud brick, the traditional building material of Egypt, should be used in modern constructions. Although he realized that traditional designs were sometimes too cramped and dark for modern housing, Fathy argued that this was not the fault of the material.

Although the palace and city of Fatehpur Sikri are remarkably well preserved, the design and decoration present a problem of interpretation. First it should be pointed out that, although the city was not inhabited for very long, at least two phases of construction can be discerned. The period during which Fatehpur Sikri was built coincided with two important events, the conquest of Gujarat in 1573 and the convening of an inter-faith conference in 1575. The conquest of Gujarat was one of Akbar's major achievements marking the Mughal domination of all northern India; it is commemorated in the gate of the mosque and in the name of the city. It seems likely that this victory may have been the impetus which changed the city from religious shrine to imperial capital. The conference of 1575 involved participants from

In 1937 Fathy held exhibitions of his work at Mansoura and Cairo which resulted in several commissions from wealthy patrons. However, these buildings were quite expensive and relied on timber for their flat roofs. With the outbreak of the Second World War and the resulting shortage of timber, he had to find a new method of roofing his houses. On a visit to Upper Egypt Fathy noticed that the Nubian villages were roofed with mud brick vaults produced without wooden centring. The method used was to lean the bricks against an end wall so that all the bricks leant against each other. Fathy employed the local Nubian builders and undertook several projects using these workers. The most important of these projects was the Nasr House in Fayyum and the tourist rest-house at Safaga.

In 1946 Fathy was approached by the Department of Antiquities who wanted to move the people of Gurna in western Luxor out of the ruins of ancient Thebes where they had been living. The Gurnis had been living in the ancient Necropolis for several generations and some lived in the tombs themselves. Nevertheless, the Department of Antiquities issued a decree stating that they wanted the 7,000 people moved to a new settlement which was to be designed by Fathy. The settlement was to contain homes for 1,000 families and include public buildings like a mosque, a covered market, schools and a theatre. The houses were built around courtyards and arranged in neighbourhood groups which had access to the main streets. Although built with traditional materials Fathy made use of earth scientists and structural and mechanical engineers to improve his designs and ensure that they worked. Part of the project was to involve the future inhabitants in the construction, both as a cost-saving measure and so that they were not alienated from their new housing.

However, the project faced considerable difficulties in implementation through the opposition of some of the Gurni Sheikhs and the slow-moving bureaucracy of the Egyptian Antiquities Department.

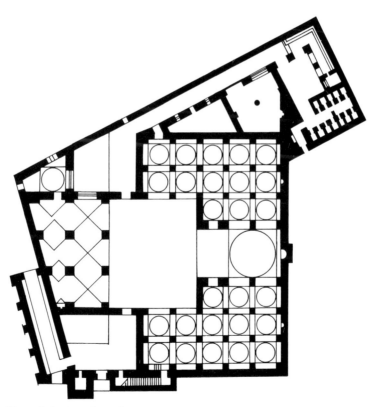

Mosque designed by Hassan Fathy, New Gurna, Egypt

In addition there was general suspicion of a project which involved traditional materials at a time when Modernism was seen as the only way to build. In the end only one-fifth of the project was completed and some parts of the village like the khan and the craft centre remain unused. Nevertheless, the mosque is well used and maintained and the Department of Antiquities has restored the theatre, belatedly realizing the value of Fathy's work. Despite the difficulties New Gurna showed the potential of mud-brick architecture and the value of training people in traditional techniques.

Other important projects carried out by Fathy in the 1950s were at Lu'luat al-Sahara in the Nile Delta and the village schools project. At Lu'lat al-Sahara houses were built in pairs, together with a mosque and a school. The village schools project involved Fathy in designing a school which was to be the prototype for village schools throughout Egypt. The design consisted of domed rooms opening on to courtyards with ventilation shafts to cool the interior during the summer. Unfortunately only two of the schools were built, one at Fares and the other at Edfu.

In 1957 Fathy left Egypt for several years to work for an architectural firm in Athens specializing in the Middle East, and during this time he designed a traditional housing scheme in Iraq. In the early 1960s Fathy returned to Egypt where he undertook two further major projects, a training centre in the Nile Valley and a new town in the Kharga oasis. Unfortunately the training centre was subsequently destroyed because of its bad location and the town known as New Bariz was abandoned because of the 1967 war.

In the 1970s Fathy began writing books about his work which were highly successful in universities throughout the world where the appeal of Modernism was wearing off. He showed that it was possible to design and build desirable residences and functional buildings which respected the traditional values of a culture and were also cheap. Since the 1970s Fathy's work in Egypt was concentrated on private houses and commissions. These buildings were constructed with increasingly sophisticated designs based on harmonic units of measurement derived from the dimensions of the human body. Probably the most important recent commission was for a Muslim community in New Mexico known as Dar al-Salam and built in 1981.

Further reading:

H. Fathy, *The Arab House in the Urban Setting: Past, Present and Future*, Fourth Arab Carreras Lecture, University of Essex, November 1970. London 1972.
—— *Architecture for the Poor*, Chicago and London 1973.
—— *Natural Energy and Vernacular Architecture*, Chicago 1985.
G. Leick, 'Hassan Fathy, architect for the poor', *Egyptian Bulletin* May 1988: 4–8.
J. M Richards, I. Serageldin and D. Rastorfer, *Hassan Fathy*, London 1985.
A. Schkifer, 'Hassan Fathy: a voyage to New Mexico', *Arts and the Islamic World* 1(1): 1982/3.

Fatimids

Caliphs who ruled North Africa, Egypt and Palestine from the tenth to the twelfth century.

The Fatimids were a religious dynasty who claimed descent from the prophet's daughter Fatima. In historical terms the Fatimids belonged to an extreme sect of Shi'a known as Ismailis who emerged as rivals to both the Umayyads of Spain and the Abbasid caliphate in Baghdad. The Fatimids' first successes were amongst the Berber tribes of North Africa who adopted the Fatimids as leaders. Their first conquest destroyed the Aghlabid rulers of Ifriqiyya (Tunisia) in 909 and replaced them with the Fatimid caliph the Mahdi Ubaid Allah. In the following years the Fatimids pursued an aggressive expansionist policy, conquering Tripoli and making raids on the French and Italian coasts. During the reign of the Caliph al-Mu'iz the empire was expanded westwards to include the whole of North Africa to the Atlantic Ocean and eastwards to Egypt and Palestine in 969. The conquest of Egypt began a new phase in Fatimid history with the foundation of Cairo as the imperial capital.

The architecture of the Fatimids can be divided into two periods, the North African period from 909 to 969 and the Egyptian period from 969 to 1171. The North African period was a time of expansion and religious extremism which can be seen in the architecture of the mosques. Examples of early Fatimid mosques are at Ajdabiya in Libiya and Mahdiya in Tunisia. The first of these was the mosque of Mahdiya, which was built like a fortress with two square corner towers flanking a single projecting monumental entrance. The mosque at Ajdabiya had a similar plan but lacks the monumental entrance façade. For ideological reasons neither of these mosques had a minaret, a feature which remained absent until the last years of Fatimid rule in Egypt.

See also: Ajdabiya, Cairo (The Fatimid Period), Libiya, Mahdiya, Tunisia

Fez

Moroccan city noted for its Islamic architecture.

Fez is located in the north-east of Morocco on either side of the Wadi Fez. The city was founded in the late eighth and early ninth century by Moulay Idris the Younger. It was divided into two halves, the east bank representing the late eighth-century city and the west bank representing the city of Moulay Idris. Each of the districts had its own congregational mosque, that on the west bank is known as the Qarawiyyin Mosque and that on the east is known as the mosque of the Andalusians.

The Qarawiyyin Mosque, founded in 859, is the most famous mosque of Morocco and attracted continuous investment by Muslim rulers. There were extensive renovations in 956 by the Umayyad caliph of Spain who also added the minaret. The building did not reach its present form and size (85 by 44 m) until 1135. The prayer hall comprises ten aisles running parallel to the qibla wall and a raised transverse aisle leading to the mihrab. The aisles are covered with gabled wooden roofs covered with roof tiles. There is a dome over the mihrab and the entrance porch in addition to the seven domes which cover the north arcade of the courtyard. The domes are made of elaborate muqarnas vaulting with zig-zag ribbing on the exterior. Inside the mosque is decorated with stucco, the most elaborate being reserved for the area in front of the mihrab. The mosque preserves its twelfth-century minbar which is regarded as one of the finest in the world. The courtyard is decorated with tile mosaic (zilij) dadoes and has a magnificent ablutions pavilion at the west. The pavilion, built in the sixteenth century, rests on eight marble columns and has a tile-covered wooden roof with overhanging eaves. The woodwork of the eaves is of exceptional quality with carved muqarnas mouldings and miniature engaged piers forming blind niches decorated with geometric interlace.

The mosque of the Andalusians has a similar plan to the Qarawiyyin Mosque although it is less well endowed. Like its twin this mosque had a minaret added by the Umayyad caliph Abd al-Rahman, although subsequent restorations were less successful. The other Great Mosque of Fez, the Jama' al-Hamra, was built in 1276 and has aisles aligned perpendicular to the qibla wall in the typical North African style.

From the thirteenth to the seventeenth centuries the madrassa became the principal form of religious architecture. The madrassas of Fez have a standard form of a two-storey courtyard building, with students' cells above and a mosque and teaching rooms below. The courtyards were usually decorated with tile mosaic and had a central pool. The most famous examples are the Saffarin, the Sahrij, the 'Attarin and the Bu 'Inaniya each of which has special features to distinguish it from its neighbours. The Bu 'Inaniya is the most unusual as it has a minaret and an early mechanical clock with gongs.

Most of the houses in Fez date from the seventeenth century or later although they preserve earlier plans. The standard construction material is either rubble stone or baked brick, with wood used for the roofs and decorative details. The usual plan is similar to the madrassas, with a rectangular courtyard and two storeys although the houses are usually less spacious.

See also: Morocco

Further reading:

D. Hill and L. Golvin, *Islamic Architecture in North Africa*, London 1976.
R. Le Tourneau, *Fez in the Age of the Marinides*, tr. B.A.Clement, Norman, USA 1961.
H. Terrasse, *La Mosquée al-Qaraouiyin à Fes*, Paris 1968.
—— *La Mosquée des Andalous à Fes*, Paris (n.d.).

Firuzabad (India)

Deserted fifteenth-century palace city in the Deccan, southern India.

The city was founded in 1400 by the Bahmani ruler Taj-al-Din Firuz Shah. The site is located on the banks of the Bhima river and consists of massive fortification walls which enclose the city on three sides. In the centre of each side are huge vaulted gateways which lead into the ruined central area. There are several buildings still standing within the city, the most impressive being the Jami

Firuzabad (Iran)

Minar i-Zarin, Firuzabad, India

Masjid which includes a huge rectangular courtyard entered via a domed gateway. Next to the Jami Masjid is the main palace area which comprises a series of interconnecting courtyards enclosed within high walls. Other standing monuments include several vaulted chambers, bath houses and a small mosque. The buildings are built in the local Sultanate style with flattened domes, bulbous finials and tapering bartered walls. There is also a notable Central Asian influence in the layout and architecture of the city

See also: Deccan, India

Further reading:

S. Digby, 'Firuzabad: Palace City of the Deccan', in G. Michelle and R. Eaton, *Oxford Studies in Islamic Art VIII*, 1992.

Firuzabad (Iran)

Sassanian capital of Iran near the modern Iranian capital of Tehran. Famous for its royal palace.

fortification

The earliest forms of fortification in Islam were probably towers of a type still seen in Arabia today, of mud brick or dry stone wall, with a tapering profile, built on a circular plan. City walls do not appear to have been common in Muhammad's time and Ta'if is the only city known to have had a wall. The conquest of Syria in the first decades of Islam brought the Arabs into contact with the forts and fortresses of the Roman *limes* (desert border). Many of these fortresses were adapted for residential or official uses, thus Qasr al-Hallabat, Udruh, and Azraq were all remodelled during the Umayyad period. This form was also adapted for new constructions, thus the palaces of Mshatta, Khirbet al-Mafjar and Qasr al-Tuba are all built in the form of fortresses with a square or rectangular enclosure protected with corner and interval towers. The palace of Qasr al-Hayr West was built around the tower of an existing (sixth-century) Byzantine monastery which included a machicolation above the gateway. This feature was later included in the gate of the palace at Qasr al-Hayr East 40 km east of the earlier one.

The influence of Sassanian architecture in this early period should also be noted – thus Qasr Kharana in Jordan is purely Sassanian in form although it is certainly an Umayyad construction. Further east in Iraq is the palace of Ukhaidhir which is the most complete example of early Islamic fortification. The palace forms a large rectangular enclosure with round corner towers and semi-circular buttresses at regular intervals. The area between each buttress comprised two tall arches built flat against the wall, above the arches there is an enclosed parapet containing vertical arrow slits and downward openings between the arches. This is the first example of continuous machicolation, a feature which did not appear in Europe until the fourteenth century.

The eighth-century walls of Baghdad were one of the greatest feats of military engineering in the Islamic world. Although there are no physical remains, descriptions indicate that the city was a vast circle enclosed within a moat and double walls. There were four gates each approached through a bent entrance. The bent entrance and the circular shape of the city are both features which appear to be copied from Central Asian architecture and were not found in contemporary Byzantine architecture.

The best surviving examples of pre-Crusader city fortifications are the wall and gates of Fatimid Cairo built in the eleventh century. There are three gates – the Bab al-Futuh, the Bab Zuwayla and the Bab al-Nasr – each of which is supposed to have been built by a different architect. Each gate consists of two towers either side of a large archway which leads into a vaulted passageway 20 m long with concealed machicolation in the roof. The lower two thirds of each gateway is solid whilst the upper part contains a vaulted room with arrow slits. Another feature of the tenth and eleventh centuries is the development of coastal forts or ribats which were designed to protect the land of Islam from Byzantine attacks. These forts have a similar design to the early Islamic palaces comprising a square or rectangular enclosure with solid buttress towers.

The arrival of the Crusaders at the end of the eleventh century revolutionized military architecture. During this period there is a fusion of European, Byzantine and Islamic principles of fortification which produced castles of enormous size and strength. European introductions were the central keep, curtain walls which follow the contours of a site and massive masonry. Although the majority of castles of the period were built by the Crusaders there are some outstanding examples of twelfth-century Ayyubid castles such as Qal'at Nimrud (Subeibe) and Qal'at Rabad (Ajlun). This new sophistication was also applied to city fortifications, thus the gateway to the citadel of Aleppo has a bent entrance with five right-angle turns approached by a bridge carried on seven arches. Elsewhere in the Islamic world fortifications were also developed in response to the increased Christian threat, thus the Almohads developed sophisticated fortifications with elaborate bent entrances.

With the defeat of the Crusaders in the East the impetus for fortress-building declined and architecture of the Mamluk period was directed mainly to civil purposes. The castles and fortifications which were built tended to be archaic in their military design although elaborate in their decoration and

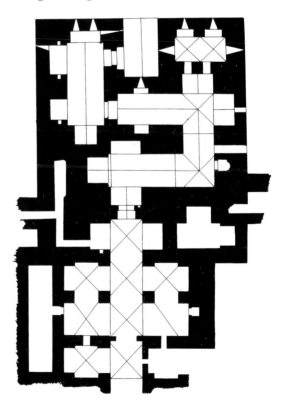

Plan of Ayyubid-period bent entrance to citadel, Aleppo

military imagery. With the introduction of firearms many of the older techniques of fortification were obsolete. From the eighteenth century onwards western techniques were adopted although these were sometimes modified to the local conditions.

See also: Aleppo, Almohads, Crusader architecture, Kharana, Qasr al-Hayr (East), Qasr al-Hayr (West), Ukhaidhir

Further reading:

K. A. C. Creswell, 'Fortification in Islam before AD 1250', *Proceedings of the British Academy* 38: 1953.

T. E. Lawrence, *Crusader Castles*, new edn. ed. R. D. Pringle, Oxford 1988.

R. D. Pringle, 'Crusader castles: the first generation', *Fortress* 1: 1989.

J. Wood, 'The fortifications of Amman citadel', *Fortress* 16: 1993.

France

France's first real contact with Islam was in the eighth century at the battle of Poitiers where the Arab forces were defeated by Charles Martel. The Arab raids into France were not part of a serious attempt to conquer the country and have left few archaeological or architectural remains. However, during the ninth century a series of Muslim Arab forts were established along the Mediterranean coast. The design of these buildings resembled the ribats of North Africa and were intended as bases for naval activity rather than as permanent settlements.

France's first modern encounter with Islam was in the late eighteenth century when Napoleon launched his expedition to Egypt. The military expedition was accompanied by a large team of scholars who introduced the concept of 'Orientalism' to Europe. Conversely, the expedition was also responsible for introducing European ideas and architecture into the region. The colonization of Algeria in the nineteenth century continued France's link with the Islamic world and was also responsible for the introduction of European architecture into North Africa.

Since the Algerian independence in the 1960s there has been a steady flow of North African immigrants to France, which thus now has a large ethnic North African population resident mostly in the larger cities (Paris, Marseilles and Lyons). The earliest mosques in France were converted churches and houses although more recently purpose-built mosques have been erected. The centre of Islamic life in Paris is the Islamic Centre which includes a mosque built in the North African style with horseshoe arches and geometric tile mosaic decoration. The mosque's minaret resembles those of Tlemcen and Marrakesh. The best-known Islamic building in Paris is the Institut du Monde Arabe built in the late 1980s in recognition of the prominent role of Arab culture in France. Although designed by Europeans the building is based on traditional Islamic principles modified for a twentieth-century European setting. The Institut is a rectangular glass building built over a steel frame and located next to the University on the banks of the Seine. One of the more unusual features of the building is the moving metal window grilles, which open and close according to the light. The movements of the window grilles are computer controlled and form geometric Islamic patterns.

Central Mosque, Paris, © *Susan Bailey*

Further reading:

J. Fremeaux, *La France et l'Islam depuis 1789*, Paris 1991.

G. Keppel, *Les Banlieus de l'Islam, Naissance d'une religion en France*, Paris 1991.

J. Novel and H. Tokka, *Institut du Monde Arabe: Une Architecture*, Paris 1990.

Fulbe

Name of West African people speaking Fulbe-related languages.

The Fulbe originated as a nomadic people inhabiting the Sahara areas of West Africa. From the fifteenth century onwards groups of Fulbe began settling in the more fertile regions south of the Sahara and integrating with resident groups. Since the seventeenth century the Fulbe were associated with orthodox Islam and inaugurated jihads in several parts of West Africa. The main areas of Fulbe settlement were the Hausa region of northern Nigeria, the Adamawa region of Cameroon and the Futa-Djallon region of Guinea.

The architectural tradition of the Fulbe originated in the circular wooden-framed tents of their nomadic lifestyle. Elements of this nomadic style are said to have been incorporated into the Hausa architecture of northern Nigeria which is a mixture Fulbe and indigenous Hausa style.

See also: Futa-Djallon, Hausa, West Africa

funduq

North African term for a small, urban shop complex. A typical funduq is a square two-storey structure built around a central courtyard with shops on one floor and store rooms on the other. Equivalent to a khan in the Middle East.

Fustat

The first Islamic capital of Egypt, now within the modern city of Cairo.

Fustat was built on the east bank of the Nile opposite the pre-Islamic Coptic settlement of Babylon. The first permanent settlement on the site was established by the Muslim general 'Amr ibn al-'As in 643. This first settlement appears to have been a huge encampment of tents arranged into tribal groups separated by open ground. In the centre of the camp was the mosque of 'Amr which is known as the oldest mosque in Egypt. Little of the original fabric of the mosque survives and in its present form it dates to 827. The settlement was not fortified until 684 when a ditch was dug around the camp in order to defend it against the Umayyad army under Marwan. During the Abbasid period Fustat was no longer the centre of government, although it was still the main commercial centre. The Fatimid conquest and the establishment of Cairo did little to alter this situation and during the tenth century Fustat was known as one of the wealthiest cities of the world. A series of famines and fires during the eleventh and early twelfth century led to the decline of the city. The Crusader siege of 1168 dealt a further blow to the city and in later periods the area of Fustat was redeveloped as a suburb of Cairo within a new wall built on the orders of Salah al-Din.

Excavations in Fustat have revealed complex street and house plans which indicate a high degree of sophistication. The basic unit appears to have been of rooms built around a square or rectangular central courtyard with a central basin. On one or two sides of the courtyard there was an open arcade of three arches, with a wide central arch and two side arches. Behind the central arch there was usually an open iwan flanked by two side rooms. On the other sides of the courtyard there was either an iwan opening directly on to the courtyard or a door to another room. In general there were few connections from one room to another and the courtyard remained the principal means of access.

See also: 'Amr, Mosque of, Cairo, Egypt

Further reading:

A. Baghat, 'Les Fouilles d'al-Foustat', *Syria* 4: 59–65, 1923.

W. B. Kubiak, *Al-Fustat: Its Foundation and Early Development*, American University in Cairo, 1987.

A. A. Ostrasz, 'The archaeological material for the study of the domestic architecture at Fustat', *African Bulletin* 26: 57–86, 1977.

G. T. Scanlon, 'Fustat expedition preliminary report 1968. Part II', *Journal of the American Research Centre in Egypt* 13: 69–89, 1976.

Futa-Djallon

Islamic region in the highlands of north-west Guinea on border with the Ivory Coast in West Africa.

Before the fifteenth century the primary residents were the Djallonke people who were sedentary agriculturalists. During the fifteenth century various groups of nomadic Fulbe arrived in the area and were absorbed into Djallonke society. During the seventeenth century more Fulbe groups with a strong attachment to Islam arrived from the Muslim state of Macina in the north-east. These newly arrived Fulbe organized themselves into a theocratic state under the direction of the religious leader Karamoko Alfa. During the nineteenth century a jihad was instigated against the non-believers of the area until the whole area was under Islamic control. The new state was divided into nine provinces each under a different leading family with a capital at Timbo.

Despite the strongly orthodox beliefs of the new state, the integration of previous generations of Fulbe into the resident pagan society meant that the architecture was essentially that of the Djallonke modified to fit the requirements of Islam. The essential architectural unit of the pre-Islamic Djallonke is the sudu, or roundhouse, a form which was also adopted for religious shrines and burials. The basic form of the sudu consists of a thatched roundhouse enclosed by concentric walls with two opposed entrances. Each entrance gives access to a semi-circular vestibule and the main central space of the building. Beds consist of moulded mud platforms set against the walls of the central inner space. Several sudu, or house units, form a family compound with a separate one for each wife. The entrance to a compound was through an entrance vestibule which was a round sudu-like construction with a doorway either side. Such vestibules were used to receive visitors in a similar manner to the more familiar entrance rooms of Islamic courtyard houses (compare for example the houses of Timbuktu). The houses of Timbo have the same basic form as traditional Djallonke housing except that the bed is placed opposite the entrance rather than to one side; they also have rectangular storage platforms supported on four posts in the centre of the room. During construction a piece of paper containing a verse of the Quran is buried under each post.

The mosques of Futa-Djallon have the same basic form as the houses although they are built on a larger scale. The earliest mosques were copies of the traditional village meeting-houses which consisted of a raised circular floor enclosed within a low mud wall above which is a steep conical thatched roof made of rafters supported by posts embedded into the wall. When a new mosque is built the older mosque is often converted into a women's area or a Quranic reading room and included within the compound of the new building. As elsewhere in the Islamic world mosques are often associated with the palace of the local ruler, thus at Fougoumba the royal audience hall was directly opposite the mosque. In the mid-nineteenth century a new concept in the architecture of mosques in the region was introduced by al-Hajj Umar who established himself as the ruler of Dingueraye. Educated as a strict Sufi, the new leader attracted a large following which transformed Dingueraye from a small village into a town of 8,000 people. As a result of this huge influx of people a city wall was built to enclose the entire settlement and a new mosque was erected. Although this mosque has not survived, its replacement built on the same site in 1883 is thought to have essentially the same design. Like earlier mosques in the region the Great Mosque at Dingueraye consists of a large thatched roundhouse with a diameter of 30 m and enclosed within a wooden fence. The thatch reaches down almost to the ground so that the ten entrances are only marked by gaps in the wooden fence. The outer wall of the mosque consists of a mud wall containing posts supporting the roof rafters. Immediately inside the outer wall there is circular arrangement of wooden pillars which also supports the roof rafters. The extraordinary arrangement of the interior consists of a square, mud-brick, box-like building in the middle which forms the sanctuary of the mosque. This mud-brick structure has three entrances on each side except for the qibla side where there is only one. The entrance on the qibla side is through an opening in the side of the mihrab and is reserved for the imam. The flat ceiling of the box is supported by rafters resting on sixteen wooden pillars arranged in four rows. In the centre there is a mud-brick pier which protrudes through the roof of the box to support a series of radiating rafters holding up the steep conical thatched roof. This design was later copied in other parts of Futa-Djallon and has now become the typical mosque form of the area. The rationale behind the Dingueraye Mosque design can be deduced from a drawing of the design by al-Hajj Umar. The drawing depicts a magic square and appears to refer only to the central square box and makes no reference to the outer circle of the thatched roof. Local religious leaders also believe that the mosque only consists of the central square

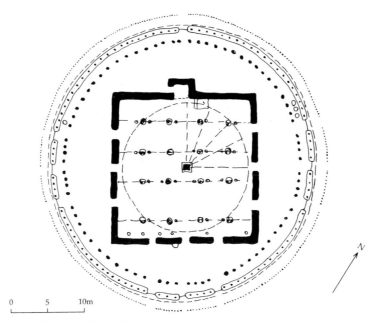

Dingueraye Mosque in Futa-Djallon region, Guinea, West Africa (after Prussin)

and that the conical thatched roof is merely for protection. This suggests the application of a standard Fulbe square mosque in a context where it was environmentally and culturally inappropriate. The thatched superstructure not only pro-tected it from rain but also made it look like an important Djallonke building rather than an alien imposition.

See also: Fulbe, West Africa

G

Gao

West African empire, which flourished in the fifteenth and sixteenth centuries, referred to by contemporary Arabic writers as Kawkaw.

The empire was founded by the Songhay groups who inhabited the banks of the Niger river in the eastern part of the present-day state of Mali. As with the other empires in the region the origin of the kingdom is shrouded in myths and legends, although there seems to be some evidence that the original capital of Gao was 100 km further south. The earliest record of Gao is from the eighth century when it is mentioned as one of the towns in contact with the Algerian city of Tahert. A tenth-century description describes the capital as composed of twin cities like the contemporary capital of Ghana and also describes the ruler as a Muslim.

Despite its strategic position on the trade routes Gao did not achieve imperial status until the fifteenth century when the empire of Mali was in decline. The first ruler to begin the expansion was Ali (1464–92) who conquered Timbuktu from the Berbers and Djenné from the disintegrating empire of Mali. Ali was followed by the most famous ruler of Gao, Askiya Muhammad, who usurped the throne from Ali's son. Askiya Muhammad consolidated the conquests of Ali and centralized the administration of the empire. He was a more convinced Muslim than Ali and made Islam the state religion as well as promoting Timbuktu as a centre of learning. In 1528 at the age of 85 Askia was deposed by his son and died ten years later in 1538. Following Askia there were a succession of short reigns between 1528 and 1591 which ended with the Moroccan invasion and the destruction of the Songhay Empire of Gao.

Fortunately the ancient capital of Gao has survived to provide some of the best examples of medieval architecture in West Africa. Three main groups of remains can be identified, Gao, Old Gao and Gao-Sané. It has been suggested that the twin-city configuration referred to in early accounts of Gao may be confirmed by the location of Gao-Sané 6 km east of the rest of the city. It is believed that Gao-Sané represents the Muslim quarter of the town due to its position facing the trade routes to North Africa. Old Gao probably represents the remains of the fourteenth-century city during the period when it was ruled by the empire of Mali. Excavations in Old Gao have revealed a large rectangular mosque (approximately 40 m wide) built of mud brick which was dated to 1325. In the centre of the west side is a deep circular mihrab (about 3 m in diameter) built of baked brick with a small doorway (a half-metre wide) on the north side. Behind the mihrab on the outside are three rectangular tombs one of which contains a headstone dated 1364. South of Old Gao is the main town which was the city of Askiya Muhhamad with its famous mausoleum contained within the courtyard of the Great Mosque. The Great Mosque is located within an area of cemeteries containing Kufic-inscribed tombstones dating from the early twelfth century. Some of the oldest tombstones were found within a subterranean vault made of baked brick similar to that used in the mihrab of the excavated mosque at Old Gao. The use of baked brick is significant in a context where they would have been very difficult to produce.

Undoubtedly the most important monument in Gao is the Great Mosque containing the tomb of Askiya Muhammad. The mosque consists of a large rectangular enclosure (45 by 50 m) with a sanctuary four bays deep. In the middle of the east wall of the sanctuary is a pair of niches one of which is the mihrab whilst the other contains a fixed minbar. The centre of the courtyard is occupied by the tomb of Askiya Muhammad, a huge pyramidical earth construction resting on a base measuring 14 by 18 m. The tomb consists of three steps or stages reaching a height of just over 10 m above ground level. A stair ramp made of split palms leads up the east side of the structure to reach the top. The appearance of the tomb is enhanced by

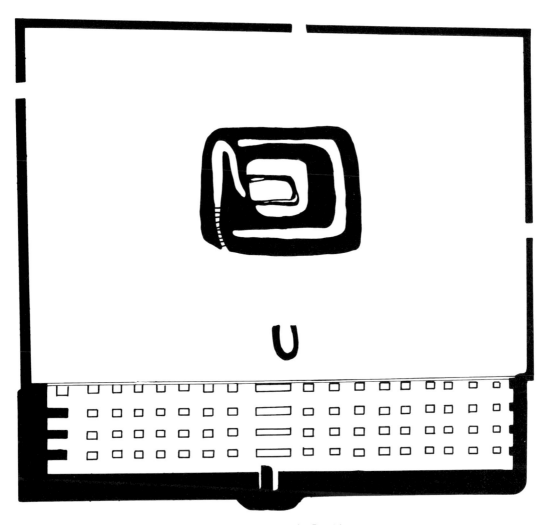

Plan of mosque and tomb of Askiya Muhammad, Gao, West Africa (after Prussin)

the many toron, or stakes, made of acacia wood which project from each side. A description of the monument from 1852 mentioned another eastern tower which was in ruins at the time; this may have been the mihrab tower which also functioned as a minaret. It seems likely that with the collapse of the eastern mihrab/minaret tower stairs were cut into the tomb of Askiya Muhammad so that this could function as the place for the call to prayer. In view of Askiya Muhammad's strong attachment to Ibadi teachings it is thought that the architectural origins of this tomb may be found in various Ibadi zawiyas in the Mzab region of southern Algeria. The design of these three-tier construc-

tions is said to derive ultimately from the minaret of the Great Mosque at Qairawan. One of the best examples is at Tidikelt in southern Algeria and consists of three superimposed stages each with a crenellated parapet. In addition to the orthodox Muslim influences on the design of the tomb, it should be noted that it also resembles the ancestral tumuli of the pre-Islamic Songhay past. This connection is reinforced by the toron projecting from the sides of the tomb.

In addition to Gao itself, there are a number of towns which contain monumental remains of the Songhay Empire. One of the best examples is the city of Tendirma in Mali built for Amar-Komdiago the brother of Askiya Muhammad in 1497. The construction of the city was carried out by Manding craftsmen under the direction of Ouahab Bari. Standing remains at Tendirma include the massive palace walls and the Great Mosque which is substantially unchanged since the Moroccan invasion of the sixteenth century. The mosque is built out of spherical mud bricks with the use of split palm and acacia wood for roof timbers. The most remarkable feature of the mosque is the mihrab tower which consists of a sloping cone with a flat surface on the side facing the mosque. Like the mausoleum of Askiya Muhammad the outer surface of the minaret is covered with projecting toron made of acacia wood. Other examples of Songhay imperial architecture can be seen in the mosques of Katsina and Birni in northern Nigeria. The Katsina minaret is particularly unusual and consists of a central square shaft with stair ramps ascending around the four sides. The minaret bears a striking similarity to the Malwiyya in Samarra although stylistically it is more closely related to the minaret of the Great Mosque in Qairawan.

See also: Songhay, West Africa

Further reading:

T. Insol, 'Looting the antiques of Mali: the story continues at Gao', *Antiquity* 67: 628–32, 1993.
——, 'A preliminary reconnaisance and survey at Gao, the Republic of Mali', *Nyame Akuma* 39; 40–3, 1993.
R. Mauny, 'La Tour et la mosquée de l'Askia Mohammed à Gao', *Notes Africaines* 47: 66–7, 1950.
—— 'Notes archéologiques au sujet de Gao', *Bulletin IFAN* 13: 837–52, 1951.
J. Sauvaget, 'Les Epitaphes royales de Gao', *Bulletin IFAN* 12: 418–40, 1950.
M.–M. Vire, 'Notes sur trois epigraphes royales de Gao', *Bulletin IFAN* 20B (3–4): 459–600, 1958.

gardens

Gardens have often been an integral feature of Islamic architectural design, particularly for palaces.

Several Umayyad palaces seem to have incorporated gardens as part of their design. At Khirbet al-Mafjar in the Jordan valley there is a large square pool with a central pavilion on columns which would have formed the centrepiece of a garden. At Qasr al-Hayr West it is likely that the immediate vicinity of the palace had a garden whilst there was a large walled garden enclosure to the west of the main building. The exact function of some of the early Islamic gardens is not always clear and some may have been purely for

producing vegetables. In Islamic Spain the garden was an integral part of the palatial design of Madinat al Zahra and reached its peak in the gardens of Granada. The development of formal gardens became an art form in Iran from at least the fourteenth century as can be seen from their frequent depiction in miniature paintings of the period. Under the Timurids gardens became a priority for royal residences which were often no more than pavilions in large formal gardens. The Mughals of India acquired their interest in gardens from the Timurids and developed the idea of a memorial garden which would surround a tomb.

From the sixteenth century garden cities became fashionable throughout the Islamic world with cities such as Isfahan in Iran or Meknes in Morocco. Further east in Java and Indonesia gardens were an essential part of the pre-Islamic Hindu tradition and continued to be built by the Muslim sultans.

Further reading:

A. Petruccioli (ed.), *The Garden as a City: The City as a Garden*, Journal of the Islamic Environmental Design Research Centre, Rome 1984.
N. Titley and F. Wood, *Oriental Gardens*, BL Humanities, 1991.

Gedi

Ruined Islamic city near Malindi in Kenya, one of the first Islamic settlements in East Africa to be systematically investigated by archaeologists starting in 1945.

Gedi is unusual as it is the only major settlement on the East African coast not to be built directly on the sea-shore — instead it is located 6 km inland and 3 km from the nearest navigable creek. The city seems to have been founded in the thirteenth century although most of the standing remains date from the fifteenth century. By the sixteenth century the city seems to have been abandoned, although it was briefly resettled in the seventeenth only to be finally abandoned after the attacks of the migrating Galla tribesmen.

The site stands on a rocky spur which dominates the surrounding countryside. The city covers an area of 45 acres and was contained within a town wall which enclosed a Great Mosque, seven smaller mosques, a palace and several private mansions, in addition to many smaller houses which must have been made of wattle and daub. The ruins also contain the remains of substantial coral stone tombs one of which carries an inscription dated to 1399.

The Great Mosque is one of the best-preserved examples of its type in East Africa. It is constructed in the typical East African style with a flat concrete roof supported on rectangular stone piers and doorways on the west and east sides. There are three rows of six piers with the middle row aligned on the central axis in line with the mihrab. The mosque has a fairly wide plan achieved by placing transverse beams between piers and spanning the distance between beams by longitudinally placed rafters. This differs from the more usual technique of placing beams longitudinally with transverse rafters as was used in the smaller mosques at Gedi and elsewhere on the coast. The mihrab is a fine example of the developed form of the early type of coastal mihrab. It is built out of dressed undersea or reef coral and set in a rectangular panel surrounded with an architrave carved in a cable pattern. The mihrab is decorated with eleven inset blue and white porcelain bowls, five in the spandrel above the niche, two in the pilasters and six in the niche itself. The edge of the mihrab is recessed five times before the niche itself which is a plain, undecorated semi-circular apse. Immediately to the east is a built-in stone minbar.

Sometime in the sixteenth century a separate area for women was screened off at the back of the mosque. To the east of the prayer hall is a veranda opening onto the ablutions court which contains a tank fed by a well, footscrapers, a latrine and a staircase to the roof. The other mosques at Gedi are all much smaller, narrower structures consisting of a simple prayer room and ablutions area to the east.

The palace of Gedi is a large complex probably built for the Sultan of Malindi. It stands amongst several other grand houses which probably housed ministers or other members of the royal family. The palace essentially consists of two main areas, the original palace and the northern annexe. It has a monumental entrance leading via a small courtyard into the main reception area, which is a long open courtyard aligned east–west. The sultan's private residence was to the south of this whilst the harem was located on the west side, although it only connects with the main palace via a small doorway from a courtyard at the back of the sultan's quarters.

The houses at Gedi are of interest because they show a development in form from the fourteenth to the sixteenth centuries and are the prototype for the more famous Swahili houses of the eighteenth century. The earliest houses consist of entrances into a long, narrow sunken courtyard from which a single entrance would lead into a reception room behind which were bedrooms and a store room. In later houses the courtyards became bigger and often an extra 'domestic' courtyard was added at the back.

See also: coral, East Africa, Kenya, Lamu

Further reading:

J. Kirkman, *The Arab City of Gedi: Excavations at the Great Mosque. Architecture and Finds*, Royal National Parks of Kenya, Oxford 1954.
—— *Gedi: The Tomb of the Dated Inscription H.802/AD 1399*, Royal Anthropological Society of Great Britain and Ireland, Occasional Paper no. 14, London 1960.
—— *Gedi: The Palace*, Studies in African History no.1, The Hague 1963.

Germany

Before the Second World War there were few Muslims in Germany although during the nineteenth century the Ottoman ambassador in Berlin established a mosque and cemetery. There were, however, a number of Islamic-type buildings in Germany influenced by the growing interest in Orientalism. The most famous example is the water-pumping station at Potsdam (1841–5) built in the form of an Egyptian Mamluk mosque. Perhaps a more suprising example is the tobacco factory at Dresden where the minarets are used as factory chimneys.

After the Second World War the German government made an arrangement with Turkey for Turks to come to Germany as temporary 'Guest workers'. By the 1970s many of these Turkish workers had become established as permanent residents although with no official status. Present estimates suggest that Germany has a Turkish minority of two to three million, many of whom live in the industrial towns of the Ruhr valley. The first mosques were usually converted houses and were architecturally indistinct from the surrounding buildings. More recently purpose-built mosques have been erected, usually in a modern Turkish style.

See also: France, Great Britain, USA

Further reading:

S. Koppelkamm, *Der imaginaire Orient: Exotische Bauten des achtzen und neunzen Jahrhunderts in Europa*, Berlin 1987.
W. A. Barbieri, 'Citizenship and Group Rights: "Guestworkers" in the Federal Republic of Germany', Unpublished PhD. dissertation, Yale University 1992.

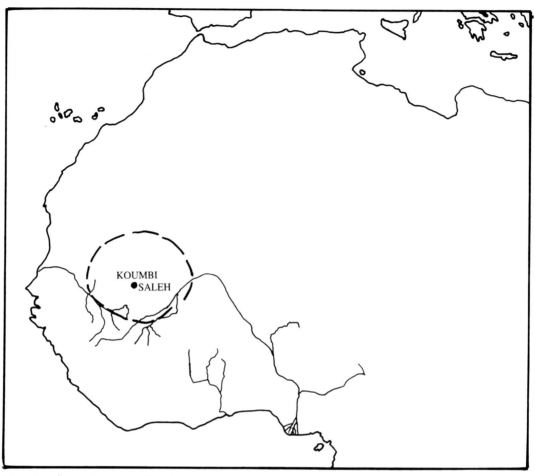

West Africa showing the empire of Ghana in the ninth century CE

Ghana

Medieval West African kingdom heavily influenced by Islam which flourished between the eighth and eleventh centuries.

Like other medieval West African kingdoms the empire of Ghana was not so much a centralized territorial entity as a network of different kinship groups, castes and age sets owing allegiance to the ruler of a powerful dynasty. Despite its rather diffuse nature the empire was well known in North Africa by the end of the eighth century and was marked on a map made before 833. The fame of the city derived from its role as the major supplier of gold which during the eighth and ninth centuries was sent via Sijilmasa and Tahert to North Africa.

Although the empire never became Muslim the ruler had a high degree of respect for Islam and many of the more important positions of government were filled by Muslims.

In 990 disruption of the trade routes led the ruler of Ghana to launch an expedition to capture the oasis city of Awdaghast from the Berbers and impose a black governor. However, in 1077 the capital of Ghana was attacked by the Berber Almoravids who massacred many of the inhabitants and forced the remainder to convert to Islam. Whilst this conquest destroyed Ghana as an empire, a reduced kingdom of this name continued to survive into the twelfth century; al-Idrisi writing in 1154 described the capital as the most extensive and thickly populated town of the blacks with the most widespread commerce. However, in 1204 there was another disaster when the town was sacked by the Sonnike ruler Sumaguru Kante. This led to the dispersion of a large number of Ghana's inhabitants and the foundation of a new settlement known as Oualata which replaced Ghana as the main caravan terminal. However, Ghana recovered and continued to function as an important trade centre until 1240 when it was conquered and incorporated into the empire of Mali. Nevertheless, Ghana continued to function as a semi-independent state within the Mali Empire and its ruler even retained the title of king.

An eleventh-century description by the Andalusian writer al-Bakri describes the capital as divided into two cities, a Muslim city and a royal city. The Muslim city had twelve mosques including a Friday mosque each with its own imam and muezzin (one who announces the call to prayer). The royal city was a pagan city containing the palace of the king within a sacred grove or wood. The houses in the city are described as being built with stone and acacia wood. The exact location of the capital is not known and there is some dispute about whether the state had a fixed capital in the modern sense. However, the site of Koumbi Saleh in Mauritania is regarded as one of the principal capitals if not the main capital.

Excavations at Koumbi Saleh, begun in 1914, have revealed a vast set of stone ruins which are still in need of full interpretation although the evidence suggests a period of occupation from the seventh to the seventeenth century. One of the most interesting discoveries is a square tomb chamber measuring just over 5 m on each side with a column recessed into each of the external corners. There were originally four openings into the chamber but three of these were subsequently blocked up leaving a single entrance on the east side. Just inside the entrance are a set of steps made of fired brick which lead down into a subterranean chamber containing spaces for three sarcophagi. Parallels have been suggested with Ibadi tombs in North Africa and the Bab Lalla Rayhana entrance to the Great Mosque of Qairawan which also employs engaged corner columns. Elsewhere excavation has revealed a row of shops connected to houses. The shops are open onto the street front whilst every other unit opens at the back onto an entrance vestibule lined with triangular niches. These vestibules consist of long narrow rooms with a bed platform at one end and stairs to another floor at the opposite end. The rooms (7 to 8 m long and 1.5 to 2 m wide) are placed side by side with two doorways in each side either side of a central pillar. The other Ghanaian city which has been excavated is the oasis city of Awdaghast also in Mauritania. The architecture here is similar to that at Koumbi Saleh with triangular niches and long narrow rooms. Although the evidence from archaeology is limited it appears that Awdaghast was inhabited from the seventh to the thirteenth century.

See also: West Africa

Gok Madrassa

The Gok Madrassa is one of the most famous buildings in the north-east Anatolian city of Sivas. Built in 1271 the building has a cruciform plan with a central open court opening onto two-storey cloisters. The most significant part of the design is the façade which comprises two corner buttress towers with a central entrance flanked by two tall minaret towers. The portal itself is recessed within a tall muqarnas niche which itself is set within a carved stone frame. Both the entrance portal and the corner buttress towers are decorated in deep relief stone carving which is characteristic of the thirteenth-century architecture of the city. The twin minarets above the entrance are built of baked brick with vertical flutes and large muqarnas corbelled balconies.

Gol Gumbaz

Mausoleum of Muhammad Adil Shah II (1627–57), one of the major Islamic monuments of India.

The tomb, located in the city of Bijapur, southern India, was built in 1659 by the famous architect, Yaqut of Dabul. The structure consists of a massive square chamber measuring nearly 50 m on each side and covered by a huge dome 37.9 m in diameter making it the largest dome in the Islamic world. The dome is supported on giant squinches supported by groined pendentives whilst outside the building is supported by domed octagonal corner towers. Each tower consists of seven storeys and the upper floor of each opens on to a round gallery which surrounds the dome.

In the centre of the chamber is a square raised podium approached by steps in the centre of each side. In the centre of the podium are the tombs of Muhammad Adil Shah II and his relations. To the west of the podium in a large apse-like projection is the mosque, also raised slightly above the floor level of the chamber.

See also: Bijapur, Deccan, India

Granada

City in south-west Spain famous as the capital of the last Muslim state in Spain.

Granada is located high up in the mountains near the Sierra Nevada and rose to prominence after the other Muslim states were defeated in the thirteenth century. During this time from 1231 to 1492 Granada was ruled by the Nasirid dynasty who survived by maintaining alliances with Christian dynasties.

Undoubtedly the most famous building in the city is the Alhambra which has a claim to being one of the most beautiful buildings of the Islamic world. The palace is located on a rocky spur which dominates the rest of the city. Although contained within a single enclosure the Alhambra is not a single palace but a complex of palaces built over hundreds of years. The earliest parts of the complex date from the twelfth century although most of the buildings were erected in the fourteenth or fifteenth centuries. On the opposite side of the valley from the Alhambra is the Generalife palace which is sometimes erroneously thought to be part of the Alhambra. Although now covered with gardens the Generalife was originally a country estate for the Nasirids.

Some remains of the eleventh-century walls are still standing together with five of the city gates, the Puerta Nueva, the Puerta de Elvira, the Puerta de Fajalauza and the Puerta Hizna Roman. Architecturally the most interesting of these gates is the Puerta Nueva which combines a bent entrance with an upward sloping ramp to slow down potential attackers. Within the walls several public buildings survive including the hammam (Bañuelo Carrera del Darro) which is one of the best examples remaining in Spain. Also within the city is the Casa del Carbón (coal exchange) formerly known as the Funduq al-Yadida (new market) which is one of the few surviving khans in Spain. It has a monumental portico decorated with plaster and decorative brickwork within which the entrance is set below a set of paired windows. The interior of the building consists of a square courtyard with three storeys of arcades on each of the four sides containing sixty rooms. In addition to public buildings several Muslim houses survive in the Albaicín Quarter of the city.

With the exception of the one in the Alhambra there are few remains of Granada's many mosques, although traces can be found in some of the churches. The church of San Salvador is built over a tenth-century mosque and remains of the ablutions court and the minaret can still be seen. The church of San Sebastian is a converted rabita, or hermitage, and is the only example of its type in Spain. It consists of a square courtyard covered with a ribbed dome supported on squinches.

See also: Alhambra, Spain

Further reading:

F. Prieto-Moreno, *Los Jardines de Granada*, Madrid 1952.
E. Sordo and W. Swaan, *Moorish Spain: Córdoba, Seville and Granada*, London 1963.

Great Britain (United Kingdom)

Britain's main source of contact with the Islamic world has been through the British Empire and in particular the Indian subcontinent. India was acquired by Britain in the eighteenth century and was one of Britain's earliest colonial acquisitions. As with most colonial encounters each side was influenced by the culture and architecture of the other. In India the British built the city of Calcutta as capital complete with Anglo-Indian mosques. In Britain the architecture of India was evoked in several buildings, the most famous of which is the Royal Pavilion at Brighton. Externally the building resembles a late Mughal palace with bulbous domes, chajjas and chatris, although internally it is decorated like a Chinese palace.

With the Independence of India in 1948 and the division of the subcontinent into Pakistan and Bangladesh a large number of immigrants came to Britain. Indians now make up the majority of Britain's Muslim population although they are mostly concentrated in cities and the larger towns. The first mosques in Britain were converted churches or houses although more recently (since 1980) many new mosques have been built, financed partly by British Muslim communities and partly by donations from oil-rich Arab countries. The best-known mosque in Britain is in Regents Park in London although other cities like Bradford also have prominent new mosques. In the typical modern British mosque there is usually an emphasis on the dome which is often covered in metal. Minarets are usually quite small and are often non-functional (i.e not used for the call to prayer).

Greece

Mountainous country in south-eastern Europe which for over 400 years formed a part of the Ottoman Empire.

The position of Greece opposite Libiya and Egypt and its exposure to the east Mediterranean sea meant that it was exposed to Muslim raids from the beginnings of Islam. Crete in particular was open to attack and was briefly occupied by Muslim forces as early as 674. Between 827 and 961 Crete was again captured by Muslim forces who used the island as a base for pirate raids against the rest of Greece. At some time during the tenth century Athens seems to have had an Arabic settlement

with its own mosque, traces of which have been excavated.

It was not, however, until the rise of the Ottomans that Greece was fully brought under Islamic rule. Different parts of Greece were incorporated into the Ottoman Empire at different times and for varying degrees of time. Thus the south and central part of the country (Peleponnesus and Ionnia) were conquered in 1460 but lost to the Venetians between 1687 and 1715 after which they were recaptured and remained part of the empire for another 100 years until the Greek War of Independence in 1821–9. Parts of northern Greece, however, were conquered by the Ottomans as early as 1360 and by 1430 the whole of the northern part of the country was under Turkish rule which lasted until 1912. There was little Turkish settlement in Greece with the exception of Thrace where colonists were brought in soon after the conquest.

There are comparatively few remains of Turkish rule in central and southern Greece although Athens contains a few notable examples. The

Fethie Cami, Athens © Cherry Pickles

oldest standing mosque in Athens is the Fethie Cami built in the late fifteenth century; the building is unusual because in plan it closely resembles an Orthodox church. The last Ottoman mosque built in Athens is the Djisdaraki Cami erected in 1759, a building with a distinctive Ottoman form, consisting of a triple-domed portico and a square domed prayer hall. In addition to mosques the Ottomans also built baths and madrassas in Athens none of which has survived although remains of the city wall built in 1788 by Ali Hadeski can still be seen. The islands of Greece, in particular Crete and Rhodes, have traces of the Ottoman occupation although as with southern mainland Greece there was no substantial Turkish settlement.

Northern Greece can be divided into three main areas, Epirus in the west near Albania, Macedonia in the middle and Thrace on the east side bordering Turkey. The area of Epirus has few traces of Turkish rule outside its capital at Ioannina and the city of Arta. At the centre of Ioannina is the fortress of Frourion which was substantially re-paired in the eighteenth century by the famous Ottoman governor Ali Pasha. Within the citadel is the mosque of Aslan Pasha built in 1688 which, with its position overlooking the lake, is one of the most romantic Turkish buildings in the Balkans. Whilst Turkish settlement in Ioannina was limited to the governor and his garrison, the town of Arta had a new Muslim suburb added to it. This suburb, now in a state of disrepair, is one of the best examples of Ottoman town planning with its mosque, imaret and hammam.

Macedonia has the highest concentration of Ot-toman monuments in Greece in the five cities of Thessaloniki, Seres, Kavalla, Yenice-i Vardar and Verria. In the regional capital, Thessaloniki, the most significant remains are the Hamsa Beg Cami and the Imaret Cami both of which date to the fifteenth century. In addition the city has three large hammams and a bedestan still standing. The other towns of Macedonia are less well known although each contains important monuments such as the aqueduct of Suleyman the Magnificent in Seres.

The oldest Ottoman monuments in Greece are to be found in the region of Thrace where there is still a significant Muslim population. One of the buildings still in use is the Komotini Mosque built in 1610 which is the only Balkan mosque to have large-scale Iznik tile decoration. Other monuments in the area include the Oruc Beg Hammam in Dimetoka built in 1398 and the Munschi Feridun Ahmed Pasha Hammam built in 1571.

See also: Ottomans

Further reading:
K. W. Arafat, 'Ottoman Athens', *Arts and the Islamic World* 4 no. 4: 1987/8.
—— 'Ottoman Ioannina', *Arts and the Islamic World* no. 20: 1991.
E. H. Ayverdi, 'Yunanistan', in *Avrupa'da Osmanli Mimari Eserleri* 4 book 5, Istanbul 1981.
M. Kiel, 'Islamic Architecture in the Balkans', *Arts and the Islamic World* 4 no. 3: 1987.
G. Soteriou, 'Arabic remains in Athens in Byzantine times', *Social Science Abstracts* 2 no. 2360: 1930.

Gujarat

Predominantly Hindu coastal region of western India with distinctive Islamic architecture.

Gujarat is a fertile low-lying region located be-tween Pakistan, Rajasthan and the Indian Ocean. The position of the region on the Indian Ocean has meant that it has always had extensive trading contacts particularly with the Arabian peninsula. It is likely that the first Muslims in Gujarat arrived sometime in the eighth century although there is little published archaeological evidence of this. The oldest standing mosques in the area are located at the old seaport of Bhadresvar in western Gujarat and have been dated to the mid-twelfth century although they may stand on older foundations.

The first Muslim conquest of the area took place at the end of the thirteenth century under the Ala al-Din the Khaliji sultan of Delhi. The earliest monument from this period is the Jami Masjid at Cambay which includes columns taken from ruined Hindu and Jain temples. The form of the mosque resembles that of the Quwwat al-Islam Mosque in Delhi with a rectangular courtyard with gateways on three sides and an arched screen in front of the sanctuary on the west side. Other early mosques built in a similar style include those of Dholka Patan and Broach all of which are located close to the coast. During the fifteenth century many mosques, tombs and other monu-ments were built in the regional capital Ahmada-bad, the most significant of which are the Jami Masjid and the tomb of Ahmad Shah. These build-ings incorporate many features from Hindu temple architecture including projecting balconies, perforated jali screens and square decorated columns. Monuments of the sixteenth century contain the same Hindu and Islamic elements combined in a more developed fashion as can be seen in the Jami Masjid of Champaner built in 1550. The Mughal conquest in the mid-sixteenth century brought Gujarat into the mainstream of architectural development. However, the architecture of the region exerted a considerable influence on the Mughal emperor Akbar, who built the city of Fatehpur Sikri in Gujarati style.

The secular architecture of Gujarat is mostly built of wood and characterized by elaborately carved screens and overhanging balconies. Another characteristic feature of the region is the use of step wells, or vavs, which consist of deep vertical shafts, approached via recessed chambers and steps. Sometimes these were very elaborate structures with multiple tiers of steps.

See also: Ahmadabad, India, Mughals, Qutb Minar

Further reading:

Z. A. Desai, 'Some Mughal inscriptions from Gujarat', *Epigraphia Indica: Arabic and Persian Supplement*, 1970, 63–92.

J. Jain-Neubauer, *The Stepwells of Gujarat in Art Historical Perspective*, New Delhi 1981.

E. Koch, '[The] Influence [of Gujarat] on Mughal architecture', in *Ahmadabad*, ed. G. Michell and S. Shah, Bombay 1988, 168–85

M. Shokooy, M. Bayani-Wolpert and N. H. Shokooy, *Bhadresvar: The Oldest Islamic Monuments in India*, part of Studies in Islamic Art and Architecture, Supplements to Muqarnas, vol. 2, Leiden 1988.

guldasta

An ornamental pinnacle in the shape of flowers.

gunbad

An Iranian and Mughal term for dome, usually used for a domed tomb.

H

Hadramawt

A large wadi in Yemen with distinctive mud-brick architecture. It runs from west to east and meets the Indian Ocean at Qishn.

The wadi is exceptionally fertile and has been settled since ancient times. The tall mud-brick tower houses, which from a distance resemble sky-scrapers are the most characteristic feature of the architecture. The form of these houses is probably derived from the stone-built tower houses of the highlands adapted into a mud-brick form for the plains at the bottom of the wadi. The best example of this architecture is the city of Shibam which has houses over eight storeys high. The exceptional height of the Shibam houses may partly be due to the wall which encloses the city, for whilst this provides protection it limits the available building land. The houses are usually built on stone founda-tions with mud-brick walls tapering from one metre at the bottom to a quarter of a metre at the top. The strongest part of the house is the stair-well which is often built of stone to the full height of the house. The exteriors have wooden window screens and ornamental relieving arches, and the upper parts of the houses are generally white-washed.

The main door for each house has a wooden latch attached to a cord enabling the door to be opened from the apartments above. The ground floors of the houses are either storerooms or shops whilst the first-floor rooms may be used for animal stalls. The second floor was used a reception area for business, and the rooms above were pri-vate apartments; the lower parts of the private rooms were functional whilst those at the top were reception rooms and open-air terraces. The reception room or majlis is usually a tall room decorated with carved plaster designs which may include a mihrab niche. At the upper levels there are often doorways to neighbouring houses so that women may visit each other without having to go out on to the streets. There are efficient waste-disposal systems with separate chutes for water and sewage. The age of the houses is difficult to determine although locally they are thought to last 300 years or more after which they will be replaced with another house on the same spot.

See also: Yemen

Further reading:

J. F. Breton, L. Badre, R. Audouin and J. Seigne, 'Le Wadi Hadramout', *Prospections*, 1978–9.

R. Lewcock, *Wadi Hadramawt and the Walled City of Shibam*, UNESCO, Paris 1986.

M. Raemakers, 'Towns and architecture in the Hadramaut', *Journal of the Royal Central Asian Society* (London) 40:246 ff., 1953.

Hagia Sophia (Aya Sophia; Church of Holy Wisdom)

Central church of Constantinople turned into a mosque after the Ottoman conquest and now a museum.

The first Hagia Sophia built in 360 by Constantine II had a timber roof and was burnt down in 404. This was replaced by a second building which was also burnt down a hundred years later. The present structure was founded in 537 although the huge central dome fell down and was replaced by the present construction in 558. The plan of the building consists of a large central dome (32 m diameter) flanked by two huge semi-domes sup-ported by smaller subsidiary domes; the two aisles are separated from the main area by a marble colonnade.

In 1453 the building was converted into a mosque by the addition of a wooden minaret; by the end of the sixteenth century the building was adorned with four tall pointed stone minarets. During the sixteenth century Selim II had his tomb built next to the building and in the seventeenth century Sultan Ahmet added a madrassa. The cathe-dral is important to Islamic architecture because its grandeur inspired Ottoman architects. The huge dome in particular impressed the Ottomans who, during the sixteenth century, built a number of mosques to rival the church of St Sophia, the most notable of which were the Süleymaniye and the Selimiye.

See also: Istanbul, Ottomans

Further reading:

W. S. George, *The Church of St Eirene at Constantinople*, Oxford 1912.

R. L. Van Nice and W. Emerson, 'Hagia Sophia and the first minaret erected after the conquest of Istanbul', *American Journal of Archaeology* 54, 1950.

Hajj routes

Special roads or routes which are taken by pilgrims on their way to Mecca.

Hajj, or pilgrimage, is one of the five pillars of Islam along with prayer five times a day, fasting, the giving of alms, and bearing witness that there is only one true God. Each Muslim is required to attempt at least once in a lifetime to visit the holy cities of Medina and Mecca. It is well known that Mecca was an important ritual centre before Islam and that it would have been visited as a shrine. Under Islam, however, the importance of visiting Mecca was greatly increased especially as the numbers of Muslims increased around the world.

Until the advent of rail and more recently air travel, the Hajj was a very arduous and risky undertaking requiring considerable preparation. Although coming from diverse locations, most pilgrims would have to make the last part of their journey through Arabia on one of several major Hajj routes. The main routes were Damascus to Mecca, Cairo to Mecca via the Sinai, Basra to Mecca, Sanca to Mecca coastal route, Sanca to Mecca inland route and Oman to Mecca via one of the Yemeni routes. Of these routes the most important were those that led from Damascus, Baghdad and Cairo. Over the centuries each of these routes developed various facilities for travellers which included wells, cisterns and dams, bridges, paved roads, markers and milestones, khans and forts. Of all the routes the Damascus route appears to be the oldest, following pre-Islamic trade routes. One of the most important stations on this route is the city of Humayma in southern Jordan where the Abbasids planned their revolution. Other early sites on this route are Khan al-Zabib, Jize and Macan, all of which contain remains of early Islamic structures associated with the Hajj. At Jise there is a huge Roman reservoir and nearby are the remains of the recently excavated Umayyad palace of Qastal which may have functioned as a royal caravanserai to receive important officials on the Hajj. Khan al-Zabib consists of a large square fortress-like building with a central courtyard and a mosque built to one side. At the oasis town of Macan there is also a huge Roman reservoir and there are signs that the nearby Roman fortress at Udruh was converted into an official Umayyad residence at this time. With the move of the caliphate from Syria to Iraq the Damascus route declined in importance, but the route was still used throughout the Ayyubid and Mamluk periods, as testified by the fourteenth-century pilgrimage itinerary of Ibn Battuta and the existence of several Mamluk forts on the route such as those at Jize and Zerka. With the Ottoman conquest of the Mamluk Empire in the sixteenth century the Hajj route was provided with new facilities and provided with fortified garrisons stationed in small forts along the route. The forts were built not only to protect the water cisterns and wells (which were repaired at the same time) but also to provide an efficient postal service for the Hajj. The forts had a simple square plan based around a central courtyard with a well in the centre. They were mostly two-storey structures with a crenellated parapet above and projecting machicolations (structures protecting openings through which to attack the enemy) on one or more sides. The forts were built to overlook the water reservoirs which were filled each year in preparation for the Hajj. It should, however, be remembered that the pilgrims would have stayed in vast encampments of tents next to the cisterns. By the eighteenth century the facilities had fallen into disrepair and the forts were inadequate protection against increased bedouin raids. In consequence the number of forts was augmented to cover most of the stops between Damascus and Mecca, and new wells, cisterns and bridges were provided. The design of the eighteenth-century forts was slightly different, with square projecting corner turrets and small gun slits. At the beginning of the twentieth century a narrow-gauge railway was built to replace the camel caravans; it used many of the same stops as the caravan route and forts were erected to protect the stations.

The decline of the Syria–Damascus Hajj route in the eighth century was largely a result of the development of a direct desert route between Baghdad and Mecca. The route was provided with

Qal'at Qatrana on the Ottoman Hajj route, Jordan

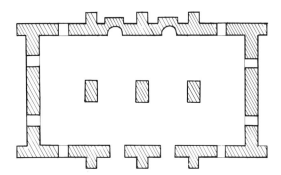

*al-Rowdah, eighteenth-century mosque on Syrian Hajj route.
Note double mihrab*

facilities paid for by Zubayda, wife of Caliph
Harun al-Rashid. Over fifty stations have been
identified on the route which is marked with milestones. The most important facilities were the
cisterns which were either square structures in
rocky ground or circular where they were built in
sand. The route included a number of stops of

varying size, the most important of which was al-
Rabadah, which has recently been excavated to
reveal a desert city in an area used to raise camels
– probably for the Hajj. Facilities at the sites
varied but usually included a mosque, a fort or
palace and several unfortified residential units. The
buildings were mostly built out of coursed stone
rubble for foundations and had a mud-brick superstructure, although occasionally buildings were
made of fired brick. Several of the mosques have
been excavated (at Zubalah, al-Qac and al-Rabadah). They generally have a courtyard leading to
the prayer hall which has a projecting mihrab and
a fixed minbar, and there is also usually the remains
of the base of a minaret. Palaces were found at
several sites (al-'Ashar, al-Shihiyat, Zubalah and al-
Qac) and consist of large rectangular or square
enclosures divided into separate inner courtyards,
which in turn may be composed of several residential units. The outer walls of the palace enclosures
are supported by solid semi-circular and circular
buttresses. On a smaller scale are the small forts
discovered on the northern part of the route which

are simple square structures built around a central courtyard with circular and semi-circular buttress towers on the outside. The houses on the route resemble the palaces in the variety of their internal arrangements; however, the basic unit seems to consist of a courtyard leading on to one or more groups of three rooms.

In more recent times the Hajj has been made by rail, sea and air and appropriate facilities have been built to accommodate modern pilgrims. One of the more famous recent buildings connected with the Hajj is the Hajj terminal at Jeddah which has won an award from the Agha Khan foundation.

Further reading:

J. S. Birks, *Across the Savannas to Mecca: The Overland Pilgrimage Route from West Africa*, London 1978.
A. D. Petersen, 'Early Ottoman forts on the Darb al-Hajj', *Levant* XXI, 97–118, 1989.
—— 'Two medieval forts on the Hajj route in Jordan', *Annual of the Department of Antiquities of Jordan*, Vol 35, 1991.
S. A. al-Rashid, *Darb Zubaydah*, Riyadh 1980.
J. Sauvaget, 'Les Caravanserais syriens du Hadjdj de Constantinople', *Ars Islamica* 4, 1937.

al-Hakim, Mosque of

One of the principal mosques of Cairo named after the Fatimid Caliph al-Hakim bi Amr Allah.

This mosque, also known as al-Anwar, 'the il-luminated', was begun in 990 under the Caliph al-'Aziz but was not completed until 12 years later under the Caliph al-Hakim. At the time of its construction this mosque was outside the city but was later incorporated within the city walls of Badr al-Jamali.

In its general design the mosque resembles those of Ibn Tulun and al-Azhar. It has a central rectangular courtyard surrounded by an arcade of pointed arches resting on brick piers. A raised transept runs from the courtyard to the mihrab. There were three domes on the qibla side, one in front of the mihrab and one in either corner. The front façade has a projecting entrance flanked by two cylindrical minarets decorated with inscriptions and carved bands. Later in 1010 the minarets were enclosed by giant brick cubes possibly because the minarets contravened a long-established Fatimid rule that the call to prayer was not to be made from a place higher than the mosque roof. The present minarets on top of the brick cubes belong to the Mamluk period.

Some of the original decoration has survived, in particular the stucco work with bands of Kufic inscriptions and stylized tree motifs. In the 1020s a ziyada was added to the south side by the caliph al-Zahir. During the Ayyubid period this mosque was the only congregational mosque in the city as the Ayyubids did not permit more than one congregational mosque within the city.

Further reading:

D. Berhens-Abouseif, *Islamic Architecture in Cairo: An Introduction*, Supplements to Muqarnas, vol. 3, Leiden 1989, 63–5.
J. M. Bloom, 'The mosque of al-Hakim in Cairo', *Muqarnas* 1: 15 ff., 1983.
K. A. C. Creswell, *The Muslim Architecture of Egypt*, Oxford 1952–60, 1: 68 ff.

hammam ('Turkish bath'; bath house)

General term used to describe both private and public bath houses. Public hammams are found throughout the Islamic world and together with the mosque are regarded as one of the essential features of an Islamic city. Private bath houses are less well known although it is known that they existed from the early Islamic period where they have been found in palaces such as Qasr al-Hayr and Ukhaidhir.

Hammams developed directly out of Byzantine bath houses such as those discovered at Avdat, and Yotvata in the Negev. One of the earliest and certainly the most famous early Islamic bath house is Qusayr Amra located in the north-eastern Jordanian desert. The building was heated by a hypocaust system supported on short brick pillars and supplied with water raised from a deep well by an animal-powered mechanism. Like other early Islamic baths Qusayr Amra does not have the frigidarium common in Roman baths although it does have an enlarged reception room, or apodyterium, decorated with frescoes in late Antique style. Other early Islamic bath houses such as Hammam al-Sarakh, 'Ayn al-Sinu and Jabal Usays have the same arrangement as Qusayr Amra with no frigidarium. The one exception to this pattern is the bath house at Khirbet al-Mafjar where the heated rooms are approached via a large hall (30 m square) resembling the classical frigidarium, with a long pool approached by steps and a mosaic floor.

There are few remains of bath houses from the period between the ninth and twelfth centuries although excavations at Nishapur have uncovered a bath house with hypocaust heating dated to the tenth/eleventh century. Sometime after the tenth century hypocausts seem to have been abandoned (in Syria at least) in favour of a system where the chimney of the furnace runs under the floor of the rooms to be heated. The effect of this innovation was that the layout of rooms was dictated by the axis of the chimney flue, and led to the warm room becoming the central room of the hammam. The typical Ayyubid hammam as it is known from Syria consists of an entrance room leading to the warm room via an intermediate unheated room. The warm room is usually octagonal with smaller hot rooms leading off at the sides. In baths built after the fifteenth century there is no intermediate room between the warm room and the changing room. As a corollary of this the size of the warm room is increased in later baths, until in eighteenth-century baths it becomes the main room. The octagonal warm room often has a central octagonal platform for massages whilst the smaller warm rooms have stone basins for washing. The warm and hot rooms never have windows but are lit instead by thick glass roundels set into the dome. A further development of the Ottoman period are twin hammams where a bath house for women and a bath house for men were set back to back to avoid the prohibition of mixed bathing. This problem is usually dealt with by having different bathing times for men and women.

See also: Khirbet al-Mafjar, Qusayr Amra

Further reading:

M. Dow, *Hammams of Palestine*, Oxford 1993.
M. Ecochard and C. Le Coeur, *Les Bains de Damas*, Beirut 1943.
E. Pauty, *Les Hammams du Caire*, Cairo 1963.
H. Terrasse, 'Trois Bains marinides du Maroc', *Mélanges*, 311–20, 1950.

haram

The private quarters of a house, sanctuary of a mosque or more generally an area set apart.

Haramayn

Term used to refer to the two holy places of Mecca and Medina. In Mamluk and Ottoman times this term was sometimes also used to refer to Jerusalem and Hebron.

haremlik

Turkish term for the private part of an Ottoman house which is only open to members of the family (from Arabic hareem).

Harran

Ancient city in south-eastern Turkey important as a centre of learning and Umayyad capital.

Harran is located in the flat plain between the Tigris and Euphrates rivers. The city was famous in early Islamic times as the centre of the pagan Sabians who worshipped the stars and achieved protected (dhimini) status in return for their astrological and scientific advice. The last Sabian temples were destroyed by the Mongol invasion of the mid-twelfth century. In 744 Caliph Marwan II established himself at Harran and made it the Umayyad capital.

The site includes the remains of a city wall, a castle and a congregational mosque. The most important monument is the Great Mosque founded by Marwan II between 744 and 750. Major modifications were carried out during the twelfth century under Salah al-Din who also fortified the citadel. The building is badly ruined, so that only the rough outline of the plan can be traced and the date of different phases is not clear. The mosque is roughly square measuring approximately 100 m per side with a rectangular courtyard to the north and the sanctuary to the south. There are two main entrances to the complex, one on the east side and one in the centre of the north side. The façade of the sanctuary consisted of nineteen arches resting on piers with engaged columns. In the centre of the façade is a wide central arch approximately in line with the deeply recessed mihrab in the south wall. Roughly in the centre of the courtyard there is an octagonal basin, above which there may have been a domed chamber supported on columns which functioned as the treasury (bayt al-mal). To the east of the north entrance is a tall square tower or minaret built in two distinct phases, the lower part is built of stone whilst the upper part is made of brick. The destruction of the mosque can be attributed to the Mongol invasion in the mid-twelfth century.

Harran is also noted for its characteristic architecture which consists of houses and storerooms covered with conical mud-brick domes.

haud or hauz

A pool or tank, often in the centre of the courtyard of a mosque.

Hausa

West African people living in northern Nigeria with a long-established distinctive architectural tradition.

Modern Hausa society is a combination of two groups of people, the Hausa themselves and the Fulbe-speaking Fulani people. The Fulani first moved into the area in the fifteenth century although it was not until the nineteenth that large-scale migrations took place. The Fulani constitute a literate Muslim class attached to the ruling élite in Hausa society. In addition to the Muslim urban populations there is also a rural population of non-Muslim Hausa known as Maguzawa. The Hausa civilization is generally agreed to have formed in about 1000 CE and comprised the cities of Daura, Kano, Gobir, Katsina, Zaria, Biram and Rano. In the nineteenth century a Fulani-led jihad established a caliphate in Hausaland with the new city of Sokoto as its capital. The main materials of Hausa architecture are oval mud bricks (tubali) and palm wood (deleb). Walls are built out of mud brick whilst palm trunks split into beams (azarori) are used for roofing. Unlike most other areas of West Africa, Hausa architecture is in the hands of a hereditary group of trained masons who are organized into guilds. These trained masons have been responsible for some of the most celebrated architecture in West Africa.

The traditional layout of a Hausa city consists of narrow winding streets set within a thick outer enclosure wall. In the older cities the outer walls have an irregular/organic shape but the walls of Sokoto, established in the nineteenth century, are square as an expression of Islamic conformity and bordered by houses which consist of courtyard compounds. In the past the street façades of the houses were left unadorned although in recent times there has been a tendency to decorate the outer façade of the entrance vestibule with embossed designs. Circular rooms with two entrances are traditionally used as entrance vestibules and are known as *zaure*. Square or rectangular rooms, called *sigifa*, are usually used for internal reception rooms. In recent times circular rooms have become less common and have been replaced with rectangular rooms with the more complex *daurin guga* dome form.

The characteristic feature of Hausa architecture is the domed room formed by a number of intersecting arches projecting from the walls of the building. The arches are made of lengths of palm wood set into the wall and projecting at increasing angles until they are horizontal at the apex of the arch where they are joined to a similar construction projecting from the opposite wall. The palm-wood frame is then covered with mud to produce smooth free-standing arches which support a ceiling made of palm-wood panels and covered with rush mats and then with a water-resistant layer of plaster, like material made out of the residue of indigo dye pits. Two main types of arch configuration are used depending on the shape of the room to be covered. The simplest form, known as the *kafin laima* vault, is used for a circular room and has all the arches or ribs meeting at a central point which is often decorated with an inset metal or ceramic bowl. The more complex vault form, known as *daurin guga*, is used for rectangular or square rooms and consists of two sets of parallel arches or ribs which intersect at the centre to form square compartments. The soffits of the arches are often decorated with abstract designs which may either be relief mouldings or painted in bright, locally produced colours.

See also: Kano, West Africa

Further reading:

S. B. Aradeon, 'Traditional Hausa architecture: the interface between structure and decoration', *Arts of the Islamic World* 5(1): 19–23, 1988.

A. Leary, 'A decorated palace in Kano', *Art and Archaeology Research Papers* 12: 11–17, 1977.

J. C. Moughtin, 'The traditional settlements of the Hausa people', *Town Planning Review* 35(1): 21–34, 1964.

—— 'The Friday mosque at Zaria city', *Savanah*, 1(2): 143–63, 1972.

L. Prussin, 'Fulani-Hausa architecture', *African Arts* 10(1), 1976.

——, 'Fulani-Hausa architecture: genesis of a style', *African Arts* 13(2): 57–65, 79–82, 85–7, 1976.

F. Schwerdtfeger, 'Housing in Zaria', *Shelter in Africa*, New York 1971.

M. G. Smith, 'The beginnings of Hausa society, AD 1000–1500', in *The Historian in Tropical Africa*, ed. J. Vanisa et al., London 1964.

H. Tukur Saad, *Between Myth and Reality: The Aesthetics of Traditional Architecture in Hausaland*, Ann Arbor University Microfilms.

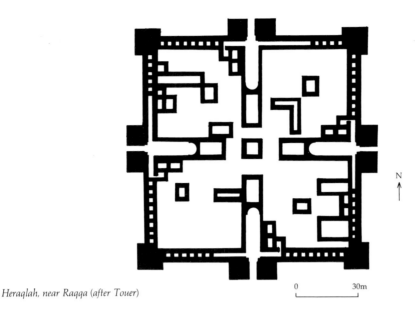

Heraqlah, near Raqqa (after Touer)

0   30m

N
↑

hayr (ha'ir)

Walled enclosures often associated with early Islamic palaces. Early examples are the enclosures at Qasr al-Hayr (East and West) and more significantly those of Samarra in Iraq. The exact function of these enclosures may vary; at Samarra they appear to be hunting reserves whereas at Qasr al-Hayr they may have a more utilitarian function.

hazarbaf

Iranian term for decorative brickwork.

hazira

A tomb contained within an enclosure which often includes a mosque. This form of tomb became popular in Timurid Iran.

Heraqlah

A square-shaped terrace-like structure with four corner towers enclosed within a small circular moat and circular wall.

This site is located in north-east Syria, 8 km west of the city of Raqqa near the Euphrates. On historical grounds this monument is reliably dated to the early ninth century, probably between 806 and 808 CE.

The monument is almost entirely built out of stone with the exception of the vaults and paving of the central structure, which are baked brick. The circular outer wall is supported by square buttresses at regular intervals and has gates at the four cardinal points (i.e. north, south, east and west). The entrances to the central building are aligned with those of the outer wall and each leads into a long vaulted hall. To the left of each entrance is a long ramp which gives access to the top of the monument. Although there are structures in the centre of the building, excavations have revealed that these cannot have been built as rooms as they have no doors or other means of access. Instead it is believed that the centre of the structure would have been filled in with earth to provide a monumental platform and that the structures must have fulfilled some symbolic or functional purpose.

The whole complex has been convincingly described as a victory monument to the Abbasid caliph Harun al-Rashid to commemorate his victory over the Byzantines at Herakleon. The size, date and geometric design is comparable with other Abbasid projects such as the octagon at Qadissiya and the Round City of Baghdad.

See also: Abbasids

Further reading:
F. Sarre and E. Herzfeld, *Archäologische Reise im Euphrat und Tigris*, Gebeit I, Berlin 1911, 161–3.

K. Touer, 'Heraqlah: a unique victory monument of Harun al-Rashid', *World Archaeology* 14(3): 1973.

Herat

City in north-west Afghanistan which became capital of the Timurid Empire in the fourteenth and fifteenth centuries.

Herat has existed since ancient times and was referred to in Greek as Aria. It was conquered by the Arabs in the seventh century but does not seem to have been fully subdued until the early eighth century. In the tenth century it was described as having four gates, a strong citadel and extensive suburbs. In the twelfth and early thirteenth century the city was developed by the Ghurids who established the Great Mosque. The city suffered under the Mongols in the thirteenth century although it began to be redeveloped by the fourteenth. In 1380 Timur entered Herat and later expelled the local ruler, this was the beginning of Herat's greatest period which lasted until the Uzbek conquest in 1508.

Timurid buildings in Herat include the Great Mosque, the madrassa and tomb of Gauhar Shad, the mausoleum of Sheikh Zadeh Abdallah and the famous shrine of Gazur Gah. The Great Mosque was established under the Ghurids in the twelfth century and contains the tomb of the Ghurid ruler Sultan Ghiyath al-Din. Although a few traces of twelfth-century stucco decoration remain, the design of the complex is mostly Timurid modified by more recent renovations. The mosque is built on a four-iwan plan with a central courtyard and an enlarged western iwan flanked with twin minarets which serves as the main prayer hall. The whole complex was decorated with polychrome tiles but these have mostly disappeared to be replaced by modern copies. The madrassa and tomb of Gauhar Shad form part of a large complex built around a musalla, or open air prayer area, measuring 106 by 64 m. The inner court had a two-storey arcade built around four iwans. The mausoleum of Gauhar Shad has a cruciform plan with the centre covered by a shallow convex dome supported by a network of pendentives and semi-domes. Above the inner dome there is a tall, ribbed outer dome resting on a cylindrical collar and covered with polychrome tiles on a blue background. Opposite the tomb of Gauhar Shad is the tomb of Sheikh Zadeh Abdallah which has a dome of similar design. The building has an octagonal plan with an large frontal iwan and side iwans added on to the south, west and east sides.

The most celebrated building in Herat is the shrine of Gazur Gah dedicated to an eleventh-century Sufi poet, Khwajeh 'Abdallah Ansari. The complex is a high-walled enclosure with a large iwan, above which is an arcade of five arches capped with two domes. The brilliance of the shrine is its original tiled decoration which consists of square geometric panels, monumental calligraphy and abstract designs.

See also: Afghanistan, Timurids

Further reading:

T. Allen, *Timurid Herat*, Wiesbaden 1983.

H. Gaube, *Iranian Cities*, New York 1979, 31–64.

F. J. Hecker, 'A fifteenth-century Chinese diplomat in Herat', *Journal of the Royal Asiatic Society*, 3rd series 3 (1): 85–91, 1993.

hosh

The courtyard of a house in Egypt or, in Palestine, used to describe houses built around a courtyard.

hujra

Small chamber or cell.

Hungary

The earliest recorded presence of Muslims in Hungary is during the ninth century of Khazars. Some of these converted to Christianity during the reign of King Stephen in the tenth century although many remained Muslim. Another Muslim (Turkic) group known as the Pecheneg was also present from the tenth century onwards. Many of these were located on the western frontier of Hungary as a defensive force for the Magyar kingdom. During the thirteenth century the Pecheneg seem to have been prosperous with large settlements the size of towns but without walls as these were forbidden to Muslim communities to prevent rebellion. By the end of the fourteenth century most Pecheneg had been forced to convert to Christianity although some remained Muslim until the beginning of the sixteenth century.

The Ottoman victory at the battle of Mohacs in 1526 renewed the Muslim presence in Hungary.

For the next 150 years, until its reconquest at the end of the seventeenth century, Hungary was a province of the Ottoman Empire. There are few buildings remaining from the period of Turkish rule although the reasons for this are unclear. One of the best-known Ottoman monuments is the tomb of Gul Baba in Buda erected between 1543 and 1548. The building is an octagonal mausoleum with a shallow domed roof covered in lead. There was once a mosque associated with the tomb but this has now disappeared. This tomb is now to be the centrepiece of an Islamic cultural centre incorporating a mosque and library.

See also: Albania, Bosnia, Bulgaria, Ottomans

Further reading:

G. Fehevari, 'A centre for Islamic culture in Hungary', *Arts of the Islamic World* 5(2) 18: 46–8, 1990.

hunkar mahfil

A royal lodge or gallery in an Ottoman mosque.

Hyderabad

Fifth largest city in India and capital of the second largest native state in British India.

The state of Hyderabad was ruled over by the Nizams of Hyderabad who were Muslims although the majority of the population was Hindu. Although conquered by the Mughals in the late seventeenth century the Nizams managed to retain their independence until 1947 when the state was taken over by Indian government troops.

The city was founded in 1591 by the fifth ruler of Golconda, Quli Qutb Saha. The city was originally known as Baghnagar (city of gardens) and later acquired the name Hyderabad. It is located on the banks of the river Musi and was laid out on a plan with the two main roads intersecting at the Char Minar at the centre of the city. To the north of the Char Minar were the palaces of the Nizam rulers which were destroyed during the Mughal conquest of 1687. Between 1724 and 1740 Mubariz Khan, the Mughal governor, supervised the construction of the city walls with fourteen gates, only two of which have survived.

Several buildings survive from the pre-Mughal period the most famous of which is the Char Minar which dominates the centre of the city. To the north-east of the Char Minar is the Mecca Masjid built out of local granite between 1614 and 1693. This is one of the largest mosques in India and the main entrance consists of five arches and four minars whilst the interior of the mosque contains two huge domes supported on monolithic columns. Directly to the north of the Char Minar is the Jami Masjid which was built in 1598 and is one of the oldest mosques in the city. This mosque forms part of a complex that included a bath house and madrassa which have survived as ruins. A better preserved complex is the Darush Shifa hospital and medical college (built in 1535) which consists of a two-storey square courtyard building with a mosque attached. Also from this early period is the Badshahi Ashurkhana which was built in 1592 as a royal house of mourning. The building is decorated with Persian-style tile mosaics and has an outer timber porch added in the late eighteenth century. Little remains of the original royal palaces although the Charkaman (Four arches) built in 1594 was originally a monumental gateway opening on to the palace grounds.

See also: Char Minar, Deccan, India

Further reading:

A. Bakshian and G. D. Schad, 'Hyderabad: shadow of empire', *History Today* 39: 19–28, Jan. 1989.

hypostyle

A flat-roofed structure supported by columns.

See also: appadana

I

Ibn Tulun Mosque

One of the oldest mosques in Egypt to have survived relatively intact. It was built by Ahmad ibn Tulun the semi-independent ruler of Egypt in 870.

The mosque formed part of the new suburb of al-Qata'ic which ibn Tulun added on to the two towns of Fustat and al-'Askar which were later incorporated into the city of Cairo. Ahmad ibn Tulun was born in Iraq and brought up at the caliph's court in Samarra and the new city of al-Qata'ic bore some resemblance to Samarra.

The mosque was begun in 876 and completed in 879. The building consists of a large rectangular enclosure with a central courtyard measuring 92 m square. Arcades two-aisles deep are ranged around three sides of the courtyard whilst on the qibla side (south-east) there are five rows of arcades. The central building is enclosed by an outer enclosure, or ziyada, on the three sides adjoining the qibla. Almost directly opposite the central mihrab is a minaret consisting of a square tower with a spiral section on the top. Access to the top of minaret is by an external staircase. At the top there is a two-storey octagonal kiosk. Whilst the octagonal kiosk and the windows on the side of the square shape appear to be of a later (thirteenth century) date there is some debate about whether the minaret is an original ninth-century structure or a later copy.

Due to its good state of preservation the Ibn Tulun Mosque provides an excellent example of ninth-century decoration and structural techniques. The most notable feature of the outer walls is the decorative openwork crenellations which resemble paper cut-outs. The courtyard façades consist of slightly pointed arches resting on rectangular piers with engaged colonettes, which is an unusual arrangement for Cairo where marble columns were usually used. Between the arches are rectangular arched niches also with engaged colonettes. Either side of each niche is a sunken rosette divided into eight lobes. A band of similar rosettes forms a cornice running around the four faces of the courtyard. Probably the most remarkable feature of the decoration is the carved stucco work which decorates the interior of the mosque. The best examples are in the soffits of the arches of the sanctuary where geometric interlace patterns are filled with stylized leaf ornament similar to Samarra stucco style B. The edges of the arches and the capitals are decorated with stucco resembling Samarra style A.

Many elements of the Ibn Tulun Mosque recall the architecture of Samarra, in particular the ziyadas, the rectangular piers and the stucco work. The minaret recalls the spiral minarets of the Great Mosque and the Abu Dulaf Mosque both because of the spiral shapes used and the positioning of the ziyada opposite the mihrab.

See also: stucco

Further reading:

K. A. C. Creswell, *A Short Account of Early Muslim Architecture*, revised and enlarged edn. J. W. Allan, Aldershot 1989, 392–406.

D. Berhens-Abouseif, *Islamic Architecture in Cairo: An Introduction*, Supplements to Muqarnas vol. 3, Leiden 1989, 51–7.

idgah

Indian term for an open-air prayer area, particularly used during festivals.

See also: musalla, namazgah

Ilkhanids

Mongol dynasty which ruled much of the eastern Islamic world from the mid-thirteenth to the mid-fourteenth century.

In 1258 Hulagau ibn Kublai Khan sacked Baghdad and killed the last Abbasid caliph al-Mu'tassim making Iraq part of the great Mongol Empire. This empire was divided into four parts of which Hulagau ruled one. Hulagau's dominions included Iran, Khurassan, Azerbayjan, Georgia, Armenia and Iraq.

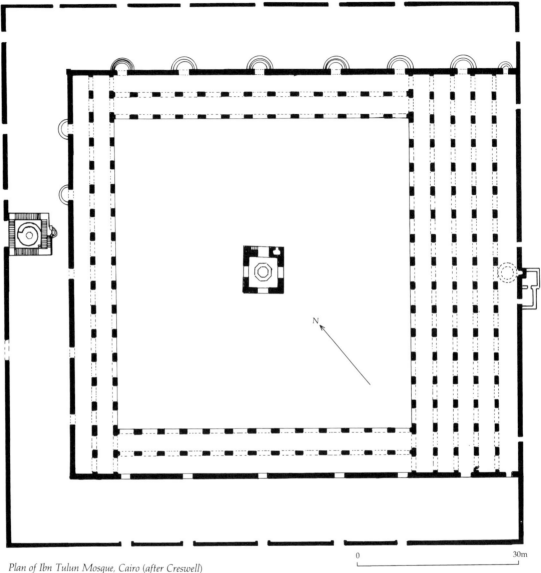

Plan of Ibn Tulun Mosque, Cairo (after Creswell)

Although the Ilkhanids rebuilt much of Baghdad, most imperial building was confined to Iran.

There are few Ilkhanid monuments which survive from before the fourteenth century. Characteristic features of Ilkhanid architecture are the massive size of monuments (which anticipates those of the Timurids), the extensive use of stucco work and the development of the transverse arch. The transverse arch was a method of covering large open areas without the use of piers or columns. The principle of the technique was to have a series of wide arches spanning the short axis of a room, these arches would then form the base for transverse vaults. Although the technique had been used before, this was the first time it was used in baked-brick architecture. One of the best examples is Khan Mirjan (1359) in Baghdad where a two-storey rectangular courtyard is covered with seven huge transverse arches.

The extant examples of imperial Ilkhanid architecture are few, although the ruins of the Mongol capital at Sultaniya give some idea of the scale of their buildings. The city was founded in 1306 and contained a huge citadel surrounded by a stone wall. Little survives of the city with the exception of the massive tomb complex of Oljetu. This is a huge octagonal building with a diameter of more than 30 m, surmounted by a massive dome covered with blue tiles. Other imperial projects were the Great Mosques of Tabriz and Varamin. The Tabriz Mosque was based around a prayer hall consisting of a single massive iwan 40 m wide and more than 80 m deep. In front of the iwan there was a courtyard which contained a madrassa and a khanqa. The Varamin Mosque is equally huge and is dominated by the strict symmetry of its axial iwans.

See also: Iran, Iraq

imamzadeh

Iranian term for venerated tomb of holy man.

imaret

Ottoman Turkish term for a kitchen which dispenses soup and bread free to the poor, students and wandering mystics (dervishes). Imarets usually form part of a larger religious complex which normally includes a mosque, madrassa and bath house (hammam).

India

The Republic of India is the largest country in south Asia and occupies the greater part of the Indian subcontinent which it shares with Pakistan and Bangladesh.

The present population of India is nearly 800 million of which almost 80 million (10 per cent) are Muslim, making it the second largest Muslim country in the world after Indonesia. Geographically India is fairly well defined, with the Himalayas to the north isolating it from the rest of Asia, whilst the Indian Ocean surrounds the country to the south. Within this vast area there are many regions each with its own languages, traditions, climate and environment, varying from the cool mountains of Kashmir to the tropical heat of the Deccan.

India differs from other parts of the Islamic world as it does not share the Roman and Sassanian traditions of the Middle East and North Africa, instead it has its own complex history which includes many different religions, cultures and ethnic groups. The most significant of these is the Hindu religion which was a highly developed culture well before the Muslim conquest and continues to be the major religion of the country. The effect of this on architecture means that Indian buildings have distinct design and building characteristics which distinguish them from Islamic buildings elsewhere. The most significant influence on architecture was the Hindu temple. Initially Hindu temples were destroyed and the remains were used to build mosques, such as the Quwwat al-Islam Mosque in Delhi which was built out of the remains of twenty-seven temples; later, however, Hindu features were copied for use in mosques and have now become characteristic of Indo-Islamic architecture. Examples of Hindu features incorporated into Islamic buildings include domed chatris, projecting chajjas and bulbous dome finials. Later on the influence of India can be seen in the mosques of south-east Asia, many of which are Indian in form.

Islam arrived in India by two routes, the overland route through Central Asia and the maritime coastal route. In general the overland route was used by Turkic and Afghan peoples who arrived in India as warriors and conquerors. These peoples established the first Muslim states in India starting in the north and later expanding to the south and east. The coastal route is less well documented and consists of the gradual development of independent Muslim trading communities along the coast in a similar manner to the establishment of Islam in East Africa. Some of the oldest established coastal communities are in Gujarat and the Malabar coast from where Islam eventually spread to south-east Asia as testified by the Gujarati gravestones found in Malaysia and Indonesia. The coastal communities were usually fairly small with no territorial or dynastic ambitions and consequently produced little monumental architecture apart from small local mosques. Occasionally there was some co-operation between the inland Muslim dynasties and the coastal Muslims as can be seen in Gujarat and the Deccan.

There are few documented remains of early Muslim coastal communities. This is partly because of the lack of archaeological work and partly because the monumental character of inland sites has taken up most of the attention of scholars. There is, however, significant historical information of Muslim coastal communities from as early as the ninth century at Quilon on the Malabar coast.

India

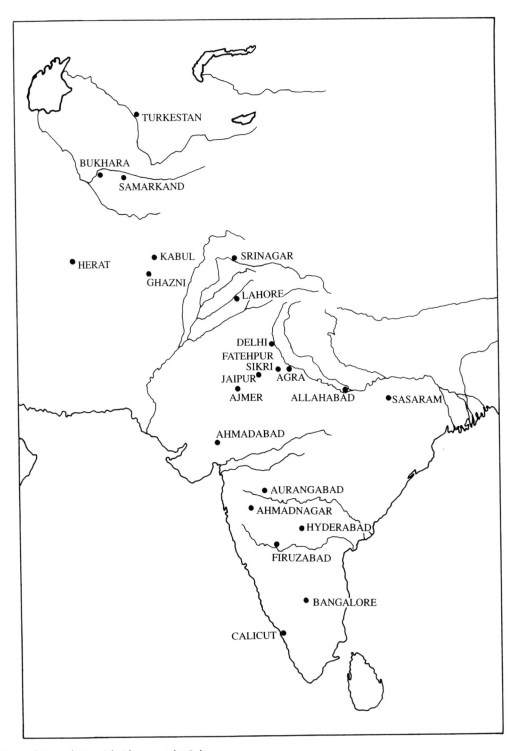

Principal sites and cities of the Islamic period in India

One of the few coastal sites with early standing remains is the old seaport of Bhadresvar which has two mid-twelfth-century mosques which pre-date the Muslim conquest of Gujarat.

The Muslim conquest of India started in the late twelfth century with the Afghan invasion led by Muhammad of Ghur who captured the Hindu stronghold of Rai Pithora, later known as Delhi (see below Pakistan for the early Islamic conquest of Sind). The death of Muhammad in 1206 left his lieutenant Qutb al-Din Aybak in control of the new Indian Muslim state. During the next 300 years much of northern India and the area of modern Pakistan was ruled by a succession of five dynasties based at Delhi. The first of these dynasties comprised the descendants of Qutb al-Din and collectively was known as the Slave dynasty. In 1290 power was seized by Jalal al-Din Firuz Shah II who was founder of the second dynasty known as the Khaliji sultans. In 1296 Jalal al-Din was murdered by his nephew who replaced him as sultan. The new sultan, Ala al-Din Muhamad Shah, reigned for seventeen years during which time he made extensive conquests in Gujarat, Rajasthan and the Deccan. However, the Khaliji dynasty was short-lived and in 1320 it was replaced by the Tughluq, named after its founder Ghiyath al-Din Tughluq. For a brief period in the mid-fourteenth century Ghiyath al-Din's successor moved the capital to Daulatabad in the Deccan, but famine and disease forced him to return to Delhi. The invasion of Timur at the end of the fourteenth century brought about the destruction of Delhi and dealt a deathly blow to the Tughluqid sultans. The last Tughluqid sultan died in 1414 leaving Delhi under the control of the Sayyid sultans who ruled as Timur's deputies. The Sayyid sultans ruled for less than forty years until 1451 when they were replaced by the Lodi kings. The end of the Delhi sultanate came in 1526 when the last Lodi king was defeated by Babur the first Mughal emperor.

The architecture of the Delhi sultanate represents a gradual evolution from an imported Afghan style using unfamiliar materials to a developed Indo-Islamic style which formed the basis of later Mughal architecture. The first building of the Delhi sultanate was the Quwwat al-Islam Mosque complex built by Qutb al-Din Aybak out of the remains of twenty-seven destroyed Hindu temples. The arcades were supported by two tiers of Hindu temple pillars placed one on top of the other to achieve the desired height. They were built in a trabeate construction and in 1199 an arched façade was added to the east side of the sanctuary to give it the familiar appearance of a mosque. However, the arches of the screen were built out of corbels rather than voussoirs whilst the decoration consisted of Quranic inscriptions contained within dense Hindu-style foliage. In the same year Qutb al-Din began the famous Qutb Minar which has become one of the potent symbols of Islam in India. Other work carried out at this time was the construction of the Great Mosque of Ajmer which like the Delhi Mosque employed re-used Hindu columns and later had an arched screen added to the front. Other notable monuments of the Slave dynasty include the tomb of Iltumish built in 1236 which includes the first use of squinches to support a dome.

Work on the Delhi Mosque continued under the Khaliji dynasty. Ala al-Din in particular devoted a great deal of attention to the mosque by extending the area of the sanctuary as well as beginning a new minaret on the same design as the Qutb Minar but more than twice the size. Unfortunately Ala al-Din was unable to finish his work and the only part completed is a monumental gateway. Other work carried out by Ala al-Din was the foundation of Siri, the second city of Delhi.

The real expansion of Sultanate architecture came during the rule of the Tughluqids in the fourteenth century. Several new cities were founded including Fathabad, Hissar and Jaunpaur as well as the third, fourth and fifth cities of Delhi. Also at this time the influence of Sultanate architecture was felt in the Deccan when Muhammad Tughluq II moved his capital to Daulatabad. Characteristic features of this architecture are massive sloping fortification walls with pointed crenellations and the development of the tomb as the focus of architectural design. One of the more important tombs is that of Khan Jahan built in 1369 which incorporates Hindu features into an Islamic form. The tomb has an octagonal domed form with chajjas, or projecting eaves, on each side and domed chatris on the roof. Another notable feature of Tughluqid architecture is the restrained use of epigraphy unlike earlier Sultanate architecture.

The monuments of the Sayyid and Lodi sultans are distinguished by their severity and lack of decoration. Nevertheless, many of the buildings are sophisticated structures like the tomb of Sikander Lodi which uses a double dome form so that the dome may have a significant form on the outside without disrupting the proportions of the interior (a technique later used in the Taj Mahal). The tomb is also the first Indian tomb to form part of a formal garden which became the established format under the Mughals. In addition to the centralized architectural styles developed during the Delhi sultanate several vigorous regional traditions also developed. The four most significant styles are those of Gujarat, Kashmir, the Deccan and Bengal. The style of Gujarat developed independently for over 200 years from its conquest by the Khaliji sultan Ala al-Din Shah in the early fourteenth century to its incorporation in the Mughal Empire in the late sixteenth century. Characteristic features of Gujarati architecture are the use of Hindu methods of decoration and construction for mosques long after they had ceased to be fashionable in Delhi. After the conquest of Gujarat, the Mughal emperor Akbar adopted this style for his most ambitious architectural project, Fatehpur Sikri. Less well known but equally distinctive is the architecture of Kashmir where the first Islamic conquest was in the mid-fourteenth century. The significant features of Kashmiri architecture are the use of wood as the main building material and tall pyramid-shaped roofs on mosques. The third major regional style is the architecture of the Deccan in southern India. Deccani architecture is characterized by massive monumental stonework, bulbous onion-shaped domes and elaborate stone carving, including vegetal forms, arched niches and medallions. Far to the east, in the region of Bengal and modern Bangladesh, a distinctive architecture developed using baked brick as the main building material. Other characteristic features of Bengal include the use of the curved do-chala and char-chala roofs which were later incorporated into imperial Mughal architecture under Shah Jahan.

See also: Bengal, Deccan, Delhi, Gujarat, Mughals

Further reading:

P. Andrews, 'The architecture and gardens of Islamic India', in *The Arts of India*, ed. B. Gray, Oxford 1981, 95–124.

P. Davies, *The Penguin Guide to the Monuments of India*, vol. 2: *Islamic Rajput and European*, London 1989.

Z. A. Desai, *Indo-Islamic Architecture*, 2nd edn. New Delhi 1986.

S. Grover, *The Architecture of India: Islamic*, New Delhi 1981.

R. Nath, *Islamic Architecture and Culture in India*, Delhi 1982.

M. Shokoohy and N. H. Shokoohy, *Hisar-i Firuza: Sultanate and Early Mughal Architecture in the District of Hisar India*, Monographs on Art and Archaeology, London 1988.

M. Shokoohy, M. Bayani-Walpert and N. H. Shokoohy, *Bhadresvar: The Oldest Islamic Monuments in India*, Studies in Islamic Art and Architecture, Supplements to Muqarnas vol. 2, Leiden 1988.

K. V. Soundara Rajan, *Islam Builds in India: Cultural Study of Islamic Architecture*, Delhi 1983.

F. Watson, *A Concise History of India*, London 1979.

A. Welch and H. Crane, 'The Tughluqs: master-builders of the Delhi Sultanate', *Muqarnas* 1: 123–66, 1983.

A. Volwahsen, *Living Architecture: Islamic Indian*, London 1970.

Indonesia

Large country in south-east Asia comprising an archipelago of over 17,000 islands stretching for over 5,000 km along the equator. The country has a large population of over 180 million of whom more than 80 per cent are Muslim, making it the most populous country in the Islamic world.

Islam reached separate parts of Indonesia at different times; it arrived in Sumatra in the thirteenth century; in the fourteenth century it was established in Java, southern Celebes, northern Moluccas and southern Borneo (Kalimantan). By the fifteenth century; it had reached the smaller islands to the east of Bali (this remained Hindu) including Lombok, Sumbawa and the northern coast of Flores.

With the exception of the mosque at Demak there are few examples of early mosques in Indonesia because they were mostly wooden and were replaced by brick or stone structures in the nineteenth century. What the wooden mosques do demonstrate is a continuity with the pre-Islamic Hindu and Buddhist past and it seems likely that for this reason they were later replaced with buildings which look more traditionally Islamic. The modern Islamic buildings of Indonesia often have more in common with India and Europe than with any indigenous Indonesian architecture. Recently, however, there have been attempts to revive traditional mosque forms by the 'Amal Bakti Muslim Pancasila' foundation which builds wooden mosques similar to the historical mosque at Demak.

See also: Java, Sumatra

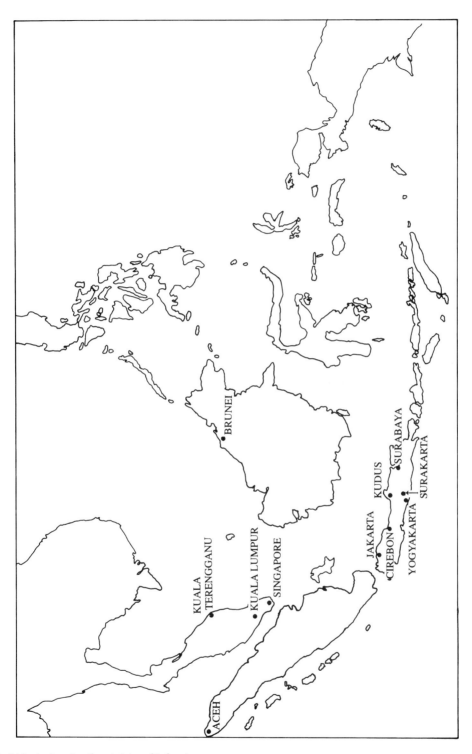

Principal Islamic sites of south-east Asia and Indonesia

Further reading:

H. I. Jessup, 'Princely pavilions: architecture as an index to court and society', *Court Arts of Indonesia*, New York 1990, chap. 3.

A. H. Johns, 'From coastal settlement to Islamic school and city: Islamization in Sumatra, the Malay Peninsula and Java', in *Indonesia: Australian Perspectives. I: Indonesia: The Making of a Culture*, ed. J. J. Fox, Canberra 1980.

N. Madjid, 'Islam on the Indonesian soil: an ongoing process of acculturation and adaptation', *Arts and the Islamic World*, 20: 67–8, 1991.

A. A. Nanji, 'Space and spirit: the contemporary expressions of buildings in Islam', *Arts and the Islamic World* 2: 63–5, 1991.

Y. Saliya, 'Mosque architecture in Indonesia: variations on a theme', *Arts and the Islamic World* 21, 1992.

Iran (Islamic Republic of Iran, formerly Persia)

Large Middle-Eastern country containing some of the most celebrated examples of Islamic architecture.

Iran is bordered on the west by Iraq and Turkey, on the east by Pakistan and Afghanistan and on the north by the former Soviet Republics of Turkmeniya and Azerbayjan. To the south the country is open to the Persian/Arabian Gulf and the Indian Ocean. The centre of the country comprises a high plateau surrounded by mountains, to the south and west are the Zagros mountains whilst to the north along the shores of the Caspian Sea are the Elbruz mountains. The majority of the population lives on the edges of the central plateau as much of the interior is fairly barren, consisting of kavir (salt marsh) and dasht (stony desert). Most of the country is fairly arid except for the north-west on the borders of the Caspian Sea where there are forests.

In addition to the present state of Iran, Iranian culture has traditionally extended into the neighbouring regions comprising the modern states of Afghanistan, Turkmeniya, Uzbekistan and Tajikistan.

History

Iran has a long history as a unified state starting with the conquests of Cyrus the Great, founder of the Achaemenid Empire in the sixth century BCE. By 525 BCE Cyrus's successor Cambyses had captured Egypt and was in control of most of the Middle East. The Achaemenid Empire was eventually destroyed by Alexander the Great in 331 BCE after which Iran was ruled by his successors known

as the Seleucids. The Seleucids were in turn overthrown by the Sassanians who ruled an empire which included most of modern Iran as well as Mesopotamia. The earliest Arab attacks on the Sassanian Empire took place in the 630s and by 637 CE the Arabs had won a major victory at the battle of Qadisiyya. Although the Sassanians were decisively defeated at the battle of Nihavand in 642 the Arab conquest was not completed until 651 when the last Sassanian emperor, Yazdigrid, was killed near Murghab in Transoxiana. However, even after the emperor's death, resistance continued whilst many parts of the country conquered by the Arabs remained under the control of Persian princes. The Arab conquest was carried out mostly by troops from the Iraqi garrison cities of Basra and Kufa, a factor which subsequently had profound influence on the politics and religion of early Islamic Iran.

For the next hundred years Iran was ruled by a series of governors appointed by the Umayyad caliphs based in Syria. The rule of the Umayyads was resented by many of the Arab troops in Iran, many of whom were influenced by the emerging Kharjirism (opposition to religious claims of the caliphate) and Shi'ism (supporters of 'Ali of Basra and Kufa. In addition a large number of Iranian converts to Islam were unhappy about their status in relation to the Arab rulers. The result of the growing opposition to the Umayyads was the Abbasid revolution which began in eastern Iran and eventually spread to most of the Islamic world. One of the consequences of the Abbasid revolution was increased Iranian influence in both the culture and administration of the caliphate. During the ninth century independent local dynasties began to emerge as rulers in several parts of Iran, the most significant of which were the Buwaihids. The Buwaihids were a Shi'a group originating from the Caspian region who eventually dominated even the Abbasid caliphs. In the ninth century eastern Iran (including the modern states of Afghanistan and Uzbekistan) was under the control of the Samanids based at Bukhara and Samarkand. In 1040 the Seljuk Turks conquered the whole of Iran and established the great Seljuk Empire. For a short period in the eleventh century a huge area from Syria to eastern Iran was nominally under the control of the Seljuks who as a Sunni group were endorsed by the religious orthodoxy and the caliphate in Baghdad. However, the unity of the

Seljuks was short lived and by the end of the eleventh century the empire was divided into a number of independent principalities. In the mid-thirteenth century Iran was conquered by the Mongols who dominated the country for the next hundred years. In the late thirteenth century the Mongol leader Ghazan Khan converted to Islam and broke away from central Mongol control. Between 1381 and 1404 Iran was subjected to another devastating Mongol invasion under the legendary Timur. The Timurid state in western Iran did not last long after Timur's death in 1405 and was replaced by the Turkoman dynasties who ruled until 1501 when they were defeated by the forces of the Saffavids under Shah Isma'il. However, in eastern Iran Timurid rule continued until 1510 when the last Timurid sultan was defeated by the Saffavids.

The Saffavids ruled Iran for more than 200 years establishing it as a unified modern state. Unlike their predecessors, the Saffavids were Shi'a and converted most of Iran to this form of Islam. By the 1730s the Saffavids were no longer able to control large areas of the country which was subjected to increasing Afghan attacks. In the 1740s the Afghans were repulsed by a Nadir Shah, ruler of a local north-eastern dynasty known as the Zands. Nadir Shah's success against the Afghans enabled him to take control of the whole of Iran, though the Saffavids remained nominally in control. In 1779 the Zands were overthrown by the leader of a Turkish dynasty known as the Qajars who ruled the country until 1924 when they were replaced by the modernizing Pahvli dynasty. In 1979 the last Pahvli ruler was overthrown and Iran became an Islamic republic.

Architecture

The building materials vary from place to place and according to the period although certain materials and techniques tend to remain predominant. For most of the Islamic period the shortage of suitable stone has meant that brick (baked or unbaked) has been the main construction material. Unbaked mud brick or pisé is generally the cheapest building material and has been used for most Iranian houses since early times. In many buildings mud brick is used in conjunction with baked brick which is employed for the more important parts of the structure. Baked (or fired) bricks were used for

more important monuments in the early Islamic period although later they were adopted for a wider range of building types. In the earliest monuments brickwork is undecorated with large expanses of plain wall in the Sassanian tradition. In later buildings decorative patterns are introduced which reach their culmination under the Seljuks with complex geometric patterns and inscriptions. Two techniques of brickwork decoration (hazarbaf) are used, one employing bricks of standard size arranged in simple patterns and the other using bricks specially cut or manufactured for the purpose. The latter technique was more suitable for inscriptions and complex motifs. Also during the Seljuk period buildings began to be decorated with glazed bricks and coloured ceramic tile inlays. During the Seljuk and Ilkhanid periods the preferred colours were turquoise, light blue and dark blue. In earlier buildings glazed tiles and bricks were set into the exterior walls of buildings to enliven the uniform earth colours of the brick and dark blue; however, during the fourteenth century the technique of tile mosaic was developed whereby large areas would be covered by tiles specially cut or shaped to form geometric and floral designs. Under the Timurids new colours were introduced including green, yellow and terracotta. The technique of tile mosaic was perfected in the fifteenth century under the Timurids who also introduced new colours including green and yellow. During the sixteenth century the Saffavids introduced overglaze painted panels using a technique known as haft-rangi (i.e. seven colours). The advantage of this technique was that it was possible to cover large areas fairly cheaply, although the quality of the colours was inferior to that produced in tile mosaics.

Cut stone architecture is rare in Iran which has no tradition of ashlar masonry to compare with that of the eastern Mediterranean. There are, however, several notable exceptions to this such as the Khuda Khana of the Friday mosque in Shiraz built in 1351. However, most stone buildings in Iran were made out of rubble stones set within a thick mortar and covered with plaster. The lack of a stone carving tradition in Iran led to the development of decorative plasterwork or stucco. The technique of stucco decoration was developed under the Sassanians, but achieved its definitive Islamic form at the Abbasid capital of Samarra in Iraq. Subsequently stucco decoration in Iran developed its own form and was used in particular for decorating mihrabs.

Wood is rarely used in Iran except in the north-west region on the borders of the Caspian Sea. Unfortunately few wooden structures survive from the earlier periods although there are several notable examples from the Saffavid period. The most famous example of wooden architecture is the porch of the Ali Qapu Palace in Isfahan which consists of a flat roof supported on huge wooden columns with muqarnas capitals. Although fairly unique because of its size the porch of the Ali Qapu Palace represents a traditional form in Iranian architecture.

Two types of building are particularly characteristic of Islamic architecture in Iran, these are mosques and tombs. In addition there is a range of secular buildings which gives some idea of the diversity of Iranian architecture. Unfortunately very little survives of Iran's Islamic architecture from before the Seljuk period so that it is difficult to trace the origin of particular building types and their relationship to Islamic architecture elsewhere.

The earliest Iranian mosques were hypostyle structures with the sanctuary located on the south-western (qibla) side of an open courtyard which was lined by arcades on the other three sides. In the absence of the marble columns used in Syria and Egypt the roof was usually supported by baked-brick piers or wooden columns. Only a few early mosques have been discovered, the most important of which are Siraf, Susa, Isfahan, Fahraj, Damghan and Nayin. The first three buildings were covered by a flat wooden roofs whilst the latter three were roofed with a system of barrel vaults supported on squat octagonal or round brick piers. The walls of these structures were initially built out of mud brick or rubble stone set in mortar and decorated with stucco.

Sometime during the eleventh century a new mosque form was introduced based on the four-iwan plan. The advent of this new building type seems to be associated with the arrival of the Seljuks. Examples of this form are found mostly in western and central Iran and include Isfahan, Basian, Zavareh, Qazvin, Yazd, Kirman and Rayy. One of the clearest examples of this new form is the mosque of Zavareh (dated to 1136) which consists of a square central courtyard with iwans in the centre of each side, behind the qibla iwan is a square domed chamber containing the mihrab.

From the Seljuk period onwards the four-iwan plan became the standard format for mosques and later developments took place within the context of this plan. Ilkhanid developments in mosque architecture were concerned with a refinement of the four-iwan plan and the increased use of decorative techniques. The problem of the four-iwan plan is that it detracts from the directional emphasis of the mihrab. One method used to strengthen this axis is the enlargement of the qibla iwan which can be seen in its most exaggerated form in the mosque of Ali Shah in Tabriz built between 1310 and 1320 where the qibla iwan was over 48 m deep and 30 m wide. Another method of strengthening the orientation is the decorative elaboration of the qibla iwan and façade (pishtaq). In the Great Mosque of Varamin built in 1322 the monumental qibla iwan is decorated with giant muqarnas, stucco inscriptions and decorative brickwork.

The collapse of Ilkhanid power in 1335 left Iran under the control of competing dynasties the most important of which was the Muzaffarids who ruled the area of Fars and Kirman. Several innovations in mosque architecture were introduced at this time which collectively have been called the Muzaffarid style. One of the most distinctive features is the use of large transverse arches which support transverse barrel vaults. This system was used in an extra prayer hall added to the Great Mosque at Yazd and the madrassa attached to the Masjid-i Jami at Isfahan. The advantage of this innovation is that large areas can be covered without intervening pillars. This period is also characterized by the growing use of tile mosaic as decoration both for the interior of mosques and for the portal façades.

In 1393 the conquests of Timur brought an abrupt end to Muzaffarid rule and marked the beginning of a period during which monumental building activity was confined to the eastern part of the Iranian world outside the borders of the present state of Iran. However, it is notable that many of the buildings erected by Timur and his successors in Samarkand and Bukhara resemble the earlier buildings of western Iran. One of the reasons for this situation is that Timurids employed craftsmen from western Iran, a fact which may also explain the comparative dearth of building activity in the west. The situation in western Iran later improved under the Qara Qoyunlu dynasty who established their capital at Tabriz. The most significant monument of the period is the Blue Mosque of Tabriz which consists of a domed central court-yard opening on to four iwans. The plan is similar to that of the early T-plan mosques of Bursa and was probably influenced by contemporary Otto-man architecture.

With the exception of Isfahan there were few major new mosques built during the Saffavid period although extensive restorations were carried out to older mosques and shrines. In particular there was an increased emphasis on the shrines of Mashad and Ardabil which were adapted for large numbers of pilgrims. At Isfahan the Saffavids built a new city based on a huge central maidan which functioned as the centre of the city. Opening on to the maidan are two mosques, the Masjid-i Shah and the Masjid-i Sheikh Luft 'Allah, one on the east and one on the south side. The maidan is aligned north–south whilst the mosques are built on a qibla axis (i.e. north-east–south-west), thus the junction between the mosques and the maidan form entrances bent to an angle of 45 degrees. The Masjid-i Sheikh is the smaller and also the more unusual mosque and comprises a single-domed chamber approached via an L-shaped corri-dor. The plan of the building lacks the central courtyard found in most earlier mosques and has more in common with domed mausoleums than the typical Iranian mosque. The Masjid-i Shah with its four-iwan plan appears more conventional al-though it has several unusual features including minarets either side of the qibla iwan, domed halls leading off the side iwans and two eight-domed prayer halls either side of the domed sanctuary area. Perhaps more surprising are the twin ma-drassas which flank the central prayer area creating a unified religious complex. The architectural unity of the complex is cleverly reinforced by the bent axis which allows a person standing in the maidan to see the entrance portal, the qibla iwan and the large central dome at the same time. The impact of this view is reinforced by the blue and turquoise glazed tilework and the twin sets of minarets flanking the entrance portal and the quibla iwan. Other mosques built under the Saffavids were generally less adventurous in their design and were built on the standard four-iwan plan.

Mosques built during the period of Zand and Qajar rule continued to be built in the classic Saffavid style but with increased emphasis on deco-ration. The most famous building attributable to the Zands is the Vakil Mosque in Shiraz, which is characterized by its vivid yellow and pink tile decoration. Several nineteenth-century Qajar mosques begin to show variations in the standard format such as entrances placed to one side and multiple minarets.

The development of commemorative tomb struc-tures mirrors that of mosques with few structures from before the eleventh century and a wide range of structures produced before the sixteenth century after which there is little innovation. Two distinct traditions of monumental tombs developed which may be described as domed mausoleums and tomb towers.

Tomb towers were generally reserved for rulers or prominent local princes and were probably a continuation of pre-Islamic Iranian practices. The degree of continuity can be seen in the tomb tower of Lajim where the commemorative inscrip-tion is in Arabic and Pahlavi. The earliest and probably the most famous commemorative tomb in Iran is the Gunbad-i Qabus built between 1006 and 1007. The tomb consists of a tall cylindrical tower 55 m high with ten angular buttresses and a conical roof. There is no decoration to relieve the stark simplicity of the brickwork except for two lines of inscription, one near the base and one below the roof. Although unusual, the monument is related to a group of Ghaznavid tomb towers produced further east in Afghanistan. During the Seljuk period the tomb tower became established as the principal type of funerary monument. Other important tomb towers include the Pir-i 'Alamdar tower (1026–7) and the Chihil Dukhtaran tower (1054–5) both in Damghan. The significance of the Damghan towers is their decorative brickwork which later became one of the standard decorative techniques on tomb towers. Also during the Seljuk period tile inlay and glazed bricks became increas-ingly popular as a form of decoration. During the Ilkhanid period the standard smooth round form of tomb towers was modified by the addition of semi-circular or angular flanges seen in buildings such as the 'Ala al-Din tomb tower in Varamin (1289). In the 'Aliabad Kishmar tomb tower semi-circular and angular flanges are combined creating a complex interplay of shadows. During the four-teenth and fifteenth century the smooth conical roof form is replaced by a pyramid form in which the conical form is made of a number of flat planes which meet at the apex.

Domed mausoleums are probably the earliest

form of commemorative tomb and can be traced back to structures such as the Qubbat al-Sulaybiyya at Samarra. These structures usually have a square or octagonal base and hemispherical dome, one of the earliest Iranian examples being the Arslan Jadhib tomb built in 1028. Another early example is the Davazdah Imam at Yazd (1036–7) which consists of a massive square chamber covered by a dome resting on an octagonal drum. During the Ilkhanid period the principle of the double dome developed with a tall outer dome concealing a lower inner dome. The purpose of the double dome arrangement was that a tall dome may attract attention to a building from the outside but is unsuitable for the smaller proportions of the interior. Under the Timurids a bulbous dome shape was developed which became characteristic of Iranian architecture and was used on many of the tombs built after the fifteenth century. In addition to the standard dome form a regional variant developed in western Iran which is linked to the Iraqi muqarnas domes.

As well as tomb towers and domed octagonal mausoleums, a third category of tomb is represented by the great shrines of Mashad, Qum and Mahan. Probably the greatest of these is the shrine of Imam Riza at Mashad which was built by the Timurids in 1418 and subsequently adorned by later Iranian dynasties. At the centre of the shrine is a great chamber covered by a bulbous glazed dome. Around the sides of the building are two tiers of glazed iwans and a monumental iwan flanked by twin minarets at the front.

Secular architecture in Iran is represented by a wide range of buildings including palaces, caravanserais, bridges, city walls, bazars, ice houses, pigeon towers and bath houses. Unfortunately most secular buildings date from the fairly recent past and their are few examples from before the Saffavid period. This is particularly true of palaces; thus the Ali Qapu Palace in Isfahan is one of the few imperial palaces to survive. Remains of earlier palaces have been found but these are mostly ruins of buildings destroyed by war or natural disasters. The Ali Qapu forms part of the imperial complex at Isfahan built by Shah Abbas in the seventeenth century. The palace is located on the west side of the central maidan and consists of a tall square building with a monumental porch at the front overlooking the maidan. The porch is more than two storeys high and is raised above the ground

on a vaulted substructure so that it functions as a huge covered viewing platform. Behind the main building of the Ali Qapu there are a series of gardens and pavilions which recall the garden palaces depicted in Persian miniature painting. However, most secular buildings such as caravanserais or bazars tend to be of more utilitarian form although sometimes they are enriched by decorative details derived from religious architecture. This process can be seen very early on in Iranian architecture in buildings such as the Seljuk caravanserai of Robat Sharaf where the entrance is decorated with elaborate brickwork and incorporates a mihrab for the use of travellers. This process continued into the nineteenth century as can be seen in the bazar entrance at Yazd which consists of three-storey triple iwans flanked by twin minarets and covered with glazed tiles. However, most caravanserais and bazars contained very little decoration beyond a foundation inscription above the gateway.

See also: badgir, Isfahan, Saffavids, Seljuks, Timurids

Further reading:

T. Allen, 'Notes on Bust', *Iran* 27: 57–66, 1989, and *Iran* 28: 23–30, 1990.
E. Beazley, 'Some vernacular buildings of the Iranian Plateau', *Iran* 15: 89–108, 1977.
—— 'The pigeon towers of Isfahan', *Iran* 4: 1–20, 1966.
L. Bier, 'The Masjid-i Sang near Darab and the Mosque of Shahr-i Ij: rock cut architecture of the Ilkhanid period', *Iran* 24: 117–30, 1986.
S. S. Blair, 'The Mongol capital of Sultaniyya, "The Imperial"', *Iran* 24: 139–52, 1986.
W. M. Clevenger, 'Some minor monuments in Khurassan', *Iran* 4: 57–64, 1966.
H. Gaube, *Iranian Cities*, New York 1979.
O. Grabar, 'The visual arts from the Arab invasions to the Saljuks', in *Cambridge History of Iran*, 1993.
—— 'The visual arts 1050–1350', in *Cambridge History of Iran*, 1993.
R. Hillenbrand, 'Saljuk dome chambers in north-west Iran', *Iran* 14: 93–102, 1976.
—— 'Safavid architecture', in *Cambridge History of Iran* 1993.
—— 'Saljuk monuments in Iran V: the Imamzada Nur Gurgan', *Iran* 25: 55–76, 1987.
L. Horne, 'Reading village plans: architecture and social change in north-eastern Iran', *Expedition* (The University Museum Magazine of Archaeology and Anthropology, University of Pennsylvania) 33(1) 1991.
A. Hutt and L. Harrow, *Islamic Architecture: Iran 1*, London 1977.
—— *Islamic Architecture: Iran 2*, London 1978.
A. K. Lambton and R. M. Savory, 'Iran (v. History)', in *Encyclopedia of Islam* (new edn.), 1954.

C. Melville, 'Historical monuments and earthquakes in Tabriz', *Iran* 19: 1981.

B. O'Kane, 'The Imamzada Husain Rida at Varamin', *Iran* 16: 175–7, 1978.

R. Pinder Wilson, 'Timurid architecture', in *Cambridge History of Iran*, 6: 728–58, 1993

R. Shani, 'On the stylistic idiosyncracies of a Saljuk stucco workshop from the region of Kashan', *Iran*, 27: 67–74, 1989.

O. Watson, 'The Masjid-i Ali Quhrud: an architectural and epigraphic survey', *Iran*, 13: 59–74, 1975.

Iraq

Large country to the north-east of Arabia and west of Iran, dominated by the twin rivers of the Tigris and Euphrates.

The present state of Iraq more or less coincides with the historical term Mesopotamia which refers to the land between the two rivers. The country may be divided into three main geographical regions: the Kurdish areas of the north, the central area between Mosul and Baghdad and the desert areas to the south and west. The Kurdish areas of the north-east are dominated by high mountains which continue into Turkey and Iran. The central area between the rivers is extremely flat, especially the southern areas and it is here that the remains of the ancient civilizations (Sumerians, Babylonians, Assyrians) have been found. The desert areas to the west are sparsely populated and have connections with the Arabic countries to the west and south.

Before the Arab conquests in the seventh century Iraq was ruled by the Sassanians from their capital at al-Mada'in or Ctesiphon. In 633 CE the Muslim Arabs crossed the Euphrates and occupied Hira; four years later at the battle of Qadisiyya the Sassanians were defeated. Initially the Arabs ruled from the old Sassanian capital but later moved to the newly established garrison town of Kufa. Basra, the other garrison city, was later built to cope with the increasing number of immigrants. Under the Umayyads the Islamic empire continued to expand, which led to the continued development of the garrison cities. In order to retain order a third, Wasit, was established midway between Kufa and Basra.

With the Abbasid revolution of 750 Iraq was established as the home of the caliphate. This shift in political power is symbolized by the building of Baghdad as a new capital in 762. Conflict between the caliph's soldiers and the local population in Baghdad resulted in the al-Mu'tassim founding a new capital further north at Samarra. For a little over fifty years Samarra was capital of the Islamic world but in 889 Caliph Mu'tamid moved back to Baghdad. Abbasid power in Iraq was smashed in 946 by the Buwaihids, a Sh'ite Persian dynasty who ruled in the name of the Abbasid caliphs. The Buwaihids spent considerable sums on building activity in Iraq, their most famous construction being the Bimaristan (hospital) built in 978 at a cost of 100,000 dinars. The Buwaihids were replaced as rulers by the Seljuks who ruled until 1154 when the long-dormant Abbasid caliphs were able to reassert their power over much of Iraq. In 1258 the Mongols sacked Baghdad putting an end to further hopes of Abbasid revival. Under the Ilkhanids Iraq was ruled by local governors, a situation which was changed when the Jalairids took over in the fourteenth century and ruled from Baghdad. In the sixteenth century Iraq was conquered by the Ottomans who incorporated it into the Ottoman Empire.

The principal building material of Iraq is mud brick whilst baked brick is used for more permanent or important structures. The abscence of suitable wood led to the development of vaults, arches and domes that could be built without wood. In the Kurdish areas of the north hewn stone set into a thick limey mortar (juss) is used as a building material. This method is also used in the desert areas of the west although mud brick is also used. The only form of wood available is the palm tree and split palm trunks are sometimes used for roofing. In the southern area near the entrance to the Gulf is a unique marshy environment where reeds are the main building material.

Architecturally the most significant time is the early Islamic period up until the tenth century. During this period five major cities were established (Kufa, Basra, Wasit, Baghdad and Samarra) which had an effect on the art and architecture of the whole Islamic world. During the medieval period Iraqi architecture generally follows that of Iran with few innovations or great monuments. One exception to this is the Harba bridge near Samarra which has a long brick inscription which is one of the finest examples of its type. Another exception is a building type known as the conical-domed mausoleum which has its origin in Iraq. The conical dome comprises a tall dome made of interlocking muqarnas vaults which has the

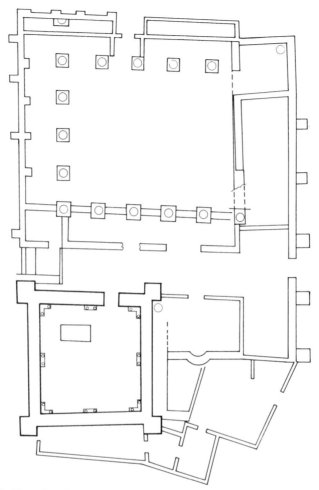

Plan of mosque and tomb of Imam Dur, Samarra, Iraq (after al-Janabi)

appearance of a honeycomb. The earliest example is the tomb of Imam Dur north of Samarra, built by the Seljuk Sharif al-Daula between 1061 and 1065. Other examples in Iraq include the Zumurrud Khatun tomb in Baghdad and the tomb of the prophet Ezekiel in Kifl. From Iraq the form spread to Syria where it was used in Damascus at the tomb and hospital of Nur al-Din.

The main development during the Ottoman period was the development of the shrines at the Shi'a holy cities of Kerbala, Khadamiya, Najaf and Samarra. The architecture of these shrines is mostly Iranian and much of the work was either paid for or built by the Saffavid shahs of Iran. Saffavid influence can also be seen outside the immediate vicinity of the shrines in the pilgrim caravanserais

between Kerbala and Najaf or in some of the bridges in the area.

See also: 'Atshan, Baghdad, Basra, Kufa, Samarra, Ukhaidhir, Wasit

Further reading:

T. al-Janabi, *Studies in Medieval Iraqi Architecture*, Baghdad 1983.

G. Reitlinger, 'Medieval antiquities west of Mosul', *Iraq* 5: 1938.

Isfahan

Capital city of Iran famous for its city planning under the Saffavids in the sixteenth century.

Isfahan is located in western Iran in an area surrounded by deserts. It is supplied with water by

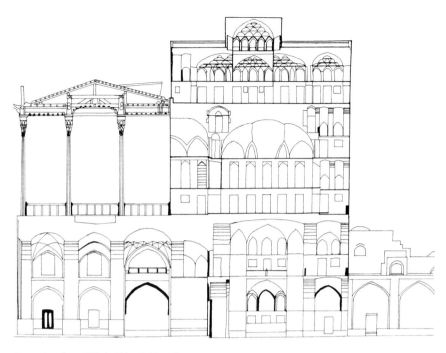

Ali Qapu gateway to palace of Shah Abbas Isfahan, Iran

the Zayandah-Rud which makes settlement in the area possible.

The main building in the city which survives from before the sixteenth century is the Great Mosque. This building was founded in 773 and comprised a prayer hall with a flat roof supported on wooden columns. Nothing remains of this structure, although large parts of the present building, including the north dome and the dome in front of the mihrab, date from the eleventh century. The north dome was built by Terkan Khatun, wife of the Seljuk ruler Malik Shah. Although now incorporated within the mosque it was originally a separate building, possibly another mosque. The most significant feature of the dome is the quality of the brickwork which is the best surviving example of Seljuk brick decoration. The dome in front of the mihrab is of similar quality although this is also decorated with stucco work. In the early twelfth century the Great Mosque was fundamentally redesigned by the creation of four axial iwans making this the earliest example of the four-iwan plan mosque which was later to be the characteristic form for Iranian mosques.

In the sixteenth century the city was completely replanned under the Saffavid ruler Shah Abbas.

The centre of this new plan was the famous maidan which is a huge rectangular open space which could be used for recreation and public displays. The principal buildings of the new capital were built around this maidan. At the south end is the Shah Mosque and facing each other near the middle of the maidan are the Luft 'Allah Mosque and the Ali Qapu or gate to the Shah's palace. At the north end there is a caravanserai and the entrance on to the bazar. To the west of the maidan there was a park area with a long boulevard leading south across the river to a country palace known as the Hazar-Jarib.

See also: Iran

Israel

See Palestine.

Istanbul (Byzantine Constantinople)

Capital city of the Byzantine and Ottoman empires, now the largest city in the modern state of Turkey.

History

Constantinople was founded by the Roman emperor Constantine in 330 CE on the site of an earlier

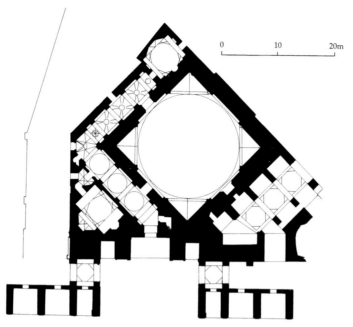

0   10   20m

Plan of seventeenth-century mosque of Luft 'Allah, Isafahan, Iran

town which traced its origins back to the Iron Age. At the centre of Constantine's city was the hippodrome, the imperial palace and the first cathedral of St Sophia (Hagia Sophia). By the fifth century the population of the city had grown so fast that Theodosius expanded the circuit of the city wall to include a large area to the west; these walls remain the boundary of the city. In 1453 the city finally fell to the Ottoman Turks after centuries of gradual Turkish advances. By the time of the final conquest the Ottomans controlled the land on both sides of the city so that it was in effect under permanent siege. The Ottoman conquest was a well-ordered operation which took several years and involved the construction of two large fortresses (Rumeli and Anadolu Hisarlar) on either side of the Bosphorus and two either side of the Dardenelles (Sultan Kale and Kilidbahir Kale) to enforce a blockade of the besieged city. The city which the Ottomans took over was in a dilapidated state with a declining population and and had little of the grandeur associated with the early Byzantine city. Much of the damage had been caused by the Fourth Crusade in the twelfth century which had been diverted from its objective and sacked Constantinople instead.

The city has a unique position on a peninsula at the point where the Bosphorus joins the Sea of Marmara. Surrounded by water on three sides, it has easy access to the Black Sea, the Aegean and the Mediterranean making it ideal as an imperial capital.

During the Ottoman period the city rapidly expanded to include the area of Galta on the opposite side of the Golden Horn and the various towns on the Asian side like Üskudar. Also during this period the banks of the Bosphorus up towards the Black Sea were gradually developed as residential areas and during the eighteenth and nineteenth centuries this became the fashionable area.

After the conquest the hippodrome (Turkish: Atmeydan) and cathedral of St Sophia remained the centre of the city with the cathedral converted into a mosque by the addition of a wooden minaret to one of the turrets. The first Ottoman palace (Eski Sarai) begun in 1454 was built between the old forum and the market area overlooking the Golden Horn. The palace was located in the middle of a park surrounded by high walls and was later abandoned as imperial residence in favour of the Topkapisarai. The new palace built on the site of the former acropolis was completed in 1472 and

Masjid Luft 'Allah, Isfahan, Iran, © *J.W. Allan,*
Ashmolean Museum

remained the centre of the empire until the twentieth century. In addition to the royal palace there were also a number of smaller palaces for notables, the most important of which is the palace of Ibrahim Pasha (now the Islamic Art Museum) located on the north side of the Atmeydan.

Architecture

The first major mosque, the Fatih Cami, was begun in 1463 although smaller mosques were built before that date and some date from before the conquest. Like the Hagia Sophia some of the earliest mosques were converted churches and those that were not (like the Yarhisar Cami) were mostly square domed units with a portico. Despite the conversion of churches in 1459 the Ottomans encouraged the former Christian inhabitants of the city to return and they were offered land grants as an incentive.

With the completion of the Fatih Cami in 1470 the city had its first imperial mosque which was followed forty years later by the Beyazit complex and sixty years later by Selim I's mosque. For nearly 100 years, until the completion of Sinan's masterpiece, the mosque of Suleyman in 1557, the Fatih Cami remained the largest and most important mosque. The Süleymaniye became most important of the imperial mosques for the rest of the Ottoman period, although the Sultan Ahmet Cami (Blue Mosque) with its position next to the Atmeydan (Hippodrome) and its six minarets attracted a lot of attention. Each of the imperial mosques was accompanied by a complex consisting of madrassas (colleges), hospices, bath houses and shops. The revenue from the shops, hammams and any other endowments was used to pay for the upkeep of the mosque and its charitable dependencies. The revenue from the Süleymaniye foundation was still large enough to pay for the upkeep of over 300 people in 1900.

The key to Istanbul's success was its many markets or bazars which continue to be some of the busiest in the Islamic world. Soon after the conquest the city was provided with two bedestans and later a third at Galata. These formed the centre of commercial life in the city with bazars growing up around each bedestan. The commercial centre of the city during the Byzantine period had been the area around Hagia Sophia but during the Ottoman period it moved to its present position near Eminönü and Sirkeci. The centre of this bazar is the bedestan established by Mehmet II which consists of a central hall covered by fifteen domes. In 1701 the bazaar around this bedestan was roofed over to become the covered bazar.

Throughout its history most of the houses of Istanbul were built of wood with stone or brick foundations and tiled roofs. The houses were built out of a wooden frame and then covered with weather boarding on the outside with shallow double pitched roofs. Houses were usually two storeys high and often had cantilevered windows projecting out over the street. The predominant use of wood caused great danger from fires and there were frequent regulations which tried to make people build in brick or stone. Before the twentieth century the skyline of Istanbul was punctuated with frequent water towers which were to be used in the event of fire.

Since Byzantine times water had come into the city along a network of channels and aqueducts from the Belgrade forest. On taking over the city the Ottomans repaired the water system building new aqueducts and dams. During his time as architect of Istanbul Sinan was in charge of the repairs to the water system and built great two-tier aqueducts, the longest of which is three-quarters of a kilometre. Later on during the eighteenth century the reservoirs were used as a place of recreation reflected in the elegant curved design of the dam known as the Valide Bend. Connected to the water system were a range of sebils (fountains) which from the eighteenth century had roofs with huge projecting eaves which came to be regarded as a characteristic feature of Turkish architecture.

See also: Ottomans

Further reading:

N. Atasoy, *Ibrahim Paşa Sarayi*, Istanbul 1972.
B. Y. Berry, 'The development of the bracket support in Turkish domestic architecture in Istanbul', *Ars Islamica* 5: 1938.
W. B. Denny, 'A sixteenth-century architectural plan of Istanbul', *Ars Orientalis* 7: 49–63, 1970.
O. Erdenen, *Istanbul çarşilari ve kapaliçarşi*, İstanbul 1965.
S. Eyice, 'Istanbul minareleri', in *Türk San'ati Tarihi ve Incelemereli*, Istanbul 1963.
J. Freely and H. Sumner-Boyd, *Strolling through Istanbul*, London 1972.
G. Goodwin, *A History of Ottoman Architecture*, London 1971.
R. L. Van Nice and W. Emerson, 'Hagia Sophia and the first minaret erected after the conquest of Istanbul', *American Journal of Archaeology* 54: Jan. 1950.

iwan

A vaulted hall, walled on three sides, with one end entirely open.

Iwans were common in the Sassanian world before Islam and rapidly became incorporated into Islamic architecture. The greatest period of diffusion was under the Seljuks in the tenth century when iwans became established as one of the basic units of Islamic architecture. One of the most typical iwan arrangements is to have four iwans opening on to a central courtyard. The first occurence of this plan is at the Assyrian site of Ashur in Iraq although this later became a typical arrangement for mosques, madrassas and palaces.

Iznik tilework

Ottoman tiles produced from the mid-sixteenth century will have a distinctive under-glaze blue colour and design.

Iznik is a town in north-west Anatolia famed for its pottery production during the Ottoman period. Under the Byzantines the town was known as Nicea and enclosed within a large circuit wall which still survives. The city was one of the first towns to be conquered by the Ottoman Turks and contains the earliest dated Ottoman mosque known as the Haci Özbek Cami.

Before 1550 the kilns of Iznik seem to have been mostly concerned with making pottery rather than tiles. Sometime around 1550 there was a change to tile production which was induced by the tiling of three great monuments, the Dome of the Rock in Jerusalem, the Süleymaniye Mosque in Damascus and the Süleymaniye complex in Istanbul. Before 1550 Ottoman tiles were hexagonal with bold cuerda sec designs, the new Iznik tiles were square and carried underglaze designs. The new shape and use of underglaze painting enabled large multi-tile compositions to be made. Another innovation of this period was the use of thick red slip as an underglaze colour which gave Iznik pottery its distinctive appearance.

See also: Istanbul, Ottomans, Süleymaniye

Further reading:

J. Raby, 'A seventeenth-century description of Iznik-Nicea', *Istanbuler Mitteilungen*, 149–88, 1976.
J. Raby and N. Atasoy, *Iznik: The Pottery of Ottoman Turkey*, London 1989.

J

jali

An Indian term for a perforated stone screen, usually with an ornamental pattern.

jami or jami masjid

A congregational mosque which can be used by all the community for Friday prayers.

jarokha

A Mughal term for a projecting covered balcony, often used for ceremonial appearances.

Java

Large island in south-east Indonesia located between Sumatra and Borneo, now forming the main island of the State of Indonesia.

The earliest traces of Islam in Java may be from as early as the eleventh century in the form of an inscribed tombstone found at Leran. However, it was not until the late fourteenth century that Islam became a major force in the politics of the island. Before the fourteenth century Islam had been a minority religion spread by Muslim sea traders from Malaysia and India. The predominant religion before the arrival of Islam was Hinduism, though some Buddhism also existed there. Central Java is covered with the remains of Hindu temples from this period, the most famous of which is Borabadur. The most important of the states in pre-Islamic Java was the kingdom of Majapahit (founded in 1293) which in the fourteenth century controlled the greater part of Indonesia and large parts of the Malay Peninsula. After the death of King Rajasanagara in 1389 the Majapahit declined rapidly mostly due to the rising power of the Malaysian state of Malacca which by this time had been converted to Islam. The Majapahit kingdom continued until the early sixteenth century when it was finally replaced by Islamic kingdoms.

Despite the political and religious defeat of the Old Javanese state, the culture of Java continued in the Islamic states that replaced it, including their architecture. The centre of Javanese cult life had always been the mountain, often surrounded by the sea. In architecture this was symbolized by artificial hills surrounded by moats, a feature found in the palaces and mosques of the new Islamic states. Three main types of monument have been identified from the Islamic period, these are palaces (*kraton*), mosques and gardens (*taman*).

Palaces

The palaces of the Islamic states developed from those of their Javanese predecessors although it is likely that the Islamic buildings also drew on some other traditions. The Javanese kratons have particular ritual significance and were built as symbolic representations of the cosmos with the king at the centre. The typical layout of the complexes reflects this symbolism with a central area surrounded by symmetrically arranged courtyards. The design of the palaces was fairly conservative and new palaces were built as copies of older palaces and were called 'putra', sons of the old palace. The palace of a particular dynasty formed the capital of a state – when the palace was abandoned and moved elsewhere the status of capital moved with it, and the former site reverted to the status of village. The Islamic palaces may be classified into two main groups: the six palaces of the Mataram dynasty, who replaced the Majapahit kings in the sixteenth century; and the palaces of the earlier Islamic kingdoms of Banten and Cirebon. In addition there were a few palaces and lesser palatial centres including the rebel palaces at Kediri and Pasuruhan and the courts at Demak and Giri.

The oldest Islamic palace in Java is the Kraton Kasepuhan (Palace of the Senior Sultan) built in 1529 by the Cirebon dynasty. This palace has a circular outer enclosure (*beteng*) which together with its monumental gates and pillar bases shows a marked affinity with the palaces of the pre-Islamic

Majapahit kings. Another early palace is that of the Banten dynasty known as the Kraton Surasowan built between 1552 and 1570. The palace is largely ruined, but remains of the rectangular outer enclosure wall with four corner towers survive, as well as a bathing fountain.

The most impressive palaces were those of the Mataram dynasty built between the seventeenth and eighteenth centuries. Not much survives of the three earliest of these palaces known as Kutha Gedhe, Kerta and Plered, although there are substantial remains of the fourth capital Kartasura abandoned in 1746. Remains at Kartasura include the outer enclosure wall (*beteng*) and the inner kraton wall both of which are made of baked red brick. However, the earliest palace of which there are extensive remains is the kraton of Kasunanan Surakarta built in 1746. This palace consists of an outer enclosure wall (*beteng*) 6 m high enclosing a rectangular area 1.8 km long by 1 km wide. The enclosure contains the inner palace in the centre and around it on either side accommodation for the palace staff and courtiers. The palace is arranged on a north–south axis with a walled courtyard (*alun-alun*) projecting on both the north and south sides. The north courtyard measured 300 m per side and was the main square of the town and centre of royal events. It was entered via a gateway in its north wall, guarded by two monster statues robbed from a nearby Hindu temple; in the centre of the courtyard were two sacred banyan trees. The south courtyard was smaller and of less importance, it contained the palace orchard and its main function seems to have been to preserve the symmetry of the north–south axis. A gateway at the back of the north courtyard (*alun-alun*) led into a smaller courtyard within the palace walls; this was the outer audience hall where the king dealt with the public. A further gateway led into two more courtyards opening on to the central courtyard of the palace which functioned as a private audience court. To the west of this was a large building known as the 'Dalem Prabasuyasa', or inner palace, which contained the ritual symbols of kingship. Either side of the central axis were residential areas: to the west the area for women and children (*kauputren*), to the east the residence of the crown prince and his family.

The palace of Yogyakarta begun in 1756 was built when the Mataram kingdom was divided in two. The basic design is identical with Kasunanan Surakarta although the east–west arrangement was reversed and the southern courtyards were more developed.

Gardens

One of the most sophisticated products of Islamic architecture in Java is the pleasure gardens (*taman*). Like Islamic gardens elsewhere the gardens of Java were an extension of the royal palaces and included architectural elements such as fountains and pavilions besides the usual flowers and trees. However, the symbolism of the Javanese gardens differs from that elsewhere in the Islamic world and is based on the dualist theme of mountain and sea derived from pre-Islamic times. This theme is represented by pavilions standing in water and centrally placed towers or artificial hills.

Although gardens were known in pre-Islamic Java none have survived and the earliest example is the Tasik Ardi in the grounds of the sixteenth-century Surasowan Palace. The gardens, however, are attributed to Sultan Agung who laid them out in the mid-seventeenth century. The garden is badly ruined, apart from the central part which has survived; this consists of a square brick tank with a two-storey stone pavilion in the centre. Other early pleasure gardens dating from the beginning of the eighteenth century can be found at the palaces of Cirebon and are composed mostly of artificial hills with caves set into them. One of the caves at the Kasepuhan garden is guarded by two lion statues and was used by the sultan as a place of meditation. A more complex garden known as Sunya Ragi is located on the outskirts of Cirebon and dates from the 1730s. Like the other gardens at Cirebon the gardens of Sunya Ragi are full of artificial hills covered with small pavilions and caves; however, here the gardens are linked by a complex set of passageways and courtyards. To the west of the mountain area was a large lake known as 'the sea' which contained an island with a central pavilion.

The most remarkable garden of Java is the famous Tamam Sari built between 1758 and 1765 next to the palace of Yogyakarta. This is the largest and most complex of all Javanese gardens, containing some fifty buildings enclosed within more than twelve walled gardens. One of the main features of the gardens is the Pula Kenanga which is a large three-storey building set in the middle of a huge basin. The building can only be reached by raft or sub-aquatic passages. One of the most remarkable buildings in the complex is the Sumur Gumulig which has been variously interpreted as a mosque and place of meditation for the sultan. The building consists of a tall two-storey structure set in the middle of the lake and it can only be reached by a sub-aquatic passage. There are two storeys inside the tower with an open central space; within this area four staircases rise from the ground floor to a central circular platform level with the second storey. A single staircase leads from the platform to the top floor which gives a view over the lake.

Mosques

The earliest mosques in Java were built from the mid-fifteenth century onwards, although there is an earlier reference to mosques in the fourteenth-century Majapahit capital. Unfortunately no early mosques have yet been discovered in Java and the oldest extant structures date from the sixteenth century.

The standard plan of a Javanese congregational mosque consists of a square enclosure with a central platform in the centre on which the main mosque building stands. The enclosure walls are usually fairly low and are decorated with inset bowls and plates from China and elsewhere and in the middle of the east side there is a monumental gate. In many of the early mosques which have survived, the central part of the mosque is further enclosed by a moat. In front of the mosque on the east side is a smaller subsidiary building called the *surambi*, used for social activities, study and the call to prayer. The sanctuary or central building of the mosque is a raised square wooden structure supported by four giant corner posts, between which small pillars take the weight of the wooden walls. The roofs are usually tiered structures made of thatch, with the number of tiers reflecting the importance of the mosque. The minimum number of tiers is two whilst the maximum is five, the top roof usually being crowned with a finial called a *mustaka*. The tiered roof structure is essential to keep these enclosed buildings cool and dry.

Sometimes the roof tiers represent a division into separate floors each of which is used for a different function; thus the lower floor may be used as the prayer room whilst the middle floor is used for study and the top floor for the call to prayer. Minarets were not introduced into Java until the end of the nineteenth century so that in mosques where there is only one storey the call to prayer is made from a veranda or from the attached *surambi*. The *surambi* was not present in the earliest mosques in Java and seems to have been introduced in the seventeenth century.

Inside the mosque there are one or two mihrabs in the west wall and a minbar made of wood, usually teak. The mihrab niches are made of brick or wood and are highly decorated with deep wood-carving derived from the pre-Islamic art of the area. In addition to the congregational mosques there are small neighbourhood mosques (*langgar*) which are small wooden structures raised up on four poles in the manner of typical Javanese houses.

Traditionally the Mesjid Agung at Demak is one of the oldest mosques in Java and is said to have been founded in 1506 although the present structure has been rebuilt and altered many times since, most recently in 1974–5. The mosque has a three-tiered roof and, unusually, a special women's prayer area separated from the main mosque by a narrow corridor. Also of an early date (sixteenth century) is the congregational mosque at Banten which is located to the west of the main square (*alun-alun lor*). The mosque has a five-tiered roof, although within the building has only three storeys. To the south of the mosque is a rectangular structure used as a social centre or meeting place (*surambi*) which was built by the Dutchman Lucas Cardeel in the seventeenth century. Within the enclosure is a tall tower also built in the Dutch style which functions as a minaret for the mosque. Nearby are the remains of another sixteenth-century mosque, also with traces of a stone tower. Both towers date to the mid-sixteenth century, which raises several questions as they pre-date the supposed introduction of minarets into Java by 300 years.

A similar question is posed by the menara and mesjid at Kudus also dated to the mid-sixteenth century. The mosque itself has been rebuilt since its foundation and represents a fairly standard mosque design. The menara or minaret consists of a tower-like brick structure with a split gateway and pottery dishes inlaid into the sides. The design of the menara resembles the lower part of East

Javanese temples and may actually be a re-used pre-Islamic structure. However, it should be pointed out that many of the earliest mosques were built with pre-Islamic features. The remains of the sixteenth-century mosque of Sendhang Dhuwur incorporate many Hindu Indonesian features in its stone- and wood-relief carving. The winged gateways present a particularly striking image of this style.

See also: Indonesia

Further reading:

H. M. Ambary, *Historical Monuments: Cerbon*, Jakarta 1982.
—— 'Laporan penelitian kepurbakalaan di Pajang (Jawa Tengah)', *Archipel* 1983, 75–84.
T. E. Behrend, 'Kraton, taman and mesjid: a brief survey and bibliographic review of Islamic antiquities in Java', *Indonesia Circle* 35: 29–55, Nov. 1984.
L. F. Brakel and H. Massarik, 'A note on the Panjuan Mosque in Cirebon', *Archipel* 23: 119–34, 1982.
K. P. H. Brongtodiningrat, *Arti Kraton Yogyakarta* (trans. R. Murdani), Yogyakarta 1978.
H. D. de Graaf, 'The origin of the Javanese mosque', *Journal of Southeast Asian History* 4(i): 1–5, 1963.
D. Lombard, 'Jardins à Java', *Arts Asiatiques* 20: 135–83, 1969.
—— 'A travers le vieux Djakarta: I. La Mosquée des Balinais', *Archipel* 3: 97–101, 1972.
T. G. T. Pigeaud, *Java in the 14th Century: A Study in Cultural History. The Nagra-Kertagama by Rakawi Prapanca of Majapahit 1365* (3 edn.), 5 vols., The Hague 1960–3.
G. F. Pijper, 'The minaret in Java', in *India Antiqua: A Volume of Studies Presented to J. P. Vogel*, Leiden 1947, 274–83.
M. C. Ricklefs, *Jogyakarta under Sultan Mangkubumi, 1749–1792: A History of Division in Java* (London Oriental Series 30), London 1974.
U. Tjandrasasmita, *Islamic Antiquities of Sendag Duwur*, Jakarta 1975.
—— 'The introduction of Islam and the growth of Moslem coastal cities in the Indonesian Archipelago', in *Dynamics of Indonesian History*, ed. H. Soebadio and M. Sarvas, Amsterdam 1978.

Jerusalem (al Quds)

Major religious city in Palestine sacred to Muslims, Jews and Christians.

Within the Muslim faith Jerusalem is regarded as the third holiest shrine and the second most important place of pilgrimage after Mecca. Muslims know Jerusalem as the city of the prophets and the place of Muhammad's night journey. The importance of the site to the Jews is that it was the site of the Temple built by Solomon in the 10th century BCE, whilst the Christians know it as the place where Christ was crucified and resurrected.

The first walled town on the site dates from the Middle Bronze Age (1800 BCE). The earliest literary reference is also from the same period when the city is mentioned as one of the enemies of Egypt. The next mention of the city is from the Amarna letters in the fourteenth century BCE. The main source for the subsequent history of the city is the Bible which describes its capture from the Jebusites under David, and the building of the Temple under Solomon.

In 70 CE the Romans destroyed the city in response to the Jewish Revolt. The site lay uninhabited for the next seventy-five years until the emperor Hadrian founded a new city known as Aelia Capitolina. Jews were specifically excluded from this new city and the area of the Temple was left undeveloped (and remained so until the Arab conquest). The layout of the present Old City of Jerusalem is approximately the same as that of the Roman town. In 324 Palestine became part of the Christian Eastern Roman Empire (Byzantium) under Constantine who founded the Church of the Holy Sepulchre in 325–6 CE. Constantine's mother took an active part in promoting the building of Christian places of worship during this period. A depiction of the city in the Madaba Mosaic Map shows it in the sixth century before the Muslim conquest. From 614 to 629 the city was in the possession of the Sassanians under Chosroes II who destroyed many Christian buildings. In 629 the city was recaptured by the Byzantines under Heraclius only to be conquered by the Muslim Arab armies ten years later. For the following 1,200 years (with the exception of the Crusader occupation) Jerusalem developed as major Islamic city although it never developed into a great commercial or administrative centre.

The main building material used for Jerusalem was stone, as wood has always been fairly scarce. The main types of stone available were limestone and Dolomite. Four types of limestone can be found in the Jerusalem region, of which two were used for building in the Islamic period. (i) Mizzi, is a hard fine-grained stone sometimes known as 'Palestinan Marble'. This occurs in two varieties, a reddish type known as mizzi ahmar from near Bethlehem and a yellowish variety from Dayr Yasin 5 km east of the city. (ii) Malaki which is less hard than mizzi but is still hard and fine grained. Outcrops were quarried to the north of the city at Solomon's Quarries and in the Kidron valley.

The development of Islamic Jerusalem can be divided into four main periods: (i) the early Islamic period from the Arab conquest to the first Crusade, (ii) the Crusader period, (iii) the Ayyubid and Mamluk periods and (iv) the Ottoman period.

Early Islamic Period

During the early Islamic period the area of the Temple Mount (Haram) was developed for the first time since Hadrian's destruction in 70 CE. The first mosque known to have been built in Jerusalem was erected by the caliph 'Umar and was described by the Christian pilgrim Arculf as 'a rectangular place of prayer ... roughly built by setting big beams on the remains of some ruins'. However, nothing of this early structure remains so that the earliest surviving structure in the city is the Dome of the Rock built by Abd al-Malik in 691. This is a large, domed octagonal structure built over the bare rock of the Temple platform, below which is a cave. Related to the Dome of the Rock is the Qubbat al-Silsila which was probably built at the same time.

To the south of the Dome of the Rock is the Aqsa Mosque which may have been started under Abd al-Malik although most of the construction was carried out under al-Walid. The mosque has been rebuilt several times subsequently although it is believed that the present structure maintains the basic layout of al-Walid's mosque. It has recently been demonstrated that the walls of the Haram were probably rebuilt at this time and provided with gateways, thus suggesting that the area was systematically developed by the Umayyads probably as a rival to the Church of the Holy Sepulchre. Further evidence for this comes from the excavations to the south of the Haram which have revealed a large Umayyad palace located at the back of the Aqsa Mosque. This follows the pattern established at other early Islamic cities such as Kufa, where the royal palace Dar al Imara is placed behind the mihrab.

Although it is known that many repairs and rebuildings were carried out during the Abbasid and Fatimid periods there was no major building programme similar to that carried out under the Umayyads.

Crusader Period

The capture of Jerusalem by the Crusaders marked an abrupt end to four and a half centuries of Muslim rule. The Crusader occupation completely changed the character of the city as the Muslim inhabitants had either been killed, fled or sold for ransom. Even most of the Christian inhabitants had fled and the Crusaders had problems repopulating the city with Europeans.

One of the first priorities of the Crusaders was to rebuild Christian churches and monuments and convert Islamic buildings to other uses. Thus the Church of the Holy Sepulchre was expanded by adding a Romanesque transept to the east side of the Rotunda. Elsewhere in the city over sixty churches were built or renovated, whilst mosques were converted into churches. The Dome of the Rock was given to the Augustinians who made it into a church whilst in 1104 Baldwin I made the Aqsa Mosque into a royal palace.

Some of the houses built during this period were similar to southern European town houses with two or three storeys above a shop or store room. However, other houses were built with courtyards in a style more familiar to the Middle East. Several suqs were built during this period and the main suq in the centre of the Old City was largely built during this period. This is a covered street with shop units either side and light openings in the roof.

The Crusades influenced the subsequent architecture of Jerusalem in several ways including the introduction of the folded cross vault and the use of cushion-shaped voussoirs.

Ayyubid and Mamluk Period

In 1188 Jerusalem was recaptured by Salah al-Din and reconverted into a Muslim city. The Haram was cleared of its Christian accretions and reconsecrated as Muslim sanctuary. The cross was removed from the top of the Dome of the Rock and replaced with a golden crescent and a wooden screen was placed around the rock below. Also at this time the famous wooden minbar of Salah al-Din was placed next to the new mihrab in the Aqsa Mosque. However, the major building projects of the Ayyubid period date mostly to the time of Salah al-Din's nephew al-Malik al-Mu'azzam Isa. During this period the most important project was rebuilding the city walls. Within the Haram certain restorations were carried out and at least two madrassas were founded, the Nahawiyya and the Mu'azzamiyya. Also the porch of the Aqsa Mosque was built during this period.

In the later Ayyubid period (first half of the thirteenth century) Jerusalem was again subjected to invasions first by the Crusaders and later by the Khwazmian Turks so that no substantial building work was carried out.

The Mamluk period lasted from 1250 to 1516 and has provided Jerusalem with some of its most beautiful and distinctive architecture. Over sixty-four major monuments survive from this period and testify to the city's wealth and confidence. The Haram in particular received a great deal of attention from the Mamluk sultans who regarded the patronage of building in this area as a royal prerogative. During this period the walls of the Haram were repaired and the interior of the west wall was provided with an arcaded portico. Several major buildings were built within the Haram, one of the more important of which is the Ashrafiyya Madrassa built on the west side. Several attempts were made to build this structure although the final attempt only took two years with masons sent from Cairo. The most impressive part is the open-sided porch, roofed with a complex folded cross vault, with alternate stones painted red to resemble ablaq.

Elsewhere within the Haram various sebils, tombs and monuments were erected. One of the most beautiful of these is the Sebil Qaitbay (built in 1482) which consists of a small three-tiered structure. The tallest part is the square base (about 5 m high), above which is a complex zone of transition (about 2 m), surmounted by a tall dome (about 3.5 m high). The exterior of the dome is carved in low relief with arabesque designs and resembles the carved masonry domes of mausoleums in Cairo, although the form of the carving suggests local workmanship.

One of the most productive reigns was that of Sultan al-Nasir Muhammad during which time the Suq al-Qattinin was built. This is the largest Mamluk complex in Jerusalem and consisted of over fifty shops with living quarters above, two bath houses and a khan.

Characteristic features of Mamluk architecture in Jerusalem include ablaq masonry in a variety of colours (black, yellow, white and red), muqarnas used in corbels, squinches and zones of transition, joggled voussoirs used for supporting arches, composite lintels and relieving arches.

Ottoman Period

One of the best-known buildings of Jerusalem is the Damascus Gate with its monumental bent entrance, crenellated parapet, machicolations, arrow slits and inscriptions. It forms part of the city wall erected by Suleyman the Magnificent between 1538 and 1541. This was one of the many building projects begun in Jerusalem at this time to renew the city's infrastructure and demonstrate that Jerusalem was now part of the Ottoman Empire. By the end of Suleyman's reign the population of Jerusalem had grown to three times its size at the beginning. Another project initiated during this period was the covering of the outside of the Dome of the Rock with Iznik tiles. This took a period of at least seven years during which several techniques of tiling were used, including cut tile-work, cuerda seca, polychrome underglaze, and blue and white underglaze. Also during this period the water system of the city was overhauled with repairs carried out to the Birket al-Sultan and Solomon's pools. Within the city this was reflected in the erection of a series of sebils (drinking fountains).

The later Ottoman period in Jerusalem has not been studied in any detail although a number of inscriptions refer to repairs and rebuilding. During the nineteenth century new suburbs grew up around the old city and there was increased European influence in the architecture.

Further reading:

M. Burgoyne, *The Architecture of Islamic Jerusalem*, Jerusalem 1976.

M. Burgoyne and D. Richards, *Mamluk Jerusalem: An Architectural Study*, London 1987.

A. Cohen, 'The walls of Jerusalem', in *Essays in Honour of Bernard Lewis: The Islamic World from Classical to Modern Times*, ed. C. E. Bosworth, C. Issawi, R. Savory and A. Udovitch, Princeton, N.J., 1989, 467–78.

K. Prag, *Jerusalem Blue Guide*, London 1989.

D. Pringle, 'Crusader architecture in Jerusalem', *Bulletin of the Anglo–Israel Archaeological Society* 10: 105–13, 1990–1.

M. Rosen-Ayalon, 'Art and architecture in Ayyubid Jerusalem', *Israel Exploration Journal* 40(4): 305–14, 1990.

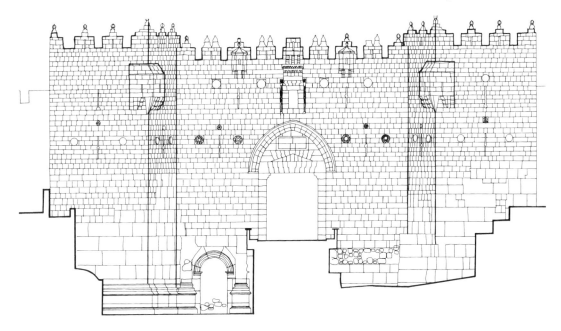

Damascus Gate with remains of Roman gate below, Jerusalem

Joggled string course

joggled voussoirs

Term used to describe a method of construction where stones in an arch or composite lintel are interlocked.

The earliest examples of joggled voussoirs are found in Roman architecture particularly in Spain and France where they are used in bridge construction. It seems that the purpose of this structural device was to strengthen lintels and arches during earthquakes, thus the arch could be pulled apart but would fall back to its original position afterwards.

The first use of joggled voussoirs in Islamic architecture is for the lintel above the entrance to the greater enclosure at Qasr al-Hayr East. Later on (twelfth century) they become characteristic of Ayyubid architecture and stones of alternating colours were used. Under the Mamluks (mid-thirteenth to early sixteenth century) they are one of the main decorative features in architecture and

are cut into very complex patterns. At this stage the patterns become more important than the structural design thus the patterns are sometimes achieved by inlaying one type of stone into another or even painting the design on.

Jordan (Hashemite Kingdom of Jordan)

Small country (88,946 square km) located at the east end of the Mediterranean, bordering Palestine, Syria, Iraq and Saudi Arabia.

Jordan can be divided into four main zones, each of which extends into neighbouring countries. In the north of the country the landscape is dominated by black basalt rock which in places forms an almost impenetrable barrier to travel. The oasis of Azraq is located on the southern edge of this region and functions as a station for eastbound

137

traffic to Iraq. The western edge of the country lies within the Jordan valley where it borders Palestine; this area is known locally as the Ghor and includes both the area of the Dead Sea and the east side of the wadi Arabah. The highland area to the east of the Dead Sea and the Jordan river is the most densely populated area of the country and includes the main cities of Amman, Irbid and Zerka. To the south and east of this region is the desert known as the Badiyya; this includes a variety of landscapes ranging from dry steppe in the north to large expanses of sandy desert in the south around Wadi Rum.

Jordan was not a fully independent state until 1946; before this period it formed part of various empires, kingdoms and lordships. Nevertheless, Jordan has one of the longest and richest archaeological sequences in the Middle East, which is reflected in architecture such as the 9,000-year-old Neolithic houses of Beidha. Probably the best-known architecture of Jordan is that of the Nabatean city of Petra which dates mostly from the period between the first century BCE and the third century CE. Here a series of magnificent façades are carved into the rose-coloured rock reflecting the wealth and connections of the Nabatean kingdom. Further north a series of cities known as the Decapolis (including Jerash, Umm Qeis, Umm al-Jemal, Pella and Amman) testify to the prosperity of this area during the Classical and Byzantine period. During the Byzantine period numerous churches with mosaics were built, the most famous of which is one at Madaba which includes a mosaic map of Palestine.

In 631 the first Arab armies invaded the prosperous lands of the Byzantine Empire. After an initial defeat at Mu'tah the Arabs eventually triumphed over the Byzantines at the battle of Yarmouk near the city of Pella. During the next 120 years Jordan was enriched with some of the finest examples of early Islamic architecture found anywhere, including the painted bath house of Qusayr Amra and the palace of Mshatta. Subsequent periods in the history of Jordan are not so well known, with the exception of the Crusader period, when magnificent strongholds were built by both Arabs and Crusaders.

The main building materials in Jordan are basalt in the north, limestone and sandstone in the central highlands and mud brick in the Jordan valley and in areas of the desert. Occasionally in the early Islamic period baked brick was employed for vaulting, although this was not repeated in the later periods. The best examples of basalt construction can be seen at Umm al-Jemal where a system of corbels supporting basalt beams was employed. Limestone was used in some of the finer architecture of Roman and early Islamic Jordan because it can be dressed to a fine finish. Mud brick does not survive well, but representative examples of mud-brick architecture can be seen in the oasis town of Ma'an.

Umayyad architecture in Jordan contains a mixture of eastern and western influences with the result that the surviving buildings represent a variety of different architectural types some of which were never repeated (i.e. the use of baked brick and stone at Mshatta and Tuba). Generally buildings from this period may be grouped into three categories: (i) those which are purely developments of Roman Byzantine architecture, (ii) those which are heavily influenced by Persian (Sassanian) architectural concepts and (iii) buildings which combine both eastern and western traditions.

Roman-Byzantine Influence

Probably the most famous Islamic building in Jordan is the bath house of Qusayr Amra located in the desert approximately 60 km west of Amman. The building stands alone apart from a small fort or caravanserai several kilometres to the north. Inside the building the walls and ceilings are decorated with a remarkable series of frescoes, including depictions of bathing women, a series of royal portraits, a hunting scene and the zodiac. Although the choice of pictures is certainly Umayyad the style of painting and the design of the bath house is purely Byzantine.

Some of the best-known Umayyad castles are re-used Roman forts or fortresses, whilst others are built in the style of Roman forts with more luxurious fittings. Qasr Hallabat is a square Roman fort 44 m per side with square corner towers. It was originally built in the second century CE to protect the Via Nova Traiana and later expanded in 212–215 CE and restored in 529. Careful excavation and analysis of the fort show that it was subsequently changed into an Umayyad residence with mosaics, painted plaster (frescoes), carved and painted wood and finely carved stucco with geometric, floral and animal motifs. To the east of the castle is a tall rectangular mosque with three entrances and a mihrab in the south wall; this building was also decorated with stucco work. Outside the forts, remains of an Umayyad agricultural settlement have been found including small houses. Approximately 3 km to the south of Hallabat is a bath house also of the Umayyad period which probably served Qasr Hallabat. The bath house is similar to that of Qasayr Amra and was decorated with painted plasterwork and stucco. Whilst the particular combination of structures and their design is characteristic of the Umayyad period (a fort converted to palace, bath house and mosque), the individual elements and building style at Hallabat are all Byzantine.

A similar structure to Hallabat is the Umayyad complex at Qastal (25 km south of Amman) which until recently was thought to have been built as a Roman or Byzantine fort. However, recent research has shown that all the main structures date from the Umayyad period. The main structure are a fort-like palace, a mosque, a bath house, reservoir, dams, cisterns, a cemetery and domestic houses. The central palace complex consists of a square fort-like building (about 68 m per side) with four round corner towers and intermediate semi-circular buttress towers. The decoration within the palace is similar to that found at Hallabat and includes mosaics, stucco work and carved stonework. Internally the building consists of a central courtyard opening on to six buyut (pl. of bayt) or houses. Probably the most impressive feature of the building

Interior of Qasr Kharana, Jordan

was the large triple-apsed audience hall, located directly above the entrance.

Sassanian Influence ('Eastern')

Structures representing strong Sassanian or eastern influences are less numerous although perhaps more striking because of their obviously foreign derivation. Perhaps the best-known building of this type is Qasr Kharana (located 50 km east of Amman on the present Baghdad–Amman highway). Kharana consists of a two-storey square-plan structure, 35 m per side, with small projecting corner towers and a projecting rounded entrance. The building is remarkable for its superb state of preservation, which includes *in situ* plasterwork on the upper floor. The building is made out of roughly shaped blocks set in a mud-based mortar with decorative courses of flat stones placed in bands running around the outside of the building. There are also small slits set within the wall which were probably for ventilation (their size and positioning means that they could not have been used as arrow slits). Internally the building is decorated with pilasters, blind niches and medallions finished in plaster. The whole appearance of the building is so different from other Umayyad structures in Jordan that scholars have tried to attribute it to the period of Sassanian occupation of the area despite an eighth-century inscription. The best parallels for Kharana are to be found in early Islamic buildings in Iraq such as Khan 'Atshan (similar size and decoration) and Qasr Khubbaz which is built using the same materials (i.e. rough stone blocks set in mud mortar).

Another building erroneously attributed to the Sassanian period is the palace on the citadel in Amman. Like Kharana the Amman citadel building exhibits unmistakable eastern influence in its architecture and layout. The best preserved part of the palace is the building known as the kiosk. This is constructed on a four-iwan plan and decorated with blind niches lined with plaster, a common feature of Sassanian and Umayyad architecture in Iraq (e.g. Ctesiphon and Ukhaidhir). The layout of the palace was huge with at least twelve courtyards arranged on a linear plan. At the opposite end of the complex from the kiosk was a large iwan leading to a cruciform-plan audience hall. All of these features are reminiscent of Mesopotamian palace arcitecture, where palaces are like small cities, containing both administrative and residential areas.

East–West Influence

Two buildings dated to the later Umayyad period (probably the reign of Walid II 743–4) represent a combination of eastern and western influences. The most obvious demonstration of these mixed influences is the use of baked brick for vaults and walls and dressed stone masonry for foundations and architectural details. The most famous of these buildings is Qasr Mshatta located 25 km to the south of Amman. This consists of a large square enclosure with four semi-circular buttress towers. The best-known feature of this palace is the southern façade which consists of a delicately carved stone frieze incorporating animals and plant motifs within a geometric scheme of giant triangles. Internally the building is divided into three longitudinal strips; only the central strip (running north–south) was developed and contains within it the entrance, the central courtyard and the audience hall. The audience hall consists of a triple-apsed room covered by a large brick dome. The layout of the palace immediately recalls that of the Abbasid palaces of Iraq such as Ukhaidhir and has led some scholars to suggest an Abbasid date for the structure. Byzantine elements are also present, however, most notably in the basilical arrangement of the approach to the triple-apsed room and in the motifs of the stonework

Although Qasr al-Tuba is in many respects similar to Mshatta it is much simpler in its decoration and is generally thought to be closer to a caravanserai than a palace. Qasr al-Tuba is the largest of the desert castles and consists of two identical halves, the southern half of which appears never to have been built. Stacks of bricks on the floor testify to the unfinished nature of the building, although it is possible that some of the structure was originally built out of mud brick. Originally there were some fine carved stone lintels at Tuba but these have now disappeared.

Medieval Period

Standing remains of the Abbasid and Fatimid period in Jordan are rare and architectural remains are mostly limited to archaeological excavations. The reasons for this are complex and related to the fall of the Umayyads and Jordan's peripheral position in relation to the Abbasid and Fatimid caliphates. The only place where significant architectural remains from this period have been uncovered are at Aqaba on Jordan's Red Sea coast. This town seems to have reached its peak of prosperity during the Abbasid and Fatimid periods, when it was a trading port in contact with Iraq, Yemen, Egypt and China. Excavations at the site have revealed a walled town (160 by 120 m approximately) with rounded buttress towers and four gateways providing access to the two main streets. Sometime during the Fatimid period mud brick replaced cut stone as the building material for many of the houses.

The Ayyubid and Mamluk periods are marked by the intrusion of the Crusaders who built castles at Karak, Shawbak and Petra to control movement between Egypt and Syria. As a result of the Crusader presence most of the well-known buildings from this period are castles and forts. Examples of Islamic forts can be seen at Azraq, Ajlun, Jise and Qasr Shebib (the Crusader castles at Karak and Shawbak were also remodelled during this period). The best example of medieval fortification can be seen at Qal'at Rabad (Ajlun) built in 1184–5. This consists of several thick walled towers with V-shaped arrow slits linked by curtain walls. The masonry of the castle consists of large blocks similar to those used by the Crusaders at Karak and Shawbak.

In addition to the large castles several smaller forts survive from the medieval period. These

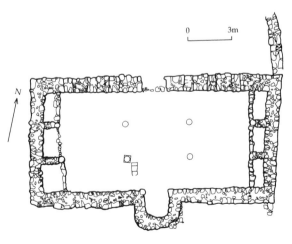

Mamluk mosque at Pella, Jordan (after Bishe)

were either built to protect the road system or as signal posts. Probably the most important route in Jordan was the pilgrimage route from Damascus to Mecca; several forts on this route have survived, notably the forts at Jise and Qasr Shebib in Zerka. Related to these forts is the Mamluk fortified khan at Aqaba. This is a rectangular structure with circular corner towers and a deep protected entrance. The form of the arch above the entrance recalls the architecture of Mamluk Egypt with its ablaq masonry and horseshoe arch.

Later Islamic Architecture

The best-known examples of early Ottoman architecture in Jordan are the Hajj forts which were built to protect the pilgrimage route from Damascus to Mecca. The earliest of the these forts were built in the sixteenth century during the reign of Suleyman the Magnificent. These were small square structures with large decorated arrow slits, projecting machicolations and large crenellated parapets. In the late eighteenth century the fort network was expanded to counter increased bedouin raids. Forts of this period are more functional and have small gun slits instead of large arrow slits, with projecting corner towers to increase the field of fire.

Other early Ottoman buildings in Jordan are difficult to date so precisely, although the fortified farmsteads at Yadudeh and Udruh probably both date from the eighteenth century.

The best examples of nineteenth-century architecture in Jordan can be seen at al-Salt west of Amman and at Umm Qeis north of Irbid. The architecture of both towns shows strong Palestinian influence. Salt in particular shares many features with Nablus. Amman, however, differs from the other cities in north Jordan as it was settled by Circassian refugees. Characteristic features of Circassian houses are the use of wood, the introduction of chimneys and small rooms.

Several mosques of the medieval period are known in Jordan, the finest of which was the twelfth-century structure at Mazar, near Mut'ah (this has now been destroyed). Mamluk mosques can also be seen at Pella and in the fort at Azraq; these are rectangular structures with flat roofs resting on arches supported by columns.

Further reading:

G. L. Harding, *The Antiquities of Jordan,* London 1967.

S. Helms, with A. V. G. Betts, W. and F. Lancaster and C. J. Lenzen, *Early Islamic Architecture of the Desert: A Bedouin Station in Eastern Jordan,* Edinburgh 1990.

A. Khammash, *Notes on the Village Architecture of Jordan,* Louisiana 1986.

R. G. Khoury, *Pella: A Brief Guide to the Antiquities,* Amman and Sydney 1988.

—— *Amman: A Brief Guide to the Antiquities,* Amman 1988.

—— *The Desert Castles: A Brief Guide to the Antiquities,* Amman 1988.

—— *Petra: A Brief Guide to the Antiquities,* Amman 1988.

A. McQuitty, 'An architectural study of the Irbid region with particular reference to a building in Irbid', *Levant* 21: 119–28, 1989.

A. D. Petersen, 'Early Ottoman forts on the Darb al-Hajj', *Levant* 21: 97–117, 1989.

—— 'Two medieval forts on the medieval Hajj route in Jordan', *Annual of the Department of Antiquities of Jordan* 35: 347–89, 1991.

K

Ka'ba

Most sacred building of Islam located in the centre of the Holy Mosque in Mecca.

In its present form the Ka'ba consists of a tall, rectangular, box-like structure 15 m high with sides measuring 10.5 m by 12 m. The building is oriented 30 degrees off the north–south axis so that

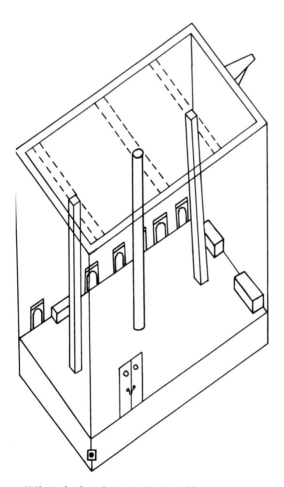

Ka'ba in the eleventh century (after Jairazbhoy)

the corners face the cardinal points. The flat roof has a gentle slope towards the north-west where there is a water spout (mizab al-rahman, or spout of mercy). The Black Stone (possibly derived from a meteorite) is built into the eastern corner of the structure. Also at the east corner is another stone known as Hajar as'ad (the lucky stone) which is touched during the circumambulation. Outside the north-west side there is a low semicircular wall which encloses an area known as the Hijr which is believed to mark the burial place of Ismail and his mother Hajar. The Ka'ba is built of large blue-grey granite blocks set in mortar resting on a base of marble. The entrance is on the north-east side and is 2 m above ground level (it is reached by a portable set of wooden steps). Inside the Ka'ba there are three tall wooden pillars which support the wooden roof which can be reached by a wooden ladder. The floor is made of marble and the ceiling is covered with cloth hangings.

According to Muslim tradition the Ka'ba was built by Ibrahim and Ismail and was the first sanctuary established on earth. This early building was simply a rectangular unroofed enclosure the height of a man. Idols were housed within the Ka'ba, the most prominent of whom were al-Lat, al-Uzza and al-Manat. Three hundred and sixty idols were arranged in a circle outside the Ka'ba forming a sacred area (Haram) where no blood could be shed. In the time of Muhammad the old Ka'ba was burnt down and it was rebuilt with the help of a man called Baqum. This new Ka'ba was built of alternate layers of stone and wood, possibly in a similar fashion to traditional Meccan houses. The height of the building was doubled and it was covered with a roof. The entrance to the building was some distance from the ground and a ladder was needed to enter it. Muhammad is said to have placed the Black Stone in its position with the help of the main tribal leaders.

In 629 after a period of exile Muhammad conquered Mecca but left the form of the Ka'ba unaltered (except for the removal of idols). In 683 during the conflict between Abd Allah Ibn Zubayr and the Umayyads the Ka'ba was destroyed by stones hurled by catapults. After the Umayyads withdrew the Ka'ba was rebuilt on a larger scale with two doors. This Ka'ba was subsequently destroyed by the Umayyad general Hajjaj bin Yusuf who rebuilt it in its previous form with only one door. This is essentially the form of the present Ka'ba although the Black Stone was removed for a period of twenty years by the Qarmathians in 929. Flood damage in 1611 necessitated its rebuilding in 1630, although the old form of the building was retained. A continuous feature of the Ka'ba's history, at least from Muhammad's time, is that the outside of the structure is covered with a huge cloth of fabric (kiswa) which is replaced annually. During the first years of Islam the old covers were not removed and new covers were placed on top. This practice was stopped in the Umayyad period as the weight of cloths was thought to threaten the stability of the Ka'ba.

See also: Mecca

Further reading:

H. A. A. Ba Salama, *Tarikh al-kab'a al mu'azzama*, 2nd printing, Jeddah 1982.

R. A. Jairazbhoy, 'The architecture of the Holy Shrine in Makkah', in *Hajj in Focus*, ed. Z. I. Khan and Y. Zaki, London 1986.

V. Strika , 'A Ka'bah picture in the Iraq Museum', *Sumer* 32: 195–201, 1976

A. J. Wensinck and J. Jomier, 'Ka'ba', in *Encyclopedia of Islam*, new edn. 4: 317–22, 1978.

Kano

Major Islamic city in the Hausa region, northern Nigeria.

Kano is the most famous of a group of cities including Zaria, Katsina, Gobir, Daura, Biram and Rano which trace their origins back to the eleventh century. At this time Kano was probably pagan, although Muslim traders may have been living there. During the fourteenth century the city was at least superficially Muslim but it was not until the end of the fifteenth century that Kano was firmly established as an Islamic town. The Kano Chronicle records how an Egyptian, Cabd al-Rahman, came to Kano to confirm Islam in the town and build a Friday mosque with a minaret there. During the eighteenth century there was a large migration of

people to Kano from the city of Agades in present-day Mali. This influx had a great effect on the culture and architecture of Kano making it into a centre of scholarship and trade.

The city is surrounded by mud-brick walls which at their maximum extent enclose an area more than 15 km in circumference. The area within the walls includes not only the city itself but agricultural and grazing land as well. The city wall is pierced by several monumental gateways, including the massive triple-arched Nasarawa Gate. Inside the city are narrow streets leading on to houses which consist of square or irregular-shaped compounds. A typical compound (or gida) is entered via a circular entrance vestibule that leads into an outer courtyard which may contain huts for unmarried sons and a reception room. At the back of the rectangular reception room is a door leading to the inner courtyard which contains the owner's house, huts for his wives, granaries, a well and a bathroom. The best houses are located within the fifteenth-century palace compound of the emir known as the Gidan Rumfa which is a large area of over 30 acres. This compound is entered via an ancient gatehouse known as the Kofar Kwaru which, with an internal height of 9 m, is the highest internal space in Kano. Within the compound are grazing land for the royal cattle, houses of retainers and public reception rooms, as well as the apartments of the ruler himself. Since the early twentieth century the internal layout of the palace has changed with circular entrance vestibules (zaure) replaced with rectangular rooms (this reflects a wider development in Hausa architecture where rectangular buildings are replacing round constructions). The most elaborately decorated part of the palace is the royal audience chamber which consists of rectangular rooms covered with domed roofs supported on intersecting arches. Both the soffits of the arches and the ceiling panels in between are decorated with brightly painted moulded abstract designs.

The famous Great Mosque of Kano (now destroyed) may be the mosque erected by Cabd al-Rahman in the fifteenth century although little of the structure remains to confirm this. One of the better known mosques of the town is the Yangoro Mosque built by the famous master-mason Bala Gwani. The mosque is divided into a series of small rectangular domed bays (2.75 by 3.35 m) resting on two-tier arches.

See also: Fulbe, Hausa, West Africa
Further reading:
D. Heathecote, 'The Princess's apartments in Kano Old Treasury', *Savanna* 2(1), 1973.
A. Leary, 'A decorated palace in Kano', *Art and Archaeology Research Papers* 12: 1–17, 1977.
H. Palmer, 'The Kano Chronicle', in *Sudanese Memoirs*, vol. 3, 1928.

kapilica

Turkish term for a specialized form of bath house, or hammam, where the building is provided with hot water from a thermal spring. Kapilicas usually have swimming pools unlike the usual Ottoman bath house.

Karaman (Laranda)

City in Konya region of Anatolia noted for its medieval architecture.

In 1071 the Byzantine city of Laranda fell to the Seljuks and remained under Muslim control until the present day, except for a brief period when it was controlled by the German emperor Frederick Barbarossa. In 1256 the city became the capital of the Karaman Oghulu who established many fine buildings in the city. In 1300 the name of the city was changed to Karaman although by 1321 the capital was moved to Konya. In 1397 the city was briefly occupied by the Ottomans but managed to regain its independence after 1402 until it was finally incorporated into the Ottoman Empire in 1415.

Undoubtedly the most famous building in Karaman is the Hatuniye Madrassa built in 1381–2 by Sultan Khatun, the wife of the Karamanid 'Ala al-Din Beg. The building has a projecting entrance portal carved in high relief and flanked by two small domed rooms. The coloured marble doorway is recessed within the portal frame and covered by a tall muqarnas hood in the Seljuk tradition. Inside there is a rectangular courtyard with a vaulted dershane and three cells on each side with an iwan flanked by two domed rooms opposite the entrance. The entrance to the domed rooms flanking the iwan are richly carved with vegetal, epigraphic and abstract motifs. Originally the interior of the madrassa was covered in hexagonal dark turquoise-green tiles although most of these have disappeared.

Other important monuments in the city include the khanqah of Sheikh 'Ala al-Din built in 1460 the imaret of Ibrahim Beg and the turbe of 'Ala al-Din. The citadel and city walls of Karaman seem to have been destroyed in the fifteenth century and the present fortifications were probably erected in the sixteenth. The present Great Mosque has been radically restored and also seems to date from the late sixteenth century.

See also: Konya, Ottomans, Seljuks, Turkey
Further reading:
J. M. Rogers, 'Laranda [Karaman] 2. Monuments', in *Encyclopedia of Islam*, 5: 678–82, 1954.

Kashmir

Isolated region of northern India famous for its wooden architecture.

Islam arrived in Kashmir in the mid-fourteenth century although it did not really become a major force until the Mughal conquest of the late sixteenth century. Wood is the standard building material with deodar (a relation of cedar) being the preferred material for monumental structures. The traditional mosque form consists of a square or rectangular timber hall covered with a pyramid-shaped roof with a pointed spire or finial. The walls are built of logs laid horizontally and intersecting at the corners. Often there was a small gallery or pavilion below the spire which could be used by the muezzin for the call to prayer. This form was also used for saints' shrines which locally are known as ziarat. After the Mughal conquest extensive royal gardens were built around Lake Dal; these were equipped with grey limestone pavilions built in the form of wooden Kashmiri mosques.

See also: India, Mughals
Further reading:
W. H. Nichols, 'Muhammadan architecture in Kashmir', *Archaeological Survey of India Annual Report*, 1906–7: 161–70.

Kenya

Country in East Africa with a significant Muslim population on the coast.

The coastal population of Kenya are part of the Swahili people who occupy the coast from Somalia to Mozambique. The origins of the Swahili culture are problematic although it has recently been shown that the Swahili are an indigenous people who converted to Islam rather than Arab colonists. Most of the settlements have their basis in the Indian Ocean trade to Arabia, India and the Far East and are consequently located next to the sea. There was, however, a strong local economy with connections to the interior which has not yet been investigated in any great detail. For example the walled city of Gedi is 6 km inland and presumably had some contact with inland tribes. It is known, too, that Kenya's fertile coast was attractive to nomadic herders and tribesmen from the north, who periodically raided and migrated southwards into Kenya causing large-scale desertion of mainland sites on the northern coast. The most famous of these nomadic groups were the Galla who raided as far south as Mombasa in the sixteenth and seventeenth centuries.

The Kenya coast contains the remains of many settlements dating from the eighth to the nineteenth century. The remains can be divided into two geographical groups – a northern group based around the Lamu archipelago, and a southern group between Gedi and Mombasa. Between these two areas there are few remains of earlier settlement, probably because there are no useful creeks or anchorages.

The Lamu archipelago is a complex series of islands and creeks which probably represents the remains of the Tana river delta before it moved further south. This heavily indented coastline provided an ideal area for coastal settlement and some of the earliest remains of Islamic trading sites have been found here. The main islands in this group are Pate, Manda and Lamu. Pate is the largest island of the group and contains the walled city of Pate which under the Nabhani kings ruled a large area of the coast during the seventeenth century. Other important sites on Pate are Faza, Siu, Tundwa and Shanga. The ruins at Shanga are mostly fourteenth century, but excavations have revealed a dense continuity of occupation which stretches back to the eighth century and includes the earliest remains of a mosque in sub-Saharan Africa. The nearby island of Manda also contains an early site (known as Manda) which is dated to the ninth century and is one of the only sites on the coast to use baked brick for construction. As well as the important early site of Manda, the island also contains the ruins of Takwa and Kitao. The island of Lamu contains the settlements of Lamu and Shella which have in recent times dominated this area of the coast. To the north there are a few sites on the mainland like Ishikani, Omwe, Mwana, Dondo and Kiunga noted for their monumental tombs. On the mainland to the south, at the mouth of the Tana river, are the sites of Mwana, Shaka and Ungwana. The site of Ungwana is famous for its congregational mosque with two parallel prayer halls which was built in several phases between the fifteenth and sixteenth centuries. The early mosque was built in the fifteenth and later in the same century a second prayer hall with three rows of piers and a domed portico was added.

The southern group of settlements are located south of the Sabaki river and are mostly mainland sites based around creeks. Immediately to the south of the Sabaki river is the town of Malindi which, although largely modern, is built over the remains of one of the main towns on the coast that flourished in the sixteenth century under Portuguese protection. Nearby is the walled city of Gedi where the Sheikh of Malindi had his residence during the fifteenth and sixteenth centuries. To the south of Gedi are the three ruined settlements of Kilifi, Mnaarani and Kitoka which collectively formed the city-state of Kilifi during the sixteenth century. Several other ancient settlements can be found next to creeks further south towards Mombasa. One of the best-known sites is Jumba La Mtwana dating mostly from the fourteenth century. Mombasa itself was an important early settlement with its deep water anchorage at Kilindi although little remains of the early settlement with the exception of a small mosque in the harbour. Mombasa island is dominated by Fort Jesus built by the Portuguese as their base on the coast and later captured and remodelled by the Omanis. One of the most intriguing monuments in Mombasa is the Mbraaki Pillar which has been dated to the eighteenth century. The pillar is a hollow cylindrical structure resembling a minaret, an idea which is reinforced by its position next to a small mosque. However, the pillar has no internal staircase and minarets are unknown in the area before the nineteenth century implying some other function. South of Mombasa towards the Tanzania border there are few early sites although there are ruined early mosques at Tiwi and Diani.

In addition to the pre-colonial Islamic architecture Kenya also contains Muslim buildings dating from the period of British rule and later. Mombasa has the largest community of Muslims on the coast and has several modern mosques which are

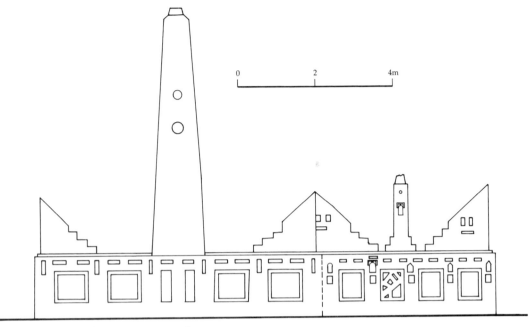

Ishikani pillar tomb, north Kenya coast (after Wilson)

still in use. Also on the main road between Mombasa and Nairobi are a series of small roadside mosques for travellers.

See also: East Africa, Gedi, Lamu

Further reading:

Azania Journal of the British Institute in Eastern Africa, 1965, ff.

J. de V. Allen and T. H. Wilson, *Swahili Houses and Tombs of the Coast of Kenya,* Art and Archaeology Research Papers, London 1979.

H. N. C. Chittick, *Manda: Excavations at an Island Port on the Kenya Coast,* British Institute in Eastern Africa Memoir no. 9, Nairobi 1984.

P. S. Garlake, *Early Islamic Architecture of the East African Coast,* British Institute in Eastern Africa Memoir no. 1, Nairobi and London 1966.

M. C. Horton, 'Early Muslim trading settlements on the East African coast: new evidence from Shanga', *Antiquaries Journal* 67: 290–323, 1987.

H. Sasoon, *Jumba La Mtwana Guide,* Mombasa 1981.

T. Wilson, *The Monumental Architecture and Archaeology North of the Tana River,* Nairobi 1978.

—— *The Monumental Architecture and Archaeology of the Central and Southern Kenyan Coast,* Nairobi, 1980.

keshk

Central Asian term used to describe mud brick buildings with square or rectangular plan and corrugated sides.

khan

Building which combines the function of hostel and trading centre. Standard features which one might expect to find in a khan are stables, store rooms, sleeping accommodation and a mosque.

The word khan is a Persian term, indicating the eastern (non-Roman) origin of this architectural form. Both the Parthians and the Nabateans built khans, the former on the eastward route to India and and the latter on the desert routes in the Negev. The earliest Islamic khans are found in Syria and date from the Umayyad period; examples include Qasr al-Hayr East and West, Khan al-Zabib and the building at Tell al-Sadiyyeh in the Jordan valley. These buildings all have a standard plan comprising a square or rectangular enclosure with rooms built around a central courtyard. During the Abbasid period khans were established on the Darb Zubayda (the pilgrimage route running through Iraq and central Arabia), although the commercial importance of these installations is not known. From the twelfth century onwards khans became a standard feature of Islamic architecture and were particularly popular under the Seljuks. During this period khans began to be established in towns where they would become centres for trade. Also at this time the caravanserai is established as a more specialized form of khan catering specifically for caravans.

During the sixteenth century Ottoman khans developed a variety of forms where the central courtyard is enclosed; some of the best examples are in Damascus and Aleppo. Also at this time khans become part of larger complexes that included a mosque, fort and bath house, as at the village of Payas near Iskenderun in Turkey.

khanqah

A monastery or hostel for sufis or dervishes.

Kharana

Early Islamic or Sassanian building in the Jordanian desert 60 km east of Amman.

Kharana is a remarkably preserved square two-storey structure with solid semi-circular and circular buttress towers. The building is made out of roughly hewn stone blocks laid in courses covered with successive layers of plaster. There are three rows of vertical slits in the walls which have been interpreted as arrow slits, although their height above the inside floor level makes this unlikely. The gateway is set between two quarter-round towers which lead into an entrance passage flanked with two long vaulted rooms that functioned as stables. Inside the building is a square courtyard with a series of undecorated rooms (for storage?) whilst on the upper floor the rooms are decorated with plaster/stucco designs similar to those at Ukhaidhir in Iraq. These include engaged pilasters, blind niches and decorative bosses. Two of the upper rooms have semi-domes resting on wide squinches at the end.

Although it was built before 710 (according to an inscription) and is Sassanian in style, the building is now generally believed to be early Islamic.

Further reading:

S. Urice, *Qasr Kharana in the Transjordan*, Durham, NC: AASDR, 1987.

khatta

An Arabic term meaning marked out (from khatt a line). This term was used by historians of the early Islamic period to describe the process of marking out new settlements or camps (amsar) such as Basra, Kufa and Fustat. The word also conveys a sense of claiming possession of a piece of land by marking out.

Further reading:

J. Akbar, 'Khatta and the territorial structure of early Muslim towns', *Muqarnas* 6: 22–32, 1989.

Khirbet al-Mafjar (Qasr Hisham)

Umayyad palace located in the Jordan valley near the ancient city of Jericho.

The palace at Khirbet al-Mafjar is a large complex comprising three main architectural elements: the mosque, the palace, and the bath house or audience hall. These are all set within a large enclosure entered by a main gateway in the outer enclosure wall. This gateway projects outwards from the enclosure wall and is set between two quarter-circular solid buttress towers. The gateway leads into a long rectangular courtyard which runs the whole length of the western side of the palace. In the centre of the courtyard is a square pool or fountain whilst towards the south end of the west wall there is another gateway leading into the central palace complex. This consists of a roughly square enclosure with solid round corner towers and semi-circular buttress towers in the middle of

Merlon at Khirbet al-Mafjar

the south, west and north walls. In the centre of this palace area is a square colonnaded courtyard with access to the ground-floor rooms. The north range consists of one large rectangular room divided into fourteen bays (two bays wide and seven long). The south range consists of five long rooms oriented north–south; in the south wall of the central room is a large concave niche which may have functioned as a mihrab. Approximately in the middle of the west colonnade is a staircase descending into a small serdab, or cellar.

In the north-west corner of the central palace is a staircase leading to a gateway which gives access to a rectangular courtyard connecting the palace to the bath house or audience hall. In the west wall there is a small opening to the outside, whilst on the east side there is a mosque. The mosque is a fairly simple rectangular structure aligned north–south and entered via a rectangular entrance vestibule on the north side. The sanctuary at the south end is three aisles wide and two bays deep with a concave mihrab niche in the centre of the south wall. In addition there is another entrance to the mosque via a staircase leading down from the upper floor of the palace to a position in the south wall of the mosque next to the mihrab.

Probably the most famous part of the palace is the audience hall or bath house which stands at the north-west corner of the complex. This was a highly sophisticated building consisting of a nine-domed hall supported on sixteen piers and flanked on all four sides by barrel-vaulted exhedrae terminating in semi-circular apses. At the south end of the hall is a pool three aisles wide and filling the three southern apses. In the centre of the east wall is a monumental doorway which leads from a small courtyard in front of the mosque. Directly opposite this doorway in the centre of the west wall is the principal apse distinguished by a huge stone chain which hung down from the arch above. At the end of the chain was a tall conical pendant which has been interpreted as a representation of an imperial

Stone decoration of Khirbet al-Mafjar, near Jericho

148

Carved stone balustrade next to pool, Khirbet al-Mafjar

Sassanian crown. In the western most apse of the north wall is a doorway into the actual bath complex which is heated by an underfloor hypercaust system. In the north-west corner of the hall is a doorway leading into a small rectangular room with an apse at the end. This room has been interpreted as the caliph's private audience room and is decorated with the famous mosaic of a lion bringing down a gazelle in front of a large tree.

The complex is mostly built out of finely dressed ashlar blocks although baked brick is used occasionally as in the bath complex. One of the most significant features of the palace is its decoration which consists of elaborately carved and painted three-dimensional stucco as well as extensive carpet-like mosaics. The stucco decoration includes representations of semi-naked women as well as male statues which are thought to represent the caliph himself.

There has been much discussion of the purpose of the palace and the function of the various rooms, most of which emphasize the evidently luxurious nature of life in the palace. It is not known exactly when the complex was built and there is no specific identification of it in early Islamic texts. The only historical evidence comes from a piece of graffiti which mentions the caliph Hisham (724–43); however, it is now generally agreed that in its final (unfinished) form the palace represents the tastes and lifestyle of al-Walid II (mid-eighth century). The solution may be that the core of the palace represented by the courtyard palace structure was built during the rule of Hisham whilst the 'bath hall' was added by his more exuberant nephew.

See also: Khirbet al-Minya, Palestine, stucco, Umayyads

Further reading:

R. Ettinghausen, *From Byzantium to Sassanian Iran and the Islamic World*, Leiden 1972.
R. W. Hamilton, *Khirbat al-Mafjar: An Arabian Mansion in the Jordan Valley*, Oxford 1959.

—— 'Who built Khirbet al-Mafjar?', *Levant* 1: 61–7, 1969.
—— 'Khirbet al-Mafjar: the bath hall reconsidered', *Levant* 10: 126–38, 1978.

Khirbet al-Minya (Hebrew: Horvat Minim; 'Ayn Minyat Hisham)

Small Umayyad palace located on the north-western shore of the Sea of Galilee (Lake Tiberias).

The palace is contained within a rectangular enclosure (66 by 73 m) oriented north–south with round corner towers and semi-circular interval towers on the south-west and north sides. In the middle of the east side is the main gate formed by two projecting half-round towers separated by the arch of the gateway. The centre of the building is occupied by a colonnaded courtyard with twin staircases giving access to an upper floor level. In the south-east corner is the mosque which is divided into twelve bays supported on piers. Next to the mosque is a triple-aisled basilical hall, whilst to the north are the residential quarters.

The buildings is built out of finely dressed limestone blocks laid in regular courses with a lower course of black basalt blocks. The top of the walls were decorated with giant stepped merlons whilst the interior was decorated with a variety of glass and stone mosaics as well as marble panels.

The building of the palace is attributed to al-Walid (705–15) on the basis of a re-used inscription set into the gateway. There is evidence that the palace continued in use at least until the end of the Umayyad period and probably, on the basis of Mamluk pottery found at the site, later. Nearby are the remains of the medieval and Ottoman site of Khan Minya which was an important post on the Damascus–Cairo trade route.

See also: Palestine, Umayyads

Further reading:

K. A. C. Creswell, *Early Muslim Architecture*, 1(2), Oxford 1969.
O. Grabar, J. Perrot, B. Ravani and M. Rosen, 'Sondages à Khirbet el-Minyeh', *Israel Exploration Journal* 10(4): 226–43, 1960.

Kilwa

Trading city on the southern coast of Tanzania which has the largest group of pre-colonial ruins in East Africa.

The name Kilwa today is used for three settlements: Kilwa Kiswani, Kilwa Kivinje and Kilwa Masoko. The ruins are confined almost exclusively to Kilwa Kiswani (on the island), whilst Kivinje and Masoko are both later settlements on the mainland.

The history of Kilwa is known from the Kilwa Chronicle which relates the history of the city from its foundation to the beginning of the Portuguese period in the sixteenth century. The earliest settlement at the site seems to have been in the eighth century although there are few standing remains from this period. At some time between the ninth and the twelfth century the settlement was taken over by a new dynasty from Shiraz in Iran who established themselves as sultans of Kilwa. The first sultan was Ali bin al-Hasan who is said to have bought the town from a pagan. The sultans of Kilwa continued to rule the town until the nineteenth century when the last sultan was deported to Zanzibar.

The wealth of the town depended on trade in ivory and other goods, but the most important commodity was gold. Gold was mined in the area of the African city of Great Zimbabwe and taken to the coast at Sofala (present-day Beira), from which it was shipped up the coast via Kilwa. There was also an overland route from Kilwa to Lake Nyasa and the Zambezi but this was always secondary to the sea routes. Sometime in the thirteenth century the sultans of Kilwa seem to have gained direct control of Sofala.

The wealth brought in by the gold trade meant that Kilwa had its own mint and was the only place in sub-Saharan Africa to issue coins. In 1332 the city was visited by Ibn Battuta who decribed it as one of the most beautiful and best-constructed towns he had visited. The wealth of Kilwa was legendary and it was mentioned by Milton in 'Paradise Lost' where it is called 'Quiloa'. However, the arrival of the Portuguese at the beginning of the sixteenth century brought an abrupt end to the prosperity of the city. During the seventeenth century the city seemed to have declined, and to have become a very small settlement, and it was only with the establishment of an Omani base there in the eighteenth century that the city again rose to prosperity. By the nineteenth century the city had again declined to a point where the administrative centre was moved to the mainland settlement of Kilwa Kivinje.

The history of the city is reflected in the surviving buildings, although it should be remembered that the number of stone buildings was small compared to a majority made out of less permanent materials. The main building materials on the island were the same as elsewhere on the coast and included reef and fossil coral used as stone, mangrove poles for wood and coconut palms for roofing. A notable feature of the medieval architecture of Kilwa is the use of domes which is not paralleled anywhere else on the East African coast at this early period. With the exception of some domes in the palace of Husuni Kubwa all of the domes in the Kilwa area are supported on squinches. Elsewhere on Kilwa buildings are covered either with barrel vaults or flat roofs made out of wood and concrete. The Makutani Palace may be an exception to this as it seems to have had a wooden roof covered with palm thatch (makuti).

The main buildings on Kilwa are the Great Mosque and the Great House, the Small Domed Mosque, the Jangwani Mosque, the palace of Husuni Kubwa and the nearby Husuni Ndogo, the Makutani palace and the Gereza fort. There are also important ruins on nearby islands including Songo Mnara, Sanje Majoma and Sanje ya Kate.

The best-known building in Kilwa is the Great Mosque which is a large complex structure dating from several periods. The building consists of two main parts, a small northern part divided into sixteen bays and a larger southern extension divided into thirty bays. The earliest phase evident at the mosque is dated to the tenth century although little survives of this above foundation level. The earliest standing area of the mosque is the northern part which dates to the eleventh or tenth century and was modified at the beginning of the thirteenth. This area was probably covered with a flat roof supported on nine timber columns. The next phase included the addition of a large cloistered courtyard to the south supported on monolithic coral stone columns and a small chamber to the south-west covered by a large dome. This was probably the sultan's personal prayer room and the dome is the largest dome on the East African coast, with a diameter of nearly 5 m. Also belonging to this period is the southern ablutions courtyard which included a well, latrines and at least three water tanks. Sometime in the

fifteenth century this arcaded southern courtyard was rebuilt and covered over with the present arrangement of domes and barrel vaults supported on composite octagonal columns, making this the largest pre-nineteenth-century mosque in East Africa.

Adjacent to the Great Mosque on the south side is the Great House which mostly dates to the same period as the latest phase of the mosque (i.e. eighteenth century). The Great House actually consists of three connected residential units each with a sunken central courtyard. Most of the complex would have been a single storey although a second floor was added to some of the central area. The purpose of the Great House is not known, but it is likely that at some stage it served as the sultan's residence judging from a royal tombstone found during excavations.

To the south-west of the Great Mosque is the Small Domed Mosque which together with the Jangwani Mosque are the only two examples of a nine-domed mosque in this area. This building probably dates from the mid-fifteenth century (it is built on an earlier structure) and contains an arrangement of vaults and domes similar to the later phase of the Great Mosque. There are only two entrances, one on the south side opposite the mihrab and one in the centre of the east side. Domes cover most of the area of the mosque except for two bays covered with barrel vaults, one next to the entrance and one in front of the mihrab. The central bays are differentiated from the side bays by being wider and by the use of barrel vaults at either end, emphasizing the north–south axis. The dominant feature of the mosque is the central dome which is crowned with an octagonal pillar and internally contains three concentric circles of Islamic glazed bowls set within the dome. The two vaults to the north and south of the central dome are also decorated with inset bowls of glazed ceramics whilst the two domes either side of it are fluted internally; the other four domes are plain internally.

The other nine-domed mosque is of approximately the same date and is known as the Jangwani Mosque; it is located to the south of the Small Domed Mosque. Although more ruinous, excavation has shown this mosque to be similar, with the same use of fluted and plain domes, and entrances only on the south and east sides.

To the east of the main group of buildings are

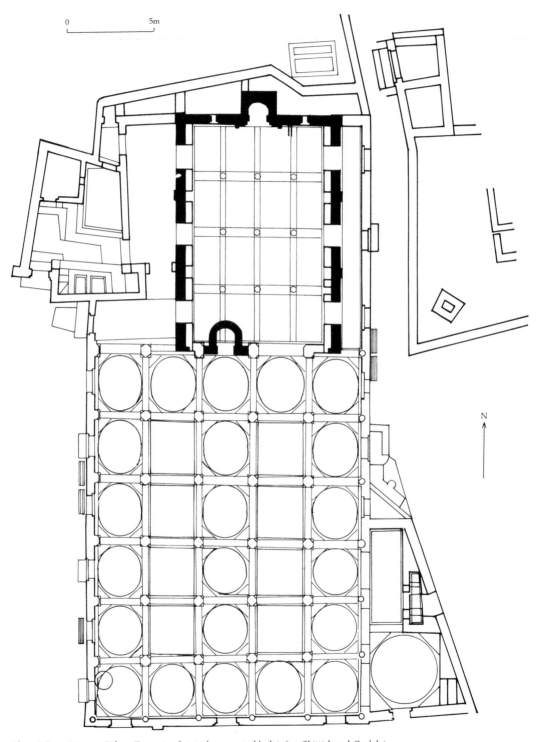

Plan of Great Mosque, Kilwa, Tanzania. Original mosque in black (after Chittick and Garlake)

the remains known as Husuni Kubwa (large Husuni) and Husuni Ndogo (small Husuni). The term Husuni derives from the Arabic term *husn* meaning fortified enclosure or fortress. Whilst this term may be appropriate for the the latter, its application to Husuni Kubwa seems unlikely for a palace complex. Husuni Kubwa is located on a coastal headland overlooking the Indian Ocean. It seems to date mostly from the late thirteenth or early fourteenth century and may well have never been completed. The complex consists of three main elements, the gateway or monumental entrance, the large south court and a complex of four court-yards which form the core of the palace. Also at the northern end of the complex there is a separate private mosque located on rocks next to the sea and reached by a staircase. The four courtyards at the northern end of the complex comprise an audience court, a domestic court, a bathing pool and a palace court. On the east side of the audience court are a flight of steps leading up to a flat-roofed pavilion which has been interpreted as the sultan's throne room. To the east of this is the domestic court which opens on to a complex of residential rooms, or *beyts*. The bathing pool con-sists of a sunken octagonal structure with steps and lobed recesses on each side. The palace court at the northern end of the palace is a sunken rectangular structure aligned north–south with steps at either end. The north set of steps leads to a further residential unit which overlooks the sea and the small mosque. It is possible that the sea mosque and the staircase represent the sultan's private entry to the palace. The royal nature of the palace is confirmed by a floriated Kufic inscription found during excavations which mentioned Sultan al-Hasn bin Sulayman.

By contrast Husuni Kubwa is a severe-looking building which fits the name Husuni (fort). It con-sists of a rectangular structure aligned north–south and measuring over 70 m long by more than 50 m wide. Thirteen evenly spaced, solid, semi-circular bastions protect the outside of the wall with one rectangular tower on the west side. The only entrance is in the middle of the south side and consists of a wide gateway leading into a gateway with the exit on the east side thus forming a bent entrance. Excavations have revealed the traces of a few structures inside but these may be later and do not give any indication of the function of the building which is unparalleled elsewhere in East

Africa and suggests an outside influence. There is little evidence for dating this structure although it is thought to be contemporary with Husuni Kubwa.

The other two important buildings on Kilwa island are also defensive structures although they seem to date mostly to the eighteenth century. The largest of these is the Makutani palace which was the residence of the sultan in the eighteenth century. This building is contained within a forti-fied enclosure known as the Makutani, which con-sists of two curtain walls fortified by square towers with embrasures. The wall was originally approxi-mately 3 m high and crenellated. Although there is no trace of a parapet this could have been built of wood like many other features of the eighteenth-century remains at Kilwa. The palace occupies a position between the two enclosure walls and appears to be built around one of the earlier towers. It is the only building on the island still to have an upper floor which contained the main residential area of the palace.

The Gereza or fort is located between the Maku-tani palace and the Great Mosque. It consists of a roughly square enclosure with two towers at oppo-site corners. Although there is some evidence that the original structure was Portuguese, the present form of the building seems to be typical of Omani forts.

In addition to sites on Kilwa island there are important sites on nearby islands. The earliest of these sites is Sanje ya Kate, an island to the south of Kilwa where there are ruins covering an area of 400 acres, including houses and a mosque. The mosque is of an early type with a mihrab niche contained in the thickness of the wall rather than projecting out of the north wall as is usual in later East African mosques. Excavations have shown that the settlement was abandoned before 1200 and most of the ruins date to the tenth century or even earlier.

To the east of Sanje ya Kate is the larger island of Songo Mnara which contains extensive ruins on its northern tip. The remains date to the fourteenth and fifteenth centuries and consist of thirty-three houses and a palace complex, as well as five mosques contained within a defensive enclosure wall. The remains at Songo Mnara are informative as they are one of the few places in East Africa where pre-eighteenth-century houses survive in any numbers. The houses have a standardized design with a monumental entrance approached by a flight of steps leading via an anteroom into a sunken courtyard, to the south of which are the main living quarters of the house.

See also: coral, East Africa, nine-domed mosque, Tanzania

Further reading:

H. N. Chittick, *A Guide to the Ruins of Kilwa with Some Notes on the Other Antiquities of the Region*, Dar es Salaam 1965.
—— *Kilwa: An Islamic City on the East African Coast*, British Institute in Eastern Africa Memoir No. 5, Nairobi 1974.
P. S. Garlake, *The Early Islamic Architecture of the East African Coast*, British Institute in Eastern Africa Memoir No. 1, Nairobi and London 1966.

kiosk (köshk)

Turkish term for a small pavilion not intended for permanent residence.

konak

Palatial Ottoman Turkish house.

The traditional Ottoman konak in western Anatolia and the Balkans is based on a four-iwan plan which is said to derive ultimately from the Cinili Kiosk in Istanbul. The plan consists of a central hall leading off to four iwans between which are enclosed rooms, often the plan is varied from this but the basic principal of a central hall with iwans is retained.

Most konaks are built of wood and have their main rooms on the upper floor with the lower floor used as a basement. The central hall is often covered with a wooden dome or a two-dimensional representation of a dome made of carved wood or paint. Sometimes the central hall is open on one side and functions as a veranda. The walls of the rooms are usually lined with sofas or long benches which are the main form of furniture. The most common form of decoration is painted ceilings, although shallow relief carving is also used. In eastern Anatolia konaks are built of stone and are built around open courtyards in the Syrian fashion; there is also a more strict division between the men's area (selamlik) and the women's area (harem).

See also: Istanbul, Ottomans, Topkapi Palace

Further reading:

N. Çakiroglu, *Kayseri Evleri*, Istanbul 1952.
D. Erginbaş, *Diyabakir Evleri*, Istanbul 1954.
L. Eser, *Kütahya Evleri*, Istanbul 1955.
E. Esin, 'An eighteenth century yali', in *Second International Congress of Turkish Art*, Naples 1965.
G. Goodwin, *A History of Ottoman Architecture*, London 1971: chap. 11, 'The Ottoman House', 428–53.
E. Kömürcüoglu, *Ankara Evleri*, Istanbul 1950.

Konya (Byzantine: Iconium)

City in southern Anatolia (Turkey) which was the capital of the Anatolian Seljuks now famous as the home of the whirling Dervishes.

Konya was established as capital in 1084 after the defeat of the Byzantines at Myriakefalon and just before the recapture of Iznik from the Crusaders. During the Byzantine period Iconium had been one of the richest Anatolian cities, a prosperity which was continued under Seljuk rule. In 1258 Konya was taken by the Mongols although it was later recaptured by the Karramanli Turks who continued to build in the Seljuk tradition. In the fifteenth century Konya was incorporated into the growing Ottoman Empire and became a regional capital.

The oldest mosque in Konya is the Alaeddin Cami built by the Seljuk sultan Alattin Keykubat between 1219 and 1221. This building stands on a hill in the centre of the city next to the remains of the Alaeddin palace. Within the mosque courtyard is an octagonal mausoleum with a tall conical (pyramid-shaped) dome which contains the remains of eight Seljuk sultans. In common with other Seljuk buildings in Konya, the entrances to the courtyard and prayer hall are surrounded by elaborate marble interlace patterns. The prayer hall is covered with a flat wooden roof supported by over forty Byzantine and classical columns. Other important Seljuk mosques in Konya include the Sahib Ata Mosque, the Iplikçili Mosque and the Ince Minareli. The Ince Minareli Mosque also has a madrassa with one of the most striking entrance façades in Seljuk architecture. This consists of a small pointed-arched doorway recessed within a huge stone frame which is covered with ornamental calligraphy. Two bands of calligraphy start either side of the doorway arch, cross over, run parallel up the centre of the portal and again cross over at

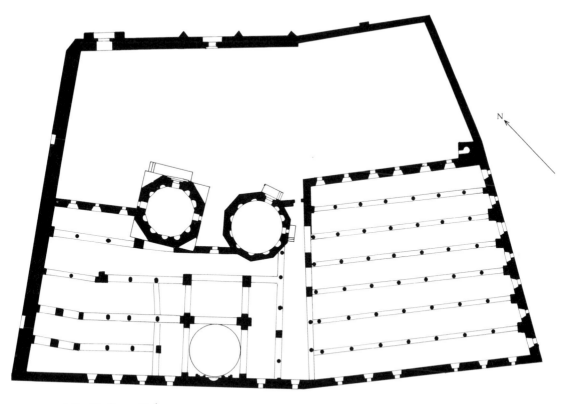

N

Mosque of Alaeddin, Konya, Turkey

the top. The edges of the frame are also decorated with calligraphic ornament whilst the areas in between are covered with stylized vegetal motifs. The Sahib Ata Cami also has a monumental portal consisting of a small pointed doorway set within a deep recess covered within a fourteen-tier muqarnas hood and flanked by bands of geometric motifs and calligraphic bands. The doorway is set between the bases of two minarets only one of which has survived as a fluted stump decorated with star patterns. Little remains of the Seljuk palaces of Konya although excavations have recovered architectural fragments indicating a rich artistic repertoire, including glazed tiles, stucco work and carved stone ornament. The decoration is noticeable for its rich figural content including depictions of birds, horses, mythical beasts and human figures. The tiles consist of eight-pointed star-shaped panels set between cross-shaped tiles.

The city's religious importance can be traced to the Sufi mystical poet Jalal al-Din Rumi who died in Konya in 1273. Jalal al-Din's tomb is the most famous building in Konya and forms part of a complex known as the Mevlana Masjid which included a mosque, madrassa, kitchen and semahane, or dance hall. The tomb itself is covered with a conical dome resting on a tall fluted cylindrical drum. The outside of the tomb and drum are covered in green tiles which distinguish it from the lead-covered roofs of the rest of the complex. Most of the complex with the exception of the tomb itself dates from the reign of Suleyman the Magnificent who added the mosque and dance hall. Next to the Mevlana complex is the Selimiye Cami commissioned by Sultan Selim II and designed by the famous architect Sinan. The mosque is unusual for the period as it has no courtyard.

See also: Ottomans, Seljuks, Turkey

kraton

General term for Javanese palaces. Derived from the Javanese root *ratu* meaning 'king', the term thus means 'residence of the king'. Sometimes the

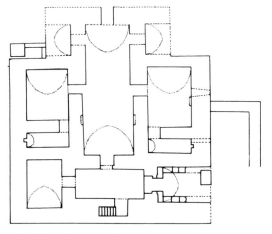

Kubadabad Palace, Beyshehir, Turkey (after Arik)

Kubadabad is located on the south-western shore of Lake Beyshehir in central Turkey. The settlement is dated by an inscription to the first half of the thirteenth century and is known to have been used by the Seljuk sultans Keykavus II and Keyhusrev III. The remains consist of more than sixteen buildings on the mainland and a separate castle or palace on an island known as Maidens' Castle. The tilework included underglaze painted star-shaped tiles with figurative scenes.

See also: Konya, Seljuks, Turkey

Further reading:

R. Arik, 'Kubad-Abad Excavations (1980–91)', *Anatolica* 18: 101–18, 1992.

K. Otto-Dorn, 'Kubadabad Kazilari 1965 On Raporu', *Turk Arkeoloji Degesi* 5.14(1–2): 237–43, 1967.

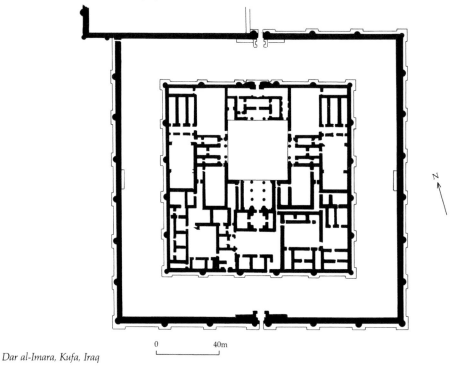

0   40m

Dar al-Imara, Kufa, Iraq

term *kadhaton* is also used which has a more specialized meaning referring to the royal quarters.

See also: Java

Kubadabad Palace

Seljuk palace famous for its glazed tilework and stucco decoration.

Kufa

Southern Iraqi city founded in the early Islamic period.

Kufa is located on the west bank of the Eurphrates near the Shi'a shrine city of Najaf. Like Baghdad, Kufa was a purely Islamic foundation, although it stood close to the Lakhimid capital of al-Hira.

After the battle of Ctesiphon and the capture of al-Mad'ain (Ctesiphon and Seleucia) the Arab armies settled in the old Sassanian capital. Soon afterwards, the armies moved to Kufa because of its pleasanter climate and strategic location on the west bank of the Euphrates (i.e. easy access to Syria and the Hijaz). In 645 Ali transferred the seat of government to Kufa. The assassination of Ali in the Great Mosque of the city in 645 brought an end to the city's role as capital.

The original city had no walls and was simply surrounded by a ditch. The principal monuments in Kufa are the Great Mosque and the Dar al-Imara, or Governor's Palace. The Great Mosque consists of a number of different phases from the early Islamic period to the present day. The first mosque on the site was laid out by a man who threw spears to each of the cardinal points to delineate a square two-spear throws long. The area was enclosed by a ditch and the only permanent architectural feature was a marble colonnade 20 m long. The columns were taken from the nearby city of al-Hira. In 670 CE the mosque was expanded and covered with a flat roof resting on stone columns. The mosque visible today has a beautiful golden dome and contains the tombs of the two saints Muslim ibn Aqeel and Hani ibn Arwa. The golden dome and tilework date to the Saffavid period (seventeenth and eighteenth centuries), although the outer wall of the mosque which is supported by twenty-eight semi-circular buttress towers probably originates in the early Islamic period.

To the south of the Great Mosque is the Dar al-Imara which was excavated by the Iraqi Antiquities Authority. The palace is enclosed by a square enclosure 170 m per side with walls 4 m wide supported by twenty semi-circular buttress towers and four round corner buttresses. In the centre of the palace there is a square (domed?) chamber approached by a vaulted hall which was probably the throne room.

See also: Dar al-Imara, Iraq

Further reading:

S. Ahmad, 'Survey of the Kufa area' (in Arabic), *Sumer* 21:229–252, 1965.

M. A. Mustafa, 'Dar al Imara at Kufa', *Sumer* 21:229–252, 1965.

——, 'Preliminary report on the excavations in Kufa during the third season', *Sumer* 19:36–65, 1963.

kuliyye

Ottoman term used to describe large complexes around mosques, which might include madrassas, libraries, khanqas, bath houses and a kitchen for the poor.

Kuwait

Small desert country located in the northern Arabia/Persian Gulf.

The first Islamic settlements in the Kuwait area were on the island of Failika and at the small port of Kathima near the modern town of Jahra. The present state of Kuwait was founded in the eighteenth century when descendants of the ruling al-Sabah family established themselves as rulers in alliance with local merchants. The prosperity of the town of Kuwait rapidly increased attracting a growing population. In 1793 the British moved their commercial base from Basra to Kuwait and in 1899 Kuwait ended its formal ties to the Ottoman authorities by signing a protection treaty with Britain. In the early part of the nineteenth century Kuwait was relatively poor with an economy reliant on a declining dhow trade and pearl fishing. After the Second World War the economy was transformed by the discovery of oil (it had actually been discovered before the war) and since then the country has seen unprecedented economic growth.

Little has survived of Kuwait's traditional architecture because of its high-speed development. The traditional building materials were rubble stone covered with thick mud plaster, mud brick and some coral stone. With the exception of date palms wood was rare, although mangrove poles imported from East Africa were used for the roofs.

Kuwait city was surrounded by a wall with five gates in the eighteenth century but this has now disappeared. Apart from the city wall Kuwait was protected by two forts, one in the city and the other on the end of the peninsula known as the Red Fort. Within the city there were a number of mosques most of which have been rebuilt several times. The oldest mosques in Kuwait are the Masjid al-Khamis built between 1772 and 1773 and the Masjid Abd al-Razzaq built in 1797. Before the nineteenth century minarets were rare and where they did exist consisted of small square towers covered with a small roof canopy.

A typical Kuwaiti merchant house was built in

the Ottoman style which reached the city from Basra. Ottoman features included projecting wooden balconies enclosed with wooden screens, or mashrabiyya, and carved wooden doorways which sometimes included European motifs. The extreme heat of the city made wind-catchers and ventilators a necessity for most houses.

Modern architecture in Kuwait is mostly in the modern international style, although there are several buildings which demonstrate some relationship to Islamic themes. The best-known example of Kuwaiti modern architecture is the water towers, consisting of tall pointed conical spires on which spherical water tanks are skewered.

See also: Bahrain, Qatar, United Arab Emirates

Further reading:

R. Lewcock and Z. Freeth, *Traditional Architecture in Kuwait and the Northern Gulf,* London 1978.

L

Lahore

Imperial Mughal capital located in the Punjab region of Pakistan.

Lahore is located in the eastern Punjab close to the Indian border and the Sikh city of Amritsar. The origins of the city are obscure although it is known that it existed as early as the tenth century. In 1021 the city was captured by Mahmud of Ghazni who demolished the fort and appointed Malik Ayaz as governor. In 1037 Malik Ayaz began construction of a new fort on the remains of the old one, which was completed in 1040. Excavation of the old fort has recently revealed a section which consists of a mud-brick wall approximately 4 m high. The new fort was also built of mud brick and consisted of a large rectangular enclosure by the banks of the river. In 1556 this fort was demolished by the Mughal emperor Akbar and replaced with a baked-brick enclosure fortified with semi-circular bastions. Akbar extended the area of the fort to the north to enclose the low lying area next to the river which was supported on vaulted sub-structures. Akbar's construction forms the core of the present fort which was added to by later Mughal emperors, as well as Sikh and British rulers of the area. The basic design of the fort is similar to the Red Fort at Delhi and the fort at Agra and consists of a huge public courtyard to the south with the private apartments and gardens to the north overlooking the river. The public courtyard known as Jahangir's Quadrangle contains some of the best examples of Akbar's architecture built in the characteristic red sandstone. The courtyard is lined by pavilions supported by massive brackets resting on twin columns. Most of the fort, however, is attributed to Akbar's successors, in particular Jahangir and Shah Jahan. Jahangir was responsible for the most magnificent example of ceramic art in Pakistan which is the 'Picture Wall'. This is an area of more than 6,000 m square decorated with human and animal figures besides the more usual geometric and figural designs. Areas

of the palace built by Shah Jahan are characterized by the use of white marble and intricate decoration. One of the most extravagant rooms in the building is the Sheesh Mahal, is a half-octagonal room decorated with mirror tiles. Outside the fort, Lahore contains a number of important Mughal buildings including the Badshahi Mosque, Jahangir's tomb, the Shalimar Bagh and the Shahdara complex. In addition to the imperial Mughal buildings there are a number of Mughal period buildings which exhibit a mixture of Mughal, Persian and local design. One of the most famous examples is the mosque of Wazir Khan built in 1634 which is profusely decorated with brightly coloured tile mosaic. At each corner of the courtyard is a thick octagonal minaret of a type which later became characteristic of Lahore. Several mosques of the late eighteenth and early nineteenth century exhibit the influence of Sikh architecture from nearby Amritsar. One of the best examples is the Sonehri Masjid (Golden Mosque) built by Bhikari Khan in 1753 which has bulbous gilded copper domes with miniature domed chatris.

See also: Mughals, Pakistan

Further reading:

M. A. Chughtai, *Badshahi Mosque*, Lahore 1972.
—— *Tarikhi Masjid*, Lahore 1974.
—— *The Wazir Khan Mosque*, Lahore 1975.
S. R. Dar, *Historical Gardens of Lahore*, 1972.
M. W. U. Khan, *Lahore and its Important Monuments*, Karachi 1964.
S. M. Latif, *Lahore: Its History, Architectural Remains and Antiquities*, Lahore 1956.

Lamu

Town on an island off the north Kenya coast, noted for its fine eighteenth- and nineteenth-century houses.

The origins of Lamu are uncertain although archaeological evidence suggests that there has been a settlement on the site since well before the sixteenth century. However, the present town of Lamu developed largely in the eighteenth and nineteenth century, eventually taking over from its

Lamu

rival city of Pate. Like all Swahili towns the wealth of Lamu was built on the Indian Ocean dhow trade and the main focus of the town is still the sea front or quay. The town is built on a gentle slope which runs down towards the sea and at its centre is the old fort constructed by the Omanis, who controlled the area from the eighteenth century onwards. Unlike most other towns Lamu has survived as a traditional Swahili town with a dense network of streets between tall stone mansions and over twenty-two mosques. In addition to the stone buildings of the town are suburbs of mud and thatch houses in which many of the population of Lamu live, as was probably the case in the past. The stone houses are built of out of coral stone and mangrove poles in the manner typical of East Africa until the twentieth century. Most were originally single storey, and upper floors were added subsequently as separate living units. The typical eighteenth-century Lamu house has a small entrance porch, or *daka*, with stone benches either side which forms the main reception area of the house. The outer porch opens on to a small inner porch (*tekani*) and at right angles to this is the

main courtyard of the house (*kiwanda*) thus forming a bent entrance to ensure privacy. Next to the inner porch, on the same side of the courtyard, is the guest room (*sabule*). Also contained within the courtyard is a bathroom or toilet, stairs to the upper floor and a semi-open kitchen covered with thatch. The main residential part of the house is located on the side of the courtyard away from the entrance and consists of a series of rooms of increasing privacy. Thus next to the courtyard is an outer living room followed by an inner living room behind which is the harem. The inner and outer living rooms are open to each other and the courtyard, whilst access to the women's area or harem (*ndani*) is via a pair of doors. The remarkable feature of these rooms is the use of decorative carved plaster and wall niches on the outward-facing walls of the living rooms and harem. The most elaborately decorated area is the harem, followed by the inner and outer living rooms. The wall niches are usually arranged in tiers and may cover the entire wall of the harem. The purposes of the niches is not fully understood although they are often used to display valuable pottery. Behind

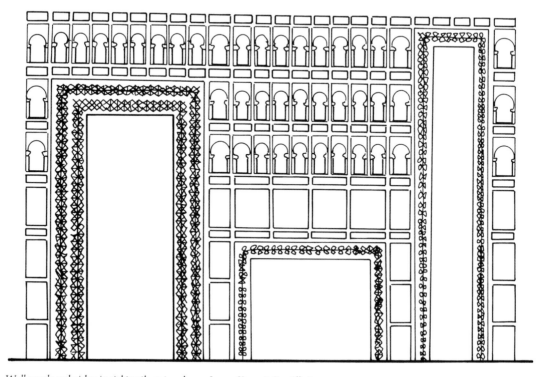

Wall panels and niches in eighteenth-century house, Lamu, Kenya (after Allen)

the harem are the inner bathroom and a room known as *nyumba ya kati* which may be for laying out and washing the dead.

Access to the upper floor is via a staircase which also has its own porch which may be used for receiving visitors. The arrangement of the upper floor is similar to downstairs except that there is no room for the dead and the kitchen is raised above the rest of the building on one side of the courtyard.

See also: coral, East Africa, Kenya

Further reading:

J. de V. Allen, *Lamu Town: A Guide*, Mombasa 1974.
J. de V. Allen and T. H. Wilson, *Swahili Houses and Tombs of Kenya*, Art and Archaeology Research Papers, London 1979.
R. L. Flemming, 'Lamu: a special Islamic townscape with no conservation plan and no policy', *Monumentum* 71–7, 1983.
U. Ghaidan, *Lamu: A Case Study of the Swahili Town*, Nairobi 1975.
U. Ghaidan and H. R. Hughes, 'Lamu, a lesson in townscape', *Architectural Review* Nov. 1973.
M. Ylvisaker, *Lamu in the Nineteenth Century: Land, Trade and Politics*, Boston 1979.

Lashkari Bazar

Ruined eleventh-century city in Afghanistan.

Lashkari Bazar is located to the north of the modern city of Bust on the east side of the Helmud river in south-west Afghanistan. The principal ruins at the city date from the Ghaznavid period in the eleventh century although there are both earlier remains from the Parthian period and later remains from the Ghurid period (twelfth to thirteenth century). In many ways the site resembles the Abbasid site of Samarra with its monumental size, its palaces, its mud-brick architecture and its elongated development alongside the river.

The citadel of Bust to the south seems to have been the first area of settlement and Lashkari Bazar seems to have been developed as a suburb or camp referred to as al–'Askar. The three principal structures at the site are the North, Centre and South palaces. The earliest of these is the Centre Palace which was probably built in the Samanid period. This is a rectangular building (32 by 52 m) with circular buttress towers at the corners. There are two storeys – a ground floor and an upper floor – although it appears that these were not connected. The largest building at the site is the South Palace which has been identified as the palace of Mahmud of Ghazni. This is a huge

structure (170 by 100 m) built around a central courtyard which opens on to four main iwans. The building is entered from the south which leads into the courtyard via a cruciform hall. At the opposite end of the courtyard is a large iwan which leads, via a passageway, into a larger one overlooking the river. This iwan which has a staircase leading down to the river has been compared to the Bab al-Amma at Samarra although it has a different form. The private quarters were arranged down the west side of the courtyard and include a small mosque at the south end (this was not accessible from the rest of the palace). The interior of the palace was richly decorated with stucco work, frescoes and carved marble panels. To the east of the palace was a large walled garden which may have contained animals.

In addition to palaces there are remains of smaller private mansions built in the same style, with iwans opening on to a courtyard. One of the more interesting features of the site is the bazar from which the site gets its name. This is a street more than 100 m long lined with small shop units (3.5 by 5 m). On one side of this street, approximately in the middle, there is courtyard building with store rooms, which was probably the office of the market inspector (muhtasib).

See also: Afghanistan, Samarra

Further reading:

T. Allen, 'Notes on Bust', *Iran. Journal of the British Institute of Persian Studies*, 26: 55–68 1988; 27: 57–66, 1989; 28: 23–30, 1990.
D. Schlumberger, M. Le Berre, J. C. Garcin and G. Casal, *Lashkari Bazar, une residence royale ghaznevide et ghoride*, Memoires de la Delegation Archéologique Française en Afghanistan, Part 1A 'L'Architecture', 1978.

Lebanon

The republic of Lebanon is located on the east coast of the Mediterranean between Palestine and Syria.

Lebanon is dominated by two geographical features, the sea and the Lebanon and Anti Lebanon mountains. The principal cities of the country are located on the coast and include the old Phoenician settlements of Tyre, Sidon, Beirut and Tripoli. The history of Lebanon in the Islamic period is similar to that of Syria with some minor variations. The main consideration is that the Lebanon mountains cut off Lebanon from the rest of Syria whilst the sea opened it up to European contact. One of the first indications of Syria's separateness occurred in the eighth century when the Christian Maronites

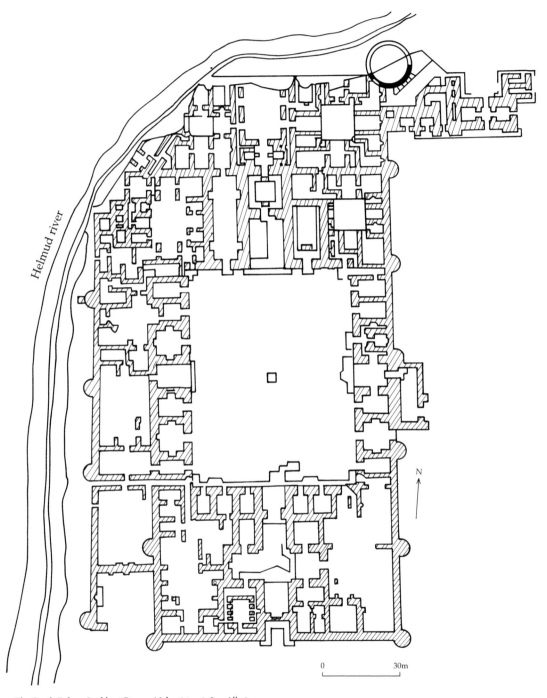

Helmud river

N

0   30m

The South Palace, Lashkari Bazar, Afghanistan (after Allen)

established an independent state in the Kadisha valley amongst the mountains of north Lebanon.

In the eleventh century dissident followers of the Fatimid caliph al–Hakim settled in the mountains of southern Lebanon and established the Druze community. During the twelfth and thirteenth centuries the country was dominated by the Crusaders who had conquered the coastal cities for use as bases in their conquest of Palestine. With the expulsion of the Crusaders in 1289 the Mamluks rebuilt cities such as Tripoli to remove all trace of the Crusader presence. In 1516 Lebanon was incorporated into the Ottoman Empire although its position enabled it to develop its own trading links with Europe. Contact with Europe was increased throughout the Ottoman period and in the eighteenth century Maronites were placed under the special protection of France. Massacres of Christians in the nineteenth century led France to press for the autonomy of Lebanon within the Ottoman Empire and from 1860 Lebanon has functioned as a semi-independent state. The country achieved full independence in 1944 at the end of the Second World War.

Stone is the principal building material in Lebanon and is used both in a dressed form and as uncut rubble. The presence of black basalt and limestone has made striped (ablaq) masonry a popular form of decoration for important buildings.

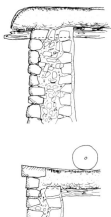

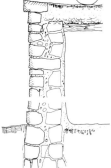

Types of wall construction, Beq'a Valley, Lebanon (after Ragette)

Wood is used as a roofing material as well as for balconies and projecting windows. Unfortunately the cedar forests of Lebanon were destroyed before the medieval period and the principal types of wood are poplar, walnut, willow and maple. Mud brick is used as a building material in the Beq'a valley where the climate is dry enough and there is suitable clay.

The only major creation of the Umayyad period was the city of Anjar which like Ramla in Palestine was intended as a new regional centre away from the predominantly Christian cities. The Mamluk period is represented by the city of Tripoli which was completely rebuilt after its conquest. Moreover, the Mamluk period left a great impression on the Christian, Druze and Muslim architecture of the country which can be seen in buildings such as the Bayt al-Din Palace.

The most distinctive feature of Lebanese architecture is seen in the houses of the coast, which display a mixture of Middle Eastern and European influence. European elements include the use of pitched wooden roofs covered with clay tiles, prominent windows and balconies (distinct from the enclosed spaces usual in Islamic domestic architecture). Middle Eastern elements include the use of the vaulted iwan (open arched room), arcades and the occasional use of domes. Mountain-houses are generally less sophisticated and are often built of roughly square blocks held together in a mud mortar. Roofs are usually flat and made of earth resting on mats supported on wooden beams. Inside, the mountain-houses may be decorated with mud plaster mixed with white lime to produce a type of stucco. This material is used to decorate walls and is also used for the construction of storage bins and hearths.

See also: Anjar, Syria, Tripoli (Lebanon)

Further reading:

F. Ragette, *Architecture in Lebanon. The Lebanese House during the 18th and 19th centuries*, New York 1980.

Libiya (Libyan Arab People's Socialist State)

Large North African country located between Tunisia and Egypt, with the Mediterranean to the north and the Sahara desert to the south.

Libiya comprises two main geographic areas, the coast and the Sahara; these areas may be further separated into several regions. The narrow coastal strip is divided into three regions: Cyrenaica in the

Bayt al-Din, Druze mansion, Lebanon © *Kerry Abbott*

east with its capital of Benghazi, the Gulf of Sirte in the centre and Tripolitania in the west. The interior desert region may be divided into several areas, the most important of which are the Jabal Nafusa in south-eastern Tripolitania, and the Fezzan in the south-east of the Libyan desert.

The present state of Libiya is largely a modern phenomenon created by Italian colonialism in the early twentieth century. Ironically, 2,000 years previously the Romans developed the regions of Cyrenaica and Tripolitania into some of the wealthiest provinces of their empire, providing grain for the Italian peninsula. During the Byzantine era the prosperity of the area continued with a population that was predominantly Christian with a large Jewish minority. The area was first conquered by Islamic forces in the mid-seventh century with the capture of Barqa (modern al-Marj) in 642 under 'Amr ibn al-As, followed in 643 by the conquest of Tripolitania. After the coastal strip was secured a further force under 'Uqba ibn Nafi was sent to take control of Zuwayla in the Fezzan. In the past it has been generally assumed that the Islamic

conquest led to the collapse of the Roman urban network but it has recently been shown that change was more gradual, with a considerable degree of continuity of settlement from the Byzantine to the early Islamic period.

During the early tenth century the power of the Abbasid caliphs in North Africa was destroyed by the radical Sh'ite Fatimid dynasty who ruled from their capital of Mahadiyya in Tunisia. During this period the importance of Libiya increased and the best examples of early Islamic architecture in the country are from this period. After the Fatimid conquest of Egypt much of North Africa, including the area of present-day Libiya, came under the control of the Berber Zirid governors. In the eleventh century North Africa was subject to a new influx known as the Banu Hilal who were supposedly dispatched by the Fatimid caliphs to reintroduce Fatimid propaganda to the rebellious Berber tribes. In the past the Hilalian invasions have been seen as the cause of North Africa's comparative backwardness in the Middle Ages. More recently this view has been modified, but the idea of the baked brick was also sometimes used. In the southern desert areas where Roman material was not so plentiful the main building material is roughly hewn stones set within a mud mortar. This use of material determined architectural forms, thus in the Jabal Nafusa area tall triangular arches were used as there was no suitable material for normal arch construction.

With the exception of the occasional building in the old Byzantine coastal cities, the first distinctive Islamic architecture in Libiya dates from the Fatimid period. During the later tenth century the Fatimids were increasingly interested in Egypt and to this end developed a number of garrison cities or staging posts on the route between Mahdiya and Egypt. Probably the best-known site is the garrison city of Ajdabiya, south-west of Benghazi, which had both a large mosque and a palace. The palace is a rectangular stone-built structure with a central courtyard flanked by suites of rooms. Directly opposite the entrance is a monumental portico which gives access to the principal rooms of the palace which are arranged in a T-plan. The mosque was a mud-brick building with stone used for the corners, piers and jambs. The mosque had a main entrance in the north-west side opposite the mihrab as well as several lateral entrances. The aisles run at right angles to the qibla wall, with the exception of the transept adjacent to the qibla wall which runs parallel (an arrangement frequent in Fatimid mosques). The mosque is important for its early evidence of a minaret which consists of a square base with an octagonal shaft, a design which later became the basis for the Mamluk minarets of Cairo.

Another early Fatimid site is the city of Madinah Sultan (Surt or Sirt) which is approximately midway between Benghazi and Tripoli. The city was enclosed by a large oval-shaped town wall with at least three gateways. One of the larger buildings uncovered during excavations was the Friday mosque which is oriented south–east (an incorrect qibla). The mosque had four gates, the most prominent of which was the monumental north gate which is of double width. Monumental gateways are a characteristic feature of Fatimid mosques and can also be seen at Mahdiya in Tunisia and in Cairo. The Madinah Sultan Mosque has a central aisle running at right angles to the qibla wall, although unusually for North Africa the rest of the aisles run parallel to the qibla wall. Some remains

Beirut house, Lebanon © *Kerry Abbott*

political weakness of the area cannot be dispelled. During the twelfth century this weakness was exploited by Roger, the Norman king of Sicily, who established a Norman kingdom in Ifriqiya which included the area of Libiya. After the expulsion of the Normans the history of Libiya is fragmented into successive dynasties controlling individual cities. For a brief period in the early sixteenth century part of Libiya was occupied by the Spanish, but they were soon displaced by the Ottomans who established naval bases on the coast to harass European shipping in the Mediterranean. During the eighteenth century Libiya was briefly ruled by the semi-independent Qarahmanli dynasty. In 1911 Libiya was again brought under European rule when the Italians invaded and established the country as an Italian colony.

The main building materials in Libiya are stone and mud brick. Re-used Roman or Byzantine stone has always been in plentiful supply so that many of the older buildings in Tripoli, Adjdabiyah or elsewhere use Roman columns and capitals. Mud brick was employed as a cheap alternative when dressed stone was not readily available, although of the original decorative scheme of the mosque have been recovered including stucco frames for coloured glass windows, red and green coloured bricks. There are traces of a subsidiary mihrab in the arcade facing the courtyard which may possibly be the remains of an eighth-century mosque which was rebuilt in 952 by the Fatimid caliph al-Muciz. Several other Fatimid establishments are known but have not yet been investigated in detail; one of the better known examples is Qasr al-Hammam near the ancient site of Leptis Magna.

Few early Islamic remains survive in Tripoli although traces of the rebuilt Umayyad fortification walls have been excavated. These were made of stone and mortar and vary between 6 and 7 m in thickness. The oldest mosque in Tripoli is the al-Naqah Mosque which was probably built by the Fatimid caliph al-Muciz in 973 although some suggest that it may be older. The present shape of the mosque is irregular indicating numerous alterations throughout history although the basic plan consists of a rectangular courtyard and a sanctuary or prayer hall covered with forty-two brick domes. Although many of the other mosques in Tripoli may have medieval origins their remains mostly date from the Ottoman period. Few important monuments of the post Fatimid medieval period in Libiya have survived although many small mosques may date to the medieval period. At the oasis site of Ujlah (Awjlah) 200 km to the south of Ajdabiya is a small twelfth-century mosque built of stone and brick. The mosque consists of at least twelve bays covered with pointed conical domes, although the most interesting feature of the building is the recessed minbar niche to the side of the mihrab (this feature is also found in East Africa and Arabia and may represent an Ibadi tradition). South of Tripoli in the area of Jabal Nafusa is a region with a high concentration of ancient mosques, many of which date from before the thirteenth century. Many of these mosques are built partially underground giving them a low profile and an organic feel accentuated by the absence of minarets. The area is also characterized by fortified store houses, known as qusur (plural of qasr), which consist of agglomerations of barrel-vaulted units contained within a defensive wall. The barrel-vaulted units are often stacked one on top of the other and are reached by ladder or ropes. During peaceful times each qasr functions as a central storage area and in times of attack the population of the village retreats into the qasr where it can withstand a long siege.

See also: Ajdabiya, Fatimids, Tripoli (Libiya)

Further reading:

A. Abdussaid, 'Early Islamic monuments at Ajdabiyah', *Libiya Antiqua* 1: 115–19, 1964.
—— 'An early mosque at Medina Sultan (Ancient Sort)', *Libiya Antiqua* 3–4: 155–60, 1967.
—— 'Barqa, modern al-Merj', *Libiya Antiqua* 8: 121–8, 1971.
J. W. Allan, 'Some mosques on the Jabal Nefusa', *Libiya Antiqua* 9–10: 147–69, 1973.
J. M. Evans, 'The traditional house in the Oasis of Ghadames', *Libyan Studies* 7: 31–40, 1976.
A. Hutt, 'Survey of Islamic sites', *Libyan Studies* 3: 5–6, 1972.
—— *Islamic Architecture: North Africa*, London 1977.
G. R. D. King, 'Islamic archaeology in Libiya 1969–1989', *Libyan Studies* 20: 193–207, 1989.
N. M. Lowick, 'The Arabic inscriptions on the mosque of Abu Macruf at Sharwas (Jebel Nefusa)', *Libyan Studies*, 5: 14–19, 1974.
A. M. Ramadan, *Reflections on Islamic Architecture in Libiya*, Tripoli 1975.
M. Shagluf, 'The Old Mosque of Ujlah', *Some Islamic Sites in Libiya*, Art and Archaeology Research Papers, London 1976, 25–8.
H. Ziegert and A. Abdussalam, 'The White Mosque at Zuila', *Libiya Antiqua* 9–10: 221–2, 1973.

M

ma'adhana

Place for the call to prayer, often identified with the minaret.

machicolation

Downward openings or slits used defending a castle or fortification.

There are three types of machicolation, a box machicolation, concealed machicolation and continuous machicolation.

A box machicolation resembles a projecting window or gallery and may also be used for this purpose. There are usually one or more slits in the floor and the box is normally located over a gate or doorway. Box machicolations were used in Roman times and their first use in Islamic structures is at Qasr al-Hayr (East and West).

Concealed machicolations are usually set into the roof above a vaulted passage leading from a gateway and are often used in conjunction with a portcullis. The first example in Islamic architecture comes from the eighth-century palace of Ukhaidhir in Iraq. These were frequently used in medieval Islamic fortifications.

Continuous machicolation consists of a parapet which is cantilevered over the front face of a wall with a series of downward openings. The earliest example of this is also at Ukhaidhir although it is not used later on in Islamic architecture.

See also: fortification

madafa

Arabic term for guest house, or room for guests.

Madinat al-Zahra'

Tenth-century palace city (now in ruins) 6 km west of Córdoba in southern Spain.

The complex was begun by Abd al-Rahman II and completed by his son al-Hakim II. The complex was named after Abd al-Rahman's favourite wife Zahra' and located near springs at the foot of the Sierra Morena. The complex was founded as a palatial residence and administrative centre away from the crowded capital at Córdoba and had a staff of 20,000 people including guards, officials and families. It was finally destroyed by fire in 1010 by the caliph's vizier al-Mansur who resented the caliph's personal residence. Material from the palace was re-used by Pedro the Cruel to build his palace in Seville.

The complex was built on three terraces surrounded by gardens with pools and water channels. On the lowest terrace is a garden pavilion built for Abd al-Rahman as a formal reception and ceremonial centre. This consisted of four pools and the pavilion itself known as the Salón Rico which has intricate decoration carved in stone to match the stucco work of the maqsura at the Great Mosque in Córdoba. This pavilion is associated with a hammam in an arrangement common to the desert palaces of Syria. Across a bridge from the Salón Rico is the main mosque of the complex with an arcaded courtyard leading on to the sanctuary five aisles deep. Next to the mosque is the Dar al-Yund (army headquarters) which consists of a cruciform basilical hall with triple-arched arcades and a ramp leading out on to the parade ground.

The upper part is occupied by the caliph's personal residence known as the Dar al-Mulk. This consisted of several apartments based around courtyards which in turn enclosed a central hall. It is likely that these apartments were at least four storeys high although they are now much damaged.

The complex is a useful example of how the Spanish Umayyads tried to copy the architecture and protocol of their more powerful ancestors. In particular the complex is thought to recall the country residence of Abd al-Rahman, the first Spanish Umayyad, at Rusafa in Syria.

See also: Córdoba, Córdoba Great Mosque, Spain

madrassa

Further reading:

F. Hernandez Gimenéz, *Madinat al Zahra': Arquitectura y Decoración*, Granada 1985.

B. Pavon Malddonao, *Memoria de la Excavación de la Mezquita de Medinat al-Zahra*, No. 50 of Excavaciones Arqueologicas en Espagne, Madrid 1966.

madrassa

Building which functions as a teaching institution primarily of Islamic sciences.

It is thought that the earliest madrassas were built by the Seljuks in eleventh-century Iran and that the design was derived either from contemporary house plans or Buddhist teaching structures, known as viharas, which survived in Afghanistan and Central Asia. The oldest extant madrassa is the Gumushtutigin Madrassa in Bosra built in 1136. This is a small structure (20 by 17 m) with a domed courtyard and two lateral iwans. However, the majority of early madrassas are found in Anatolia where two main types occur, based either on an open or a closed courtyard building. The domed madrassas are usually smaller buildings whilst those with an open courtyard are generally larger and have central iwans surrounded by arcades. The first Egyptian madrassas date from after 1160 when Sunni orthodoxy was returned to the country. The significance of the Egyptian madrassas is the four-iwan plan where each iwan represented one of the four orthodox schools of law. This design later spread to other countries and can be seen in the Mustansriya Madrassa in Baghdad. Another significant development which took place in Egypt is the madrassa becoming the dominant architectural form with mosques adopting their four-iwan plan.

Although it is traditionally thought that madrassas provide sleeping and working accommodation for students, the extant examples show that this was not a rule and it is only later on that student facilities became an accepted part of a madrassa.

mahal

Arabic term for place or location. In Mughal architecture it is used to describe the palace pavilion, or more specifically the women's quarters.

Mahdiya

Fatimid capital of North Africa located on the east coast of Tunisia.

The city of Mahdiya occupies a defensive position on the peninsula of Ras Mahdi. The city was established in 913 by the Fatimid Mahdi (leader) 'Ubaid Allah on the site of the destroyed Carthiginian port of Zella. The city functioned as a port from which the Fatimids were able to launch their campaign to conquer Egypt.

Architecturally the most significant building in the town is the Great Mosque built in 916. This is the earliest surviving example of a Fatimid mosque. The design of the mosque differs considerably from earlier North African mosques as it had no minarets and only one monumental entrance giving it the appearance of a fortress rather than a mosque. This view is reinforced by the massive square corner buttresses and the stark simplicity of the design. The internal layout of the mosque is similar to earlier mosques of the region with nine aisles running perpendicular to the qibla wall and a transverse aisle parallel with the qibla wall. In the eleventh century erosion by the sea destroyed the original qibla wall which was subsequently rebuilt further back thus reducing the space of the prayer hall.

See also: Ajdabiya, Fatimids, Tunisia

Further reading:

A. Lezine, *Mahdiyya: Recherches d'Archéologie Islamiques*, Paris 1965.

maidan

A large open space, or square, for ceremonial functions.

Malaysia

Predominantly Muslim country in south-east Asia divided into two parts, the southern half of the Malay peninsula and the northern part of Borneo.

It seems likely that Islam came to Malaysia as early as the ninth century although at present there is no archaeological confirmation of this. The earliest record of Islam in Malaysia is the Trengganu Stone dated to 1303 or 1386. The stone is written in Malay with Arabic script and records various regulations of Islamic law.

Before the fourteenth century the southern half of the Malay peninsula was home to a series of small weak states which were dominated by their northern neighbours of Cambodia and Thailand and later by the Indonesian kingdom of Majapahit. By 1403, however, the first king of Malacca had established himself as ruler of the southern Malay peninsula with the support of the Chinese emperor. The king of Malacca made several friendly visits to the Chinese emperor in return for support against the Thai kingdom of Ayudhya which was encroaching on the northern part of the peninsula. At this time (in the 1420s) the king of Malacca converted from Hinduism to Islam making Malacca the main centre of Islamic culture in south-east Asia. Under Chinese protection the state of Malacca grew to become the most powerful in the area with its control of the strategic straits of Malacca which were the main route for commerce between China and the west. By the end of the fifteenth century Malacca's position was threatened by the Portuguese who saw it as a threat to their further eastward expansion. In the early sixteenth century China withdrew its naval support of Malacca and in 1511 the sultanate of Malacca was finally defeated.

The Portuguese victory was the start of a long period of colonial rule first by the Portuguese, followed by the Dutch after 1641 and finally by the British from 1824 until 1957. Despite the crusading zeal of the Portuguese the Malay inhabitants remained Muslim throughout the colonial period.

Unfortunately there are few architectural remains from the pre-Portuguese period and these are mostly Buddhist or Hindu, although the surviving fortifications of Malacca may be Islamic. Most pre-nineteenth-century mosques in Malaysia were built of wood and have not survived very well. The oldest mosque in Malaysia is generally agreed to be the Masjid Kampaung Laut in the state of Kelantan built in the sixteenth century. The mosque was moved from its original location in 1970 after serious floods damaged its structure. The mosque stands on a square raised platform and has a three-tier pyramid roof with each tier separated by a gap to allow air circulation. A similar mosque was built at Demak in Indonesia by the same group of Muslim traders. Another early mosque is the Masjid Trengkera in Malacca built in the early eighteenth century (1728). This is a four-tier structure on a square base with a polygonal six-storey minaret. The form of the minaret resembles a pagoda and suggests strong Chinese influence. Most early Malaysian mosques have neither minarets nor mihrabs although these were often added in the nineteenth century. The window frames were usually decorated with bands of Quranic calligraphy and there are often elaborately carved minbars and Quran stands.

The colonization of Malaysia by Britain in the nineteenth century introduced a new Anglo–Indian stone- and brick-built mosque form. These mosques are characterized by the use of domes, crenellations and arched windows which locally are characterized as 'Moorish architecture'. One of the best examples of this architecture is the Headquarters of the Malayan Railway Company which is covered with onion domes with arched windows and striped masonry. This architecture which can also be seen in Singapore seems to be derived primarily from south India.

Since Independence in 1957 there have been attempts to move away from this Anglo–Indian architecture to buildings that are more traditionally Malay. The model for such buildings is usually the traditional form of Malay houses – wooden buildings with tall thatched roofs in three or more tiers. One of the earliest examples of this post-colonial architecture is the National Museum at Kuala Lumpur which uses traditional roof forms, although many of the other elements are built in a modern international style. More successful as an evocation of the traditional style is the Bank of Bumipatra which is based on the traditional Kelantan house design. The building has a huge three-tiered roof on a rectangular base.

See also: Indonesia, Java, Singapore

Further reading:

G. Haidar, 'On the crest of the hill: The International Institute of Islamic Thought and Civilization, Kuala Lumpur', *Arts and the Islamic World* 21: 14–18, 1992.

A. Lamb, 'Miscellaneous papers on early Hindu-Buddhist settlement in northern Malaya and southern Thailand', *Federation Museums Journal* NS 6: 1961.

Wan Hussein Azmi, 'Islam di Malaysia-Kedatangan dan Perkembangan (Abad 7–20 m)', *Tamadun Islam di Malaysia*, Kuala Lumpur 1980.

O. bm. Yatim, 'Islamic arts in Malaysia', *Arts and the Islamic World* 1(2): 1993.

Zainal Abidin Wahid (ed.), *Glimpses of Malaysian History*, Kuala Lumpur 1980.

S. S. Zubir, 'Identity and architecture in Malaysia', *Arts and the Islamic World* 5(1): 74–6, 1988.

Maldives

A group of over 2,000 islands off the south–west coast of Sri Lanka which now forms an independent republic with its capital at Male.

The inhabitants of the Maldives have been Muslim

since 1153 when they were converted by a Berber known as Abu al-Barakat. The language of the islands is Dihevi which is related to Sinhalese although it is written in a script based on Arabic numerals.

The houses are made out of coral stone and coconut wood; the stone is used to build a platform and the wood is used for the superstructure. As experienced boat builders the Maldivians were able to build wooden houses without nails and make very tight joints. Ibn Battuta visited the islands twice in 1343 and 1346 and gave an account of the construction of houses. The house was built around a hall which opened on to the reception room, known as the malem, where the owner of the house would receive his male friends. At the back of the malem was another door which opened on to the rest of the house forbidden to guests.

There are many mosques on the islands; at present Male has thirty-three including the main mosque known as the Hukuru Meskit (Great Mosque). The standard mosque plan which seems to have remained the same since the seventeenth century consists of a stone building raised on a rectangular platform with an entrance at the east end and a rectangular recess at the west end. Near the entrance is a well set within a paved area with a path leading to the mosque entrance to keep feet clean after washing. Many of the mosques are built of stone although some are built out of wood like the houses. Each mosque is surrounded by a graveyard on three sides with tombstones made of finely dressed coral blocks (rounded stones represent women and pointed stones represent men). In general Maldivian mosques do not have mihrabs although they are oriented towards Mecca and have a square recess at the qibla end. Minarets are also unusual although the Hukuru Meskit has a thick cylindrical tower which functions as a minaret.

See also: coral

Further reading:

J. Carswell, 'Mosques and tombs in the Maldive Islands', *Art and Archaeology Research Papers* 9: 26–30, 1976.
—— 'China and Islam in the Maldive Islands', *Transactions of the Oriental Ceramic Society* 41: 121–98, 1975–6.

Mali

Islamic West African empire which flourished during the thirteenth and fourteenth centuries.

The date of the first emergence of the kingdom of Mali is not known although there are references to it as early as the ninth century. However, it was not until the thirteenth century that the kingdom achieved the status of empire through the conquest of a number of rival states. The medieval empire of Mali was formed out of the unification of two distinct Manding groups, an established northern group and a more recent southern group. The unification was achieved by the famous Mali hero Sundiata who defeated Sumaguru Kante, lord of Susu in 1234 and then went on to conquer Ghana, Gangaran and the gold-producing area of Bambuko. The ruling clan, from which the king was selected, was the Keita clan of the northern group which traced its ancestry back to Bilal, the first black follower of the prophet. The empire had two distinct capitals: Kangaba, the religious capital, and Niani, capital of the Keita clan and birthplace of Sundiata. Although some branches of the Mali dynasty were Muslim fairly early on, it was not until the thirteenth century that the kings were Muslim.

After Sundiata the most famous king of Mali was Mansa Musa who made a legendary pilgrimage to Mecca in 1324–5. Although previous kings of Mali had made the pilgrimage to Mecca the journey of Mansa Musa made a particularly big impression because he dispersed large quantities of gold on the way. The amount of gold given away was so large that a contemporary account said that the value of gold in Egypt depreciated considerably after his arrival. In consequence of this the fame of Mansa Musa and Mali spread all over the Islamic world and beyond, so that Mali even appeared on contemporary European maps for the first time. When Mansa Musa returned to Mali he was accompanied by several North African travellers amongst whom was Abu Ishaq al-Saheli a poet from Andalusia who is credited with the introduction of a new style into West African architecture.

Mansa Musa was succeeded by Maghan I (1337–41) about whom little is known except that he had acted as regent for Mansa Musa during his absence on pilgrimage. In 1341 Maghan was succeeded by Mansa Musa's brother Sulayman who reorganized the empire and financial system in order to recover from the excessive expenditure of his brother. Sulayman was the ruler at the time of Ibn Battuta's visit in 1353 so that there is quite a detailed description of his rule including the king's friendly relations with the Marinid sultans of Morocco. Ibn Khaldun traced the careers of the next

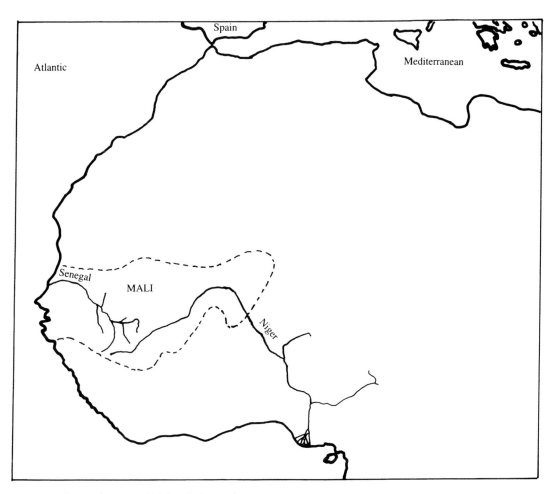

West Africa, showing the empire of Mali in the fourteenth century CE

five kings until the beginning of the fifteenth century, when the kingdom had been seriously weakened by civil wars and was no longer in a position to control all its dependencies which gradually were lost to rival kingdoms. One of the most formidable of these rivals was the Songhay kingdom of Gao or Kawkaw based on the banks of the Niger east of Mali. The arrival of the Portuguese during the fifteenth century introduced another new factor into the politics of the region. The ruler of Mali sought the assistance of these newcomers to fight off African rivals but they were unable to prevent the continuing disintegration of Malian power. In the 1590s the Moroccans occupied Djenné and the rulers of Mali were unable to retake the town. However, the greatly reduced kingdom of Mali continued to survive until 1670 when it was finally destroyed.

Despite its fame there are few architectural remains of the empire of Mali and one is forced to rely mostly on contemporary Arabic descriptions and rather complex oral traditions. At the spiritual capital of Kangaba there is little that remains from the medieval period with the exception of the giant linke (baobab) tree which marks the ancestral centre of the Mali Empire. There are several descriptions of the political capital at Niani, one of the best is that of the fourteenth-century writer al-Umari.

'[The capital] extends in length and breadth to a distance of approximately one barid (postal stage). It is not surrounded by a wall and most of it is scattered . . . . The town is surrounded on four sides by the "Nile" .... The buildings of this town are made of iwad or clay like the walls of the gardens of Damascus. This consists of building two thirds of a cubit (approximately 30 cm) in clay, then leaving it to dry, then building above it in the same way ... and so on until it is complete. The roofs are of wood and reeds and are generally domed or conical, in the form of cupolas of camel-backs, similar to the arch-shaped openings of vaults.'

Ibn Battuta's description of 1353 is not so full although he does indicate that he reached the city by boat and that it had a separate quarter for white merchants. He then describes the king's palace in some detail, in particular the audience hall which may be the same as that built by Abu Ishaq al–Saheli a decade or two earlier. The audience hall is contained within the palace and consists of a square domed chamber with triple-arched windows in each side. The windows are filled with wooden lattice work or grilles covered in silver and gold leaf (mashrabiyya?). Ibn Khaldun probably describing the same building notes that it was 'solidly built and faced with plaster; because such buildings are unknown in his [the sultan's] country'. Obvious parallels for this building can be found in the architecture of fourteenth-century North Africa and Spain (compare for example the Salón del Trono in the Alhambra). Next to the palace was a large open area used as a mosque or place of prayer.

The location of Mali's capital is unknown although it may be the site of Niani-en-Sankrani in Guinea occupied between the sixth and seventeenth centuries. Archaeological work at the site has revealed a large complex with a fortified royal compound, several residential areas, a metal-working centre and many cemeteries. A possible mosque site and Muslim cemetery have been identified near the royal complex which consists of a large square courtyard (20 m per side) and a smaller circular structure. The residential structures at the site consist of roundhouses built of mud with stone foundations.

See also: Djenné, Manding, West Africa

Further reading:

H. Haselberger, 'Architekturskizzen aus der Republic Mali Ergebnisse der DIAFE 190709 des Frobenius Institut', *International Archives of Ethnography* 50(1): 244–80, 1966.

J. Hunwick, 'The mid-fourteenth-century capital of Mali', *Journal of African History* 14(2): 195–206, 1973.

Mamluks

Term applied to the architecture of Greater Syria and Egypt between 1250 and 1516. During this period the area was ruled by the Mamluk sultans based in Cairo.

The word 'mamluk' is an Arabic term for slave and was applied to soldiers who, although non-Muslim by birth, had been captured as children, converted to Islam and trained to fight on behalf of their owners. The Mamluk sultanate had its origins in such slave soldiers, usually of Turkic or Mongol origin, who were used as guards by the Ayyubid sultans and princes. Gradually the Mamluks increased their power and by 1250 their position was so strong that they were able to depose and appoint sultans. In 1260 one of these soldiers, Baybars, became the first Mamluk sultan starting a tradition that was to endure for the next 250 years.

The Mamluk sultanate can be divided into two periods; the first lasted from 1250 to 1382 and is known as the Bahri (sea-based) Mamluk period because the dominant Mamluks were based on Roda island in the Nile delta. The second period from 1382 to 1517 is known as the Burji Mamluk period because those in power came from the Citadel in Cairo (burj is Arabic for tower). This period is sometimes also called the Circassian period, as most of the sultans were of Circassian origin.

The Mamluks were able to seize and retain power primarily through their superior military organization and training. This was demonstrated in 1260 when Sultan Baybars was able to halt the westward advance of the Mongols at the battle of 'Ayn Jalut in Palestine. Similarly the Mamluks continued to fight the Crusaders who by this time were confined to the coast of Syria. The main battles against the Crusaders took place under Sultan Qalaoun and his son Khalil, who in 1291 captured the cities of Acre, Tyre, Sidon, Beirut and Tripoli ending the Crusader presence in the Levant.

Mamluk architecture reflects the confidence derived from its military successes and is one of the most distinctive Islamic styles of building. The main source for Mamluk architecture was the buildings of the Ayyubids and in some senses the Mamluk style is simply a development of that of the Ayyubids. However, the Mamluks were also influenced by other styles, in particular Italian and Andalusian architecture.

As with Ayyubid architecture there is a significant difference between Syrian and Egyptian Mamluk architecture, which can be explained by the availability of materials and differing traditions of building. In Egypt brick remained an important material of construction up until the fifteenth century, whereas in Syria it was seldom used. Other differences can be detected in decorative details such as the type of arch used in muqarnas mouldings (in Egypt they are angular points whereas in Syria they have a rounded profile). Another factor which created different styles was Cairo's position as capital city which meant that its buildings tended to be grander and more highly decorated than those of Syria. Jerusalem is interesting in this respect as its position midway between Damascus and Cairo made it susceptible to influences from both Syria and Egypt.

There are, however, several features which are characteristic of buildings throughout the area under Mamluk control. These can be considered under three headings: surface decoration, layout and planning, and structural elements.

Surface Decoration

The most characteristic feature of Mamluk architecture (and art in general) is the use of heraldic blazons. These are usually round discs divided into three fields with various emblems (e.g. cup, horn, disc, etc.) set into the middle. Each sultan and group of Mamluks had their own blazon which would be applied to any objects belonging to the group including buildings. As well as providing dating evidence these blazons give a useful insight into how the Mamluk regime operated. Another related decoration employed on buildings was monumental calligraphy in Naskhi script, this would usually state the name and rank of a building's founder.

The usual surface for both blazons and calligraphy is ashlar masonry, although plaster and wood are also sometimes used. Other decorative motifs employed are geometric and floral patterns which are often interlaced. Ceramic tile decoration is rare, although coloured glass mosaics and inlaid marble are occasionally used for mihrabs and other places of special importance. One decorative feature to spread from Syria to Egypt is the use of ablaq

(alternating layers of different colours, or shades of masonry); this was used in Syria in Ayyubid times but is not found in Egypt until 1300 (it is possible that this idea may have Italian origins). Mashrabiyya screens of turned wood were also used for interiors.

Structural Elements

In addition to surface decoration many structural elements were developed into decorative features. Openings, in particular doorways, became subjects for elaboration and frequently consisted of a monumental frame or panel and a recessed niche for the door covered with a muqarnas vault. Another example of such elaboration is the joggled voussoir where the stones of an arch were cut so as to interlock and provide increased strength to the arch. Usually the effect is enhanced by using ablaq techniques. Sometimes this becomes purely surface decoration when the actual voussoirs are not inter-cut and there is simply an interlocking façade. Another decorative effect created with openings was the horsehoe arch which was introduced during this period.

Buildings were generally roofed with cross vaults although sometimes plain barrel vaults were used. In Jerusalem an elaborate form of vault called the folded cross vault was developed from Ayyubid military architecture. This is basically a cross vault with a large circular hole in the roof over which a wooden clerestory or other feature could be added. Domes were common in buildings of this period and could be made from a variety of materials including baked brick, wood and stone. Wooden domes were often used in houses and palaces because they were lighter and easier to build, although mausoleums tended to be covered with brick or stone domes. In fourteenth-century Cairo, masonry domes carved with arabesque designs became a fashionable method of covering tombs.

Layout and Planning

The growth of cities during the Mamluk period meant that most types of building, even palaces, were located within the fabric of a city. The result of this was that buildings were often built on an irregular-shaped plot because of the shortage of space. Many Mamluk buildings which

Doorway of Serai al-Takiyya. Mamluk period, Jerusalem (after Burgoyne)

seem to be square and symmetrical are built on irregular ground plans. The architects were able to make the buildings appear square by a variety of techniques such as horizontal lines (ablaq) and controlled access (passageways) which distort perspective. A related problem was that narrow streets tend to detract from the visual impact of a building

façade. This was overcome by use of recessed entrances, domes, and projecting corners which have a cumulative effect of a staggered façade which can be viewed from the side.

The military nature of Mamluk rule affected society in many ways although it did not have much effect on architecture. The main reason for this was that so many fortresses had been built by the Ayyubids and Crusaders that there was generally no need to build new castles when existing fortifications could be repaired. Also with the advance of the Mongols the nature of warfare changed so that speed and communications became more important than the defence and capture of strongholds. As a consequence of this the Mamluks invested instead in an efficient system of communication based on small forts, fire beacons and pigeon lofts. This system was kept separate from the usual trade network of khans and caravanserais and was regarded as part of the Mamluks' military organization.

Building Types

Some of the most distinctive buildings of the Mamluk period are the many religious foundations. Most cities already had Friday mosques so that these were seldom built during this period. The Great Mosque in Tripoli is one exception to this and was built soon after the city was taken from the Crusaders, it has a traditional plan based around a central courtyard with single arcades on three sides and a double arcade on the qibla side. More typical of the period are the many religious institutions such as madrassas, zawiyas and khanqas built to counter the spread of Shi'ism. In Cairo these were often built to a cruciform plan which developed from the four-iwan madrassa where each iwan represents one of the schools of law. Many of these buildings also had some political purpose, thus they were often built as memorials to a particular Sultan or were used as centres for training officials. During this period it was common for the tomb of the founder to be incorporated into the building, this applied to mosques, madrassas and even hospitals.

Madrassas became a common feature in most cities and were used to train administrators. Jerusalem in particular seems to have been developed as a training ground for Mamluk clergy and officials and the area around the Haram was extensively developed (Mecca was too far from Cairo to be developed in this way and in any case was not directly under Mamluk control).

The stability provided by the Mamluk regime was a stimulus to trade and numerous suqs, khans and caravanserais can be dated to this period. The Suq al-Qattanin (Cotton Market) in Jerusalem is one of the best preserved Mamluk city markets. It

was built on the orders of Sultan al-Nasir Muhammad in 1336 as a huge complex with over fifty shop units, two bath houses and a khan. Each shop is a small cross-vaulted room opening onto the covered street with another room (for storage or accommodation) located above with a separate access. Although the highest concentration of suqs and khans was in the cities there was also an extensive network of roadside khans and caravanserais. Some of these buildings were quite large as they were not restricted by the competition for space evident in city buildings. Khan Yunis in Ghaza is a huge complex built in 1387 on the main road between Egypt and Syria. The plan comprises a huge central courtyard (perhaps with a building in the centre) with accommodation and storage units around the sides and a domed mosque with a minaret next to the gateway.

See also: ablaq, joggled voussoirs, mashrabiyya

Further reading:

There are several books devoted to Mamluk cities; the most useful of these are:

M. H. Burgoyne and D. Richards, *Mamluk Jerusalem: An Architectural Study*, Essex 1987.

J. C. Garlin, J. Revault, B. Maury and M. Zakariya, *Palais et maisons du Caire: Époque mamelouke*, Paris 1982.

H. Salam-Liebech, *The Architecture of Mamluk Tripoli*, Harvard 1983.

Other useful works are:

M. Abu Khalaf, 'Khan Yunnus and the khans of Palestine', *Levant* 15: 178–86, 1983.

J. C. Kessler, *The Carved Masonry Domes of Cairo*, London 1976.

J. Sauvaget, *La Poste aux Chevaux dans l'empire des Mamlouks*, Paris 1941.

Manda

Island trading port on the north Kenya coast in East Africa.

This is the largest early Islamic complex in the Lamu archipelago and one of the largest on the coast. The earliest occupation seems to have been in the mid-eighth century and to have continued until the sixteenth when it was noted by the Portuguese.

The earliest structures at the site were made with timber posts and walls of wattle and daub. During the tenth century the settlement expanded on to an area of land reclaimed from the sea by sea walls built from huge coral blocks. Sometime in the tenth century the wooden structures were replaced with stone buildings made out of reef coral. Also during the tenth century some buildings were made out of two types of baked brick, a locally made variety and rarer imported brick (possibly from Oman). The only tenth-century building completely excavated is known as the 'House of Cisterns' and consists of a large courtyard building entered via a flight of seven steps.

Buildings erected after the thirteenth century used fossil coral instead of the reef coral of earlier structures. Ruins surviving from the later period of occupation include several houses, a town wall, two mosques and several monumental tombs.

See also: coral, East Africa, Kenya, Shanga

Further reading:

H. N. Chittick, *Manda: Excavations at an Island Port on the Kenya Coast*, British Institute in Eastern Africa Memoir 9, in 2 vols., Nairobi 1984.

M. C. Horton, 'Asiatic colonization of the East African coast: the Manda evidence', *Journal of the Royal Asiatic Society* pt. 2: 201–12, 1986.

mandal

Mughal term for a pavilion or house.

manding (Mande)

West African language group which formed the ruling class of the empire of Mali, now used to describe one of the dominant urban architectural styles of the region.

The current distribution of the Manding peoples covers an area including southern Mali, Burkina Faso and the Ivory Coast. Prominent cities with Manding architecture include Mopti, Djenné, Ségou, Bobo Dioulasso, Wa and Kong.

Characteristic features of Manding architecture are the use of mud brick, conical towers with projecting toron, and elaborate decorated entrance façades. Mud is the traditional building material of the area and is used in several forms, either as spherical hand-rolled lumps or as rectangular or cylindrical bricks. Conical towers may either occur as buttresses or as towers marking the position of a mihrab in a mosque. It is thought that the conical towers derive from the pre-Islamic ancestral pillars of the region whilst the use of toron traditionally suggests continual rebirth. Whilst the façades of mosques and palaces are often decorated with earthen pillars and projecting toron, the decoration of house façades is normally restricted to the entrances. Some of the most elaborate entrance façades can be found at Djenné in Mali which is

usually considered the birthplace of the Manding style. A traditional façade will consist of three levels contained within two parallel buttresses. The first two levels correspond to the two storeys inside the house whilst the third level corresponds to the roof level parapet. The first level consists of the doorway covered by a steep sloping sill above which is the second level containing a rectangular panel with a square window in the middle. The third level consists of a line of projecting toron made of split palm, a panel containing four pillared niches and four pointed crenellations on the top.

See also: Djenné, Mali, Sudan, West Africa

Further reading:

L. Prussin, 'Sudanese architecture and the Manding', *African Arts* 3(4): 12–19 and 64–7, 1970.

manzil

Arabic term for house or way station (literally 'a place to stay').

maq'ad

Projecting balcony overlooking a courtyard in Egyptian houses.

maqbara

Graveyard.

maqsura

Screen which encloses the area of the mihrab and minbar in early mosques.

The origin of the screens was to protect the caliph from assassination attempts during praying. There also may have been some spiritual connotation similar to the chancel screen in churches. They were often wooden screens decorated with carvings or interlocking turned pieces of wood (mashrabiyya).

Marakesh

Southern capital of Morocco.

Marakesh is on a wide plain located 40 km from the High Atlas. It was founded by the Almoravid ruler Yusf ibn Tashfin in 1062, although there are few buildings which have survived from this period. The best surviving example is the dome of the Almoravid palace; built of baked brick covered with plaster, the dome rests on a square brick base. The area immediately below the drum is pierced with twenty-four multifoil niches, whilst the dome itself is decorated with interlaced arches in relief and zig-zag patterns on the top. Inside the dome has an entirely different configuration and consists of an eight-pointed star rising to a muqarnas dome.

Remains from the Almohad period (twelfth to thirteenth century) include the Kutubiyya Mosque, the Kasba Mosque and the Bab Agnau. The Kutubiyya Mosque is built in the traditional Almohad style with the lateral arcades of the courtyard forming an integral part of the prayer hall. The mosque has a minaret more than 60 m high, decorated with windows and blind niches with interlaced arches; at the top there is a small kiosk covered with a fluted dome. The parapet is decorated with ceramic tile inlays and stepped merlons. The minaret is ascended by a ramp which is built around a hollow square core. The core contains a series of six vaulted rooms, one on each storey and each with a different form of vault (the design is similar to the Giralda tower in Seville). The Kasba Mosque is a square building containing five courtyards, four subsidiary and one central. The minaret is decorated in a similar style to the Kutubiyya and inside there is a staircase built around a central core. The Bab Agnau is part of the massive Almohad fortifications which stretch around the city for a distance of over 10 km. The gateway is built of brick and comprises a wide opening covered with a pointed horseshoe arch. The inner arch is framed by a magnificent round horseshoe arch decorated with a bold interlaced pattern. The intrados of the arch is decorated with bold stylized flora, and the whole is enclosed within a giant rectangular frame with a Kufic inscription.

The city has three madrassas the oldest of which is the Bin Yusuf Madrassa built as a mosque in the twelfth century and converted in the sixteenth. The town also contains the tombs of various Moroccan rulers, including that of Yusuf ibn Tashfin founder of the Almoravid dynasty, and the tomb of the seven saints which is still the object of an annual pilgrimage.

There are several palaces within the city, the oldest of which is the Dar al Makhzan founded by the Almohads but considerably altered in the sixteenth century. The city also contains historic gardens, the most important being the Mamounia, originally laid out in the seventeenth century.

See also: Morocco

Mardin

City in south-east Anatolia (Turkey) associated with the Artukid dynasty during the medieval period.

Mardin is located in a strategic position on a rocky spur overlooking the crossroads between east–west and north–south routes. The city is dominated by the fortress which has stood on this site since Roman times. During the Islamic period the castle has been extensively repaired several times, first by the Hamdanids in the ninth century, later by the Artukids and more recently by the Ottomans. From 1104 to 1408 the city became the principal stronghold of the Artukids who resisted successive attacks by the Ayyubids, the Mongols and the Timurids.

The buildings of the town are terraced into the hillside and all have magnificent views over the Mesopotamian plain. The main building stone is brilliant white limestone which provides a dazzling contrast to the grey-black basalt which characterizes the surrounding region.

Several important buildings survive from the Artukid period including the Great Mosque, a hammam and several madrassas. The prayer hall of the Great Mosque is a multi-domed unit in the usual Artukid style whilst the minaret is a tall cylindrical tower with elaborately carved cartouches. One of the most striking buildings in the city is the Kasim Pasha Madrassa built in 1445 by the Aq-qoyunulu ruler Kasim b. Jahangir. There are also several important churches and monasteries in the region.

See also: Turkey

maristan

Hospital.

marqad

Tombstone.

mashhad

Shrine, or commemorative mosque.

mashrabiyya

Wooden grille or grate used to cover windows or balconies.

The word is derived from the niches used to store vessels of drinking water. The grilles are traditionally made from short lengths of turned wood joined together through polygonal blocks so that

Star-shaped mashrabiyya

they form large areas of lattice-like patterns. The patterns formed by the lattice work vary from place to place although commonly the main lines of the grille are at a 45 degree angle. Mashrabiyya can also be made of metalwork although this is more rare and was usually reserved for the houses of the very rich or public buildings.

masjid

Mosque.

mastaba

Bench or platform.

mathara

Place of ritual ablution.

mazar

Mausoleum or shrine.

Mecca (Makka)

The most sacred city of Islam located in western Saudi Arabia.

The city of Mecca lies about 70 km inland from the Red Sea port of Jeddah. It is built in a hollow in the mountains known as Batn Mecca. The oldest part of the city contains the Holy Mosque and the Ka'ba and is known as al-Batha. Rainfall is extremely scarce and unpredictable; in ancient times water was supplied by a series of wells, the most important of which is the well of Zamzam within the holy precinct. Despite the aridity of the area the city's position makes it prone to flash floods which are diverted by a series of dams and channels which deflect water away from the city centre.

History

In pre-Islamic times Mecca was known as a sacred site and was referred to as Maccorba in the time of Ptolemy. The first permanent settlements on the site were made in the fifth century CE by the Quraysh tribe. By the sixth century the city appears to have become a great trading centre profiting from the caravan trade between the Mediterranean and the Indian Ocean. In 570 the prophet Muhammad was born in Mecca, by the year 610 he had begun to preach the message revealed to him as Quran. Muhammad's teaching annoyed the prominent merchants of the town so that in 622 he was compelled to leave for the city of Medina. (This event is known as the Hejira or migration and is the starting point for the Muslim calendar.) In Medina Muhammad attracted a large following who were able to attack the Meccan caravans. By 630 Muhammad and his followers (the Muslims) had defeated Mecca and converted most of its inhabitants to Islam. In the following years Medina became capital of the new Islamic state whilst Mecca retained its position as religious centre and centre of pilgrimage.

For a brief period between 680 and 692 Mecca became the capital of a rival caliphate established by Abd Allah Ibn Zubayr who controlled most of Arabia and Iraq. During the Abbasid period huge sums of money were spent on developing the city. In the tenth century the decline of the caliphate allowed the Qarmathians (a radical anti-establishment group) to sack Mecca and carry off the Black Stone to their base in Bahrain. The Black Stone

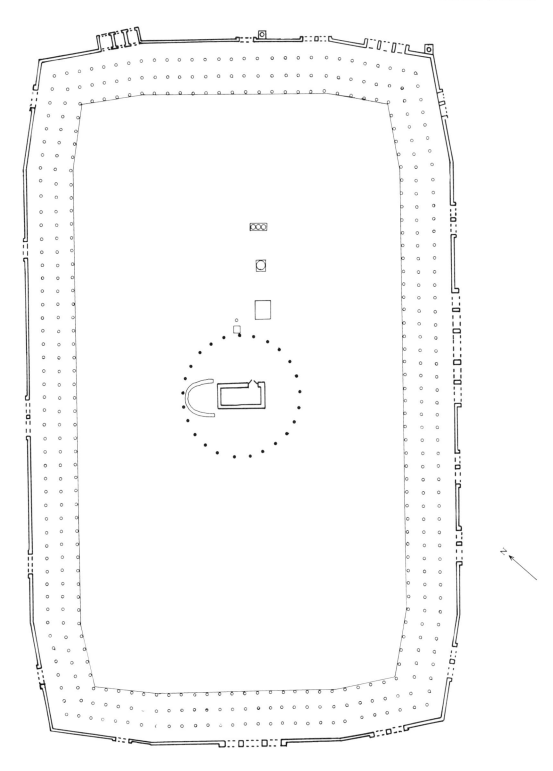

The Haram, Mecca (after Jairazbhoy)

was later returned and Mecca continued to develop as a religious centre.

From the late tenth century to the beginning of the nineteenth century Mecca was ruled by the Sharifs of Mecca who attempted to remain independent of the dominant powers of the time. In 1929 Mecca became part of the Kingdom of Saudi Arabia.

Architecture

The most important building in Mecca is the Holy Mosque of Mecca which contains the Ka'ba, a tall box-like structure which stands in a courtyard in the centre of the mosque. The Ka'ba is pre-Islamic in origin although at the beginning of the Islamic period it became established as the main object of pilgrimages to Mecca.

The area around the Ka'ba was first enclosed by a wall in 638 in order to create an open space for the tawaf (circumambulation). In 646 the area was enlarged with a new enclosure wall with arcades opening on to the courtyard. In 684 under Abd Allah Ibn Zubayr the mosque was further enlarged and decorated with marble and mosaic decoration. In 709 the Umayyad caliph al-Walid covered the arcades of the mosque with a teak roof resting on marble columns. A further enlargement was carried out by the Abbasid caliph al-Mansur between 754 and 757, and it was at this time that the first minaret was built. For the next 700 years numerous modifications were carried out although no major alterations to the form of the building occurred until the Ottoman period in the sixteenth century. The best medieval description of the mosque is by Ibn Jubayr who visited it in 1183. He describes a roofed arcade around a central courtyard decorated with large merlons and stucco decoration.

Major renovations were carried out in 1564 under the direction of the Ottoman sultan Suleyman the Magnificent who replaced the flat roofs of the arcades with stone domes and rebuilt the minarets. The next major rebuilding took place in the twentieth century under Saudi rule and made the Holy Mosque of Mecca the largest mosque in the world. In its present form the mosque has seven minarets, two-storey arcades around the enlarged courtyard and a covered street (Ma'sa) between the hills of al-Safa and al-Marwa (1920s).

Other features within the Holy Mosque include the well of Zamzam and the Maqam Ibrahim. According to Muslim tradition the well of Zamzam sprang up when Hajar (the wife of Ibrahim) was looking for water for her child Ishmael. In the ninth century the well was covered with a vaulted roof by the Abbasid caliph al-Mu'tassim. The form of the building was changed several times in the following centuries the most enduring of which was that built by the Ottomans in the seventeenth century. In addition to its function as a cover of the well the Maqam Zamzam also functioned as a base for Shafi theologians. Hanbali, Hanafi and Malaki theologians each had their own maqam within the courtyard which were also rebuilt at this time. In the 1950s all these maqams were removed by the Saudi authorities to make more space for the circumambulation of the Ka'ba. The Maqam of Zamzam was replaced by two underground ablutions rooms fed by the well of Zamzam. The Maqam Ibrahim contains a stone with two footprints which are thought to be those of Ibrahim. This building was restored by the Saudi authorities in the 1950s.

In its present form Mecca is predominantly a modern city although it does contain a few houses from the Ottoman period (eighteenth century or later). Traditional Meccan houses are generally tall (three to four storeys) with projecting wooden windows (mashrabiyya) and flat roofs enclosed by walls 2 m high. The extreme heat of the city in the summer (50 degrees celsius) means that the houses are equipped with airshafts which allow hot air to escape. Most of the houses in Mecca are dual purpose, serving as family homes and as pilgrim hostels during the season of the Hajj.

The main building materials used in Meccan houses are stone, brick and wood. Two types of stone are used, finely dressed stone and rubble stone. The dressed stone (sandstone or granite) is used for decorative panels around doorways and windows that often incorporate decorative niches. Rubble stone is used for load-bearing walls which are usually two stones wide and laid in rough courses of mud-based mortar. At regular intervals (between 50 and 70 cm) there are layers of wood (usually palm or mangrove) which improves the load-bearing capacity of the walls. The windows are made of hardwood (usually teak) and are highly decorated. Windows may be either flat panels with openings protected by screens or elaborated structures resting on carved brackets. Brick is used in

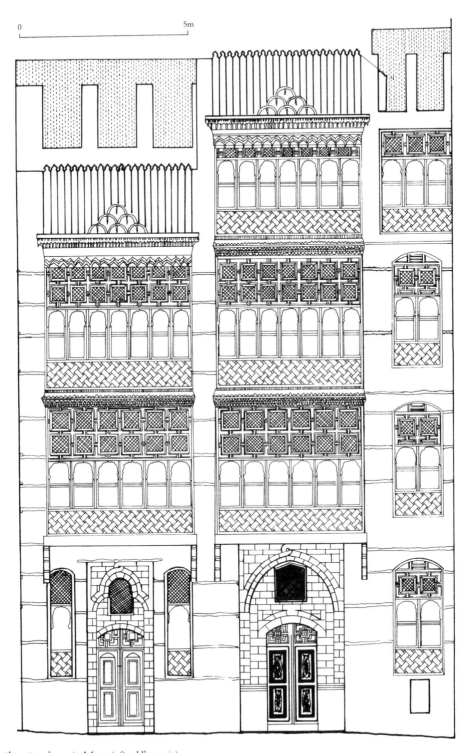

0   5m

Eighteenth-century house in Mecca (after Ulluenegin)

walls which enclose the terraces or roof gardens on the top of each house. The brick is locally made and laid in a decorative pattern which leaves holes for ventilation.

See also: Hajj routes, Ka'ba, Medina, Saudi Arabia

Further reading:

E. Esin, *Mecca the Blessed, Medinah the Radiant*, London 1963.

R. A. Jairazbhoy, 'The architecture of the Holy Shrine in Makkah', in *Hajj in Focus*, ed. Z. I. Khan and Y. Zaki, London 1986, 151–70.

G. R. D. King, *The Historical Mosques of Saudi Arabia*, London and New York 1986, 19–26.

N. and B. Uluenegin, 'Homes of Old Makkah', *Aramco World* 44(4): 20–9, 1993.

M. Watt, A. J. Wensinck, C. E. Bosworth, R. B. Winder and D. King, 'Makka', *Encyclopedia of Islam* 6: 144–87, 1991.

A. Yusef, 'Al-Haramain: a development study', *Hajj in Focus*, ed. Z. I. Khan and Y. Zaki, London 1986, 171–80.

medina

Literally 'city'. This term is often used in North Africa to describe the older part of the city.

Medina (Madina al-Monawwara)

Second most sacred city of Islam located in the Hijaz region of Saudi Arabia.

The city of Medina stands in a fertile oasis 360 km north of Mecca and 160 km east of the Red Sea. In pre-Islamic times the city was known as Yathrib although by the early years of Islam it was also referred to as Medina. The original city of Medina comprised a series of small settlements dispersed over a wide plain. The spaces between the settlements were filled with fruit gardens, fields and date-palm groves. Each settlement was protected by a number of forts or towers which at the beginning of Islam are said to have numbered more than 200. At the time of Muhammad's arrival in Medina (the first year of the Hejira) the town had a large Judaeo-Arabic population in addition to the pagan Arab population. The first Muslim converts in Medina were converted by Muhammad whilst they were on a pilgrimage to Mecca. In 622 Muslim pilgrims from Medina invited Muhammad to come to their city to escape the growing hostility of the Meccan hierarchy. With Muham-

mad's arrival in Medina the city became the capital of an expanding Muslim Empire. After Muhammad's death Abu Bakr was appointed as caliph and continued to rule from Medina as did his two successors Umar and Uthman. Under Ali the newly established town of Kufa replaced Medina as the capital. Medina remained in a secondary position under the Umayyads although they did develop it as a religious centre.

The first city wall was built around the centre of Medina in 974 in preparation for a Fatimid attack. In 1162 a larger area was enclosed by a wall with towers and gates erected by Nur al-Din Zangi. After the Ottoman conquest of the Hijaz in the sixteenth century the Ottoman sultan Suleyman the Magnificent enclosed the city in a new wall 12 m high made of granite and basalt blocks. Suleyman was also responsible for building an aqueduct which brought water into the city from the south. In the 1860s the Ottoman sultan Abd al-Aziz increased the height of the walls to 25 m. During the twentieth century the walls were gradually removed as they were thought to be of no further use.

The most important building in Medina is the Mosque of the Prophet Muhammad. When Muhammad arrived in 622 he was given a plot of land on which to build his house and prayer area (the first mosque). The mosque was a rectangular enclosure (35 by 30 m) with covered areas at the south and north ends. The house of Muhammad and his wives was built on the outside of the east wall. Originally Muhammad and his followers prayed towards Jerusalem but after a revelation the direction of prayer was changed to Mecca in the south. In 629 the mosque was extended on the north, south and west sides to form a square enclosure. In its earliest form the mosque had no mihrab although there was a wooden minbar of three steps which was used by the prophet for preaching the Quran. After his death Muhammad was buried in his house in the room of one of his wives. Subsequently the caliphs Abu Bakr and Umar were buried in the same place. During the reign of Umar the palm trunks were replaced with stone columns and a new roof of teak was added.

The first major rebuilding of the mosque was carried out during the reign of the Umayyad caliph al-Walid. Walid more than doubled the size of the mosque and incorporated the room contain-

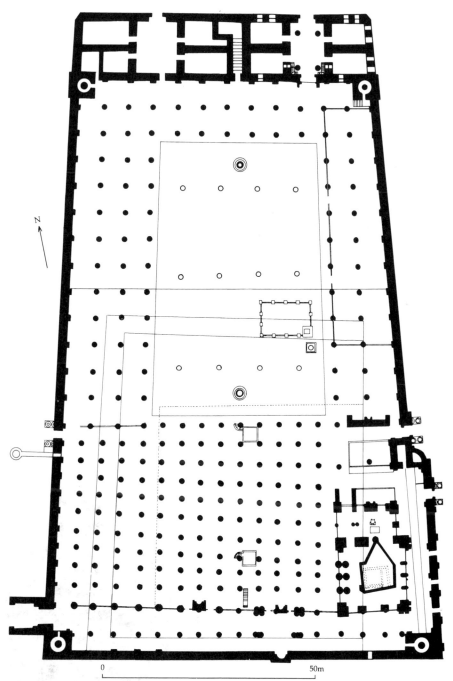

The mosque of the Prophet, Medina; with tomb of Muhammad in lower right-hand corner (after Sauvaget)

ing the graves into the body of the mosque. To prevent any confusion with the Ka'ba in Mecca the enclosure around the graves was of an irregular shape. Walid also added a mihrab and four minarets to the structure of the mosque and embellished the interior of the mosque with mosaic and marble decoration. The mosque was further enlarged under the Abbasid caliphs in 781 by al-Mahdi and in 862 by al-Muawakkil. In 1256 the mosque suffered from a major fire which destroyed the roof, the Quran of Uthman and the minbar of the prophet. The mosque was rebuilt by the Egyptian Mamluk sultan Baybars who established a tradition of Mamluk restoration work on the mosque. In 1279 the Mamluk sultan Qala'un added a wooden dome over the tomb of the prophet. In 1467 this was replaced by a stone dome under the directions of Qayt Bay who also replaced the maqsura.

The Ottoman conquest of the city in the sixteenth century introduced a new architectural style into the Medina Mosque. One of the first modifications was the mihrab Suleymani added by Suleyman the Magnificent. Later on in the sixteenth century the mosque was extended to the west and a new minaret was added. The present green dome over the tomb of the prophet was added in 1818 under the Ottoman sultan Mahmud II. In the 1920s the mosque became the responsibility of the Saudi rulers who undertook various repairs and restorations. In 1951 the Saudi government initiated the largest programme of expansion in the mosque's history making the total mosque area 22,955 m square. In 1973 a huge new court was added on to the west side of the mosque to cope with the increasing number of pilgrims.

Like Mecca, the city of Medina is mostly a modern concrete construction. By analogy with the Prophet's mosque it is known that in the early days of Islam the houses were built of mud brick with palm wood used for roofing and pillars. The advent of Islam brought new wealth to the city and may have encouraged the development of stone architecture. Certainly by the beginning of the Ottoman period stone was in use on a large enough scale to be employed for the city walls. The traditional house form in Mecca appears to have been a courtyard house three or four storeys high built out of granite or basalt. Water was relatively more plentiful than at Mecca and each house had its own well. According to reports, some of the houses had columned halls opening on to bathing pools.

Further reading:

G. R. D. King, *Historical Mosques of Saudi Arabia*, London and New York 1986.

J. Sauvaget, *La Mosquée Omeyyade de Medine. Études sur les origines architecturales de la mosquée et de la basilique*, Paris 1947.

W. M. Watt and R. B. Winder, 'Al-Madina', *Encyclopaedia of Islam*, new edn., 5: 994–1007, 1986.

A. Youssef, 'Al Haramain: a development study', in *Hajj in Focus*, ed. Z. I. Khan and Y. Zaki, London 1986.

Meknes

Former capital of Morocco located on a high plateau between Fez and Rabat.

The city of Meknes was founded by the Almoravids in the eleventh century, before that period the site was occupied by a cluster of small villages. The city suffered from the Almohad conquest in 1150, although it was later restored and in the thirteenth century was provided with an aqueduct, bridges and a madrassa. The city reached its peak under the Sa'adians who adopted it as their capital in the seventeenth century. Under the sultan Moulay Ismail the city was enclosed by a triple wall with a perimeter of more than 30 km pierced by twenty gates. To the south of the city is a huge separate enclosure reserved for the sultan which contains two palaces, one for the sultan and one for his wives and 500 concubines. The palaces were built as a series of gardens connected by pavilions supported on marble columns. There are a total of forty-five separate pavilions within the grounds, as well as four mosques and twenty domed tombs containing the graves of sultans and their families. To support the palace there was a huge granary, store house, stables, an army camp and palatial residences for the officials.

See also: Morocco

Mérida

City in south-west Spain noted for its Roman ruins and early Islamic fortress.

The fortress is located next to the river Guadiana and the famous Roman bridge. It is probably a continuation of an older structure, although it was substantially altered to its present form in 835 according to an inscription found in the fortress (now in the local museum). It is similar to sixth- and seventh-century Byzantine forts of North Africa although the arches above the gateways are horseshoe-shaped indicating their Islamic provenance.

The fortress is essentially a large square enclo-

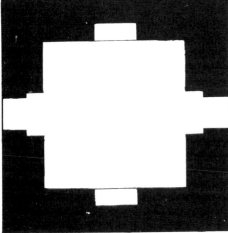

Tomb of Sultan Sanjar, Merv, Turkmenistan (after Pugachenkara)

sure (130 m per side) with solid rectangular buttress towers and three gateways. The gateway leading from the Roman bridge is in the form of a gatehouse flanked by two massive towers. The only contemporary structure within the fortress is a cistern which took water directly from the river via a tunnel. Entry to the cistern is from a barrel-vaulted corridor with staircases at either end and doorways in the side which lead to the cistern. The jambs of the doorways and other parts of the cistern include re-used Visigothic building stones.

See also: Spain

Further reading:

K. A. C. Creswell, *A Short Account of Early Muslim Architecture*, revised and enlarged ed. J. W. Allan, Aldershot 1989, 302.

G. Goodwin, *Islamic Spain*, Architectural Guides for Travellers, London 1990, 125–6.

Merv (also Marw or Marv)

Ancient city in the Central Asian republic of Turkmenistan. Also called Merv al-Shahijan or Royal Merv to distinguish it from the city of the same name in modern Afghanistan.

The city is located in the Merv oasis fed by the Murghab river. During the early Islamic period it functioned as one of the chief cities of Khurassan and under the Abbasids was capital of the east. During the eighth century the centre of the town gradually moved from its old Sassanian site of Gyaur Kala to a new site which is now known as Sultan Kala. In 1070 the Seljuk sultan Malikshah rebuilt the city wall which remains as one of the finest examples of medieval fortification. Other remains from the Seljuk period include the mausoleum of Sultan Sanjar which is a domed structure standing on a square base measuring 27 m per side. The Mongol invasions caused severe damage

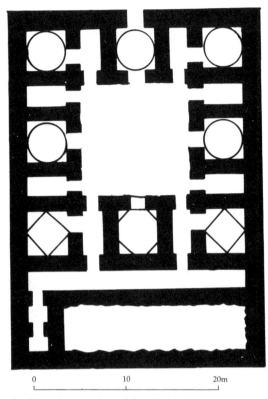

Pre-thirteenth-century house, Merv, Turkmenistan

Mihrab built in 1227 of dressed limestone, Great Mosque, Silvan

to the city which never fully recovered. Under the Timurid sultan Shah Rukh attempts were made to revive the fortunes of the city. The city dam was rebuilt to restore the irrigation system but this was only partially successful. Also the city of this period was built on a different site known as Abd Allah Khan Kalla.

Further reading:

G. Herrman, V. Masson, K. Kurbansakhatov, et. al., 'The International Merv Project, preliminary report on the First Season', *Iran* 31: 39–62, 1993.

E. O'Donovan, *The Merv Oasis and Adventures East of the Caspian During the Years 1879–81*, London 1882.

G. A. Pugachenkava, 'Puti razvitiya arkhitekturi Iuzhnogo Turkmenistana pori rabovladeniya', *Trudi Iuzhno-Turkmenistanskoi Arkheologicheskoi Ekspeditsii* 6: Moscow, 1958.

mescit

Turkish term for a small mosque without a minbar, equivalent to the Arabic term masjid.

mihrab

Niche or marker used to indicate the direction of prayer usually in a mosque.

A mihrab is usually a niche set into the middle of the qibla wall of a building in order to indicate the direction of Mecca. The earliest mosques do not appear to have had mihrabs and instead the whole qibla wall was used to indicate the direction of Mecca. Sometimes a painted mark or a tree stump would be used to reinforce the direction. In the cave beneath the rock in the Dome of the Rock there is a marble plaque with a blind niche carved into it which, if contemporary with the rest of the structure, may be dated to 692 making it the oldest surviving mihrab. The first concave mihrab appears to have been inserted into the Prophet's Mosque at Medina during some restorations carried out by the Umayyad caliph al-Walid I in 706. Excavations at Wasit in Iraq have confirmed this date for the introduction of the first concave mihrab where there are two superimposed mosques; the lower one datable to the seventh century has no mihrab whilst the upper mosque has a concave mihrab.

Mihrab of mausoleum of Iltumish, Delhi

Mihrab, Kilwa-Kivinje, Tanzania

In addition to its function as a directional indicator it is thought that the first mihrab niches had a ceremonial or ritual function associated with symbols of royalty. Certainly the mihrab became a focus for architectural decoration and was often embellished with the latest artistic techniques (e.g. stucco, polychrome glazed tiles, carved woodwork, glass mosaic, marble inlay). The designs were usually epigraphic and often geometric or vegetal, but never with any suggestion of figurative imagery. The area in front of the mihrab was also emphasized, either by a maqsura immediately in front of the mihrab or a raised aisle leading from the courtyard to the niche. In later mosques, especially in Bengal, multiple mihrabs are set into the qibla wall, thus diffusing any hierarchy of sanctity.

There is also an early association of mihrab and minbar, with the minbar placed next to the mihrab possibly to lend spiritual authority to the sermon. In some areas such as East Africa the mihrab is linked to a recessed minbar niche so that the imam climbs the minbar by entering a door in the side of the mihrab. This arrangement, however, is extremely unusual as the mihrab should be kept free of any mystical connotations.

mimar

Islamic term for architect.

minaret

Tower-like structure usually associated with mosques or other religious buildings.

Although the mosques of Damascus, Fustat and Medina had towers during the Umayyad period it is now generally agreed that the minaret was introduced during the Abbasid period (i.e. after 750 CE). Six mosques dated to the early ninth century all have a single tower or minaret attached to the wall opposite the mihrab. The purpose of the minaret in these mosques was to demonstrate the power of Abbasid religious authority. Those opposed to Abbasid power would not adopt this symbol of conformity, thus Fatimid mosques did not have towers. Although later minarets appear to have become synonymous with Islamic architecture they have never been entirely universal. In parts of Iran, East Africa, Arabia and much of the Far East many mosques were built without them. In such places the call to prayer is either made from the courtyard of the mosque or from the roof.

The form of minarets differs throughout the Islamic world. A brief summary of the form in each area is required.

Egypt

In post-Fatimid Egypt minarets developed into a complex and distinctive form. Each tower is composed of three distinct zones: a square section at the bottom, an octagonal middle section and a dome on the top. The zone of transition between each section is covered with a band of muqarnas decoration. In earlier structures the square shaft was tall and the dome was ornate, later the central octagonal section became longer whilst the square shaft was reduced to a square socle at the base. During the fourteenth century the dome at the top was modified into the form of a stone bulb.

Another feature of the post-Fatimid period (after the twelfth century CE) is the increase in the number of buildings which had minarets. Whereas under the Abbasids minarets had been restricted to congregational mosques, during the Mamluk period all kinds of buildings could have minarets including smaller mosques, tombs, khanqas and madrassas.

Syria

The traditional Syrian minaret consists of a square plan tower built of stone. The form is thought to derive from the traditional Syrian church tower of the Byzantine period. The tower standing opposite the mihrab in the Great Mosque of Damascus is the oldest minaret in Syria, dating from the early ninth century, although the upper part may have been rebuilt several times. Another early Syrian minaret is that of the Great Mosque at Harran

(now in modern Turkey) built sometime between the eighth and eleventh centuries. It is built of large dressed ashlar blocks with a cyma reversa moulding at 16 m above ground level. Generally during the Ottoman period the square tower was abandoned in favour of the octagonal or cylindrical minaret.

North Africa and Spain

North Africa and Spain share the square tower form with Syria and are thought to derive from the same source – Syrian church towers. In time this design was adapted by Christians in Spain for use as church bell towers.

The earliest minaret in North Africa is that of the Great Mosque of Qayrawan built in 836. This massive tower with battered walls is over 31 m high with a square base 10.6 m per side. The lower 4 m are built of large re-used stone blocks whilst the upper sections are built of smaller long slabs which resemble baked bricks. The smaller minaret at Sfax also dated to the ninth century was probably modelled on that at Qayrawan.

Several early minarets survive in Spain including that belonging to the congregational mosque in Seville and that of the mosque at Medina al-Zahra. However, the most impressive early minaret is that of Abd al-Rahman of Córdoba completed in 968 and now encased within the church tower. The minaret is 8.5 m square at the base, 47 m high and contains two independent staircases. Related minarets are those of the Qarawiyyin Mosque in Fez (built 955) and the mosque of the Andalusians at Fez (built 956) although both are smaller than that at Córdoba.

The Almoravids and early Almohads followed Fatimid precedent in not building minarets. The earliest Almohad tower is at the mosque of Timnal which is unusual both for its positioning (behind the mihrab) and its relatively short height of 15 m. It appears that the architect sought to make it appear tall from outside without it being visible from the courtyard of the mosque. However, later Almohad minarets were tall, impressive structures such as that of the Kutubiyya Mosque which is 67 m tall and 12.5 m per side at the base. The exterior is decorated with panels of decorative motifs around paired sets of windows. The top is decorated with with serrated crenellations, a band of polychrome tilework and three gilded copper balls.

In the same tradition are the minarets of the

Great Mosque of Seville (built 1184), the unfinished minaret of the mosque of Hassan at Rabat and the minaret of the Qasaba Mosque in Marrakesh.

Iran

The oldest known minaret in Iran is that of the congregational mosque at Siraf dated to the ninth century. It is known that many minarets were built during the tenth century although the only the survivors are the minarets at Fahraj and Nayin. The minaret at Fahraj has a tapering cylindrical form and a projecting balcony. The minaret attached to the Friday mosque at Nayin consists of a tall tapering brick shaft, the lower part of which is octagonal in plan whilst the upper part is cylindrical. The shaft is decorated with a simple chevron pattern using diagonally laid bricks. A similarly ancient miharet is attached to the Tarik-Khana in Damghan built in 1026. Like the minaret at Nayin it is decorated with bricks bonded in different ways, although here the decoration is more complex containing seven bands of diamond patterns.

The cylindrical minaret form, which was developed in Iran, spread over a huge area with the Seljuk conquests of Syria, Anatolia, Iraq, Afghanistan and India. Some of the structures were severe plain brick shafts whilst others were highly decorated with complex brick patterns. A variation of the standard from was the introduction of various forms of cylindrical fluting. The Jar Kurgan minaret has semi-circular fluting whilst the minaret of Ghazna attributed to Masud II has angular flutes. Minarets of this type may be interpreted as victory towers rather than as religious towers in the strict sense. Probably the most surprising example of this type of tower is the Jam minaret. This 60 m high tower stands in a secluded valley in Afghanistan and is decorated with monumental calligraphy celebrating the victory of the Ghurid sultan. It is significant that the Qutb Minar in Delhi was built by a Turkish general who served in the army of the Ghurid sultan who built the Jam minaret.

Iraq

Probably the earliest standing minaret in Iraq is the manar al-Mujida located in the desert northwest of Kufa. This has a cylindrical shaft 7 m high on a square base with a spiral staircase inside. The structure is not associated with any mosque but is dated to the Umayyad period (before 750 CE) on the basis of its plain brick decoration and association with nearby structures.

The most famous minarets in Iraq are the giant spiral minarets of Samarra both of which are dated to the ninth century. The larger of these, known as the Malwiyya, stands away from the rear of the Great Mosque at Samarra. The other minaret stands in the same position near the Abu Dulaf Mosque. Although it is generally believed that the form of these minarets is derived from the ziggurat (e.g. Khorsabad) their relationship to the topography of Samarra is often not considered. As the Great Mosque at Samarra was the largest mosque in the world it would have needed a correspondingly tall minaret. To have built a cylindrical minaret 50 m high would have been both impractical and visually unimpressive within the vast horizontal spaces of Samarra. However, a giant spiral minaret contains enough mass in relation to its height to make a significant visual impact.

The spiral minarets of Samarra were never copied, except in the mosque of Ibn Tulun in Egypt which copies many other features from Samarra. In the Ibn Tulun minaret the top part has a small spiral ramp reminiscent of the minarets of Samarra.

Later minarets in Iraq are versions of Iranian Seljuk minarets although Iraq seems to have developed its own local schools. Thus, the minaret of the Friday mosque in Mosul (known locally as al-Hadba) is decorated with complex geometric patterns and seems to be related to other minarets in the vicinity such as Mardin, Sinjar and Irbil.

India

Minarets were never universally adopted in India and where they were built they were not necessarily used for the call to prayer.

The most famous minaret in India is the Qutb Minar attached to the Kuwwat al-Islam Mosque in Delhi which was begun in 1189. This tower has four storeys marked by balconies supported on bands of muqarnas corbels. The upper storey was rebuilt in 1368. An interesting feature is the alternation of circular and angular flutes which relates it to similar minarets of Jam and Ghazna in Afghanistan.

With the exception of Gujarat and Burhanpur in

Khandesh functional minarets attached to mosques did not become popular until the Mughal period. In Gujarat and Burhanpur minarets were always built in pairs flanking the central iwan as in Iran. These minarets were cylindrical constructions with internal staircases with intermediate balconies leading to conical roofs. Elsewhere before the Mughal period solid tower-like buttresses were attached to the corners of mosques.

The first minarets of the Mughal period are the four seventeenth-century towers flanking Akbar's tomb at Sikandara. These are tapering white marble constructions with two intermediate balconies and an open canopy on top. The lower stages of these towers are fluted. Later Mughal minarets copied this form with some variation in the decoration of the shaft.

Ottoman Minarets

The earliest minarets in Anatolia were built by the Seljuks. Often these were pairs of towers with a stone base and a brick shaft. Some mosques however were built with single minarets such as the Alaeddin Mosque at Konya.

The combination of tall pointed minarets and large lead covered domes gives Ottoman architecture its distinctive form. In most mosques in the Ottoman Empire this was achieved with a single minaret attached to the corner of a mosque. However, in the major cities of the empire mosques were built with two, four or even six minarets. At some point it seems to have been established that only a reigning sultan could erect more than one minaret per mosque. A characteristic feature of these minarets is the use of multiple balconies which was first developed in the Uç Şerefeli Mosque in Edirne which was built in 1447.

Arabia

Outside Mecca and Medina minarets were fairly rare before the nineteenth century. The few minarets that do survive are either square or circular in plan often with a slightly tapering profile. In southern Yemen the larger mosques occasionally have large minarets to distinguish them from the tall tower houses. In northern Yemen minarets are rare outside the capital San'a. The minarets of San'a are similar to those of medieval Cairo although the external decoration is characteristically Yemeni.

East Africa

With the exception of the thirteenth-century mosque of Fakhr al-Din in Mogadishu (Somalia) minarets dating from before the nineteenth century are rare. Nineteenth-century minarets include those of Mombasa and the Shella minaret on Lamu island.

One of the most curious structures in the area is the Mbraaki pillar dated to circa 1700. This 14 m-high structure has no means of access to the interior although it is believed to be hollow. At the foot of the minaret a mosque was excavated which is believed to be of the same period making this the oldest minaret in Kenya.

West Africa

The earliest minarets are those of the ninth- to thirteenth-century settlements at Koumbi Saleh and Tegadoust. Excavated remains indicate that these had large square minarets. During the thirteenth and fourteenth centuries the characteristic West African minaret developed. These minarets have a massive square structure with tapering sides and projecting wooden beams (torons). One of the most famous minarets is that of the Kano Great Mosque (destroyed 1937) which was over 20 m high on a square base with battered sides. The Fulani reformers of the nineteenth century objected to the use of minarets and replaced many of them with staircase minarets.

Far East

Minarets are not a traditional feature of Far Eastern Islamic architecture and have only recently been introduced on a large scale. In western China minarets usually take the form of squat pagoda-like structures, with a few exceptions such as the minaret of the Huaisheng Mosque in Guangzhou which is a tall tapering cylinder 20 m high.

See also: East Africa, Cairo, India, Iran, Iraq, Mosque, Syria, West Africa.

Further reading:

D. Berens-Abouseif, *The Minarets of Cairo*, Cairo 1985.
J. Bloom, *Minaret: Symbol of Islam*, Oxford 1989.

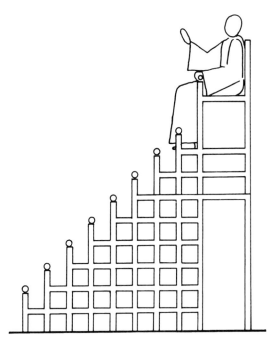

Umayyad minbar in the mosque of the Prophet, Medina (after Sauvaget)

K. A. C. Creswell, 'The evolution of the minaret with special reference to Egypt', *Burlington Magazine* 48, 1926: 134–40, 252–8, 290–8.

R. Hillenbrand, *Islamic Architecture: Form, Function and Meaning*, Edinburgh 1994.

B. O'Kane, 'Seljuk minarets: some new data', *Annales islamologiques* 20, 1994: 85–101.

G. F. Pijper, 'The Minaret in Java', *India Antiqua: A Volume of Essays Presented to Jean Phillipe Vogel*, Leiden 1947.

minbar

Type of pulpit usually found in mosques from which prayers, speeches and religious guidance are given. The minbar is situated to the right of the mihrab and consists of a raised platform reached by a set of steps, often there is a door at the entrance to the steps and a dome or canopy above the platform.

The minbar is one of the earliest architectural features to be identified with Islam. The earliest historical reference to a minbar states that in 629 the Prophet made a minbar from which he used to preach to the people. This minbar consisted of two steps and a seat (mak'ad) and resembled a throne. After the death of the Prophet the minbar was used by caliphs and governors as a symbol of authority. This continued under the last few years of Umayyad rule until in 750 CE the caliph Mu'Awiya ordered that all the mosques of Egypt be provided with minbars. This process was repeated in other Islamic lands so that by the beginning of the Abbasid period the minbar's function as a pulpit was universally established.

Most minbars are made of wood and are highly decorated whilst those made of stone or brick tend to be much simpler and often comprise a bare platform reached by three to five steps. The earliest extant wooden minbar is that in the Great Mosque in Qairawan which is said to have originated in Baghdad. It is a fairly simple design without a gate or canopy and consists of seventeen steps leading up to a platform. This minbar is made of plane tree and decorated with 200 carved panels and strips of unequal size. Although it has been restored several times most of the decoration seems to be Umayyad, consisting of diverse motifs held together within a rigid framework in a manner similar to that used at Mshatta.

In the Fatimid period minbars are built with a doorway at the entrance to the stairway and a domed canopy above the platform. The best example of this type is that in the Aqsa mosque in Jerusalem built for Nur al-Din in 1168. An example of this style in stone is the minbar in the mosque of Sultan Hasan (1356–63). Over the doorway to the minbar and also in the mihrab of this mosque muqarnas carving is used. Later on muqarnas remains an important decorative element in minbar design and is used particularly on minbar domes.

Most early minbars in Persia and Afghanistan were destroyed by the Mongol invasions; however, from the Timurid period we have several examples. One of the most impressive of these is that in the Djawahr Shah Agah in Meshed (constructed between 1436 and 1446). Structural elements in this minbar are subordinated to the covering of pentagonal and star-shaped panels with tendrils in relief, which has the overall effect of a woven carpet.

In Ottoman Turkey although most minbars were made of wood some of the most important were built of marble. Thus in the Selimiye Cami in Edirne there is a tall minbar of Marmara marble which is widely regarded as the finest in Turkey. The form of this minbar with its solid portal, its steep stairs and tall hood are all characteristic Ottoman features.

In India almost all minbars are built of stone and

are often elaborately carved. In Gujarat and Ah-madabad minbars are in the form of pavilions on four piers. In Hyderabad, to the south, the minbars are heavier and plainer, with no canopies or portals.

The Swahili mosques of the East African coast usually have simple stone mihrabs. At Sanje Ya Kate in southern Tanzania there is a sixteenth-century mosque with a unique minbar set into the wall. This is entered through an opening in the qibla wall from which the stairs lead to a niche next to the mihrab.

Mogadishu

Capital of Somalia located on the southern coast.

Mogadishu was established as a trading city some-time before the twelfth century although no early remains have yet been discovered. There are a number of historic mosques in the old quarter of the city which mostly date from the nineteenth century or later. The principal mosque of the town is the mosque of Fakhr al-Din dated to the thir-teenth century. This is the most sophisticated exam-ple of mosque architecture in East Africa and demonstrates architectural planning. The mosque has a narrow courtyard which opens on to a portico of five bays, the central bay of which is covered with a fluted dome. Entry into the prayer hall is through doorways decorated with marble panels. The prayer hall is divided into nine bays covered with a panelled ceiling with a central dome. The mihrab is carved out of north Indian marble and carries a date of 1269. The mosque also has a minaret which is the earliest occurrence of this feature in East Africa (minarets only become wide-spread from the nineteenth century).

See also: East Africa, Somalia

Monastir

Important medieval city on the east coast of Tunisia.

At present Monastir is on the coast, but in early Islamic times it was probably a peninsula or island. Monastir was one of the coastal cities developed by the Aghlabids during the ninth century. The city contains the remains of three ribats or fortified monasteries the earliest of which is the great ribat of Harthma ibn A'iyan founded in 796. The Great Mosque of the city was built in the ninth century although most of the structure dates to the tenth century or later.

See also: Aghlabids, Tunisia

Morocco (Arabic: Maghrib)

Country at the north-west corner of Africa with an Atlantic and Mediterranean coast.

The country may be divided into three main re-gions, the coastal plains, the Atlas mountains and the Sahara desert. The majority of the population lives on the plains with a smaller, more rural population in the mountains. The Sahara is sparsely inhabited.

Traditionally Islam first reached Morocco during the conquest of the Arab general 'Uqba who reached the shores of the Atlantic in 684. However, it seems likely that the first real conquest, as opposed to a temporary raid, took place at the beginning of the eighth century under the general Musa ibn Nusayr. The predominantly Berber popu-lation was quickly converted to Islam and took part in the Muslim conquest of Spain. After the initial success of the Spanish conquest the Berbers were disappointed with their share of the land allocations, in addition many were affected by the doctrines of Kharijism which represented a devia-tion from orthodox Islam. By 740 the situation had become critical and there was a rebellion against the Umayyads. A Syrian army sent to restore order was defeated in 742 leaving Morocco independent of central control. For the next forty years there was a period of anarchy with several Berber groups vying for power. In 788 the Idrissids emerged as the victors and were able to establish an independent monarchy which lasted until the end of the tenth century when it became a victim of Fatimid and Umayyad (Spanish) rivalry. During the eleventh century the country was taken over by the Almoravids who ruled an empire which included southern Spain and much of north-west Africa. In the mid-twelfth century the Almoravids were displaced by the Almohads who conquered a vast territory from the southern Sahara to central Spain. The Almohad Empire collapsed in the mid-thirteenth century to be replaced by the Marinids who ruled an area roughly equivalent to modern Morocco although there were constant attempts to expand eastward. Local unrest and increasing European interest in Morocco led to the collapse of the Marinids in the fifteenth century. A period of anarchy was followed by a reaction against Christian occupation of the coast which was embod-

Dome of Baru Din, Great Mosque, Marakesh, Morocco

ied in the Sa'dian dynasty. The Sa'dians who claimed descent from the Idrisids lasted until the mid-seventeenth century when they were defeated by the 'Alawids. The 'Alawids also had a semi-religious basis claiming their descent from 'Ali, members of this dynasty still rule the country.

A large variety of materials are used in historic and traditional Moroccan architecture. This partly reflects the variety of the natural landscape which includes extremely high mountains, fertile plains and arid desert. Another important factor is the influence of Spanish architecture which was re-inforced by the Christian reconquest which drove Muslims southwards into Morocco. The coastal cities of the north inherited the Byzantine system of construction in stone and baked brick. In the Atlas mountains mud pisé and rubble stone construction were the predominant materials although these were often covered with plaster. Overlapping gutter-shaped tiles with a characteristic blue-green colour were used for the roofs of important buildings and may represent Spanish influence. Small monochrome tiles were used for floors, as dadoes for courtyards and sometimes as decoration for

whole façades. Wood was relatively plentiful, cedar, cork and oak from the Atlas mountains was used for a variety of functions including roofing timber, supports for projecting windows, panelled ceilings and decorative mashrabiyya screens. The quality of wood carving is extremely high and resembles that of Muslim Spain. Stucco was extensively used for decorative features such as multifoil arches and decorative panels.

There are few examples of Moroccan Islamic architecture from before the eleventh century and those which do survive have been extensively altered. The most important city for the early period is Fez which was established as a capital in 807 by Moulay Idris the Younger. Very little survives of the early city although it is known that it had an advanced water system which supplied water for domestic use. Architecturally the most significant buildings in the town are the Qarawi-yyin and the Andalusian mosques which were both built in the ninth century. The form of these mosques with aisles running parallel to the qibla wall cut by an axial aisle is a Syrian–Umayyad plan. Later mosques in Morocco follow the more usual North African practice of aisles perpendicular to the qibla. No mosques of the Almoravid period have survived with the exception of the Great Mosque of Taza which was considerably remodelled in later periods.

Remains of the Almohad period are more plentiful and include the Kutubiya and Kasba mosques in Marakesh, the Hassan Mosque in Rabat and the Great Mosque of Timnal. The earliest of these is the mosque of Timnal which is built out of mud pisé and baked brick. The prayer hall has nine aisles perpendicular to the qibla wall and one aisle parallel to the qibla wall, an arrangement which was to become standard. The unusual feature of the building is the incorporation of the mihrab into the base of the minaret. This arrangement was not used in subsequent mosques although huge decorative minarets became one of the characteristic features of Almohad architecture. The most impressive example is the unfinished mosque of Hassan in Rabat begun in 1196. This vast mosque measures 140 by 185 m and includes three rectangular courtyards. The minaret, at the north end of the building (opposite the mihrab), has a massive square base measuring 16 m per side containing a ramp which rises around a square core. Although the tower is only 44 m high its is known that its projected

Khirbet al-Mafjar, mosaic in diwan

the Great Mosque of Al-Mansura in Tlemcen (Algeria), within Morocco their chief concern was the building of madrassas in which they excelled. Fez in particular contains a large number of Marinid madrassas the most famous of which are the 'Attarin, the Sahrij and the Bu 'Inaniya. The standard plan comprises rooms arranged around a rectangular courtyard with a central pool and decorated with tile mosaic and stucco work. The main focus of each madrassa is the prayer room which opens on to one of the shorter sides of the courtyard.

Another development of the Marinid period is the funerary complex which sees its first expression in the necropolis of Challa near Rabat built in the

Khirbet al-Mafjar, mosaic in diwan (detail)

height would have been approximately 70 m. The exterior of the tower is decorated with a variety of blind niches with cusped arches and a network of lozenges.

Although the Marinids were responsible for

fourteenth century. The complex is a large garden enclosed by a high wall fortified with buttress towers and an Almohad-style gateway. Within the complex there are tombs set within extensive areas of vegetation. There are two funerary mosques within the complex both with square decorated minarets in the Almohad style. In the sixteenth and seventeenth centuries the Sa'adians built a similar type of complex but on a grander scale with decoration of unparalleled ornateness. A different type of funerary–memorial complex is represented by the city of Moulay Idriss built by the Sa'adian ruler Moulay Ismail in the seventeenth century. Here the tomb of Idris I forms the centre of a sacred city which is restricted to Muslims.

The domestic architecture of Morocco represents a wide variety of architectural forms from semi-permanent camps to the luxurious courtyard villas of Fez, Rabat, Marakesh and Meknes. The simplest form of dwelling is the thatched hut or gourbi which may either be rectangular with a pitched roof or circular in plan with a conical roof. In the Atlas mountains there are villages of semi-permanent huts built around a central keep, or kasba. Sometimes these are purely for storage (tiremt) and have no accommodation although there is usually a guard's house. Some of the more developed villages formed walled enclosures with the keep functioning as a residence for the ruling family. City houses were enclosed courtyard structures with little external decoration. Inside the wealthier houses contain some of the most eloquent examples of Islamic decoration and recall the splendour of Muslim Spain.

See also: Almohads, Fez, Marakesh, Meknes, Rabat

Further reading:

R. Landau, *The Kasbas of Southern Morocco*, London 1969.

mosaics

Inlay of small tiles or stones used for decoration of walls or floors.

The use of mosaics in Islam is derived directly from Roman and Byzantine architecture where their most common function was to decorate churches and public buildings. It is known that many mosaics in the early Islamic period were carried out by Byzantine craftsmen and artists. Two main types of mosaic can be distinguished, those used for floors and those used for walls. Floor mosaics were made out of coloured fragments of stone or marble and were often arranged as patterns. Wall mosaics were often made out of specially manufactured tesserae of glass and were usually arranged as illustrative scenes.

Examples of floor mosaics have been found in excavations of the earliest Islamic structures in Syria and Palestine which were often converted Byzantine buildings. Floor mosaics usually lack any figural depictions of animals or humans and it is noticeable that many churches had the figural parts of the mosaics removed or scrambled during the Islamic period. Nevertheless, private palaces such as Qasr al-Hayr in Syria and Khirbet al-Mafjar had figural mosaics on the floor. It has been argued that figural representation on the floor was permitted as it was not in a respectful situation and could be walked over. The most famous example is the apse of the audience hall at Khirbet al-Mafjar which has a depiction of a lion attacking a deer in front of a tree.

Wall mosaics are more elaborate than those on the floor and are often gilded with gold leaf. The oldest example of wall mosaics in Islamic architecture is the decoration of the Dome of the Rock in Jerusalem, dated by an inscription to 691 CE. The motifs used include both Sassanian (winged crowns) and Byzantine (jewelled vases) themes held together within an arabesque foliage. Other early Islamic wall mosaics are those of the Great Mosque in Damascus which depict houses and gardens next to a river but significantly no people or animals. Although mosaic was primarily a technique employed in the Mediterranean area it was occasionally used further east in Iraq and Iran. Some of the best examples have been found at the palace of al-Quwair in Samarra. Generally mosaics declined in importance after the tenth century, although in Egypt glass mosaics were used for the decoration of mihrabs as late as the thirteenth century (see for example the mausoleum of Shajar-at al Durr in Cairo). From the eleventh century onwards mosaics were replaced by glazed tilework in most parts of the Islamic world.

See also: pietra dura, tilework, Umayyads

mosque

Building used for Muslim prayer, the principal unit of Islamic architecture.

The first mosque was the house of the Prophet Muhammad in Medina. This was a simple rectangular (53 by 56 m) enclosure containing rooms for the Prophet and his wives and a shaded area on the south side of the courtyard which could be used for prayer in the direction of Mecca. This building became the model for subsequent mosques which had the same basic courtyard layout with a prayer area against the qibla wall. An early development of this basic plan was the provision of shade on the other three sides of the courtyard, forming a basic plan which has become known as the Arab-plan mosque. The roofs of the prayer area (sanctuary or musalla) were supported by columns which were either made of wood (palm trunks in the Medina Mosque) or later on of re-used columns. From the ninth century onwards columns began to replace piers as the main form of roof support and domes were introduced as a roofing method.

Several features which were later to become standard features of mosques were introduced at an early stage. The first of these is the minbar, or pulpit, which was used by Muhammad to give sermons. A later introduction was the mihrab or prayer niche which was first introduced by the Umayyad caliph al-Walid in the eighth century. Other features include the ablutions facilities and a central pool or fountain and the minaret which

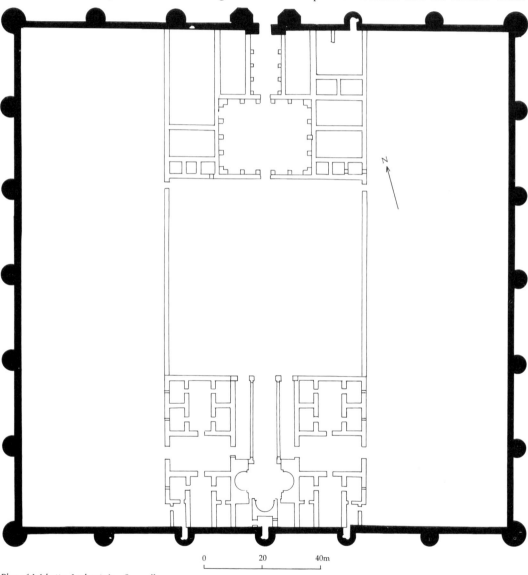

Plan of Mshatta, Jordan (after Creswell)

seems to make its first appearance in the Abbasid period. Also during this formative period the maqsura was introduced which was designed to provide privacy and protection to the ruler and also possibly to give him added mystery. This sense of mystery may have been reinforced by the placing of the royal palace or Dar al-Imara at the back of the mosque behind the qibla wall often with a connecting door.

The details of mosques in different areas of the Islamic world were dictated by local building traditions and materials, although the basic form remained the same until the eleventh century when the Seljuks introduced new architectural forms based specifically on the dome and the iwan. Although these had been known in Sassanian times and had been used in mosque architecture, they had not been used to alter the basic plan of the mosque. However, the Seljuks introduced the idea of four iwans set into the middle of each courtyard façade, as seen in the twelfth-century mosques of Isfahan, Zawara and Simnan. This arrangement became the standard form for the Iranian mosque and was later adopted for madrassas.

See also: Aqsa, Cairo, China, Damascus, East Africa, Fatimids, India, Indonesia, Iran, Iraq, Java, Malaysia, Mughals, nine-domed mosques, Ottomans, Spain, Turkey, West Africa

Mshatta

One of the most famous desert castles of the early Islamic period.

The palace of Mshatta is located on the border of the desert in Jordan (about 25 km south-west of Amman). It is generally dated to the late Umayyad period (the reign of Walid II) although an Abbasid date has also been suggested.

The palace consists of a large square enclosure with four semi-circular buttress towers. Outside the enclosure are the remains of a large bath house which has recently been excavated. The best-known feature of this palace is the southern façade which consists of a delicately carved stone frieze incorporating animal and plant motifs within a geometric scheme of twenty giant triangles (this façade is now in Berlin). Internally the building is divided into three longitudinal strips of equal size; only the central strip (running north–south) was developed, and contains within it the entrance, the

central courtyard and the audience hall. The area immediately inside the entrance has only foundations to mark the positions of rooms which were arranged symmetrically on either side of a central axis. This consists of a narrow vaulted passageway leading to a small square courtyard, on one side of which is the small palace mosque. This courtyard opens on to a large central courtyard (including a rectangular pond) at the other side of which is the heart of the palace. This consists of three iwans, the central iwan leading to the throne room (audience hall) and the side iwans leading to housing units (buyut – pl. of bayt) either side of the audience hall. The audience hall consists of a triple-apsed room covered by a large brick dome.

The importance of the palace for architectural historians is that it combines western (Roman and Byzantine) elements with features derived from the art of the Sassanians. The decorative frieze at the front of the building is one of the best examples of this combination. The vine leaves and naturalistic depictions of animals resembles Byzantine art although the decoration also includes popular Sassanian motifs such as the senmurv, a dragon-like mythological beast, and griffin. The most significant eastern feature of the design is thought to be the way the geometric pattern of giant triangles dictates the nature and space of the more naturalistic ornament.

Other eastern features found at Mshatta include the use of brickwork for vaults and the layout of the palace which resembles that of early Islamic buildings in Iraq (cf. Abbasid palaces at Ukaidhir and Samarra). However, Byzantine elements are also present, most notably in the basilical arrangement of the approach to the triple-apsed room and in the motifs of the stonework.

Further reading:

K. A. C. Creswell, E. M. A. Vol 1 Part 2, 578–622

O. Grabar, 'The date and meaning of Mshatta', *Dumbarton Oaks Papers*, 41: 243–8, 1987.

R. Hillenbrand, 'Islamic art at the crossroads; East versus West at Mshatta', in *Essays in Honour of Katharina Otto-Dorn*, Malibu 1981, 63–86.

mud brick

Traditional building material in much of the Middle East, India and North Africa. It is likely that in the past the majority of buildings in an Islamic city were made of this material. Mud brick has only recently been superseded by concrete as a cheap and versatile building material and is still used in many areas.

The traditional form of a mud brick is a large flat square slab produced by filling a wooden mould with mud or clay of the preferred type. In some areas the shape of the bricks is varied; thus in Djenné, West Africa, conical bricks were used until quite recently. Often some additional material (temper) such as straw is added to the brick to give it increased strength. The brick is then left to bake in the sun for several days until it is very hard and can be used for building. The bricks are laid in the normal manner, with layers of mud mortar used to bind the bricks together. When a mud-brick wall is completed it is usually coated with a layer of water-resistant mud plaster. In order to avoid the problems of water erosion mud-brick buildings are often built on stone footings or have overhanging roofs with water run-off directed into special channels. Mud brick also requires a certain amount of maintenance usually in the form of annual replastering.

Mud brick has several advantages over more modern materials: it has better thermal insulation (warmer in winter and cooler in summer), it is cheaper, it can be produced locally and it is environmentally less harmful. Recently there have been attempts to revive the use of mud brick through special projects such as those instigated by Hassan Fathy in Egypt.

See also: Djenné; Fathy, Hassan

Mughals

The Mughals were an Indian Islamic dynasty which ruled most of northern India (including the area of present-day Pakistan) from the beginning of the six-teenth to the mid-eighteenth century. As patrons of architecture the Mughals commissioned some of the finest buildings known to the world including the Red Fort at Delhi and the Taj Mahal.

History

The earliest Muslim presence in India dates from 712 with the Arab conquest of Sind which was a part of the original eastward expansion of Islam. However, it was not until the eleventh century that Muslim warriors first penetrated to the Indian heartland under the leadership of Mahmud of Ghazni. For the next 150 years the Punjab and Lahore were part of the Ghaznavid Empire although the Rajput princes of Rajasthan prevented further penetration into the subcontinent. In 1192 an Afghan sultan, Mahmud of Ghur, defeated an alliance of Rajput princes and captured Delhi, one of their principal cities. Although Mahmud soon left India he made his Mamluk (slave) general Qutb al-Din Aibak governor of Delhi. For the next 300 years this part of India was ruled by various competing Islamic dynasties including the Timurids.

The first Mughal ruler was Babur who traced his descent on his mother's side from Chengiz Khan and on his father's side from Timur (Tamuralne). Babur was a Central Asian prince who ruled the area of Fargahna but had some claim to Samarkand which he repeatedly tried to capture. In addition to his dream of taking Samarkand Babur also believed he had some claim to the Delhi sultanate through his Timurid ancestors. At the battle of Paniput in 1526 Babur defeated Ibrahim Lodi, the Muslim sultan of Delhi, with a small force which had, however, the additional advantage of artillery and gunpowder. A year later this victory was consolidated by Babur's defeat of the combined forces of the Rajput princes at Khanuna. Three years later, in 1530, Babur died at Agra leaving the sultanate to his son Humayun. Despite the enormous advantages bequeathed by his father Humayun did not have his father's ruthlessness and in 1540 lost the throne to the Bengali ruler Sher Khan. For the next fifteen years Delhi was ruled by Sher Khan and after his death by his son Islam Sher Sur. Humayun had lost the throne mostly through the treachery of his brothers and it was only after he had defeated them by recapturing Kabul and Kandahar in 1545 that he was in a position to retake Delhi which he did in 1555 defeating Sher Sur. Unfortunately Humayun was only able to enjoy his position for a year as he died in 1556 falling down a stairway in his library in Delhi.

Humayun left the empire to his 13-year-old son Akbar and his Turcoman guardian Bairam Khan. For the next four years the prince and his guardian had to fight off rival claims to the throne whilst securing the boundaries of the kingdom. Akbar's first concern on assuming full power was the pacification of the Rajput princes who constantly threatened the Delhi sultanate. In 1562 Akbar married the daughter of the Raja of Amber (the nearest Rajput state to Delhi later known as Jaipur) who became the mother of the Sultan's heir Jahangir. This was the beginning of a policy that he continued with other Rajput princes so that by the end of his reign all were under his overlordship although with varying degrees of independence. In addition to marital alliances and diplomacy Akbar also gained territory by force conquering Gujarat in 1573, Bengal in 1576, Kashmir in the 1586, Sind and Baluchistan between 1591 and 1595. The southern part of India was added in the latter part of his reign and included Berar and part of Ahmadnagar.

Akbar's territorial victories were consolidated by an efficient system of government with a paid non-hereditary civil service. In addition Akbar abolished the 'jizya', poll tax payable by Hindus and other non-Muslims, in order to integrate and unify the differing peoples of his expanding empire in the same way that the Rajput dominions had been incorporated. Religious toleration became a central principle of Akbar's government to the extent that in 1570 he convened a conference between the different religions at his newly established city of Fatehpur Sikri. The conference included scholars from Hindu and Muslim sects as well as Jains, Zoroastrians and Catholic Jesuits from Goa. The result was a new religion conceived by Akbar himself and known as Din Ilahi (Divine Faith) which drew elements from all the sects. Although the religion was not successful it shows Akbar's concern to create an empire free from religious divisions. Akbar died in 1605 leaving the empire to his son Jahangir who had recently been in open revolt of his father. On his accession to the throne Jahangir left his son Shah Jahan in charge of the military campaigns, a pattern which was later repeated when as emperor Shah Jahan delegated control of the south to his son Aurangzeb. Both Jahangir and later Shah Jahan continued the policies of Akbar so that the empire remained relatively stable despite more or less constant warfare in the south of the country. Shah Jahan failed in his attempt to create a united Sunni state incorporating India with Central Asia, but managed to keep the empire more or less intact for his son Aurangzeb.

The last of the great Mughals, Aurangzeb, departed from the pattern of government set by Akbar and precipitated the decline of the empire. Aurangzeb devoted a great deal of energy and manpower to continuing the conquest of the south of India at the expense of all other policies. The empire reached its greatest extent during this period and included the whole subcontinent with the exception of the southern tip. However, this brought increased problems of communication and military control which the empire was not able to manage. These problems were exacerbated by Aurangzeb's fanatical Muslim zeal which meant that he reversed the policy of religious tolerance exercised by his great-grandfather by introducing the poll tax (jizya) for non-Muslims. Similarly he encouraged the destruction of Hindu temples and other religious shrines and his southern conquests became one of the greatest iconoclastic excursions in India's history. Although Aurangzeb may have been a pious Muslim, this policy was not successful in an empire which depended on the co-operation and toleration of different ethnic and religious groups. Perhaps the best example of Aurangzeb's policy was the Great Mosque built to tower over the Hindu holy city of Banares.

With Aurangzeb's death at the age of 90 in 1707 the empire passed to his son Bahadur Shah who only lived another five years. During the next half-century the rapidly disintegrating empire was ruled by eight sultans. The weakness of the empire was shown in 1739 when Delhi was sacked by the Persian emperor Nadir Shah who carried off the peacock throne along with countless other treasures. The latter part of the century witnessed the conflict between a variety of forces including the Mughals, the Hindu Marathas and the British East India Company. In 1803 the East India company occupied Delhi and Agra thus ending Mughal power in India. For the next half-century the powerless Mughals were retained by the British as 'Kings of Delhi'. Finally in 1857 the last Mughal Bahadur Shah II was stripped of even this title and was removed from Delhi for his part in the sepoy mutiny.

Architecture

Mughal architecture was derived from three main sources: native Indian Islamic, Persian Central Asian and local Hindu architecture. It is difficult to determine the extent to which any feature or building type used by the Mughals derives from any of these particular sources, partly because earlier Indian Islamic architecture contains both Hindu and Islamic elements. What is clear, however, is that Mughal architecture does incorporate many elements from local Hindu architecture, in particular the art of the Rajput palaces. Distinctive Hindu features incorporated into Mughal architecture include trabeate stone construction, richly ornamented carved piers and columns, and shallow arches made out of corbels rather than voussoirs. In addition there are particular constructions usually associated with Hindu buildings, including chatris, chajjas and jarokhas, which became characteristic of Mughal architecture. A chatri is a domed kiosk resting on pillars which in Hindu architecture is used as a cenotaph but in Islamic architecture is placed as decoration on top of mosques, palaces and tombs. A chatri is a sloping stone overhang at roof level, used to deflect rain water away from the walls of a building and usually supported on heavy carved corbels. A jarokha is a projecting balcony supported on corbels with a hood resting on columns. Whilst all of these features may be paralleled elsewhere in Islam, the particular form which they assume in Mughal architecture shows a clear derivation from local Hindu architecture. In addition to Hindu features there are some elements derived from the pre-existing Islamic architecture of India. The best example is the curved do-chala roof derived from Bengali huts which was first used in this stone form in the sultanate architecture of Bengal. Another Indo-Islamic feature is the cusped arch which can be found in the pre-Mughal architecture of Delhi and Gujarat.

Obvious Persian influences in Mughal architecture are the extensive use of tilework, the iwan as a central feature in mosques, the use of domes, the charbagh, or garden, divided into four and the four-centrepoint arch. The form of buildings and some of the decorative motifs also suggests obvious Persian influence.

The materials used for Mughal architecture varies widely depending on the region and the type of construction. As with most other areas, many of the original buildings have not survived because they were made of less permanent materials such as wood, as well as having been subject to deliberate destruction as a result of wars or rebuilding. However, the material which stands out as characteristic of Mughal architecture is the use of a hard, deep-red sandstone. This material is very strong under compression and so can be used for trabeate construction where roofs are made of flat stone slabs supported on stone columns. When domes were built these were sometimes constructed in the Persian tradition using squinches or pendentives, but more commonly they rested on horizontal flat beams laid over the corners of the structure. Despite its strength and hardness the Indian masons trained in the Hindu tradition of building ornate temples were able to carve this sandstone with intricate details as seen in the columns of the Jami Masjid in Delhi. White marble is the other type of stone often associated with Mughal architecture. It is first used in conjunction with red sandstone as a stone cladding for the front of monumental buildings such as the tomb of Humayun in Delhi where it is used as an inlay and outline for the red sandstone ground. Later, during the reign of Shah Jahan in the seventeenth century, white marble facing was used to cover entire buildings, the best-known example of which is the Taj Mahal. In addition to the fine-cut stone masonry used for façades coursed rubble stone construction was used for the majority of walls. Baked brick was also used for some elements of the construction like domes and arches although this was usually covered with plaster or facing stones.

Decoration of buildings was carried out using a variety of techniques including ceramic tilework, carved and inlaid stonework, pietra dura inlay with coloured and semi-precious stones. Tilework was applied to the exterior of buildings in the Persian manner using Chinese, Persian and Indian tiles. Two main types of tile were used – cuerda sec using coloured glazes, and tile mosaic which used cut pieces of monochrome tiles to produce a pattern. Mughal architecture excels in the quality of its carved stonework, from shallow relief depictions of flowers to intricate pierced-marble screens known as jalis. It has previously been thought that the pietra dura work in Mughal architecture was an Italian introduction because Shah Jahan used some Italian examples of the technique in his palace in Delhi, however this technique had an independent development in India which is obvious when the Italian panels are compared with Indian examples. The main types of building designed for the sultans included palaces and forts, mosques, tombs and gardens. The range of buildings indicates the image the emperors wished to project of themselves as all-powerful rulers close to heaven. One of the most important types of building was the fortified palace as seen at Delhi, Agra, Ajmer,

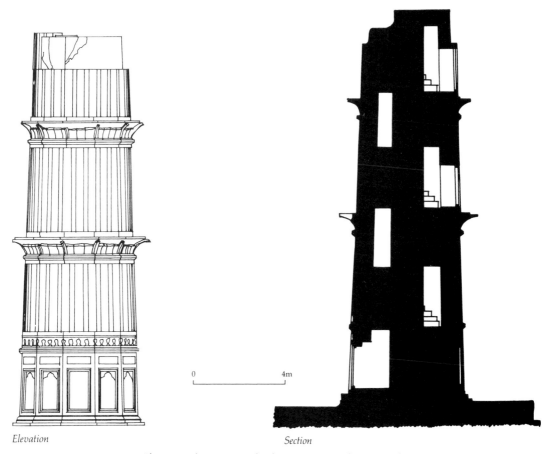

Elevation

Section

0   4m

Elevation and section of Hashtsal Minar (1634), India (after Koch)

Fatehpur Sikri and Lahore. Although differing sub-stantially in details the palaces share a common overall design where severe external walls conceal a series of courtyards, pavilions and gardens which convey an impression of paradise on earth. The standard plan was of a monumental outer gate which leads inside to another gate known as the 'Hathai Pol' where visitors dismount from elephants. From here there was access to the Diwan-i Amm or public audience hall behind which were the private areas of the palace. The private areas of the palace were usually raised up above the rest of the complex for increased privacy and to catch any breezes in the summer heat. This part of the palace usually included a private audience hall, a bath house, several courtyards with pavilions based around pools and a separate area for the women, known as the zenana. On one side of this private area was a tower projecting from the outer walls known as the Mussaman Burj (octagonal tower) from which the emperor appeared once a day to show that he was still alive.

Babur, the first Mughal emperor, only reigned for four years, during which time he was too busy securing his empire to spend time on major build-ing projects like palaces and instead governed from tented encampments. The earliest Mughal palace is the Purana Qila in Delhi built by Hu-mayun and continued by the Bengali usurpers Sher Sur and Islam Sur. The palace is surrounded by a huge wall 1.5 km long with three huge gateways. Each gateway consists of an arched opening flanked by two huge semi-circular bastion towers with battered walls, arrow slits and pointed crenella-tions. Little remains of the original structures inside the fort with the exception of the mosque and a domed octagonal pavilion known as the Sher Mandal so that it is not possible to tell much about the building's layout. The next imperial palace to be built was Akbar's fort at Agra where enough remains to show that it was the basic model for subsequent Mughal palaces. The palace is built next to the river Jumna and is surrounded by huge walls fortified with semi-circular towers. There are two gates, an outer gate with a drawbridge and complex bent entrance leading to an inner gate called the Hathai Pol where visitors were required to dismount from their elephants. Most of the buildings inside the complex belong to Akbar's successor Shah Jahan with the exception of the court known as the Jahangiri Mahal. This structure was built in the style of a Hindu Rajput palace with carved stone beams and giant corbels supporting chajjas. This tendency is carried further in Akbar's new city of Fatehpur Sikri founded in 1570 where the whole palace is overwhelmingly Hindu in its form with Islamic elements reduced to a minimum. Of the same period is the fort at Ajmer in Rajasthan, this is much smaller than the imperial palaces and consists of a rectangular courtyard enclosure measuring 85 by 75 m with four octagonal corner towers and a half-octagonal gateway. In the centre of the courtyard is a rectangular pavilion built of yellow stone and divided into nine chambers in the form of a Hindu mandala. Hindu elements were also predominant in Akbar's other palaces at Allahabad and Lahore although little of Akbar's original work survives at either of these palaces.

The palaces of Shah Jahan by contrast have a more familiar Islamic appearance as can be seen in his modifications to Akbar's fort at Agra where he added several new courtyards, the most famous of which is the Anguri Bagh (grape garden). This is a square garden divided into four sections with a central rectangular pool with lobed sides which provides water for the garden. The garden is surrounded by various pavilions the most prominent of which are the Khas Mahal (private audience hall) and the Sheesh Mahal (glass pavilion). Although these pavilions have many of the same Hindu features seen in Akbar's architecture (i.e domed chatris and chajjas) they are less prominent and tempered with more Islamic forms like lobed arches and the curved Bengali do-chala roofs. In addition the white marble facing of the buildings produces a new lighter appearance which is not found in the earlier buildings of Akbar or in Hindu architecture. The most lavishly decorated building

of the palace is the Mussaman Burj which overlooks the river at the east side of the palace. The tower has an octagonal copper dome and inside is lined with carved marble dadoes, pietra dura inlay, pierced screens above the doorways and decorative rows of niches. From inside there is an uninterrupted view of the river and the Taj Mahal built by Shah Jahan for his wife Mumtaz Mahal.

In 1638 Shah Jahan chose the site of his new city at Delhi based around his palace which became known as the Red Fort. By 1648 the fort was completed at a cost of ten million rupees. The layout and design of the Red Fort bears a striking resemblance to the Agra Fort on which it was probably based. Like the Agra Fort, the Red Fort has rectangular open pavilions with cusped arches, white marble dadoes carved in relief and pietra dura work. However, the Red Fort has a more regular symmetrical design, reflecting the fact that it was planned and built mostly by one patron (with a few additions by Aurangzeb) unlike the Agra Fort which gradually developed under two emperors. The most magnificent of the rooms at the Red Fort is the Diwan-i Amm or public reception room where the enthroned emperor would receive audiences. This room was approached from the main gate via an arcaded passageway, a large courtyard, another gateway and an even larger courtyard so that visitors were suitably awed by the time they reached the emperor. The room consists of a hypostyle hall nine bays wide and three bays deep supported by twelve-sided columns spanned by cusped arches. The throne occupies a special position in the middle of the back wall and consists of a raised platform covered by a dome supported on columns. The area behind the throne is decorated by pietra dura panels imported from Italy. Within the palace is the Diwan-i Khass or private audience hall which is equally lavishly decorated and originally had a silver-clad ceiling inlaid with gold.

Unlike the palaces, the mosques of the Mughals were built to accommodate the public and were thus more restrained in their decoration although equally monumental. Delhi contains some of the earliest examples of Mughal mosques in India which clearly show their derivation from earlier Sultanate mosques. The Mahdi Masjid is one of the earliest examples of a Mughal mosque and its architecture resembles that of the Lodi sultanate which preceded the Mughals. The mosque is built like a small fort with corner turrets and a monumental gateway built in the style of Lodi tombs. The arrangement inside is unique and consists of a rectangular courtyard with two prayer halls at the qibla end either side of a central piece of blank wall. Nearby is the Jamali Kamali Masjid built between 1528 and 1536 which has a more distinctively Mughal appearance. The building is faced in red sandstone with white stone outlining the details to relieve the intensity of the red. The sanctuary façade consists of an arcade of four centrepoint arches resting on thick piers; the heaviness of the façade is relieved by rosettes in the spandrels of the arches, two-tier blind arches on the piers and a row of smaller blind arches running in a line above the arches. The central arch leading on to the mihrab is the same size as the other arches but is emphasized by a tall pishtak-like façade with engaged columns. The area behind this arch is covered by a squat masonry dome typical of Rajput and earlier Sultanate architecture.

The earliest surviving imperial Mughal mosque is the Qala-i-Kuhna Masjid in the Old Fort (Purana Qila) in Delhi although ironically it was begun in 1541 during the Shah Sur period. Like the Jamali Kamali Masjid the sanctuary of this mosque consists of five bays running north–south parallel to the qibla with the central bay emphasized by a dome. The arrangement of the arcade is the same although here the arches are set within taller pointed arches of differing sizes to lighten the appearance of the façade. The next imperial mosque is attributable to Akbar's reign and rather surprisingly shows more signs of Hindu influence than mosques of the earlier period. This is the mosque of Fatehpur Sikri, the palace city built by Akbar in the 1570s, where Hindu influence was at its most pronounced. The basic plan of the mosque conforms to the established pattern of Mughal mosques with a large courtyard surrounded by an arcade and a centrally placed iwan set into the arcade of the sanctuary on the west side of the courtyard. However, the details of the mosque are mostly Hindu in their associations, from the richly carved columns and corbelled arches in the arcades and the sanctuary to the domed chatris lining the roof. With the reign of Jahangir and later Shah Jahan the appearance of mosques returns to a more overtly Islamic form. In the Jami Masjid of Shahjahanabad built in 1650 the use of Hindu elements is

drastically reduced to two chatris on the roof whilst other more Islamic feature such as the minarets, the central iwan and cusped arches assume a higher prominence. The domes have a taller pointed appearance familiar in Islamic buildings elsewhere instead of the squat Hindu style domes used in earlier Mughal mosques. The design of the Shahjahanabad Jami Masjid was a major influence on later Indian mosque architecture with its use of three domes over the sanctuary in conjunction with a raised central arch, or iwan, and engaged minarets. During the reign of Aurangzeb this form was developed as the standard mosque form. The Moti Masjid (Pearl Mosque) built by Aurangzeb in the Red Fort at Delhi was too small to incorporate all the features found at the Jami Masjid but incorporated a three-domed sanctuary with a raised central arch and mini-domed pillars projecting out of the roof to resemble minarets. In the Badshahi Mosque in Lahore built by Aurangzeb in 1674 the pattern of the Jami Masjid was copied with the addition of more minarets making a total of eight.

An important function of imperial Mughal architecture was to overawe people with the power, wealth and sophistication of the sultans; in no area was this more effective than in the design and construction of the sultans' tombs. The earliest tombs of the Mughal period resemble those of the previous Muslim sultans of Delhi and typically consist of an octagonal domed structure sometimes surrounded by an open veranda. One of the first Mughal examples is the tomb of Adham Khan built by Akbar for his wet nurse and her son who was killed in a palace dispute. Another example of this tomb type is the mausoleum of Sher Shah Sur at Sasaram built before 1540. This has the same basic plan as the Adham Khan tomb with a central domed octagonal chamber surrounded by an octagonal arcade with three arches per side. The tomb is made more elaborate, however, by its location in the middle of a specially made moat and its use of domed chatris to mark the corners of each side of the octagon. Other related tombs with a similar design include the tomb of Sayyid Lodi (1517), the tomb of Isa Khan in Delhi.

Later Mughal tombs were also based on an octagonal form but instead of sides of equal length four of the sides were shortened thus producing a square shape with cut off corners. An early example of this type is the Afsarwala tomb in

Delhi, situated in the garden of the Arab serai near the tomb of Humayun. Humayun's tomb built in the 1560s is the first example of the imperial Mughal tomb complexes which came to character- ize the splendour of the dynasty (Babur was buried in a simple garden grave and later his remains were transferred to Kabul). Humayun's tomb is composed of four-square octagonal shapes built on two storeys around an octagonal domed space. Between each octagon is a deep iwan giving access to the central domed space which contains the tomb of Humayun. The central structure is sur- rounded with arcades forming a low square with chamfered corners. In turn this central structure is set in the middle of a square garden divided into quarters which are further subdivided into thirty- two separate sections. The tomb of Humayun was a model for later Mughal tombs, although the tomb of his immediate successor Akbar differs greatly from this model. Akbar's tomb, located in the district of Sikandara (8 km outside Agra) was begun in 1605 and completed seven years later. It is not known whether Akbar took any part in the design of the tomb although it is known that his son Jahangir may have altered the original design. The outer part of the building is a rectangular structure with engaged octagonal towers at each corner and a tall iwan in the centre of each side. The central part of the complex is very different from any other tomb as it lacks a central dome. It consists of a five-storey pavilion with an open rectangular courtyard at the top containing a tomb-like cenotaph. This architecture is character- istic of Akbar's reign and can be compared with the Panch Mahal in the palace at Fatehpur Sikri where there is also a conglomeration of pavilions five storeys high. The outer form of the complex can be compared with the tomb of Itimad-ud- Daulah's tomb completed in 1628 which consists of a low building with a square plan and short engaged octagonal corner towers. In the centre, raised one storey above the rest of the structure, is a vaulted pavilion.

The classic form of tomb was returned to for the Taj Mahal built by Shah Jahan for his wife Mumtaz Mahal who died in 1631. The basic form of the tomb recalls that of Humayun's tomb at Delhi and consists of four octagonal structures joined together by iwans and grouped around a central domed area. As in Humayun's tomb the central building is two storeys high, but here the central dome is more than double the height of the rest of the structure. Instead of being surrounded by arcades the lower part of the structure is raised on a terrace, the sides of which are marked by blind arcades. At each corner of the square terrace is a tapering cylindrical minaret on an octagonal base. The basic forms used in the Taj Mahal were re-used in later tombs but never with the same success. The Bibi ka Maqbara tomb, built less than forty years later, has the same design as the Taj Mahal but the octagonal minarets are thicker and higher in proportion to the central complex which consequently loses some of its significance. A later tomb in this tradition is that built for Safdar Jang in 1753. In this building the minarets are incorpo- rated into the central structure as engaged corner turrets whilst the terrace becomes an arcaded substructure.

One of the most important aspects of Mughal architecture was the design of gardens which pro- vided the setting for tombs and palaces or stood on their own as places for relaxation. Babur, author of the first Mughal architecture, was a lover of gardens and laid out several after his conquest of Delhi. One of the earliest Mughal gardens is known as the Rambagh or Aram Bagh in Agra and was planned by Babur. Although the original form of the garden may have been altered the narrow water channels are indicative of its early date. The usual form of Mughal gardens was derived from the Persian char bagh which consists of a square walled garden divided into four equal units around a central feature usually a pool or fountain. The geometric form of gardens meant that the plant borders assumed a certain importance as can be seen at the Anguri Bagh in Agra Fort where the flower beds are made of interlocking cusped squares like a jigsaw puzzle. Also the form of gardens meant that the plants were usually kept quite low so that the shape of the arrangement was visible. In Kashmir Mughal gardens assumed a less formal and more natural appearance, with tall trees and shrubs and architecture hidden within the garden rather than dominating it as was the case with the more formal gardens of Delhi and Agra. At Srinagar there were once several hundred gardens built around the Dal Lake although only a few still remain. One of the most famous of these is the Shalimar Bagh laid out during the reign of Jahangir in 1619. The form of the garden echoed that of palace architecture and consisted of a terraced system where the garden was divided into three parts; the lowest part was accessible to the public, the middle section was for the emperor and his friends, whilst the highest part (which was totally out of view) contained the zenana, or women's private area. In the centre of the women's area, in the middle of a formal pool, is the Black Pavilion built by Shah Jahan. The building has a three-tiered tiled roof and is built in the style of local Kashmiri wooden mosques.

Like his ancestor Babur, Aurangzeb was more concerned with garden architecture than the construction of palaces. One of the most impressive of these gardens was that of Fatehbad near Agra which although now largely derelict contains a central arcaded pavilion surrounded by a crenellated wall with a monumental entrance.

Public buildings of the Mughal period were usually of a utilitarian design with very little embellishment. The roads were one of the primary concerns of the Mughal administration and during the 1570s Akbar initiated a programme of road improvements including the provision of milestones, wells, reservoirs and caravanserais. The best examples of this are the caravanserais built at Chata near Mathura and Chaparghat. These buildings have a fairly uniform design consisting of a large rectangular enclosure with octagonal corner towers. Inside there are iwans leading on to cells along the side of the walls. The cells are usually arranged in pairs with a connecting door in between, thus forming units of four (two iwans and two closed rooms). In addition to the standard rooms there are usually at least two larger sets of rooms for more important travellers. Most caravanserais have one entrance; where there are two these are usually opposite each other. Sometimes the central axis of the caravanserais are built as bazars for the visiting merchants. The only areas of architectural elaboration are the gates or mosques which were attached to the buildings. One of the most magnificently decorated gateways is that of the Nur Mahal caravanserai by Nur Jahan between 1618 and 1620. Its design resembles funerary and mosque architecture of the period, with a central iwan flanked by three tiers of side iwans; however, the decoration, which consists of carved human, animal and mythical figures, is more reminiscent of palatial architecture of the period.

Milestones, known as kos minar (small towers), were used to mark the roads. These are usually very plain structures with an octagonal base and a tapering cylindrical shaft. One of the main routes which received attention during Akbar's reign was the Agra to Ajmer pilgrimage route which was provided with road markers and small resthouses. Under Jahangir the improvement of roads continued with trees planted on the road from Agra to Bengal, the construction of wells and kos minar on the road from Agra to Lahore and the provision of small stations on the Pir Panjal pass into Kashmir. During the reign of Aurangzeb the roadside facilities were extended and improved, with particular attention paid to the roads between Agra and Aurangabad and Lahore to Kabul. Repairs carried out on bridges, caravanserais and roadside mosques were paid for out of the emperor's private income.

See also: Fatehpur Sikri, Taj Mahal

Further reading:

C. Ascher, 'The Mughal and post-Mughal periods', in *The Islamic Heritage of Bengal*, G. Michell, Paris 1984.

H. Crane, 'The patronage of Zahir al-Din Babur and the origins of Mughal architecture', *Bulletin of the Asia Institute* NS 1: 95–110, 1987.

S. Crowe, S. Haywood and S. Jelicoe, *The Gardens of Mughal India*, London 1972.

Z. A. Dessai, 'Mughal architecture in the Deccan', in *History of Medieval Deccan: 1295–1724* 2, ed. H. K. Sherwani and P. M. Joshi, Hyderabad 1974, 305–14.

J. Dickie, 'The Mughal garden: gateway to paradise', *Muqarnas* 3: 128–37, 1985.

A. N. Khan, *The Hiran Minar and Baradari Shaikhpura: A Hunting Resort of the Mughal Emperors*, Lahore 1980.

I. A. Khan, 'New light on the history of two early Mughal monuments of Bayana', *Muqarnas* 6: 55–82, 1990.

W. G. Klingelhofer, 'The Jahangari Mahal of the Agra Fort: expression and experience in early Mughal architecture', *Muqarnas* 5: 153–69, 1988.

E. Koch, *Mughal Architecture*, Munich 1991.

—— *The Hunting Palaces of Shah Jahan* (forthcoming).

G. D. Lowry, 'Humayun's Tomb: form, function and meaning in early Mughal architecture', *Muqarnas* 4: 133–48, 1987.

K. K. Muhammad, 'The houses of the nobility in Mughal India', *Islamic Culture* 60(3): 81–104, 1986.

R. Nath, *History of Mughal Architecture (i) (Babur to Humayun)*, New Delhi 1982.

—— *History of Mughal Architecture (ii) (Akbar)*, New Delhi 1982.

S. Parihar, *Mughal Monuments in the Punjab and the Haryana*, New Delhi 1985.

G. H. R. Tillotson, *The Rajput Palaces; The Development of an Architectural Style 1450–1750*, New Haven, Conn., and London 1987.

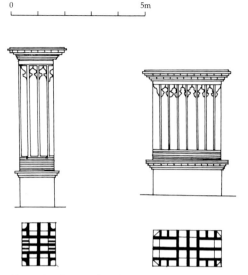
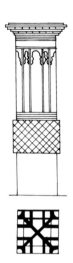
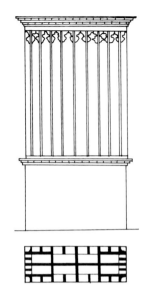

Types of mulqaf (wind-catchers) (after Kay and Zandi)

—— *Mughal India*, Architectural Guides for Travellers, London 1990.
F. Watson, *A Concise History of India*, London 1979.

muhtasib

A municipal officer responsible for public morals and regulation of markets.

An important duty of the muhtasib was the supervision of building construction which involved regulation and inspection of materials. The uniform size of materials used in construction was ensured by the use of wooden templates which were kept in the mosque. The muhtasib was also responsible for checking mould boxes used for baked bricks and mud bricks to check that these were not distorted. Raw mud bricks were not allowed to be used until they had whitened. Also the muhtasib ensured that builders kept stockpiles of the correct spare materials such as bricks for lining wells, floor bricks, and fire bricks for ovens.

mulqaf

Arabic term for wind-catcher.

See also: badgir

muqarnas

System of projecting niches used for zones of transition and for architectural decoration.

Muqarnas is one of the most characteristic features of Islamic architecture and is used throughout most of the Muslim world (in North Africa a related system known as muqarbaras is also used). Muqarnas is usually associated with domes, doorways and niches, although it is often applied to other architectural features and is sometimes used as an ornamental band on a flat surface.

The earliest examples of muqarnas so far discovered were found at Nishapur in eastern Iran and date to the late ninth or early tenth century. These consist of fragments of stucco niches with carved and painted decoration which were found within domestic buildings. Of a similarly early date are fragments of painted stucco muqarnas belonging to a bath house of the Abbasid or Fatimid period at Fustat in Egypt. The wide dispersion of muqarnas at this early date (ninth–tenth century) suggests that its origin was somewhere in the centre of the Islamic world, probably Baghdad.

During the eleventh century muqarnas spread to most parts of the Middle East (from Egypt to Central Asia) whilst in the western Islamic World a similar device called muqarbaras was also used. The earliest use of muqarnas seems to have been on the inside of buildings in association with domes and vaults. The first use of muqarnas on the exterior of a building is on the tomb of Ladjin in Mazandaran built in 1022 where two superimposed rows are used as decoration. Some of the most

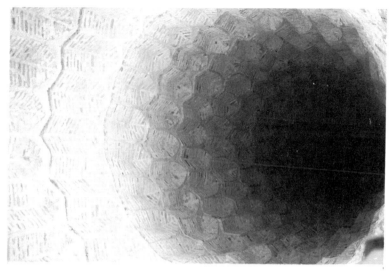

Interior of muqarnas dome, Mashad al-Shams, Hilla, Iraq

Exterior of muqarnas dome, Mashad al-Shams, Hilla, Iraq

impressive examples of muqarnas on the exterior of buildings are where it is used as corbelling for balconies on minarets. One of the best examples of such muqarnas corbelling is found on the minaret of Suq al-Ghazzal in Baghdad dated to the thirteenth century. The base of the minaret is encased in a thick sleeve of muqarnas corbelling above which there is a short shaft which supports a giant six-tiered band of muqarnas corbelling which forms a platform for the balcony.

Generally, however, the most elaborate muqarnas are associated with domes. Some of the earliest and simplest forms of muqarnas can be found in the eleventh-century mausoleums at Aswan in Egypt. One example consists of an arched squinch divided into three lobes on the bottom with a small single niche on top. In Iraq the same device was taken to its most extreme form with the development of conical domes made of muqarnas. The oldest surviving example is the mausoleum of Imam Dur north of Samarra. This dome is extraordinary both for its height (over 25 m) and its profuse, almost organic, muqarnas plaster decoration.

One of the most common uses of muqarnas was for column capitals. Before the eleventh century Islamic buildings would rely on re-used classical and Byzantine capitals or copies of these forms. Muqarnas was particularly suited for use in capitals as it lends itself to the transition from circular column to the square section of an arch and was uniquely Islamic in form. In Ottoman architecture, where Turkish triangles performed the same function as muqarnas pendentives and squinches, muqarnas was still employed for portals, niches, column capitals and other decorative features.

It is in its use for domes and vaults that muqarnas was to have its most significant impact. By providing a diffused method of transition from flat to curved, muqarnas zones of transition were able to break down the distinction between vertical and curved, domed and horizontal. The best examples of this can be seen in conical domes such as that at Natanz in Iran where the roof emerges not as a hemispherical dome but as a multi-faceted prism-like series of surfaces.

The almost universal adoption of muqarnas as architectural decoration meant that it was also adapted for woodwork such as mosque furniture. The minbar of Nur al-Din built for the Aqsa Mosque in Jerusalem had three bands of tiered muqarnas on a canopy above the foot of the stairs.

In Iraq, Iran and the eastern Islamic world the most suitable materials for muqarnas construction were plaster and baked brick. Both materials have the advantage of being light whilst bricks have the additional advantage of being made to a standard dimension which is useful when repeating the complex geometric alignments necessary for muqarnas. Plaster also has the advantage that it can easily be decorated by carving or painting. In Syria and Egypt the first muqarnas domes were made from plaster suspended from a wooden frame within an outer dome made out of stone. The most famous example of this technique is the dome in Nur al-Din's maristan built in 1154. Later muqarnas stone domes were made, the best examples of which belong to fifteenth-century Egypt.

The first muqarnas was made purely out of interlocking cut niches but fairly early on 'dripping' stalactites were developed. These are thin downward projections from the cut side of the niche which give the illusion of arches suspended in mid-air. These stalactite niches are some of the most elaborate form of muqarnas which defy attempts at two-dimensional representation.

There are several theories about the origins of muqarnas. Generally the decorative origin and function is favoured over the suggestion that muqarnas was the solution to a particular structural problem. The reason for this conclusion is that some of the earliest examples of muqarnas found were decorative plaster bands, although equally early are examples of muqarnas squinches from Egypt. Whilst certainly muqarnas did have a decorative function, from the beginning its early and frequent association with domes and pendentives suggests that the form had structural associations. The tiered form of muqarnas means that the thrust of the dome could be directed downwards into the corner of a building without adding the extra weight of a pendentive. On the other hand muqarnas squinches are a way of providing a greater span without having to build large heavy arches. In general muqarnas tends to blur the distinction between squinch and pendentive and provides a more subtle transition from square to octagon. A view which combines both decorative and structural functions suggests that the origins of muqarnas may be found in Islamic theology which promotes an occasionalist view of the universe whereby the continued existence of anything is dependent on the will of God. Muqarnas is then a way of expressing this view of the universe where the dome appears to stand without visible support.

Further reading:

J. Bloom, 'The introduction of the muqarnas in Egypt', *Muqarnas* 5, 1988.

O. Grabar, *The Formation of Islamic Art* (revised and enlarged edition), Yale University Press: New Haven and London 1987.

musalla

Literally a place where prayer is performed, although in practice it has come to refer to large open spaces outside cities for that purpose.

The prime function of a musalla is to provide additional space for prayer during festivals such as Ramadhan. Sometimes they are referred to as 'Festival Mosques', and in India, Iran and Ottoman Turkey they are referred to by the term *namazgah*. Sometimes a musalla is no more than an open space marked out with a line which indicates the direction of Mecca (the qibla), although more often it will include a long wall on the qibla side which may include a mihrab. Sometimes musalla reached advanced stages of building with an arcade covering the qibla wall (as recorded at Bahrain) and elaborately decorated mihrabs such as that of Mashad. The usual position of a musalla was outside the city gates although they are occasionally within the city as in Abbasid Samarra.

N

nahr

Canal or river.

namazgah

Turkish and Persian term for an open-air prayer place often used by the army. Sometimes these are quite elaborately built with a minbar and a standing mihrab.

naqqar khana

Mughal term for a drum house or place for an orchestra during ceremonies.

Natanz, shrine of Abd al-Samad

Sufi funerary complex at Natanz in western Iran.

Natanz is located on the edge of the Dasht-i Kavir desert 60 km south-east of Kashan. This is a large funerary complex which has grown up organically around the tomb of Abd al-Samad, a follower of the famous Sufi saint Abu Said who died in 1049. The central feature of the site is the octagonal tomb around which is built a four-iwan congregational mosque dated to 1309. Internally the tomb is a cruciform chamber which is converted to an octagon at roof level. The roof is a blue-tiled octagonal pyramid dome outside and internally comprises a tall muqarnas vault. Another important structure at the site is the khanqa or dervish hostel built in 1317 which is located to the south-west of the tomb. Only the portal of this structure survives with a large muqarnas semi-dome.

Nilometer

Device located on Roda island, Egypt for measuring the rise of the Nile during the period of inundation.

This structure was built in 861–2 CE during the reign of Caliph al-Mutawakil. The purpose of the device is to measure the level of the flood to work out the amount of tax due to the government (a higher flood level indicates a higher yield). The structure consists of a ·2 m square stone-lined pit 13.14 m deep connected to the Nile by three tunnels. In the centre of the square pit is a tall octagonal column divided into cubits each of which is subdivided into twenty-four smaller units. A staircase runs down the four sides so that the central column could be read. The floor at the bottom was made of cedar beams. Approximately halfway up there are four pointed relieving arches, one on each side of the pit. The arches are of a two-centred type used in Gothic architecture in Europe during the fourteenth century. The curves of the arches are emphasized by two bands of moulding whilst above there are foliated kufic inscriptions which contain Quranic passages referring to crops and harvests.

Further reading:

K. A. C. Creswell, *A Short Account of Early Muslim Architecture*, revised and enlarged edn. J. W. Allan, Aldershot 1989, 383–5.

nine-domed mosque

This is a type of mosque roofed by nine domes of equal size.

Although the distribution of this building type is very wide (it is found as far apart as East Africa, Bangladesh, Central Asia and North Africa) it does not occur in great numbers in any one area. The earliest extant examples date from the ninth century CE, whilst there are few buildings of this type later than the sixteenth century.

Most nine-domed mosques are fairly small (usually 10–15 m square) though substantially built. It is common for these buildings to be open on two, three or even four sides but it is rare for them to have a sahn or minaret. Sometimes the central row of domes is raised to emphasize the mihrab axis.

There are two theories about the origin of this type of mosque. The older theory originated by Creswell asserts that the mosque is derived from the earliest forms of Islamic funerary monuments,

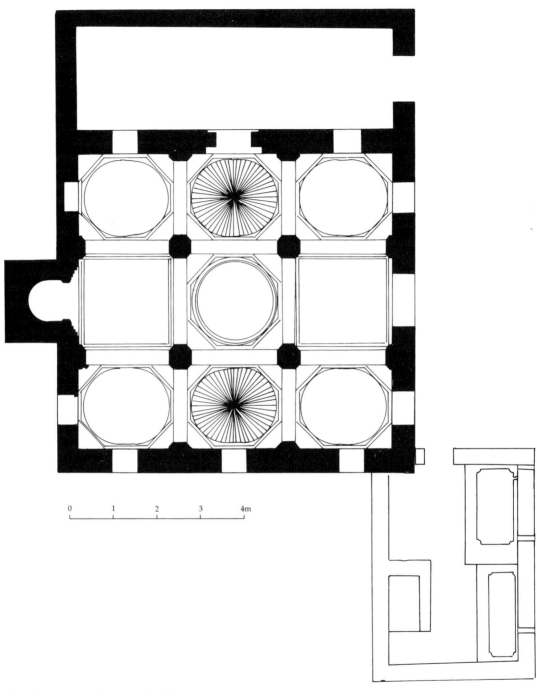

Nine-domed mosque, Kilwa (after Garlake)

such as the Qubbat al-Sulaybiyya at Samarra, which were domed and had open sides. More recently it has been suggested that the type derives from honorific buildings such as Khirbet al-Mafjar.

Whilst the origin of the design may be disputed it is clear that many of the mosques were associated with tombs or burials so that it is reasonable to suggest that they should be regarded as memorial mosques. Important examples can be found at Kilwa, Fustat, and Toledo.

Further reading:

K. A. C. Creswell, *Muslim Architecture of Egypt I*, Oxford 1952, 11–13.

R. Ettinghausen, *From Byzantium to Sassanian Iran and the Islamic World*, London 1972, 57–8.

G. R. H. King, 'The nine bay domed mosque in Islam', *Madrider Mitteilungen* 30: 1989.

Nishapur

Famous medieval city located in the Khurassan region of eastern Iran.

Nishapur was founded in Sassanian times as 'New Shapur' and rose to prominence in early Islamic times as capital of the Tahirid dynasty in the ninth century. The city was at the height of its prosperity and importance under the Samanid dynasty in the tenth century. In 1037 the city was captured by the Seljuks and remained a part of that empire until 1153 when it was sacked by the Ghuzz. Despite the sacking and several earthquakes the city continued to function until 1221 when it was sacked by the Mongols. A modern city of the same name has grown up near the site based around an eighteenth-century shrine.

Although no standing architecture remains at the site, excavation has revealed extensive architectural remains together with a large number of finds making this one of the best examples of a medieval Islamic city. The remains were found mostly within three mounds known as Tepe Madrasseh, Sabz Pushan and Qanat Tepe. There is no evidence of occupation at any of the sites before the eighth century indicating that the Sassanian city may have been elsewhere. The main materials of construction were mud brick (*khist*) and trodden earth or pisé (*chineh*) and baked brick. Wood was used as a strengthening material in walls as well as for columns. Many of the walls were covered with stucco and painted plaster panels (frescoes). The remains of several mosques were found on the site all with rectangular recessed mihrabs. At Tepe Madrasseh remains of a prayer-hall iwan were found together with the base of a minaret. The minaret had an octagonal shaft and was built of yellow fired bricks with decorated with shallow vertical slots. Elsewhere on the site columns built of baked brick were also decorated with slots. At Qanat Tepe remains of a mosque were found close to the remains of a bath house. The bath house had hypocaust heating, a plunge pool and a nine-sided octagonal basin in the centre. The most remarkable feature of the bath house was the frescoes which included representations of human figures. At Sabz Pushan remains of small houses were found which included centrally placed sunken fireplaces made from earthenware jars set into the ground. Among the most important finds at the site were the remains of eleven muqarnas panels excavated from a cellar. These were prefabricated plaster panels which would have been attached to the zone of transition in the roof of the cellar and are some of the earliest evidence for the use of muqarnas.

O

ocak

Turkish word for a chimney hood, also used to designate a unit of Ottoman troops of Janissaries. The typical Ottoman ocak consists of a tall conical hood set against the inside wall of a building. Some of the best examples can be found in the kitchens in the Topkapisarai.

See also: Ottomans

Oman

The sultanate of Oman is located in the south-east corner of the Arabian peninsula and borders on the Indian Ocean.

It is the third largest country in Arabia after Saudi Arabia and Yemen and comprises five distinct geographical regions, the Musandam peninsula, the Batinah coastal strip, the Hajjar mountains, the Naj desert and Dhofar. The Musandam peninsula is separate from the rest of the country and comprises a rocky headland adjacent to the straits of Hormuz. The Batinah coastal strip is located between the sea and the mountains in the northern part of the country and varies between 20 and 25 km wide, this is the most densely populated region of Oman. The Hajjar mountains are a very distinctive feature; running in a belt parallel to the coast in the northern part of the country, they are the source of most of Oman's water. The Naj desert, comprising several areas including the Wahiba sands, separates the northern mountains from those of the south and its population is mostly nomadic. Dhofar is a mountainous region in the south of the country with a tropical climate and is the only part of Arabia to experience a summer monsoon.

Until the discovery of oil Oman's economy was based upon a number of natural resources, the most important of which were copper from the mountains in the north and frankincense from Dhofar. Also Oman's position on the Indian Ocean meant that it was able to establish a long-distance maritime trade based on the monsoons of the Indian Ocean. In addition, fishing and dates have remained important components of Oman's economy even after the discovery of oil.

The earliest settled communities in Oman have been dated to 3000 BCE and by 2000 BCE copper was being exported to Mesopotamia. In the fourth century BCE Oman was occupied by the Persians who remained in control of the country until the advent of Islam in 630 CE. Under Islam Oman's trading network flourished and included East Africa, India and the Far East. During this period various coastal towns grew up, the most important of which were Sohar, Qalhat and Dhofar (al-Balid). In 1503 the coastal towns were captured and occupied by the Portuguese. As a result the towns of the interior, the most important of which were Nizwa and Bahla, grew in power and influence. By 1650 the Portuguese had been expelled by the Ya'ariba leader, Sultan bin Sayf, who rebuilt the fort at Nizwa. Internal conflicts allowed a Persian invasion in 1743 but this was brought to an end by Ahmad ibn Sa'id governor of Sohar who was elected imam in 1743. He was the founder of the Al Bu Sa'id dynasty which continues to rule Oman today.

In 1730 Oman had acquired the island of Zanzibar and by the 1830s Sultan Sa'id ibn Sultan had built a new capital in Zanzibar. From 1856 Oman and Zanzibar were ruled by two branches of the same family.

For various reasons Oman was not modernized until the 1970s, which has meant that traditional architecture has survived here better than in most of the other Gulf states. The main building materials employed in Oman are mud brick, baked brick, stone, mangrove poles, palm trees and lime (used for mortar and plaster). The particular combination of materials employed depends on the region and type of building.

Baked brick is used fairly infrequently in Oman and is confined mostly to the port of Sohar. Baked bricks were first used in the early Islamic city and were also used in houses of the nineteenth century although it is not certain if bricks were still made in nineteenth-century Oman or imported from elsewhere. Occasionally baked bricks are found incorporated into buildings outside Sohar such as the arches of the Great Mosque in Bahla or in the columns of the mosque of the Samad quarter in Nizwa. Mud brick on the other hand is more common and is frequently used in the oasis towns of the interior. It is usually used in conjunction with mud mortar and plaster sometimes mixed with lime. Mangrove poles imported from East Africa are frequently used for roofing in the houses of the coast. Palm trunks are also used for roofing there and for inland parts of the country. Palm fronds and trunks are also used for less permanent structures on the coast. Several types of stone are used for building in Oman; amongst the more common types are coral blocks on the north coast, coastal limestone in Dhofar and roughly hewn blocks of igneous rock in the mountains. Lime for use in mortars is either made from burning limestone or coral blocks.

The architecture of Oman can be divided into several types based on the type of building, the materials used and the location. The main groups are houses, mosques, forts and mansions.

Until recently the most common form of architecture on the coast was the palm-frond house which may take several forms from a single-room temporary dwelling used for the date harvest to a large enclosure incorporating winter and summer rooms. The basic unit of construction is a rectangular room measuring approximately 3 by 5.5 m. The walls are made from stems (zur) tied together to form a panel whilst the main form of support are palm trunks placed externally. The winter houses have flat roofs whereas the summer houses have pitched roofs and are called Khaymah (tent). Often houses made of other materials have palm-frond roofs or verandas.

Mud-brick houses are found throughout Oman, although they are most common in oasis towns. They are usually built with very shallow foundations or directly on to the ground, and the first metre or so is often built out of irregular stones to serve as a base for the mud-brick superstructure. Simple mud-brick houses have pitched palm-frond (barristi) roofs whilst the larger houses have flat earth roofs supported by palm trunks or mangrove poles. Some of the larger mud-brick houses are three storeys high.

Stone-built houses are common on the coast or in the mountains. One of the simplest forms is a type of coral house found in the Batinah. These are built out of rough lumps of coral rag which are plastered over with mud; the roofs are usually made of palm fronds; locally these are called kerin. In Salalah and the Dhofar coast houses are made out of roughly squared limestone blocks which are laid in courses and interspersed with wooden tie-beams. Usually, however, stone buildings in Oman are made out of rough-hewn stones laid in successive bands approximately half a metre high and covered with a plaster surface, producing walls with layers of overlapping plaster coats.

Mosques are mostly built out of stone or mud brick with flat roofs. Minarets are rare in Oman before the nineteenth century. A fairly common feature in Omani mosques is the combination of mihrab and minbar, where the minbar is entered through an opening in the mihrab (this feature is also found in other parts of the Indian Ocean littoral such as East Africa and Yemen). In the north of Oman mosque roofs are usually supported by arches resting on cylindrical columns, in Dhofar the columns are usually octagonal. Built shrines do not occur in the Ibadi region of the north but are fairly common in the predominantly Sunni region of Dhofar where they usually have pointed domes.

Fortified buildings are one of the most noticeable features of Omani architecture. Most settlements, however small, have some form of fortified structure. There are two main types of fortified building in Oman, the sur or fortified enclosure and the citadel. A sur is a fortified enclosure which is used on a temporary basis during raids or other disturbances, consequently the design of such enclosures is fairly simple and consists of a roughly square enclosure which may or may not have a tower. On the other hand the citadels or forts of the main towns are fairly sophisticated structures designed for use with artillery. The most famous forts in Oman are at Nizwa, Ibra, Izki, Mudhairib and al-Rustaq. These buildings were influenced by the Portuguese forts of the sixteenth and seventeenth centuries, although they also included local developments such as the use of two diagonally opposed towers linked by thick curtain walls.

One of the consequences of Oman's vast trading links was the growth of a wealthy mercantile class who were able to build mansions. Some of these are located within coastal cities such as Sur or

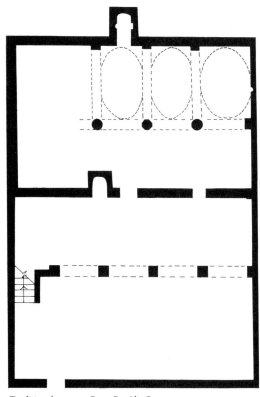

Traditional mosque, Banu Bu Ali, Oman

Muscat, whilst others are rural dwellings set in their own grounds such as Bayt Na'man on the Batinah plain. Common features found in mansions and in more important houses include elaborately carved doorways, pre-cast stucco mouldings around doorways and recesses, and painted wooden ceilings. Such buildings often have a private prayer room, a light well (shamsiya) and ventilation slits above the windows.

Further reading:

The most useful works on the architecture and archaeology of Oman can be found in the *Journal of Oman Studies*, including those listed below.

P. and G. Bonnenfant and Salim ibn Hamad ibn Sulaiman al-Hathri, 'Architecture and social history at Mudayrib', 3: 107–35, 1977.

P. M. Costa, 'The study of the city of Zafar (al-Balid)', 5: 111–50, 1979.

—— 'Studies on the built environment of the Batinah', 8(2): 1985.

—— 'Bayt Na'man, a seventeenth-century mansion of the Batinah', 8(2): 195–210, 1985.

P. M. Costa and S. Kite, 'The architecture of Salalah and the Dhofar littoral', 7: 131–53, 1985.

E. Enrico, 'Introduction to Omani architecture of the sixteenth, seventeenth and eighteenth centuries', 6(2): 291–306, 1983.

E. Galdieri, 'A masterpiece of Omani 17th-century architecture. The palace of Imam Bilarab Sultan al-Yaariba at Jabrin', 1: 167–79, 1975.

M. Kerveran, C. LeCouer-Grandmaison, M. Soubeyran and A. Vialatte de Pemille, 'Suhari houses', 6(2): 307–16, 1983.

Ottomans (Turkish: Osmanli)

Major Islamic dynasty based in Turkey which at its height controlled a vast area including all of modern Turkey, the Balkans and much of the Middle East and North Africa.

The origins of the Ottoman dynasty can be traced back as far as their thirteenth-century founder Othman (Osman). Othman was a leader of a branch of the Qayïgh clan which was part of the Turkic Öghuz tribe originally from Central Asia. The Öghuz was amongst those Turkic groups who had fled west with the Mongol invasions of the thirteenth century and now threatened the ailing Byzantine Empire. Originally the Ottomans had been based around the southern city of Konya but later moved north-west to the area of Bursa later known in Turkish as the Hüdavendigâr (royal) region. The position of the Ottomans on the border with Byzantine territory meant that they constantly attracted fresh Turkic warriors (ghazis) willing to fight the Christians. The constant warfare and arrival of new soldiers meant that the emerging Ottoman state developed a strong military organization and tradition which enabled it gradually to take over rival Turkish states in the vicinity. In 1357 a new phase in Ottoman expansion was achieved by crossing the Dardanelles into Europe and fighting the divided Balkan Christians. By 1366 the Balkan provinces had become so important to the Ottoman state that the capital was moved from Bursa to Edirne. Another result of the move into Europe was that instead of relying on the Turkic warriors the army was now formed by Christians who had been captured as children and converted to Islam. The advantage of this new method was that the religious orthodoxy and absolute allegiance of the soldiers could be ensured. The new troops known as Janissaries were the élite force of the growing empire; at the same time a system of feudal land grants was adopted for the Ottoman cavalry. In 1394 Ottoman control of the

Open-air mosque, Ras al-Junayz, Oman

Balkan provinces was recognized when Bayazit was granted the title Sultan of Rum by the Abbasid caliph in Cairo. A major setback occurred in 1402 when a second Mongol invasion led by Timur (Tamurlane) conquered much of Anatolia and defeated the Ottoman sultan at Ankara. However, Timurid success was short lived and soon the Ottomans were able to regain control of much of their territory in Anatolia. The major event of the fifteenth century was the capture of Constantinople (later known as Istanbul) and the defeat of the Byzantine Empire by Mehmet the Conqueror in 1453.

Having consolidated their position in Anatolia during the fifteenth century by the beginning of the sixteenth century the Ottomans were able to launch a major offensive in Europe and the Middle East. In 1517 the defeat of the Mamluks brought Syria and Egypt into the Ottoman Empire and in 1526 Hungary was brought under Ottoman control. For the next century and a half the Ottomans were the world's foremost Islamic power and undisputed rulers of most of the eastern Mediterranean. As orthodox Sunnis the Ottomans established contacts with their co-religionists the Mughals of India although the distance was too great for any meaningful co-operation beyond sending a few Turkish ships against the Portuguese in the Indian Ocean.

The siege of Vienna in 1683 marked the high point of their military power in Europe and their defeat marked the beginning of an irreversible decline which continued into the eighteenth century. Nevertheless, Turkey remained a major power during the nineteenth century despite the loss of large amounts of territory to local leaders in Europe

Ottomans (Turkish: Osmanli)

Bibi Miriyam, domed thirteenth-century mausoleum, Qalhat, Oman

and the Middle East. Turkey's disastrous participation in the First World War led to the loss of its remaining Arab provinces and a European attempt to take control of Anatolia. European expansionism in turn prompted a reaction in Turkey which led to the rise of the Young Turks and the abolition of the Ottoman sultanate in 1922.

For over 500 years the Ottomans ruled an area now occupied by more than fifteen modern states so that Ottoman buildings now represent a sizeable proportion of the historic architecture of the region. The Ottoman presence in these areas was marked by the erection of imperial structures such as fortresses, mosques and khans which preserve a remarkable degree of uniformity despite the large distances involved. However this picture must be modified by two observations, first that direct Ottoman control over some areas was limited to relatively short periods and second that Ottoman architecture was subject to local influences. The first observation may be illustrated by the case of Iraq where constant warfare with the Saffavids meant that Ottoman control fluctuated throughout the sixteenth, seventeenth and eighteenth centuries and was only firmly established in the nineteenth century. The consequence of this is that Iraq contains few distinctively Ottoman buildings from before the nineteenth century. The second observa-

tion is important as it calls for a distinction between buildings in the imperial style and locally derived buildings – thus an imperial mosque in Damascus (e.g. the Tekkiye) may differ from a local mosque in the Syrian style. Even in the case of imperial Ottoman buildings concessions were made to local taste; thus the Sinan Pasha Cami in Cairo is Ottoman in plan but has distinct Egyptian features like the use of muqarnas above the windows, the short minaret and the use of ablaq masonry. Sometimes local styles affected the imperial style – thus the tall domes of Syria and Egypt influenced the 'baroque' buildings of seventeenth-century Istanbul.

The heartland of the Ottoman Empire was western Anatolia and Thrace and it was in this area that the imperial style developed out of Byzantine and Seljuk architectural traditions. The Byzantine tradition is characterized by domes, baked brick and tiles, the Seljuk by iwans, carved stonework and the use of spolia. The main building materials used in Ottoman architecture were baked bricks and tiles, cut limestone, marble and wood, whilst glazed tiles and glass (coloured and plain) were used for decoration.

The use of baked brick in Ottoman architecture was inherited directly from Byzantine practice which in turn was copied from earlier Roman work. Brick is used on a much greater scale in early Ottoman buildings than those of the later period possibly in imitation of contemporary Byzantine practice which used bricks until the beginning of the fourteenth century when they were no longer available. The usual brick form was a flat square of varying dimensions, the Ottomans had a much wider range of brick sizes than the Byzantines whose bricks were of a standard size although better in quality. The standard Byzantine construction technique, copied in early Ottoman buildings, was rubble and brick construction where the size of bricks determined the thickness of the walls. Often layers of brick alternate with layers of cut stone thus the Haci Özbek Cami at Iznik is built of triple layers of brick alternating with layers of individual cut stone blocks separated by single vertically laid bricks. The ratio of layers of brick to layers of stone does not seem to have been standard for every building and in some cases the thickness of layers varies in the same building. In general, however, three layers of brick to one of stone was fairly usual during most periods. The standardized size of bricks and their lightness compared with stone also made them ideal material for the construction of domes, barrel vaults and arches. When stone replaced brick and stone as the main facing material, bricks continued to be used for arches, domes and vaults. In early Ottoman buildings tiles were used to cover the outside of the dome although from the sixteenth century onwards lead was increasingly used.

The walls of Ottoman buildings were built with a rubble stone core enclosed by a facing of stone or brick and stone. In some of the earlier buildings rubble stone was used on the exterior of buildings either contained within layers of brick or plastered over. Later on the use of cut limestone became more usual, first in conjunction with brick and later on its own. Immediately after the conquest of Constantinople there seems to have been a reversion to brick and stone due to a shortage of cut limestone. However, from the beginning of the sixteenth century onwards most important buildings were faced in cut stone, although subsidiary structures continued to use brick and stone. The quality of masonry in Ottoman buildings is extraordinary due to its precision and smoothness which gave buildings a monumentality not easily achieved with brick and stone.

In addition to limestone Ottoman buildings used large quantities of antique and Byzantine marble both as columns and for decoration. During the sixteenth century there were large numbers of disused Byzantine churches which were used as quarries for marble columns thus the Ottoman buildings of this period tend to use more columns than earlier or later periods. The hardest form of marble available was porphyry, which is twice as hard as granite, although this was only used rarely as it tended to crack. New marble seems only to have been available from the quarries at Marmara although there was enough ancient marble available to fulfil most needs. Sometimes, however, there seems to have been an acute shortage of marble; thus the tomb of Suleyman was built using fake red and green marble. Fake marble was often used for voussoirs of arches where the weight of real marble would cause structural problems. Fake marble voussoirs were usually made of brick and covered with plaster which was then painted.

Wood was essential in the construction of Ottoman buildings and was used for the centring of vaults and domes, for tie-beams and as scaffolding. In addition wood was used for projecting galleries and also for pitched wooden roofs, although these were less common than brick domes in monumental buildings. In domestic architecture, however, wood was the predominant material and most of the houses of Istanbul were built entirely out of wood.

One of the most distinctive features of imperial Ottoman architecture is its use of polychrome glazed tiles as wall decoration. Glazed tiles were used by the Ottomans as early as thirteenth century at the Yeşil Cami at Iznik although it was not until the fifteenth century that the first of the famous Iznik tiles were produced. During the sixteenth century Iznik tiles replaced marble as the main form of decoration in mosques thus in the Ivaz Efendi Cami in Istanbul tilework columns are placed either side of the mihrab instead of the usual marble columns.

The windows of mosques were often decorated with stained glass set into thick plasterwork frames. Coloured glass made with a high proportion of lead was mostly imported from Europe and clipped to the sizes required. Although coloured glass was used more often, the architect Sinan preferred to use clear glass and altered the structural arrangement of buildings to introduce the maximum amount of light into the interior.

Ottomans (Turkish: Osmanli)

Sixteenth-century Ottoman fortress at Ras al-ʿAyn, Israel/Palestine

Ottoman architecture can be divided into three major periods which roughly correspond to historical developments. The early period between the thirteenth and mid-fifteenth century was the period before the capture of Constantinople in 1453 and characterized by the transition from a small principality to a sultanate. The second period from the capture of Constantinople (Istanbul) to the mid-sixteenth century is regarded as the classical Ottoman period and saw the most brilliant developments in arts and technology to match the spectacular Ottoman victories in Europe, North Africa and the Middle East. The third period from the end of the sixteenth century to the twentieth century is known for political and economic decline, matched in architecture by weaker forms on a smaller scale and the increasing influence of Europe.

Early Period

Possibly the oldest Ottoman building is the Etrugrul Mescit in Söğüt 40 km south-east of Iznik which dates from the first years of the fourteenth century. The mosque has been significantly altered by the addition of a minaret and tall arched windows although its essential form of a tall cube capped by a dome remains unchanged. More authentic and better dated is the Haci Özbek Cami at

Iznik which is dated to 1333, two years after the capture of the city from the Byzantines. Like the mosque at Söğüt the Haci Özbek Cami is a small cube covered with an almost hemispherical dome (radius 4 m) resting on a zone of Turkish triangles. The original portico was on the west side (i.e. at right angles to the qibla) and consisted of three bays resting on two marble columns. Two of the bays were covered by barrel vaults, whilst that above the entrance was covered with a cross vault; the north and south sides of the portico were walled in as protection against the wind. Other early Ottoman mosques include the Alaettin Cami at Bursa and the Orhan Ghazi Cami at Bilecik. The Aleattin Cami was built in 1335 after the Ottoman capture of Bursa and is of a similar form and size to the Haci Özbek Cami except that the portico and entrance is on the north side in line with the mihrab. The Orhan Ghazi also has a similar plan but here the size of the prayer hall is increased by four large (approximately 9 by 2.5 m) arched recesses which make it twice as large as the Haci Özbek Cami whose dome is approximately the same size. The walls are pierced with windows and the mihrab is flanked by two large windows in an arrangement which became standard in later Ottoman mosques. The Orhan Ghazi Mosque also has a detached minaret which may be the oldest surviving Ottoman minaret.

The next major development in Ottoman mosque architecture is the Yeşil Cami at Iznik built in the late fourteenth century (1378–92). This is one of the first buildings for which the name of the architect is known (Haci bin Musa). The portico consists of three long bays set side by side with a high fluted dome in the central bay. The portico is open on three sides with the entrance in the middle of the north side formed by a stone door frame. The portico leads into the main part of the mosque which contains a rectangular vestibule and a prayer hall. The vestibule is an arcade of three bays resting on two thick columns and opening into the main prayer hall. The central bay of the arcade is covered by a fluted dome and is flanked by two flat-topped cross vaults. The prayer hall is the usual square domed unit although its diameter is slightly larger (11 m) and the vestibule on the north side appears to increase its floor area. The Seljuk-style brick minaret is set on the north-west side of the mosque, a position which became traditional in Ottoman mosques.

The capture of Bursa in 1325 led to its growth as the Ottoman capital city with mosques, khans, public baths and madrassas. A result of this centralizing process was the development of new, more specialized, architectural forms. The most remarkable changes occurred in mosque architecture with Orhan's royal mosque which is an adaptation of the Ottoman square domed unit to a Seljuk madrassa plan. The building consists of a central domed courtyard opening on to three domed chambers one either side on the east and west and a larger one on the south side. The building is entered via a five-bay portico and a small vestibule. The plan is ultimately derived from the Iranian four-iwan plan although the northern iwan has been reduced to a shallow vestibule. The side rooms were used as teaching areas as the building was also a zawiya, or convent, and the main room to the south is the prayer hall. The courtyard dome is higher than that of the prayer hall and originally had an occulus or hole at the apex to let in light and air. This plan was later used by Orhan's successor Murat for the famous Hüdavendigâr Mosque which he built just outside Bursa at Çekirge. This extraordinary two-storey building combines two functions, a zawiya on the ground floor and a madrassa on top. The combination seems particularly surprising when it is realized that the zawiya represents a mystical form of Islam

and the madrassa represents orthodox Sunni Islam which would generally have been opposed to mystical sects. This combination suggests a royal attempt to incorporate reconciled mystical and orthodox forces in the service of the Ottoman state.

The zawiya on the ground floor has the same basic T-plan as Orhan's mosque with a central domed courtyard leading off to iwans; however, in this building the iwans are vaults instead of domes and the mihrab projects out of the south wall of the southern iwan. The walls of the central courtyard and the prayer hall are raised up above the upper floor thus forming a two-storey courtyard. The upper floor is reached by twin staircases either side of the main entrance which lead upwards to a five-bay portico directly above that on the ground floor. Five entrances lead off the portico into the body of the madrassa which also has a four-iwan plan around a central courtyard. The centre of the courtyard is occupied by the prayer hall and courtyard from the ground floor and so is reduced to a vaulted walkway with windows opening on to the courtyard below. To the north of the upper courtyard between the staircases is a vaulted iwan which is the main entrance to the upper floor. Either side of the courtyard are six vaulted cells whilst at the south end there is a domed room directly above the mihrab on the ground floor. The same T-plan is used for the mosque of Murat's successor Beyazit, built between 1391 and 1395. Modifications in this mosque include the positioning of the lateral iwans along the side of the prayer hall, or in other words the prayer hall is brought into the body of the mosque instead of projecting beyond it. This building is also noted for its portico which is regarded as the first monumental Ottoman portico because of its height and the use of wide stilted arches to create an elevated and open space separate from the mosque inside. The Yeşil Cami built in 1412 has essentially the same plan although the portico was not completed.

In addition to the royal mosque Beyazit also built the first great Ottoman congregational mosque or Ulu Cami at Bursa. The building was begun in 1396 and completed four years later in 1400. Before this period congregational mosques had usually been re-used Byzantine churches. The Ulu Cami represents a different design concept from either the square domed unit or the Bursa T-plan mosques and is more closely related to the ancient mosques of Syria, Egypt and Iraq. The Ulu Cami consists of a large rectangular enclosure five bays wide by four bays deep (63 by 50 m) and roofed by twenty domes resting on twelve massive central piers. The mihrab is centrally placed and is on the same axis as the main doorway. In the second bay in front of the mihrab is the courtyard represented by an open dome above a sunken pool. The mosque has two minarets, one on the north-east and one on the north-west corner of the mosque; the north-east minaret was added later by Mehmet I, some time after 1413. Mehmet also built a smaller version of the Bursa Ulu Cami at Edirne known as the Eski (old) Cami which consists of nine domes.

The climax of the first period of Ottoman architecture was the Yeşil Cami at Bursa which was part of a complex built for Mehmet I. The complex consists of a mosque, madrassa, bath house (hammam), an imaret, or kitchen, and the turba (tomb) of Mehmet. Earlier sultans had built complexes such as that of Beyazit or Orhan, but this is the best preserved example of its type. The madrassa has a standard form consisting of cells on three sides and a domed prayer hall on the south side. The kitchen and bath house are both rectangular domed structures whilst the turba is an octagonal domed building located high up above the rest of the complex. The mosque is of the familiar Bursa T-plan design and closely resembles that of the Beyazit complex. The chief differences are the use of brilliant green tiles to decorate the interior and royal boxes or loggias which overlook the internal domed courtyard.

The development of mosques and religious buildings is paralleled in secular architecture by the evolution of classical Ottoman forms from the Seljuk period. The clearest examples of this are bridges, which in the early period are graceful structures with a high central arch flanked by two lower arches, whereas those of the later period are more heavily built in the Roman style, with a succession of evenly spaced arches resting on massive piers. Several bath houses survive from this period particularly in Bursa which contains simple structures like the Çekige Hammam and complex double-domed structures like the Bey Hammam. The plan of these bath houses develops from a single-domed area leading off to two or three smaller domed or vaulted chambers to a building consisting of one or two large domed areas which open on to a series of small cells arranged around a cruciform covered courtyard.

Classical Period

The second period of Ottoman architecture, often referred to as the 'Classical' period, has its origins in the Üç Şerefeli Cami in Edirne built by Murat II and completed in 1447 six years before the conquest of Constantinople. The Üç Şerefeli Mosque had its origins in the fourteenth-century Ulu Cami of Manisa which was visited by Murat II sometime before 1437. The Ulu Cami of Manisa differs from others of the time in having a large central dome in front of the mihrab covering a space equivalent to nine bays. The Manisa Ulu Cami is also unusual because the central courtyard is separated from the main body of the mosque and is not covered by a dome as in the Bursa tradition. Both of these features were found in the Üç Şerefeli Mosque built over seventy years later. However, the dome of the Edirne mosque is much larger and measures over 24 m in diameter, more than double that of its Manisa prototype. Also in the Edirne mosque, the size of the central courtyard is increased so that it resembles those of Syria and Egypt rather than the internal courtyards of the Bursa tradition. However, the arcade on the south side of the courtyard adjacent to the sanctuary of the mosque is raised up in the manner of earlier Ottoman porticoes (e.g. Beyazit Cami in Bursa). The exterior of the building is distinguished by four minarets placed outside each corner of the courtyard. The two north minarets have one balcony (şeref) each whilst the south-east minaret has two balconies and the massive north-west minaret (from which the mosque gets its name) has three balconies each with its own spiral staircase.

The conquest of Constantinople in 1453 exposed Ottoman architects to a whole new range of buildings, the most important of which is the Hagia Sophia (Aya Sophia) which was immediately converted into a mosque by the addition of a wooden minaret to one of the corner turrets. The new concepts introduced by the Üç Şerefeli were not immediately incorporated into Ottoman buildings, and the first mosques were either converted churches or single-domed units in the traditional style. The first major complex to include these features was the Mehmet Fatih Cami built for Murat II between 1463 and 1470. Unfortunately the complex suffered an earthquake in 1766 and the main part of the mosque collapsed so that the present building is an eighteenth-century replica built on the same foundations. The most notable feature of the Fatih Cami was its 26 m dome which for the next hundred years was the largest dome in the empire with the exception of the Hagia Sophia dome of 32 m. The internal arrangement of the Fatih Cami consisted of a large central dome combined with a semi-dome of similar diameter flanked on two sides by three smaller domes and a half dome. This huge area (approximately 40 by 58 m) is entirely open except for two massive piers either side of the semi-dome and two smaller piers either side of the main dome. Outside the mosque is the original rectangular courtyard built to the same design as the Üç Şerefeli Cami courtyard although here there are only two minarets placed against the north wall of the mosque. In addition to the mosque itself the Fatih Cami is remarkable for the ordered geometry of the vast complex which surrounds it. The complex is located on an artificially levelled terrace with the western part of the complex raised up on a vaulted substructure. To the west and east of the mosque are eight orthodox madrassas, four on the west and four on the east side. The design of the madrassas is uniform and consists of nineteen cells arranged around three sides of a rectangular arcaded courtyard with a domed teaching room (dershane) on the fourth side. The complex also includes a hospital and a hostel for travellers and dervishes built on a similar plan to the madrassas.

The next major imperial complex was built by Beyazit II at Edirne in 1484. This complex is the major monument to Beyazit's reign and significantly is not in Istanbul, which was dominated by Mehmet's complex, but at Edirne the former capital. The mosque at the centre of the complex combined the new concepts of courtyard and large domes with older ideas of the single-domed unit and the incorporation of tabhanes (hostels for dervishes). The central area of the mosque is a single square unit covered with a dome of 20 m diameter. Flanking this central area but separate from it are two square nine-domed tabhanes (one on either side). Although separate from the central area the tabhanes are definitely part of the mosque as they are both incorporated into the south side of the courtyard and each has a minaret attached

on the exposed north corner. The rest of the complex includes the elements found in earlier structures, although here the buildings are specifically directed towards medical facilities, thus there is a hospital, asylum and medical college as well as the usual kitchen, bath house and bakery. The main hospital building is hexagonal and consists of series of iwans opening on to a central hexagonal hall covered by a dome. Another complex built by Beyazit at Amasya also contains a building which departs from the traditional square form of Ottoman architecture. This is the Kapiaga Madrassa which is an octagonal building built around a central arcaded courtyard.

Although Beyazit's complex at Edirne is the largest monument to his reign, probably the finest is his mosque in Istanbul begun in 1491. The building has a cruciform plan consisting of the square domed sanctuary, a square courtyard of equal size and two small rectangular wings projecting out of the sides. Like the Edirne mosque these wings were officially tabhanes although unlike Edirne they are not separated from the main area of the mosque by walls suggesting resting rooms rather than hostels. The architectural achievement of this mosque is the incorporation of a second semi-dome so that the large central dome (in this case only 17 m diameter) is balanced by a semi-dome either side, one above the door and the other above the mihrab. Either side of this central domed area are rows of four domes balancing the space of the central area. Like other imperial mosques before it with the exception of the Üç Şerefeli Mosque, this building has two minarets placed at the northern corners of the covered area. The next major mosque to be erected in Istanbul was the Selim I Cami completed in 1522 during the reign of Suleyman the Magnificent. The building comprised a single-domed space flanked by tabhanes and opening on to a rectangular arcaded courtyard. The main dome has a diameter of 24.5 m and was the largest Ottoman dome of the time. However, the design of the building with its single dome covering a square area recalled earlier Ottoman mosques and represented no significant architectural advance. The real advance came with Sinan, whose designs ensured him a place as the foremost of Ottoman architects.

Sinan's first major project was the mosque of Şehzade built for Suleyman the Magnificent in memory of his son Şehzade who died at the age of 22. The mosque was begun in 1543 and completed five years later. The main feature of the design was the quatrefoil arrangement of domes based on the use of a single central dome flanked by four semi-domes, one on each side. The idea was not entirely new and had been used before in the Fatih Pasha Cami at Diyarbakir and Piri Pasha Mosque at Hasköy. Sinan's achievement was to translate this plan into a large scale and reduce to a minimum the obstruction of piers to create an open space horizontally and vertically. The domes rest on four huge central piers and sixteen wall piers and four major corner piers which also functioned as buttresses for the outward thrust of the domes. The size and proportions of the domed area are matched by those of the courtyard, a symmetry which is improved by the absence of the tabhane rooms of the Beyazit and Selim mosques.

Sinan's next major work was the mosque of Suleyman the Magnificent begun in 1550 and known as the Süleymaniye. This building and its associated complex was Sinan's largest commission and took seven years to build. Like the Fatih complex the Süleymaniye is located on a large artificially levelled terrace and has foundations which reach 12 m into the ground. At the centre the complex consists of the mosque in the middle with a courtyard to the north and a tomb garden to the south all enclosed within a wall defining the mosque precincts (cf. ziyada). Outside this enclosure are the usual buildings of an imperial complex including a hospital, medical college, hospice, advanced religious college, primary school, soup kitchen and bath house. In the north-east corner of the complex there is a small garden containing the tomb of Sinan who was buried there thirty years after the completion of this complex. The mosque at the centre of the complex was covered by a large central dome (26 m diameter) contained within two semi-domes instead of the four used at Şehazade's complex. Either side of the central dome are a series smaller domes alternating in size from 5 to 10 m in diameter. The same principal of four massive central piers and several external piers is used here as in the Şehzade Mosque although here the arrangement of the outer piers is more complex — on the south (qibla) side they are on the outside as buttresses whilst on the north side abutting the courtyard they are inside the mosque to enable a neat join with the courtyard portico.

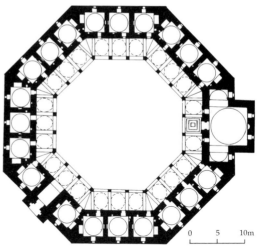

Kapiaga Madrassa, Amasya, Turkey (sixteenth century)

Several other of Sinan's buildings stand out including the Rüstem Pasha Cami noted for its profusion of Iznik tilework, the Mirimah Pasha Cami and the Zal Mahmut Pasha complex. However, undoubtedly Sinan's greatest achievement is the Selimiye Cami in Edirne built between 1569 and 1575. This building, with a dome of equal dimensions to that of Hagia Sophia, is regarded as the supreme achievement of Ottoman architecture. The brilliance of the building relies on the enormous size of the dome which is emphasized by the use of giant squinches or exhedra instead of the semi-domes used earlier at the Süleymaniye or the Şehzade Mosque. In the earlier buildings the semi-domes tended to break up the interior space whereas the giant squinches emphasize the circular space. The central dome and its supporting domes rest on eight huge circular piers which are detached from the exterior walls and appear as free-standing columns although they are actually tied to huge external piers of buttresses. The mihrab space is emphasized by placing it in an apse-like half-dome which projects out of the mosque between the two southern piers. Like the Üç Şerefeli Cami the Selimiye is equipped with four minarets, two on the north side of the dome and two at the north end of the courtyard. Although Sinan continued for another thirteen years after the completion of the Selimiye, his most important work had already been done.

In contrast to the advances of religious architecture, secular buildings of the period are fairly conservative and tend to stick to established forms. Where there is development this is often influenced by mosque architecture; thus the Haseki Hürrem Hammam in Istanbul designed by Sinan owes much of its grandeur to its tall domes inspired by contemporary mosques. Civil engineering, including bridges and forts, is characterized by solid construction and austere design reminiscent of Roman architecture. This can be seen in Rumeli Hisar, the fortress built by Mehmet II to control the Bosphorus before the conquest of Constantinople. The building consists of a huge enclosure (approximately 220 by 100 m) formed by three huge towers (two semicircular and one polygonal) linked by a tall crenellated wall strengthened by interval towers or bastions. The interior was filled with a mosque and a large number of wooden buildings which have now disappeared. The bastions and towers represent a variety of different shapes and designs which suggest that the fortress was built by a number of individuals working to a broad general design rather than a detailed architect's plan. Bridges on the other hand tended to be built to a standard plan which was applied to a variety of situations. The most famous bridge of the period is that of Büyükçekmice to the west of Istanbul; built by Sinan in 1566, it consists of a series of four humped bridges resting on three artificial islands. At the west end of the bridge there is a rectangular caravanserai covered with a wooden gabled roof. Other important caravanserais of the period include the Sokollu Mehmed Pasha Caravanserai at Lüleburgaz and the Selim II complex at Payas in eastern Anatolia both built by Sinan. One area where secular architecture was innovative and influential was in the imperial palace or Topkapisarai. This building was established as the centre of imperial power soon after Mehmed II entered Istanbul and remained the centre until the collapse of Ottoman power in the twentieth century. Several parts of the fifteenth-century palace remain, the most important of which is the Çinili Kiosk built in 1473. This pavilion, based on a four-iwan plan, was designed by a Persian architect and decorated with blue glazed bricks in Timurid style. The building influenced much of the subsequent domestic architecture of Istanbul, in particular some of the Bosphorus mansions.

Later Period

In the last years of the sixteenth century and the first years of the seventeenth century Ottoman architecture continued to use the forms and style developed by Sinan during the Classical period. Thus the Yeni Valide complex built by Sinan's successor Davut is a copy of the Şehzade Mosque with a few alterations to the size and shape of the courtyard. The most famous building in this late classical style is the Sultan Ahmet Cami in Istanbul also known as the Blue Mosque begun in 1609 and completed in 1617. The most distinctive feature of this building is the use of six minarets instead of the previous maximum of four. It is roofed with the quatrefoil design used in the Şehzade Cami with four huge cylindrical fluted piers supporting the 23.5 m dome (considerably smaller than the Selimiye). The plan has several weaknesses, the most notable of which is the way the mihrab is placed in the middle of a flat wall without any architectural emphasis. Also the portico is not raised to the level of the central domed area thus making the mosque and courtyard seem like two independent units rather than a gradual development of mass.

From the end of the sixteenth century slavish copying of the Classical style was gradually replaced; characteristic features of the new style are flamboyant decoration, increased use of windows and curves, and growing European influences. The most famous example is the Nuruosmaniye Cami in Istanbul completed in 1755. The plan of this building is still based on the square covered by a dome but the strict geometry of the Classical period is modified, thus there are small projecting wings either end of the qibla wall and the mihrab is located in a curved apse in a manner similar to that of the Selimiye in Edirne although here the apse is curved. The recessed porches, which in earlier mosques would have been filled with muqarnas mouldings, are here filled with carved acanthus leaves. The most striking feature of the building is the courtyard which is built in a curved D-shape with the straight side forming the portico of the mosque. The courtyard is also unusual because the domes above the two north entrances are pierced with a series of arched windows which add to the light coming from the trefoil arched windows at the sides. The absence of a central fountain and the positioning of the mosque on an irregular-shaped terrace add to the surprise of this building. Other eighteenth- and nineteenth-century mosques, however, retained the strict square geometry which was now prescribed by the religious orthodoxy as the necessary form for a mosque. Thus the Laleli Cami and complex built ten years later in 1783 has a conventional plan, although this is modified by making the prayer hall rectangular instead of square, by cutting off the two side aisles either side of the main dome and making them into external arcades. The apse form of the mihrab area used in the Nuruosmaniye is retained although here it has a square form similar to the Selimiye in Edirne instead of the curved form of the Nuruosmaniye. The Laleli is also noticeable for its use of Ionic capitals instead of the muqarnas capitals preferred in the Classical period.

Several methods were used to break away from the enforced geometry of the square domed unit; one method was to give an undulating curved form to the outer edges of domes. This was a technique which was first used on the wooden roofs of sebils (fountains) and kiosks such as that on the tomb of Mehmet II rebuilt in 1784. The use of this technique on mosque domes can be seen on the Beylerbey Cami of 1778 and in an extravagant form at the Iliyas Bey Cami built in 1812. Similar techniques were used for windows and arches which had undulating curves hung as drapery in the European manner. Outside the strict boundaries of orthodoxy there was more room for experimentation, thus the Küçük Efendi complex in Istanbul was built for dervishes and has a radical plan. The building, completed in 1825, consists of an oval structure which combines a mosque and dervish dance hall.

The nineteenth century saw the emergence of new building forms and types influenced by Europe. The most successful of these new forms was the clock tower which by the beginning of the First World War had been established in Ottoman cities throughout the empire. The earliest example was a three-storey wooden tower outside the Nusretiye Cami in Istanbul, other early examples are at Yozgat and Adana. The extent of European influence can be seen in the decision to move the royal residence from the Topkapisarai in old Istanbul to the newly fashionable banks of the Bosphorus. The new residence known as the Dolmabahçe Palace was built in 1853 in the European Classical style with a colonnaded façade looking out over the water. The palace stretches out along the side of the Bosphorus in a series of blocks or wings, the most famous of which is the throne room measuring 44 by 46 m.

Increased European interest in Ottoman and Seljuk architecture also stimulated an interest in revivalist architecture. One of the earliest examples of revivalism in Turkish architecture is the palace of Ishak Pasha at Dogubayazit in eastern Anatolia completed in 1784. This imposing building, set against the backdrop of Mount Ararat, recalls the Seljuk architecture of eastern Anatolia with carved animals and huge monumental doorways. However, this building is exceptional and it is not until the late nineteenth and early twentieth centuries that revivalism becomes established as a style in Ottoman art. Notable examples are the Vakif Han built by Kemalettin in 1914 and the Istanbul main post office built in 1909. Both these buildings incorporate medieval and early Ottoman features in buildings made using modern methods and materials.

See also: Albania, Bosnia, Bulgaria, Bursa, Byzantine architecture, Cairo, Cyprus, Edirne, Greece, Iraq, Istanbul, Iznik, Jordan, Lebanon, Palestine, Sinan, Syria, Turkey

Further reading:

O. Aslanapa, *Turkish Art and Architecture*, London 1971.

Y. Bingöl, *Der Ishak Pascha Palast in Dogubayazit am Berg Ararat*, Berlin 1982.

M. Cezar, *Typical Commercial Buildings of the Ottoman Classical Period and the Ottoman Construction System*, Istanbul 1983.

A. Gabriel, *Les Monuments turcs d'anatolie*, 2 vols., Paris 1931–4.

—— *Châteaux turcs du Bosphore*, Paris 1943.

—— *Une Capitale turque, Brousse*, Paris 1958.

G. Goodwin, *A History of Ottoman Architecture*, London 1971.

—— *Ottoman Turkey*, London 1977.

A. Kuran, *The Mosque in Early Ottoman Architecture*, Chicago 1968.

J. M. Rogers and R. M. Ward, *Suleyman the Magnificent*, London 1988.

I. Utkular, *Çanakkale Bogazinda Fatih Keleleri*, Istanbul 1954.

Oualata (also known as Walata, Iwalatan and Birou)

Important trading city in south-west Mauritania.

The collapse of the empire of Ghana in 1224 led refugees from Awdaghast to found a new city in the small village of Birou. The new city was called Oualata and contained immigrants from several ethnic groups including Berbers, Islamized Soninke and Massufa nomads. The Berbers were the religious leaders as well as the merchants whilst the Soninke provided craftsmen and the Massufa nomads acted as caravan leaders and guides. The rise of the empire of Mali and the subsequent shift of political power to the south strengthened the position of Oualata as a regional centre and as a terminus for trans-Saharan caravans. The main partner for this desert trade was the city of Siji-massa from which goods would be traded to Fez and Tlemcen in Morocco.

During the fourteenth century Mansa Musa started his famous pilgrimage from Oualata and on his return brought with him the famous architect and poet al-Saheli who built an audience hall there. In 1352 the city was visited by Ibn Battuta who stayed there for seven weeks. He described the city as a cosmopolitan trading and intellectual centre under the administration of the empire of Mali. In the sixteenth century a new component was added to the city's ethnic composition with the arrival of the Arabic Beni Hassan tribe. The lasting result of this was the adoption of Hassaniya, a mixed Arabic Berber language which became the main language of commerce in the city. The other main language of Oualata is the Soninke language of Azer.

The buildings of Oualata are made of stone with roofs made of split-palm beams and palm-frond matting overlaid with earth. The houses consist of a central courtyard entered through an inner and outer vestibule. There are often two storeys in the houses with the upper floor reached by an external staircase in the courtyard. All the rooms lead directly off from the courtyard which is the centre of activity and contains beds for the servants. The stone walls of the houses are covered with a thick layer of mud plaster (banco) on both the outside and the inside. This technique is unique to Oualata and distinguishes it from other Berber towns of Mauritania suggesting the influence of non-Berber architecture from further south. This idea is strengthened by the fact that the mud rendering is carried out by the women of the society. The most remarkable feature of the earthen rendering is the application of striking white-painted designs around the doorways, windows and niches of the courtyard. It is noticeable that the designs are restricted to the interior of the courtyards and are not visible from the outside, consisting of ara-besque medallions and chain motifs executed in thick but precise white lines. The most elaborate decoration is reserved for the doorway of the senior wife's room where a number of different motifs are used to produce a highly ornate design. The doorways are made of wooden planks with wooden locks and are decorated with Moroccan brass medallions. Either side of the doorway are elaborately carved wooden pillars, or asnads, which are used as calabash supports. The pillars are set into an earthen base made in the shape of a small stepped pyramid but at the top divide into three branches. Similar pillars are found in Berber tents and their presence in these houses are reminders of a nomadic past. Inside, the rooms are fairly bare except for a large canopied platform bed hung with tapestries and mats.

See also: Agades, Timbuktu, West Africa

Further reading:

G. J. Duchemin, 'A propos des decorations murales des habitations de Oualata (Mauretanie)', *Bulletin IFAN* 12(4): 1095–110, 1950.

O. Du Puigaudeau, 'Contribution à l'étude du symbolisme dans le décor mural et l'artisanat de Walat', *Bulletin IFAN* 19(1–2): 137–83, 1957.

P

Pakistan

Predominantly Muslim country in the north-west corner of the Indian subcontinent.

Pakistan is located in a strategic position with Afghanistan and Iran to the west, India to the east, the Sinkiang region of China to the north and the Indian Ocean to the south. Running down the centre of the country from the Chinese border to the Indian Ocean is the Indus river which unites the diverse regions and cultures through which it passes. In the north and west the country is dominated by the highest mountains in the world and includes parts of Himalayas, the Hindu Kush and the Karakoram mountain ranges. Officially the country is divided into five regions, the Northern Areas, the North-West Frontier, the Punjab, Baluchistan and Sind. Each region has its own languages and cultures reflecting a complex historical development. Most of the population lives in the Indus valley which comprises the states of Punjab and Sind. The valley is home to one of the world's oldest civilizations based on the cities of Mohenjodaro and Harrapa which flourished more than 4,000 years ago. During the fourth century BCE the northern part of the country was conquered by Alexander the Great who established a Macedonian garrison at Taxilla. The Greeks were soon defeated by the Mauryans who later introduced Buddhism as the state religion. For the next 400 years or more the region was the centre of a Graeco-Indian Buddhist culture illustrated by the great stupas of Taxilla. During the fifth century CE there was a period of Hindu revival under the Gupta dynasty, remains of which can be seen in Hindu and Jain stone shrines.

The first Muslims in Pakistan were probably Arab seafarers taking part in the extensive Indian Ocean trade network. However, the first Muslim conquest of the area was by Mohammad ibn al-Qasim who captured the region of Sind in 711. For the next one and a half centuries Sind was ruled by Umayyad and later Abbasid governors until 873 when the province broke away from the caliphate. The province was now divided into several independent city states the most important of which were Multan and Mansurah. During the tenth century Sind developed as an important centre of Ismaili and Khariji thought which was brought to an abrupt end by the invasions of Mahmud of Ghazni between 1004 and 1008. Several years later the province of Punjab, then under Hindu control, was captured by Mahmud who established a fort and mint at Lahore. For the next 150 years much of the present area of Pakistan was under Ghaznavid control, until the invasions of Mahmud of Ghur at the end of the twelfth century. Mahmud's deputy Qutb al-Din Aybak soon took over and ruled the Punjab from his Indian capital of Delhi. For the following 300 years with a few exceptions Pakistan was under the control of the various dynasties ruling from Delhi the most significant of which was the Tughluqs. In the sixteenth century the Punjab was incorporated into the Mughal Empire and Lahore became one of the three main cities of the empire. For a period of about fifty years in the early nineteenth century the Punjab was under the control of the Sikhs although by the end of the century it was firmly incorporated into British India. In 1947 the Muslim parts of India comprising the modern states of Pakistan and Bangladesh were made independent as one country despite the great distances separating them. In 1970 the country separated into two independent states, Pakistan and Bangladesh.

The range of building materials and techniques used in Pakistan reflects both the variety of its natural environment and its long cultural history. The scarcity of suitable building stone in the Indus valley has meant that mud or clay has always been the main building material. Mud may be used in several forms: as mud brick, baked brick or pisé. Mud brick was first used in the cities of Harrapa and Mohenjodaro over 4,000 years ago and continues to be used in many of the villages of the

Punjab today. Baked brick is used for more permanent structures such as wells, important houses or mosques whilst pisé is used for structures which need to be built cheaply and quickly. On the coast of Sind mud is used as a thick plaster over a wooden frame to produce wattle-and-daub constructions. In the mountains of the North-West Frontier the typical form of construction consists of rubble stone walls set in mud mortar and covered over with a mud-plaster finish. These buildings are covered with flat roofs made of timber branches overlaid with matting and then covered with earth. The only region where timber is plentiful is in the northern region of the Swat valley where there are dense pine forests. The architecture of this region is similar to its Indian neighbour, Kashmir with finely carved wooden mosques covered by pagoda-style roofs.

Archaeological work in Sind has revealed the remains of several early Islamic sites, the most significant of which is Bhambore, thought to be the ancient city of Debal. The city was divided into two parts and enclosed with a defensive wall fortified with semi-circular buttress towers. Probably the most important discovery is the congregational mosque with a large central courtyard and no mihrab. The absence of a mihrab confirms the

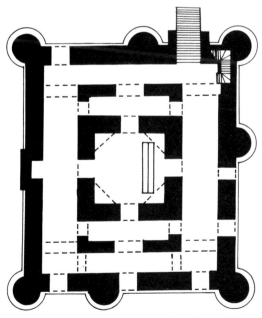

Plan of tomb of Khalid Walid at Kabriwala, Pakistan (after Mumtaz)

early date of the building given by an inscription dated to 727.

Medieval architecture in Pakistan is best represented by the funerary and religious buildings of Multan and Uchch in the Punjab. There are few remains from the Ghaznavid period apart from the twelfth-century tomb of Khaliq Walid or Khalid Walid near Multan. The tomb consists of a rectangular baked-brick enclosure containing a square domed chamber. The outer enclosure wall is strengthened with semi-circular buttress towers and includes a rectangular projection marking the position of the mihrab in the west wall. Inside, the mihrab consists of a rectangular recess covered with an arched hood and framed by bands of inscriptions cut into the brickwork. In the centre of the recess is a blind niche set between pilasters and crowned with a trefoil arch. The design of this mausoleum represents the first stage in the evolution of the medieval tombs of Multan which culminated in the tomb of Shah Rukn-i Alam built during the reign of Ghiyas al-Din Tughluq. In the latter tomb the outer walls no longer form an enclosure but are wrapped around the central octagonal tomb. Externally the walls slope inward and are strengthened at the corners by tapering domed turrets providing a counter thrust to the weight of the dome. The distinctive sloping walls and corner turrets of this tomb were later repeated in the Tughluqid architecture of Delhi.

Another architectural tradition is represented by the flat-roofed tombs and mosques of Uchch a small city to the south of Multan. A typical Uchch mosque consists of a rectangular hall with wooden pillars supporting beams resting on carved brackets. The areas between the beams are covered with wooden boards which are usually painted in yellow or white against a bright orange or red ground. The walls of the buildings are usually made of baked brick covered in decorative cut plaster. Most buildings of this type are entered via a projecting wooden porch also supported on wooden columns. Prominent buildings of this type are the tombs of Jalal Din Surkh Bukhari, Abu Hanifa and Rajan Qattal.

During the sixteenth century most of the area of modern Pakistan was brought under Mughal rule. In general imperial Mughal architecture was restricted to Lahore, whilst the rest of the country developed its own regional style. One exception to this general rule is the fort at Attock in the

North-West Province built by Akbar as a defence against invasion from the west. The fort is built on a hillside between the Indus and Kabul rivers and consists of a huge enclosure wall fortified by projecting machicolations and large round bastions. Other buildings at Attock include the garden and palace of Akbar which are small structures hidden amongst the hills. Certainly the most developed expression of Mughal architecture in Pakistan is the fort at Lahore built by Akbar in 1556 on the banks of the river Ravi. The plan of the Lahore fort resembles those of Agra and Delhi with its riverside position and its arrangement of gardens and pavilions. The fort is entered via a main gateway leading into a large rectangular courtyard with the imperial reception hall (diwan-i amm) in the centre of the wall opposite the entrance. Behind the reception hall is the private area of the palace divided into courtyards and gardens overlooking the river. Apart from the fort the most important imperial building in the city is the Badshahi Mosque built by Aurangzeb in 1674. The mosque has the same general plan as that of the Jami Masjid in Delhi although the Badshahi Mosque is much larger. Other imperial Mughal buildings in

Lahore include the tomb of Jahangir, the Shahdara complex and the Shalamar Bagh.

In addition to the imperial Mughal complexes, Lahore also contains some of the finest examples of the regional Mughal style which is a mixture of Mughal forms with local and Persian modifications. Characteristic features of this style are the use of brightly coloured tile mosaics, thick octagonal minarets, wide flattened domes and arches. Probably the finest example of tile mosaic (kashi) is the Picture Wall in the fort at Lahore which includes both animal and human figures. Probably more representative of the local style is the tilework of the Wazir Khan Mosque, where all surfaces are covered with floral and geometric designs in coloured tiles. This mosque also has the earliest examples of the thick octagonal minarets which later became characteristic features of Lahore architecture.

Outside Lahore, Mughal-period architecture may be divided into a number of local styles, the most significant of which is that of Sind. The architecture of Sind was heavily influenced by the neighbouring state of Gujarat in India which consists of heavily carved trabeate stone buildings. Some of the finest examples can be found in the Makli cemetery in

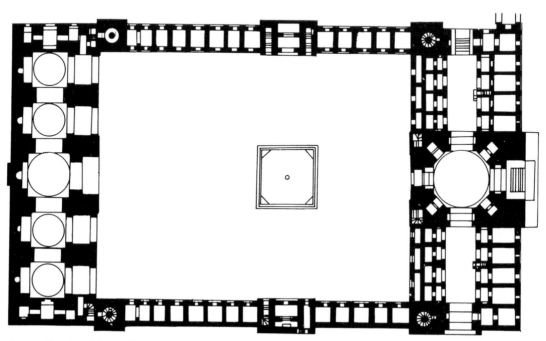

Seventeenth-century Mosque of Wazir Khan, Lahore, Pakistan (after Mumtaz)

lower Sind, where exuberantly carved tombs are covered by corbelled domed canopies resting on square carved monolithic columns. Sind is also noted for its geometric tile mosaics which may have been the inspiration for the more naturalistic tilework of Lahore. Some of the best examples of tilework can be seen in the monuments of Hyderabad and Thatta in upper Sind. Other characteristic features of architecture in this region are the use of multiple blind niches on outer walls and elaborately shaped crenellations. During the period of British rule the architecture of Pakistan was represented by an eclectic mixture of European, Hindu and Mughal styles. Immediately after Independence, Pakistani architecture developed under the influence of Modernism which saw its culmination in the establishment of a new capital at Islamabad in 1960. Although the design of Islamabad was based on religious and national criteria it did not include provision for a national mosque. This situation was rectified in 1970 when work began on the Shah Faisal Masjid which is a huge structure covered with a roof in the form of a truncated pyramid flanked by four tall pointed minarets.

See also: Banbhore, India, Lahore, mihrab, Mughals

Further reading:

A. H. Dani, *Thatta-Islamic Architecture*, Islamabad 1982.

J. Kalter, *The Arts and Crafts of the Swat Valley: Living Traditions in the Hindu Kush*, London 1991.

A. N. Khan, *Uchch History and Architecture*, Islamabad 1983.

F. A. Khan, *Architecture and Art Treasures in Pakistan*, Karachi.

K. K. Mumtaz, *Architecture in Pakistan*, London 1985.

A. B. Rajput, *Architecture in Pakistan*, Karachi 1963.

N. I. Siddiqui, *Thatta*, Karachi 1963.

Palestine

Small country on the eastern shore of the Mediterranean comprising an area of 26,650 square km.

Physically it is divided into four main regions; a low-lying coastal strip along the Mediterranean, a central hilly or mountainous area running north to south through the centre of the country, the Jordan Rift Valley containing the Sea of Galilee and the Dead Sea, and the Negev desert which covers most of the southern part of the country.

Until 1918, when it was conquered by Britain, the country was part of the Ottoman Empire. At present the land is divided between the state of Israel and the occupied territories of Gaza and the West Bank. Israel is a new state created in 1948 with a largely immigrant population, whose architecture is alien to the region. However the people of Gaza and the West Bank are mostly the indigenous inhabitants of the country, whose architecture has developed within the landscape for at least the last two thousand years.

Palestine was one of the first areas to be conquered by the Arab armies of Islam in 637 and from that point onwards has remained one of the main centres of Islamic culture. For some time during the seventh century Muslims were expected to pray towards Jerusalem rather than Mecca, thus establishing Jerusalem's position as one of the holiest sites of Islam. However, throughout the Umayyad period the culture of the area remained predominantly Byzantine and there was only gradual change to a new Islamic culture. With the Abbasid revolution in 750 Palestine was no longer near the centre of the empire and consequently was exposed to a number of competing forces including the Tulunids and Ikhshids. In the tenth century Palestine came under the control of the Fatimids who ruled the area from their newly founded capital at Cairo. During the following century the country was fought over by Byzantines and the Fatimids, but it was eventually conquered by the European Crusaders at the end of the eleventh century. For the next two hundred years, parts of Palestine were ruled by a series of Crusader kings. The Crusaders were gradually expelled through a series of wars conducted first by the Ayyubids under Nur al-Din and Salah al-Din, and later by the Mamluks under Baybars and his successors. Cultural, spiritual and commercial life flourished under the Mamluks until the late fifteenth century when internal problems and external pressures allowed the conquest of the area by the Ottoman Turks in 1516. For the next four hundred years Palestine was part of the Ottoman province of Damascus. However, during this period various local governors were able to achieve semi-independent status. During the eighteenth century Dhahir al 'Umar ruled a large area of northern Palestine and amassed a great deal of wealth from the cotton trade. Dhahir was succeeded by Ahmad al-Jazzar Pasha the governor of Sidon who re-established the city of Acre as one of the major ports of the Mediterranean. During the nineteenth century the country was subjected to increasing European influence with colonies established in Haifa and Jerusalem. The British defeat of the Ottomans in 1918 led to the establishment of the British Mandate which ruled the country until 1948. In 1948 Palestine was divided between Jordan, Israel and Egypt; in 1968 Israel occupied the entire country.

The main building materials in Palestine are stone and unbaked mud brick. Wood and baked brick are hardly ever used. Three main types of stone are used, depending on the region of the country. Along the Mediterranean coast kurkar, a silicous limestone, is used for building. This has the property that it can easily be cut from the outcrops near the seashore, although it also weathers easily and is difficult to dress to a fine finish. Both the cities of Acre and Jaffa are built of this material. In the northern part of the Jordan Rift Valley and around the Sea of Galilee, basalt blocks are used in construction. Basalt is extremely hard and is consequently difficult to cut or carve, although once shaped it does not weather much. As a consequence basalt is often used in combination with limestone which is used for architectural details. The cities of Tiberias and Beisan (Bet Shean) have the best examples of basalt architecture. The best-quality building stone comes from the central hilly region. In this area various types of limestone can be found. Limestone is fairly easy to cut and does not erode as much as kurkar stone. Limestone cut and dressed to a fine finish is known as ashlar masonry and is used in some of the finest buildings in the country. Limestone occurs in a variety of colours from white to honey yellow and pink; some of the best examples can be found in Jerusalem, Hebron and Ramla. In addition various types of marble are obtained from the hills around Jerusalem, whilst Dolomite (hard limestone with magnesium) is used in areas of Galilee.

Until recently a large number of buildings were made out of mud brick and pisé particularly in the Jordan valley and the coastal plain where building stone was not so readily available as in the hills. Mud brick has the advantages of being cheap, easy to work with good thermal insulating properties. Unfortunately mud brick also requires a high degree of maintenance and it has mostly been replaced with reinforced concrete which has some of the same plastic qualities. The best examples of mud-brick architecture still surviving are in Jericho, where a wide variety of buildings, including mosques and cinemas, are built out of this material.

Early Islamic Period

Undoubtedly the most famous building in Palestine is the Dome of the Rock built by the caliph Abd al-Malik in 691. The significance of this building extends beyond its immediate architectural design to its symbolic function of demonstrating the presence of Islam and its status as a major religion in Jerusalem, home to both Christianity and Judaism. Together with the Aqsa Mosque and the Royal Palace to the south of the Haram, Jerusalem's place as a religious and cultural centre of Islam was established.

However, the capital of Palestine during the Umayyad and Abbasid periods was not Jerusalem but Ramla. Like Basra, Kufa and Wasit, Ramla was one of the new towns established in the first years of the Arab conquests. Today little survives of the early Islamic city with the exception of two large underground cisterns, one below the congregational mosque (Jami' al-Abiyad) and one outside the city to the west. Generally, however, the major cities of the Byzantine period continued to be the major settlements; thus archaeology has demonstrated the continued occupation of Lydda, Beisan, Tiberias Gaza, Caesarea and Acre into the Umayyad and Abbasid periods. As much of the population remained Christian, churches continued to be built during the period.

Outside the cities and in the Negev a number of new settlements were built in the early Islamic period. Some of these were agricultural centres, whilst others were palaces and mansions for the new élite. The best known of these is the Umayyad palace of Khirbet al-Mafjar near Jericho in the Jordan valley (known locally as Hisham's palace although it has now been reliably attributed to Walid II). This building was modelled on a Roman bath house and was lavishly decorated with mosaics and stucco. The stucco includes representations of semi-naked women and is unique in Islamic art. A similar but smaller structure was built at the south end of Lake Tiberias (the Sea of Galilee) in an area of hot springs. The original building was a Roman fort although this was substantially rebuilt during the Umayyad period to resemble a palace, with mosaics etc.

In the Negev large numbers of early Islamic sites have been found, which indicate a growth in the settlement of the area. This parallels the increased building activity in the deserts of Jordan, Iraq and Saudi Arabia and may be linked to a shift in emphasis towards Arabia in the early Islamic period.

Increasing political tension and fragmentation in the later Abbasid and Fatimid periods meant that few major monuments can be dated to this period. Significantly two large monuments in Palestine which can be dated to this period (tenth and eleventh centuries) are fortified structures built to guard against an impending Byzantine invasion. One of these buildings, Kefar Lam is built on the north coast south of Haifa and the other, Mina al-Qal'a (now known as Ashdod Yam) is located on the southern coast near Ashdod. Both are built of thin slabs of kurkar stone (laid in a manner resembling brick construction) forming large rectangular enclosures with solid corner towers and semi-circular buttresses. The fort at Ashdod was fairly luxurious and includes a line of marble columns in the centre re-used from the classical site of Ashdod. Outside the fort at Ashdod there are the remains of a domed building which has been interpreted as a bath house. The domes are supported on shell-like squinches (characteristic of the Fatimid period) with pierced holes for light.

Crusader Period

The Crusader conquest of Palestine had a profound influence on the appearance of the country. In Jerusalem the Aqsa Mosque was converted into a palace by Baldwin I and the Dome of the Rock was converted into an Augustinian church. In the countryside numerous castles, tower houses and churches testify to the Crusader presence. The castles guarding prominent positions are perhaps the best-known architectural legacy of the Crusades. The most famous in Palestine are Monfort and Belvoir, although there are numerous smaller fortresses throughout the area. Typically a Crusader castle consisted of a square or rectangular tower surrounded by thick enclosing walls. The enclosure walls would follow the shape of the land unlike the regular shapes of the earlier Islamic forts. Many of the features found in Crusader fortification were later re-used in Arab castles such as Ajlun (Qal'at Rabad) and Nimrud.

Whilst the Crusader castles controlled the land physically, the spiritual possession of the holy land was marked by the construction of hundreds of churches. In Jerusalem alone there were sixty, some of which were built on the ruins of Byzantine churches. The churches were distinguished with fine carved capitals and sculptures.

With the Muslim reconquest of Jerusalem in 1187 the Crusader presence was reduced to the area around Acre, which for the next hundred years (until it too fell in 1191) was the centre of the Crusader kingdoms, and was enriched with some of the finest Crusader architecture in the Middle East.

The Crusades influenced the architecture of Palestine in two ways: directly through the copying of techniques and the re-use of buildings, and indirectly through the development of the counter-Crusade. The direct influence is seen in the adaptation of certain techniques for Islamic buildings such as cushion-shaped voussoirs and folded cross vaults, all of which can be found in the Mamluk buildings of Jerusalem. One of the best examples of this influence can be seen in the minaret of the Great Mosque of Ramla, which resembles a Crusader church tower. The indirect influence can be seen in the development of a propaganda expressed through monumental inscriptions and carved devices. One of the most famous examples of the latter, of the lion of Baybars catching a mouse, is depicted on the Lion Gate in Jerusalem (this can also be seen at Jisr Jindas between Ramla and Lydda).

Mamluk Era

Mamluk rule in Palestine produced some of the best examples of medieval architecture in the Middle East, with a proliferation of religious buildings including mosques, madrassas, khanqas and commemorative mausoleums. Jerusalem in particular was provided with a large number of religious buildings as befitted Islam's holiest shrine after Mecca and Medina. Mamluk architecture in Jerusalem was characterized by the use of joggled voussoirs, ablaq masonry, muqarnas mouldings and coloured marble inlays. In Ramla, the Great Mosque was rebuilt and the Crusader church was converted into a mosque.

One of the more beautiful Mamluk buildings of Palestine is the tomb of Abu Hoeira near Yabne (modern Yavne). This consists of a triple-domed portico and a central area covered by a large dome set on squinches. The decoration is restrained and restricted to the areas around the doorway and mihrab which are decorated with inlaid marble and inscriptions.

A characteristic feature of the Mamluk period was the revitalization of the road systems which were provided with khans, mosques and bridges. Examples of Mamluk khans include Khan al-Tujjar, Khan al-Minya, Jaljuliyya, Ramla and Lydda. Probably the most impressive of these is Khan Yunis at Ghaza built out of ablaq masonry with a mosque and minaret included in its design. Several Mamluk bridges survive in Palestine, the most impressive of which is Jisr Jindas, decorated with an inscription flanked by two lions (other bridges include Jisr Banat Yaqub and a bridge at Beisan).

Ottoman Conquest

The Ottoman conquest of Palestine in 1516 introduced new architectural concepts, although these were only gradually adopted and never became universal. The most obvious symbol of the Ottoman conquest was the redevelopment of Jerusalem; this included rebuilding the walls, tiling the Dome of the Rock and renovating the city's water supply.

The city of Acre, rebuilt in the eighteenth century, is the best example of a complete Ottoman city in Palestine. It has several khans, at least two bath houses, three main suqs, at least ten mosques and a citadel. The wealth of the city was expressed in the mosque of al-Jazzar Pasha and the large bath complex known as Hammam al-Basha. The mosque was modelled on those of Istanbul with a large central dome and a pencil-like minaret. The baths were extensively decorated with Armenian tiles and inlaid marble floors. The houses of Acre were two, three- or even four-storeyed structures with painted wooden ceilings.

Important cities during the Ottoman period included Hebron, Nablus, Ramla, Jaffa, Safed, Tiberias and Acre (from the eighteenth century onwards). Most of the cities were surrounded by walls, the best surviving example of which are the walls of Tiberias rebuilt by Dhahir al 'Umar. The walls of Acre date mostly from the late eighteenth century and are of Italian design.

The houses of Ottoman Palestine varied depending on the region in which they were located. There are few or no remains of the mud-brick houses of the coastal plain although the stone houses of the villages have survived well until recent times. The predominant form of roofing for stone houses was the dome made by filling a room with earth, covering this with a reed mat and then building the dome over the top. During the eighteenth century domes were often decorated with carved plaster usually in the form of swirls, rosettes and semi-circles. In Galilee, buildings were roofed by using transverse stone arches to support short beams over which a roof could be laid.

Outside Jerusalem Ottoman control was established through a series of forts garrisoned by Janissaries (imperial Ottoman troops). These fortresses were large square or rectangular structures with square corner towers; surviving examples can be seen at Ras al-Ain near Tel Aviv, Khan al-Tujjar near Kefar Kanna and Qal'at Burak south of Jerusalem.

See also: Abbasids, al-Aqsa Mosque, Dome of the Rock, Fatimids, Jersalem, Khirbet al-Mafjar, Khirbet al-Minya, Mamluks, Ottomans, Ramla, Umayyads

Further reading:

S. Amiry and V. Tamari, *Palestinian Village Architecture*, London 1990.
T. Canaan, *Mohammedan Saints and Santuaries in Palestine*, Jerusalem 1927.
——— *The Palestinian Arab House*, Jerusalem 1933.
L. Mayer, *Some Principal Muslim Religious Buildings in Israel*, Jerusalem 1950.

Persia

See Iran.

Philippines

Country composed of a group of islands on the east side of the South China Sea between Taiwan, Indonesia and Malaysia.

The country consists of two main islands, Mindanao in the south and Luzon in the north and more than twenty smaller islands. The south-western islands have a large Muslim population whereas the northern ones are predominantly Roman Catholic. Filipino Muslims share much in common with their Indonesian and Malaysian neighbours who first introduced Islam to the Philippines. The first areas to be converted to Islam were the islands of the Sulu archipelago between the fourteenth and fifteenth centuries. By the mid-sixteenth century Muslim missionaries from Borneo were working on the island of Luzon. However, earlier in 1522 the islands were discovered by the Spanish who established their first permanent settlement in 1565 and in 1571 founded the capital of Manila. There was some conflict with the newly established Muslim sultanates of Luzon but the Spanish won with their superior firepower. Nevertheless, the south-western part of the Philippines remained Muslim despite constant attempts to defeat them by the Spanish. The Muslims of the islands were given the name Moros by the Spanish who associated them with the Muslims of North Africa. Throughout the seventeenth, eighteenth and nineteenth centuries the Spanish tried unsuccessfully to conquer the Moro people. When the Philippines passed into American control in 1898 the Americans continued the Spanish policy of trying to subdue the Muslims of the south-west. In 1913 the Moros were finally defeated by superior American arms and a peace treaty was signed. The peace treaty was a success as it allowed the Muslims complete control over their own affairs and equality with the Catholic Filipinos.

The earliest physical evidence of Islam in the Philippines is a tombstone on the island of Jolo which has been provisionally dated to 1310. Oral history recounts how Islam was brought to the island of Jolo by Tuan ul Makdum (later called Sharif Aulia) who built 'a house for religious worship'. Later, in 1380 he built another mosque at Tubig Indangan on Simunul island south of Jolo. This mosque, considerably altered, is now known as the oldest mosque in the Philippines. A photograph of the building taken in 1923 shows a square wooden structure open on one side with remains of a two-tier coconut-palm thatch roof. The mosque was comprehensively rebuilt in the 1970s with concrete walls and a two-tier tin roof.

Islam came to the island of Mindanao in the fifteenth century and several mosques on the shores of Lake Lanao may have been founded in this early period, although no early remains seem to have survived. One of the oldest mosques is the Taraka Mosque in Lanao del Sur which is a square structure with a three-tier tin roof and painted abstract designs on the walls. Another early mosque is the Ranggar in Karigongan which consists of a simple square room with bamboo walls and a pyramid roof. A later development is represented by the insertion of an onion-shaped dome on an octagonal drum in the centre of the roof also found in one of the Lake Lanao mosques. This design reaches its climax in one of the Lanao mosques where there is a central onion dome flanked by four pagoda-like minarets. It is generally assumed that the use of domes reflects Indian influence via Malaysia and Indonesia, although it may also be through Chinese influence. After the Second World War, since Filipinos have been able to travel to Mecca, a new Middle-Eastern mosque style is noticeable in the Philippines. One of the more notable examples is the mosque of Jolo town on Jolo island which consists of a large rectangular prayer hall with a central dome and four flanking minarets. Probably the most famous mosque in the Philippines is the Quiapo Mosque in Manila which has an arcaded courtyard containing a fountain and a domed prayer hall.

Other examples of Islamic architecture in the Maranao area include royal residences and fortifications. Royal residences are known as 'torogan' and consist of raised platforms with tall sloping roofs. Inside, a torogan consists of one room with the king's bed in the centre and a small bedroom for the royal daughters. Sometimes the daughters' room (known as a lamin) is located in a separate room above the main roof of the torogan. Islamic forts (kota) were used to resist the Spanish and later American attempts to convert the Maranao Muslims to Christianity. Kotas consist of earthworks reinforced with wooden stakes.

See also: Indonesia, Java, Malaysia, Sumatra

Further reading:

A. Abbahil, 'The Maranao Mosque: its origins, structure and community role', *Danslan Quarterly* 1(20):85–103, 1980.

E. G. Giron, 'A mosque in Quiapo', in *Philippine Panorama*, 1977, 5–6.

P. Gowing, *Muslim Filipinos: Heritage and Horizon*, Quezon City, Philippines 1979.

W. Klassen, *Architecture in the Philippines*, Cebu, Philippines 1986, 125–52.

pisé

A form of mud brick where the brick is moulded in situ on a wall.

This technique is quicker than mud-brick construction because larger bricks can be produced which could not be transported under normal circumstances. Because pisé allows high-speed (and therefore cheaper) construction it was often used for large-scale works such as enclosures or city walls.

pishtaq

Iranian term for a portal projecting from the façade of a building.

This device is most common in Anatolian and Iranian architecture although it also occurs in India. In its most characteristic form this consists of a high arch set within a rectangular frame, which may be decorated with bands of calligraphy, glazed tilework, geometric and vegetal designs.

Q

qa'a

A reception hall in Cairene houses.

qabr

A grave. It may also refer to the structure erected above the grave.

qabrstan

An Iranian term for a cemetery, equivalent to maqbara.

Qairawan

City in north-west Tunisia which functioned as the capital of the province of Ifriqiyya (roughly equivalent to modern Tunisia) during the early Islamic period.

Qairawan was founded in 670 by 'Uqba ibn Nafi, the Arab general in command of the Muslim conquest of North Africa. The principal monument in the city is the Great Mosque also known as the mosque of Sidi 'Uqba after the general who founded it. The first mosque on the site was begun immediately after the Arab conquest and consisted of a square enclosure containing a courtyard and prayer hall or sanctuary. This first building was made of mud brick and had to be restored in 695. There was another major reconstruction in 724–43 when a minaret was added. The present minaret was

Great Mosque, Qairawan, Tunisia, © *Creswell Archive; Ashmolean Museum*

added by the Aghlabids in 836. It is a giant three-tier structure built of baked bricks on a base of re-used ashlar blocks. At present the minaret stands on the north wall of the courtyard but in the ninth century it would have been outside the mosque courtyard in a manner similar to the contemporary Abbasid mosques of Samarra.

The mosque took its present form from the major rebuilding which took place under the Aghlabids which was completed in 862. The present mosque enclosure forms a large rectangle measuring 125 by 85 m. The prayer hall is one third of the mosque area and comprises seventeen aisles perpendicular to the qibla wall with another aisle parallel to the wall. Aghlabid modifications included the present mihrab, the dome in front of the mihrab and the minbar. The mihrab niche is lined with perforated marble panels decorated with vegetal designs. Surrounding the mihrab are a series of polychrome lustre tiles which are believed to have been imported from Baghdad. The dome covering the area in front of the mihrab is built of stone and rests on a drum supported by large shell-shaped squinches. The dome has a gadrooned form which internally takes the form of thin radiating ribs. The inside of the drum is circular and decorated with a series of sixteen blind niches and eight arched windows. The minbar is the oldest in existence and consists of a high staircase with a series of intricately carved panels on the side decorated with geometric and stylized vegetal designs. The present maqsura (screen) was added in restorations of the eleventh century. Further restorations were carried out in 1294 when the arches of the arcades were remodelled and the projecting portal of Bab Lalla Rayhana was added. Other Aghlabid monuments at Qairawan include the Mosque of the Three Gates, and the famous polygonal cisterns or artificial lakes. Outside Qairawan three satellite cities were established known as al-Abbasiya, Raqqada and Sabra al-Mansuriyya. Nothing remains of Abasiyya, although at Raqqada there are huge reservoirs and the remains of a large palace built of baked brick. Other cities with Aghlabid monuments include Tunis, Susa, Sfax and Monastir. In 1052 the city was enclosed with a crenellated brick wall which was extensively restored in the eighteenth century.

See also: Aghlabids, Monastir, Sfax, Susa, Tunis, Tunisia

Further reading:

L. W. Boothe, 'The Great Mosque of Qirouan', *Oriental Art New Series* 16:321–36, 1970.

L. Golvin, 'Quelques réflexions sur la Grande Mosquée de Kairouan à la période des Aghlabides', *Revue de l'Occident musulmans et de la Méditerranée,* 1968.

qal'a

Castle, fortress or citadel.

Qal'at Banu Hammad

Eleventh-century capital of the Hammadids located in the mountains to the south of Algiers.

The city was founded in 1007 by Hammad ibn Buluggin, although it did not become capital until 1015 when Hammad withdrew his allegiance from the Fatimids. Excavations at the site have revealed the plan of the Great Mosque and three palaces. The buildings were constructed of roughly squared stones laid in courses which were originally covered in plaster. The Great Mosque was built in the North African style with its aisle running perpendicular to the qibla wall. Opposite the qibla wall is a square minaret 25 m high, with large blind niches which were originally decorated with coloured glazed tiles. The remains of the palaces indicate a high degree of wealth and probably an elaborate ceremonial function. One of the palaces is built around a cruciform tower containing ramps which led to a domed pavilion on the top. Another palace was built around a rectangular pond or lake measuring 65 by 45 m. The palaces were decorated with stucco which included early examples of muqarnas decoration.

See also: Algeria

Further reading:

L. Golvin, *Recherches Archéologiques à la Qal'a des Banu Hammad,* CNRS, Paris 1965.

A. Lezine, 'Le Minaret de la Qal'a des Banu Hammad', *Bulletin d'Archéologie Algérienne* 2:261–70, 1966–7.

qanat

Subterranean canal system usually used to bring water some distance from a river or mountains. Access to the qanat is by vertical shafts at regular distances.

qasaba

Central part of a town or citadel.

qasr

Palace or mansion.

Qasr al-Hayr East (Qasr al-Hayr al-Sharqi)

Settlement in the Syrian desert built by the Umayyads in 730 CE.

Qasr al-Hayr East is located 80 km east of Palmyra and 80 km south of Dayr al-Zor on the Euphrates. The Qasr represents a large complex which may be divided into four main groups: the small enclosure, the large enclosure, the bath house and the outer enclosure.

The small enclosure is a square building, approximately 70 m per side, with two solid semi-circular buttress towers on each side and four round towers at the corners. The entrance is on the western side through a monumental gateway flanked by two half-round towers. The lintel of the gateway is made of joggled voussoirs above which there is a relieving arch outlined by a continous moulding which also runs along the front of the towers. Either side of the relieving arch there are shallow recessed niches with engaged side columns. At the top of the gateway is a panelled frieze, in the centre of which there is a projecting machicolation. Inside there is a courtyard with a central pool around which there is a columned arcade or portico. On the north, east and south sides the rooms are arranged in groups of three with a central room and two rooms either side. At the north- and south-east corners there are small rooms with latrines set into the wall. On the west side there are two long vaulted rooms either side of the gateway which includes a mihrab in its south wall. The pattern of the upper floor is similar to the ground floor. The building probably funtioned as a khan.

The large enclosure has a similar plan to the small enclosure but is much larger, measuring 167 m per side. This building also differs in having four axial entrances leading into a large central courtyard lined with an arcade. The internal plan comprises twelve structural units, eight of which (two per side) are courtyard buildings. Three of the four corner units seem to have been open areas, whilst the south-east corner contains a small mosque with a raised central aisle. One of the courtyard buildings on the east side appears to have been an industrial building for the production of olive oil (i.e. presses

and vats). The function of the building is not clear although it may have been a governor's residence.

The bath house comprises a triple-aisled hall with cold plunge pools, a series of three hot rooms and a warm room with a heated pool. The complex included a furnace, latrines and two service rooms. There were two separate sets of latrines and two entrances which implies there may have been some sexual segregation.

The outer enclosure from which the complex derives its name (Hayr) is a vast wall of irregular shape which stretches for more than 15 km. The wall is approximately 1 m wide and is buttressed internally and externally with solid semi-circular buttresses. Four gates were discovered, each contained within pairs of circular buttress towers. The purpose of the enclosure is debated, although it may have been partially for water conservation, for agriculture and animals (domestic or wild?).

See also: Qasr al-Hayr West, Syria, Ummayads

Further reading:

O. Grabar, R. Holod, J. Knutstad and W. Trousdale, *A City in the Desert: Qasr al-Hayr East*, Harvard Middle Eastern Monographs 22/24, 1978.

Qasr al-Hayr West (Qasr al-Hayr al-Gharbi)

Umayyad palace and settlement in the Syrian desert.

Qasr al-Hayr was built by the Umayyad caliph al-Walid in 728. It is located in the Syrian desert 40 km east of Palmyra and 40 km west of Qasr al-Hayr East. The complex comprises a khan, a palace, a bath house, mills and various hydraulic installations.

The khan is a square courtyard structure with two projecting wings to the east, on the side of the entrance. The foundations of the building were of stone but the upper parts (with the exception of the stone doorway) were of mud brick and have not survived. The southern wing on the outside is a small mosque with the mihrab in the centre of the south wall; the north wing has a water trough against the wall and may have been a stable or place for watering animals. The entrance to the khan is through a large rectangular doorway above which is an Arabic inscription with the date of construction 727. Internally the khan comprises a series of rooms around a colonnaded central courtyard.

The palace is one of the most luxurious examples

Qasr al-Hayr West (Qasr al-Hayr al-Gharbi)

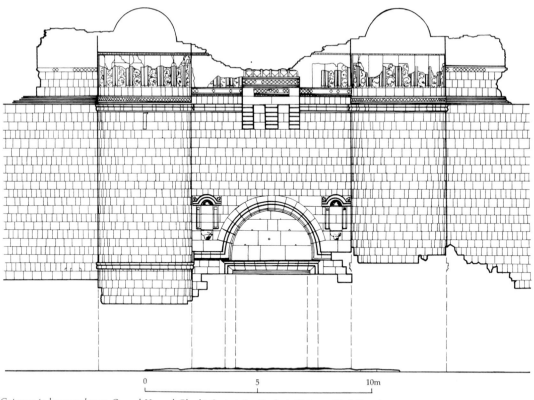

Gateway to lesser enclosure, Qasr al-Hayr al-Gharbi, Syria (after Grabar). Note machicolation above gate

of Umayyad palatial architecture. The structure, which is approximately square, is built on to a pre-existing Byzantine monastic tower dating from the sixth century. The tower is built of massive dressed masonry whereas the rest of the palace is built of mud brick on stone foundation. Above the entrance to the tower are the remains of a box machicolation which may have been the example for the gateway at Qasr al-Hayr East. The main part of the palace comprises a square enclosure with solid semi-circular buttress towers and round corner towers built around a paved courtyard. There are eight living-units, or bayts (two per side), each comprising a central hall leading out on either side to a set of side rooms including a latrine. The most impressive feature of the building is the arched gateway set between two half-round towers. The outer façade was decorated with panels of elaborate stucco which are now in the Damascus museum. The lower part of the decoration is large panels of vegetation arranged in geometric patterns, above which is a smaller set of panels

containing vegetal ornament within squares, circles and diamonds. Above the panels is a row of blind niches with alternating round and pointed arches; the top was made up of stepped merlons or crenelations. The interior of the gatehouse above the entrance was probably a palatial domed reception hall decorated with frescoes. Inside the palace the arcade around the courtyard was decorated with carved stucco animals whilst at the base of the staircase there were frescoes containing naked women and hunting scenes.

Immediately to the north of the palace there is a bath house, a fairly small building containing a vaulted hall with benches around the side and three warm rooms. An unusual feature is that a mosque was attached to the south side of the dressing hall.

The entire complex of Qasr al-Hayr al-Gharbi relied on a water system ultimately derived from a dam 15 km distant. There are two main canals, one leading to the palace and bath house and the other leading via a cistern to the khan, some mills and then a huge rectangular enclosure containing a network of small irrigation channels. The irrigation channels are also fed by a large semi-circular barrage which collects water from the hill.

See also: Qasr al-Hayr East, Syria, Umayyads

Further reading:

D. Schlumberger (ed.), *Qasr el-Heir el Gharbi*, Paris 1986.

Qasr al-Tuba

Unfinished Umayyad complex in south-east Jordan.

Qasr al-Tuba is a large rectangular enclosure divided into three strips; only the west wing appears to have been completed, although there are traces of mud-brick structures elsewhere in the complex. Like Mshatta the remaining parts of the building are made of ashlar masonry with baked brick used for the barrel-vaulted roofs. There is a dam and several wells associated with the qasr but no other

Stone and brick construction, Qasr al-Tuba, Jordan

Slightly pointed doorway arches, Qasr al-Tuba, Jordan

Qasr al-Tuba, Jordan

structures have been identified. The purpose of the building is not clear but it may have been connected with the Wadi Sirhan caravan route.

Qatar

A peninsula on the east coast of Arabia projecting northwards into the Gulf.

Although it used to be dependent on pearl diving and fishing, today the main economy of the State of Qatar is oil. The country is predominantly desert with few natural water resources. It is ruled by the Amir of Qatar from the capital Doha.

Until recently permanent architecture has been confined to one or two towns and several semi-permanent encampments. Archaeological excavations at Ras Abrak has revealed the presence of several semi-permanent seasonal encampments. One of these has been interpreted as a fish-curing complex and consisted of two roughly rectangular rooms linked by a sheltered courtyard containing fireplaces and a cairn. The entire complex was built out of thin limestone slabs laid without mortar although there may have been a superstructure built out of some less durable material.

On the northern tip of the country are the remains of a small town, al-Huwailah. At present the site is largely in ruins but the main features can be distinguished, including a fort surrounded by several stone houses. Around this central complex are the remains of further structures which were probably huts built of palm fronds and were the main form of accommodation in the town.

Recent development has meant that little survives of the traditional town of Doha with the exception of the Old Amiri Palace which has recently been restored and is now used as a museum. This is a large complex containing quarters for several families. There are three gatehouses and two public reception rooms (an inner and outer majlis). The main material for construction is coral blocks (both in the form of lumps and thin slabs) used in conjunction with mangrove poles in a panel--and-frame construction. For ornamental purposes carved teak and mahogany from India were used.

Further reading:

B. DeCardi, *Qatar Archaeological Report: Excavations*, Oxford 1973.
G. R. H. Wright, *The Old Amiri Palace Doha, Qatar*, Qatar 1975.

qibla

Direction of Mecca which determines the direction of prayer.

The qibla is the prime factor in the orientation of mosques and is usually marked by a mihrab (or more in India). Many early mosques were not built to a correct qibla orientation, as has been demonstrated in the excavations of the Great Mosque of Wasit, where three different qibla orientations are recorded. It is believed that idea of qibla orientation is derived from the Jewish practice of indicating the direction of Jerusalem in synagogues.

qubba

Literally 'dome', often used to refer to a domed mausoleum which contains the grave of a saint or some important personage.

The earliest surviving example of this type of structure is the Qubbat al-Sulaybiyya at Samarra which is octagonal. Another early example is the tomb of Ismail the Samanid in Balkh which is a square structure with a hemispherical dome. Also dated to the ninth century are large numbers of domed mausoleums at Aswan in southern Egypt. From the eleventh century this type of structure becomes widespread in the Islamic world and is now one of the most common building types.

Qusayr Amra

Umayyad bath house complex in the eastern desert of Jordan famous for its painted frescoes.

The building was probably built by the Umayyad caliph al-Walid between 712 and 715. It comprises three main parts, a hall or undressing room, three heated rooms and a well-house to the north. The hall is divided into four parts, the main hall, an alcove and two small rooms either side. The entire hall (including the two side rooms) is roofed by three barrel vaults resting on transverse arches. The walls of both the main hall and the two side rooms are covered in frescoes whilst the floors were covered with marble, except in the side rooms where there were floor mosaics. The subjects of the frescoes differ according to their position; thus the main hall is decorated with hunting scenes and semi-naked women on the soffits of the arches. The alcove is decorated with six figures representing the defeated enemies of Islam. The two rooms leading to the hot room are decorated

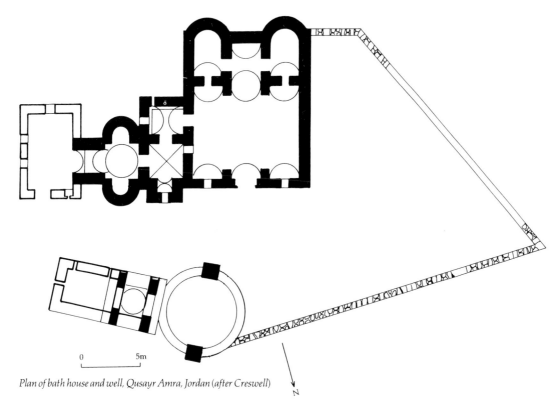

Plan of bath house and well, Qusayr Amra, Jordan (after Creswell)

N

with bathing women whilst the dome of the hot room is painted with a representation of the zodiac. The zodiac representation is the earliest surviving example of a domed representation of the stars and is of fundamental importance to the history of science.

The exact function of Qusayr Amra is not known although it seems to have been a princely desert retreat with formal associations (e.g. the audience hall).

See also: hammam, Jordan, Umayyads

Qutb Minar and Mosque

Famous twelfth-century minaret and mosque complex in Delhi, northern India.

The complex commemorates the first Islamic conquest of Delhi by Muhammad of Ghur in 1193. The mosque was built in the centre of the Hindu fort of Rai Pithora built earlier in the twelfth century by the Chauhan Rajputs. The area occupied by the mosque in the centre of the citadel is known as Lal Kot and was built by the Tomar Rajputs in the eleventh century. The mosque was begun by Qutb al-Din the first Islamic sultan of Delhi and is all that remains of the first Islamic city.

The Mosque

The present buildings are contained within a large, partially ruined, rectangular enclosure approximately 225 by 125 m. The enclosure is a multi-period complex containing three major phases of Islamic building, the earliest of which is dated to between 1193 and 1198. Twenty-seven Hindu and Jain temples were demolished to make room for the first mosque, which was called 'The Might of Islam' (Quwwatu'l Islam); however, the remains of the temples were used to provide building materials for the mosque, in particular the columns used in the arcades of the courtyard. This consists of a rectangular enclosure built on an east–west axis with the qibla pointing west towards Mecca. The courtyard is entered from two entrances on the north–south sides and a larger domed entrance to the east. Inside, the courtyard is bordered on three sides by arcades whilst on the west side is the sanctuary separated from the courtyard by a screen. The screen contains five arches, of which the central arch is the highest; it is framed by a decorative border which combines Quranic inscriptions with dense vegetal carving and the spandrels of the arches are decorated with interlocking pierced discs. Standing in the courtyard directly in front of the central arch is an iron pillar 12 m high which was made for the Hindu god Vishnu in the fourth century CE. The columns supporting the arcades are made of finely carved red sandstone and consist of alternate square and round sections carved with various Hindu motifs, such as the bell and chain, as well as some figural sculpture. Because the columns were not sufficiently tall for the mosque they were placed one on top of the other to double the height. The arcades and sanctuary are covered with a trabeate roof where the columns support flat beams resting on brackets. The area immediately in front of the mihrab was covered by a large dome although this has now disappeared. The first stage of the Qutb Minar can also be attributed to this initial phase of construction.

The second stage of the mosque was carried out in the early thirteenth century by Iltumish, who extended the mosque laterally and completed the work of his father on the Qutb Minar. The lateral extension of the mosque was carried out by extending the screen north and south and adding an outer enclosure, or courtyard, which included the Qutb Minar in the south-east corner. The arcades of the extension were built in the same way as the inner enclosure and used columns which were specially carved to resemble the two-tier Hindu temple columns used in the first mosque. Iltumish was also responsible for commissioning his own tomb, which was begun the year before his death. The tomb is located outside the mosque to the west and consists of a square chamber covered with a dome, now collapsed. The interior is extravagantly decorated with carvings in red sandstone which included Hindu motifs intertwined with passages of Quranic calligraphy. In the centre of the building is Iltumish's tomb whilst to the west are three mihrab niches.

The third major phase of the mosque complex was carried out by Ala al-Din Khaliji, the fourteenth sultan of Delhi, between 1296 and 1316. Like his predecessor Ala al-Din decided to increase the area of the original mosque by extending the length of the screen to the north thus enclosing an area more than double the size of the previous extension. At the same time Ala al-Din also began

work on another minaret on the same pattern as the Qutb Minar which is known as the Alai Minar. For various reasons Ala al-Din was not able to complete either of these ambitious projects leaving the stump of a minaret and in the north part of the unfinished new courtyard. However, in 1311 he was able to complete a new monumental gateway to the complex known as the Alai Darwaza which linked the west wall of Iltumish's complex with the completed west wall of his new courtyard. The gateway consists of a large square domed chamber with a tall pointed arch in the north and south sides. The gateway is faced in red sandstone inlaid with bands of white marble and is completely covered in carved designs and epigraphic bands. The south façade of the chamber consists of a tall pointed arch in the centre, flanked on each side by a window covered with a pierced stone screen (jalis) and a blind arch of similar design. Above the two arches either side of the main arch are two flat rectangular panels each divided in two and containing a small square blind niche. The arches of the façade are decorated with spiky projecting tassels whilst the jambs of the arches are made up of engaged columns similar to those used to support the arcades.

East of the Alai Darwaza is a small square domed tomb built by the Turkestani Imam Zamin. This is the latest building at the site dating to 1538.

The Minar

Although subsequently copied in various ways, the Qutb Minar is a unique building which announces the arrival of Islam in India. The minar comprises a tall tapering cylindrical tower standing on a circular base with five storeys which together reach a height of 72.5 m. Each of the storeys is reached by an internal spiral staircase which leads to the balconies which are supported on muqarnas corbels. The most characteristic feature of the building is the corrugated angular and rounded fluting on the shaft which forms the basis for many later imitations. The first part of the tower was built by Qutb al-Din who died in 1210 leaving only one storey completed. This is the thickest part of the tower with a base diameter of 14 m tapering to 9 m at the first balcony. This part of the minaret is built with alternating sharp-angled and rounded fluting (twelve of each type) which are decorated with bands of inscriptions. Between 1211 and 1236 the tower was completed by Iltumish with three more storeys, each with a different pattern of fluting. The second storey added by Iltumish has rounded flutes, the third storey has angular flutes and the fourth storey was plain. During the fourteenth century the top of the building was damaged by lightning and in 1369 Firuz Shah repaired the damage to the top and added an extra storey. The diameter at the fifth storey is only 2.7 m making a reduction from an area of 44 square metres at the base to 8.5 m at the top.

The design of the Qutb Minar and in particular the fluting have clear antecedents and parallels in Afghan architecture; thus the first storey built by Qutb al-Din may be compared to the twelfth-century tower at Khwaja Siyah Push in Sistan which has eight semi-circular flutes alternating with eight shallow-angled flutes. Similarly the round flutes of the second storey may be compared with those of the early twelfth-century Jar Kurgan tower in Uzbekistan.

The effect of the tower on later Indian architecture is significant, influencing not only towers but the decoration of columns and domes. The earliest known direct copy is the Alai Minar in the same complex which was begun by Ala al-Din Khaliji in the early fourteenth century; it had twice the base area of the Qutb Minar and was projected to be twice the height. Although it was never completed, the base can still be seen and is circular, with square flutes and a tapering cylindrical shaft with sharp-angled flutes. An earlier example of the influence of the Qutb Minar can be found in the paired minarets on top of the early thirteenth-century gateway of Araha-i-Din Mosque at Ajmer. However, the most complete copy is the Hashtsal Minar near Palam built for Shar Jahan and completed in 1634. The top of the building has been damaged, as have the two collar-like balconies of which only the projecting supports remain, so that its present height is 17 m. Like its ancient model the Hashtsal Minaret is decorated with alternating round and angled flutes although there is no attempt to recreate the muqarnas mouldings which support the balconies of the Qutb Minar. There is no mosque associated with the tower and it seems likely that this was a hunting monument consciously recalling the victory connotations of the Qutb Minar.

See also: Delhi, India, minaret

Further reading:

T. W. Arnold and K. Fischer, 'Kutb Minar', *Encyclopedia of Islam*, 1954.

A. B. M. Hussain, *The Manara in Indo-Muslim Architecture*, Dacca 1970.

E. Koch, 'The copies of the Qutb Minar', *Iran* 29: 95–108, 1991.

J. A. Page, *An Historical Memoir on the Qutb*, Delhi (originally published in *Memoirs of the Archaeological Survey of India* 22. 1926), reprinted New Delhi, Delhi 1970.

R

Rabat

Capital of Morocco located on the Atlantic coast.

The city of Rabat is located at the mouth of the Bou Regreg river. Rabat stands on the south side of the river and the twin city of Sale occupies the north bank. Although there was probably a Roman settlement on the site, the present city of Rabat was founded in the twelfth century by the Almohad ruler Sultan Abd al-Mumin as a depot and launching point for the Almohad conquest of Spain. The city still retains parts of its twelfth-century walls including two monumental Almohad gateways. The façade of the gateways consists of a central entrance with a slightly pointed horseshoe arch with spandrels decorated with bold interlace designs. Both gateways form bent entrances, the Udayya gate has a passage which runs along the side of the wall before opening into the town, whilst the Bab Ruwah has a complicated zig-zag pattern with blind passages.

The most famous monument in Rabat is the mosque of Hassan begun in 1196 after the Almohad victory over Alfonso VIII at Alarcos in Spain. The mosque would have been one of the largest in the Islamic world but construction ceased after the death of Ya'qub al-Mansur in 1199. The plan of the mosque can still be discerned and consists of a huge rectangle 140 by 185 m with three courtyards and a huge minaret in the middle of the north side opposite the qibla wall. The unfinished minaret is 40 m high, but if completed it would have reached a height of over 70 m. The tower is built in the characteristic Almohad style with a square central core around which a ramp rises to reach the top. Within the central core are a series of vaulted rooms, one on each storey, each with a different form of vault. The exterior of the tower is decorated with windows set within blind niches with multi-foil and cusped arches, the upper part of the tower is covered with a network of interlaced arches.

The current main mosque of the city was built by the Marinids in the thirteenth century and stands opposite a madrassa built in the same period. The Kasba des Ouadias forms an enclosure within the city which contains houses and a twelfth-century mosque. To the south of the city is the fortified necropolis of Challa built by the Marinids in the fourteenth century.

See also: Almohads, Morocco

Ramla

Capital of Palestine in the early Islamic period.

Ramla is located in the southern coastal plain of Palestine roughly equidistant between Gaza and

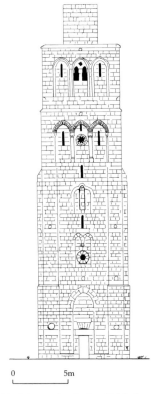

Tower of White Mosque, Ramla, Israel/Palestine

Jerusalem. The city was founded in 712 by the Umayyad caliph Sulayman as an alternative to nearby Lydda which had a predominantly Christian population.

Little remains from the early Islamic period, although the White Mosque to the north-east of the modern town preserves the shape of the Umayyad mosque, whilst the cistern known as Birket al-ʾAnaziya was built during the reign of the Abbasid caliph Harun al-Rashid. The city suffered from a series of earthquakes and the Crusader occupation of the twelfth century so that by the Mamluk period (1250s) it was at least a quarter of its former size. Although the White Mosque was rebuilt by Sultan Baybars, this area of the town never recovered. Instead, the south-east part of the city became the centre of the town with the Crusader church of St John functioning as the Great Mosque. This has remained the town centre to the present day and contains a number of interesting Mamluk and Ottoman buildings.

See also: Mamluks, Palestine

Further reading:

M. Ben-Dov and M. Rosen Ayalon, 'Ramla', in *New Encyclopaedia of Excavations in the Holy Land*, Jerusalem 1993.

A. D. Petersen, 'A preliminary report on a survey of historic buildings in Ramla', *Levant* 25: 1995, 75–101.

Raqqa

Prominent Abbasid and medieval city located on the Euphrates river in Syria.

Raqqa was founded by Alexander the Great and was known as Leontopolis in the Byzantine period. In 639 the town was captured by the Arabs and renamed Raqqa. In 772 the Abbasid caliph al-Mansur founded a new city, west of the old one, which he enclosed with a wall similar to that of Baghdad, with an inner and an outer wall and a moat or ditch. The remains of the walls can still be seen and form a rounded enclosure with a straight wall on the south side. The inner wall still survives to a height of 10 m in places and is studded with half-round towers at regular intervals. There is a gap of 20 m between this and the outer wall of which little survives. In the middle of the enclosure are the remains of the Great Mosque which was built in 772. This is a huge rectangular enclosure measuring 90 by 110 m, with a large central courtyard containing a minaret of later date (twelfth century).

The outer walls of the mosque are made of mud brick supported by solid semi-circular buttress towers. The prayer hall consisted of three arcades supported on cylindrical piers, whilst the other three sides were lined with double arcades. The building was decorated with stucco, traces of which survive.

The famous Baghdad gate which stands at the south-east corner of the city is now thought to date to the twelfth century. It is a baked-brick construction with a main gateway set below a row of two-tier blind niches separated by engaged columns. The gateway itself and the upper tier of arches are of a four-centrepoint design which makes its first appearance in the late ninth century at Samarra.

See also: Abbasids, Baghdad, Samarra, Syria

Further reading:

J.-C. Heusch and M. Meinecke, 'Grabungen im abbasidischen Palastareal von ar-Raqqa/ar-Rafiqa', *Damaszener Mitteilungen* 2: 85-105, 1985.

M. al-Khalaf, 'Die abbasidische Stadtmauer von ar-Raqqa/ar Rafiqa', *Damaszener Mitteilungen* 2: 122–31, 1985.

J. Warren, 'The date of the Baghdad Gate at Raqqa', *Art and Archaeology Research Papers* XIII: 22–3, 1978.

rauza

Persian term for mausoleum.

Red Fort (Lal Qila)

Mughal palace in Delhi built by the Mughal emperor Shah Jahan between 1638 and 1648.

The building derives its name from the use of red sandstone as the main building material. The palace forms the core of Shah Jahan's new city of Shahjahanabad. The fort is located next to the Jumna river and surrounded on all four sides by a high crenellated wall which on the landward side is enclosed within a moat. The two main entrances to the palace are the Lahore and Delhi gates both of which were enlarged by Jahan's successor Aurangzeb. The internal layout of the palace is symmetrical and was probably based on that of the Agra fort. The Lahore gate was the main form of public access and leads into a large square with the imperial audience hall on the opposite side. The private apartments were made up of a series of pavilions and gardens arranged in a rigid geometry. The decoration of the palace is of outstanding quality and refinement and with the Alhambra is one of the finest examples of Islamic palatial architecture. Decorative techniques include painting, gilding, pietra dura (stone inlay) gilding and white marble carved in shallow relief.

See also: Agra, Delhi, India, Lahore, Mughals, Taj Mahal

riad

North African term for a walled garden.

ribat

Fortified enclosure for religious warriors, common in North Africa in the early Islamic period.

A typical ribat is located near the coast and partially functions as a look-out post. Usually ribats are square or rectangular courtyard structures, two storeys high, with storage rooms and stables on the ground floor and sleeping accomodation and a mosque on the upper floor. Later ribats seem to have lost their military function. Important examples are at Sfax, Monastir and Sousse in Tunisia.

See also: Tunisia

Ribat-i Sharaf

Royal Seljuk caravanserai on the road between Nishapur and Merv.

This building was founded in 1114 as a royal caravanserai and expanded in 1156 when it was used as a semi-permanent residence for Sultan Sanjar and his wife who were held under house arrest by the Öghuz Turks. The first part of the structure is a square enclosure built around a central courtyard with a central iwan in each side leading to a domed room. The extension is half the size and is built on to the front of the original structure. The building was decorated with elaborate stucco work and a monumental entrance pishtaq flanked with twin blind niches.

riwaq

Arcade or portico open on at least one side.

S

sabil

See sebil.

Saffavid

Dynasty of Kurdish origin which ruled Iran during the sixteenth and seventeenth centuries.

Although the founder of the dynasty was probably a Sunni, the Saffavids later became Shi'a and adopted this as a state religion. Little remains of the early architecture of the Saffavids who established capitals first at Tabriz and later at Qazvin. The little that does survive indicates that they continued the architectural forms established by their predecessors the Timurids. Thus the Saffavids continued to use the complex vaulting forms, with networks of arches, squinches and pendentives, developed under the Timurids. An early example of a Saffavid building is the tomb of Harun-i Vilayat which although Timurid in form has an emphasis on exterior tile decoration. This was a feature which was developed in later Saffavid architecture where the architectural form seems to be subordinated to the tile patterns.

The most productive period of Saffavid architecture began in 1598 with Shah Tahmasp's decision to redesign Isfahan as an imperial capital. The centre of the new developments was the Maidan-i-Shah which is a rectangular square or park around which was built the palace, the principal mosques and the principal bazar of the city. The main characteristics of this architecture was the layout and planning with the mosques built at a deliberate angle to the maidan to show off both their monumental portals (pishtaq iwans) and their glazed domes. Similarly the main gate of the palace, the Ali Qapu, was made into a pavilion overlooking the Maidan-i-Shah from which the shah's palace could be seen. The emphasis on accessibility is also demonstrated in the tomb complexes, where the outside faces are pierced with arches instead of

forbidding walls. This is also seen on utilitarian structures such as the famous Pol-i-Khaju bridge built in 1650. This bridge, which links Isfahan to the southern palace, is 110 m long and has two tiers of arcades which provide shelter from the summer heat. Another characteristic of the architecture is the use of lighter materials such as wood, stucco, paint and tiles, and an increasing emphasis on gardens. However, this may appear to be a development simply because earlier structures of this type have not survived.

Outside Isfahan buildings such as caravanserais are generally larger and plainer than their predecessors indicating the growth of commercial traffic.

See also: Iran, Isfahan

sahn

Courtyard of a mosque.

Samarkand

Timurid capital located in the Central Asian state of Uzbekistan.

Samarkand is located on the banks of the Zeravshan river approximately 200 km east of Bukhara. Next to the present city are the ruins of Afrasiyab which was the site of the city from 500 BCE until the Mongol destruction of 1220 CE. In the eighth century the city was sacked by the Arab general Qutaiba bin Muslim. After the Arab conquest a new city was built to the south-west with Afrasiyab remaining as an industrial quarter specializing in the production of paper for which it was famous. Excavations have revealed workshops for pottery and glass in addition to a large mosque which was burnt during the Mongol invasion.

Samarkand once again rose to international prominence in 1369 when it was captured by the Mongol emperor Timur and chosen as his capital. Timur enclosed the city with a wall 7 km long and established his citadel and palace in the western part of the city. There are few monuments which survive from the reign of Timur partly because he was more concerned with conquest than architecture and partly because he was more interested in a more ephemeral type of architecture represented by gardens, pavilions and tents. Contemporary accounts describe a series of magnificent gardens with three-storey pavilions made of wood and decorated with porcelain and marble. One of the most splendid examples of this type of architecture must have been the tented encampment erected to celebrate the wedding of Timur's grandsons. It comprised 20,000 tents arranged into streets in a meadow on the banks of the Zeravshan river. The most magnificent tent was that of Timur which was 100 m square with a central dome supported on twelve giant tent poles above which was a square wooden turret.

Two major monuments have survived from Timur's reign, however; these are the Bibi Khanum Mosque and the mausoleum of Gur-i Amir. The Bibi Khanum Mosque is a massive building begun in 1399, after Timur's conquest of India. It forms a rectangle 160 by 200 m built around a huge central courtyard, entered via a monumental portal iwan flanked by twin towers. Either side of the central courtyard there were shallow iwans leading into prayer halls roofed with fluted domes covered in blue glazed tiles. The main prayer hall/sanctuary with its massive tiled dome is hidden behind a huge pishtaq iwan 40 m high and flanked with twin towers more than 50 m high. Unfortunately the speed of construction together with the massive size of the mosque combined to make it unstable and it started to disintegrate as soon as it was built. The other major monument surviving from Timur's time is the mausoleum of Gur-i Amir built by Timur for his grandson Muhamad Sultan between 1403 and 1404. This tomb eventually housed Timur himself after his death on campaign in 1405. The tomb is built on an octagonal plan and is crowned with a bulbous dome resting on a muqarnas band set on an octagonal drum. The interior of the tomb is square with deeply recessed arches set into the middle of each side. The dome is supported on a network of eight intersecting arches supported by corner squinches. On the floor of the tomb are the cenotaphs of Timur's descendants, the tomb of Timur is marked by a huge green jade slab.

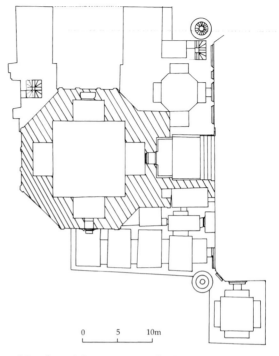

0   5   10m

Mausoleum of Gur-i Amir, Samarkand, Uzbekistan

Other funerary monuments erected by Timur were part of a mausoleum complex known as the Shah i-Zinda. The complex was built around the shrine of Quthman ibn Abbas whose tomb stood at the end of a narrow lane approached by a set of thirty-six stone steps. The shrine of Quthman is approached through a series of anterooms decorated with stucco and covered with a roof resting on carved wooden columns. Either side of the lane leading to the shrine there are a total of sixteen tombs representing the development of tomb architecture. The royal tombs are of two types: a square type with a main façade and polygonal type with two or more entrances. The oldest tomb, that of Timur's niece, Shad i Mulk, is of the first type with a large screen which hides the ribbed dome behind. The screen is contained within two engaged columns and frames a large recessed portal decorated with muqarnas mouldings and glazed tiles inset within carved mouldings. The tomb of Shihrin Bika Aka was built some ten years later and also has a screen façade although this is decorated with tile mosaic, a new technique imported from Persia. This tomb also has a more advanced dome design which has a slightly bulbous form resting on a sixteen-sided drum.

The centre of the city was the Registan, although no buildings of Timur's period survive in this square, considered the finest in Central Asia. The oldest building in the Registan is the madrassa of Ulugh Beg built between 1417 and 1420. The madrassa has the typical Timurid form with a huge entrance iwan (pishtaq) set into an entrance façade flanked with twin minarets. The entire surface of the façade and minarets is decorated with blue, turquoise and yellow tile mosaic against a background of yellow/buff baked brick. One of the notable features of the decoration is the use of giant calligraphic patterns in complex geometric arrangements. The interior of the madrassa consisted of a courtyard surrounded by two storeys of cells and teaching rooms designed to accommodate 100 students. Ulugh Beg's love of learning is further demonstrated by his observatory which was a three-storey tiled structure nearly 50 m in diameter cut into the hillside. In the middle of the building was a deep slit 40 m long which contained a sextant with an arc of 63 m. With this instrument Ulugh Beg was able to produce the first precise map of the stars and planets.

Opposite the Ulugh Beg Madrassa in the Registan is the Shirdar Madrassa which has the same general form even though it was built 200 years later in the seventeenth century. On the third side of the square is the Tilakar Mosque and Madrassa also built in the seventeenth century. This building has the largest façade, which is over 120 m long with a massive entrance iwan (pishtaq) flanked on either side by two storeys of open arches facing on to the square and domed cylindrical corner turrets. Inside, the mosque is decorated with multiple layers of gold painted on to a blue background.

See also: Bukhara, Timurids, Uzbekistan

Further reading:

J. Lawton and F. Venturi, *Samarkand and Bukhara*, London 1991.

A. L. Mongait, *Archaeology in the U.S.S.R.*, trans. M. W. Thomson, Pelican, London 1961.

N. B. Nemtseva, 'The origins and architectural development of the Shah i Zinda', trans. with additions by J. M. Rogers and A. Yasin, *Iran* 15: 51–74, 1977.

R. Pinder-Wilson, 'Timurid architecture', in *Cambridge History of Iran* 6, 1993.

D. N. Wilber, 'The Timurid court: life in gardens and tents', *Iran* 27: 127–134, 1979.

Samarra

Abbasid capital in central Iraq.

Samarra is now recognized as the largest archaeological site in the world and stretches for over 40 km along the banks of the Tigris. Although there were settlements in the area of Samarra before the Abbasid period, it was not established as capital until 836 CE when the Abbasid caliph al-Mu'tassim decided to set up a new city following clashes between his troops and the local population of Baghdad. The city remained capital for fifty-six years and was home to eight caliphs, until 892 when the capital was moved back to Baghdad.

The predominant building material in Samarra was mud brick and pisé with baked brick reserved for more important structures (i.e. the Great Mosque and the Bab al-Amma). Houses and palaces were decorated with carved and moulded stucco panels, and Samarra provides the earliest examples of bevelled stucco decoration. Some of the palaces were also decorated with wall paintings and glass mosaic although none of this remains in situ.

The modern town of Samarra is located approximately in the centre of the Abbasid city. Immediately to the north-west of the city, on the west bank of the Tigris, is the Jausaq al-Khaqani which for most of the time was the caliph's palace and was always his official residence. It was built by one of al-Mu'tasim's Turkish generals and reflects features of Central Asian influence such as wall paintings with Bactrian camels. The palace is a vast complex, including a mosque, a polo ground and a horse-racing track. On the west side of the palace, facing the river, there is a monumental gateway or portal known as the Bab al-Amma, or public gate. This structure was probably an official entrance and a place for public audiences. Directly to the east of the palace is the Great Mosque of Samarra with its spiral minaret (the Malwiyya). Measuring over 240 by 160 m this is one of the largest mosques in the world. It is built entirely of baked brick although marble columns on brick piles originally supported the roof. The outer wall of the mosque is supported by four corner towers and twenty semi-circular bastions resting on square bases. The curtain wall is entirely plain except for a frieze which runs between the bastions, each section consisting of six bevelled squares with shallow concave discs in the centre. The Malwiyya,

Qubbat al-Sulaybiyya, Samarra, Iraq

Great Mosque above and smaller mosque in foreground, Samarra, Iraq

or spiral minaret, is 52 m high and may have been influenced by earlier Mesopotamian ziggurats.

In the north of Samarra are the remains of an extension to the city built by Caliph al-Mutawakkil in an attempt to found a new city. This new area had a palace, garrisons and a congregational mosque known as the Abu Dulaf. The Abu Dulaf Mosque is a smaller version of the Great Mosque and has a spiral minaret 19 m high. On the west bank of the Tigris is the Ashiq Palace, one of the last buildings made before the capital was relocated in Baghdad. The palace is built on a vaulted substructure or terrace so that it can overlook the Tigris. The building forms a high rectangle with the outer walls decorated by a series of blind niches. One of the distinctive features of the palace is the use of the four-centrepoint arch for the first time in Islamic architecture.

South of the modern town of Samarra are a number of major structures, including the palaces of al-Istabulat, al-Balkuwara and Musharrahat. In addition, there is a huge octagonal enclosure, each side of which is half a kilometre long, known as the octagon of Qadisiyya. This probably represents the remains of an unfinished city started by Harun al-Rashid in the eighth century.

See also: Abbasids, Baghdad, Iraq

Further reading:

A. Northedge, 'Planning Samarra', *Iraq* 47: 109–28, 1985.
—— 'The Palace of Istabulat', *Archéologie islamique* 4: 1993.
A. Northedge and R. Falkner, 'The 1986 survey season at Samarra', *Iraq* 49: 143–74, 1987.
A. Northedge, T. J. Wilkinson and R. Falkner, 'Survey and excavations at Samarra 1989', *Iraq* 52: 121–48.

San'a

Capital city of Yemen.

The city is located on a high plateau 2,200 m above sea level. Above the city is Jabal Nuqum which acts as a collecting point for clouds and consequently precipitation. San'a seems to have risen to prominence in the third century CE although an earlier settlement probably existed on the site.

San'a has thirty-four historic mosques, the oldest of which is the Great Mosque which is said to have been founded on the orders of Muhammad during his lifetime. This early mosque was extended northwards during the Umayyad period on the orders of Caliph al-Walid. Subsequent restorations were carried out in the twelfth, thirteenth and sixteenth centuries, although the basic form of the building appears to have remained the same. In its present form the mosque consists of a large rectangle measuring 66 by 78 m with six gateways, one at the south, four on the east and west sides and one in the north wall next to the mihrab. The external walls are built of large blocks of squared basalt with a central core of rubble. The courses of the wall are marked by narrow ridges (approxi-

mately 0.5 cm wide) formed by the faces of the stones leaning outwards. This is a masonry technique characteristic of pre-Islamic Yemeni architecture. In the centre of the mosque there is a square courtyard surrounded by arcades, four on the south side, three on the east and west sides and five on the north (qibla) side. The arcades have a flat wooden roof supported by arches resting either on columns or on circular stone piers. In the centre of the courtyard is a square box-shaped structure covered with a dome known as Sinan Pashas Qubbah. Although it was built in the early seventeenth century, its form and position suggest it may have earlier antecedents. There are two minarets, one in the south-east corner of the courtyard and the other at the east side of the mosque next to the outer wall. They both seem to date from the thirteenth century but may have been restored later. The mosque has four mihrabs, three subsidiary ones at its south end and a main mihrab to the left of centre in the north wall. The area above the mihrab is roofed by five corbelled wooden domes, a central dome and four smaller side domes. In the centre of each dome is a block of alabaster which would have functioned as a skylight.

Other early mosques in San'a include the Jabbanah Musalla, the Tawus Mosque, the mosque of al-Jala and the Jami al-Tawashi. The Jabbanah Musalla is an open-air prayer area which is said to date from the time of Muhammad, although it has been extended in later times. The other early mosques are rectangular box-like structures with hypostyle roofs and recall pre-Islamic Yemeni temples. Mosques of the twelfth century and later are influenced by the architecture of Egypt and Syria. This influence can be seen in the use of arches and domes, which are rare features in the traditional architecture of Yemen. After the Ottoman occupation of the sixteenth century, mosques were built with large central domes and domed arcades.

The domestic architecture of San'a is represented by tall tower houses built of stone and decorated with white plasterwork around the windows and coloured glass in the reception rooms (mafraj) at the top of the house.

See also: Yemen

Further reading:

R. B. Serjeant and R. Lewcock (eds.), *San'a. An Arabian*

Mosque, San'a, Yemen, © Charles Aithie

Islamic City, World of Islam Festival Trust, London 1983.

saqaqa

Water tank for ritual ablutions.

sardivan

Fountain in the centre of a mosque courtyard.

Sassanians

Iranian dynasty which ruled from 226 CE to the Arab conquest in 651.

The Sassanians controlled the eastern half of what became the Umayyad and Abbasid empires. Unlike their Byzantine rivals, the Sassanians were completely destroyed by the Arab invasions. Nevertheless, Sassanian traditions continued to have great importance, particularly during the Abbasid period in the eighth and ninth centuries. This influence is symbolized by the great arched iwan (Taq i Khusrau) at Ctesiphon which, like the Hagia Sophia in Constantinople, provided an example for Islamic architects. The influence of the Sassanians on Islamic architecture can even be seen in Syria Palestine in the Umayyad period thus the mosaics of the Dome of the Rock are decorated with Sassanian symbols of royalty. More tangible evidence is found at Qasr Kharana which is purely Sassanian in design although it appears to date from the Islamic period. Other examples of Sassanian influence are the stepped merlons found at Umayyad palaces such as Khirbet al-Minya or the stucco work of Khirbet al-Mafjar.

The architecture of Iraq at this period is a continuation of Sassanian practice with baked brick and roughly coursed stone set in thick mortar as the main building materials. Buildings such as Khan 'Atshan and Ukhaidhir are very similar to Sassanian buildings in their design, although constructional details such as the development of the pointed arch and the use of machicolations indicates new developments. In eastern Iran the influence of Sassanian culture remained longer, thus some ninth-century buildings have inscriptions in Pahlavi (Sassanian script) and Arabic.

See also: Abbasids, 'Atshan, Byzantine architecture, Samarra, Ukhaidhir, Umayyads

Saudi Arabia

One of the largest countries in the Middle East occupying the greater part of the Arabian peninsula.

To the north the country is bordered by the states of Jordan, Iraq and Kuwait, whilst to the south are Yemen and Oman. On the west side is the Red Sea and on the east the coast of the Arabian Gulf, with the Gulf states of Bahrain, Qatar and the United Arab Emirates. The country is divided into three provinces: Western Province comprising the Hijaz and the Tihama, Central Province comprising Najd and the Empty Quarter, and Eastern Province comprising the oasis of al-Hassa and the towns of the Arabian Gulf.

Before Islam the principal settlements were the trading cities of the Hijaz which included Yathrib (Medina), Medain Saleh and Mecca. The establishment of Islam guaranteed Mecca's position as both a trading city and centre of the Muslim world. For a period of approximately 300 years after the death of Muhammad Arabia enjoyed an unprecedented economic growth and settlements like al-Rabadah grew from small settlements into major towns. During this time Arabia had the largest area of settlement until modern times. During the Middle Ages (1000–1500) the lack of central authority meant that Arabia was again a marginal area, only enlivened by pilgrim routes and secondary trade routes. With the growth of the Ottoman Empire in the sixteenth century Arabia became strategically important both for religious reasons (Mecca and Medina) and strategic reasons (growing European presence in the Indian Ocean). The increasing involvement of the Turks in the area provoked a reaction both within Arabia and from outside. The reaction from within Arabia led to the creation of the first Saudi state by Muhammad ibn Saud and Muhammad ibn Abd al-Wahhab. The state began in Najd in the 1740s and gradually expanded so that by the beginning of the nineteenth century successful attacks had been mounted against Kerbala in Iraq and Mecca in the Hijaz. The growing power of the Saudis was viewed with alarm by the Ottomans, who launched a campaign which led to the execution of the Saudi ruler. During the nineteenth century the Saudis gradually reasserted themselves spreading over large areas of Arabia. With the defeat of the Turks in the First World War the Saudis were able to make great gains and in the 1920s were able to take control of the Hijaz. Oil wealth has added to the strength of the kingdom which is now one of the oldest monarchies in the Middle East.

A variety of materials are employed in the traditional architecture of Saudi Arabia, these may be divided into three groups, stone, wood and mud. Mud is the commonest building material and may either be used as mud brick, pisé or as mud plaster for stone walls. Mud brick is the principal construction material in central Arabia as well as in the oasis towns of the eastern and western provinces. In northern Najd mud brick has recently replaced stone as the principal material of construction; the reasons for this are not known, although mud brick may be more versatile.

Stone is predominantly used in the mountainous regions of the Hijaz and 'Asir province and formerly in the northern Najd. Dressed stonework and ashlar masonry are uncommon in most of Saudi Arabia with the exception of the older cities of the Hijaz. The usual method of stone construction in most of the country is stone slabs laid in rough courses without mortar. True arches are rare in traditional stone architecture and the usual means of covering an opening are with a lintel or corbelled arch. Sometimes the outer surfaces are plastered with mud plaster or lime plaster where it is available. In the mountains of 'Asir layers of projecting flat stones are set into the walls to deflect rainfall away from their coating of mud plaster.

On the east and west coasts coral forms the principal building material. This may either be fossil or reef coral depending on preference and availability. Coral walls are usually coated with a hard white lime plaster, which is sometimes carved into elaborate stucco patterns.

Wood is an essential component of traditional architecture despite its natural scarcity in the arid desert environment. The date palm is the main source of wood in much of the country and is used for roofing and lintels. Tamarisk wood is also used but is more scarce and difficult to find in suitable lengths. On the coasts imported mangrove wood is used for roofs and strengthening in walls.

Hijaz

Historically the cities of the Hijaz have been the main cultural centres of Arabia, but recently Riyadh has grown in significance. The principal towns of the Hijaz are Mecca, Medina and Jeddah, in addition there are a number of smaller towns such as Tabuk and al-'Ula. As religious cities Mecca and Medina are responsible for bringing a large number of pilgrims to the area and have a cosmopolitan population. However, Jeddah as the port of Mecca has grown to be the main city of the Hijaz and until recently has been the main commercial centre of Saudi Arabia. The architecture of the Hijaz is particularly subject to outside influences, thus settlements of al-'Ula, Tabuk and al-Wajh developed as a result of the pilgrim routes. The medieval khan of Qasr Zurayb near al-Wajh is a clear example of this external influence.

Tihama and 'Asir

The Tihama is located in the south-west corner of Saudi Arabia and comprises two distinct regions, the hot humid coastal plain and the high mountains of 'Asir. The architecture of the coastal plain is of two types, town houses and rural houses. The town houses are built of coral and are usually rectangular single-storey buildings with a courtyard. Rural houses are made of wood and thatch and are related to the architecture of nearby East Africa. The architecture of the mountains is built of stone and is related to the mountain architecture of Yemen.

Najd

The Najd is a plateau in the centre of Arabia south of the Nafud desert. The principal areas of occupation are clustered around the Jabal Tuwayq and include Riyadh, the present capital of the country as well as Ha'il, the nineteenth-century capital. North of the Nafud desert is the oasis town of Dumat al-Jandal which has a mosque attributed to the second caliph, 'Umar ibn al-Khattab (634–44).

Al–Hassa

The great oasis of al-Hassa stands about 60 km from the coast of the Arabian Gulf. The architecture of the area is predominantly stone and mud, although its position near the coast means that it is open to outside influences, the most obvious of which is the white plaster decoration used to create stucco panels and decorative arches. During the sixteenth century the oasis was occupied by the Ottoman Turks in an attempt to curb Saffavid or Portuguese ambitions in the area, and Ottoman influence may still be seen in Hufuf, the principal town of the oasis. The mosque of Ibrahim has a large central dome resting on four large squinches and a domed portico similar to classical Ottoman mosques. Nevertheless, the mosque is not Ottoman in details such as the muqarnas hood of the mihrab or the use of polylobed arches.

The Gulf Coast

The Gulf coast includes the towns of al-Jubayl, al-Qatif and the modern city of Dhahran. As on the west coast coral is the traditional building material although it is used in a different form. One of the notable features of this architecture is the use of thin coral panels held between piers. Also the buildings of this region are distinguished by their use of decorative arches and ornamental plasterwork.

See also: Ka'ba, Mecca, Medina

Further reading:

G. R. D. King, 'Traditional architecture in Najd, Saudi Arabia', *Proceedings of the Tenth Seminar for Arabian Studies*, London 1976, 90–100.

—— 'Islamic architecture in Eastern Arabia', *Proceedings of the Eleventh Seminar for Arabian Studies*, London 1977, 15–28.

—— *Historical Mosques of Saudi Arabia*, London and New York 1986.

—— 'Building methods and materials in western Saudi Arabia', *Proceedings of the Seminar for Arabian Studies*, vol. 19 1989.

T. Prochazka, 'The architecture of the Saudi Arabian south west', *Proceedings of the Tenth Seminar for Arabian Studies*, London 1976, 120–33.

Sawma'a

Minaret.

sebil

Turkish term for a drinking fountain. Also used to refer to a small kiosk with attendant who dispenses water, or sherbet, from behind a grille.

Selimiye

Ottoman mosque at Edirne in European Turkey considered to be the culmination of Ottoman architecture.

The mosque forms the centre of a complex which includes a madrassa (college), a Quran reading room and a huge covered market, the proceeds of which paid for the upkeep of the mosque. This complex, built by the famous architect Sinan, is generally considered to be his greatest work. The mosque consists of two rectangular areas of equal size placed side by side; the northern area is the courtyard and portico and the southern area comprises the prayer hall of the mosque covered by a huge dome, 32 m in diameter. The dome is the same size as that of the Hagia Sophia, thus achieving the Ottoman ambition of building a mosque of equal size and brilliance to the Ottoman masterpiece. Instead of using half-domes of the same radius placed at the sides of the central dome as was usual in earlier mosques, Sinan used smaller corner domes which function as giant squinches. The dome rests on an octagon formed by eight massive cylindrical fluted piers which project through the roof to act as stabilizing turrets for the fenestrated drum. The significance of the design is that it breaks away from the square domed area which had remained the dominant principal in Ottoman mosque architecture.

Like the Süleymaniye and the Üç Şerefeli Mosque, the Selimiye has four minarets, but here they are placed at each corner of the mosque rather than at the corners of the courtyard as had happened previously. At 68 m these are the tallest Ottoman minarets and with their central positioning emphasize the pyramid-like mass of the dome.

The mosque is built mainly of yellow sandstone although red sandstone is also used for voussoirs in arches and for outlining architectural details. The interior of the building is provided with traditional mosque furniture, the most impressive of which is the tall marble minbar. The sides of the minbar are decorated with a carved geometric interlace pattern based on a twelve-pointed star and circle. Directly below the dome is the square muezzin's gallery resting on an arcade of wide-lobed arches, and below this is a small marble fountain emphasizing the central axis of the dome. The mihrab is contained within a square, apse-like area and covered by a small semi-dome which emphasizes its position. The royal prayer room is located on an upper gallery in the north-west corner of the mosque as was traditional in Ottoman architecture. The royal area is heavily decorated with Iznik tile panels and stained-glass windows, whilst the south window forms the mihrab niche.

See also: Edirne, Ottomans, Sinan, Süleymaniye

Seljuks

Turkish dynasty which ruled much of Anatolia, Syria, Iraq, Iran and Central Asia during the eleventh century.

The Seljuks were a division of the Kiniq clan of Öghuz Turks who originated in the steppes north of the Aral Sea. Originally they were hired as soldiers to take part in the internal feuding of Khurassan and eastern Iran. In 1038 the leader Tughril Beg gained control of all Khurassan and had himself proclaimed sultan at Nishapur. As Sunni Muslims the Seljuks wanted to restore orthodoxy to the central Islamic lands and in 1055 Tughril defeated the Sh'ia Buwaihids who ruled from Baghdad. Further victories followed with the defeat of the Byzantines at Manzikert in 1071 and

the defeat of the Qarakhanids in Central Asia in the late eleventh century. The unified Seljuk state did not last much beyond the beginning of the twelfth century, partly owing to its pattern of inheritance and partly because the areas covered were too diverse.

During the twelfth century the empire broke up into a number of independent principalities which can be classified into three main groups: a western group comprising Anatolia, a central group covering Syria and Iraq, and an eastern group including Iran and and Central Asia.

Seljuk architecture is characterized by the rapid transmission of ideas and forms. During this period many of the characteristic forms of Islamic architecture become common everywhere, thus madrassas, memorial tombs and khans were built from Central Asia to western Anatolia. Iwans became one of the principal architectural units and were used both for religious and secular buildings. In Iran and the eastern areas decorative brickwork and elaborate stucco ornamentation are common, whilst in Anatolia these decorative themes were translated into stone.

The homeland of Seljuk architecture was Iran, where the first permanent Seljuk structures were built. Unfortunately the Mongol invasions destroyed most of these buildings and only a few remain. In 1063 Isfahan was established as capital of the Great Seljuk Empire under Alp Arslan and parts of the Great Mosque date to this period. The most significant alteration carried out in the early twelfth century was the conversion of the building into a four-iwan plan mosque. Another mosque-type introduced at this time was the kiosk mosque, consisting of a domed space with three open sides and wall containing a mihrab on the qibla side. The architecture of this period was also characterized by memorial tombs which were usually octagonal structures with domed roofs. The most impressive example of tomb architecture is the mausoleum of Sultan Sanjar at Merv, a massive building measuring 27 m square with a huge double dome resting on squinches and muqarnas pendentives.

In Syria and Iraq the surviving monuments are represented by madrassas and tombs. The madrassas such as the Mustansiriya in Baghdad or the Muristan in Damascus were built to a four-iwan plan, while the tombs were characterized by conical muqarnas domes.

The greatest number of surviving Seljuk monuments are in Anatolia. Characteristic features of

Seljuk architecture in the region are elaborate stone portal façades carved in deep relief, small courtyards which are sometimes covered (to cope with the cold climate), and the introduction of tiles as architectural decoration.

The first mosques built in Anatolia copied the layout of Syrian mosques thus the mosques of Diyarbakir (1091), Dunaysir (1204) and Silvan (1152) have a design based in that of the Great Mosque in Damascus. Later on the design changes, so that in buildings such as the Great Mosque at Harout and the Kolluk Mosque at Kayseri the courtyard is reduced to a small area in the centre of a large prayer hall. Other mosques were built with an iwan on the qibla side of the courtyard which leads into a domed prayer hall. Another development of the period is the introduction of wooden mosques which may have been common in Central Asia at the time (no examples survive from there). These are large halls with flat roofs supported on wooden columns with muqarnas capitals. The Eshrefoglu Mosque at Beyshehir has this form but has a separate brick dome resting on columns in front of the mihrab and an open bay in the centre recalling the courtyard of earlier mosques.

Like the mosques, the Seljuk madrassas of Anatolia were built around small courtyards which were sometimes roofed with domes or vaults. The central court was often surrounded with arcades, with an iwan on the qibla side functioning as the prayer hall. The mausoleums were like those of Central Asia with an octagonal plan and conical roofs.

See also: Baghdad, Damascus, Iran, Iraq, Isfahan, Merv, Nishapur, Syria

semahane

Literally 'dance hall'; an Ottoman Turkish term for a room used for dervishes to dance. The typical Ottoman semahane was an octagonal domed room often attached to a mosque. The most famous is the Mevlana dervish centre in Konya.

serai

Turkish term for a palace.

serdab

Sunken courtyard opening on to underground rooms used to escape the heat of the day. Serdabs are of pre-Islamic Iranian origin but were rapidly incorporated into Islamic architecture. One of the earliest examples is in the palace of Khirbet al-Mafjar.

şeref

Ottoman term for the balcony on a minaret. Most minarets only have one balcony, although some of the more important mosques have minarets with up to three, the most famous example being the Üç Şerefeli Mosque in Edirne.

Seville (Arabic: Ishbiliyya)

City in south-west Spain originally capital of the Muslim province of al-Andalus (Spain) and later one of main centres of Islamic culture in Spain.

Before the coming of Islam, Seville was the first capital of the Visigoths until they moved to Toledo. It was captured by the Arabs in the eighth century and remained a Muslim city until the early thirteenth century when it was taken by the Christian armies of Ferdinand III. Despite this change Seville remained an important centre of Mudéjar architecture throughout the Middle Ages.

During the Islamic period the city was known for silk weaving and scholarship and was the home to the famous physician and philosopher Averroës. Unfortunately little remains of the early Islamic city, although traces of the Almohad and Almoravid city remain along with fine examples of Mudéjar craftsmanship.

Parts of the first Umayyad mosque founded in 859 can be found in the church of San Salvador. These remains include arcades resting on columns (now sunk deep into the ground) and the minaret which may be the oldest surviving Muslim building in Spain. The present cathedral of Santa Maria de la Sede is built on the site of the Almohad Great Mosque built in 1172. The mosque itself no longer exists but the minaret known as La Giralda still dominates the city's main square. The tower took fourteen years to build and is over 50 m high. The tower has a square base and shaft (like all minarets in Spain) and has ramps inside instead of staircases. The interior contains seven chambers, one on each storey, each with a different type of vault. Each face of the exterior is divided into three vertical strips or decorative panels. Each floor has a centrally placed pair of windows with a single column in the middle and either side of the windows are paired niches of similar design. Above the windows and niches is a delicate net-like diamond pattern executed in elaborate brickwork. The tower bears a strong resemblance to the Kutubiyya minaret in Marakesh also built by the Almohads.

Little remains of the original defences of the city which contained twelve gates and 116 interval towers, although the remaining parts have been recently restored. The Torre del Oro, a twelve-sided tower, represents the latest phase of Muslim fortifications. The best example of Mudéjar architecture in Seville is the Alcazar which was rebuilt as the palace of Pedro the Cruel in the fourteenth century. Many of the masons and carpenters were hired from Granada thus explaining some of the similarity between the lavish decoration and intricate design of this palace and the Alhambra. The palace also re-used some of the columns and other building materials taken from Madinat al-Zahra' after its destruction in 1010. The palace contains a series of courtyards or patios which are decorated with intricate carved stonework arcades and polychrome tile dadoes. The most famous of these courtyards is the Patio de las Doncellas which has an arcade composed of multi-lobed arches resting on twin columns, above which is a diaper pattern similar to that of the Giralda Minaret. The highlight of the palace is the Salón de los Embajadores which is covered with an amazing wooden dome decorated with star patterns and supported on intricate wooden muqarnas squinches.

See also: Alhambra, Córdoba, Mudéjar, Spain

Sfax

Walled city located on the east coast of Tunisia.

Sfax rose to prominence under the Aghlabids in the ninth century. The city walls, built in the late seventh century, were renewed in the ninth and provided with huge square and polygonal towers. The Great Mosque is similar to that of Qairawan and is the only mosque to have the same arrangement of a square minaret on the north side aligned with the mihrab.

See also: Aghlabids, Tunisia

Shanga

Islamic trading city in the Lamu archipelago off the north Kenya coast, East Africa.

Shanga is one of the most intensively investigated early Islamic sites in East Africa with an occupation stretching from the mid-eighth to the fourteenth century. It is not mentioned in any major historical sources except for a passing reference in the Pate Chronicle, so that all information comes from excavations carried out in recent years.

The earliest phase, dated to the eighth century, is represented by a large rectangular wooden enclosure containing a well and surrounded by roundhouses made of wattle and daub on timber frames. In the second period (ninth–tenth century) a rectangular wooden mosque was built in the central area. Whilst roundhouses continued to be built on the west, on the east side the houses were now rectangular. In the third phase (tenth–eleventh century) the enclosure and mosque were rebuilt in coral stone and a monumental stone building was erected in the centre. At this same time many of the houses outside were also built out of coral stone. The fourth and fifth periods, lasting from the eleventh to the end of the twelfth century, is marked by the decline of the settlement and the

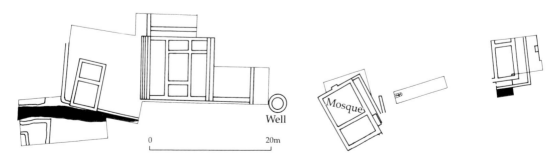

Plan of ninth-century monumental buildings, Shanga, Kenya (after Horton)

reintroduction of wooden architecture in the centre of the site. The sixth phase of occupation (early fourteenth to fifteenth centuries) is represented by the reintroduction of stone buildings using a new technique of fossil coral instead of the previous reef coral. Many of the ruins of this period still survive, and consist of remains of over 200 houses, three mosques and a large number of tombs.

See also: coral, East Africa, Kenya, Manda

Further reading:

M. C. Horton, *Shanga: An Interim Report*, National Museums of Kenya, Nairobi 1981.
—— 'Early Muslim trading settlements on the East African coast: new evidence from Shanga', *Antiquaries Journal* 67: 290–323, 1987.

Shahr-i Sabz

Town in Uzbekistan, Central Asia, which Timur tried to make his capital in the fourteenth century.

The city or town forms a rectangular enclosure surrounded by a wall approximately 4 km in circumference and in places up to 5 m thick. The main ruins at the site are the monumental entrance to Timur's palace (the Ak Saray, 'White Palace') and the Dar al-Siyadat. Although incomplete it can be seen that the entrance arch would have been more than 50 m high and 22 m wide, making it one of the largest archways in the Islamic world. The interior of the iwan and the towers flanking it are decorated with light and dark blue-glazed bricks forming a geometric carpet-like pattern which includes the names Allah, Muhammad, Ali and Othman in large square calligraphy. An archaeological analysis of the site has shown that the portal would have been preceded by a huge open space 70–80 m long which would have emphasized the massive proportions of the building. Inside the entrance, the palace would have comprised a large courtyard with a central pool and audience hall on the same axis as the entrance. The royal cemetery known as the Dar al-Siyadat contained the tomb of Jahangir (with a tall domed roof) and the tomb intended for Timur himself (this had a conical roof on a cruciform plan). Other buildings preserved at the site include the baths and the bazar. The bazar comprises four main streets which converge on a central crossroads covered with a dome.

shish mahal

Mughal term for a room decorated with mirror mosaics.

Sicily

Large island south of Italy, occupied by Muslim Arabs for 200 years.

The first Arab conquest in Sicily was the capture of Mazara in 827 by the Aghlabid governors of Ifriqiyya (roughly equivalent to modern Tunisia). The conquest of the island was not complete until 75 years later, although immigration began immediately. In 1061 the island was captured by the Normans and became the centre of a flourishing Byzantine, Islamic and Norman culture.

There are few architectural remains of the Islamic period because most buildings were rebuilt or remodelled later under the Normans. Indeed, many of the most important Arab buildings were themselves converted Byzantine structures; thus the cathedral of the capital at Palermo was converted into the Great Mosque by the Arabs and subsequently became a Norman cathedral. There are only two entirely Muslim structures which have survived. These are La Favara Castle (Arabic al-Fawwara) and the eleventh-century baths of Cefala 30 km outside Palermo.

Probably the most significant traces of Islamic architecture are found in the buildings of the Norman kingdom, when Arab craftsmen and designs continued to be used. Probably the most striking example of this is the Cappella Palatina with its painted wooden ceiling. To the south of Palermo the Norman king built a royal park in the Islamic style, with palaces and hunting lodges. One of the best preserved palaces is the Ziza Palace built by William II (1166–89). This rectangular structure is built in the form of an Islamic reception hall with a central cruciform reception room flanked by smaller rooms. The building is decorated with muqarnas corbels, rows of blind niches and a fountain which runs in a narrow channel through the palace.

See also: Aghlabids

Further reading:

G. Marçais, *L'architecture musulmane d'Occident: Tunisie, Algerie, Maroc, Espagne et Sicile*, Paris 1955.

Sinan (Koca Sinan; 1491–1588)

Famous Ottoman architect responsible for transforming Ottoman architecture from a traditional discipline into a conscious art form.

Sinan was born a Christian in the Karaman region of south-east Anatolia and at the age of 21 was recruited into the Janissaries (special Ottoman force selected from subject Christian populations). As part of his training Sinan worked as a carpenter and engineer on building sites in Istanbul. As a soldier Sinan fought for the emperor in Rhodes, Belgrade, Baghdad and Moldavia, rising rapidly to the position of Commander of the Royal Guard. During this period Sinan may have worked as a military engineer converting churches into mosques and building bridges. Sinan's first recorded building is the Hüsrev Pasha Cami in Aleppo built between 1536 and 1537. This complex consists of a single-domed mosque with a small rectangular courtyard and two madrassas located on an irregular-shaped site. The mosque's tall dome is pierced by sixteen windows and supported by buttresses. In order to compensate for the height of the dome Sinan built the portico wider than the mosque adding an extra bay at each end. This solution causes problems for the positioning of the windows and the pendentives of the portico domes which clash.

In 1538 at the age of 47 Sinan was appointed as the chief architect of Istanbul by Suleyman the Magnificent. During the next fifty years Sinan built over 300 buildings, recorded by his friend and biographer Mustafa Sâ'i. Sinan's first task as chief architect was the construction of a women's hospital for Suleyman's Russian wife. The complex known as the Haseki Hürrem was built on an irregular site and consisted of a hospital, hostel, mosque and medical school (Tip medrese). Although the building may not have been started by Sinan and has been subsequently altered, it conveys an impression of his ability to manage a difficult site and produce an impressive, functioning building. This ability is more clearly expressed in the tomb of the Grand Admiral Hayrettin Barbaros built in 1541. This is a tall octagonal chamber covered with a dome and pierced by two sets of windows, an upper level and a lower level. The lower-level windows are rectangular, covered with lintels under relieving arches, whilst those of the upper level are covered with shallow four-pointed arches. The exterior of the building is very plain, except for the windows and two plain mouldings marking the transition from wall to drum and from drum to dome. The severe impression created is modified by the high quality of workmanship and the harmonic proportions.

Sinan's first major work is the Şehzade Cami in Istanbul built in memory of Suleyman's son and the heir to the throne who died at the age of 22. The complex, begun in 1543 and completed five years later, contains a madrassa, an imaret (hospice) and a Quran school besides the mosque and the tomb of Şehzade. The mosque consists of two equal squares comprising a courtyard and domed prayer room. The most notable feature of the design is the use of four semi-domes to expand the interior space, for although this plan had been used earlier at Diyarbakir this was the first time it had been used in an imperial mosque. The arches carrying the large central dome rest on four giant piers which rise up above roof level to act as buttresses for the drum of the dome. This design later became a standard solution to the limitations imposed by the size of domes in Ottoman mosques. Another important innovation was the development of the façades at the side of the mosque and courtyard. This was achieved by placing doorways at the side of the building thus giving the it a cross-axial arrangement. This was important in large complexes where the north façade was not necessarily the most important and certainly not the longest side of the building. The tomb of Şehzade stands alone in a garden to the south of the mosque. This tomb has the same basic form as the Admiral Barbaros tomb although here the austerity is replaced with intense beauty. The dome is composed of fluted ribs, whilst the top of the octagon is marked by ornate crenellations supported on muqarnas corbelling. The interior of the tomb is covered with yellow, blue and green Iznik tiles and light is filtered through stained-glass windows.

Sinan's next important commission was the mosque of Suleyman's daughter Mirimah at Üsküdar known as the Iskele Cami (Harbour Mosque). This was the first of three commissions for Mirimah and her husband Rüstem Pasha the Grand Vizier. The Iskele Cami is built on a raised platform to protect it from the water and has a double portico instead of a courtyard because of lack of space. The double portico is an idea which was also used at the Rüstem Pasha mosques at Tekirdag and Eminönü, both in Istanbul, and later became a standard format for lesser mosques.

Sinan's largest project at this time was the mosque complex of Suleyman which was to be the largest purpose-built mosque in Istanbul. This building known as the Süleymaniye established Sinan's reputation as the foremost of Ottoman architects and is the place which he chose for his own tomb. The complex covers a huge area (about 330 by 200 m) of sloping ground overlooking the Bosphorus with the mosque at the centre. Characteristically Sinan was able to turn the difficulties of the terrain to his advantage by building the complex on several levels. Thus the two madrassas on the east side of the complex are built in steps down the hillside, whilst the mosque itself is built on a huge artificial platform with vaulted substructures on the east side. The mosque itself uses many of the features of the Şehzade Cami such as the lateral entrances, but in place of the cruciform plan there is a central dome between two semi-domes. The mass of the central dome is emphasized by the four minarets, a feature only previously seen at the Üç Şerefli Cami in Edirne.

Although the Süleymaniye was probably Sinan's largest building complex, it was not his greatest work; this was the Selimiye Cami in Edirne begun nearly twenty years later. The Selimiye built between 1569 and 1575 incorporates many of the features of the Süleymaniye but abandons the system of large semi-domes at the side of the dome in favour of giant squinches placed at the corners. Also the system of four central piers is replaced by eight piers arranged in an octagon with the result that the building has an airiness and space unparalleled in Islamic or Western architecture. The main dome has the same diameter as that of Hagia Sophia and thus achieves the Ottoman ambition of constructing a building equal to the highest achievement of the Byzantines.

Whilst working on the Selimiye Sinan continued to produce a variety of smaller buildings, for example the Sokollu Mehmet Pasha Cami in Istanbul which, like many of his other famous works, was built on a steep hillside. Again Sinan was able to exploit the site by building the courtyard out on to an artificial terrace with an entrance from below. This technique had been used before at the Iskele Cami and the Rüstem Pasha Cami, but not as effectively as here, where a wide staircase leads up into the middle of the courtyard facing the sardivan (fountain).

After the completion of the Selimiye in 1575

Sinan lived for a further thirteen years and continued to design buildings, though is likely that many of these were not visited by him. When he died at the age of 97 Sinan was interred in the tomb he had built for himself next to the Süleymaniye. This is an open canopy covered by a vault set in a garden which originally contained his house. At the end of the garden is a small octagonal domed fountain which had earlier been the cause of a dispute. Sinan's epitaph was written by his friend Mustapha Sâ'i and only mentions one of his works, the four-humped bridge at Büyükçekmice.

Art historians have spent a considerable amount of time discussing Sinan's contribution to architecture and particular his relationship to the Renaissance. There was a considerable amount of contact between Italy and the Ottoman Empire at this stage, as can be seen from invitations to Leonardo da Vinci and later Michelangelo to build a bridge across the Golden Horn. Despite this contact and the similarities between the work of Alberti and Sinan it should be noted that their objectives were different. In Renaissance buildings there was a tension between humanity and God; in those of Sinan there was a single purpose – to mirror a single and infinite Divinity.

See also: Ottomans, Selimiye, Süleymaniye

Further reading:

Ahmet Refik, *Mimar Sinan*, Istanbul 1931.
A. Gabriel, 'Le maître-architecte Sinan', in *La Turquie Kemaliste* 16, Ankara 1936.
G. Goodwin, *A History of Ottoman Architecture*, London 1971.
—— *Sinan*, London 1992.
A. Güler, J. Freely and A. R. Burrelli, *Sinan: Architect of Süleyman the Magnificent and the Ottoman Golden Age*, London 1992.
A. Kuran, M. Niksarli and A. Güler, *Sinan: The Grand Old Master of Ottoman Architecture*, Istanbul 1987.
A. Petruccioli (ed.), *Mimar Sinan: The Urban Vision* (Journal of the Islamic Environmental Design Research Centre), Rome 1988.
A. Stratton, *Sinan*, London 1972.

Singapore

City-state on southern tip of the Malay peninsular with a mixed population of Malays, Chinese and Indians, as well as a small Arab minority.

The earliest mosques in Singapore were built of wood and thatch; during the nineteenth century these were replaced with brick structures. The most important mosque in Singapore is known as the Sultan Mosque and was originally built between 1823 and 1824 with a grant of $3,000 from the British East India Company. The original mosque was demolished in the 1920s to make way for the present structure built by the British firm Swan and Maclaren in 1928. The building has two large onion-shaped domes, a polygonal minaret and crenellations to enliven the façade. Either side of the prayer hall are separate areas for women.

The oldest surviving mosque in Singapore is the Jamae Mosque, which was built on the site of an earlier structure between 1826 and 1835. Its main feature is the façade, which is flanked by two square towers. Each tower is divided into seven mini-storeys linked by decorative crenellations in the form of a mini-gateway. Of similar design is the Nagore Durgha shrine built between 1828 and 1830 which also has two miniature towers either side of a miniaturized entrance façade located on top of the real entrance. It seems likely that these mosque façades may derive from the Char Minar in Hyderabad, south India. A simpler design is represented by the Tamil al Abrar Mosque built in the 1850s where the entrance is flanked by two pillars. Other early mosques include the Abdul Gafoor Mosque (1850s) and the Hajjah Fatimah Mosque (1930) both of which combine European (British) elements with Indian design.

See also: India, Indonesia, Malaysia

Further reading:

J. Beamish and J. Ferguson, *A History of Singapore Architecture: The Making of a City*, Singapore 1985.
Monuments Board of Singapore, *Preservation of Singapore National Monuments*, Singapore 1985.

Siraf

Major early Islamic port city located on the Iranian side of the Arabian/Persian Gulf.

The city contains some of the earliest examples of Islamic architecture excavated in Iran. The most significant discovery is the congregational mosque, a huge rectangular structure with a central courtyard set on a raised podium. There is a single entrance reached by a set of steps on the east side opposite the qibla, next to which is the square base of a mihrab. The first phase of the mosque, dated to the early ninth century, has three arcades parallel to the qibla wall forming the prayer hall, and a single arcade on the other three sides. In the second phase (dated to 850) two more arcades

were added to the prayer hall and the single arcades on the other three sides were made double. In both phases the mihrab was a simple rectangular niche set into the middle of the qibla wall. Several smaller mosques were also discovered, each with a rectangular mihrab projecting on to the outside of the building.

See also: Abbasids, Iran, Iraq, Samarra

Further reading:

D. Whitehouse, *Siraf II. The Congregational Mosque and Other Mosques from the Ninth to the Twelfth Centuries*, The British Institute for Persian Studies.

Somalia

Somalia is located on the coast of East Africa directly below the Arabian peninsula.

The landscape of the country is predominantly semi-arid bush with mountains in the north near the border with Ethiopia. The coastal plain is similar to that of Kenya further south, with mangroves and coastal reefs.

Islam seems to have spread to Somalia through Muslim traders who established trading stations and urban centres along the coast between the seventh and the twelfth centuries CE. From the twelfth century the coastal towns had become independent Muslim sultanates fighting the Ethiopian Christians who controlled the interior. From the tenth century the Somalis of the interior gradually adopted Islam and became attached to the coastal towns. During the nineteenth and twentieth centuries Somalia was divided between Italian, British and French administrations before achieving independence in 1960.

The Islamic architecture of Somalia is similar to that of Kenya, with coral used as the main material for permanent buildings. The principal urban centre is Mogadishu which also has some of the oldest mosques, the most famous of which is the mosque of Fakhr al-Din built in the thirteenth century. Further south are a number of ancient urban settlements, the most important of which are Merka, Munghia, Barawa and Bur Gao. Most of the mosques of Merka are eighteenth century or later, although the tomb of Sheikh Uthman Hassan may date to the thirteenth century. Munghia consists of a large roughly square enclosure (about 200 m per side) built of earth with a facing of stone. Approximately in the centre there is a raised mound with the remains of a mosque on

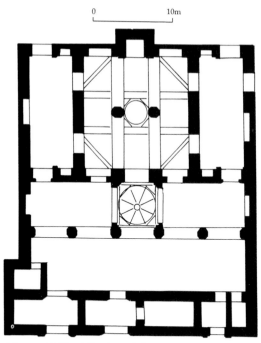

Mosque of Fakhr al-Din, Mogadishu, Somalia (after Garlake)

top. Although the mosque is badly damaged, it seems to consist of a central rectangular hall flanked by two side aisles. The mihrab in the centre of the north wall has a fluted semi-dome and, together with the pottery found there, suggests a twelfth-century foundation for the site. Although Barawa was probably founded at a similar date, the earliest buildings in the town date from the eighteenth century. One of these, a mosque, has a square minaret with elaborate carved woodwork. Probably the largest early site on the coast is Bur Gao whose are contained within a huge enclosure similar to that of Munghia. The principal standing structure on the site is a square building covered with a low domical vault. The site also contains a number of pillar tombs similar to those of north Kenya.

See also: East Africa, Kenya

Further reading:

N. Chittick, 'An archaeological reconnaissance of the southern Somali coast', *Azania* 4: 115–30, 1969.
H. C. Sanservino, 'Archaeological remains on the southern Somali coast', *Azania* 18: 151–64, 1983.

Songhay

The people who inhabit the banks of the Niger river

between Gao and Dendi in West Africa.

The Songhay people were the ruling population of the empire of Gao during the fifteenth and sixteenth centuries. Some of them were Muslim before the eleventh century but some have remained pagan to the present day. Little is known of early Songhay architecture, although ancestor-worship seems to have been expressed through earthen burial mounds. Elements of this tradition seem to have been incorporated in Islamic monuments where prominent people are buried within solid-earth pyramid-like constructions, the most famous of which is the tomb of Askiya Muhammad at Gao.

See also: Gao, West Africa

South Africa

The Muslim community of South Africa seems to have originated from south-east Asia, mostly Malaysia. The Malays were mostly brought to South Africa as slaves in the eighteenth century, although some came freely as political exiles Although they were allowed to remain Muslim they were not able to worship publicly until 1804. Before that time prayer was carried out within houses or in the open air. The first purpose-built mosque was the Auwal Mosque in Cape Town built at the beginning of the eighteenth century. In its earliest form the mosque lacked a minaret and resembled a chapel from the exterior. Inside, there were two courtyards, a kitchen and storage rooms as well as a prayer hall. For planning reasons the building was not oriented to face Mecca; instead the mihrab inside was built at an angle to the rest of the building to correct this.

Further reading:

F. R. Bradlow and M. C. Cairns, *The Early Cape Muslims: A Study of their Mosques, Genealogy and Origins*, Cape Town 1978.

Spain (Arabic: al-Andalus)

Large country in south-western Europe occupying the greater part of the Iberian peninsula and known in Arabic as al-Andalus.

Large parts of this country were Muslim from the arrival of the Arab armies in 711 to the fall of the amirate of Granada in 1492. Before the arrival of the first Arab armies Spain was ruled by the

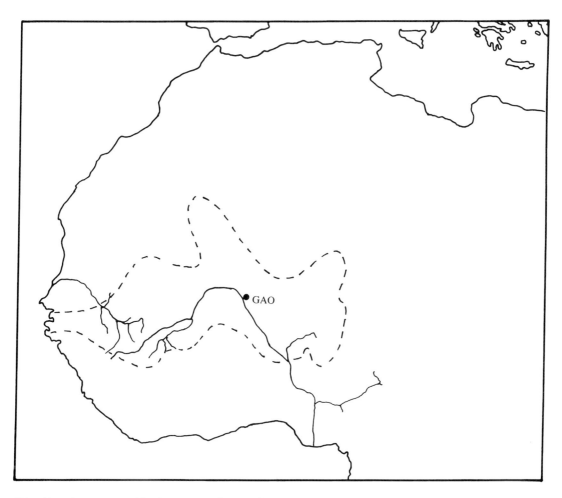

West Africa showing extent of Songhay empire in the sixteenth century

Visigoths, warrior nomads from east of Europe who had recently been converted to Christianity. They in turn had taken over the country after the collapse of the Byzantine rule which was a direct continuation of Roman suzerainty in the country. At the time of the Arab invasions the Visigothic kingdom was weak and their king Roderick was not universally acknowledged.

The Arab conquest was carried out by Musa the commander of North Africa and his semilegendary lieutenant Tariq. Within a year Toledo, the Visigothic capital, had been captured. The speed of the conquest alarmed the caliph who in 716 summoned the commander and his general to return. Nevertheless, the conquest continued northwards and by the 730s had reached central France where it was finally checked by Charles Martel at a battle between Poitiers and Tours. The only area of Spain which withstood the invasion was the region of Asturias in the Cantabrian mountains of the northwest. Until the 750s the province was ruled by governors sent by the Umayyad caliphs. The Abbasid revolution had led to the killing of all members of the Umayyad dynasty with the exception of Abd al-Rahman who escaped via North Africa to Spain where he defeated the resident governor Yusuf in a battle near Toledo. For the next 270 years the country was ruled by the Umayyad descendants of Abd al-Rahman. The most famous member of this dynasty was Abd al-Rahman III who reigned for fifty years between 912 and 961. It was during this reign that the title of the ruler

263

Spain (Arabic: al-Andalus)

Islamic Spain in the eighth century

was changed from amir to caliph and 'Commander of the Faithful' in order to counter the claims of the Fatimid caliphate. During this period the capital was Córdoba which became one of the brightest centres of culture in the Islamic world. Despite this high level of sophistication, the dynasty itself was prone to internal divisions and finally collapsed in 1031.

For the next half century Spain was divided into at least twenty-three independent principalities, known as the Muluk al-Tawaif, each with its own court and ruler. The size of these principalities varied greatly, with some ruling a single city whilst others like the Aftasids in south-west Spain ruled large areas of the country. Despite political disunity the Islamic culture of Spain thrived during this period. Nevertheless, the Christians of the north-west were able to exploit divisions amongst the Muslims to conquer extensive territories. The capture of Toledo by Alfonso VI of Castile in 1085 showed the weakness of these principalities and encouraged the conquest of the Almoravids in 1090.

The Almoravids were a dynasty of fanatical fundamentalist Berbers from North Africa. Under their leader Yusuf, the Almoravids invaded Spain and stemmed the tide of Christian conquest. From their newly established capital of Marakesh the Almoravids now ruled a huge area from present-day Senegal to Spain.

In 1145 the Almoravids, weakened by disunity, were replaced by the Almohads, another fanatical Berber group who managed to challenge the Christian advance. By 1212, however, the Almohads were driven from Spain by a coalition of Christian rulers. This left Granada as the only Muslim province to survive the Christian invasions. Granada was ruled by the Nasirid dynasty which maintained the area as a centre of cultural and scientific excellence with the Alhambra at its centre. The Nasirids were finally ousted from their position in 1492 by the united forces of Castile and Aragon under Ferdinand and Isabella.

Despite the political defeat of Islam in Spain Muslims continued to live in the country until the seventeenth century when they were all expelled. Nevertheless, traces of Islamic presence survive in the culture and architecture of Spain.

In many ways the landscape of Spain is similar to that of North Africa with its aridity, high mountains and endless desert-like plains. Communication from one part to another is hindered by precipitous valleys, high mountains and the three major rivers of the Ebro, Tagus and the Duero.

The building materials of Islamic Spain reflect the availability of natural resources and the diversity of cultural influences. The main materials used are wood, stone and baked brick, although mud brick was also used. Unlike many parts of the Middle East, Spain had plentiful supplies of timber suitable for building including both pine and oak. Wood was usually used for roofs which were normally gabled and covered with baked clay tiles, although occasionally wooden domes were also used. The pine roofs of the Great Mosque in Córdoba reflect the plentiful supplies of wood in medieval Spain. Stone was used for walls either in the form of ashlar masonry or in the form of coursed rubble. Often masonry was re-used from earlier Roman or Visigothic structures, although fine stone carving continued. One of the most distinctive features of Spanish Islamic architecture is the use of brick which, like ashlar masonry, was a direct continuation of Roman building methods. Sometimes stone was encased in brick in the same manner as Byzantine fortifications.

Notable features of Spanish Islamic architecture include horseshoe arches, paired windows with a central column, construction in brick and stone, polychrome tiles, intricate carved stucco work and overlapping arches. Several terms are used to describe Islamic-type architecture in Spain each of which has a particular meaning. The best-known term is 'Moorish' which is often used to refer to Islamic architecture in general although it more properly should be used to describe the architecture of the Moors or Berbers of North Africa. The less well-known term Mudéjar refers to architecture carried out for Christian patrons by Muslim craftsmen. Mudéjar architecture uses many of the most characteristic features of Islamic architecture including Arabic calligraphy and the horseshoe arch. Many of Christian Spain's most beautiful churches and palaces were built by Mudéjar craftsmen and the tradition was carried on into the new world. A related style is known as Mozarabic which refers

to the architecture of Christian buildings under Muslim rule. In addition to its influence on Christian buildings, Islamic architecture also influenced the substantial Jewish community in Spain so that many synagogues in Spain were built in an Islamic style (the best examples are in Toledo, see below).

The range of buildings surviving from the Islamic period in Spain is quite large and includes castles, fortifications, mosques, churches and synagogues, palaces, bridges, hammams, mills, villages and towns. The most numerous remains are castles and fortifications which can be found throughout the country and from all periods from the eighth to the fifteenth century. These are often difficult to date precisely and most were subsequently re-used after the Christian reconquest. One of the best examples of early fortification are the walls and square battered towers of the castle known as Baños de la Encina near Jaén in Andalusía. Here the gate is sandwiched between two towers and protected by machicolation and a portcullis. Later on fortifications were protected by bent entrances where the gateway was perpendicular to the walls, thus exposing attackers to fire from three sides. A later development of fortifications was the albarrani tower which was located outside the city walls but connected to it by a bridge so that defenders were able to outflank their attackers. Often albarrani towers were built to protect buildings outside the walls without the added expense and inconvenience of changing the line of the city wall; thus at Calatrava la Vieja the tower was built to protect a nearby watermill. In addition to the major fortifications hundreds of small towers and forts were built all over the peninsula to defend borders and coasts. These were often small isolated towers built of cheap local materials such as mud brick or coursed rubble, although sometimes they were sophisticated structures dominating the countryside like the castle of Belmez near Córdoba.

Most of the mosques of Spain were converted into churches after the reconquest, some with very little alteration and others where the architecture was profoundly damaged as in the case of the Great Mosque of Córdoba where a cathedral was built in the middle of the structure in the sixteenth century. Characteristic features of Spanish mosques are square minarets and large mihrabs which are sometimes like a separate room. Where decoration has survived intact it is usually very elaborate and includes carved plaster and woodwork.

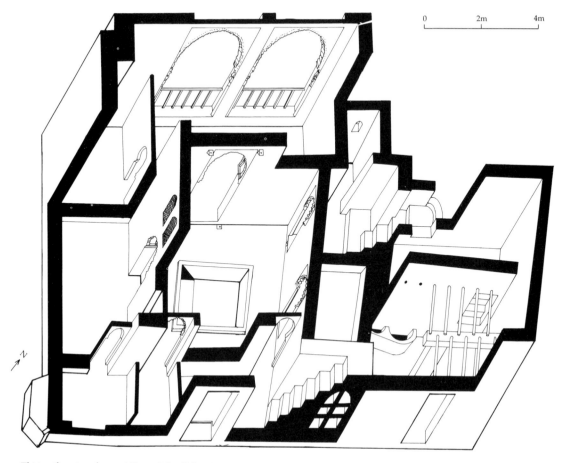

0   2m   4m

Thirteenth-century house at Siyasa (after Palazon)

Palaces fared better after the reconquest and some of the finest examples of Islamic palaces can be found in Spain such as the Alhambra and the Generalife. The Islamic palatial tradition was continued after the reconquest with palaces which are almost entirely Islamic in conception, like that of Pedro the Cruel in the Alcazar at Seville. Another type of Islamic building often associated with palaces is the hammam. Few of these have survived in Spain although fine examples can be seen at Ronda and Granada. Bridges and mills are less easy to distinguish as Muslim work, although many examples survive. It is thought that some of the water mills near Córdoba may be related to the great water wheels of Syria. In addition to specific buildings and monuments many towns and villages retain the layout and appearance of Islamic times. Some of the more important cities with

substantial traces of Islamic architecture are Córdoba, Seville, Granada, Toledo and Zaragoza, but many other towns and cities contain traces of Islamic buildings including Madrid and Asturias (starting-point of the reconquest).

The area conquered by the Arabs in the eighth century still contained many remains of the Roman and Byzantine civilizations which proceeded the Visigothic conquest, and many of the basic techniques of construction remained the same throughout the Islamic period. The contribution of the Visigoths to Islamic architecture is poorly documented although it is thought that the ubiquitous horseshoe arch may be derived from Visigothic architecture. The distinctive features of Islamic buildings in Spain may in part reflect its early incorporation into the Islamic caliphate and its distance from the centre of the empire. The most notable influences from within Islam are from North Africa and Syria. The North African influence is easy to explain through its proximity and the successive invasions of Berber tribes under the Almohads and the Almoravids, the most famous example being the Giralda tower in Seville. Syrian architecture, however, influenced Spain through the Umayyad dynasty who sought to recall their homeland and assert their legitimacy through copying Syrian buildings and hiring Syrian architects. The most striking example of this is the city of Madinat al-Zahra' near Córdoba which is meant to recall the desert palaces of the Umayyads and in particular Rusafa.

Other notable influences were Byzantine architecture, both through remains of Byzantine structures in Spain and through the friendship between the Byzantine emperors and the Umayyad rulers, born out of a mutual dislike of the Fatimids.

See also: Alhambra, Córdoba, Córdoba Great Mosque, Granada, Seville, Toledo, Zaragoza

Further reading:

G. Goodwin, *Islamic Spain,* Architectural Guides for Travellers, London 1990. (This is the best available general guide in English.)

M. Asin, *Guadalajara Medieval, Arte y Arqueología Arabe y Mudéjar,* C.S.I.C. Madrid 1984.

C. Esco, J. Giraut and P. Senac, *Arqueología Islamica de la Marca Superior de al-Andalus,* Huesca 1988.

C. Ewart, 'Tipología de la mezquita en Occidente de los Amayas a los Almohades', Congreso de Arqueología Medieval Española, 1: 180–204, Madrid 1987.

E. Lambert, *Art Musulman et Art Chrétien dans la Péninsule Ibérique,* Paris and Toulouse 1958.

B. Pavón-Maldoado, *Les Almenas Decorativas Hispano Musulmanas,* Madrid 1967.

F. Prieto-Moreno, *Los Jardines de Granada,* Madrid 1952.

E. Sordo and W. Swaan, *Moorish Spain: Córdoba, Seville and Granada,* trans. I. Michael, London 1963.

J. Zozaya, 'Islamic fortifications in Spain; some aspects', Papers in Iberian Archaeology, B.A.R. 193, Oxford 1984.

squinch

Small arch in the corner of a building that converts a square space to an octagonal area which may then be covered with a dome.

stucco

Decorative plasterwork used in architecture.

Stucco is primarily an invention of the Iranian world where it was used in the absence of suitable stone for carving. It has a long history which can be traced back as far as Parthian times, when it was used to cover rubble masonry. During the Sassanian period stucco continued to be used to enliven surfaces on buildings made of baked brick or mud brick. By the sixth century stucco was used in the eastern Mediterranean although it was mostly a characteristic of Iranian architecture. The advent of Islam led to an unparalleled growth in its use throughout the Middle East and North Africa. Many of the earliest Islamic monuments employ stucco as the main form of decoration, as dadoes, ceiling decoration or sculpture. Usually the stucco was carved or moulded, although it was often painted as well.

The most adventurous uses of stucco can be found in the Umayyad palaces of Syria and Palestine. At Khirbet al-Mafjar in the Jordan valley the lavish decoration includes painted stucco statues of semi-naked bathing girls and stucco representation of the caliph himself. However, usually stucco was

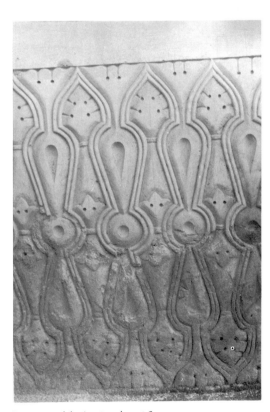

Stucco in serdab of main palace at Samarra

restricted to its original function of covering walls and ceilings with carved or moulded patterns. The largest corpus of stucco work from the early Islamic period has been found at the Abbasid capital of Samarra in Iraq. The stucco from this site has been divided into three groups or styles which may represent a chronological development. Style 'A' consists of vine leaves and vegetal forms derived from the Byzantine architecture of Syria–Palestine; style 'B' is a more abstract version of this; and style 'C' is entirely abstract with no recognizable representational forms. The first two styles appear to be carved, but the third style was produced by wooden moulds. The Samarra styles are significant as they reappear later in buildings such as the Ibn Tulun Mosque where the soffits of the arches are decorated with style 'B' ornament. After the collapse of the Abbasid caliphate stucco continued to be one of the main forms of decoration and spread throughout the Islamic world to India, Anatolia and Spain.

See also: Khirbet al-Mafjar, Samarra

Sudan

The Republic of Sudan is the largest country in Africa and spans the area between North Africa and sub-Saharan Africa.

Like Egypt, Sudan owes its existence to the Nile, which flows through the country from Kenya in the south to Egypt in the north. The western part of the country forms part of the Sahara desert whilst the area east of the Nile is divided between the Ethiopian Highlands and the Red Sea.

Although Islam is the official religion, Muslims only make up two-thirds of the population, the rest of whom are either Christian (4 per cent) or have tribal religions. Historically northern Sudan has always been dominated by its Egyptian neighbour to the north, nevertheless, throughout the medieval period (seventh to sixteenth centuries) a number of Christian urban centres such as Meroe and Kush have flourished. Islam became the principal religion of north Sudan in the early nineteenth century after the invasions of the Egyptian ruler Muhammad Ali. In the late nineteenth century there was a revolt against Turkish Egyptian rule which led to the establishment of a quasi-religious state ruled by the Mahdi. This state lasted for sixteen years until 1898 when the country was incorporated into the British Empire.

The materials of construction used in the Sudan vary greatly depending on the region and the people. On the Red Sea coast in the north of the country coral is the traditional material for permanent buildings, whereas in those parts bordering on the Nile, including Khartoum, mud is principally used.

There are few Islamic buildings in Sudan which date from before the nineteenth century, except in the Red Sea port of Suakin. This city which lies to the south of Port Sudan flourished under the Ottomans from the sixteenth century. Now almost entirely abandoned, Suakin provides a useful indication of the historic urban architecture of the Red Sea coast which has elsewhere mostly disappeared. The houses, many of them up to three storeys high, are built of coral slabs taken from the coastal foreshore.

In the Nile valley houses are traditionally built around two or three sides of a large central courtyard or compound. The standard method of construction is horizontal courses of mud and dung mixed with small stones and later covered with a plaster of smooth mud (jalus). The most striking feature of traditional houses in the area is the painted decoration made of mud- and lime-based pigments. Usually the outer façades of the houses are decorated with particular emphasis on the doors, whilst inside a principal reception room is also decorated.

See also: East Africa, Egypt, Somalia

Süleymaniye

Ottoman mosque complex in Istanbul built for Suleyman the Magnificent between 1550 and 1557.

The complex consisted of a hospital, medical school, hospice, soup kitchen, primary school, four madrassas (colleges), shops and coffee houses in addition to the mosque itself. The complex is built on an artificial platform on top of a hill that overlooks the Bosphorus; to the east the ground slopes away rapidly. The mosque precinct contains three main areas, the mosque itself in the centre, a courtyard to the north and a tomb garden to the south which contains the tomb of Suleyman and his wife. The mosque is covered with a large central dome (25 m diameter) with two large semidomes of equal radius, one above the north entrance and one above the mihrab. The central area is flanked by side aisles covered by small domes of alternating size. Like that of its predecessor the Şehzade Cami, the central dome rests on four huge central piers placed in a square. The whole building is illuminated with more than a hundred windows and grilles, many of which are filled with stained glass made by the celebrated Ottoman glass-maker Ibrahim Şarhoş. Outside at each corner of the courtyard are four minarets with balconies supported on muqarnas corbels. This is the first Ottoman building in Istanbul to have four minarets, although previously the Üç Şerefeli in Edirne also had four. The sides of the building are enlivened with several entrances (three on each side) approached by steps and two-tier arcaded galleries placed between the outer corner buttresses.

The tomb garden behind the mosque contains a large cemetery which has grown up around the tombs of Suleyman and Roxelane. Both tombs are octagonal structures in the traditional Ottoman fashion, although Suleyman's tomb unusually faces east instead of north. Roxelane's tomb is smaller and placed to one side of Suleyman's tomb which stands in the middle of the garden. The interiors of both tombs are decorated with Iznik tiles, although Roxelane's tomb is significantly less grand. Suleyman's tomb is surrounded by a colonnaded veranda with a porch on the east side. This arrangement is echoed internally where Suleyman's sarcophagus is surrounded by a circular colonnade.

The arrangement of the complex outside the mosque precinct consists of an L-shaped arrangement of buildings on the north-west side and a smaller group to the east. The eastern complex is built on a steep hill so the madrassas are stepped into the hillside. On the north-west corner of the complex is the tomb of the architect Sinan.

See also: Istanbul, Ottomans, Sinan

Sultan Hasan Mosque

Large madrassa, mosque and tomb complex in Cairo built by the Mamluk sultan Hasan.

This building was erected between 1356 and 1361 next to the Citadel of Cairo. The cost of the project was so high that it was never fully completed and Sultan Hasan himself was murdered and his body hidden, so that he was never buried in the mausoleum. It is a huge complex, measuring 65 by 140 m, and four storeys high, making it one of the largest mosques in Cairo. The main function of the building was as a madrassa with tomb attached but its size and the beauty of its prayer hall meant that it was recognized as a congregational mosque as well.

The basic plan of the building consists of a central courtyard leading off into four large iwans. The largest iwan is the prayer hall and behind this is the domed mausoleum. As this was a madrassa for the four rites of Sunni law there were four separate courtyards, one for each of the rites. Around each of these courtyards were the students' rooms arranged in four tiers. Many of the rooms were equipped with latrines and those facing the street had large windows.

The arch of the main iwan, or prayer hall, is very large and certainly the largest of its kind in Cairo. An inscription runs around the three walls of the iwan in an ornate Kufic on a background of floral scrolls which includes Chinese lotus flowers. The mausoleum is entered through a doorway to one side of the mihrab and consists of a domed chamber 21 m square and 30 m high. The original dome was wooden and has not survived, although the muqarnas wooden pendentives which carried it remain.

One of the most important aspects of the Sultan Hasan complex is the treatment of the external façades. Given its prominent position next to the citadel and the size of the complex it was important that its exterior reflected this. Each of the three sides of the mausoleum which projects on the south-east side of the complex consists of a central medallion around which are ranged four sets of windows, two above and two below. The most famous façade of the structure is that containing the entrance on the north side. The entrance-way itself consists of a large recess covered with an extravagant muqarnas vault which is comparable with that of the Gök Madrassa in Turkey. The doorway is set at an angle to the rest of the façade so that it can be seen when approaching along the street. The façade to the right of the doorway consists of long rectangular recesses extending four storeys from the base of the building to the top, each recess containing windows from the students' rooms. The height of this arrangement and its simplicity give this façade a strangely modern appearance.

Further reading:

D. Berhens-Abouseif, *Islamic Architecture in Cairo: An Introduction*, Supplements to Muqarnas, 3: 122–8, Leiden 1989.

J. M. Rogers, 'Seljuk influence in the monuments of Cairo', *Kunst des Orients* 7: 40 ff., 1970–1.

Sumatra

Most westerly large Indonesian island located west of the Malay peninsula and east of Java.

The first evidence for Islam in Indonesia comes from late thirteenth-century accounts of Marco Polo and Chinese documents which state that the region of Aceh on the northern tip of Sumatra was ruled by Muslim kingdoms. At this time the southern part of Sumatra was ruled by the Javanese kingdom of Majpahit which came to control most of the area of present-day Indonesia. Nevertheless, the Muslim states in the north of Sumatra began to spread, converting first the coastal peoples and only later the central area of Melayu. It was from Sumatra that Islam reached the Malay peninsula and gradually spread into Java itself. The Portuguese victory over Malacca in the early sixteenth century meant that Aceh once again became the main centre of Islam in the area. During the seventeenth century Sumatra was dominated by the ruler of Aceh, Iskandar Muda (1607–36) who had artillery, elephant and horse cavalry and a navy capable of carrying 700 men. The rule of Iskandar Muda's successor Iskandar Thani Alauddin Mughayat Syah (1636–41) was a period of cultural renaissance with several books written about the life of the court.

Unfortunately few early Islamic buildings survive in Sumatra probably because they were built of wood and frequently replaced. The earliest mosque of which records survive is the Masjid Agung Baiturrahman at Banda Aceh on the northern tip of Sumatra. It is likely that the present building stands on the site of one of the earliest mosques in Indonesia; however, the first records of the building (1612) describe an Indo-Islamic structure designed with the help of Dutch engineers. The building had three domes which were increased to five after a fire. However, it is likely that most early mosque forms were related to the traditional Sumatran house design. A recent example is the Rao-Rao Mosque in Batu Sangkar (west Sumatra) with an Indo-Islamic façade behind which is wooden mosque with a complex Sumatran roof-type known as rumah-adhat. This consists of a three-tiered pyramid roof construction with a small kiosk on top crowned with a tall finial.

The houses of Sumatra are one of the most distinctive features of the island and are world famous as examples of vernacular architecture. There are many regional house forms representing different cultural traditions, many of which predate Islam. The basic form of a Sumatran house consists of a building, set on upright piles driven into the ground, above which is a huge pitched roof. Wood is used for the piles and framework of the house, bamboo poles for the roof and the walls. Distinctively Islamic house types include the houses of Aceh, Minangkabu, Batak Mandailing and Lampung regions. The traditional Aceh house has a fairly basic design consisting of a rectangular platform resting on piles with a longitudinal gabled roof. Aceh houses are usually divided into three with the central area reserved for sleeping. The entrance is usually in the middle of one of the long sides and the gable ends are often decorated with geometric or other non-representational designs. The designs are either painted or carved, sometimes as fretwork panels. The most celebrated Sumatran house type is that of Minangkabu which has the entrance set in the middle of the long side. The roofs of the house are made up of a succession of pointed gables resembling the prow of a ship; the decoration is similar to that of the Aceh houses but may also include inset mirror work. The Batak Mandailing houses are similar to those of Minangkabu with roof ridges that sag in the middle and point upwards at the ends. The southern part of Sumatra, the Lampung area, is heavily influenced by neighbouring Java and Malaysia, and its houses are mostly of the coastal type.

Several palaces survive on Sumatra, the oldest of which is the seventeenth-century Aceh palace known as Dar al-Dunya. The building shares many characteristics with the Javanese palaces, or kratons, with many references to Hindu cosmology and little relationship to Islamic design. The Dar al-Dunya palace has the same north–south axis and three successive courtyards found in Java and, like the palaces of Yogyakarta and Surakarta, has a large formal garden. In the centre of the garden is a mountain-shaped structure with caves and ledges for meditation similar to the mountain representations of Java (e.g. Sunya Ragi). Nineteenth-century palaces show increasing Islamic and European influence, although there is still little relationship to the traditional wooden architecture of the island. The palace of Istana Maimun at Medan is laid out in a formal European style enlivened with arcades of horseshoe arches and crenellations.

See also: Indonesia, Java

Further reading:

E. M. Loeb, *Sumatra its History and People*, Oxford 1935.

D. Lombard, *Le Sultunat d'atjéh au temps d'iskandar Muda 1607–1636*, Publications de l'École Française d'extrême-Orient, 51, Paris 1967.

G. Serjeant, 'House form and decoration in Sumatra', *Art and Archaeology Research Papers* no. 12, 1977.

Susa

Tunisian coastal city noted for its ninth-century Aghlabid buildings.

Under the Byzantines the city was known as Justinianopolis in honour of Justinian who rebuilt it after the Vandal destruction. In 689 CE it was captured by the Arabs and became one of the principal ports for the Aghlabid conquest of Sicily. In 827 the city was refortified with ramparts and walls built in the Byzantine style. Important Aghlabid buildings within the city include the ribat built or restored by Ziyadat Allah in 821, the Bu

Fatata Mosque built in 840 and the Great Mosque established in 859.

See also: Aghlabids, Tunisia

Syria (Arabic: al-Sham)

Geographically Syria may be defined as the northern part of Arabia between the Mediterranean and the Euphrates river. This area includes Lebanon, Palestine and Jordan as well as the modern state of Syria. Politically Syria refers to the modern state of Syria which roughly corresponds to the northern part of the geographical area of Syria excluding the mountains of Lebanon and including parts of the Jazira between the Euphrates and the Tigris. (Here the term Syria will be used to identify the area of the modern Arab Republic.) The majority of Syria's population lives within 100 km of the Mediterranean whilst there is lesser concentration of people along the Euphrates river valley. The area between the coastal strip and the Euphrates is sparsely populated semi-desert.

Syria was relatively densely populated in Roman and Byzantine times, with large cities such as

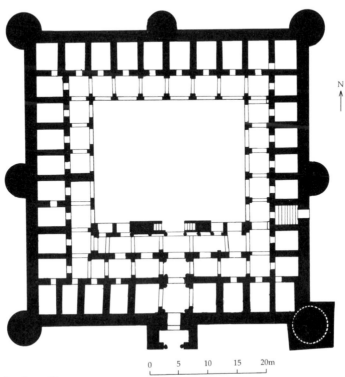

Ribat at Susa, Tunisia (after Creswell)

Syria (Arabic: al–Sham)

Muqarnas dome, Hospital of Nur al-Din, Damascus, Syria,
© *Rebecca Foote*

Palmyra, Rusafa and Sergiopolis developing in the eastern part of the country. Traditionally it has been thought that the Arab conquest of the seventh century bought an end to this wealthy urbanization. Recent studies, however, have shown that there was a more complex sequence of events, which led to the growth of different parts of the country and different areas of cities. What is certain is that the eastern part of the country, in particular Damascus and Raqqa were developed in the Umayyad and early Abbasid periods. Damascus flourished under the Umayyads who established it as the capital of their vast empire. The topography of Damascus changed very little from late Byzantine times and the only major addition was the construction of the Great Mosque. Elsewhere cities such as Palmyra, Bostra and Raqqa continued to be inhabited with few changes from the Byzantine plan. However, a major change in the Umayyad period was the development of desert settlements such as Qasr al-Hayr (East and West). These

settlements relied on the increased trade and mobility offered by a situation where both eastern and western parts of the desert were united under Islamic rule. The Abbasid revolution in the mid-eighth century brought about a radical change in the orientation of the Islamic world, where the lands of the former Sassanian Empire became central and the west declined in importance. The result in Syria was a decline in wealth and urbanization exacerbated by the growth of a rival caliphate (the Fatimids) in Egypt. During the ninth and tenth centuries Syria was in the middle of a three-way conflict between the Abbasids and their successors, the Fatimids and the Byzantines.

During the eleventh century the Seljuk Turks established themselves in the north of the country. By the end of the eleventh century the Great Seljuk Empire had divided into a number of independent principalities, or Atabegs. The arrival of the Crusaders in the early twelfth century imposed a sense of unity on the Muslim principalities which made itself felt under Salah al-Din and his Ayyubid successors. During the thirteenth century Syria was subjected to a series of Mongol invasions which were repulsed by the Mamluks who had replaced the Ayyubids as rulers of Syria. There were further Mongol raids in the fifteenth century led by the Central Asian ruler Timur. Despite the successive waves of invaders Syria seems to have been prosperous in the Middle Ages and some of the finest artistic and architectural works were carried out during this period.

In 1516 the Mamluks were defeated and Syria was incorporated into the Ottoman Empire. The country thrived during the first century of Ottoman rule with many khans established in the major cities as well in the countryside. The Ottoman Hajj (pilgrimage) route to Mecca was of great importance during this period with Damascus established as the starting-point. During the eighteenth century Europeans seem to have become increasingly involved in the commerce of the region. Cotton was of particular importance and many Europeans established consulates in the coastal cities in order to control this trade. In the nineteenth century there seems to have been an economic decline with less European trade and increasing interference from Egypt, culminating in the invasion of 1831. Administrative reforms were introduced in the latter part of the nineteenth century which led to Syria being regarded as one of the most advanced parts of the Ottoman Empire. The collapse of Turkish rule in 1918 led to the creation of a French protectorate which formed the basis of the modern independent republic.

The building materials used in Syria vary depending on the area and type of settlement. On the Mediterranean coast houses are generally stone built, often of ashlar masonry; their general appearance is that of Lebanese houses. In the mountains buildings are made out of rubble stone with mud mortar, their roofs made of wooden beams covered with matting and an exterior coating of earth. The region of the Hauran in the south-east is predominantly basalt desert with no trees. Basalt has been the main material of construction since ancient times and many traditional houses re-use ancient material because of its indestructibility and the difficulty of carving new basalt blocks. One of the principal forms of house construction is to have transverse arches carrying short basalt beams which form the roof. Houses in the Aleppo region are built of mud brick with conical mud domes resembling beehives. Several buildings joined together within a courtyard form a single house. In central Syria the traditional house is a rectangular mud-brick building with a flat roof. These houses are usually surrounded by a courtyard wall which may also include animal pens. In addition to permanent settlements many people are traditionally nomadic or semi-nomadic. Black goat-hair tents are the principal form of bedouin tent used in the region. The main cities also have their own methods of construction which differ from those of the countryside.

See also: Aleppo, Basra, Damascus, Lebanon, Qasr al-Hayr East, Qasr al-Hayr West, Raqqa

T

tabhane

Turkish term for the hostel attached to a mosque where travellers (usually dervishes and mystics) could live free for three days. In early Ottoman mosques these formed separate chambers although they were later incorporated into the main body of the mosque.

Taj Mahal

Major Islamic tomb complex built by the Mughal emperor at Agra in India.

The Taj Mahal was begun by Shah Jahan in 1631 and took over twenty years to build. The tomb was built for Shah Jahan's wife Arjumand Banu Begam (also known as Mumtaz Mahal) who he married in 1612 before he was made emperor. She was the niece of Jahangir's wife Nur Jahan and granddaughter of his famous Persian minister Iltimad al-Daulah. Mumtaz Mahal was the emperor's favourite wife and during nineteen years of marriage she bore him fourteen children. Her death whilst accompanying him on a campaign in the Deccan caused the emperor great sorrow and inspired him to build the most beautiful tomb complex in the world.

Although unique in its size and beauty, the Taj Mahal forms part of a series of imperial Mughal tombs of which it is undoubtedly the greatest. The earliest Mughal tombs copied those of their Islamic predecessors the Lodi sultans of Delhi and were octagonal domed structures surrounded by arcades. Another popular tomb form in the early Mughal period was the square chamber-tomb as seen in the 'Barber's tomb' in Delhi. Later on in the Mughal period the two forms were combined to produce octagonal tombs with four sides shorter than the others, thus producing a square with the corners cut off. In the tomb of Humayun at Delhi four of these 'square' octagons were assembled around a central octagonal space which was then covered with a dome. The area between the octagons was bridged by iwans which formed the main access points to the central domed area. This is essentially the same design that was used in the Taj Mahal. In Humayun's tomb, however, the central area is surrounded on four sides by an arcade of pointed arches at ground level and is made of red sandstone with marble inlay, neither of which features are found in the Taj Mahal. Similarly the dome on the roof is lower set than in the Taj Mahal so that it does not produce a dominant upright form but rather a pyramidal one.

The Taj Mahal is located on a terrace on the banks of the Jumna river and can be seen from the emperor's palace in the Agra Fort. The building is part of a complex which included many buildings beside the central tomb and garden; to the south is a complex known as the 'chauk-i jilau khana', or ceremonial forecourt, which was flanked by four courtyards (two on each side) containing apartments for the tomb attendants; directly south of these is a further area divided into four caravanserais by two intersecting streets, and south of this are two more caravanserais and a bazar built around a square. A residential area grew up around this complex which was known as Mumtazabad. The revenue of this village together with that of thirty other villages in the vicinity was devoted to the upkeep of the building.

Like many other Mughal memorial tombs the Taj Mahal was incorporated into a formal garden of the Persian char bagh form where a square garden wall encloses a garden divided equally into four. In most tomb complexes the tomb forms the centre of the garden with the four parts arranged equally around it. In the case of the Taj Mahal, however, a square pool forms the centre of the garden whilst the tomb building was located at the far end of it, overlooking the river. The walls of the garden tomb complex are strengthened by six octagonal towers capped with domed chatris. The gate to the complex consists of a large rectangular structure with engaged corner turrets placed in the middle of a tall wall which effectively screens the

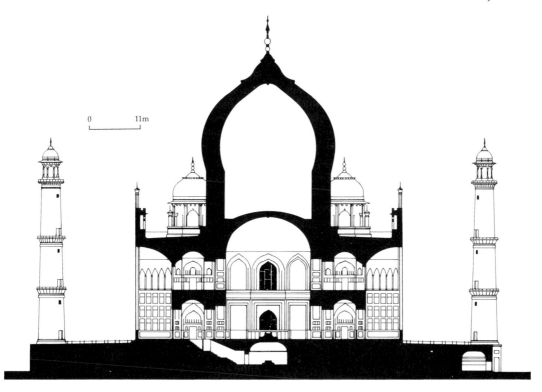

Section through Taj Mahal (after Tillotson)

Taj Mahal from view until the visitor has passed through the gate. The effect of this is enhanced by the fact that the outer buildings of the complex and the gateway are built and faced in red sandstone whereas the tomb and minarets are faced in white marble.

The central part of the complex is raised on a rectangular podium decorated with arcades of blind niches. At each corner of the podium is an octagonal base for a minaret whilst the tomb stands in the centre. The gate is directly in line with the centre of the dome on the tomb, a symmetry which is emphasized by the minarets, two either side of the tomb. Each minaret is a tall (42 m), slightly tapering, cylindrical structure with two intermediate balconies and an open domed pavilion (chatri) on the top. Long pools divide the garden into four parts, one running east–west and the other running north–south from the gate to the Taj Mahal. At either end of the east–west axis are large triple-domed buildings with a central iwan. The building on the west side is a mosque whilst that to the east is known as the 'jawab', or echo, as

it has no other function than to balance the view with the mosque on the other side. The north–south pools further emphasize the central axis of the gateway and dome.

The Taj Mahal has the same basic form as Humayun's tomb and consists of four octagons arranged around a central domed space. The façade of the tomb consists of a tall central iwan framed by a pishtaq which contains a frame of Quranic calligraphy flanked on each side by four smaller iwans, two on each storey. The iwans are all composed of four centre-pointed arches with pietra dura decoration in the spandrels. The corners of the building are cut off or chamfered with projecting pillars marking the change from one face to another. The central dome is flanked by four large domed chatris supported on piers between lobed arches. The domes on the chatris and the central dome represent a synthesis of Persian and Indian architecture where the bulbous form of the dome is derived from Persian Timurid architecture and the finial and its lotus base derive ultimately from Hindu temple architecture.

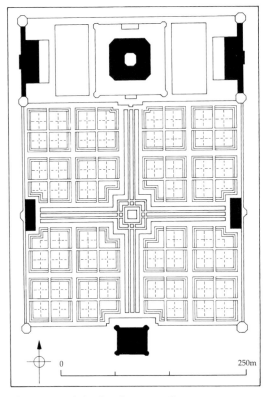

Plan of Taj Mahal and gardens (after Tillotson)

The central dome of the Taj Mahal is very tall (the finial is 73 m above ground level) and is raised up above the pishtaqs of the surrounding iwans by a tall circular drum about 15 m high. The dome is composed of two parts, an inner dome and an outer shell. The inner dome is approximately the same height as the iwans whilst the outer dome towers above. The use of an inner dome keeps the height of the inner space in proportion whilst the outer dome makes the height of the building correspond to its mass and with the minarets makes building stand out visually. Directly below the centre of the dome is the cenotaph of Mumtaz Mahal and next to it that of her husband Shah Jahan. The actual tombs, however, are in a vault or cave directly beneath the cenotaphs. The cenotaphs in the main chamber are surrounded by an octagonal pierced screen with two gates with pietra dura inlay on the posts. The walls of the interior are divided into blind arches alternating with arched doorways which give access to the four circular side chambers. Around

each of the arches is a frame of Quranic inscriptions whilst the marble dadoes are also lavishly decorated with naturalistic depictions of flowers in low relief. The whole arrangement of the tomb, in particular the octagonal screen and the cave beneath, recalls the arrangement of the Dome of the Rock in Jerusalem. The reasons for this are probably coincidental and may simply reflect the fact that whilst octagonal mausoleums are rare in the Middle East they were common in India and there was no religious awareness of its significance.

As the finest example of Mughal funerary architecture it is not surprising that the design of the Taj Mahal was subsequently copied and developed in later tombs. The most obvious copy is the tomb of Rabi'a Daurani in Aurangabad built in 1660 which has the same arrangement of a central tomb on a podium with minarets at each corner. The Aurangabad tomb, however, is different because the central building is square instead of octagonal and the minarets are thicker and taller in proportion to the central structure. A more interesting version of this design is the tomb of Safdar Jang in Delhi built in 1753. This building is also square like the tomb at Aurangabad, but here the minarets are attached to the central structure instead of standing apart at the corners of the terrace. Instead of white marble the building is faced in red sandstone with white marble inlay.

See also: Mughals

Further reading:

W. F. Begley, 'Amanat Khan and the calligraphy on the Taj Mahal', *Kunst des Orients* 12: 5–39, 1978–9.
—— 'The myth of the Taj Mahal and a new theory about its symbolic meaning', *The Art Bulletin* 61: 7–37, 1979.
W. E. Begley and Z. A. Desai, *Taj Mahal: The Illumined Tomb: An Anthology of Seventeenth Century Mughal and European Documentary Sources*, The Agha Khan Program for Islamic Architecture, Cambridge, Mass. 1989.
D. Brandenburg, *Der Taj Mahal in Agra*, Berlin 1969.
S. Gole, 'From Tamerlane to the Taj Mahal', in *Islamic Art and Architecture: Essays in Honour of of Katherina Otto–Dorn 1*, ed. A. Daneshavari, 1981, 43–50.
R. A. Jairazbhoy, 'The Taj Mahal in the context of East and West: a study in comparative method', *Journal of the Warburg and Courtauld Institutes* 24: 59–88, 1961.
R. Nath, *The Immortal Taj Mahal: The Evolution of the Tomb in Mughal Architecture*, New Delhi 1972.

talar

Iranian term for a hypostyle wooden hall which proceeds through the main part of a building.

taman

Indonesian term for a pleasure garden, usually associated with the royal palaces, or kraton. Taman gardens usually have a central tower, or artificial mountain, surrounded or approached by water, which in pre-Islamic tradition symbolizes mountain and sea.

See also: Java, kraton

Tanzania

Country in East Africa bordering on the Indian Ocean with a substantial Swahili-speaking Muslim population on the coast.

Tanzania forms part of the Islamic coast of East Africa which stretches from Somalia in the north to Mozambique in the south. Before 1970 the country was known as Tanganyika but following independence it united with Zanzibar to form the present state of Tanzania with its capital at Dar es Salaam. However, the two former countries retain autonomy and only the former territory of Tanganyika will be dealt with here (see separate entry for Zanzibar).

The earliest Islamic settlements in Tanzania can be traced back to at least the eighth century CE and appear to be related to the Indian Ocean dhow trade. The famous site of Kilwa on an island off the south coast contains traces of ninth-century Islamic structures, but unfortunately these are too fragmentary to reconstruct their form beyond establishing that they were built of mud over wooden frames. However, from the tenth-century levels of the site remains were found of an early stone mosque which, although not fully excavated, appears to conform to the same plan as early mosques elsewhere on the coast (e.g. the use of coursed coral blocks). Apart from archaeological sites the majority of Islamic monuments on the coast date from the period before 1200. The earliest standing monuments on the coast are the early mosque at Kaole and the mosque at Sanje ya Kati.

The ruins at Kaole consist of about fifteen tombs, two of which have pillars, and two mosques. The early mosque dates from the thirteenth century whilst the later one was probably built sometime in the sixteenth century. The early mosque has several unusual features not found later. It consists of a rectangular hall approximately 4 by 6 m north–south. Originally there was a set of masonry columns running down the centre of the structure which would have supported a flat roof. Access to the flat roof is by means of a staircase at the south end of the building. Either side of the central prayer hall were narrow side aisles (about 1 m wide) which were later enlarged. Architecturally the most interesting feature of the building is the mihrab. The mihrab arch consists of a plain border approximately 20 cm wide with a round arch containing a pointed niche at the apex. The panelled apse of the mihrab which projects out of the wall is probably a later fourteenth-century addition and it is likely that the original mihrab was set within the thickness of the wall. The mihrab arch is built out of roughly squared blocks covered with plaster to produce a smooth finish. This is an unusual technique which is not found in later mosques where the mihrab is usually made out of dressed coral blocks. The ablution area of the mosque is situated to the south of the prayer hall rather than to the east which became more usual later. The ablution area consists of a square well next to a rectangular tank covered with a barrel vault and a rectangular foot scraping area. Both the barrel vault and the footscraper consist of raw blocks of coral set in mortar, features which are unusual and may be a sign of early mosques.

The later mosque of Kaole is larger than its earlier neighbour and consisted of a central prayer hall supported by two rows of wooden columns. Each column was sunk deep into the ground and was encased in an octagonal masonry collar where it met the plastered floor of the mosque. Like the early mosque, the ablutions area is at the south end of the building which is unusual in mosques of this date and may well result from the influence of the earlier structure.

Other important medieval sites in Tanzania include the ruins at Kilwa, Tongoni, Kunduchi and Mafia island. The ruins of Kilwa form a group on their own noted for the dense concentration of buildings and independent architectural development. Kilwa is the only place on the coast where dome construction was widespread and the only place where a significant continuity of occupation can be traced from the thirteenth to the sixteenth century.

Tongoni (from Swahili meaning 'ruins') is located on the north coast of Tanzania near the mouth of the Pangani river. The settlement, originally known as Mtangata, was founded in the fourteenth century and flourished until the arrival of the Portuguese in the sixteenth century, although it continued to be inhabited until the eighteenth, when it was finally abandoned. Remains at the site include a mosque and over forty tombs, of which nearly half are pillar tombs, which makes it the largest concentration of this form of monument on the coast. Only one of these pillars is still standing, although the size and shapes of fallen pillars can be worked out. Most of the pillars are cylindrical, although some have square and octagonal sections and nearly all have concave recesses or indentations which contained imported ceramic bowls (usually Chinese celadon ware). The mosque consists of a narrow central prayer hall, with a roof supported on a central row of four columns and two side aisles. Accessible through open archways at the south end is a transverse room which may have been used as a separate area for women.

The ruins of Kunduchi are located next to a creek 20 km north of Dar es Salaam. The earliest remains at the site date from the fourteenth century which continued in use until the nineteenth century. The standing remains consist of a mosque and cemetery containing pillar tombs. The mosque was built in the fifteenth century, although most of the pillar tombs are from the eighteenth, which represents one of the latest groups of pillar tombs.

The island of Mafia is located at the end of the Rufiji delta about 15 km offshore. There are extensive remains of several eighteenth- and nineteenth-century settlements on the island. The most famous of these, known as Kua, contains five mosques (at least) and the remains of many eighteenth-century houses. The mosques have a variety of mihrab types which were developed in later nineteenth-century mosques. The mihrabs at Kua include apses decorated with blind arcades and an early example of a recessed stepped minbar in the Friday mosque. The houses at Kua are unique on the East African coast and consist of two identical halves with a single entrance. A typical house is entered through

Nine-domed mosque, Kilwa, Tanzania. Note pillar above central dome

a single gateway leading into a long transverse room; behind this is a doorway leading to two separate L-shaped passages which lead into a long reception room that opens on to a courtyard on one side and a small private room (harem) on the inner side. Sometimes there are additional buildings in the courtyard and sometimes there are two separate entrances. It is thought that the two identical halves may represent the family houses of two wives rather than a men's and a women's section. Nineteenth- and twentieth-century Islamic architecture in Tanzania is best represented in the cities of Bagamoyo and Dar es Salaam. Bagamoyo was the capital of German East Africa before the First World War and contains the various elements associated with a small colonial capital. The architecture is an interesting mixture of styles including Omani Arab, German, German Orientalist (i.e. Ottoman) and Swahili. Many of the more important government buildings are built in the style of Omani palaces with external verandas and carved wooden doors — the important addition of steel girders enabling larger spaces to be covered without support. After the defeat of the Germans in the First World War, Dar es Salaam replaced Bagamoyo as capital. Like the Germans in Bagamoyo the British in Dar es Salaam built official buildings in an Oriental style with modern materials; some of the more notable ones are the National Museum with its Turkish tiles and the old hospital.

See also: East Africa, Kilwa, Zanzibar

Further reading:

H. N. Chittick, *Annual Reports of the Department of Antiquities*, Dar es Salaam 1958–64.

G. S. P. Freeman-Grenville, *The Medieval History of the Coast of Tanganyika*, London 1962.

P. S. Garlake, *The Early Islamic Architecture of the East African Coast*, Memoir No. 1 of the British Institute in Eastern Africa, London and Nairobi 1966.

Tanganyika Notes and Records, Dar es Salaam 1959 onwards.

taq

Iranian term for an arch.

tekke

Also known as a dergah, a tekke is a lodge for dervishes. Tekkes are a frequent occurrence in Turkish architecture and are usually part of a complex which includes a mosque and memorial tomb. They may be regarded as the counterpart of the more orthodox madrassa. A tekke often consists of a number of individual cells which are used as shelters for the dervishes.

See also: Edirne, Ottomans, Turkey

tilework

Glazed tiles are one of the most characteristic features of Islamic architecture.

Three distinct tile formats were developed which may be characterized as single tiles, composite tile panels and tile mosaics. Single tiles are complete compositions which may include abstract designs or figural representation but are independent of other tiles. Composite tile panels consist of several tiles carrying a design or picture which together form a complete composition. Tile mosaics are made of many pieces of monochrome coloured tile which are joined together to form a picture. There is also a fourth category which consists of three-dimensional glazed ceramics which are used to form architectural features such as mihrabs. The decoration of tiles may be classified according to the various techniques used, which are similar to those used on pottery. The simplest technique is to paint a tile with a monochrome glaze before firing. Extra colours may be added by coating the glaze with lustre after the first firing and then firing the tile a second time at a lower temperature. More complex polychrome tiles may be produced by using a technique known as 'cuerda seca' which uses coloured glazes separated by outlines made of a greasy substance which burns away after firing. Other techniques include overglaze painting (known as 'minai'), underglaze painting and relief moulded designs.

The earliest dated examples of Islamic tiles are those around the mihrab of the Great Mosque of Qairawan which were produced in Iraq sometime before 862 CE. These are square tiles (21 cm per side) decorated with abstract and vegetal forms in polychrome and monochrome lustre on a white ground. From the eleventh century onwards tiles replaced mosaics as the main form of wall decoration in many parts of the Islamic world. Three main tile-making traditions can be distinguished: these are Spain and North Africa, Turkey and Iran.

In Seljuk Iran the exterior surfaces of brick buildings were enlivened by blue-green glazed bricks or tiles whilst alternating star- and cross-shaped minai tiles were used to decorate interiors. Other techniques developed during the Seljuk period include tile mosaics and decorative inscriptions which were generally restricted to blue, black, turquoise and green as the main pigments. In the fourteenth century potters working in Tabriz developed the cuerda seca technique which enabled them to adopt complex Chinese patterns. This technique continued to be used during the Saffavid period and it was not until the nineteenth century that underglaze painting was introduced to Iranian tilework. The tilework of Iran also influenced the architecture of India to the east, in particular the area of present-day Pakistan. Generally Indian glazed tilework was restricted to tile mosaics and can be seen in the magnificent 'Picture Wall' at Lahore Fort. Indian craftsmen took the tile mosaic one stage further when they developed the technique of mirror mosaics which was later adopted in Iran.

In Spain and North Africa a technique of tile mosaic, known as zilij, was developed using yellow, green, blue and turquoise tiles. In the eighteenth century the Ottomans introduced the techniques of polychrome panels made of square or rectangular tiles. One of the main centres of production was Tunis, where tiles were decorated with green, yellow and blue designs. Before the fifteenth century several different formats of tile decoration were used in Anatolia which included tile mosaic, hexagonal, octagonal, star- and cross-shaped tiles. In the fourteenth century the Ottomans adopted the Persian technique of cuerda seca for the brilliant green tiles which characterize early Ottoman mosques such as the Yeşil Cami in Bursa. However, the most significant development came in the sixteenth century when the potteries of Iznik began producing tilework for imperial use. The achievement of Iznik potters was to produce tiles with underglaze colours which remained stable under the glaze. Characteristic colours of Iznik tiles are blue, turquoise and red against a white background.

See also: Iznik, tilework

Further reading:

J. Hedgecoe and S. S. Damulji, *Zillij: The Art of Moroccan Ceramics*, New York, NY 1993.
J. M. Scarce, 'Function and decoration in Qajar tilework', *Persian Art and Culture of the 18th and 19th Centuries*, Edinburgh 1979.

Timbuktu (also known as Tombouctou)

Famous Islamic trading city in Mali, West Africa.

Timbuktu is located on the southern edge of the Sahara several kilometres north of the Niger river. According to tradition the city originated as a nomadic Tuareg encampment in the twelfth century. The encampment would have consisted of tents made out of acacia wood frames covered over with mats and animal-skin canopies. In 1325 the city was conquered by Mansa Musa who incorporated it into the empire of Mali. During this period the famous Andalusian poet and architect Abu Ishaq al-Saheli visited the city and built a mosque there. Several years later in 1333 the city was burnt and pillaged in an attack by Mossi tribesmen from Yatenga (present-day Upper Volta) although it was later rebuilt by Sulayman the emperor of Mali. The rule of Mali ended in the fifteenth century and for the next forty years the city was controlled by Tuareg nomads until its annexation by Ali the ruler of Gao in 1468. During this time Timbuktu became the main centre for the trade with North Africa and enjoyed its greatest period of prosperity. This was brought to an abrupt end with the Moroccan invasion of 1591, although the city managed to remain more or less independent until 1787 when it passed into the control of the Tuareg. In the nineteenth century the city was incorporated into the Fulbe state of Massina and remained under nominal Fulbe control until the advent of French colonialism in the late nineteenth century. Despite these conquests by various groups and dynasties, Timbuktu remained substantially independent for most of its history due to its position on the border of the desert.

The first known European visitor was Caillié who wrote the following description of the city in 1828: 'The city of Timbuktu forms a sort of triangle, measuring about three miles in circuit. The houses are large, but not high, consisting entirely of a ground floor. In some a sort of water closet is constructed above the entrance.' The city has retained this triangular configuration into recent times although new houses have been built around the central core. The city is divided into five districts, or quarters, traditionally inhabited by different ethnic groups – the Ba Dinde, the Saré-kaina, the Bella Faraji, the Sankoré and the Dijingueré Ber. The Dijingueré Ber quarter is generally thought to be the oldest Muslim part of the city and in earlier times may have been separated from the rest of the town with its own city wall. The Saré-kaina quarter, also known as the Sané-gungu quarter, is the area inhabited by the rulers and political élite; in this area are the largest houses and also the remains of the Moroccan kasbah built on the site of the Songhay royal palace. The Sankoré quarter in the north-west tip of the city is the area formerly inhabited by the Berber tribes and is said to have been founded by Sidi Mahmoud a sixteenth-century immigrant from Oualata. The main material of construction in Timbuktu is mud brick, although stone is used for strengthening the walls and in important places such as doorways. Early nineteenth-century descriptions of the city describe the making of hand-rolled round bricks which are then baked in the sun. Roofs are made of split palm beams and palm-frond matting which is then covered with earth. Construction is in the hands of a group of

Songhay-speaking people known as the 'gabibi' who are also responsible for gravedigging.

The major monuments of the city are the three ancient mosques each located in a different quarter of the city. Reputedly the oldest building is the Sankoré Mosque, which was founded by a woman during one of the periods of Tuareg rule, possibly during the thirteenth century. The building was subsequently repaired, rebuilt and developed so that in its present form it consists of an irregular form based around a square central courtyard. This courtyard seems to represent an early phase of the mosque's development as it conforms to the dimensions of the courtyard built by Qadi al-Aqib in 1581. On the south-east corner of the mosque is a small, square, entrance vestibule built during Fulbe rule in the nineteenth century to serve as a Shar'ia court. The mosque contains two mihrabs, a small one in the east wall of the interior courtyard and a larger one in the east wall of the sanctuary. The larger mihrab is located north of the centre of the

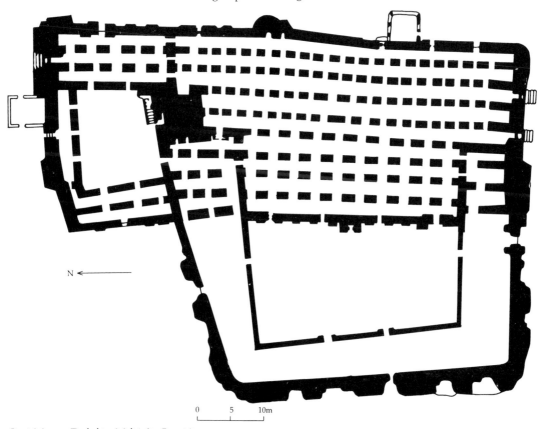

N ←

0 5 10m

Great Mosque, Timbuktu, Mali (after Prussin)

east wall and externally consists of a tower-like conical projection similar to that of the Dijinguéré Ber Mosque. The dominant feature of the building is the minaret on the south side of the courtyard, consisting of a large stepped pyramid similar to that of the mausoleum of Askiya Muhammad at Gao. However, the Sankoré minaret is slightly smaller and has an internal staircase instead of external stair ramps as at Gao.

The most famous mosque in Timbuktu is the Dijinguéré Ber Mosque, which was built between 1324 and 1327 by Mansa Musa emperor of Mali after his return from the Hajj. The mosque is attributed to the architect Abu Isahq al-Saheli who built a royal audience chamber at the same time. Today there is no trace of the audience chamber which may have resembled that of the capital at Niani described by contemporary Arab travellers. Like most other ancient buildings in the city the mosque underwent several successive stages of construction and repairs. As it stands at present the plan of mosque consists of a roughly rectangular sanctuary with a small internal courtyard at the northern end and a large double-walled external courtyard on the western side. The oldest part of the mosque is generally agreed to be the western part of the sanctuary. In this part there are round arches made of dressed limestone supporting the roof, a feature not found elsewhere in West Africa until the colonial period. Like the Sankoré Mosque the Dijinguéré Ber has two towers, a conical mihrab tower with projecting toron (acacia wood stakes) and a tapering square minaret adjacent to the interior courtyard.

The third ancient mosque in Timbuktu is the small complex in the centre of the city known as the mosque of Sidi Yahyia built in the mid-fifteenth century. This consists of a rectangular sanctuary attached to a short, square, tapering minaret enclosed within a large outer courtyard. The sanctuary is four bays deep and has three entrances on the short northern side and two entrances in the eastern wall either side of the wide shallow central mihrab. According to tradition, the first imam of the mosque is buried under the minaret, a concept that parallels the stepped pyramid minarets of the Gao and Sankoré mosques.

The houses of Timbuktu are either single-storey or two-storey courtyard houses. The two-storey houses tend to be more elaborate and are mostly confined to the Sané-gungu quarter inhabited by

the chief merchants. From the outside the houses are generally quite plain with shallow square buttresses dividing the wall into panels. The doorways are fairly simple with wooden doors decorated with Moroccan brass bosses, although this has been superseded by snipped tin decoration. Above the main doorway is a single window, decorated, containing a Moroccan-style hardwood grille. Each grille consists of two parts, opening shutters recessed within a horseshoe arch on the top and the wooden grille below made of intersecting wooden strips (cf. mashrabiyya). The houses are entered via an outer and inner vestibule which leads out on to a square courtyard from which the other rooms of the house can be reached. In a two-storey building there are men's rooms either side of the courtyard, whilst in a single-storey house the single men's room is to the right of the entrance. In larger houses there is usually a secondary courtyard for women behind the main courtyard. In two-storey houses latrines are usually on the upper floor above a sealed latrine shaft (sekudar).

See also: Agades, Oualata, West Africa

Further reading:

R. J. and S. K. McIntosh, 'Archaeological reconnaisance in the region of Timbuktu, Mali', *National Geographic Research* 2: 302–19, 1986.

L. Prussin, *Hatumere: Islamic Design in West Africa*, Berkeley 1986.

Timurids

Central Asian dynasty founded by Timur which flourished from the end of the fourteenth century to the end of the fifteenth.

Timur was born a member of the Barlas tribe and claimed descent from the Mongol Khan Chatagay. By 1370 Timur had gained control of Samarkand and Balkh after which he spent ten years consolidating his control of Central Asia. From 1381 Timur extended the range of his operations and managed to gain control of Iran, Iraq, Syria, the Caucasus and Delhi. In 1402 Timur's excursions into Anatolia brought him into conflict with the Ottoman sultan Bayazit whom he defeated and captured at the battle of Ankara. One of the results of these wide-ranging conquests was the collection of skilled craftsmen from all over the Middle East who were used to enrich the new capital at Samarkand. Timur died in 1405 and was succeeded by his son Shah Rukh who ruled the empire from Herat where he had been governor during the reign of Timur.

Samarkand was ruled by Shah Rukh's son Ulugh Beg whilst Fars was ruled first by his nephew Ibrahim. By the mid-fifteenth century the western provinces were mostly lost to the Turkmans leaving Herat as capital of a much diminished empire which continued until 1507 when it was taken over by the Turkmans.

The main building material employed for imperial monuments was baked brick although dressed stone was used in Azerbayjan. The standard brick form was square (24–27 cm per side and 4–7 cm thick) whilst cut or moulded bricks were relatively rare compared with earlier periods. Mortar was usually quick-setting gypsum plaster rather than the more common lime plaster. The standard method of exterior decoration was tile revetments which were on a larger scale than in previous periods. Two main forms of tilework were used, tile mosaic, with individual coloured pieces cut to form patterns, and underglaze-painted tiles known as 'haft rangi' (seven colours). The underglaze-painted tiles tended to be of a lower quality but were useful for covering large areas. A large variety of arch forms were used including round, two-, three-, and four-centre arches, although the most common was the three-centred arch with a high crown, where the height of the arch was more than half the height of the entire opening. A large variety of domes and vaults were employed which displays the wide range of influences in Timurid architecture. One of the most significant vaulting forms employed was based on the use of wide transverse arches spanning between parallel walls. Vaults of various forms were then built to cover the area between each transverse arch to produce a large vaulted area. The vaults used to span the arches included tunnel or barrel vaults, stellar vaults and cross vaults, all of which produce characteristic humps on the roofs of buildings.

Dome forms became increasingly distinctive under the Timurids with the development of double-shell domes where there is an outer dome and a shallower inner dome. The characteristic outer dome form consists of a tall 'melon-shaped' structure set on a high drum and decorated with ribs covered in decorative tilework.

The most characteristic feature of Timurid imperial buildings is their massive scale, emphasized by huge entrance portals and thick minarets covered in tile decoration. Internally the buildings are slightly less well organized and they often have a large variety of smaller rooms whose relationship to the overall plan is not always evident. The most famous of the Timurid monuments are the shrine of Ahmed Yasavi at Turkestan (Yasi) in Khazakstan and the Masjid Jami' at Samarkand. The monuments are quite similar in their scale and conception with huge portal iwans behind which rise characteristic melon-shaped domes on high collars or drums. The Ahmed Yasavi tomb was built by Timur for his son Jahangir whilst the Masjid Jami' at Samarkand was built to commemorate the Timurid capture of Delhi. Other monumental projects carried out by Timur include the mausoleums at Shahrisbaz (his first capital) for his father Taraghay and the Gur-i-Amir for his son Muhammad Sultan at Samarkand. In addition Timur undertook massive civil engineering projects including building the towns of Baylaqan, Shahrukhiya and Iryah, the citadels and walls of Ghazui, Balkh and Samarkand.

The later Timurid buildings of Herat in Afghanistan mirror those of the early Timurid Empire, although many were destroyed in the nineteenth century. One of the most celebrated buildings in Herat was the mosque and madrassa built by the architect Qavam al-Din for the wife of Shah Rukh. Little is left of the complex except for two minarets at diagonally opposite corners of the mosque and a minaret and iwan from the madrassa. The best preserved Timurid structure in Herat is the shrine of the mystic of Khwajeh 'Abdallah Ansari at Gazur Gah. The complex is built on the plan of a four-iwan madrassa and oriented to the qibla (i.e. east–west) with the entrance in the centre of the west façade. The entrance portal consists of a large iwan, half-octagonal in plan, leading into the rectangular central courtyard. There is a mosque and cells for mystics at the western end, whilst at the eastern end is a shallow iwan set into a tall pishtaq.

See also: Herat, Iran, Samarkand

Further reading:

L. Golombek and D. L. Wilber, *The Timurid Architecture of Iran and Turan*, Princeton, NJ 1988.

B. O'Kane, *Timurid Architecture in Khurassan*, Costa Mesa, CA 1987.

Tlemcen

City in western Algeria noted for its medieval architecture.

Tlemcen was founded in the eighth century on the ruins of the Roman city of Pomaria although it did not rise to prominence until the Almoravid period in the eleventh century. The most important Almoravid contribution to the city was the Great Mosque which survives in the centre of the town. The prayer hall consists of thirteen aisles running perpendicular to the qibla wall and covered with pitched tile roofs. Like other Almoravid mosques the courtyard arcades of the Great Mosque open directly into the prayer hall. The minaret which stands opposite the qibla was added in 1136. The most astonishing feature of the mosque is the lavish decoration in the area of the mihrab which includes stone panels with intricately carved stylized flora. Covering the area in front of the mihrab is a magnificent perforated dome carried on sixteen brick ribs and four small squinches. Between the ribs there is an intricate stucco latticework of stylized floral motifs whilst at the apex of the dome is a small muqarnas cupola. The entire dome is covered by a tiled roof on the exterior.

The other important mosque in Tlemcen is the al-'Ubbad Mosque built by the Marinid sultan Abu al-Hasan in 1339. The mosque is raised on a plinth and approached by a monumental staircase leading to a ceremonial projecting porch with an entrance hall behind it. The entrance hall leads on to a small courtyard behind which is the prayer hall. The whole structure is covered with opulent decoration in the form of carved stucco work, glazed tiles and delicately carved stone.

See also: Algeria

Toledo

City in central Spain famous as first Arab capital of Spain and later major Islamic and Christian city.

Toledo was the capital of the Visigoths until its capture in 712 CE by the Arabs, who used the city as their capital until they moved to Córdoba in 717. The city remained an important frontier city until its capture by the Christians in 1085, and even after this Muslims and Jews continued to make important contributions to the intellectual life of the city with translations of scientific treatises.

Despite its fairly early conquest by the Christians, substantial remains of the Islamic period are still standing, together with some notable examples of Mudéjar architecture. The walls of the city contain many early sections including the Bab al-Qantara (c. 850) which is thought to be the earliest use of a bent entrance in Spanish fortifications. Access to this gate is via a bridge known as the Puente de Alcantara (866–71) which has a magnificent high-sprung central arch similar to those of Seljuk bridges in Anatolia. Probably the most famous gate of the city is the Old Bisagra Gate (also known as Puerta de Alfonso VI) through which El Cid entered the city in 1085. The gate is a monumental structure built out of huge uneven blocks near the ground and smaller pieces of coursed rubble near the top. The gateway is flanked by two blind niches with pointed horseshoe arches resting on engaged columns. The gateway itself is recessed behind a wide arched machicolation and consists of a round horseshoe arch with a huge stone lintel spanning the width between the two imposts.

Within the city there are several important religious buildings which are Cristo de la Luz (mosque of Bab al-Mardum), Santa María La Blanca (a former synagogue), the Sinagoga del Transito and the cathedral. The mosque of Bab al-Mardum is a nine-domed mosque with a raised central dome built in 999. Originally there were triple entrances on three sides with a mihrab on the south side. Three of the outer faces are made of brick and decorated with a band of Kufic inscriptions, below which is a geometric panel above decorative intersecting round horseshoe arches.

The church of Santa María La Blanca was built as a synagogue in 1250 and contains four rows of arches supported on octagonal brick piers with capitals decorated with fir cones and punctuate scrolls. More well known is the Sinagoga del Transito built in 1357 during the reign of Pedro the Cruel. The building is lavishly decorated with carved plaster and woodwork, with Arabic and Hebrew inscriptions and coloured tiles. The cathedral of Toledo was once the Great Mosque of the city and possibly contains the remains of a large Córdoba-style mihrab, now the octagonal chapel of Ildefonso.

See also: Córdoba, Granada, Mudéjar, Seville, Spain, Zaragoza

Tomb of the Abbasid caliphs (Cairo)

Mid-thirteenth-century tomb in Cairo containing tombs of the Abbasid caliphs who were taken there after the Mongol sack of Baghdad.

The date of the tomb is not known; some attribute it to the Ayyubid period whilst others believe it was built by the Mamluk sultan Baybars in the 1260s. The complex is one of the most highly decorated buildings to have survived in Cairo with finely carved stucco and painted Kufic inscriptions. The mihrab is a keel-arched niche, with a central medallion from which lines radiated to form a muqarnas frame to the opening. The dome is supported on two-tier muqarnas squinches between which are carved niches and windows.

Topkapi Palace

Imperial Ottoman palace in Istanbul founded by Mehmet II in 1459.

The Topkapi replaces an early royal palace that was established between the old forum and the Golden Horn. This early palace was built predominantly of wood and surrounded by a high wall.

The Topkapi Palace is located on the old Byzantine acropolis and overlooks the Sea of Marmara and the Bosphorus. The building consists of four great courtyards built over a period of four hundred years. Most of the early buildings in the palace were probably built of wood and have not survived the great fires of 1574 and 1665. Fifteenth-century buildings which have survived include the kitchens, the treasury, the physician's building and the Çinili Kiosk. The kitchens on the south side of the second court consist of a long building covered with huge domed chimneys and ventilators. There are several other kitchens in the palace including a separate women's kitchen, a hospital kitchen and several smaller private ones. The treasury is built as a long six-domed hall in the form of a small bedestan and is located in the second court. One of the most unusual buildings of this period is the Physician's Tower, a square building with extremely thick walls and a small chamber on the top. It has been suggested that the lower building was a drug store whilst the upper room was the doctor's office. Outside the main area of the palace but within the outer walls is the celebrated Çinili Kiosk. Designed by a Persian architect, this has many Persian features such as the wide arches. It is set on a raised platform reached by external steps and has a four-iwan plan with a tall dome above the centre.

During the sixteenth century the architect Sinan carried out extensive work at the palace including building (or rebuilding) the vaults supporting the east end. Other work carried out at this period was the building of Murat III's bedchamber next

to a heated outdoor pool. Unfortunately another fire in 1574 destroyed large areas of the palace which had to be rebuilt. This was taken as a chance to remodel much of the palace including the kitchens and the wooden quarters of the Halberdiers (halberd carriers) which were completely rebuilt at this time. A second fire in 1665 led to another period of rebuilding and refurbishment particularly of the harem area. Important buildings from the seventeenth century include the Baghdad Kiosk erected to celebrate the reconquest of that city.

During the early eighteenth century the palace was redecorated in the Ottoman baroque style. A new bath house for the sultan and a palace school were built at this time, both of which include lavish decoration in the European style. In 1789 Selim III became sultan and instituted a series of apartments or salons in the French Rococo style. These buildings had large European glazed windows and were decorated in ornate painted plasterwork. In the mid-nineteenth century the sultans moved to a new palace (the Dolmabahçe) on the banks of the Bosphorus which was more fashionable and not cluttered with associations of the past.

See also: Istanbul, Ottomans

Further reading:

F. Davis, *The Palace of Topkapi in Istanbul*, New York 1971.
B. Miller, *Beyond the Sublime Porte; The Grand Seraglio of Stamboul*, New York 1970.

toron

West African term for projecting wooden stakes used in mud-brick architecture especially in minarets.

The preferred material is acacia wood although split palm is sometimes also used. It is generally agreed that toron have a practical purpose as fixed scaffolding for mud-brick structures which need constant maintenance, although they may also have a symbolic and aesthetic function. Symbolically the use of projecting wooden branches relates the structure to a tree which in West African tradition is a symbol of renewal and rebirth, an idea strengthened by the fact that toron are primarily associated with religious structures. Aesthetically toron may be compared to the horns used in hunting towers (as in e.g. Manara Umm al-Qaroun in Iraq, or the Hiran Manar at Fatehpur Sikri).

See also: Manding, West Africa

Tripoli (Lebanon)

Tripoli is located on the north coast of Lebanon and in the medieval period was the principal port.

Tripoli has a long history of settlement although it first became a city in 358 BCE under the Phoenicians. The city was captured by the Muslim Arabs in the early seventh century CE and became a flourishing Arab seaport until 1109, when it was captured by the Crusaders. For nearly 200 years Tripoli was one of the principal Crusader ports and was one of the last Crusader cities to be recaptured by the Muslims. The city was finally retaken in 1289 and an ambitious programme of reconstruction was initiated. The Mamluk city was built on a new site slightly inland from the Crusader city. Tripoli flourished during this period with a series of nine mosques, sixteen madrassas and five khans constructed before the Ottoman conquest of the sixteenth century. The principal mosque of the city (the Great Mosque) was built in 1294 and includes a Crusader tower which was converted into a minaret. The city remains one of the best examples of Mamluk planning and architecture outside Egypt.

See also: Lebanon, Mamluks

Further reading:

H. Salam-Liebich, *The Architecture of the Mamluk City of Tripoli*, Cambridge, Mass. 1983.

Tripoli (Libiya)

Capital city of Libiya located on the Mediterranean coast.

The name Tripoli derives from the Roman term for the three cities of Tripolitania, which were Leptis Magna, Oea and Sabratha. The present city of Tripoli is built on the site of Oea.

Tripoli was first conquered by the Arab armies of Camr ibn al-As in 643 CE. The captured Byzantine city had a wall which was pulled down by the Arab conquerors and later rebuilt at the end of the Umayyad period. The remains of the Umayyad wall have recently been discovered by archaeologists who have identified a stone wall 6–7 m wide.

Apart from the Umayyad wall there are few remains of the early Islamic period in the city. The oldest mosque is the al-Naqah Mosque which has been interpreted as the mosque of Camr ibn al-As, although it is more likely that it was built by the Fatimid caliph al-Muciz in 973. The al-Naqah Mosque is roughly rectangular, measuring approximately 20 by 40 m, and divided between the courtyard and the sanctuary. The sanctuary is covered by forty-two brick domes supported on columns, some of which have Roman capitals. The mihrab is in the middle of south-east side of the courtyard and has a slight turn to the east to correct the misalignment of the original building.

Most of the other remains in Tripoli date from the Ottoman period when the city was the most westerly Turkish port. The present city walls date from the sixteenth century as testified by Turkish inscriptions on some of the gates. One of the oldest Ottoman buildings is the mosque of Darghut, governor of Tripoli and Turkish commander, who died in 1564 during the siege of Malta. The mosque has a T-shaped plan with a central area divided into fifteen domed bays flanked by two six-bay annexes recalling the tabhanes of Ottoman mosques elsewhere. Behind the qibla wall is a square domed room which contains the tomb of Darghut Pasha. To the south-west of the mosque is a bath house which is built on the remains of Darghut's palace. The most celebrated Turkish mosque is that of Ahmad Pasha al-Qarahmanli built by the semi-independent Turkish governor in 1736. The mosque is located in the middle of a square complex which includes a madrassa, graveyard and the tomb of Ahmad Pasha. The sanctuary consists of a square area covered with twenty-five domes (i.e. five arcades of five bays). There is no courtyard but there is an L-shaped ambulatory on the north-west and south-west sides. In addition there is a raised gallery at first floor level opening on to a wooden balcony which runs around three sides of the sanctuary. The whole building is decorated with fine green, yellow and blue tiles imported from Tunis.

In addition to mosques Tripoli contains many examples of Ottoman houses and funduqs. The houses are usually two-storey structures built around a central colonnaded courtyard and are decorated with polychrome tile and stucco decoration. A typical funduq has a similar design, consisting of a two-storey structure built around a central courtyard. The lower floors are usually used for storage and the upper floor for shop units. There also used to be many bath houses, but only three of these have survived.

See also: Libiya, Ottomans, Tunis

Further reading:

M. Brett, 'Tripoli at the beginning of the fourteenth century AD/ eighth century A.H.', *Libyan Studies* 9: 55–9, 1978.
K. McLachlan, 'Tripoli – city, oasis and hinterland – reflections on the old city 1551 to the present', *Libyan Studies* 9: 53–4, 1978.
M. Warfelli, 'The old city of Tripoli', in *Some Islamic Sites in Libiya: Tripoli Ajdabiyah and Uljah*, Art and Archaeology Research Papers, London 1976.

Tulunids

Dynasty which ruled over Egypt and Syria in the late ninth and early tenth century.

The dynasty was founded by Ahmed ibn Tulun the son of a Turkic soldier from Bukhara who was based at the Abbasid capital of Samarra. Ahmed was originally sent to Egypt as deputy to the governor but soon acquired the governorship himself. As governor of Egypt Ahmed soon extended his power to Syria and Palestine whilst the Abbasids were distracted by rebellions in lower Iraq.

Ahmed's son and successor Khumarawayah received official recognition of his position from the caliph when he was granted Syria and Egypt in return for an annual tribute of 300,000 dinars. By the time of Khumarawayah's death in 896 the empire was weakened by extravagance and internal revolts. Three more Tulunid rulers followed but in the next ten years their situation was so weakened that in 906 an Abbasid general was able to take over Egypt and put an end to Tulunid rule.

Architecturally the most significant member of the dynasty is Ahmed ibn Tulun who established a new city as his capital in Egypt. This city was known as al-Qat'ic and was effectively an addition to Fustat. The city was famous for its similarity to the great Abbasid capital of Samarra. Not much remains of Ahmed's city but it is known to have had a triple-arched public entrance like the Bab al-Amma at Samarra, a polo ground, race track and park for wild animals. Ahmed also built structures useful to the general population such as a 60,000-dinar hospital. However, the only monuments remaining are the congregational mosque of Ibn Tulun and an aqueduct. The mosque displays certain similarities to the congregational mosques of Samarra, in particular the minarets. The aqueduct is built of brick and has a large inlet tower at the village of Basatin about two miles south of the citadel.

Ahmed's son Khumarawayah is known to have built a beautiful palace with a golden hall decorated with sheets of gold carrying representations of himself and his wife. Not surprisingly the palace has not survived.

Further reading:

K. A. C. Creswell, *A Short Account of Early Muslim Architecture*, ed. by J. Allen, Aldershot 1989.
P. K. Hitti, *History of the Arabs*, 10th edn., London 1970, 452–5.
C. E. Bosworth, *The Islamic Dynasties*, revised paperback edn., Edinburgh 1980, 43–4.

Tunis

Capital city of Tunisia since the thirteenth century.

Although smaller than that of Qairawan, the Great Mosque of Tunis (known as the Zaituna Mosque) has a similar history and design. The first mosque on the site was built in 732 to be replaced in 863 with the Aghlabid structure which forms the core of the present mosque. The prayer hall consists of fifteen aisles running east–west (i.e. perpendicular to the qibla wall) with the mihrab at the end of the central aisle, which is both wider and taller than the other aisles and surmounted by a dome at the end next to the mihrab; there is also a dome over the entrance, but this was added later, in the eleventh century. Both domes are ribbed and rest on shell squinches like the domes of the Great Mosque of Qairawan. The Tunis mosque is also famous for its role as a university. Next to it is an ablutions courtyard constructed by the Hafisid rulers in the fourteenth century which is one of the best examples of Tunisian decorative architecture. In the centre of the courtyard is an octagonal fountain and the whole area is decorated with white marble with black marble inlay.

Other important mosques in Tunis are the Qasr Mosque built in the twelfth century and the mosque of the Kasba built in the thirteenth century. The latter is interesting as one of the best examples of Andalusian influence in Tunisian architecture with its decorated minaret and ornate stucco decoration.

Tunis also contains a number of eighteenth-century palaces.

See also: Aghlabids, Tunisia

Tunisia

Further reading:

J. Revault, *Palais et demeurres de Tunis (XVIe et XVIIe siècles)*, Paris 1967.

—— *Palais et demeurres de Tunis (XVIIIe et XIXe siècles)*, Paris 1971.

Tunisia

North African country named after its capital Tunis.

Tunisia is a predominantly coastal country located between Algeria and Libiya. Northwards, a short distance across the sea, is the island of Sicily. Physically the country can be divided into three regions, a forested mountainous area to the north, a central plain watered by the Wadi Mejerda and a drier mountainous region to the south.

Tunisia has a long history of settlement starting with the Phoenician ports of the ninth century BCE. The greatest of these ports developed into the city of Carthage which dominated the trade of the Mediterranean until it was destroyed by the Romans in 146 CE. For a short period after the collapse of Roman rule the country was taken over by the Vandals until they were expelled by the Byzantines who ruled the country up to the time of the Arab conquest in 640. During the early Islamic period the country was known as Ifriqiyya with its capital at Qairawan. In the ninth century the country was ruled by the semi-autonomous Aghlabid dynasty who undertook the conquest of Sicily. During the tenth century the country became a base for the Fatimids before they moved to Egypt in 969. Tunisia's prominent position in Islamic history was brought to an end in the mid-eleventh century by the invasions of the Banu Hilal from northern Egypt. In a reversal of history the Normans of Sicily occupied the country for a short period in the mid-twelfth century until they were expelled by the Almohads. Following the Almohad victory Tunisia was ruled by a local dynasty known as the Hafisids who remained in power until the sixteenth century. In 1574, after a struggle between the Turks and the Spanish, the Turks gained the upper hand and Tunisia was incorporated into the Ottoman Empire. During the eighteenth century the country was ruled by a local dynasty known as the Husseinis, who, with increasing French help, ruled the country up to 1945 when Tunisia became an independent republic.

The main building material in Tunisia is stone which may either be finely dressed ashlar or smaller squared blocks. Baked brick was used, particularly in the early Islamic period for buildings like the Great Mosque at Qairawan. Roman and Byzantine material, in particular columns, formed one of the major building materials for early Islamic buildings. As elsewhere in North Africa the horseshoe arch was the dominant arch form in monumental architecture. A certain amount of wood was available for roofs although generally buildings were covered with stone vaults. From the fifteenth century onwards glazed tiles became a common architectural feature which has survived until the twentieth century.

Tunisia is noted for the large number of religious buildings surviving from before the tenth century. The oldest Islamic monument in Tunisia is the Great Mosque of Qairawan which was built in 670 by 'Uqba ibn Nafi. Little remains of this early mosque which was rebuilt more than three times until 862 when it reached its present form under

Ribal of Susa, Tunisia © Creswell Archive, Ashmolean Museum

the Aghlabid ruler Abu Ibrahim Ahmad. The plan of this building became a model for later Tunisian mosques. The standard form comprises aisles running perpendicular to the qibla wall with a raised aisle in the centre leading to a domed cupola in front of the mihrab. In addition there is usually one (or more) aisle running parallel to the qibla wall forming a T-plan. Examples of this style include the Great Mosques of Tunis, Susa, Mahadiya, Monastir and Sfax – only the Great Mosque of Tozeur differs from it, with aisles running parallel to the qibla wall. This mosque form remained remarkably constant and even continued after the Ottoman conquest although there are examples of mosques of pure Ottoman form such as the Sidi Mahriz Mosque in Tunis.

Other religious structures include the ribat or fortified convent, an architectural form particularly characteristic of Tunisia. One of the best examples is the Ribat of Susa which was built by the Aghlabid ruler Ziyadat Allah in 821. This consists of a square building (95 m per side) with a central courtyard, towers at the corners and a monumental entrance. Three of the corner towers are circular whilst the fourth is square and forms a base for a cylindrical watchtower. The ground floor contains numerous rooms opening from the courtyard whilst on the first floor above the entrance there is a large prayer hall covered with barrel-vaulted aisles perpendicular to the mihrab. Other examples include the three ribats of Monastir, the oldest of which was founded in 796.

There is a wide variety of traditional house types in Tunisia from the bedouin tent to sophisticated courtyard villas. In southern Tunisia there are fortified settlements (qusur) which contain several tiers of barrel-vaulted rooms (ghorfas) arranged around a courtyard. The appearance of these structures is quite organic and resembles a beehive. Most of the time they are used for storage, but they could be used as dwellings in times of trouble. The standard form of village house is a windowless, flat-roofed structure, with a central courtyard used for animals. Town houses are a developed form of the village house; they are often two storeys high and decorated with polychrome glazed tiles. The houses of Tozeur are noted for their decorative brickwork façades. In Tunis there are a number of eighteenth-century Ottoman palaces and mansions. These are usually multiple courtyard structures with extrava-gant decoration which is a mixture of Islamic and European style.

See also: Aghlabids, Qairawan, Tunis

Further reading:

A. Lezine, *Architecture de l'Ifriqiyya: recherche sur les monuments aghlabides*, CNRS, Paris 1966.

G. Marçais, 'Recherches d'archéologie musulmane en Tunisie', *Bulletin de la Société Française des Fouilles Archéologiques* 5: 38–46, 1923–4.

turba (or turbe)

Mausoleum.

Turkey

The Republic of Turkey occupies a position between Asia and Europe and comprises Anatolia and Turkish Thrace.

Turkey is a large country open to the sea on three sides with the land route to the Middle East and Asia on the fourth side. The country may be divided roughly into five areas, each with a different environment and culture. West of Istanbul is Turkish Thrace, a green area with many connections with the Balkans. The northern part of the country stretching along the Black Sea coast is heavily wooded, with a high rainfall and cultural connections with Russia, Ukraine and other former Soviet Republics. The central area, where the capital Ankara is situated, is known as the Anatolian plain and has an extreme climate which produces snow in the winter and very hot summers. This area is largely inhabited by rural farmers although there are also Turkish nomads with tents. To the south and west is the Aegean and Mediterranean coast which has a mild climate and rich classical heritage. To the east, on the borders of Iraq and Iran, is a harsh mountainous area with a mixed population of Kurds, Armenians and Turks. Historically Turkey's position has meant that it has often been the scene of conflict between East and West, although the corollary of this is that it has also become extremely wealthy through East–West trade. Until the eleventh century most of Turkey was controlled by the Byzantine Empire which ruled from its capital at Constantinople (later Istanbul). During the ninth century there were regular Muslim raids which were sometimes quite successful. One of the largest raids was that of 838 when the city of Amorium was occupied and marble columns were taken back and used at Samarra. However, not until the eleventh century did the Byzantines, who had already lost the Middle East and North Africa to Islam, begin to lose large amounts of territory to the recently converted Seljuk Turks. In the early thirteenth century the Byzantines suffered a further blow when Constantinople was sacked by the soldiers of the Fourth Crusade. By the beginning of the fourteenth century Byzantine control was reduced to the area around Constantinople and Trabzon to the east on the Black Sea. In 1453 Constantinople was taken by the Ottomans who by the early sixteenth century controlled all of modern Turkey as well as large areas beyond its borders. In 1922 the Ottoman sultanate was abolished and replaced by the Turkish Republic under Mustafa Kemal Attaturk who instituted a policy of modernization and secularism.

The traditional architecture of Turkey reflects this varied landscape and rich history with many regional styles. A large range of building materials are employed including mud and baked brick, wood, stone and nomad tents.

The traditional Turkic nomad tent is known as a yurt and consists of a round wooden frame covered with a skin or hair tent. In south-western Anatolia the traditional Arabic type is found, comprising a black goat-hair tent which is supported with wooden poles and long ropes anchored with pegs. Mud brick is employed predominantly in the south-east of the country and in central Anatolia. At the town of Harran near the Syrian border houses are built out of one or more square mud-brick units, capped with flat-topped or pointed conical domes. In central Anatolia rectangular houses are built out of mud brick with stone foundations and roofs of wood and mud. The houses have thick walls with few windows to conserve heat in the winter and remain cool in the summer. Rooms are heated by open dung fires with a hole in the roof or an earthenware jar as a chimney. The roofs are built with roughly shaped timber branches up to 4 m long laid perpendicular to the walls of the house and covered with a layer of thatch which is then covered with mud. The mud on the roof is kept flat and waterproof with a section of column or other cylindrical stone which is rolled over the roof.

Baked brick in Turkey derives from two independent traditions, the Byzantine and the Persian Seljuk tradition. During the Byzantine era baked brick was one of the main building materials, especially in the cities of western Anatolia. This tradition continued into the Ottoman period and bricks are still one of the main building materials alongside the ubiquitous concrete. The usual method of using the flat tile-like bricks was in combination with rubble stone or dressed stone construction in alternate layers. Seljuk Persian brickwork was restricted in its impact on eastern Anatolia because of the strong stone-carving tradition already prevalent there. However, baked brick was often used in minarets in the west where it was sometimes arranged in decorative patterns in a manner alien to Byzantine practice. Glazed bricks are another technique imported into Anatolia by the Seljuks, although the most famous example is the Çinili Kiosk in the Topkapi Palace which was built by a Timurid architect.

In north-western Turkey and on the coast of the Black Sea wood is fairly plentiful and is the main building material. It is used in a number of ways from all-timber constructions to buildings with stone or brick walls and a wooden superstructure. Some of the oldest surviving wooden structures are Seljuk-period mosques which have been preserved because of their religious importance. A good example is the Aslan Cami in Ankara which has walls built of re-used stone and brick and an interior made of wooden columns supporting a flat roof made of wooden beams. However, most wooden structures are not more than 250 years old so that a large part of the architectural tradition is lost. The standard form of a traditional wooden town house consists of a stone basement, on top of which is built a rectangular platform cantilevered to project out above the street. Although the basement may be irregular, this is corrected on the upper floors where the cantilevering is used to produce a rectangular shape. Windows are often built to project an extra half-metre or more beyond the façade to give views along the street. Many houses are three storeys high including the basement, although it is likely that in the past most were one or two storeys high. In Istanbul many of the houses are clad in external weather-boarding, but elsewhere the walls of the houses are made of lath and plaster. Inside the grander houses the ceilings are often decorated with painted scenes on plaster or wood.

Stone buildings represent the largest group of

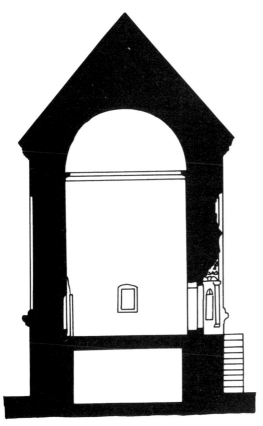

Donner Kumbet, Kayseri, Turkey

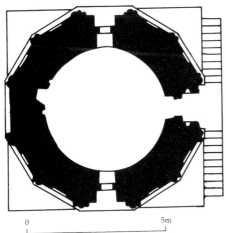

Donner Kumbet, Kayseri, Turkey

historical buildings in Turkey from the eighth-century mosque at Harran to the eighteenth-century baroque mosques of Istanbul. The material used varies according to the region; thus in Diyarbakir black basalt is used whereas in Edirne red sandstone is employed in conjunction with yellow limestone. The most basic form of stone construction can be found in the Gourami region near Kayseri where houses are built out of the abandoned caves previously used by Christians. The houses may either consists of a cave on its own or a cave with a stone-built arched porch. Some of the most sophisticated stonework is found in the carved doorways of the Seljuk period in Konya, Nigde, Erzerum, Kayseri and Sivas. Probably the most spectacular example is the doorway of the Gök Madrassa in Sivas which combines intricate calligraphy and floral designs with bold carved borders. Ottoman stonework by contrast tends to be fairly austere with a restrained use of carved decoration relying instead on the form and mass of the building.

See also: Bursa, Byzantine architecture, Diyarbakir, Edirne, Istanbul, Konyo, Seljuks, Ottomans

Turkmenistan

Mausoleum Kounia Urgench, Turkmenistan © *StJohn Simpson*

Further reading:

K. A. Aru, *Türk Hamamlari Etüdü*, Istanbul 1949.
Ö. Bakirer, *Selçuklu Öncesi ve Selçuklu Dönemi Anadolu Mimarisinde Tugla Kullani*, Ankara 1981.
G. Goodwin, *A History of Ottoman Architecture*, London 1971.
R. Holod and A. Evin, *Modern Turkish Architecture*, Philadelphia 1984.
F. Seton Lloyd and D. Storm Rice, *Alanya ('Alaiyya)*, London 1958.
S. Ögel, *Anadolu Selçuklulari'nin Taş Tezyinati* (*Anatolian Seljuk Stone Ornamentation*), Ankara 1987.
R. M. Riefstahl, *Turkish Architecture in South Western Anatolia*, Cambridge, Mass. 1931.
M. Sözen, *Anadolu Medreseleri Selçuklular ve Beylikler Devri*, vols. Istanbul 1970–2.
—— *Anadolu'da Akkoyonulu Mimarisi* (*Anatolian Aqqounulu Architecture*) Istanbul 1981.
M. Sözen and M. Tapan, *50 Yilin Türk Mimarisi* (*50 Years of Turkish Architecture*), Istanbul 1973.
B. Ünsal, *Turkish Islamic Architecture in Seljuk and Ottoman Times 1071–1923*, London 1973.

Turkmenistan

Former Soviet Central Asian Republic which lies to the east of the Caspian Sea and to the north of Afghanistan and Iran.

Geographically Turkmenistan is defined by the Koppet Dag mountains along its southern border with Iran and to the north by the Amu Darya (Oxus) river which separates it from Uzbekistan.

Mausoleum, Kouria-Urgeuch, Turkmenistan

The Kara Kum desert covers the central part of Turkmenistan dividing the country into north and south. Before the construction of the Kara Kum canal at the beginning of this century habitation in southern Turkmenistan was only possible at oases where rivers from the Koppet Dag mountains disappeared into the sands of the Kara Kum. The most famous of these desert oases was the ancient city of Merv (qv) fed by the Murghab river.

Mud brick is the principal construction material although fired brick is used for monumental architecture. To the north along the Amu Darya wood is often used for columns and roofs.

Buildings of the early Islamic period, from the eighth to eleventh centuries CE, are mostly found in the area around Merv although there may also be isolated buildings of the period in the Kara Kum desert. Many buildings of the eleventh to thirteenth century Seljuk period have survived in particular at Serakhs on the border with Afghanistan, at Mestorian in the south-west and at Urgench on the border with Uzbekistan. These are mostly religious buildings characterized by elaborate brick decoration, epigraphic bands, the use of stucco, and the combination of mud brick with fired brick. Buildings of the later medieval period are more difficult to identify, although the city of Bairam Ali near Merv preserves the layout and walls of a fifteenth- to sixteenth-century Timurid city. Probably the most significant Islamic building of later periods is the Great Mosque of Anau, destroyed by an earthquake in 1948, most of which dates to the seventeenth century. The mosque comprises a huge domed iwan flanked by twin minarets and two smaller domed chambers on either side of the courtyard. The façade of the iwan was decorated with polychrome tiles depicting dragons and elaborate decorative brickwork.

After the Russian conquest in the nineteenth century Islamic forms were used in buildings of Russian design such as the Tsar's hunting lodge at Bairam Ali which employs domes, crenellations and minaret-like pinnacles. This tradition was continued into the Soviet period with buildings such as the Academy of Sciences where the arcades are decorated with pseudo-epigraphic brickwork.

See also: Central Asia, Merv

Further reading:

G. A. Pugachenkava, 'Puti razvitiya arkhitekturi Iuzhnogo Turkmenistana pori rabovladeniya', *Trudi Iuzhno-Turkmenistanskoi Arkheologicheskoi Ekspeditsii* 6, 1958.

U

Ukhaidhir

Early Abbasid palace in the desert of south-western Iraq.

The palace stands in the desert west of the city of Kerbala and east of the oasis of Shithatha. The building is made out of rough-hewn limestone blocks and mud plaster with baked brick used for roofing vaults, resembling earlier Sassanian structures (cf. Kharana in Jordan). The palace may be divided into two structural phases, a central palace core and an outer enclosure wall added slightly later. The exterior curtain wall is composed of tall blind niches alternating with solid semi-circular buttress towers. On top of the wall there was a parapet which was cantilevered over the niches allowing a continuous series of slits (machicolation) which could protect the lower parts of the wall from attack. The main gateway is set between two quarter-round towers and contains a slot for a portcullis. To the right of the entrance on the outside there is a large stable block. The central

core of the palace contains a mosque, a bath house and a main reception hall. The upper floor is reached by ramps running up at right angles to the axis of the main gateway. There are small tunnels running over the main vaults which provided cooling and ventilation.

Recent survey work in the vicinity of Ukhaidhir has demonstrated the development of the area during the early Isalmic period, starting with the small palace at Tulul Ukhaidhir several kilometres to the north of the main palace. In addition there is an outer mud-brick enclosure containing a variety of mud-brick buildings which are now only visible as humps.

See also: Abbasids: Atshan, Khan; Iraq; Sassanians

Further reading:

G. Bell, *Palace and Mosque at Ukhaidhir: A Study in Early Muhammadan Architecture*, Oxford 1914.
B. Finnster and J. Schmidt, *Sasaidische und fruhislamische Ruinem im Iraq, Baghdader Mitteilungen* 8, Berlin 1976.

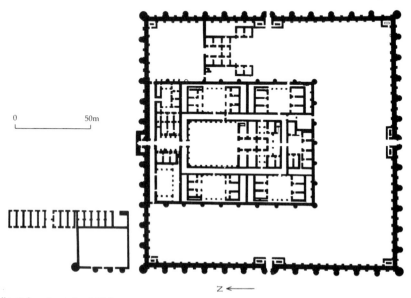

Plan of Ukhaidhir Palace, Iraq (after Mehdi)

ulu cami

Turkish term for a congregational or Friday mosque.

Umayyads

The dynasty of Umayyad caliphs was based in Syria and ruled the Islamic world from 660 to 750 CE.

Under the Umayyads the Islamic state was transformed from a theocracy to an Arab monarchy. In 661 Ali, the last Orthodox caliph was murdered and Mu'awiya, the governor of Syria, became the first Umayyad caliph. Mu'awiya provided the centralization essential for the survival and continuing expansion of the Arab Empire. At its height Umayyad rule extended from the Atlantic coast of North Africa to India and from Central Asia to the Yemen. The administration of conquered provinces was usually left intact, so that the tax accounts for Syria, for example, continued to be kept in Greek. Socially, however, Umayyad rule was characterized by the domination of Arabs.

The success of the Umayyad caliphate carried within it the seeds of its own destruction. Because the economic and social structure of the empire was dependent on the conquest of new lands, any setbacks or reverses caused resentment and dissatisfaction throughout the regime. Similarly the secular nature of the dynasty aroused opposition amongst those in favour of a more theocratic state. In 747 a revolution against the Umayyads began in Khurassan and soon spread throughout the eastern part of the empire. By 750 the Umayyad regime had been defeated to be replaced by the Abbasids who ruled from Iraq. Only one branch of the Umayyads survived by fleeing to Spain where the dynasty continued to rule until 1051 CE.

Almost all surviving Umayyad monuments are in Syria and Palestine whence the dynasty derived most of its support. As the Arabs did not have an architectural tradition suited to the needs of a great empire, they adopted the building methods of the defeated Sassanian and Byzantine empires. Because they ruled from Syria, Byzantine influence was stronger, although Sassanian elements became increasingly important. In many cases Byzantine or even Roman buildings were simply taken over with little or no modification. However, the conquests did provide some innovation both in terms of building types and in the prominence given to decoration.

The most important building projects undertaken during the Umayyad era included mosques, palaces and cities. Mosques were obviously an important element in the expansion of the Islamic state although the speed of the conquests meant that these were often temporary structures or converted churches. New cities were built in answer to specific requirements, such as the need for an administrative centre rather than for dynastic propaganda as in the Abbasid period. The most characteristic type of building is the 'Desert Palace' built as a residence for the ruling élite.

The earliest Islamic cities were garrison towns such as Basra and Kufa, built as centres for the conquest of Khurassan and Central Asia. The Umayyads continued this policy of building cities which were little more than giant military camps, although significantly these were unfortified. The most important city of this type was Wasit built in 701 by Yussuf ibn al-Hajjaj the Umayyad governor of Iraq. Architecturally these cities were important because they were divided according to tribal groups, each with its own masjid, which prefigures similar divisions in later Arab cities. Trade was also a powerful stimulus for the foundation and growth of cities in the early Islamic period. The frontiers of the Islamic state were particularly conducive to the growth of cities in North Africa and in eastern Iran military camps quickly grew into trading cities.

Mosques were an essential part of early Islamic government as they provided a meeting place at which important announcements could be made. Early on two separate mosque-building traditions developed; in Syria this was based on the conversion of churches whilst in Iraq mosques developed out of square enclosures used for prayer. The earliest Iraqi mosque for which we have archaeological evidence is the Friday mosque at Wasit built to a square plan with a hypostyle roof. The oldest Islamic building in the west is the Dome of the Rock built by Abd al-Malik in 691. However, this building is a sanctuary rather than a mosque and its influence on later Islamic architecture is limited.

More important in terms of mosque development is the Great Mosque in Damascus built by the caliph al-Walid in 705 CE. This building is modelled on Syrian churches, which after the conquest were used as mosques. Churches were converted to mosques by blocking up the west door and piercing the north wall with doorways, creating a building with a lateral axis perpendicular to the direction of prayer. Mosques built in the same style as Damascus include Qasr al-Hayr, Qusayr Hallabat, Raqqa, Balis, Diyarbakir and Der'a. Other developments in religious architecture in the Umayyad period include the introduction of the mihrab and the minaret.

In secular building the most important constructions of the Umayyad period were the desert palaces of Syria and Palestine. Some of these buildings were new foundations, whilst others were Roman or Byzantine forts converted to meet the needs of the new Arab rulers. Significantly, most of these buildings were abandoned soon after the fall of the Umayyad regime and they remain as monuments to the wealth and tastes of the dynasty. Their size and scale vary enormously, from the small and lavishly decorated bath house of Qusayr Amrah to the great fortified city–palace of Qasr al-Hayr al-Sharqi. From the outside most of these buildings resemble fortresses; thus the main entrance of Qasr al-Hayr al-Sharqi is protected by two tall semi-circular towers and a machicolice. In some of the palaces the effect of the fortifications is softened by great decorative friezes, as at Mshatta, Qasr al-Hayr al-Gharbi and Khirbet al-Mafjar. Most of these palaces include a bath house and a mosque as well as living accommodation arranged according to the bayt system. Each palace comprised a number of bayts, each of which would house a family or tribal unit. There is very little differentiation between the rooms within each bayt, so they were probably used simply as shelters in a similar manner to a bedouin tent with no permanent fixtures.

The building techniques employed by the Umayyads were as diverse as the regions they conquered, so that major projects would employ workmen of several different nationalities. At its most conservative Umayyad architecture is indistinguishable from either Byzantine or Sassanian work but usually there is a combination of eastern and western elements which produce an unmistakably Islamic building. One of the best examples of this mixture is to be found at Mshatta where the walls are of cut stone in the Syrian tradition, the vaults are constructed in the Mesopotamian fashion and the decorative carving is a mixture of Byzantine and Coptic motifs.

The most common building materials used in this period were stone, wood and brick. In Syria the majority of buildings were constructed out of cut stone or ashlar masonry. The quality of Umayyad masonry is generally very high with sharp edges, tight joins and large blocks producing buildings with a monumentality unsurpassed in later Islamic building. Ashlar masonry is particularly suited to the construction of large vertical surfaces which can be enlivened by carving, as on the entrance façade at Mshatta. With the exception of basalt most stone is unsuitable for roofing large areas and only small spans could be roofed with barrel vaulting. In general Umayyad architecture avoided the problem of intersecting vaults so that most buildings were either made up of small units or roofed in wood.

In Syria, timber from the forests of Lebanon was often used for roofing. Roofs were either shallow, pitched structures supported by wooden trusses, as in the Great Mosque of Damascus, or occasionally wooden domes, as in the Dome of the Rock or the Aqsa Mosque. Timber was also used for centring, scaffolding, tie-beams and mosque furniture such as minbars.

Although brick architecture was common to both the Byzantine and Sassanian empires its use in Umayyad architecture was limited to the eastern part of the empire. The availability of suitable stone in Syria meant that bricks were rarely used there even in Byzantine times. When bricks were used in Syria it is significant that the Mesopotamian style was used with thin joints, rather than the thick layers of mortar used in the Byzantine tradition. Examples of this are found at Qasr al-Tuba and Mshatta. In Iraq both baked brick and mud brick were used extensively. Often baked brick was used for pillars, vaults and the lower courses of walls whilst mud brick was used for the upper parts. Examples can be seen at Wasit and Usqaf Bani Junayd.

Umayyad architecture can be distinguished from that of earlier periods by its use of decorative techniques. None of these was new but the variety and scale of decorative effects was far greater than ever before. The most important decorative methods employed were mosaic, wall painting, sculpture and relief carving.

Although it is probable that most Umayyad mosaics were made by Byzantine craftsmen, the motifs used and the choice of designs usually indicate an Islamic influence. The earliest Islamic mosaics are those in the Dome of the Rock, which consist of gold and polychrome tesserae in representations of Byzantine and Sassanian royal jewels. The Great Mosque in Damascus contains a very important group of mosaics depicting an ideal city which, significantly, is devoid of people. This is due to the ban on figural representation in mosques and is a good example of Byzantine art adapted for Islamic purposes. Even in the desert palaces mosaics usually avoided figures, although occasionally, as at Khirbet al-Mafjar, there are representations of animals.

In addition to floor mosaics most Umayyad palaces were decorated with frescoes, usually on walls, although occasionally on floors, as at Qasr al-Hayr al-Gharbi. The best preserved paintings are those at Qusayr Amrah which include representations of a great hunt, half-naked dancing girls and a famous portrait of six rulers of the world.

Sculptures are found at a number of desert palaces, most notably Khirbet al-Mafjar and Qasr al-Hayr al-Gharbi. Both eastern and western sculptural traditions were used, although the medium was usually stucco rather than stone. Because stucco is not free-standing, sculptures were usually incorporated into some structural feature of a building such as the entrance.

See also: bayt, masjid, mihrab, minaret

Further reading:

K. A. C. Creswell, *A Short Account of Early Muslim Architecture*, ed. by J. Allen, Aldershot 1989.

R. Ettinghausen, *From Byzantium to Sassanian Iran and the Islamic World*, Leiden 1976.

R. Hillenbrand, 'La dolce vita in Early Islamic Syria: the evidence of later Umayyad palaces', *Art History* 5(1): 1–35, 1982.

H. N. Kennedy, *The Prophet and the Age of the Caliphates: The Islamic Near East from the Sixth to the Eleventh Century*, London and New York 1986.

United Arab Emirates (UAE)

Federation composed of the seven emirates of Fujairah, Ajman, Ras al-Khaimah, Abu Dhabi, Dubai, Umm al-Quwain and Sharjah. The country previously known as the Trucial Coast is located on the Arabian side of the Gulf between Qatar and Oman. The eastern part of the country bordering on Oman is mountainous whilst the western part is flat sandy coastal plain.

The traditional materials of construction in the emirates are coral, mud brick, dry stone and wood

and thatch. Coral obtained from the coastal reefs is the prime building material on the coast. Two forms are used, irregular rubble blocks set into a thick mortar known as 'sarooj' and thin coral slabs used as panels between load-bearing pillars. Mangrove wood obtained from East Africa is used both as strengthening for walls and for roof beams. The maximum length of mangrove poles is 3.5 m which imposes a rigid geometry on the coastal houses. Ceilings resting on the mangrove beams are made of planks of date-palm wood and are sometimes painted.

In oasis towns, such as al-Cain on the Omani border, houses are built out of mud brick with split-palm beams used for roofing in a manner common throughout the Arabian peninsula. Often the lower parts of the walls are built from large stone blocks to strengthen the buildings against water and wind erosion. The most ephemeral buildings are those built of palm fronds and wood, although it is likely that in the past these may have been the commonest form of dwelling. Palm-frond, or barasti, houses are usually built on a wooden frame made out of mangrove poles, split-palm trunk or any other available wood. The palm fronds are used in two forms, either as straight poles (approximately 1 m long) stripped of their leaves used for creating screens or with the leaves still on for roof thatch. The shape of palm-frond houses varies from square or rectangular flat-roofed buildings to triangular tent-like structures.

In the mountains in the east of the country houses are built out of irregular-shaped blocks laid without mortar; inside, the walls of the houses may be plastered with mud. The flat roofs are made out of palm fronds or any other locally available wood. Sometimes the houses are built into the ground, with triangular pitched roofs made of palm wood. Most of the stone houses are rectangular, although in the central mountains of the UAE round stone houses are also found, with roofs made of mountain bushes.

Before the twentieth century the emirates depended on trade and fishing for their primary income. Each town was located on a creek or peninsula with easy access to the sea and a hinterland used for agriculture. The most famous of these towns (now disappeared) is Julfar which had extensive trade links with East Africa, India and the Far East during the seventeenth and eighteenth centuries. The location of the emirates on the coast

Traditional house, UAE. Note wind-tower (mulqaf) (after Kay and Zandi)

of the Gulf has also meant that the country was heavily influenced by it neighbour Iran. This influence can be seen in the Bastakia quarter of Dubai which developed as an outpost of the Iranian city of Bastak. Today the Bastakiya quarter is notable for its wind-towers, which are a characteristic feature of central Iranian towns.

There are few old mosques standing in the UAE and those that do survive are mostly in the smaller villages. This is because the larger mosques of the towns have undergone constant renovation and renewal so that the main mosques are now dazzling new structures. Reputedly the oldest mosque in the emirates is the mosque of Bidiya on the east coast, near the site of the battle of Dibba which established Islam in the area. This mosque is a rectangular building with a large central pillar supporting four flat-topped domes with pointed finials. The deep-set mihrab projects out of the back of the mosque and is flanked by a fixed minbar of four steps. Until recently minarets were fairly unusual in the UAE although in the east there are a number of small coastal mosques with squat minarets capped with unusual pointed domes.

Like many of the other countries of the Arabian peninsula the emirates have a number of forts and watch-towers built to protect the urban populations. Each of the seven emirates had its own forts which are now in varying states of repair. The oldest of these is the Husn of Abu Dhabi originally built in the eighteenth century to protect the city's well. The emirate of al-Cain has six forts built by the Nahyan family around the Buraimi oasis between 1830 and 1910. Most of the forts have now been restored and converted into museums.

The most sophisticated houses in the UAE are found in the coastal towns where there was enough wealth and outside influence to build on a large scale. The typical house of a wealthy coastal family consists of a two-storey structure built around a central courtyard. From the outside the houses are generally quite plain, although sometimes the upper parts of the walls were decorated with crenellations and the wind-towers were decorated with elaborate arches. Inside, the rooms opening on to the courtyard were decorated with carved stucco panels or grilles, sometimes containing stained glass.

The phenomenal growth of the emirates since

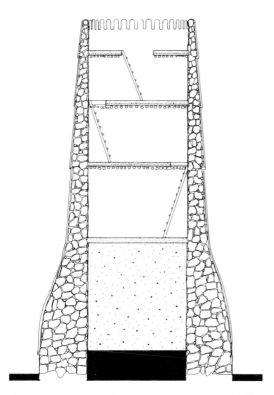

Defensive tower, UAE. Note lower part of tower is filled with sand (after Kay and Zandi)

the Second World War has meant that many of the older historical and traditional buildings were destroyed. In recent times, however (since the 1970s), there has been a concerted effort to protect and restore historical buildings. One of the most successful projects has been the restoration of the abandoned nineteenth-century palace of Sheikh Saeed, ruler of Dubai from 1912 to 1958. The present architecture of the UAE represents a wide variety of Islamic styles indicating both the wealth and cosmopolitan nature of the country.

See also: Bahrain, Oman, Qatar

Further reading:

A. Coles and J. Jackson, 'A windtower house in Dubai', *Art and Archaeology Research Papers*, 1975.

W. Dostal, *The Traditional Architecture of Ras al-Khaimah,* Dubai 1983.

S. Kay, 'Richness of style in UAE mosques', *Arts and the Islamic World*, 3(4), 1985–6.

S. Kay and D. Zandi, *Architectural Heritage of the Gulf,* Dubai 1991.

A. al-Tajir, 'Traditional architecture of the UAE', *Arts and the Islamic World* 3(4): 68ff., 1985–6.

United States of America (USA)

Islamic architecture in America can be divided into three distinct types, buildings for Muslim Americans, Orientalist buildings built by non-Muslims to evoke the spirit of the Orient, and buildings in the Spanish-American style which recalls the Mudéjar architecture of Spain.

American cities with large Muslim populations include New York, Chicago, Detroit and Los Angeles, all of which have several mosques. The architecture of these mosques generally reflects the ethnic origin of the main Muslim group in the area, thus there are Albanian mosques in the four cities with large Albanian populations. In recent times the influx of students from oil-rich countries into colleges in the United States has led to a number of mosques being built on campuses. One of the most ambitious projects is the headquarters of the Islamic Society of North America (ISNA) at Plainfields, Indiana, begun in 1975. Although not yet complete, the centre will eventually include a mosque, accommodation for 500 students, a refectory, a library for 100,000 volumes and recreational facilities. Another notable Islamic student centre is that of the University of Arkansas at Johesboro financed by a patron from Saudi Arabia. The main building of the centre is a mosque with a small courtyard and a square-shafted minaret. There is a separate women's section or gallery on the upper floor which is reached by external and internal staircases. The building is faced in dark and light coloured brick and the façade is decorated with a calligraphic brick frieze. Both the Arkansas and the Indiana centres are undoubtedly modern buildings which reflect traditional Islamic architecture. By contrast the Dar al-Salam centre at Abiquiu in New Mexico, designed by the Egyptian architect Hassan Fathy, is built with traditional materials and techniques. The complex consists of a mosque, madrassa and several accommodation blocks, all built out of mud brick known locally as adobe (from the Arabic al-toub). The building is covered with barrel vaults and domes and decorated with crenellations and carved woodwork. As well as being a religious centre Dar al-Salam will also function as a centre for traditional architecture and technology.

Orientalist architecture in the USA is primarily a feature of the early twentieth century and is a product of the incredible wealth of America combined with cinema-inspired fantasy (e.g. *The Thief* of Baghdad). This can be seen in the numerous cinemas built in the Moorish palace style with names like the Alhambra. The most complete examples of this Islamic fantasy architecture is the city of Opa-Locka conceived as 'the Baghdad of south Florida'. The buildings have horseshoe-shaped windows, minarets, domes and crenellations. The most important building is the city hall, built as a fortified citadel with thick crenellated enclosure walls. This building is covered with five large domes and framed by four minarets (three small cylindrical towers and one huge octagonal tower). Other Islamic-style buildings in the city include the railway station, the archery club, the archaeological museum and the Opa Locka hotel.

The discovery of the New World and the expulsion of Muslims from Spain occurred in the same year, 1492. The result was that a large number of Muslims converted to Christianity and emigrated to the New World where their skills were used in the development of New Spain. Mudéjar (forced Muslim converts to Christianity) style architecture in America is found mostly in Mexico and Central America, although it can also be seen in the south and west of the USA in Texas, New Mexico and California.

See also: Mudéjar, Spain

Further reading:

N. Ardalan, 'Architects in America design for Islamic cultures', *Arts and the Islamic World* 3(3): 46–50, 1985.

F. S. Fitzgerald Bush, *A Dream of Araby* (n.d.).

C. Hotchkiss Malt, 'Opa–Locka: American city with Islamic design', *Arts and the Islamic World*, 1(3): 33–6, 1983.

A. Schleifer, 'Hassan Fathy: a voyage to New Mexico', *Arts and the Islamic World* 1(1): 1982/3.

Urgench

Ancient capital of Khorezm in western Uzbekistan.

Urgench was established as the Mongol capital in the early fourteenth century. The most prominent remains at the site is the tomb of Turabek Khanum dated to 1320. This has a massive portal with a muqarnas vault. Outside, the tomb has a polygonal plan whilst the interior is hexagonal.

Uzbekistan

Independent Central Asian Republic with a predominantly Muslim population.

Uzbekistan occupies a vast area between Afghanistan, Turkmenistan and Khazakstan; most of this area is desert, semi-desert or steppe. The main areas of occupation are the western area of Khorezm, where the river Amu Dar'ya enters the Aral Sea, and the cities of Bukhara and Samarkand on the Zeravshan river. The population of the Republic is predominantly Uzbek (Turkic) although Persian was the main language in the early Islamic period.

The main source of prosperity for this region is the trans-continental trade route between China, India, the Middle East and Europe known as the Silk Route. The trade led to the establishment of urban centres on the edge of the deserts of Central Asia. From the second century this trade was controlled by the Kushans, a semi-nomadic people from Chinese Central Asia. The Kushans built up a vast empire which controlled most of the trade passing through Central Asia. In the fourth century the Sassanians took control of the western part of the trade routes and reduced the Kushans to a series of independent principalities. The central part of the route was controlled by the Soghdians who occupied Samarkand and Bukhara. The first Arab raids occurred in the mid-seventh century, although it was not until the beginning of the eighth century that any real conquests were made with the capture of Bukhara and Samarkand. By the mid-eighth century most of the region was under Arab control. By the ninth century a Persian dynasty known as the Samanids was in control of both Bukhara and Samarkand. The Samanids were nominally vassals of the Abbasids although they acted independently. During this period Islam gradually replaced Buddhism, Manichaeism and Zorastrianism as the main religion of the area. At the end of the tenth century the Samanids were replaced by the Karakhanid Turks who established Samarkand as their capital. During the eleventh century the Seljuk Turks rapidly expanded westwards from their base in the region of Khorezm in western Uzbekistan. The region of Khorezm was left under the rule of the Khorezmshas who were vassals of the Seljuks. In 1077 the Khorezmshas declared themselves independent, establishing their capital at Urgench. By the twelfth century the Khorezmshas had gained control of most of Central

Asia. This period of great prosperity was interrupted by the Mongol invasions of the early thirteenth century. The earliest period of Mongol rule in the region was not characterized as successful, although under the Timurids in the fourteenth and fifteenth centuries it entered one of the most brilliant periods of history. In the sixteenth century the region was conquered by the Uzbeks who now form the majority of the population.

The main building materials are mud brick and pisé, baked brick and wood. Stone is generally not available for use as a building material. In addition to the fixed buildings temporary or mobile dwellings (yurt) are made of felt over a wooden frame. For traditional houses throughout the region mud brick and pisé are most commonly used. Some of the best examples of mud architecture are the fortified walls which surround most settlements from small villages to major cities such as Bukhara. Important buildings such as mosques, madrassas and mausoleums were sometimes built of baked brick. In premodern times the standard brick form was a square tile 5–7 cm thick. These were used in a variety of decorative patterns produced by placing bricks in alternating groups vertically and horizontally. From the twelfth century glazed bricks were used and eventually became common in the fifteenth century under the Timurids. Although wood has always been rare, especially in the eastern parts of Uzbekistan, it was used for roofs and occasionally for columns, especially in mosques and palaces. Some of the best examples of wooden architecture are in Khiva and include carved wooden columns with muqarnas capitals and bulbous lotus bases resembling lotus buds. Wooden ceilings are often painted.

The majority of Islamic monuments in Uzbekistan are found in Bukhara and Samarkand whilst Khiva is a good example of traditional nineteenth-century architecture. Outside these cities the most important monuments in the country are at Shahr-i Sabz, the village which Timur tried to make his capital.

See also: Bukhara, Samarkand, Shahr-i Sabz, Timurids

W

wakala

Urban building combining the functions of khan, warehouse and market.

waqf

A charitable endowment often intended for the upkeep of a religious building, educational establishment or hospital.

Wasit

Capital of Iraq during the Umayyad period.

Wasit lies south-east of the modern town of Kut in southern Iraq. It was founded in 701 CE by al-Hajjaj, governor of Iraq, as a garrison town to replace Kufa and Basra which had been demilitarized after a revolt against the Umayyads. In 874 another Friday mosque was built by the Turkish general Musa ibn Bugha in the eastern part of the city. The devastation wrought by the Mongols in the thirteenth century and by Timur in the fourteenth hastened the decline of a city that was no longer on the main trade routes due to a change in the course of the Tigris.

The first mosque on the site was built by al-Hajjaj in 703; measuring 100 m per side, it was located next to the governor's residence. Iraqi excavations revealed two superimposed mosques, the earlier of which had no mihrab. This confirms the early date of the mosque, as the first concave mihrab was introduced by al-Walid in 707–9 in the mosque of Medina.

There are also the remains of a thirteenth-century madrassa on the site, consisting of a monumental portal flanked by twin minarets with fluted brick decoration.

West Africa

Region of Africa comprising the modern states of Mali, Mauritania, Senegal, Niger, Nigeria, Cameroon, Burkina Faso, Guinea and Ghana.

Known to medieval geographers as the Sudan, this area extends from the Sahara desert in the north to the mouth of the Niger river in the south, and from Atlantic in the west to Lake Chad in the east. The region was subject to the influence of Islam from the eighth or ninth century onwards and by the nineteenth century large areas were Islamicized.

West Africa can be divided into four main zones, the Sahara, the Sahel, the Savannah and the rain forests. The largest zone is the Sahara desert which extends from the Atlas mountains in Morocco and Algeria to the Senegal river. Until recent times the vast dunes and extreme temperatures of this desert have formed an impenetrable barrier to all except the nomadic tribes which inhabit the area. South of the desert is band of semi-arid country known as the Sahel (Arabic for 'coast') where there is an intermittent vegetation of scrub and occasional small trees. Below this is the Savannah region characterized by a rich growth of grass and plentiful seasonal rainfall. Further south near the coast, especially in Nigeria, Benin, Togo and Ghana, are the dense rain-forests. In recent times the area of the Sahara and the Sahel have been increasing at the expense of the Savannah, probably due to human activity. The best example of this phenomenon is the area occupied by the empire of Ghana which in medieval times was rich grassland and is now desert.

History

The means by which Islam penetrated into West Africa was via the trade routes from North Africa. The main goods involved in the trade included gold, slaves, ivory and gum from West Africa and manufactured goods from the Mediterranean area. This trade was a continuation of pre-Islamic Roman and Byzantine trade routes and was in the hands of the Berber tribes of the Sahara. Already by the end of the seventh century there are accounts of Muslim traders from North Africa and Egypt in the markets of the Sudan. By the end of the eighth

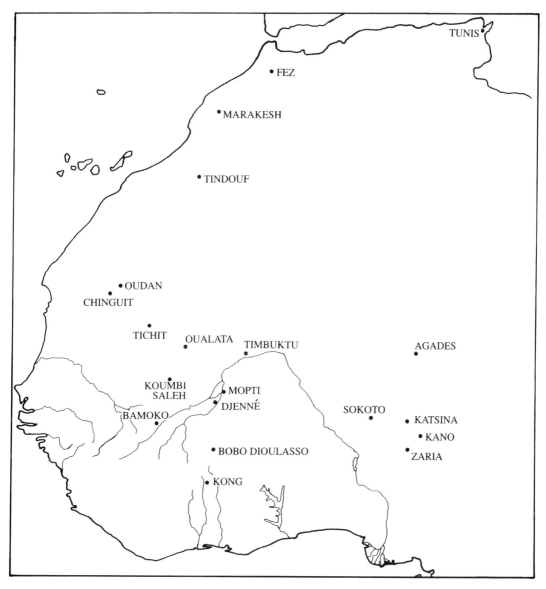

Principal Islamic sites of West Africa

century the northern part of the trade was controlled by the semi-independent Berber dynasties of
the Rustamids in Morocco and the Idrisids in
western Algeria. These dynasties controlled the
northern termini of the West African routes at
Sijimassa and Tahert and were able to collect taxes
from this lucrative trade. It was this trade which
was one of the motivating forces behind the rise
of the Fatimids in North Africa. With the support

of Berber tribes the Fatimids gained control of most
of North Africa in the ninth century and by the
tenth century were in a strong enough position to
take control of Egypt, Africa's wealthiest province.

The role of the Berbers in the dissemination of
Islam amongst the peoples of the Sudan was critical, particularly in the area of present-day Mauritania. The Berbers in this area are known as the
Sanhadja or Muthalamin and were the ancestors of

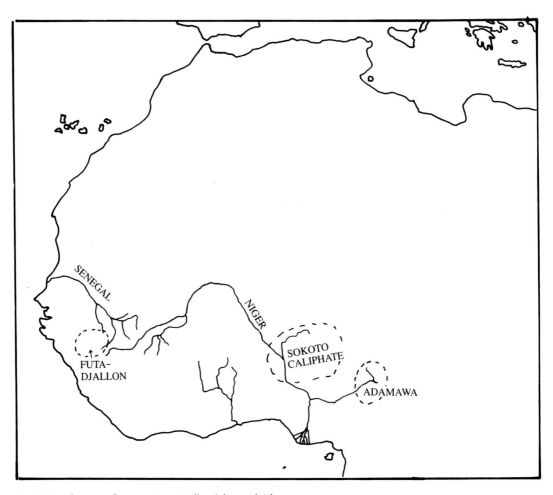

West Africa showing Fulbe areas of Futa-Djallon, Sokoto and Adamawa

the Almoravids who invaded Spain in the eleventh century. They comprised three main tribal groups, the Lamtuna, Massufa and Godala, who were allied into a loose confederation. The most prominent of these groups was the Lamtuna who arrived in the area in the eighth century and captured the oasis city of Awdaghast in Mauritania. By the tenth century most of the Sanhadja leaders had adopted Islam which they used to wage a jihad against the southern kingdoms.

The southern part of West Africa below the Sahel was dominated by the three great empires of Ghana, Mali and Gao. Each of these empires was composed of a particular language group; thus Ghana was controlled by Soninke-speaking peoples, Mali by Manding peoples and Gao by Song-hay people. These were not empires in the modern sense but rather confederations of language and kinship groups which owed allegiance to a central ruler whose capital was often mobile. The empires are difficult to define in territorial terms as they had differing degrees of control over different peoples over a wide area. The key to the rise and fall of these empires was the control of the gold trade with North Africa.

Ghana controlled an area roughly equivalent to south-eastern Mauritania and south-western Mali and flourished between the ninth and eleventh centuries. During this period Ghana was the main opposition to the Sanhadja Berbers of western Mauritania and in 990 captured the Berber city of Awdaghast. Although it was a pagan country there were large numbers of Muslims in Ghana's administration and by the eleventh century the capital was divided into two cities, a Muslim city and a pagan royal city. In spite of this the Almoravid Berbers launched a jihad against the empire and in 1077 destroyed the capital and forced the survivors to convert to Islam. A reconstituted kingdom of Ghana managed to survive until 1240 when it was incorporated into the empire of Mali.

The rise of Mali was due to a number of factors including the decline of the empire of Ghana and the discovery of a new oriferous (gold producing) region on the Niger river. The Mali Empire was formed by the unification of two groups of Manding peoples in the thirteenth century, and was located south of Ghana on the banks of the Niger, although it later took control of much of the former empire of Ghana. Unlike Ghana's, the ruler of Mali was a Muslim although most of the people within the empire remained pagan. The most famous of Mali's rulers was Mansa Musa who made a pilgrimage to Mecca in 1324 during which he gave away large quantities of gold. By the end of the fifteenth century Mali was in decline due to the devastating effects of rival claimants to the throne, a shift in trade patterns and increasing attacks from the Tuareg and Mossi. The empire which grew to replace the power of Mali was the Songhay Empire of Gao, with its centre on the banks of the Niger in the east of the modern state of Mali. Gao had a long history stretching back to the ninth century when it was an important kingdom on the route to Tahert in Algeria and Ghana and Silgilmasa to the west. By the ninth century the ruler of Gao was Muslim, although it is probable that this was merely one of the king's religions. During the thirteenth and fourteenth centuries Gao became subject to the empire of Mali; when this declined at the end of the fourteenth century Gao began taking over some of the outer dependencies of Mali. By the end of the 1460s Ali, the founder of the Songhay Empire, had taken Djenné and Timbuktu thus gaining control of some of the principal trading towns of the Sahel. Ali was succeeded by Askiya Muhammad who consolidated his territorial conquests and introduced Islam as the state religion. The empire flourished for the next hundred years until the Moroccan conquest of 1591.

In addition to the medieval empires which dominated West Africa there are a number of trading cities on the border of the Sahara desert which, although sometimes incorporated into empires, were essentially independent. The most important of these cities were, from east to west, Oualata, Timbuktu and Agades. Oualata in western Mauritania rose to prominence in the thirteenth century after the collapse of Ghana when it was populated by refugees from Awdaghast and other cities. The city was predominantly Ibadi with a mixed Arab Berber population and was one of the principal towns trading with Sijilmasa in Morocco. Further west, in the modern state of Mali, is the famous city of Timbuktu, established as a nomadic Tuareg encampment in the twelfth century. During the fifteenth century under Songhay rule the city became the principal intellectual and religious centre in West Africa. The city has a mixed population of predominantly Berber origin although there are significant numbers of Soninke and Manding.

Whilst the medieval period in West Africa was dominated by the great empires the period after the sixteenth century was characterized by the emergence of smaller independent cities and kingdoms. The post-medieval period is also notable for the integration of Islam into local culture. Whereas Islam had previously been the religion of foreign traders and local rulers who adopted Islam as another attribute of kingship, it now became the religion of whole groups and villages. In the nineteenth century this was partially achieved through jihads or holy wars, but the more common method of diffusion was through the urbanized trade networks. The widespread adoption of Islam throughout West Africa meant that the nature of the religion itself was modified to conform to local ritual requirements. In most cases this meant that local rituals and cultures were adapted to serve Islamic requirements, although in other cases (such as among the Ashante) this meant the adaptation of Islamic forms for use in essentially pagan societies.

Islamic West Africa south of the Sahel can be divided into two main language groups, the Mande-speaking peoples of Mali, Burkina Faso, Ivory Coast and Ghana, and the Fulbe-speaking peoples of northern Nigeria and Futa-Djallon in Guinea. The Mande-speaking peoples occupy roughly the same area as the empire of Mali, although the main cities of the post-medieval era are further east than the old capitals of Kangaba and Niani. The main Manding cities are Mopti, Djenné, Ségou, Bobo Dioulasso, Wa and Kong, each of which functioned as independent or semi-independent states in the eighteenth and nine-teenth centuries. The most famous of these cities is Djenné whose origins may be traced back to the thirteenth century. Although the city did not rise to prominence until the sixteenth century, by the nineteenth century it was one of the main towns in West Africa. Less well known but equally impor-tant in the propagation of Islam was the city of Kong established by immigrants from Ségou and Djenné in the eighteenth century. Kong was lo-cated further south on the edges of the equatorial forest (present-day Ivory Coast) and developed as a centre of Islamic scholarship and commerce for the surrounding area.

The Fulbe-speaking people occupy two distinct areas either side of the area dominated by the Mande peoples. First to be settled by Fulbe-speak-ing people was the Hausa area of north Nigeria where they arrived as Muslim clerics in the fif-teenth century. Hausaland already had an estab-lished, partially Muslim, society dating from the beginning of the eleventh century, comprising seven independent city-states. These cities, known as bakwoi, were Dauro, Kano, Gobir, Katsina, Zaria, Biram and Rano. Kano and Katsina already had an Islamic tradition and it was these cities that the Fulbe developed into a seat of Islamic learning and culture. Although Hausaland was subjected to sub-sequent waves of influence, most notably Songhay rule in the sixteenth century and large-scale immi-gration from Agades in the eighteenth, the Fulbe continued to arrive both as clerics and pastoralists. In the nineteenth century the urbanized Fulbe instigated a jihad for Islamic reform in the Hausa states. The result was a new state based on the recently founded capital of Sokoto, known as the Sokoto caliphate. The success of the Sokoto caliphate encouraged Fulbe in the neighbouring region of Adamawa (present-day Cameroon) to carry out a similar jihad from their newly estab-lished capital of Yolo. The jihad was similarly successful and Adamawa was eventually included within the Sokoto caliphate.

Two thousand kilometres further west is the other area of Fulbe domination in the Futa-Djallon region of Guinea. The early Fulbe migrations into this area were peaceful and were accompanied with intermarriage with the native Djallonke people. From the late seventeenth century onwards there was an intensification of the immigration

until the eighteenth century when it was organized into a jihad. By the end of the eighteenth century Fulbe control of the area was complete with a capital established at Timbo.

Architecture

The Islamic architecture of West Africa reflects the complexities and diversities of its history as well as the differing natural environments. In the past, analysis of the architecture of the area has tended to concentrate on the influence of North Africa and the Middle East rather than to examine the indigenous cultures and architecture of the area. Three main sources of influence were identified each of which ignored the possibility of local invention or development. The most far-fetched idea was that the monumental architecture of the region was developed from the dynastic architec-ture of Egypt and was transmitted by the migration of Songhay people from the upper Nile to the Niger. The second explanation attributes the entire West African architectural tradition to the Andalu-sian poet and architect al-Saheli who accompanied Mansa Musa on his return from the Hajj in 1324. Whilst there is some information that al-Saheli did design an audience hall it is unlikely that this or any other work he may have carried out created an architectural style for the whole region. The third suggestion is that the Moroccan invasion of 1591 was the primary influence on the subsequent architecture of the region. Whilst the Moroccan invasion was certainly accompanied by builders and craftsmen and may have had some influence this was not sufficient to create a complex and distinct architectural style. More recently scholars have emphasized the architectural styles and beliefs of indigenous pagan cultures as influences on the later Islamic architecture of the region.

A wide variety of building materials and tech-niques are used over this vast region. The tech-niques are largely defined by the material, which may be grouped into three basic types, stone, mud and wood. Stone predominates in the western Sahara and Sahel and tends to be associated with Berber architecture. The best examples of stone cities are found in Mauritania at sites like Chinguit, Oudan, Tijika, Qasr el Barka and Tichit. Excavation has shown that Koumbi Saleh, the capital of ancient Ghana, and its sister city Awdaghast were also built of stone. Many of these sites were originally founded as ribats, although they later grew into large trading cities. The commonest method of building in stone in the area uses split limestone in dry-stone wall constructions. The limestone used in the buildings comes in several colours from green and yellow to rose, depending on local availability. The outer faces are usually left unplastered although at Tichit the inner surfaces are coated in clay and a mud mortar is used for some of the walls (at Oualata both the inner and outer surfaces are covered in mud plaster). A characteristic feature of this masonry is the use of triangular niches sometimes arranged to form composite triangular features. Also common are projecting corbels, bands of triangular niches forming chevron patterns and battered walls. The roof and ceilings are usually built of split date-palm trunks arranged diagonally over the corners, forming a square shape in the centre which is then covered by further split-palm beams arranged longitudinally. Above the beams, is placed a woven matting of split palm fronds, on top of which a layer of earth is spread. Although in the cities the buildings are built to a rectangular or square plan, many of the buildings in villages are built with a round plan or with rounded corners. Even in Chinguit itself many of the houses are built with the external corners rounded off.

Whilst stone is the building material of the western Sahara, mud is the characteristic building material of the southern Sahel and the Savannah areas. Sometimes mud is used in combination with stone as at Timbuktu and Oualata, suggesting either the integration of two cultural traditions or the interface between two different environments. At Oualata the buildings are essentially dry-stone constructions covered with layers of mud plaster which serve no structural function. The effect of the mud-plaster coverings is to make the buildings look like mud-brick structures suggesting a cultural tradition originating from the southern Savannah regions grafted on to an existing Berber architecture. This suggestion is strengthened by the make-up of the population, a mixture of Berber and Soninke people. Inside the houses of Oualata, the areas around doorways and niches are decorated with brilliant white wall paintings in the form of arabesque medallions. The use of the mixture of mud and stone at Timbuktu is very different from the practice at Oualata; thus the buildings have a rubble-stone core held together by mud mortar

and plaster. The quality of the stones used at Timbuktu mean that it would not be possible to build houses solely out of stone, thus the mud plaster and mortar here perform a structural function whilst the stone is used for strength. In many Timbuktu houses exposed limestone is used for corner quoins and door jambs and the building of any house starts with the laying out of four corner stones. The decoration of buildings at Timbuktu suggests a close relationship with the stone-built Berber cities of Mauritania; thus the triangular niches and chevron bands are here executed in mud brick. This architectural similarity is paralleled in the ceilings and roofs which employ the same method of diagonally split palm beams. The preference for stone architecture is most clearly expressed on the interior of the oldest part of the Djingueré Ber Mosque where round 'Roman' arches made of dressed limestone are used to support the roof. The distinction between stone and mud-brick architecture in Timbuktu is observed by the builders who are divided into two castes depending on which material they use. It seems likely that there was a pre-existing mud-architecture tradition in the area which was developed by the incoming Berber population who were unable to find their normal building materials. The city of Agades was founded as a Berber city and one might expect it to be built of stone especially as the surrounding Berber villages consist of rectangular stone structures with Oualata-style ceilings. However, the city itself is made almost entirely of mud and resembles the Hausa architecture of north Nigeria. The reason for this could perhaps be attributed to the city's abandonment in the eighteenth century and it should be noted that a sixteenth-century traveller described the city as built in the Berber style. The subsequent rebuilding of the city in the nineteenth century was by people from north Nigeria which may explain its close relationship to Hausa architecture.

Mud either as brick or as pisé is associated with the greatest examples of West Africa's monumental architecture such as the mosque of Djenné or the minaret of Agades. The area most suited to mud-brick architecture is the Savannah region where there is enough water to make bricks, plaster and pisé yet not too much rain to dissolve the dried mud walls. Mud architecture lends itself to the creation of plastic sculptural forms on fairly simple structures, thus a simple rectangular façade can be enlivened by the addition of crenellations, engaged pillars and decorative panels. The traditional methods of mud architecture vary from one town to another; thus in Djenné cylindrical mud-bricks are used whereas in other towns simple dried-earth lumps will be used as the building material. Stylistically there are two main groups of mud architecture, a western tradition originating in the Manding cities of modern Mali and a more easterly tradition in the Hausa cities of north Nigeria.

The western style, often referred to as the 'Sudan style', can trace its origins to the city of Djenné in Mali. This architecture is characterized by the elaborate decorated façades of houses which emphasize verticality by the use of crenellations, engaged pillars and division into several registers. Mosques are distinguished by large minaret-like towers above the mihrab and tapering buttresses terminating in cone-shaped pinnacles. The mihrab towers are usually covered with projecting wooden stakes, known as 'toron'. These stakes were often found all around the walls of a mosque and functioned as scaffolding although they may also have some ritual significance. The most famous building in Djenné is the Great Mosque built in 1909 on the ruins of the previous mosque. It was meant to be a replica but differed considerably from the ruined original which had been recorded before its destruction. The new mosque was built with French funding and guidance from French military engineers and was used by the French as a basis for a neo-Sudanese style. Thus in 1935 the French Administration at Mopti built a new Friday mosque, using the new Great Mosque of Djenné as a model. Although the new Sudan style was based on the pre-colonial style it emphasized symmetry and monumentality at the expense of tradition and ritual.

Like the western tradition of mud architecture the origin of the eastern tradition can be traced to one main town, which in the case of Hausa architecture is Kano. Externally Hausa architecture is plainer than its western counterpart, although inside it displays a wide variety of decorative motifs. Hausa buildings are distinguished by their extensive use of wood and may be regarded as timber-frame buildings as opposed to the more pure mud-brick architecture in the west. The origins of this style are thought to derive from mat-frame tents where the mat-walls are gradually replaced with earth walls. The advantages of this can be seen in the use of one of the most characteristic features of Hausa architecture, the ribbed dome. This consists of a number of ribs converging in the centre and covered over with palm-frond matting. These domes may be set on a square or circular base producing either a single central point or a central square at the intersection of the ribs. The wooden ribs (usually acacia wood) are then plastered with mud to produce free-standing arches which are decorated with abstract designs. Flat roofs are achieved by building light mud walls on top of the ribs between the centre and the outer wall, making the ribs into giant armatures or brackets with a curved inner profile. South of the Hausa area in the region of Adamawa the concept of mud-brick architecture with flat roofs is modified by the use of conical thatched roofs. This adaptation is necessary in a region where high rainfall makes flat roofs impracticable. One of the more interesting results of this is that in order to preserve the appearance of an Islamic rectangular or square house façades are built on to the front of thatched buildings. These stage-like façades built of mud are enlivened by the use of elaborate arabesque designs above projecting doorways.

Further west, in the Futa-Djallon region of Guinea, wood and thatch replaces mud as the main building material. The buildings of this region consist of circular huts covered with huge conical thatched roofs supported by large central poles. The lower part of the roof is supported by shorter poles contained within a circular outer wall. The eaves of the thatched roof project beyond the line of the outer wall so that from the outside the walls and entrances are barely visible. Mosques in the region are built in the same manner as the houses, but inside the hut there is a flat-roofed rectangular mud-walled building with a mihrab in the east wall. According to local tradition the mosque is only the square building inside whilst the outer thatched building is merely for protection. This arrangement further strengthens the idea that in West Africa Islam can only be represented by rectangular or square architecture of mud or stone.

Further reading:

R. M. A. Bedaux, 'Tellem, reconnaissance d'une culture de l'ouest african au moyen âge: recherches architectoniques', *Journal de la Société des Africanistes* 42: 103–85, 1972.

R. Bravmann, *Islam and Tribal Art in West Africa*, Cambridge 1974.

N. David, 'The Fulani compound and the archaeologist', *World Archaeology* 3: 111–31, 1971.

S. Denyer, *African Traditional Architecture*, New York 1978.

A. D. Hyland, *Traditional Forms of Architecture in Ghana*, Kumasi 1975.

D. Jacques–Meunie, *Cités anciennes de Mauritanie*, Paris 1961.

R. J. McIntosh, 'Archaeology and mud wall decay in a West African village', *World Archaeology* 6: 154–71, 1974.

B. Mallen and C. Benedetti, 'Afro-Brazilian mosques', *Mimar* 29: 1988.

L. Prussin, 'The architecture of Islam in West Africa', *African Arts* 1(2): 32–25 and 70–4, 1968.

—— 'Sudanese architecture and the Manding', *African Arts* 3(4): 12–19 and 64–7, 1970.

—— 'Contribution à l'étude du cadre historique de la technologie de la construction dans l'Ouest africain', *Journal de la Société des Africanistes* 40: 175–8, 1970.

—— 'West African mud granaries', *Paideuma* 18: 144–69, 1972.

—— 'Building technologies in the West African savannah', *Le Sol, la parole et l'écrit, mélanges en hommage à Raymond Maury*, Paris 1981.

—— *Hatumere: Islamic Design in West Africa*, Berkeley 1986.

J. Sacht, 'Sur la diffusion des formes d'architecture religieuse musulmane à travers le Sahara', *Travaux de l'Institut de Recherches Sahariennes* 11(1): 11–27, 1954.

M.-M. Vire, 'Stèles funéraires musulmanes soudano-sahariennes', *Bulletin IFAN* 21 в (3–4): 459–600, 1959.

Y

Yasavi (Shrine of Ahmed Yasavi)

Shrine built by Timur for his son Jahangir between 1397 and 1399.

The shrine is located in the city of Turkestan (modern Yasi) in the Republic of Kazakhstan. The building is oriented north–south on a rectangular ground plan (65.5 by 46.5 m) with portals at the south and north ends. The main doorway is the magnificent south portal which is flanked by huge cylindrical corner towers or minarets over 20 m high. Behind the portal is the dome of the prayer hall rising to a height of over 37 m. At the other end of the structure is the north façade in the centre of which is the entrance to the mausoleum. The mausoleum is capped by a tall 'melon-shaped' ribbed dome set on a high cylindrical drum. Externally the building is well articulated with its two entrance façades, domes and an extensive covering of tilework. Internally, however, there is less feeling of unity beyond the principal rooms: leading off from the prayer hall and mausoleum are many smaller rooms with different vaulting systems which do not seem integrated in an overall design.

Yemen

Second largest country in Arabia located in the south-west of the Arabian peninsula.

The country comprises three main inhabited regions, the highlands, the coastal plain and the Wadi Hadramat. The mountains of the highlands are extremely high (up to 4,000 m) giving the region a moderate temperature and relatively high rainfall. The favourable climate makes this the most fertile part of southern Arabia with intensive cultivation of tropical plants in the wadis and in steep mountain terraces. The coastal plain is extremely hot and fairly arid, with little potential for agriculture; traditionally the main occupations have been fishing and trade. The Wadi Hadramat is a wide valley 160 km long which runs from west to east, roughly parallel with Gulf of Aden. The valley is very fertile with a system of dams and terraces which catch the water from the twice-yearly monsoon.

In pre-Islamic times Yemen was the home to advanced cultures which traded with the great civilizations of Mesopotamia, Egypt and Syria. The best known are the Sabeans who flourished between the tenth and the first centuries BCE. The Sabeans were responsible for the Marib Dam, one of the greatest engineering feats of the ancient world. In the first century BCE the Sabeans were replaced by the Himyarite clan who ruled the area until the sixth century CE. By the early sixth century Judaism had become established as the official religion as a counter to the missionary activity of the Byzantines. In 575 Sassanian interest in the country culminated in its conquest and annexation as a Persian satrapy.

The history of Yemen under the first caliphs is confused but it is clear that there was some conversion to Islam during the seventh century. During the Abbasid period (eighth to ninth centuries) there appears to have been a division with Shafi orthodox Sunnis on the coast and Zayidi Shi'a in the highlands. This division reflected older tribal rivalries and does not exactly mirror similar movements elsewhere in the caliphate. During the ninth century Yemen was ruled by a number of competing dynasties the most prominent of which were the Zayidis, the Rassids and the Yafurids. The Rassids were a dynasty of imams claiming descent from the prophet and they continued to rule parts of the country until 1962. In 1174 Yemen was conquered by the Ayyubids seeking a haven from the turmoil of northern Arabia brought about by the Crusaders. In 1230 Nur al-Din 'Umar the deputy of the Ayyubid ruler declared himself independent and started a new dynasty known as the Rasulids, who ruled until the mid-fifteenth century when they were replaced by the Tahirids.

The Tahirids remained in power till the early sixteenth century when increasing European interest in the area resulted in two successive invasions

Mosque near Ta'iz, Yemen, ©Charles Aithie

by Muslim powers determined to prevent a Christian presence in the land of Islam. The first invasion by the Mamluks was of short duration and achieved little. A year later after their defeat of the Mamluks the Ottomans launched an invasion and by 1547 they were established in the capital, San'a. Ottoman rule lasted until 1602 when the Zayidi imams once again established themselves as rulers of San'a. The Ottomans invaded for a second time in 1872 and remained in at least partial control until their defeat at the end of the First World War. With the defeat of the Turks the Zayidi imams once again took power until they were deposed in 1962. The post-sixteenth-century history of south Yemen is slightly different and is dominated by the rivalry of two tribal groups, the Kathiris and the Qu'aitis.

The traditional building materials in Yemen are stone, coral, mud brick, baked brick, wood and stucco. Stone is the principal building material in the highland regions, although mud brick and baked brick are also used for the upper parts of the tall houses. The quality of stonework varies from massive dressed sandstone blocks used in the more important buildings of San'a to roughly squared blocks of stone laid in rough courses for village houses. Coral is the principal building material in

coastal towns where it is used in conjunction with hard white lime plaster. Mud brick is used throughout the country but is employed to its greatest effect in the Wadi Hadramat where structures over eight storeys high are built of mud brick. Baked brick is comparatively more rare and is used for the upper parts of buildings in the principal cities of San'a and Zabid. Decorative brickwork appears to have been introduced to Yemen during the Ayyubid period (twelfth century) as can be seen from the brick minaret of the Great Mosque in Zabid. As in the rest of Arabia suitable building wood is very scarce and is usually imported from Africa or India. Yemeni woodwork is of extremely high quality and the panelled ceilings are some of the best in the Islamic world. Stucco work is also highly developed with elaborate arches, decorative panels and delicate calligraphy all executed in fine white stucco. One of the most important uses of stucco is for the elaborate windows of coloured glass which characterize Yemeni houses.

The religious architecture of Yemen may be divided into three types of building, mosques, madrassas and tombs. The earliest mosques in Yemen are cubical mosques and hypostyle halls, both of which may be directly related to pre-Islamic temple architecture in the country. The typical cubical mosque consists of a tall rectangular chamber with a flat wooden roof supported by two rows of three columns. These mosques are usually windowless, although they may have windows placed high up near the ceiling. Some of the earliest examples of this type of mosque may actually be converted temples, as seems to be the case with the mosque of Tamur restored in 1089. Hypostyle halls also appear in Yemeni temple architecture and appear to form an early mosque type. Early examples include the Great Mosque of Zabid and the mosque of Sulayman ibn Daud in Marib. These buildings differ from the early mosques of the Hijaz and Syria–Palestine which opened on to large open courtyards. The earliest example of the courtyard mosque in Yemen is the Great Mosque of San'a which traditionally was planned by Muhammad although in its present form seems to date from the time of Abd al-Malik (early eighth century).

The Ayyubid invasion of the twelfth century introduced many new features into Yemeni architecture, the most significant of which was the dome. The earliest domed mosques had a large central

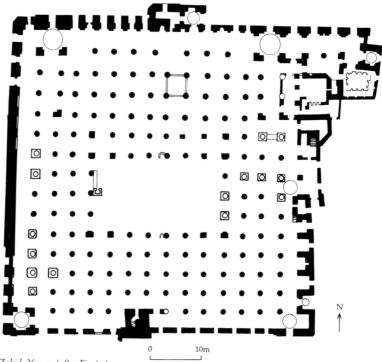

Great Mosque of Zabid, Yemen (after Finster)

dome flanked by smaller domed bays either side. Another innovation of this period is the decorative brick minaret such as that of al-Mahjam which consists of a square socle with an octagonal shaft which is faceted lower down and has a large diaper pattern on the upper shaft. A characteristic feature of Yemeni mosques of this period (twelfth to fifteenth centuries) is a domed tower-like structure marking the position of the mihrab. The Ottoman conquest of the sixteenth century introduced a new form of domed mosque comprising a large domed area with a multiple-domed portico. One of the best examples of this type is the mosque of Mustafa Pasha in Ta'iz built in 1554. Despite the Ottoman form of this building the execution is entirely Yemeni with stucco decoration and a thick cylindrical minaret.

The Ayyubids were responsible for introducing the madrassa as an architectural type, although the form in Yemen differed from that found elsewhere in the Islamic world. The main distinguishing feature is that Yemeni madrassas had no accommodation for students and teachers. Many Yemeni madrassas simply comprised a mosque with a teaching hall opposite. One of the finest examples of

Yemeni Islamic architecture is the Ashrafiyya Madrassa in Ta'iz which comprises a mosque, a teaching hall, a Quran school and a library arranged around an internal courtyard. Another innovation of the Ayyubid period was the domed mausoleum which was used to commemorate deceased imams and rulers. The earliest examples date from the thirteenth century and comprise square domed structures open on three sides, the fourth side containing the mihrab. Probably the most elaborately decorated structures are the tombs of Sa'da which have extravagantly decorated domes covered with calligraphic and geometric designs executed in painted stucco.

The richness of Yemeni religious architecture is matched in the domestic architecture of the towns and some of the villages. One of the most characteristic building forms is that of the tower houses which in San'a and the highlands are built of stone and brick but in the Wadi Hadramat are extravagantly tall mud-brick structures. The external walls of these houses are normally battered, with their thickness decreasing with height. The windows are usually decorated with wooden grilles which are often plain but can become quite elaborate. In

Al-mudhafar Mosque with Ashrafiyya Mosque in the background, Ta'iz, Yemen, ©Charles Aithie

San'a and the highlands the exterior of the buildings are also decorated with geometric brickwork
and white stucco borders around the windows.
The design of these buildings varies with regions
and the date of construction, although they have
the same basic plan. Each house has a single door
which opens on to the street. Inside there is a
passageway or hall opening on to various rooms of
utilitarian function (storage, animal pens etc.). At
the end of the hallway there is a staircase leading
up to the first floor. Depending on the height of
the house the living quarters may start at the first
or the third floor. In the upper storeys there are
bedrooms, bathrooms and pillared reception rooms
which often open on to terraces. The room at the
top of the house is usually a large reception hall
(mufraj) with two tiers of windows. The upper row

of windows in the mufraj usually comprise elaborate stucco tracery filled in with coloured glass
(green, blue, red and yellow). At the top of the
house are parapets, sometimes with arrow slits for
defence.

See also: Hadramawt, San'a

Further reading:

P. Costa, 'Islamic religious buildings in Yemen', *Proceedings
of the 8th Seminar for Arabian Studies 1974*, London
1975.

B. Finster, 'An outline of the history of Islamic religious
architecture in Yemen', *Muqarnas: An Annual on Islamic
Art and Architecture* 9: 124–47, 1992.

L. Golvin and M. C. Fromont, *Architecture et urbanisme
d'une cité de haute montagne en République arabe du Yemen*,
Éditions de Recherche sur les Civilisations, Mémoire
no. 30, Paris 1984.

R. B. Lewcock and G. R. Smith, 'Two early mosques in

A funduq in Thula, Yemen (after Golvin and Fromont)

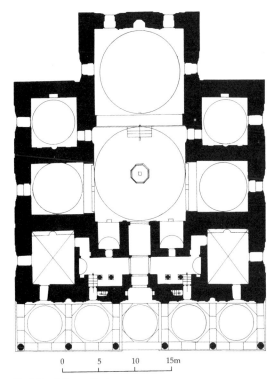

Yeşil Cami, Bursa, Turkey

the Yemen, a preliminary report', *Art and Archaeology Research Papers*, 1973.
—— 'Three early mosques in the Yemen', *Oriental Art*, NS 20: 1974.
Naval Intelligence Division, *Western Arabia and the Red Sea*, Geographical Handbook Series, BR 527, Oxford 1946.
U. Scerrato, G. Ventrane and P. Cuneo, 'Report on the third campaign for the typological survey of the Islamic religious architecture of the Yemen', *East and West*, 36(4): 1986

Yeşil Cami (The Green Mosque)

Imperial Ottoman mosque in Bursa famed for its green tile decoration.

The Yeşil Cami is part of a large complex built by Sultan Mehmet and completed in 1420. The complex is one of the last in a series of royal mosque complexes in Bursa starting with the Orhaniya in the fourteenth century and ending with the Muradiye completed in 1447. The complex includes a mosque, madrassa, bath house, soup kitchen and the tomb of Mehmet.

The mosque is built in the Bursa T-plan style which is based on the four-iwan plan of Seljuk madrassas. In Bursa mosques the entrance iwan becomes reduced to a small entrance vestibule leaving a T-shaped building with a central courtyard flanked by side rooms (iwans) and with a large prayer hall in front. The central courtyard is covered with a dome which has an oculus, or round hole, in the roof to let in light and air. In most of the Bursa T-plan mosques the entrance is preceded by a three- or five-domed portico, which is a feature borrowed from the usual Ottoman single-domed mosque. In the Yeşil Cami, however, the portico is missing as Mehmet died before this could be added. The entrance façade of the mosque contains eight windows, one pair either side of the door on the ground floor and four on the upper floor. Each of the ground-floor windows consists of a rectangular grilled opening inset into a richly carved arched frame which itself is set into a recessed panel. Between each pair of windows there is a deeply recessed minbar with a muqarnas hood. The upper windows are set into rectangular panels and are entirely open except for a low carved balustrade. Only the two central windows are real; the other two serve no purpose except to balance the composition of the façade. The entrance opens into a small vestibule from which stairs lead up to the celebrated royal gallery. On the ground floor the vestibule opens into the domed central courtyard which is flanked on either side by small domed alcoves. To the south of the courtyard under a large arch is the domed prayer hall with its magnificent muqarnas hooded mihrab surrounded by a tilework frame.

The most noticeable feature of the interior is the extensive use of polychrome glazed tiles. Until the seventeenth century the outer surface of the domes were covered in green tiles giving the mosque its name. The tiles carry a variety of patterns including flowers, calligraphic inscriptions, geometric interlace as well as motifs executed in three dimensions like the tile bosses in the royal gallery. The tilework of the mosque is reproduced in Mehmet's tomb, which is located on a hill above the mosque.

See also: Bursa, Ottomans

yurt

Circular tent used in Turkey and Central Asia. It is made out of a portable wooden frame covered with skin or felt.

Z

zanana

Mughal term used to describe the women's quarters in a palace or house.

Zanzibar

Large island off the east coast of Africa; together with the island of Pemba it forms an autonomous part of Tanzania. The capital of Zanzibar is Zanzibar town and the capital of Pemba is Chake.

Zanzibar is a low-lying coral island covered with coconut palms and famed for its cultivation of spices, in particular cloves. Pemba on the other hand is a true island lying on rock away from the continental shelf. The island rises much higher out of the water and has a deeply indented coastline with many remains of ancient settlement. Remains of pre-Islamic sites have been found on both Zanzibar and Pemba although the nature of settlement at these sites has yet to be clarified.

Zanzibar

Zanzibar has a long history of Islamic settlement starting in the eighth century at the trading site of Unguja Ukuu on the southern part of the island where a hoard of gold Abbasid coins was found. Unfortunately no traces of early structures have been discovered at this site although there is a later mosque there. The earliest known structure on the island is the Kizimkazi Mosque which is dated by an inscription to 1107 CE and consists of a rectangular structure with three columns running down the centre to support the roof, which would have been flat. Although it was restored in the eighteenth century, excavations have shown that the basic form of the mosque dates back to the twelfth. South of the mosque are traces of domestic occupation and a stone tomb within an enclosure wall. Jongowe on Tumbatu island north-west of Zanzibar island contains one of the largest groups of remains on the island, covering an area of 25

hectares. The site has a long history with its own chronicle and was mentioned by Yakut. The present remains consist of a mosque and a group of houses dated to the twelfth and thirteenth centuries. The best-preserved building is the mosque which stands in an irregular enclosure next to the sea. It has a rectangular shape with a deep mihrab projecting from the north end and eight arched doorways, four on the west and four on east side. On the east side there is a side aisle next to the sea with its own mihrab. Both mihrabs are fairly plain structures built of cut reef coral. Also on Tumbatu island is the site of Gomani which has important examples of local tombs dated to 1400 CE. In the sixteenth century Zanzibar was occupied by the Portuguese who established farmsteads on the island and built a church in Zanzibar town which was later converted into an Omani fort. There are a few remains of Islamic buildings from the eighteenth century with the exception of some of the Kizimkazi ruins and the mosque and tombs of Shakani. From the beginning of the eighteenth century Portuguese power in the area declined in favour of the Omanis who took over many of the former Portuguese bases. By 1832 the Omani position in Zanzibar was so secure that Sultan Sayyid Sa'id moved his capital from Muscat to Zanzibar. This move meant that a whole new series of buildings were erected to house the new sultans and their administration. One of the first Omani buildings in Zanzibar was the Mtoni Palace built for Sayyid Sa'id in 1830 which is about 5 km north of Zanzibar town. Although the palace is much ruined, substantial remains are still standing including the harem, the domed bath block containing hot and cold water plunges and the sultan's personal mosque on the beach. Nearby is the Marhubi Palace, built in 1880 by Sayyid Barghash and enclosed in over 50 hectares of gardens. Although the palace was burnt down in 1890 the bath complex still stands which includes domed baths, pavilions, water storage tanks and an aqueduct. Other buildings with bath complexes are the country houses of Kidichi and Kizimbai – the Kidichi baths have beautiful examples of Persian stucco work on the interior. Approximately 10 km north of Zanzibar town are the ruins of Chuini Palace also built by Sayyid Barghash. The building is several storeys high and consists of a central core containing rooms opening out to balconies on each side which are supported with massive cylindrical columns. Other Omani palaces on Zanzibar are Beit al-Ras and the Dunga Palace both built around 1850.

The town of Zanzibar is known as the 'Stone Town' to distinguish it from the newer suburbs. Most of the buildings in the old town date to the nineteenth century and are notable for their highly decorative wooden doorways. The centre of the town contains the various ministries of the sultanate built in the eighteenth and nineteenth centuries. These buildings have the same form of some of the palaces with a multi-storey central block surrounded on all sides by extensive verandas. One of the more recent palaces, the Beit al-Ajcib, is built in the same style but the verandas are supported with imported iron columns. The Portuguese church in the centre was converted into a fort with four towers by the Omanis in 1800. One of the more unusual buildings is the public baths (Hamani) built out of brick and coral stone by Sayyid Barghash in 1880 which are the only known public baths of this type in East Africa. Another notable building in Zanzibar town is the National Museum completed in 1925 to the design of a British architect working in the Oriental style, which resembles the Hagia Sophia in Istanbul.

Pemba

Pemba has many more archaeological sites than Zanzibar and even today it is more populous than its neighbour. The earliest site so far discovered is at Mtambwe Mkuu dated to the eleventh century, although this has no early standing structures. Some of the earliest structures on the island are found at Ras Mkumbuu which is one of the largest sites on the East African coast. The remains date to the fourteenth century and consist of a mosque, a number of pillar tombs and many houses, of which four are still standing. The mosque is a large structure four aisles wide and five bays deep, supported on three rows of four rectangular piers. The mihrab is centrally placed and aligned with the central row of columns and there is a tower entered from a doorway to the east of the mihrab. This is one of the few pre-nineteenth-century examples of a minaret in East Africa, although it seems likely that the tower was not very tall. (Other fourteenth-century mosques on Pemba include Shamiani, Mtangani, Mduni and Mkia wa Ngombe.) On the east coast of Pemba are the remains of Pujini which are famous as the only pre-Portuguese fortifications on the East African coast. The fortifications date to approximately 1400 CE and comprise a square area enclosed by walls and ramparts containing houses and a barrack block.

The capital, Chake, contains a nineteenth-century Swahili fort and the Bohra Mosque. The Bohra Mosque dates to the early twentieth century and was built by the Bohra Indians of Pemba. The mosque is a two-storey structure containing a prayer hall below and a Quran school above and is one of the few examples of Indian Muslim architecture in East Africa.

See also: coral, East Africa, Tanzania

Further Reading:

F. Aalund, 'Zanzibar old stone town', *Monumentum* 143–59, 1983.

M. C. Horton and C. M. Clark, *Zanzibar Archaeological Survey 1984–5*, Zanzibar 1985.

M. C. Horton, C. M. Clarke and Y. Staelens, *Zanzibar Museums Project 1986*, Zanzibar 1986.

J. S. Kirkman, 'Excavations at Ras Mkumbuu on the island of Pemba', *Tanjanyika Notes and Records* 1: 94–101, 1959.

A. Prins, *The Swahili-Speaking Peoples of Zanzibar and the East African Coast*, London 1964.

Zaragoza

City in north-west Spain which was Muslim from the eighth to the twelfth century and which continued as a centre of Mudéjar culture.

During the Islamic period the town was settled by Berbers from North Africa who in the eleventh century were ruled over by their own Dhu Nunid amirs. The city finally fell to Alfonso VI of León and Castile in 1085.

Few remains of the Islamic period survive with the exception of Parts of the city walls and parts of the Aljafería palace. The Islamic parts of the city walls have been dated to the late ninth century whilst the most visible parts are Mudéjar work.

The most well-known part of Zaragoza is the fortified palace complex known as the Aljafería.

The outer walls of this structure have recently been restored and may be Islamic, the main gate is a round horseshoe arch between two semi-circular bastions. Remains of the mosque can be found incorporated into a later church. Inside, there is a square room covered by a dome and a mihrab with a horseshoe arch covered by a semi-dome as in the mosque at Córdoba.

Within the palace most of the building is Mudéjar and consists of a series of courtyards decorated with arches and pools leading to the royal hall. The arches are cusped and rest on pairs of columns with re-used Islamic capitals. Between the arches the building is decorated with ornate interlacing strapwork and vegetal motifs.

Many of the churches of the city also contain much Mudéjar work. The cathedral, known as La Seo, has an interesting mixture of Islamic-style blind niches and diaper-patterned brickwork with Gothic windows.

See also: Córdoba, Granada, Seville, Spain

Further reading:

G. Goodwin, *Islamic Spain*, Architectural Guides for Travellers, London 1990, 131–7.

zawiya

Literally 'a corner': often the place where a holy man both lived and was buried.

zigara

Mausoleum (literally 'place of visitation').

zilij

North African term for glazed tiles, usually applied to tile mosaics used for dadoes in houses and mosques. Predominant colours are orange, green and white.

ziyada

Outer enclosure or extension of mosque common to congregational mosques in the early Islamic period.

The name is derived from an Arabic term meaning an addition or increase in size. The best surviving examples of ziyadas can be found in Samarra at the Great Mosque (847) and the Abu Dulaf Mosque (861) and also at the mosque of Ibn Tulun in Cairo. The earliest example is at the Great Mosque at Samarra where an outer enclosure surrounds the mosque on the east, north and west sides (i.e. not on the qibla side). This enclosure is surrounded by an even larger rectangle which encloses all four sides of the mosque although the south side is narrower than the other sides. The area covered by the mosque and its ziyadas amounts to 17 hectares. Likewise the mosque of Abu Dulaf which copies the Great Mosque in many ways also has two ziyadas or enclosures.

The mosque of Ibn Tulun provides the best-preserved example of a ziyada. Like the mosques at Samarra the ziyada encloses the mosque on the three sides away from the qibla. The enclosure wall resembles that of the mosque itself with its niches and crenellations. Each wall is pierced with several doorways which led from adjoining markets. Although no remains have been traced, four historical sources imply that latrines and places for ablution were located within the ziyada.

The origin of the ziyada is likely to have been the outer *temenos* of pre-Islamic shrines or sanctuaries where the temple was separated from the secular city by an outer enclosure. Ziyadas are not usually found on the qibla side of a mosque as this position was reserved for the Dar al-Imara.

Further reading:

K. A. C. Creswell, *A Short Account of Early Muslim Architecture*, revised and enlarged edn. J. W. Allan, Aldershot 1989, 395–6.

ziyaret

Venerated shrine or mausoleum.

zulla

Arabic term for shaded area. Used to refer to sanctuary or covered part of mosque.

Appendix

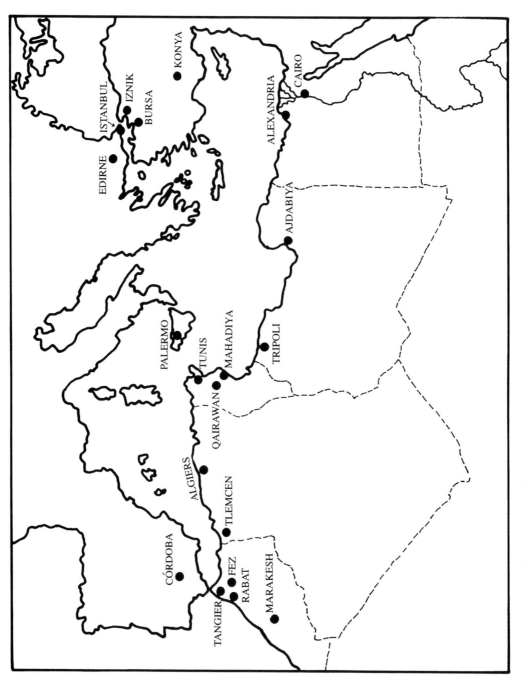

The Mediterranean World showing principal historic cities and sites

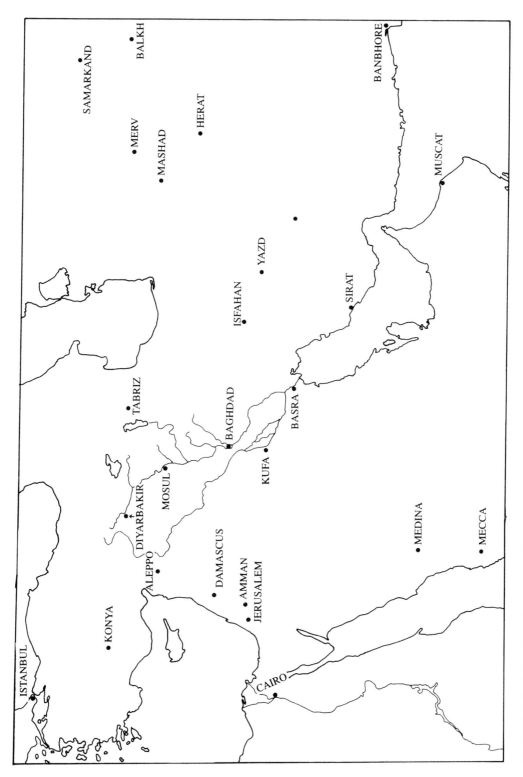

The Middle East and Central Asia showing principal historic cities and sites

Index

Index

Index

Index

Index

Index

Index

Index

Index

Index

Index